Giancarlo Gandolfo

International Economics II

International Monetary Theory and
Open-Economy Macroeconomics

Second, Revised Edition

With 54 Figures

Springer-Verlag
Berlin Heidelberg New York
London Paris Tokyo
Hong Kong Barcelona
Budapest

Professor Dr. Giancarlo Gandolfo
University of Rome "La Sapienza"
Faculty of Economics and Commerce
Via Castro Laurenziano 9
I-00161 Rome

ISBN 3-540-58687-3 Springer-Verlag Berlin Heidelberg New York Tokyo
ISBN 0-387-17978-X 1st Edition Springer-Verlag New York Berlin Heidelberg Tokyo

This work is subject to copyright. All rights are reserved, whether the whole or part of the material is concerned, specifically the rights of translation, reprinting, re-use of illustrations, recitation, broadcasting, reproduction on microfilms or in other ways, and storage in data banks. Duplication of this publication or parts thereof is only permitted under the provisions of the German Copyright Law of September 9, 1965, in its current version, and permission for use must always be obtained from Springer-Verlag. Violations are liable for prosecution under the German Copyright Law.

© Springer-Verlag Berlin Heidelberg 1987, 1995
Printed in Germany

The use of registered names, trademarks, etc. in this publication does not imply, even in the absence of a specific statement, that such names are exempt from the relevant protective laws and regulations and therefore free for general use.

Typesetting: Elsner & Behrens GmbH, Oftersheim
42/2202 - 5 4 3 2 1 0 - Printed on acid-free paper

*To the memory of my father
Edgardo Gandolfo*

Preface to the First Edition

There is no lack of good international economics textbooks ranging from the elementary to the advanced, so that an additional drop in this ocean calls for an explanation. In the present writer's opinion, there seems still to be room for a textbook which can be used in both undergraduate and graduate courses, and which contains a wide range of topics, including those usually omitted from other textbooks. These are the intentions behind the present book, which is an outcrop from undergraduate and graduate courses in international economics that the author has been holding at the University of Rome since 1974, and from his ongoing research work in this field. Accordingly the work is organized as two-books-in-one by distributing the material between text and appendices.

The treatment in the body of this book is directed to undergraduate students and is mainly confined to graphic analysis and to some elementary algebra, but it is assumed that the reader will have a good knowledge of basic microeconomics and macroeconomics (so that the usual review material on production functions, indifference curves, standard Keynesian model, etc., etc. has been omitted). Each chapter is followed by an appendix in which the treatment is mainly mathematical, and where (i) the topics explained in the text are treated at a level suitable for advanced undergraduate or first-year graduate students and (ii) generalizations and/or topics not treated in the text (including some of those at the frontiers of research) are formally examined.

The appendices can be read independently of the text and can, therefore, also be used by students who already know "graphic" international economics and want to learn something about its mathematical counterpart. Of course the connections between text and appendices are carefully indicated, so that the latter can be used as mathematical appendices by the student who has mastered the text, and the text can be used as a literary and graphic exposition of the results derived mathematically in the appendices by the student who has mastered these. The appendices require a working knowledge of calculus, matrix algebra, optimization methods, and dynamic analysis for stability purposes.

The traditional distinction between the pure theory of international trade and international monetary theory is maintained; note that, although trade theory is treated (in Book I) before turning to international monetary theory (in Book II), there is enough independence in the two parts to make it possible for a teacher who so prefers to deal with international monetary matters before trade matters. In any case, one chapter briefly indicates the problems that arise when one tries to integrate these two branches of international economics, a topic which is usually omitted from comparable textbooks. Other topics treated here which are seldom present — at least not simultaneously present — in international economics textbooks include: international trade under uncertainty; illegal transactions in international trade (a theory of smuggling); Dutch disease and de-industrialization; neo-Ricardian versus orthodox theories of international trade; imported intermediate goods in the multiplier mechanism; international transmission of perturbations in n-country models; the new Cambridge school of economic policy; integration between portfolio and macroeconomic equilibrium under fixed and flexible exchange rates; the inflation-devaluation vicious circle; etc. The bibliographies appended to each chapter, though far from exhaustive, may seem unduly long for a textbook, but they have been compiled to serve a double purpose. They aim to help all those who wish to read the original sources (both classic and very recent) to find these: in fact, many (though not all) items in these lists are quoted throughout. And secondly they can be a teaching aid insofar as they can help the teacher to prepare selected reading lists.

International economics — and especially international monetary theory — is in a state of flux. The author has tried to give a balanced treatment of the various approaches, in the belief that they all have something to teach us. This undogmatic and eclectic presentation will, it is hoped, have the advantage of serving a wider audience than the believers in one specific creed, thus leaving the reader free to form a personal opinion and to choose an approach without ignoring the others. The book is mainly analytical, and no detailed description of the international monetary system and of its evolution over time has been included. This is a deliberate omission, made for various reasons. A single chapter on this topic would not suffice and, furthermore, it would quickly become obsolete, given the rapid succession of events occurring in our time. The student interested in these matters would do best to read one of the several good books available of the institutional-descriptive type.

It should however be stressed that this decision does not at all mean that the real world has been excluded. Firstly, the author has given a very brief treatment of the key events of the international monetary system since the second world war, so as to provide the minimum amount of information necessary to set the theoretical problems against their institutional and historical background. Thus, for example, when dealing with optimum currency areas a treatment of the EMS (European Monetary System) is included, and when dealing with the issue of fixed versus flexible exchange rates, a concise evaluation of the experience of the managed float is given. Secondly, the results of empirical tests of some of the theories of international trade and finance are briefly discussed. However, by stressing the analytical aspects, the author hopes to give the student the tools for an understanding of facts and policies — tools that will survive the circumstances of the passing day.

In writing this textbook I have been fortunate enough to benefit from comments, criticism, and suggestions coming from all levels. The students of my international economics courses, who served as guinea pigs in my testing of this material throughout the years, performed their task admirably well by indicating unclear points and suggesting amendments, and they even survived the experiment!

Colleagues who have been using my lecture notes in other universities were kind enough to let me know their own reactions as well as those of their students.

I am particularly indebted to Flavio Casprini, with whom I have discussed this work in detail ever since the preparatory planning phase down to a close scrutiny of the final version. I am also very grateful to Pietro Carlo Padoan, Maria Luisa Petit and Francesca Sanna Randaccio, who read the entire first draft with painstaking care and made innumerable and invaluable comments. Helpful observations on single points came from Claudio Gnesutta, Cristina Mastropasqua, Giancarlo Martinengo and Ferruccio Marzano. Derrick Plant went through the entire final version to check my English: as he is a wonderful linguist but not a mathematical economist, I must apologize for having caused him many a nightmare in forests swarming with such horrible creatures as Jacobians, Hessians, and the like (he was particularly awed by the Jacobians). It goes without saying that none of the persons mentioned has any responsibility for possible deficiencies that might remain.

Last, but not least, I wish to thank Anna Maria Olivari who, in addition to carrying out all the secretarial work, transformed my scribblings into beautiful typescripts. Her collaboration has been indispensable for the completion of this work.

University of Rome "La Sapienza"
Summer 1986   Giancarlo Gandolfo

Preface to the Soft-Cover Edition

The present soft-cover edition, which follows the one-volume hard-cover one, has been published in two independent volumes with the intention of making the book more suitable for teaching purposes.

University of Rome "La Sapienza"
Spring 1987   Giancarlo Gandolfo

Preface to the Second Edition

This new edition maintains the same structure of the first edition, but has been updated and enriched. The comments and recommendations of colleagues and students, and my use of the first edition, suggested the introduction of new topics and the expansion of existing ones. In addition to the new material, there is of course the standard set of revisions: a better explanation of several difficult points, the updating of the institutional material and of the references, and the correction of misprints.

The main innovations in Vol. I are the "new" protectionism and the "new" trade theories. The new protectionism was already briefly mentioned (under the title "Other impediments to free trade") in the previous edition, but the increasing importance of these forms of protectionism and the emergence of the "political economy" of protectionism required a new and deeper treatment (see section 5.9). A chapter was already devoted to the new trade theory (Chapter 8), but the increasing importance of (models of) trade based on increasing returns, imperfect competition, cross-hauling, etc., suggested a complete revision of this chapter to give a detailed treatment of such developments.

More innovations are contained in Vol. II, perhaps reflecting the fact that international monetary economics, more than trade theory, is in a state of flux. The frequent use, in this volume and in international monetary economics writings in general, of the various interest-rate parity conditions and related topics (efficiency of the foreign exchange market, capital mobility and asset substitutability, etc.) suggested the detailed and unified exposition in the new section 10.7. The treatment of exchange-rate determination has been expanded: it now includes simultaneous models and a review of empirical studies. A new chapter (Chapter 19) has been introduced to cover the theory and practice of monetary integration, including the European Monetary System (previously dealt with in Chapter 18) and the prospective European Monetary Union. The previous Chapter 19 (now Chapter 20) has been completely revised and rewritten; this is also reflected in the new title. It now includes, amongst others, important topics such as international capital transfers, international policy coordination, proposals for the management of exchange rates (target zones, etc.).

I owe helpful comments to Giuseppe De Arcangelis, Daniela Federici, Jürgen Heubes, Piercarlo Padoan, Giovanna Paladino, Yang Qian, Luca Ricci, Laura Sabani, Karlhans Sauernheimer. I am particularly indebted to Francesca

Sanna Randaccio, who has made very useful suggestions as regards the new parts and has read the whole first edition with painstaking care, spotting many points that needed clarification. None of the persons mentioned has any responsibility for possible deficiencies that might remain.

University of Rome "La Sapienza"
February 1994

Giancarlo Gandolfo

Table of Contents

Index of Tables		XVIII
Index of Figures		XIX
10	The foreign exchange market	3
10.1	Introduction	3
10.2	The spot exchange market	6
10.3	The forward exchange market and swap transactions	8
10.3.1	Introduction	8
10.3.2	Various covering alternatives; forward premium and discount	10
10.3.3	Covered interest arbitrage	13
10.3.4	Swap transactions	14
10.4	The transactors in the foreign exchange market	16
10.4.1	A digression on speculation	16
10.4.2	Other transactors	20
10.5	The various exchange-rate regimes	21
10.5.1	The two extremes	21
10.5.2	The Bretton Woods system	22
10.5.3	Other limited-flexibility systems	23
10.5.4	The current nonsystem	25
10.6	Euro-dollars and Xeno-currencies: an introduction	29
10.7	International interest-rate parity conditions, and the foreign exchange market	30
10.7.1	Covered interest parity (CIP)	31
10.7.2	Uncovered interest parity (UIP)	31
10.7.3	Uncovered interest parity with risk premium	32
10.7.4	Real interest parity	33
10.7.5	Efficiency of the foreign exchange market	34
10.7.6	Perfect capital mobility, perfect asset substitutability, and interest parity conditions	35
Appendix		36
A.10.1	N-point arbitrage	36
A.10.2	On the measure of the approximation error of the interest differential	38
A.10.3	Marginal conditions and portfolio selection theory in speculative equilibrium	38
A.10.3.1	Proof of the marginal conditions	39
A.10.3.2	Marginal conditions and portfolio selection theory	43
A.10.4	Expectations, interest, parity and market efficiency	46
A.10.4.1	Rational expectations and market efficiency	46
A.10.4.2	The Peso problem	48
A.10.4.3	The Siegel paradox	48
References		49

XIV   Table of Contents

11 Balance of payments and national accounts 50
    11.1   Balance-of-payments accounting and presentation 50
    11.1.1   Introduction 50
    11.1.2   Accounting principles 52
    11.1.3   Standard components 57
    11.1.3.I   Current account 57
    11.1.3.II   Capital account 60
    11.2   The meaning of "surplus", "deficit", and "equilibrium"
                in the balance of payments 63
    11.3   The balance of payments and national accounts 67
    11.4   The international adjustment process and open-economy
                macroeconomics: an overview 73
    Appendix 76
    A.11.1   The presentation of the US balance of payments 76
    A.11.2   Illegal transactions in the balance of payments 84
    References 86

12 The role of the exchange rate in the adjustment process
    in a partial equilibrium framework 87
    12.1   Introduction 87
    12.2   Critical elasticities and the so-called Marshall-Lerner condition . . 89
    12.2.1   The balance of payments in domestic currency 90
    12.2.2   The balance of payments in foreign currency 93
    12.2.3   Partial vs total elasticities 94
    12.2.4   A note on terminology 95
    12.3   The equilibrium exchange rate; multiple equilibria and stability . . 96
    12.3.1   Derivation of the demand and supply schedules; stability . . . 97
    12.3.2   Multiple equilibria 102
    12.3.3   Monetary authorities' intervention to peg the exchange rate . 103
    12.4   Interrelations between the spot and forward exchange rate . . 104
    12.4.1   The various excess demand schedules 104
    12.4.2   Forward market equilibrium and the spot rate 108
    12.4.3   The monetary authorities' intervention 109
    Appendix 110
    A.12.1   The critical elasticities condition 110
    A.12.1.1   The simple case 111
    A.12.1.2   The general case 113
    A.12.1.3   Effects on the terms of trade 118
    A.12.2   The stability of the foreign exchange market 118
    A.12.3   A framework for the simultaneous determination of the spot
                and forward exchange rate 119
    References 122

13 The role of income changes in the adjustment process 123
    13.1   Introduction 123
    13.2   The multiplier without foreign repercussions and the balance
                of payments 124
    13.2.1   The basic model 124
    13.2.2   Balance-of-payments adjustment in the case of an exogenous
                increase in exports 127
    13.2.3   Balance-of-payments adjustment in the case of an exogenous
                increase in imports 129
    13.3   Foreign repercussions 131
    13.3.1   A simplified two-country model 131
    13.3.2   An alternative graphic representation and stability analysis . . . 132

13.3.3	Multipliers and balance-of-payments adjustment	135
13.4	Intermediate goods and the multiplier	137
13.4.1	Introductory remarks	137
13.4.2	Different requirements of intermediate goods	138
13.4.3	Identical requirements of intermediate goods	139
13.4.4	Some empirical results	141
Appendix		142
A.13.1	The multiplier without foreign repercussions	142
A.13.1.1	Basic results	142
A.13.1.2	The balance of payments	144
A.13.2	The multiplier with foreign repercussions	145
A.13.2.1	The basic model	145
A.13.2.2	Stability analysis	147
A.13.2.3	The various multipliers: a comparison	149
A.13.2.4	The balance of payments	150
A.13.3	Foreign repercussions in a n-country model	150
A.13.3.1	The general model	150
A.13.3.2	Stability analysis	152
A.13.3.3	Comparative statics. A comparison between the various multipliers	153
A.13.3.4	The balance of payments	155
A.13.4	Concluding remarks. The empirical relevance of the foreign multiplier	156
References		158

14 The absorption approach and interactions between exchange rate and income in the adjustment process ... 159

14.1	The absorption approach	159
14.2	Elasticities versus absorption: controversy and synthesis	161
14.3	A dynamic model of interaction between exchange rate and income in the adjustment process	164
14.3.1	The basic model	164
14.3.2	A graphic representation	166
14.3.3	Stability and comparative statics	168
14.3.4	The J-curve	172
Appendix		173
A.14.1	Alexander's synthesis	173
A.14.2	A simplified version of the Laursen and Metzler model	174
A.14.2.1	The RR and BB schedules	175
A.14.2.2	The dynamics of the system	176
A.14.2.3	Comparative statics	177
A.14.3	The J-curve	178
A.14.4	The original two-country version of the Laursen and Metzler model	181
A.14.4.1	The basic model	181
A.14.4.2	Stability	183
A.14.4.3	Comparative statics	184
References		186

15 Money and other assets in the adjustment process under fixed exchange rates . 187

15.1	Introduction	187
15.2	The classical (Humean) price-specie-flow mechanism	187
15.2.1	Introductory remarks	187
15.2.2	A simple model of the classical theory	190
15.2.3	Concluding remarks	195
15.3	The monetary approach to the balance of payments	196
15.3.1	The basic propositions and implications	196

15.3.2	A simple model	200
15.3.3	Concluding remarks	204
15.4	Macroeconomic equilibrium in a standard Keynesian-type open model	205
15.4.1	Introductory remarks: The Mundell-Fleming model	205
15.4.2	Graphic representation of the equilibrium conditions	207
15.4.3	Simultaneous real, monetary and external equilibrium; stability	210
15.4.3.1	Observations and qualifications	214
15.4.4	Comparative statics	217
15.5	Monetary and fiscal policy for external and internal balance. The assignment problem. The coordination problem	220
15.5.1	Introductory remarks	220
15.5.2	Internal and external balance and the assignment problem	222
15.5.2.1	Observations and qualifications	225
15.5.3	The policy coordination problem across countries	227
15.6	Portfolio equilibrium in an open economy	230
15.6.1	Introduction	230
15.6.2	Asset stock adjustment in a partial equilibrium framework	230
15.6.3	Portfolio equilibrium and macroeconomic equilibrium	234
15.6.3.1	Introductory remarks	234
15.6.3.2	A simple model	235
15.6.3.3	Momentary and long-run equilibrium	238
Appendix		241
A.15.1	A formal interpretation of the classical theory	241
A.15.2	The monetary approach to the balance of payments	243
A.15.2.1	A simple model	243
A.15.2.2	A two-country model	244
A.15.2.3	The effects of a devaluation	247
A.15.3	Macroeconomic equilibrium in a standard Keynesian-type open model	248
A.15.3.1	The slopes of the various schedules	248
A.15.3.2	The study of dynamic stability	249
A.15.3.3	Comparative statics	251
A.15.4	Monetary and fiscal policy and internal and external balance	254
A.15.4.1	The static model	254
A.15.4.2	The assignment problem	256
A.15.5	The problem of coordination	258
A.15.5.1	The basic model	258
A.15.5.2	International coordination compared to simple pairing	260
A.15.5.3	International coordination compared to internal coordination	262
A.15.6	Portfolio equilibrium in an open economy	263
A.15.6.1	The case of partial equilibrium	263
A.15.6.2	Portfolio and macroeconomic equilibrium	265
A.15.6.2.1	The dynamics of the long-run equilibrium	266
A.15.6.2.2	The stability conditions	268
References		272
16 Money and other assets in the adjustment process under flexible exchange rates		273
16.1	Introduction	273
16.2	The critical elasticities condition is neither necessary nor sufficient	273
16.2.1	The basic model	274
16.2.2	Non-necessity and non-sufficiency of the critical elasticities condition	277
16.3	Monetary and fiscal policy for internal and external balance in the standard Keynesian macroeconomic model, and the choice of instruments	279
16.3.1	Perfect capital mobility	279

16.3.2	The normal case	282
16.4	The alleged insulating power of flexible exchange rates and the international propagation of disturbances	284
16.4.1	The alleged insulating power	284
16.4.2	The propagation of disturbances in a simple model	285
16.4.3	The propagation of disturbances in a two-country model	287
16.5	The new Cambridge school of economic policy	289
16.5.1	Introductory remarks	289
16.5.2	The basic model	290
16.5.3	Observations and qualifications; other versions	292
16.6	Portfolio and macroeconomic equilibrium in an open economy	295
16.6.1	Introductory remarks	295
16.6.2	The basic model	297
16.6.3	Static expectations	300
16.6.4	Rational expectations and overshooting	303
Appendix		305
A.16.1	The critical elasticities condition is neither necessary nor sufficient	305
A.16.2	On the choice of policy instruments	307
A.16.2.1	Fiscal policy	307
A.16.2.2	Monetary policy	309
A.16.3	On the alleged insulating power of flexible exchange rates and the propagation of disturbances	312
A.16.3.1	The one-country model	312
A.16.3.2	The two-country model	315
A.16.4	The new Cambridge school	318
A.16.4.1	The basic model	318
A.16.4.2	An extension	322
A.16.5	Portfolio and macroeconomic equilibrium	324
A.16.5.1	The basic model	324
A.16.5.2	Static expectations	327
A.16.5.2.1	Short-run equilibrium	327
A.16.5.2.2	Long-run equilibrium	329
A.16.5.3	Rational expectations	334
A.16.6	Forward market intervention	336
References		337
17 International capital movements and other problems		338
17.1	Introduction	338
17.2	Short-term capital movements and foreign-exchange speculation	338
17.2.1	The main types of short-term capital movements	338
17.2.2	Flexible exchange rates and speculation	340
17.3	Long-term capital movements	343
17.4	The transfer problem	346
17.4.1	Introductory remarks	346
17.4.2	The traditional setting	347
17.4.3	Observations and qualifications	351
17.5	Exports, growth, and the balance of payments	353
17.5.1	Export-led growth	354
17.5.2	Growth and the balance of payments	357
Appendix		359
A.17.1	Speculation	359
A.17.2	The transfer problem	361
A.17.3	Exports, growth, and the balance of payments	363
References		366

18 The exchange rate ... 367
- 18.1 Introduction ... 367
- 18.2 The traditional arguments ... 367
- 18.3 The experience of the managed float ... 370
- 18.3.1 Introduction ... 370
- 18.3.2 New light on an old debate? ... 371
- 18.4 The vicious circle of depreciation-inflation ... 374
- 18.4.1 Introductory remarks ... 374
- 18.4.2 The depreciation-inflation circle ... 375
- 18.4.3 Is the circle really vicious? ... 377
- 18.5 Exchange-rate determination: theory ... 378
- 18.5.1 The purchasing-power-parity theory ... 378
- 18.5.2 The traditional flow approach ... 380
- 18.5.3 The modern approach: money and assets in the determination of the exchange rate ... 381
- 18.5.3.1 Introductory remarks ... 381
- 18.5.3.2 The monetary approach ... 381
- 18.5.3.3 The portfolio approach ... 383
- 18.5.3.4 Interaction between current and capital accounts ... 384
- 18.5.4 The exchange rate in macroeconometric models ... 386
- 18.6 Exchange-rate determination: empirical studies ... 389
- 18.6.1 Introduction ... 389
- 18.6.2 The reactions to Meese and Rogoff, and the way out ... 391
- 18.6.3 An economy-wide model beats the random walk ... 392
- Appendix ... 393
- A.18.1 A disequilibrium model of real and financial accumulation in an open economy ... 393
- A.18.2 The modern approach to exchange-rate determination ... 394
- A.18.2.1 The monetary approach ... 394
- A.18.2.2 The portfolio approach ... 395
- A.18.2.3 Empirical studies ... 397
- A.18.2.4 Currency substitution ... 400
- References ... 401

19 The theory of monetary integration and the European Monetary System ... 403
- 19.1 Introduction ... 403
- 19.2 The theory of optimum currency areas ... 404
- 19.2.1 The traditional approach ... 405
- 19.2.2 The cost-benefit approach ... 407
- 19.2.3 The common monetary unit and the basket-currency ... 410
- 19.3 The common monetary policy prerequisite ... 412
- 19.4 The single-currency problem ... 413
- 19.5 The European Monetary System ... 416
- 19.5.1 Introduction ... 416
- 19.5.2 The ECU ... 418
- 19.5.3 The indicator of divergence ... 423
- 19.5.4 Monetary cooperation within the EMS ... 425
- 19.5.5 The EMS and the theory of optimum currency areas ... 427
- 19.6 Towards the European Monetary Union? ... 429
- 19.6.1 The Maastricht treaty and the gradual approach to monetary union ... 429
- 19.6.2 The institutional aspects ... 431
- 19.6.3 Conclusion ... 434
- Appendix ... 434
- A.19.1 Fiscal policy in a monetary union ... 434
- A.19.2 Some properties of basket-currencies in general and of the indicator of divergence in particular ... 439

A.19.2.1	The basket-currency	439
A.19.2.1.1	The sum of the weights	439
A.19.2.1.2	Solution for the quantities	440
A.19.2.1.3	Other properties	441
A.19.2.2	The indicator of divergence	444
A.19.2.3	The asymmetry in the bilateral margins	445
References		447

20 Problems of the international monetary system ... 448

20.1	Key events in the postwar international monetary system	448
20.1.1	Introductory remarks	448
20.1.2	Convertibility	450
20.1.3	Euro-dollars	450
20.1.4	Special Drawing Rights	452
20.1.5	Collapse of Bretton Woods	457
20.1.6	Petrodollars	459
20.1.7	Demonetization of gold	460
20.1.8	The EMS	462
20.1.9	The international debt crisis	462
20.2	International liquidity and the demand for international reserves	464
20.2.1	Introductory remarks	464
20.2.2	The descriptive approach	465
20.2.3	The optimizing approach	468
20.2.4	The problem of the composition of international reserves	470
20.3	The traditional analysis of Euro-markets	472
20.3.1	General remarks and the simple multipliers	472
20.3.2	More sophisticated multipliers	474
20.4	The portfolio approach to Euro-markets	476
20.5	An evaluation of the costs and benefits of Xeno-markets	478
20.6	International capital flows and foreign exchange crises	481
20.6.1	Introduction	481
20.6.2	The basic case	482
20.6.3	Exchange rate expectations and the credibility problem	482
20.6.4	The Tobin tax	484
20.7	International policy coordination	484
20.7.1	Policy optimization, game theory, and international coordination	484
20.7.2	The problem of the reference model and the obstacles to coordination	488
20.8	Proposals for the international management of exchange rates	490
20.8.1	Introduction	490
20.8.2	McKinnon's global monetary objective	491
20.8.3	John Williamson's target zones	491
Appendix		493
A.20.1	The optimum level of international reserves and the theory of economic policy	493
A.20.1.1	The cost-benefit approach	493
A.20.1.2	The maximization of a welfare function	494
A.20.1.3	Intertemporal maximization and the normative theory of economic policy	496
A.20.2	The composition of international reserves	501
A.20.3	A portfolio model of the euro-market	504
A.20.4	Capital liberalization and foreign exchange crises	508
A.20.4.1	Introduction	508
A.20.4.2	The actual specification	509
A.20.4.3	The method of analysis	511
A.20.5	The policy coordination problem	511
A.20.6	Target zones	513
References		516

21 The problem of integration between the pure theory of international trade
  and international monetary economics 517
  21.1   Introduction 517
  21.2   An epistemological problem 518
  References 519

Bibliography 521

Name Index 545

Subject Index 551

General Overview of International Economics I

The Pure Theory of International Trade

Index of Tables

Index of Figures

1 Introduction

2 The classical (Ricardo-Torrens) theory of comparative costs

3 The neoclassical theory of international trade

4 The Heckscher-Ohlin model

5 Tariffs, protection, economic integration

6 International trade and economic growth

7 Some refinements of the orthodox theory

8 The new theories of international trade

9 Neo-Ricardian theories of international trade

Bibliography

Name Index

Subject Index

Index of Tables

Table 10.1	Exchange rate arrangements, as of September 30, 1993	26
11.1	Entries in the balance of payments accounts in the five typical cases	57
11.2	A simplified accounting framework for real and financial flows	67
A.11.1	Summary of US international transactions – seasonally adjusted (millions of dollars)	77
A.11.2	US international transactions (millions of dollars)	78
12.1	Exchange-rate depreciation and balance of payments: a numerical example	92
13.1	Coefficients of imports of intermediate goods and open economy multipliers	142
14.1	Effects of a devaluation according to the absorption approach	160
16.1	Non-necessity of the critical elasticities condition	277
16.2	Non-sufficiency of the critical elasticities condition	278
19.1	Composition of the ECU, central weights and rates, threshold of divergence	421
19.2	Grid of bilateral parities in the EMS and compulsory intervention points (as of 2nd August 1993)	422
19.3	Convergence Indicators, 1991–94	433
20.1	Estimated Xenocurrency market size (at end of period, billions of dollars) and growth rates	451
20.2	World international reserves and their composition (millions of US dollars at end of period)	454
20.3	Payoff matrix of the international policy game	485
A.20.1	Optimal and actual currency composition of foreign exchange reserves, 1976 and 1980 (per cent)	503

Index of Figures

Figure 12.1	Various forms of the supply curve of foreign exchange and stability .	100
12.2	Multiple equilibria and stability	103
12.3	Pegging of the exchange rate and monetary authorities' intervention	103
12.4	The arbitrageurs' excess demand for forward exchange	106
12.5	Commercial traders' excess demand for forward exchange . . .	107
12.6	Speculators' excess demand for forward exchange	107
12.7	Determination of the equilibrium in the forward market	108
13.1	The multiplier without foreign repercussions and the balance of payments	128
13.2	The balance of payments and national income: exogenous increase in exports	128
13.3	The balance of payments and national income: exogenous increase in imports, case (i)	130
13.4	The balance of payments and national income: exogenous increase in imports, case (ii)	131
13.5	The multiplier with foreign repercussions	132
13.6	The multiplier with foreign repercussions: alternative representation and stability analysis	134
14.1	Flexible exchange rates and the level of income: the real-equilibrium schedule	167
14.2	Flexible exchange rates and the level of income: the balance-of-payments schedule	167
14.3	Flexible exchange rates and the level of income: a dynamic analysis of the adjustment process	170
14.4	Flexible exchange rates and the level of income: effect of an exogenous increase in domestic demand	171
15.1	Graphic representation of the classical theory of the adjustment mechanism of the balance of payments	193
15.2	A diagram of the adjustment mechanism according to the MABP	202
15.3	Effects of a devaluation according to the MABP	203
15.4	Macroeconomic equilibrium under fixed exchange rates: the real-equilibrium schedule	207
15.5	Macroeconomic equilibrium under fixed exchange rates: the external balance schedule	207
15.6	Macroeconomic equilibrium under fixed exchange rates: the monetary equilibrium schedule	209
15.7	Variations in the quantity of money and shifts in the LL schedule	209
15.8	Determination of real and balance-of-payments equilibrium . . .	211
15.9	Determination of general macroeconomic equilibrium in an open economy under fixed exchange rates	211
15.10	General macroeconomic equilibrium in an open economy under fixed rates: dynamic analysis of the adjustment process . .	213
15.11	The burden of interest payments and the BB schedule	216

15.12	Effects of an exogenous variation of domestic expenditure (case 1)	.	218
15.13	Effects of an exogenous variation of domestic expenditure (case 2)	.	218
15.14	Effects of an exogenous variation in exports		219
15.15	Internal and external balance and monetary and fiscal policy under fixed exchange rate		223
15.16	Internal and external balance and monetary and fiscal policy under fixed exchange rates: the assignment problem		225
15.17	Determination of portfolio equilibrium in an open economy	. .	232
15.18	Monetary policy, portfolio equilibrium and capital movements	.	233
16.1	Macroeconomic equilibrium under flexible exchange rates: the dynamics of the adjustment process		275
16.2	Perfect capital mobility and monetary policy		280
16.3	Perfect capital mobility and fiscal policy		281
16.4	Imperfect capital mobility and fiscal policy: first case		282
16.5	Imperfect capital mobility and fiscal policy: second case		283
16.6	International transmission of perturbations under fixed exchange rates		286
16.7	Static expectations: short-run equilibrium and economic policy	.	301
16.8	Rational expectations: short-run equilibrium and economic policy.		303
16.9	Rational expectations and long-run equilibrium		304
16.10	Rational expectations, "news", and overshoothing		305
17.1	An example of destabilizing speculation		341
17.2	An example of profitable and destabilizing speculation		342
17.3	The transfer problem in the context of the standard macroeconomic model under fixed exchange rates		352
17.4	Growth and the balance of payments according to the MABP	. .	358
18.1	Interaction between the current account and the capital account	.	385
20.1	The portfolio approach to the Euro-market		477
20.2	The Hamada diagram		486
20.3	Game theory and the gains from coordination		488
A.20.1	The dynamics of the optimum reserve level		499

International Monetary Economics
and Open-Economy Macroeconomics

10 The Foreign Exchange Market

10.1 Introduction

By its very nature, the pure theory of international trade treated in Book I does not require any reference to money nor to the money prices of goods (expressed in terms of one or other of the national currencies: US dollar, UK pound, Italian lira, etc.). This derives from the fact (see Chap. 1) that the distinctive feature of the pure theory of international trade is the assumption that trade takes place in the form of barter, or that money, if present, is only a veil, having no influence on the underlying real variables but serving only as a reference unit, the numéraire. An important consequence of this assumption is that, as we have seen (for example, in Sect. 3.3) the international accounts of any country vis-à-vis all the others invariably balance: that is, no balance-of-payments problem exists.

International monetary theory (which is essentially of a macroeconomic nature) deals with the problems deriving from balance-of-payments disequilibria in a monetary economy, and in particular with the automatic adjustment mechanisms and the adjustment policies concerning the balance of payments; with the relationships between the balance of payments and other macroeconomic variables; with the various exchange-rate regimes; with the problems of international liquidity and other problems of the international monetary systems; and so on (for details see Sect. 11.4).

It is then self-evident that as soon as one comes to grips with the problems of international monetary economics it becomes indispensable to account for the fact that virtually every country has its own monetary unit (currency) and that most international trade is not barter trade but is carried out by exchanging goods for one or another currency. Besides, there are international economic transactions[1] of a purely financial character, which, therefore, involve different currencies.

From all the above the necessity arises of a *foreign exchange market*, that is, of a market where the various national currencies can be exchanged (bought and

---

[1] An economic transaction is the transfer from one economic agent (individual, corporate body, etc.) to another of title to a good, the rendering of a service, or title to assets, having economic value. It includes both real transfers (i.e., transfer of title to goods or rendering of services) and financial transfers (i.e. of money, credits and financial assets in general). Transactions can either involve a payment, whatever the form (bilateral transfers) or not (unilateral transfers, such as gifts). As we shall see in detail in the next chapter, what qualifies an economic transaction as international is the fact that the parties are residents of different countries.

sold) for one another. The foreign exchange market, like any other concept of market used in economic theory, is not a precise physical place. It is actually formed — apart from institutional characteristics which we shall not go into — by banks, brokers and other authorized agents (who are linked by telephone, telex, computer, etc.), to whom economic agents apply to buy and sell the various currencies; thus it has an international rather than national dimension, although in the actual quotation of the foreign exchange rates it is customary to refer to typical places (financial centres) such as New York, London, Paris, Zurich, Milan, Tokyo, Frankfurt, etc.

We must now define the concept of *(foreign) exchange rate*. It is a price, and to be exact the price of one currency in terms of another. Since two currencies are involved, there are two different ways of giving the quotation of foreign exchange. One is called the *price quotation system*, and defines the exchange rate as the *number of units of domestic currency per unit of foreign currency* (taking the USA as the home country, we have, say, $ 1.4285 per British pound, $ 0.004931 per Japanese yen, $ 0.0005714 per Italian lira, etc.); this amounts to defining the exchange rate as the *price of foreign currency in terms of domestic currency*.

The other one is called the *volume quotation system*, and defines the exchange rate as the *number of units of foreign currency per unit of domestic currency* and is, obviously, the reciprocal of the previous one (again taking the USA as the home country, we would have 0.700035 British pounds per US dollar, 202.7986 Japanese yen per US dollar, 1750.09 Italian lire per US dollar, etc.); with this definition the exchange rate is the *price of domestic currency in terms of foreign currency*.

The latter system is used by Great Britain and a few other countries; all the other countries use the former.

We shall adopt the prevailing definition, and a good piece of advice to the reader is always to ascertain which definition is being (explicitly or implicitly) adopted, to avoid confusion. The same concept, in fact, will be expressed in opposite ways according to the definition used. Let us consider for example the concept of "depreciation of currency x": this means that currency x is worth less in terms of foreign currency, namely that a greater amount of currency x is required to buy one unit of foreign currency, and, conversely, that a lower amount of foreign currency is required to buy one unit of currency x. Therefore the concept of depreciation of currency x is expressed as an *increase* in its exchange rate if we use the price quotation system (to continue with the example of the US dollar, we have, say, $ 1.45 instead of $ 1.4285 per British pound, etc.) and as a *decrease* in its exchange rate, if we use the volume quotation system (0.689655 instead of 0.700035 British pounds per US dollar, etc.). By the same token, expressions such as "a fall in the exchange rate" or "currency x is falling" are ambiguous if the definition used is not specified. Since many important books and articles in the field of exchange rates have been written and are being written in English by authors using the volume quotation system and by others using the price quotation system, the danger of confusion is not to be underrated.

It should now be pointed out that, as there are various monetary instruments which can be used to exchange two currencies, the respective exchange rate may be different: the exchange rate for cash, for example, is different from that for cheques and from that for bank transfer orders; further distinctions can be present within the same instrument (the exchange rate for banknotes, for example, may be different from that for coins or for different denominations of notes; the exchange rate for a bank transfer order can be different according as the transfer takes place by an ordinary draft or by telex, etc.). These differences depend on various elements, such as the costs of transferring funds, the carrying costs in a broad sense (if a bank keeps foreign currency in the form of banknotes in its vaults instead of in the form of demand deposits with a foreign bank, it not only loses interest but has to bear custody costs, etc.).

These differences are however very slight, so that henceforth we shall argue as if there were only one exchange rate for each foreign currency, thus also neglecting the *bid-offer spread*, that is, the spread which exists at the same moment and for the same monetary instrument, between the buying and selling price of the same currency in the foreign exchange market.

To conclude this introductory section, we must explain another difference: that between the *spot* exchange rate and the *forward* exchange rate. The former is that applied to the exchange of two currencies on the spot, that is, for immediate delivery. In practice the currencies do not materially pass from hand to hand except in certain cases, such as the exchange of banknotes; what usually takes place is the exchange of drawings on demand deposits[2] denominated in the two currencies.

The *forward* exchange rate is that applied to the agreement for a future exchange of two currencies at an agreed date (for instance, in three months' time). In other words, we are in the presence of a contract which stipulates the exchange of two currencies at a prescribed future date but at a price (the forward exchange rate) which is fixed in advance (as is the amount) at the moment of the stipulation of the contract. When the contract expires, or, to be exact, two days before the expiry date, it becomes automatically a spot contract, but of course the price remains that fixed at the moment of the stipulation.

The forward exchange rate is quoted for various delivery dates (one week; 1-, 3-, 6-months; etc.; rarely for more than one year ahead) and for the main currencies: not all currencies, in fact, have a forward market.

The spot and the forward market together constitute the *foreign exchange market*.

Since the exchange rate is, as we have seen, a price which is quoted on a market, the problem comes immediately to mind of whether the exchange rate (spot and forward) is determined in accordance with the law of supply and demand, much as the price of a commodity is determined on the relative market. The problem is very complicated, as it involves the whole of international monetary theory and also depends on the institutional setting; therefore we shall deal with it later, after having introduced the necessary notions (for a general treatment see Sect. 18.5; preliminary treatments are given in Sects. 12.3, 14.3, 16.2, 16.6).

---

[2] To avoid confusion, the reader should note that *demand deposit* is here taken to mean a deposit with a bank from which money can be drawn without previous notice and on which cheques can be drawn (synonyms in various countries are: current account deposit, checking deposit, sight deposit).

10.2 The Spot Exchange Market

Given n currencies, $n-1$ bilateral (spot) exchange rates of each one vis-à-vis all the others will be defined, thus $n(n-1)$ exchange rates in total. The spot exchange market, however, by way of the so-called *arbitrage* on currencies, enables one to determine all the exchange rates by knowing only $(n-1)$ of them. In other words, arbitrage[3] succeeds in causing actual exchange rates to practically coincide with the values which satisfy certain simple mathematical relations which, from the theoretical point of view, exist between them. Arbitrage can be defined as the simultaneous buying and selling of foreign currencies to profit from discrepancies between exchange rates existing at the same moment in different financial centres.

Let us first consider the mathematical relations and then the arbitrage activity.

To begin with, the exchange rate of currency i for currency j and the exchange rate of currency j for currency i are — theoretically — the reciprocal of each other: this enables us to reduce the exchange rates from $n(n-1)$ to $n(n-1)/2$. If we denote by r_{ji} the exchange rate of currency i ($i=1,2,...,n$) with respect to currency j ($j=1,2,...,n; j \neq i$) in the ith financial centre, that is, given the definition adopted, the number of units of currency i exchanged for one unit of currency j[4] (price of currency j in terms of currency i), the *consistency condition* requires that

$$r_{sk} r_{ks} = 1, \tag{10.1}$$

where k and s are any two currencies. In fact, the consistency condition (also called *neutrality condition*) means that by starting with any given quantity of currency k, exchanging it for currency s and then exchanging the resulting amount of currency s for currency k, one must end up with the same initial quantity of currency k. More precisely, starting with x units of currency k and selling it in financial center s for currency s we obtain xr_{ks} units of currency s; if we then sell this amount of currency s in financial center k for currency k we end up with $(xr_{ks})r_{sk}$ units of currency k. The consistency condition $x=(xr_{ks})r_{sk}$ must therefore hold; if we divide through by x and rearrange terms we obtain Eq. (10.1). From this equation it immediately follows that

$$r_{sk} = 1/r_{ks}, \quad r_{ks} = 1/r_{sk}, \tag{10.2}$$

which is our initial statement.

If, to take an example, the exchange rate between the German mark (DM) and the US dollar ($) is 2 in Frankfurt (DM 2 for $ 1), mathematically the $/DM exchange rate in New York is 1/2 ($ 0.5 for DM 1). What ensures that the exchange rate between the two currencies in New York is 1/2 – given the exchange rate of 2 between them in Frankfurt – is indeed arbitrage, which in such cases is called *two-point arbitrage*, as two financial centres are involved. Let us

---

[3] Since, as we shall see in the following sections, there are other types of arbitrage, it is to be understood that here "arbitrage" means arbitrage on foreign currencies.

[4] The reader should note that the order of the subscripts is merely conventional, so that many authors (as here) use r_{ji} to denote the price of currency j in terms of currency i, whereas others follow the reverse order and use r_{ij} to denote the same concept. It is therefore important for the reader to check carefully which convention is adopted.

10.2 The Spot Exchange Market

assume, for example, that while the DM/$ exchange rate in Frankfurt is 2, the exchange rate in New York is $0.51 for DM 1. Then the arbitrageur can buy DM with $ in Frankfurt and sell them for $ in New York, thus obtaining a profit of $0.01 per DM, which is the difference between the selling ($0.51) and buying ($0.5) dollar price of one DM. If, say, the arbitrageur buys DM 2,000,000 in Frankfurt, the expense is $1,000,000; by selling DM 2,000,000 in New York the revenue is $1,020,000 with a profit of $20,000 (in fact equal to 0.01 times 2,000,000). It should also be noted that, since everything occurs almost instantaneously and simultaneously on the computer, telephone, telex, or other such means of communication, this arbitrage does not tie up capital, so that no cost of financing is involved and, also, no exchange risk is incurred; the cost is the fee for the utilization of the telephone or other lines.

In this way opposite pressures are put on the mark in Frankfurt and in New York: the additional demand for marks (supply of dollars) in the former financial centre brings about an appreciation of the mark with respect to the dollar there, and the additional supply of marks (demand for dollars) in the latter brings about a depreciation of the mark with respect to the dollar there, that is, an appreciation of the dollar with respect to the mark. This continues as long as arbitrage is no longer profitable, that is, when the exchange rates between the two currencies in the two financial centres have been brought to the point where they satisfy the condition of neutrality.

In practice this condition is never exactly satisfied, because of possible friction and time-lags (such as, for example, transaction costs, different business hours, different time zones, etc.), but in normal times the discrepancies are so small as to be negligible for our purposes.

Having examined the relations between the bilateral exchanges rates, we must now introduce the notion of *indirect* or *cross* *(exchange) rate*. The cross rate of currency i with respect to currency j indicates how many units of currency i exchange *indirectly* (this is, through the purchase and sale of a third currency, m) for one unit of currency j. More precisely, with one unit of currency j one can purchase r_{jm} units of currency m in financial centre j; by selling this amount of currency m for currency i in financial centre i at the exchange rate r_{mi}, one obtains $r_{jm}r_{mi}$ units of currency i. The indirect rate between currency i and currency j is thus $r_{jm}r_{mi}$. The consistency (or neutrality) condition obviously requires that the indirect and direct rates should be equal, and as the direct rate of currency i with respect to currency j is r_{ji}, the mathematical relation which must hold is

$$r_{ji} = r_{jm}r_{mi}, \tag{10.3}$$

for any triplet of (different) indexes i,j,m. This condition can also be written — recalling that, from (10.2), we have $r_{ji}=1/r_{ij}, r_{mi}=1/r_{im}$ — as

$$r_{ji}r_{im}r_{mj}=1 \text{ or } r_{ij}r_{jm}r_{mi}=1. \tag{10.4}$$

If, for example, the French franc/US $ rate in Paris is 8 (eight francs for one dollar) and the Italian lira/French franc rate in Milan is 219 (i.e. 219 lire for one franc), the lira/$ cross rate in Milan is $219 \times 8 = 1752$ (i.e. 1752 lire for one dollar). It is still arbitrage, this time in the form of *three-point* or *triangular arbitrage* (as three financial centres are involved), which *equalizes the direct and indirect exchange rate*. If, to continue our example, the direct lira/$ rate is 1700, the arbitrageur will (a) buy dollars with lire, say $ 1 million with lire 1.7 bn (since two-point arbitrage is already working, it will make no difference whether this operation is carried out in New York or Milan); (b) sell $ 1 million in Paris for FF 8 million; (c) sell FF 8 million in Milan for lire 1.752 bn thus obtaining a profit of lire 52 million.

The considerations made above on the almost instantaneousness and negligible cost of the various operations also explain why these will continue until the direct and indirect exchange rates are brought into line, so as to cause the profit to disappear. This will, of course, occur when, and only when, the direct exchange rate between any two currencies coincides with all the possible cross rates between them. In practice this equalization is never perfect, for the same reasons as in the case of two-point arbitrage, but here too we can ignore these discrepancies.

It can readily be checked that the cross rates between any pair of currencies (i,j) are $n-2$: in fact, as there are n currencies, it is possible to exchange currencies i and j indirectly through any one of the other $(n-2)$ currencies. And, since all these cross rates must equal the only direct rate between currencies i and j, it can easily be shown that it is sufficient to know the $n-1$ direct rates of one currency vis-à-vis all the others to be able to determine the full set of (direct) exchange rates among the n currencies. Let us in fact assume that we know the $n-1$ direct rates of one currency, say currency 1, vis-à-vis all the others: that is, we know the rates $r_{21}, r_{31}, \ldots, r_{n1}$. From Eq. (10.3) we have, letting $i=1$,

$$r_{j1} = r_{jm} r_{m1}, \qquad (10.5)$$

for any pair of different subscripts j, m. From Eq. (10.5) we immediately get

$$r_{jm} = r_{j1}/r_{m1}, \qquad (10.6)$$

whence, account being taken of Eq. (10.3),

$$r_{mj} = 1/r_{jm} = r_{m1}/r_{j1}. \qquad (10.7)$$

Now, since the rates r_{j1} and r_{m1} are known by assumption, from Eqs. (10.6) and (10.7) it is possible to determine all the direct exchange rates between all pairs of currencies (m,j) and therefore the full set of bilateral exchange rates. This completes the proof of the statement made at the beginning of this section.

10.3 The Forward Exchange Market and Swap Transactions

10.3.1 Introduction

The main function of the forward exchange market is to allow economic agents engaged in international transactions (whether these are commercial or financial) to cover themselves against the *exchange risk* deriving from possible future variations in the spot exchange rate[5]. If, in fact, the spot exchange rate were permanently and rigidly fixed, the agent who has in the future to make or receive a payment in foreign currency (or, more generally, who has liabilities and/or assets in foreign currency) does not incur any exchange risk, as he already knows how much he will pay or receive (or, more generally, the value of his liabilities and assets) in terms of his own national currency. But when exchange rates are bound to change through time, as is usually the case (see below, Sect. 10.5, for the various exchange rate systems), an exchange rate risk arises.

From the point of view of the agent who has to make a future payment in foreign currency (for example, an importer who will have to pay in three months' time for the goods imported now), the risk is that the exchange rate will have depreciated at the time of the payment, in which case he will have to pay out a greater amount of domestic currency to purchase the required amount of foreign currency. From the point of view of the agent who is to receive a future payment in foreign currency (for example, an exporter who will be paid in three months' time for the goods exported now) the risk is that the exchange rate will have appreciated at the time of the payment, in which case he will get a smaller amount of domestic currency from the sale of the given amount of foreign currency.

Naturally the agent who has to make a future payment in foreign currency will benefit from an appreciation of the domestic currency and, similarly, a depreciation will benefit the agent who is to receive a future payment in foreign currency. But, if we exclude the category of speculators (see below, Sect. 10.4), the average economic agent is usually risk averse, in the sense that, as he is incapable of predicting the future behaviour of the exchange rate and considers future appreciations and depreciations to be equally likely, he will assign a greater weight to the eventuality of a loss than a gain deriving from future variations in the exchange rate.

The average operator, therefore, will seek cover against the exchange risk, that is, he will *hedge*[6]. In general, hedging against an asset is the activity of making sure to have a zero net position (that is, neither a net asset nor a net liability position) in that asset. As we are considering foreign exchange, to hedge means to have an exact balance between liabilities and assets in foreign currency[7], that is, in financial jargon, to have no *open* position in foreign exchange, neither a *long* position (more assets than liabilities in foreign currency) nor a *short* position (more liabilites than assets in foreign currency). A particular case of a zero net position in foreign exchange is, of course, to have zero assets and zero liabilities. This can be obtained, for example, by stipulating all contracts in domestic

---

[5] Here, as well as subsequently, "spot exchange rate" is used to denote a generic spot exchange rate belonging to the set of all spot exchange rates.

[6] Some writers (see, for example, Einzig, 1961, 1966) distinguish between covering and hedging. "Covering" (by means of forward exchange) is an arrangement to safeguard against the exchange risk on a payment of a definite amount to be made or received on a definite date in connection with a self-liquidating commercial or financial transaction. "Hedging" (by means of forward exchange) is an arrangement to safeguard against an indefinite and indirect exchange risk arising from the existence of assets or liabilities, whose value is liable to be affected by changes in spot rates. More often, however, no distinction is made and hedging (in the broad sense) is taken to include all operations to safeguard against the exchange risk, however it arises.

[7] Of course, this exact balance must hold for each foreign currency considered separately.

currency. But this hardly solves the problem, because for the other party the contract will then necessarily be in foreign currency, and this party will have to hedge.

Now, one way to cover against the exchange risk is through the forward exchange market. The agent who has to make a payment in foreign currency at a known future date can at once purchase the necessary amount of foreign currency forward: since the price (the forward exchange rate) is fixed now, the future behaviour of the spot exchange rate is irrelevant for the agent; the liability position (the obligation to make the future payment) in foreign currency has been exactly balanced by the asset position (the claim to the given amount of foreign exchange at the maturity of the forward contract). Similarly, the agent who is to receive a payment in foreign currency at a known future date can at once sell the given amount of foreign currency forward.

There are, however, other ways of hedging; the main possibilities will be briefly examined and then compared, in Sect. 10.3.2.

10.3.2 Various Covering Alternatives; Forward Premium and Discount

Let us consider the case of an economic agent who has to make a payment at a given future date (the case of the agent who is to receive a future payment is a mirror-image of this). Let us also list the main opportunities for cover, including the forward cover mentioned above. The possibilities are these:

(a) The agent can buy the foreign exchange forward. In this case he will not have to pay out a single cent now, because the settlement of the forward contract will be made at the prescribed future date[8].
(b) The agent can pay immediately, that is, purchase the foreign exchange spot and settle his debt in advance. To evaluate this alternative we must examine its costs and benefits. On the side of costs we must count the opportunity cost of (domestic) funds, that is, the fact that the economic agent forgoes the domestic interest rate on his funds for the delay granted in payment (if he owns the funds) or has to pay the domestic interest rate to borrow the funds now (if he does not own the funds). For the sake of simplicity, we ignore the spread between the lending and borrowing interest rates, so that the costs are the same whether the agent owns the funds or not. On the side of benefits, we have the discount that the foreign creditor (like any other creditor) allows because of the advance payment; this discount will be related to the foreign interest rate (the creditor's domestic interest rate). For the sake of simplicity, we assume that the percentage discount is equal to the full amount of the foreign interest rate and that the calculation is made by using the exact formula $x[1/(1+i_f)]$ instead of the approximate commercial formula $x-i_f x = x(1-i_f)$, where x is the amount of foreign currency due in the future and i_f is the foreign interest rate (referring to the given period of time).

---
[8] We are abstracting from possible domestic regulations requiring the immediate deposit of a certain proportion of the value (in domestic currency) of the forward contract.

(c) The agent can buy the foreign exchange spot immediately, invest it in the foreign country from now till the maturity of the debt and pay the debt at maturity (*spot covering*). The costs are the same as in the previous case; on the side of benefits we must count the interest earned by the agent by investing the foreign exchange abroad.

In practice things do not go so smoothly (think, for example, of foreign drafts which are discounted and rediscounted, etc.), but at the cost of some simplification they can be fitted into these three alternatives.

In order to compare these three alternatives[9], besides the domestic and foreign interest rates, we must also know the exact amount of the divergence between the forward exchange rate and the (current) spot exchange rate. For this we need to define the concept of forward *premium* and *discount*. A *forward premium* denotes that the currency under consideration is dearer (of course in terms of foreign currency) for future delivery than for immediate delivery, that is, it is dearer forward than spot. A *forward discount* denotes the opposite situation, i.e. the currency is cheaper forward than spot. The higher or lower value of the currency forward than spot is usually measured in terms of the (absolute or proportional) deviation of the forward exchange rate with respect to the spot exchange rate[10]. This is one of the cases where it is most important to have a clear idea in one's mind of how exchange rates are quoted (see Sect. 10.1). If the price quotation system is used, the higher value of the currency forward than spot means that the forward exchange rate is *lower* than the spot exchange rate, and the lower value of a currency forward than spot means that the forward exchange rate is *higher* than the spot rate. But if the volume quotation system is used the opposite is true: the higher (lower) value of a currency on the forward than on the spot foreign exchange market means that the forward exchange rate is *higher* (*lower*, respectively) than the spot rate. If, say, the $ in New York is dearer forward than spot with respect to the DM, this means that fewer dollars are required to buy the same amount of marks (or, to put it the other way round, that more marks can be bought with the same amount of dollars) on the forward than on the spot exchange market, so that if the USA uses the price quotation system, in New York the $/DM forward exchange rate will be lower than the spot rate, whereas if the USA used the other system, the opposite will be true.

Therefore in the case of the price quotation system the forward *premium* will be measured by a *negative* number (the difference forward minus spot exchange rate is, in fact, negative) and the forward *discount* by a *positive* number. This apparently counterintuitive numerical definition (intuitively it would seem more

---

[9] In the case of an agent who is to receive a payment in the future the alternatives are: (a) sell the foreign exchange forward; (b) allow a discount to the foreign debtor so as to obtain an advance payment, and immediately sell the foreign exchange spot; (c) discount the credit with a bank and immediately sell the foreign exchange spot.

[10] We observe, incidentally, that in the foreign exchange quotations the forward exchange rates are usually quoted implicitly, that is, by quoting the premium or discount, either absolute or proportional. When the forward exchange rate is quoted explicitly as a price, it is sometimes called an *outright forward exchange rate*. We also observe, as a matter of terminology, that when the spot price of an asset exceeds (falls short of) its forward price, a *backwardation* (*contango*, respectively) is said to occur.

natural to associate premium with a positive number and discount with a negative one) is presumably due to the fact that this terminology seems to have originated in England, where the volume quotation system is used, so that by subtracting the spot from the forward exchange rate one obtains a positive (negative) number in the case of a premium (discount). Be this as it may, having adopted the price quotation system and letting r denote the generic spot exchange rate and r^F the corresponding forward rate of a currency, the *proportional* difference between them,

$$\frac{r^F - r}{r}, \tag{10.8}$$

gives a measure of the forward premium (if negative) and discount (if positive). As there are different maturities for forward contracts, in practice the proportional difference (10.8) is given on a per annum basis by multiplying it by a suitable factor (if, for example, we are considering the 3-month forward rate, the factor is 4) and as a percentage by multiplying by 100. The reason why the *forward margin* (a margin is a premium or a discount) is expressed in this proportional form is that, in this way, *we give it the dimension of an interest rate* and can use it to make comparisons with the (domestic and foreign) interest rates; expression (10.8) is, in fact, sometimes called an *implicit interest rate* in the forward transaction.

So equipped, we can go back to compare the various alternatives. We first show that alternatives (b) and (c) are equivalent. We have already seen that the costs are equivalent; as regards the benefits, we can assume that the discount made by the foreign creditor for advance payment (case b) is percentually equal to the interest rate that our debtor might earn on foreign currency invested in the creditor's country (case c). More precisely, let i_h and i_f be the home and the foreign interest rate respectively, referring to the period considered in the transaction (if, for example, the delay in payment is three months, these rates will refer to a quarter), and x the amount of the debt in foreign currency. With alternative (b), thanks to the discount allowed by the foreign creditor, it is sufficient to purchase an amount $x/(1+i_f)$ of foreign currency now; the same is true with alternative (c), because by purchasing an amount $x(1+i_f)$ of foreign currency now and investing it in the creditor's country for the given period at the interest rate i_f, the amount $[x/(1+i_f)](1+i_f) = x$ will be obtained at the maturity of the debt. The purchase of this amount of foreign currency spot requires the immediate outlay of an amount $r[x/(1+i_f)]$ of domestic currency.

Therefore, if we consider the opportunity cost of domestic funds (interest foregone on owned funds, or paid on borrowed funds), referring to the period considered, the *total* net cost of the operation in cases (b) and (c), referring to the maturity date of the debt, is obtained by adding this opportunity cost to the sum calculated above. Thus we have

$$\frac{rx}{1+i_f}(1+i_h). \tag{10.9}$$

Let us now consider case (a): the agent under consideration will have to pay out the sum $r^F x$ in domestic currency when the debt falls due. It is then obvious that alternative (a) will be better than, the same as, or worse than the other one [since (b) and (c) are equivalent, there are actually two alternatives] according as

$$r^F x \lesseqqgtr \frac{rx}{1+i_f}(1+i_h). \tag{10.10}$$

If we divide through by rx we have

$$\frac{r^F}{r} \lesseqqgtr \frac{1+i_h}{1+i_f}, \tag{10.11}$$

whence, by subtracting unity from both sides,

$$\frac{r^F - r}{r} \lesseqqgtr \frac{i_h - i_f}{1+i_f}, \tag{10.12}$$

On the left-hand side we meet our old friend, the *forward margin*; the numerator of the fraction on the right-hand side is the *interest (rate) differential* between the domestic and the foreign economy. Formula (10.12) is often simplified by ignoring the denominator, but this is legitimate only when i_f is very small (for a precise determination of the degree of approximation, see Sect. A.10.2). The *condition of indifference* between the alternatives then occurs when the forward margin equals the interest rate differential.

It is interesting to observe that an absolutely identical condition holds in the case of *covered interest arbitrage*, to which we now turn.

10.3.3 Covered Interest Arbitrage

In general, *interest arbitrage* is an operation that aims to benefit from the short-term employment of liquid funds in the financial centre where the yield is highest: we are in the presence of economic agents engaged in purely financial operations. As, however, these agents are not speculators (on whom, see Sect. 10.4), they will cover themselves against exchange risk (by having recourse to the forward exchange market), hence the denomination of *covered* interest arbitrage. Since Keynes (1923) is credited with the first precise treatment of this problem, the theory is also referred to as the Keynesian theory of covered interest arbitrage.

Let us consider, for example, an agent who has to place a certain amount of domestic currency short-term. For each unit[11] of domestic currency placed at home short-term, he will obtain, after the stipulated period has elapsed, the amount $(1+i_h)$, where i_h is referred to this same period. Alternatively, the agent can buy foreign currency spot and place it abroad for the same period of time: as $(1/r)$ of foreign currency is obtained per unit of domestic currency, he will obtain $(1/r)(1+i_f)$ of foreign currency at the end of the period, where i_f is the foreign

---

[11] By considering a unit of domestic currency, we are implicitly assuming that the interest rates are independent of the amount of funds placed or that this amount is not so huge as to give its owner the power to influence market interest rates significantly.

interest rate referring to this same period. To eliminate any exchange risk, the agent can now sell that amount of foreign currency forward: thus he will obtain, after the stipulated period has elapsed, the amount $r^F(1/r)(1+i_f)$ of domestic currency with no exchange risk.

Now, if, for the sake of simplicity, we assume that the costs of the operations are equal, it is obvious that the agent will place the funds at home or abroad according as $(1+i_h) \gtreqless r^F(1/r)(1+i_f)$, whilst he will be indifferent in the case of equality. Since — as can be easily checked — the same conditions hold when the arbitrageur does not own the funds but has to borrow them, or when the funds are in foreign currency, it follows that funds will flow in (inward arbitrage), have no incentive to move, flow out (outward arbitrage) according as

$$1+i_h \gtreqless \frac{r^F}{r}(1+i_f), \qquad (10.13)$$

If we divide through by $(1+i_f)$ and exchange sides, this condition can be written as

$$\frac{r^F}{r} \lesseqgtr \frac{1+i_h}{1+i_f}, \qquad (10.14)$$

whence, by subtracting one from both sides,

$$\frac{r^F-r}{r} \lesseqgtr \frac{i_h-i_f}{1+i_f}, \qquad (10.15)$$

which coincides with (10.12), of course when both refer to the same period of time (as we said above, the computations are usualy normalized on a per annum basis). The condition of equality in (10.15), that is when funds have no incentive to move from where they are placed, is called the *neutrality condition* and the forward rate is said to be at *interest parity* or simply that *interest parity* prevails[12], and the corresponding forward exchange rate is called the *parity forward rate*. Sometimes it is wrongly called *equilibrium condition*: in fact, as we shall see in Sect. 12.4, the foreign exchange market can be in equilibrium even if the neutrality condition does not occur.

10.3.4 Swap Transactions

The presence of the forward exchange market beside the spot exchange market, allows hybrid spot and forward transactions such as *swap*[13] contracts. A swap is a

---

[12] When there is a difference between the forward margin and the interest rate differential such that funds tend to flow in (out), we say that there is an *intrinsic* premium (discount) for the domestic currency.

[13] The swap contracts we are dealing with take place between private agents and are different from swap agreements between central banks, in which the latter exchange their respective currencies between themselves (by crediting the respective accounts held with one another: for example, the Bank of England credits the Bank of Italy's account with 100 million pounds, and the Bank of Italy credits the Bank of England's account with 220 billion lire), usually with the obligation to make a reverse operation after a certain period of time.

transaction in which two currencies are exchanged in the spot market and, simultaneously, they are exchanged in the forward market in the opposite direction. At first sight the swap contract would not seem to have wide potential use: on the contrary, its market is more important than the outright forward exchange market, second only to that for spot exchange.

An obvious example of swap transaction is that deriving from the covered interest arbitrage operations treated in Sect. 10.3.3. If we assume, for instance, that the condition for an outward arbitrage occurs, the arbitrageur will buy foreign exchange spot and simultaneously sell it forward[14].

Another example is related to the cash management of multinational corporations. Suppose that a parent company in the US has an excess of liquidity in dollars, which is likely to persist for three months, whereas a subsidiary in England has a temporary shortage of liquidity in pounds, which is likely to last for three months. In such a situation the parent company can sell dollars for pounds spot and lend these to the subsidiary, at the same time selling pounds for dollars forward so as to cover the repayment of the debt by the subsidiary. This is a swap transaction in the pound/dollar market.

Swap transactions are also carried out by banks themselves, to eliminate possible mismatches in the currency composition of their assets and liabilities. A bank, for example, may have — for a time horizon of three months — a $ 50 million excess of dollar loans over dollar deposits, and, simultaneously, an excess of deposits in pounds over loans in pounds of equivalent value. In such a situation the bank can sell the excess of pounds for $ 50 million spot and simultaneously buy the same amount of pounds for dollars three months forward so as to cover against the exchange risk. Alternatively, the bank could have lent the pound equivalent of $ 50 million, and borrowed $ 50 million, in the interbank money market.

Swap transactions involve two exchange rates (the spot and the forward rate); in practice a *swap rate* is quoted, which is a price difference, namely, the difference between the spot and forward rates quoted for the two transactions which form the swap transaction (this difference is quoted in absolute rather than percentage terms).

We conclude the section by observing that in the forward exchange market the same type of arbitrage operations on foreign exchange takes place as described in relation to the spot market (see Sect. 10.2), so that the direct and indirect (or cross) forward rates come to coincide.

In the forward, as well as in the spot, exchange market, various categories of economic agents operate, some of whom we have already mentioned; it is now time to classify them more precisely.

---

[14] More precisely, since the arbitrageur not only covers the capital, but also the accrued interest, against the exchange risk, the quantity of foreign currency sold forward will exceed the quantity of it bought spot by an amount equal to the interest on the latter accrued abroad.

10.4 The Transactors in the Foreign Exchange Market

It is as well to point out at the beginning that the classification of the various transactors will be made on a *functional* rather than personal or institutional basis. In fact, the same economic agent can be a different transactor at different times or even belong to different functional categories of transactors simultaneously: for example, an exporter who does not hedge in the hope of a depreciation of his domestic currency is simultaneously a trader and a speculator. A possible classification is based on three categories (within which it is possible to perform further subdivisions): non-speculators, speculators, and monetary authorities. To put this classification into proper perspective, a digression on speculative activity is in order.

10.4.1 A Digression on Speculation

In general, speculation may be defined as the purchase (sale) of goods, assets, etc. with a view to re-sale (re-purchase) at a later date, where the motive behind such action is the expectation of a gain deriving from a change in the relevant prices relatively to the ruling price and not a gain accruing through their use, transformation, transfer between different markets, etc. (Kaldor, 1939).

The first rigorous formulation of the equilibrium of speculative activity in a broad sense (that is, referred to a generic real or financial asset) is attributed to Keynes (1936) and was subsequently elaborated by Kaldor (1939) and Tsiang (1958), who applied it to foreign exchange speculation.

Keynes does not explicitly refer to speculative activity but considers an asset holder whose equilibrium is determined in accordance with well-known marginal principles deriving from optimizing behaviour. Let us introduce the following elements (all expressed as marginal proportional rates referred to the same unit of time):

(i) q, the marginal yield of the asset as such, which accrues by assisting some process of production or supplying services to a consumer, etc.;
(ii) c, the marginal carrying cost of the asset (exclusive of the rate of interest), deriving from the mere passage of time (wastage, storage costs, etc.) irrespective of its being used to produce a yield[15];
(iii) l, the liquidity premium, which is the value of the power of disposal over an asset during a period, that is, the price which people are willing to pay for the potential convenience or security given by this power of disposal (exclusive of yield or carrying cost).

The sum $(q-c+l)$ is called by Keynes the *own-rate of interest* of the asset[16]. To this Keynes adds a fourth element, i.e.

---

[15] Sometimes it is doubtful whether certain elements of cost are to be included in c or deducted from q (for example, depreciation of a house deriving from its use ought to be deducted from q, but depreciation deriving from atmospheric agents ought to be included in c). This, however, is irrelevant for the result, as only the difference $(q-c)$ matters: see below.

[16] To be precise, it is an own-rate of interest when q etc. are expressed in terms of the asset as the standard of value, and an *own-rate of money-interest* when they are expressed in terms of money: see Keynes (1936). Our treatment is, of course, in terms of money.

(iv) a, the expected rate of appreciation (or depreciation) of the asset during the period considered. By defining $a=$ (expected price minus current price)/current price, the rate will be positive (negative) in the case of an expected appreciation (depreciation) of the asset. The quantity $(a+q-c+l)$ can therefore be defined as the (overall) *marginal net yield of the asset*.

Therefore an economic agent who can obtain an interest rate i[17] by placing his funds on the money market (or can borrow then at the same rate) will prefer to place them in the asset under consideration if

$$a+q-c+l>i, \qquad (10.16)$$

and is in equilibrium when

$$a+q-c+l=i, \qquad (10.17)$$

where it is understood that i is referred to the same period as a,q,c,l.

The right-hand side of Eq. (10.17) can be considered as a marginal cost (in the case of owned funds it is an opportunity cost). If one prefers, it is possible to shift c to the right-hand side and consider the sum $(c+i)$ as the marginal cost, but it seems more illuminating to use the original formulation, though it is largely a matter of definition.

We must now account for the fact that the investment opportunities include a variety of assets, in which case the asset holder's equilibrium requires the equalization of the net marginal yield of each asset to the interest rate:

$$a_u+q_u-c_u+l_u=i, \; u=1,2,...,n, \qquad (10.18)$$

where the subscript u denotes the asset. This condition is intuitive; see, however, Sects. A.10.3.1 and A.10.3.2 for a rigorous proof and for a discussion of the relationships between this traditional treatment and the modern theory of portfolio selection.

Kaldor (1939) applied condition (10.17) to speculative activity in the broad sense (as defined above), but modified it to the following form (our δ is his r)

$$EP-CP=i+c-q+\delta, \qquad (10.19)$$

where EP and CP are the expected price and current price respectively, and δ is a *risk premium*. With respect to Keynes's formulation, we note the appearance of δ and the disappearance of l. As regards δ, Kaldor observes that the presence of a risk premium is necessary to account for the fact that expectations are uncertain. The greater the dispersion of expectations and the greater the size of commitments (i.e. the size of speculative stocks), the greater will be this premium. The term l has been omitted by Kaldor but, as Tsiang (1958) observes, it can be included in δ with a negative sign. He also observes that Kaldor's formulation of the left-hand

---

[17] The relevant interest rate is the short-term rate of interest, since speculation is essentially a short-term commitment (Kaldor, 1939).

side of (10.19) is a simplification[18] because — as we are dealing with *rates* — the expected rate of appreciation at time t is

$$a_t = \frac{EP_t - CP_t}{CP_t}. \tag{10.20}$$

We shall, therefore, write Eq. (10.19) in the precise form

$$\frac{EP_t - CP_t}{CP_t} = i_t + c_t - q_t + \delta_t. \tag{10.19.1}$$

The application of (10.19.1) to foreign exchange speculation made by Tsiang presents no difficulty. Since we are using the price quotation system, EP_t and CP_t can be interpreted immediately as the expected (spot) exchange rate and the current (spot) exchange rate respectively. As regards the other element in the formula, we begin by observing that the carrying cost is negligible and for all practical purposes can be omitted. Secondly, as we are dealing with short-term assets in foreign currency, the marginal yield q can be identified with the foreign short-term interest rate. Finally, the possible liquidity premium l (which can by no means be secondary when the speculator is also engaged in foreign trade) is included with negative sign in δ. We thus obtain the relation

$$\frac{\tilde{r}_t - r_t}{r_t} = i_{ht} - i_{ft} + \delta_t, \tag{10.21}$$

where $\tilde{r}_t, r_t$ denote the expected and current spot exchange rates respectively, and i_{ht}, i_{ft} are the short-term interest rates at home and abroad (referring to the period considered by the speculator). If the left-hand side of (10.21) is greater (smaller) than the right-hand side, the speculator will increase (decrease) his speculative stocks in foreign currency by purchasing (selling) foreign currency spot, until the two sides are brought into equality.

In general, the agent who expects an increase in the price of an asset is called a *bull*, whereas a *bear* is one who expects a decrease in the price of an asset. Therefore, a bull in foreign currency ($\tilde{r}_t > r_t$) will normally buy foreign currency (have a long position) and a bear ($\tilde{r}_t < r_t$) will normally sell foreign currency (have a short position); both *deliberately incur an exchange risk to profit from the expected variation in the exchange rate*. We have inserted "normally" because the right-hand side of Eq. (10.21) has an important role to play; if, for example, i_{ht} is sufficiently higher than i_{ft} so as to offset $\tilde{r}_t$ being greater than r_t, no bullish speculation will occur, etc. These considerations will be taken up again in subsequent chapters (see, for example, Sect. 15.5.2.1).

We have so far dealt with speculation on *spot* foreign exchange, besides which a *forward* exchange speculation also exists. The latter derives from a divergence between the *current forward rate* and the *expected spot rate* of a currency. If the

---

[18] This simplification is justified if we put the current price at the starting period (period zero) at one and consider only a vicinity of the starting period, so that

$$(EP_t - CP_t)/CP_t \cong (EP_t - CP_t)/CP_0 = EP_t - CP_t.$$

expected spot rate is higher than the current forward rate, it is advantageous for the speculator to buy foreign currency forward, as he expects that, when the forward contract matures, he will be able to sell the foreign currency spot at a price (the expected spot rate) higher than the price that he knows he will pay for it (the current forward rate). In the opposite case, namely if the expected spot rate is lower than the current forward rate, it is advantageous for the speculator to sell foreign currency forward, in the expectation of being able to buy it, at delivery time, at a price (the expected spot rate) lower than the price that he knows he will be paid for delivering it (the current forward rate).

We have talked of delivery etc. In practice, the parties of a forward exchange speculative transaction settle the *difference* between the forward exchange rate and the spot exchange rate existing at maturity, multiplied by the amount of currency contemplated in the forward contract. It should also be noted that, in principle, forward speculation *does not require the availability of funds* (neither command over cash nor access to credit facilities) at the moment the contract is stipulated, by the very nature of the forward contract (both payment and delivery are to be made at a future date). In practice banks often require the transactor in forward exchange to put down a given percentage of the contract as collateral[19]; this percentage depends, amongst other things, on the efficiency and development of the forward market, and on possible binding instructions of central banks.

We must at this point examine whether a situation is possible in which only spot speculation or only forward speculation is present. According to some authors (see, for example, Spraos, 1953), there is a line of indifference between speculating spot and speculating forward, which coincides with the same neutrality condition already examined above in relation to covered interest arbitrage. This opinion hardly seems convincing, in the sense that there would be a reason for such a line of indifference (as in the case of covered interest arbitrage), if the two types of speculation were mutually exclusive, that is, if the funds employed in spot speculation could not be used in forward speculation, and vice versa. But, as we have shown, forward speculation, unlike spot, does *not* require the availability of funds at the moment when the speculator opens a position (unless the bank requires him to put down a percentage of the contract); thus it is possible for a speculator to employ his available funds in spot speculation *and* to open a speculative position forward at the same time. Therefore it is reasonable to think that the two types of speculation can coexist.

According to other writers (see, for example, Tsiang, 1959), speculation is only forward, not in the sense that spot speculation does not exist, but in the sense that any spot speculative activity can be considered as the combination of a covered interest arbitrage and forward speculation. If, for example, an agent speculates by purchasing spot foreign exchange instead of forward exchange, this is equivalent to acting first as a covered interest arbitrageur, who purchases spot exchange against the sale of the same amount of forward exchange, and then as a forward speculator, who purchases the forward exchange from himself (in the

---

[19] When no such percentage is required, the forward speculator does not incur any interest cost, so that — with reference to the general formulation of speculative equilibrium and since in any case no interest gain is involved — only the risk premium will be relevant. If, on the contrary, a percentage is required, the opportunity cost of the tied funds will have to be taken into account.

former capacity) on the expectation that the future spot exchange rate will be higher than the current forward rate, thus yielding him a speculative gain. Similar considerations can be made in the case of a speculative sale of spot exchange. This is undoubtedly true, but we do not believe that such an artificial division is helpful in the analysis of speculation, so that we shall consider the two types of speculation separately.

As regards the problem of how to identify a speculator, the fact that we use a functional classification exempts us from singling out a category of individuals or institutions, an impossibile task because, among other things, speculative activity may occasionally be carried out by agents for whom it is not the main activity. Banks and other financial institutions, brokers, (all acting on their own account and not on account of customers), multinational corporations and any other agent who has an efficient network of information may be a speculator. Even agents classified as nonspeculators can functionally be speculators: the typical example is that of importers and exporters who change the timing of their payments and receipts to get the benefit of expected variations in the exchange rate. If, for instance, a depreciation is expected, and traders do not hedge on the forward market, and, on the contrary, not only pay their debts in advance, but also pay in advance for goods that they are due to receive in the future (as importers), and delay the collection of payment for the goods already delivered (as exporters), then we are in the presence of speculative activities (speculative exploitation of the *leads and lags* of trade). Uncovered interest arbitrage when there are expectations of changes in the future spot rate also involves a speculative position, etc.

The problems deriving from the presence of speculators will be dealt with in subsequent chapters, especially Sects. 17.2 and 18.2.

10.4.2 Other Transactors

A second functional category is that of *non-speculators*. This category includes exporters and importers of goods and services, businesses which carry out investment abroad (for the precise definition of foreign investment see Chap. 11), individual or institutional savers who wish to diversify their portfolios between national and foreign assets on the basis of considerations of risk and yield (excluding speculative gains), arbitrageurs, etc.

Finally we have the *monetary authorities*. These are the institutions (usually the central banks, but also exchange equalization agencies, etc.) to which the management of the international reserves (for a precise definition of which, see Sect. 11.1.3.II) of the relative country is attributed. Monetary authorities can intervene in the foreign exchange market both by exchanging (buying and selling) foreign currencies for their own, and by taking various administrative measures (for example, by obliging residents to make an advance deposit – see Sect. 5.5.5 – or by reducing the periods of time allowed for anticipating payments and for delaying receipts of foreign exchange, etc.). Since the forms of this kind of intervention differ according to the various exchange rate regimes, we shall now consider these.

10.5 The Various Exchange-Rate Regimes

In theory a large number of exchange-rate regimes are possible, because between the two extremes of perfectly *rigid* (or *fixed*) and perfectly (freely) *flexible* exchange rates there exists a range of intermediate regimes of *limited flexibility*. A detailed treatment is outside the scope of the present work, so that we shall briefly deal with the main regimes, beginning by the two extremes. It is as well to state at the outset that our treatment will be purely descriptive, with no discussion of the pros and cons of the various regimes, for which see Sects. 18.2 and ff.

10.5.1 The Two Extremes

One extreme is given by perfectly and freely flexible exchange rates[20]. This system is characterized by the fact that the monetary authorities of the country which adopt it do *not* intervene in the foreign exchange market. Therefore the exchange rate (both spot and forward) of the currency with respect to any foreign currency is left completely free to fluctuate in either direction and by any amount on the basis of the demands for and supplies of foreign exchange coming from all the other operators described in the previous section.

The other extreme is given by rigidly fixed exchange rates. Here various cases are to be distinguished. The first and oldest is the *gold standard*, where each national currency has a precisely fixed gold content (for our purposes it is irrelevant whether gold materially circulates in the form of gold coins or wheter circulation is made of paper currency which can be immediately converted into gold on demand). In this case the exchange rate between any two currencies is automatically and rigidly fixed by the ratio between the gold content of the two currencies (which is called the *mint parity*): if, in fact, it were different, a profit could be made by shipping gold between the two countries concerned. Let us assume, for example, that the gold content of the pound sterling and the French franc is 0.0030 and 0.0003 ounces of gold respectively: the exchange rate between the two currencies is $0.0030/0.0003 = 10$, that is, 10 francs to the pound. If, in fact, the monetary authorities stated a different rate, for example, 11 francs to the pound, anyone could sell pounds for francs, give these to the French central bank in exchange for gold, ship the gold to England and obtain pounds in exchange for it, thus ending up with 10% more pounds (with one pound one gets 11 francs and then $11 \times 0.0003 = 0.0033$ ounces of gold in France, which are worth £1.1 in England). As long as the exchange rate is out of line with the gold content ratio, the outflow of gold from France would continue, a situation which cannot be maintained: either the monetary authorities halt it by administrative measures (for example by suspending convertibility, in which case we have gone off the gold standard system) or are compelled to fix the rate at 10 francs to the pound. It is clear that we would arrive at the same result if the exchange rate were

---

[20] Sometimes this is also called a regime of floating exchanges, whereas "flexible exchange" is used to indicate a system under which exchange parities are liable to relatively frequent changes (see, for example, Einzig, 1966). To avoid confusion we shall stick to the terminology given in the text.

lower, for example 9.9 francs to the pound (gold would flow from England to France, etc.).

To be precise, the exchange rate can diverge from mint parity within certain margins — called the *gold points* — which depend on the cost of transport and insurance of the gold shipped from one country to another. It is self-evident, in fact, that the operations described above are not profitable if these costs exceed the gain deriving from the divergence between the exchange rate and mint parity.

Conceptually similar to the gold standard is the *gold exchange standard*, in which, without itself buying and selling gold, a country stands ready to buy or sell a particular foreign exchange which is fully convertible into gold. This system enables the international economy to economize gold with respect to the gold standard, because the ultimate requests for conversion into gold of the convertible foreign currency are normally only a fraction of the latter. It must be emphasized that, for this system to be a *true* gold exchange standard, the convertibility of the foreign currency must be free and full, so that it can be demanded and obtained by any agent. In this case the system is equivalent to the gold standard. If, on the contrary, the convertibility is restricted, for example solely to the requests from central banks, we are in the presence of a *limping* gold exchange standard, in which case the automatic mechanisms governing the gold standard no longer operate, and the concept itself of convertibility has to be redefined: now convertibility simply means that private agents have the right to freely exchange the various currencies between each other at fixes rates. When convertibility into gold is completely eliminated, even between central banks, we have a *pure exchange standard*, in which a country buys and sells foreign exchange (or a stipulated foreign currency) at fixed rates.

10.5.2 The Bretton Woods System

The exchange rate system that was put into being after the end of World War II and which is called the Bretton Woods system (after the name of the New Hampshire town where the negotiations took place and where the final agreement was signed in 1944), belonged to the category of the limping gold exchange standard with important modifications. To synthesize to the utmost, each country declared a *par value* or *parity* of its own currency in terms of gold, from which the bilateral parities automatically derived. However, at that time, the only currency convertible into gold — at the fixed price of $ 35 per ounce of gold — was the US dollar, which in this sense became the *key currency*. The convertibility of the other currencies into dollars qualified the system as a gold exchange standard, limping because the convertibility of dollars into gold was restricted to the requests from central banks.

The member countries were required to stand ready to maintain the declared parity in the foreign exchange market by buying and selling foreign exchange (usually dollars, which thus became the main *intervention currency*); more precisely, the actual exchange rate could vary only within the so-called *support* (or *intervention*) *points*, which were initially set at 1 percent above or below parity.

The modifications consisted in the fact that parity, notwithstanding the obligation to defend it, was not immutable, but could be changed in the case of "fundamental disequilibrium" in accordance with certain rules: changes up to 10% could be made at the discretion of the country, whilst for greater changes the country had first to notify the IMF (the International Monetary Fund, which is one of the international organizations set up by the Bretton Woods agreement) and obtain its assent.

The obligation to maintain the declared parity together with the possibility of changing it gave the system the name of *adjustable peg*. The idea behind it was a compromise between rigidly fixed and freely flexible exchange rates, and it is clear that the greater or lesser extent to which it approached either system depended essentially on the interpretation of the rules for changing parity. The prevailing interpretation was restrictive, in the sense that parity was to be defended at all costs and changed only when it was unavoidable, but this point will be taken up again in Sect. 18.2.

In any case, the defence of a given parity requires a continuous intervention of the monetary authorities of the country in the foreign exchange market: the authorities stand ready to meet both the market's excess demand for foreign exchange and the market's excess supply when these arise[21]. If, for example, at the given parity the market's demand for foreign exchange is higher than the supply by a certain amount, the monetary authorities must intervene by supplying the market with that amount, because if they did not do so, the pressure of excess demand for foreign exchange would cause a depreciation in the exchange rate. And vice versa in the case of an excess supply of foreign exchange on the market.

So much as regards the spot exchange market. As regards the forward market, the Bretton Woods system did not contemplate a similar obligation to intervene. For an examination of the advisability of such an intervention, see Sect. 12.4.3.

The Bretton Woods system collapsed with the declaration of the *de jure*[22] inconvertibility into gold of the US dollar on August 15, 1971. It was replaced by a situation in which many countries adopt a regime of *managed* or *dirty float*, where no officially declared parities exist (except for possible agreements among specific countries, such as the European countries forming the European Monetary System, on which see Sect. 18.7) and the exchange rates float, albeit with more or less pronounced interventions on the part of the monetary authorities. The managed float belongs to the category of limited-flexibility exchange-rate systems, of which we now give a classification.

10.5.3 Other Limited-Flexibility Systems

The Bretton Woods system could also be classified as a limited-flexibility system, though — as we saw in Sect. 10.5.2 — it was nearer to the fixed exchange-rate

---

[21] The alternative to this intervention is to act on other macroeconomic variables of the system, so as to eliminate or reduce the excess demand, or to introduce administrative controls on foreign exchange. In the latter case, the foreign exchange is rationed by the monetary authorities and economic agents cannot freely engage in international transactions.

[22] It was *de jure*, but the dollar had already been inconvertible *de facto* for various years. The amount of officially held dollars by non-US central banks was, in fact, much greater than the official US gold reserve, and the system was able to keep going only because these central banks did not actually demand the conversion of dollars into gold. Therefore a *de facto "dollar standard"* prevailed: see Sects. 18.4 and 19.1.

extreme. There are four other main types of intermediate systems, of which three have been implemented at one time or another, and one is purely theoretical.

(a) The *Crawling Peg* (also called gliding parities; sliding parities; shiftable parities). This system consists in replacing the abrupt parity changes of the adjustable peg with a gradual modification of parity; the permissible deviation of the exchange rate from parity is maintained within narrow limits (usually $\pm 1\%$). The parity can vary by a maximum prescribed amount during the time unit chosen, for example by 2 or 3 per cent during a year, as originally suggested by J. E. Meade (1964), J. Williamson (1965), and others[23]. This change is also subjected to a short-run constraint, in the sense that the parity cannot vary by more than 1/52 of the yearly amount per week.

This system can give rise to several variants, according to (i) the rules for changing the parity, and (ii) the indicators that have to be monitored in order to ascertain the need for a parity change. On the basis of (i) we have the *discretionary variant* (whether to change the parity within the prescribed limits is entirely at the discretion of the monetary authorities), the *automatic variant* (the monetary authorities are obliged to change the parity if, and only if, certain indicators reach certain critical levels), the *presumptive variant* (the signals of the indicators are a presumption that the monetary authorities should change the parity but have no obligation to do so).

Whichever the variant, all proponents agree that countries should *maintain interest rate differentials* sufficient to prevent such creeping changes in parities from giving rise to capital flows: if, for example, the currency of a country is depreciating at 2% per annum, that country's interest rate should be kept two percentage points above the foreign interest rate.

As regards the indicators, among the many which have been suggested, we can mention: disequilibrium in the balance of payments; change in international reserves; relative inflation rates; a moving average of the previous spot exchange rates.

One kind of crawling peg is adopted, for example, by Chile, Colombia, Madagascar (see Table 10.1 below), but it should be noted that the maximum possible rate of variation in the exchange rate is enormously higher than the 2–3 percent originally suggested.

(b) *Wider Band* (also called widened band). The basic idea is to broaden the band of permitted variation in the exchange rate around parity (i.e. the range between the intervention points, which should be officially declared), while maintaining a fixed but adjustable parity; according to its first modern proponent (Halm, 1965), traces can be found in Robert Torrens. The main variants concern the rules for changing the parity. One variant proposes that the parity (and with it the entire band) should be changed gradually, according to the same rules as for the crawling peg (this case is defined as a "movable band" or "gliding band").

---

[23] According to Williamson (1981, p. 4), the idea originally came from Harrod, who proposed it in 1933.

Another variant proposes, on the contrary, discrete jumps (like the adjustable peg) but with a delayed official declaration of the change. More precisely, when — as a consequence of an irreversible move of the exchange rate to one or other of the margins of the band — the need for a parity change arises, the monetary authorities should change it, but announce the change only after a certain period of time, taking care so to define the new parity as to make the old margin (where the exchange rate was stuck) fall inside the new band. The delay in the announcement (which is meant to have an anti-speculative purpose) has suggested the name "delayed peg" for this variant.

Whether the monetary authorities should intervene or not, when the exchange rate fluctuates within the band, also comes under discussion: according to one opinion, no such intervention should be carried out, so as to allow the system to behave as an ideal freely flexible exchange-rate system within the margins. Others, on the contrary, argue that intervention should take place within the margins to offset abnormal movements before it is too late.

A recent example of this type of system is the EMS (European Monetary System), on which see Sect. 18.7.

(c) *Managed or Dirty Float.* In this system the exchange rates are flexible, so that no officially declared parities exist, but the monetary authorities intervene more or less intensely to manage the float. A practically infinite range of alternatives exists as regards the criteria for this management (see also Sect. 18.4.2). At one end of the spectrum, official intervention may be limited to smoothing out exchange-rate movements: this is the case nearest to the freely flexible regime. At the other end of the spectrum, monetary authorities may pursue a very active intervention policy with the aim of driving the exchange rate towards what they consider an appropriate value: in this case managed floating will resemble a pegged-rate system. An appropriate exchange rate may be estimated by the authorities as an equilibrium exchange rate (see Sect. 18.8) or as an exchange rate consistent with their general economic policy objectives.

As we said above, after the collapse of the Bretton Woods system many countries chose a managed float system. As to the current situation see below, Sect. 10.5.4.

(d) *Oscillating Exchange Rates.* This is a system which involves a widened band *plus* precise rules for intervention which make the exchange rate oscillate within the margins so as to encourage stabilizing, and discourage destabilizing, speculation. It was proposed by the present writer in conjunction with B. Cutilli in 1963 (Cutilli and Gandolfo, 1963; see also Cutilli and Gandolfo, 1972, 1973), but has not been taken up in either academic or official circles, so that — as this is a textbook — we omit its treatment and refer the reader to the works cited.

10.5.4 The Current Nonsystem

After the collapse of the Bretton Woods system, no other replaced it, if by system we mean a coherent set of rules (rights and obligations) and a precise exchange-rate regime universally adopted. Williamson (1976) aptly coined the name "nonsystem" to denote the current situation. In fact, the situation at the moment

Table 10.1. Exchange rate arrangements, as of September 30, 1993[a]

Currency pegged to

US Dollar	French Franc	Russian Ruble	Other currency	SDR	Other composite[b]
Angola	Benin	Armenia	Bhutan (Indian Rupee)	Libya	Algeria
Antigua & Barbuda	Burkina Faso	Azerbaijan		Myanmar	Austria
Argentina	Cameroon	Belarus	Estonia (Deutsche Mark)	Rwanda	Bangladesh
Bahamas, The	C. African Rep.	Kazakhstan		Seychelles	Botswana
Barbados	Chad	Turkmenistan			Burundi
Belize	Comoros		Kiribati (Australian Dollar)		Cape Verde
Djibouti	Congo				Cyprus
Dominica	Côte d'Ivoire		Lesotho (South African Rand)		Fiji
Grenada	Equatorial Guinea				Hungary
Iraq	Gabon				Iceland
Liberia	Mali		Namibia (South African Rand)		Jordan
Marshall Islands	Niger				Kenya
Oman	Senegal				Kuwait
Panama	Togo		San Marino (Italian Lira)		Malawi
St. Kitts & Nevis					Malta
St. Lucia			Swaziland (South African Rand)		Mauritania
St. Vincent and the Grenadines					Mauritius
Suriname					Morocco
Syrian Arab Rep.					Nepal
Yemen, Republic of					Papua New Guinea
					Solomon Islands
					Thailand
					Tonga
					Vanuatu
					Western Samoa
					Zimbabwe

[a] For members with dual or multiple exchange markets, the arrangement shown is that in the major market.
[b] Comprises currencies which are pegged to various "baskets" of currencies of the members' own choice, as distinct from the SDR basket.
[c] Exchange rates of all currencies have shown limited flexibility in terms of the U.S. dollar.
[d] Refers to the cooperative arrangement maintained under the European Monetary System.
[e] Includes exchange arrangements under which the exchange rate adjusted at relatively frequent intervals, on the basis of indicators determined by the respective member countries.

10.5 The Various Exchange-Rate Regimes

Flexibility limited in terms of a single currency or group of currencies		More flexible		
Single currency[c]	Cooperative arrangements[d]	Adjusted according to a set of indicators[e]	Other managed floating	Independently floating
Bahrain	Belgium	Chile	Cambodia	Afghanistan, Islamic State of
Qatar	Denmark	Colombia	China, P.R.	Albania
Saudi Arabia	France	Madagascar	Croatia	Australia
United Arab Emirates	Germany	Nicaragua	Ecuador	Bolivia
	Ireland		Egypt	Brazil
	Luxembourg		Greece	Bulgaria
	Netherlands		Guinea	Canada
	Portugal		Guinea-Bissau	Costa Rica
	Spain		Indonesia	Dominican Rep.
			Israel	El Salvador
			Korea	Ethiopia
			Lao P.D. Rep	Finland
			Malaysia	Gambia, The
			Maldives	Georgia
			Mexico	Ghana
			Pakistan	Guatemala
			Poland	Guyana
			Sao Tome & Principe	Haiti
			Singapore	Honduras
			Slovenia	India
			Somalia	Iran, I. R. of
			Sri Lanka	Italy
			Tunisia	Jamaica
			Turkey	Japan
			Uruguay	Kyrgyz Rep.
			Venezuela	Latvia
			Viet Nam	Lebanon
				Lithuania
				Moldova
				Mongolia
				Mozambique
				New Zealand
				Nigeria
				Norway
				Paraguay
				Peru
				Philippines
				Romania
				Russia
				Sierra Leone
				South Africa
				Sudan
				Sweden
				Switzerland
				Tanzania
				Trinidad and Tobago
				Uganda
				Ukraine
				United Kingdom
				United States
				Zaïre
				Zambia

of going to the press, is that each country can choose the exchange-rate regime that it prefers and notify its choice to the IMF, so that various regimes coexist. Some countries peg their exchange rate to a reference currency (usually the dollar, but also the French franc and other currencies) with zero or very narrow margins; naturally they will follow the reference currency's regime with respect to the other countries. Then there are other countries which peg their currency to a composite currency[24] such as, for example, the IMF's Special Drawing Right (SDR). Groups of countries enter into monetary agreements to form currency areas, by maintaining fixed but adjustable exchange rates among themselves (margins are usually wider than in the Bretton Woods system); an example is the EMS (European Monetary System: see Sect. 19.5). The situation is further complicated by the fact that a country may adopt different exchange-rate regimes with respect to different foreign countries: for example, a country adhering to a currency area such as the EMS keeps fixed but adjustable exchange rates (with widened margins) with respect to the partner countries and a managed float with respect to outside countries. Just to give an idea of the complexity of the current nonsystem we reproduce from the IMF's *International Financial Statistics* a table showing the exchange rate arrangements existing in 1993.

The presence of floating exchange rates makes it difficult to ascertain the behaviour of the external value of a currency. In fact, whilst in a fixed exchange-rate regime it is sufficient to consider the declared par value, in a floating regime a currency may simultaneously depreciate with respect to one (or more) foreign currency and appreciate with respect to another (or several others). In such a situation it is necessary to have recourse to an index number, in which the bilateral exchange rates of the currency under consideration with respect to all other currencies enter with suitable weights. This index is called an *effective exchange rate*[25] and is given by the formula

$$r_{ei} = \sum_{j=1/j \neq i}^{n} w_j r_{ji}, \qquad (10.22)$$

where

r_{ei} = effective exchange rate of currency i,
r_{ji} = exchange rate of currency i with respect to currency j,
w_j = weight given to currency j in the construction of the index; it goes without saying that, by definition, the sum of the weights equals one.

---

[24] A composite currency, also called a "basket-currency" is an artificial currency consisting of predetermined amounts of various currencies. Another example of a basket-currency is the ECU (European Currency Unit). On the characteristics of basket currencies in general see Sect. 19.2.3; on the ECU see Sect. 19.5.2; on the SDR see Sect. 20.1.4.

[25] Usually the effective exchange rate is given as an index number with a base of 100 and presented in such a way that an increase (decrease) in it means an appreciation (depreciation) of the currency under consideration with respect to the other currencies as a whole.

It is self-evident that it is not possible to determine the weights unambiguously; this is an ambiguity inherent in the very concept of index number. Many effective exchange rates thus exist in theory; usually, however, the weights are related to the share of the foreign trade of country i with country j in the total foreign trade of country i. Effective exchange rates are computed and published by the IMF, by central banks, by private banks (such as the Morgan Guaranty Trust Co. of New York), etc.

We conclude this section by stressing again that we have deliberately abstained from giving a comparative evaluation of the various exchange-rate regimes. The reason is that such an evaluation requires familiarity with notions (adjustment processes of the balance of payments, macroeconomic equilibrium in an open economy, etc.), which will be dealt with in the following chapters. Thus the comparative evaluation of the different exchange-rate regimes, which has led to hot debates in the literature, has to be deferred (see Sects. 18.2–18.4).

10.6 Euro-Dollars and Xeno-Currencies: An Introduction

The description of foreign exchange transactions given in the previous sections is the traditional one. The situation has, however, been complicated by the development, since the late 1950s, of an international money market of a completely new type: the so-called *Euro-dollar* system, subsequently extended to other currencies.

In the traditional system, economic agents can obtain loans, hold deposits, etc., in a currency, say currency j, only with country j's banks so that, for example, a German resident can hold dollar deposits only with the US banking system. *Euro-dollars* are, on the contrary, dollar deposits with European banks. The Euro-dollar market began in fact with dollar deposits placed with European banks[26] and used by these to grant loans in dollars. Note that, in general, a European bank can also accept deposits and grant loans denominated in currencies other than the dollar (and, of course, different from the currency of the country where the bank is resident); so that the denomination *Euro-currencies* has been coined (these include the Euro-dollar, Euro-mark, Euro-sterling, Euro-yen, etc.). Still more generally, since similar operations can be carried out by banks outside Europe (Asia-dollars, etc.), the general denomination *Xeno-currencies* (from the Greek xenos = foreigner) has been suggested by F. Machlup (1972, p. 120) to indicate deposits and loans denominated in currencies other than that of the country in which the bank is located.

As regards the Euro-dollar market, various reasons have been put forward to explain its birth. According to some, the origin lies in an initiative of the Soviet Union which, during the Korean war, fearing that its dollar deposits in the US might be frozen by the US government, found it convenient to shift these dollar accounts to Europe, largely to London. Others believe that the initiative was taken by London banks which, in order to avoid the restrictions on the credit to foreign

---

[26] By European banks we mean banks "resident" in Europe (in accordance with the definition of resident which will be examined in detail in Sect. 11.1). Thus a European bank can also be a subsidiary of a US bank.

trade imposed in the UK in 1957, induced the official agencies of the Soviet Union to deposit their dollar holdings in London by granting favourable interest rates. Still another factor is believed to be the US Federal Reserve System's Regulation Q, which fixed the rates of interest paid on time deposits, but which did not apply to time deposits owned by nonresidents. Thus New York banks began to compete for nonresidents' deposits, the interest rates on these rose about 0.25% above the ceiling in 1958−9, and London banks were induced to bid for dollar deposits which in turn they re-lent to New York banks. A practical factor may also have had its importance: due to the difference in time zones, European and US banks are open simultaneously only for a short time in the day, so that Europeans who had to borrow or lend dollars found it convenient to do this directly in London rather than in New York through a London bank.

Be this as it may, the enormous growth of the Xeno-currency markets with their own interest rates etc., has greatly complicated the international financial market: let it suffice to think of the greater complexity of interest arbitrage operations and of the birth of new types of international banking transactions. As regards these, they can be classified in four main types: *onshore-foreign*, *offshore-foreign*, *offshore-internal*, and *offshore-onshore*. The first word of each pair refers to the currency in which the bank is transacting: if it is that of the country in which the bank is resident the transaction is *onshore*, whilst if it is the currency of another country the transaction is *offshore*. The second word refers to the residence of the customer (borrower or lender): the customer is *internal* if resident in the same country as the bank, *foreign* if resident in a country different from that where the bank is resident and also different from the country which issues the currency being transacted; in fact, the customer is *onshore* if resident in the country issuing the currency.

Before the birth of Xeno-currencies, international banking transactions were entirely of the *onshore-foreign* type: an example of an onshore-foreign deposit is a deposit in dollars placed with Chase Manhattan, New York, by a non-US resident. The growth of offshore deposits related to Xeno-currencies has given rise to the multiplication of the three other types of international banking transactions.

An example of an *offshore-foreign* deposit is a deposit in D-marks placed with a Swiss bank by a French resident.

An example of an *offshore-internal* deposit is a deposit in pounds sterling placed with a Dutch bank by a Dutch resident.

Finally, an example of an *offshore-onshore* deposit is a deposit in US dollars placed by a US resident with a Japanese bank.

For a treatment of Xeno-markets, both to explain their multiplication analytically and to examine their impact on national monetary policies, see Sects. 20.1.3 and 20.3–20.5.

10.7 International Interest-Rate Parity Conditions, and the Foreign Exchange Market

The relations between interest rates (domestic and foreign) and exchange rates (spot and forward) explained in Sects. 10.3 and 10.4, are very important and

10.7.1 Covered Interest Parity (CIP)

This is the condition deriving from covered interest-rate arbitrage, explained in Sect. 10.3.2. It holds when there is no incentive for arbitrage funds to flow in or out, namely when

$$\frac{1+i_h}{1+i_f} = \frac{r^F}{r}, \tag{10.23}$$

whence

$$\frac{i_h - i_f}{1+i_f} = \frac{r^F - r}{r}. \tag{10.24}$$

These equations can be written in alternative specifications, that are often used in the literature. From the algebra of logarithms we recall that $\ln(1+x) \simeq x$ for small x; if we let $x = (y-z)/z$ we have $\ln[1+(y-z)/z] \simeq (y-z)/z$. Now, if we take the logarithms of both members of Eq. (10.23), we get

$$\ln(1+i_h) - \ln(1+i_f) = \ln(r^F/r), \tag{10.25}$$

whence, using the approximations to the logarithms just recalled,

$$i_h - i_f = \frac{r^F - r}{r}, \tag{10.26}$$

or

$$i_h = i_f + \frac{r^F - r}{r}, \tag{10.27}$$

i.e. the interest differential equals the forward margin, or the domestic interest rate equals the foreign interest rate plus the (positive or negative) forward margin. The same relations can be obtained from (10.24) by neglecting the denominator of the fraction on the left-hand side. A precise measure of the approximation error made using (10.26) instead of (10.24) is given in Sect. A.10.2.

Equations (10.26) and (10.27) are the *covered interest parity* (CIP) conditions.

10.7.2 Uncovered Interest Parity (UIP)

Let us consider an agent who holds deterministic (or certain) exchange-rate expectations, namely is sure of the exactness of his expectations about the future value of the spot exchange rate. Alternatively we can assume that the agent is *risk neutral,* namely is indifferent to seeking forward cover because, unlike arbitrageurs, only cares about the yield of his funds and not about the risk. Suppose that such an agent has to place a certain amount of funds short-term, that we assume to be denominated in domestic currency (if they are denominated in foreign currency the result will not change). He will consider the alternative between:

a) investing his funds at home (earning the interest rate i_h), or
b) converting them into foreign currency at the current spot exchange rate r, placing them abroad (earning the interest rate i_f), and converting them (principal plus interest accrued) back into domestic currency at the end of the period considered, using the expected spot exchange rate ($\tilde{r}$) to carry out this conversion.

The agent will be indifferent between the two alternatives when

$$(1 + i_h) = \left[\frac{1}{r}(1 + i_f)\right]\tilde{r}, \tag{10.28}$$

where the interest rates and expectations are referred to the same time horizon. If the two sides of Eq. (10.28) are not equal, the agent can earn a profit by shifting funds in or out of the country according as the left-hand side of Eq. (10.28) is greater or smaller than the right-hand side.

If we divide both members of (10.28) by $(1+i_f)$, we get

$$\frac{1+i_h}{1+i_f} = \frac{\tilde{r}}{r}, \tag{10.29}$$

whence, subtracting one from both members,

$$\frac{i_h - i_f}{1+i_f} = \frac{\tilde{r}-r}{r}. \tag{10.30}$$

From these relations we obtain, using the logarithmic approximation explained in Sect. 10.7.1,

$$i_h - i_f = \frac{\tilde{r}-r}{r}, \tag{10.31}$$

or

$$i_h = i_f + \frac{\tilde{r}-r}{r}, \tag{10.32}$$

This condition, according to which the interest differential is equal to the expected variation in the spot exchange rate or, equivalently, the domestic interest rate equals the foreign interest rate plus the expected variation in the exchange rate, is called the *uncovered interest parity (UIP)* condition.

10.7.3 Uncovered Interest Parity with Risk Premium

Both deterministic expectations and risk neutrality are rather strong assumptions, so that in the normal case of agents who are uncertain about the future value of the exchange rate and/or are risk averse, a risk coefficient or *risk premium* has to be introduced. The reasoning is the same as that used in relation to foreign-exchange speculators – see Sect. 10.4.1, in particular Eq. (10.21). Thus we have

$$i_h = i_f + \frac{\tilde{r}-r}{r} + \delta, \tag{10.33}$$

where δ is the risk coefficient or risk premium, expressed in proportional or percentage terms like the other variables appearing in the equation. It is not surprising that (10.33) is equal to (10.21): the motivations are different, but the underlying economic calculations are the same. In fact, for speculators the main element of profit is the expected change in the exchange rate, and the interest rates enter the picture rationally to compare the alternatives. For financial investors the main element of profit is the interest differential, and the expected variation in the exchange rate enters the picture rationally to compare the alternatives. The final result is in any case the same.

10.7.4 Real Interest Parity

The interest rates so far considered are nominal rates. It may however be interesting to reason in terms of *real* interest rates. According to the well-known Fisher definition, real and nominal interest rates are related by the expected inflation rate (naturally referred to the same time horizon as the interest rates). More precisely,

$$i_{Rh} = i_h - \frac{\tilde{p}_h - p_h}{p_h}, \tag{10.34}$$

where i_{Rh} is the real interest rate and $(\tilde{p}_h - p_h)/p_h$ is the expected inflation rate. A similar definition holds for the rest-of-the-world real interest rate, namely

$$i_{Rf} = i_f - \frac{\tilde{p}_f - p_f}{p_f}. \tag{10.35}$$

Let us now consider the uncovered interest parity condition (10.32), that we report here for the reader's convenience,

$$i_h = i_f + \frac{\tilde{r} - r}{r},$$

and assume that purchasing power parity (PPP) holds. PPP will be dealt with at some length in Sect. 18.5.1, and if we apply it to expected changes, one of its implications is that the expected variation in the exchange rate equals the difference between the expected inflation rates in the two countries, namely

$$\frac{\tilde{r} - r}{r} = \frac{\tilde{p} - p_h}{p_h} - \frac{\tilde{p}_f - p_f}{p_f}. \tag{10.36}$$

This relation is also called *ex ante* PPP, since it is obtained applying the expectation operator to (the relative version of) PPP. If we now substitute the expected variation in the exchange rate, as given by Eq. (10.36), into the UIP condition, and use the definitions (10.34) and (10.35), we get the relation

$$i_{Rh} = i_{Rf}, \tag{10.37}$$

which is called *real interest parity*. It should be noted that, if we accept the orthodox neoclassical theory, according to which the real interest rate equals the marginal productivity of capital, Eq. (10.37) is equivalent to the equalization of the price of the factor "capital" (see Vol. I, Sect. 4.3). It is then interesting to observe that, if we *assume* from the beginning that factor-price equalization holds (i.e., Eq. (10.37) becomes our initial assumption), then – by reasoning backwards – we *prove* PPP as a *result* of the analysis (see Sect. 18.5.1).

10.7.5 Efficiency of the Foreign Exchange Market

According to the generally accepted definition of Fama (1970, 1976), a market is efficient when it fully uses all available information or, equivalently, when current prices fully reflect all available information and so there are no unexploited profit opportunities (there are various degrees of efficiency, but they need not concern us here). Then, by definition, in an efficient foreign exchange market both covered and uncovered interest parity must hold.

We heve in fact seen (Sect. 10.3.3) that, if there is a discrepancy between the two sides of the CIP equation, it will be possible to make profits by shifting funds at home or abroad, according to the sign of the discrepancy. But, if assume perfect capital mobility (so that no impediment exists to capital flows), such a profit opportunity cannot exist if the market is efficient.

Similarly, a risk-neutral agent will be able to make profits by shifting funds at home or abroad, as the case may be, if the UIP condition (10.32) does not hold. If the agent is risk averse or has uncertain expectations, we shall have to consider the possible discrepancy between the two sides of Eq. (10.33). This last observation also holds for speculators, as we have shown in Sects. 10.4.1 and 10.7.4.

If we assume the interest rates as given, in the foreign exchange market the variables that must reflect the available information are the spot (both current and expected) and forward exchange rate. Hence, since both CIP and UIP hold if the market is efficient, we have

$$\frac{r^F - r}{r} = \frac{\tilde{r} - r}{r} \tag{10.38}$$

from which

$$r^F = \tilde{r}, \tag{10.39}$$

namely the forward exchange rate and the expected spot exchange rate (both referred to the same time horizon) coincide. In a stochastic context (see Sect. A.10.4) it turns out that the forward exchange rate is an unbiased and efficient predictor of the future spot exchange rate.

In the case of risk premium, using (10.26) and (10.33) we get

$$\frac{r^F - r}{r} = \frac{\tilde{r} - r}{r} + \delta, \tag{10.40}$$

namely the forward margin is equal to the sum of the expected variation in the spot exchange rate and the risk coefficient. In terms of levels we have

$$r^F = \tilde{r} + RP, \tag{10.41}$$

where $RP = \delta r$ is the risk premium in levels.

The assumption of efficiency of the foreign exchange market, together with the various parity conditions, has been subjected to innumerable empirical studies. These have generally not given favourable results for either the market efficiency hypothesis or the parity conditions (see, for example, the surveys by MacDonald and Taylor, 1989, 1990, and by Froot and Thaler, 1990).

10.7.6 Perfect Capital Mobility, Perfect Asset Substitutability, and Interest Parity Conditions

From the theoretical point of view the verification of the interest parity conditions requires *perfect capital mobility,* by which we mean that asset holders are completely free instantaneously to move them abroad or to repatriate them. Imperfect capital mobility could derive, e.g., from administrative obstacles such as controls on capital movements, from high transaction costs, and so on. Asset holders can thus instantaneously realize the desired portfolio composition by moving their funds. An equivalent way of saying this is that the speed of adjustment of the actual to the desired portfolio is infinite, so that the adjustment of the actual to the desired portfolio is instantaneous. It follows that the current portfolio is always equal to the desired one.

Perfect capital mobility thus implies covered interest parity: the domestic interest rate is equal to the foreign interest rate plus the forward margin. It does not, however, necessarily imply interest parity, unless a further assumption is introduced: the assumption of *perfect substitutability* between domestic and foreign assets. This means that asset holders are indifferent as to the composition (in terms of domestic and foreign bonds) of their portfolios so long as the expected yield of domestic and foreign bonds (of equivalent characteristics such as maturity, safety, etc.) is identical when expressed in a common numéraire. Taking for example the domestic currency as numéraire, the expected yield of domestic bonds is the domestic interest rate, while the expected yield of foreign bonds is the foreign interest rate, to which the expected variation in the exchange rate must be added algebraically (to account for the expected capital gains or losses when the foreign currency is transformed into domestic currency). But this is exactly the uncovered interest parity condition.

When domestic and foreign assets are not perfect substitutes, UIP cannot hold, but uncovered interest parity with risk premium will hold. The factors that, besides exchange risk, make domestic and foreign bonds imperfect substitutes are, amongst others, political risk, the risk of default, the risk of the introduction of controls on capital movements, liquidity considerations, and so on.

It is now as well to clarify a point. Perfect capital mobility plus perfect asset substitutability imply, as we have just seen, that both CIP and UIP hold, namely $i_h = i_f + (r^F - r)/r = i_f + (\tilde{r} - r)/r$. It is however often stated that perfect capital mobility plus perfect asset substitutability imply that the domestic interest rate cannot deviate from the foreign interest rate, i.e. $i_h = i_f$. This is not automatically true, unless further assumptions are made. More precisely, the additional property of (nominal) interest rate equalization requires that the agents involved expect the future spot exchange rate to remain equal to its current value *(static expectations)*. This amounts to assuming $\tilde{r} = r$ and so, since there is no perceived exchange risk, the forward exchange rate is also equal to the current spot exchange rate, $r^F = r$.

In the case of fixed exchange rates for this to hold it is sufficient that the various agents are convinced of the fixity of the exchange rate: the current spot exchange rate, in other words, is *credible*. In the case of flexible exchange rates, static expectations are a bit less plausible. However, they remain valid in the case of agents who do not hold any particular expectation about the future spot exchange rate, i.e. hold appreciations and depreciations in the exchange rate as equally likely. If so, the best forecast is exactly $\tilde{r}=r$. More technically, this means that agents implicitly assume a (driftless) *random walk,* namely a relation of the type $\tilde{r}=r+\varepsilon$, where ε is a random variable with zero mean, finite variance, and zero autocovariance.

It should be stressed, in conclusion, that the distinction between perfect capital mobility and perfect asset substitutability (advocated by Dornbusch and Krugman, 1976, and endorsed, for example, by Frankel, 1983), is not generally accepted. Other authors, in fact (for example, Mundell, 1963, p. 475; MacDonald, 1988, Sect. 2.5) include in the notion of perfect capital mobility not only instantaneous portfolio adjustment, but also perfect asset substitutability. We agree with Dornbusch and Krugman and with Frankel in considering the distinction between the two notions important and useful, so that we accept it (see, for example, Sect. 18.5.3.1).

Appendix

A.10.1 *N*-Point Arbitrage

In Sect. 10.2 we have described 2- and 3-point arbitrage and shown how these keep bilateral exchange rates equal to (or very near to) their theoretical values. But one might well ask whether more complicated forms of arbitrage involving more than three currencies (in general *n*) are possible. The answer is theoretically in the affirmative, but negative in practice, as the arbitrage activity involving more than three centres is in reality extremely rare. This does not derive from the complexity of the calculations, which increases as the number of centres involved increases[27], but from an important theorem, according to which *if three-point arbitrage is not profitable, then k-point arbitrage (k=4,5,...,n) will not be profitable either.*

We begin by noting that, as in the case of three currencies treated in the text, also in the *n*-currency case if one starts with one unit of a currency and exchanges it successively for all the other currencies in turn so as to return to the initial currency, one must end up exactly with the initial unit. Thus the following condition must hold

$$r_{ji}r_{im}r_{ms}...r_{vz}r_{zj}=1, \qquad (\text{A.10.1})$$

where $j,i,m,s,...,v,z$ run from 1 to *n* and are different among themselves. Equation (A.10.1) is a generalization of Eq. (10.4).

The proof of the theorem can be given by induction, showing that if $(k-1)$-point arbitrage is not profitable, then *k*-point arbitrage is not profitable either

---

[27] In fact, this would not be a problem today. Any programmable pocket calculator, not to speak of home or personal computers, can easily and immediately perform all the required calculations for *n*-point arbitrage.

(Chacholiades, 1971, 1978). Let us then assume that the left-hand side of (A.10.1) involves k financial centres: if we eliminate one, for example the i-th, we have $(k-1)$-point arbitrage and, as this is assumed not to be profitable, it must be true that

$$r_{jm}r_{ms}...r_{vz}r_{zj}=1. \tag{A.10.2}$$

Now, if k-point arbitrage were profitable, Eq. (A.10.1) would not hold, that is

$$r_{ji}r_{im}r_{ms}...r_{vz}r_{zj}=\alpha, \ \alpha \neq 1. \tag{A.10.3}$$

Dividing (A.10.3) by (A.10.2) we have

$$\frac{r_{ji}r_{im}}{r_{jm}}=\alpha, \tag{A.10.4}$$

that is, as $r_{jm}=1/r_{mj}$ by Eq. (10.2) (two-point arbitrage),

$$r_{ji}r_{im}r_{mj}=\alpha, \tag{A.10.5}$$

Now, if three-point arbitrage is not profitable, Eq. (10.4) holds, which is given here for the reader's convenience

$$r_{ji}r_{im}r_{mj}=1. \tag{A.10.6}$$

Therefore in Eq. (A.10.5) α must necessarily equal 1. Thus (A.10.3) cannot hold and (A.10.1) is verified, so that k-point arbitrage is not profitable.

It follows, by mathematical induction, that when 3-point arbitrage is not profitable, 4-, 5-,...,n-point arbitrage is also non-profitable.

In the text we mentioned the existence of forward arbitrage and it is easy to see, by replacing r with r^F, that the theorem demonstrated above holds for forward exchange as well. Another interesting theorem is that *if three-point spot arbitrage and (two-point) covered interest arbitrage are not profitable, then three-point forward arbitrage is not profitable either.* In fact, three-point spot arbitrage insures that (A.10.6) holds, whilst the non-profitability of (two-point) covered interest arbitrage insures the following conditions (which can be immediately derived from Eqs. (10.14) in the text)

$$\frac{r^F_{ji}}{r_{ji}}=\frac{1+i_i}{1+i_j}, \ \frac{r^F_{im}}{r_{im}}=\frac{1+i_m}{1+i_i}, \ \frac{r^F_{mj}}{r_{mj}}=\frac{1+i_j}{1+i_m}. \tag{A.10.7}$$

From (A.10.7) we have

$$r_{ji}=\frac{1+i_j}{1+i_i}r^F_{ji}, \ r_{im}=\frac{1+i_i}{1+i_m}r^F_{im}, \ r_{mj}=\frac{1+i_m}{1+i_j}r^F_{mj}, \tag{A.10.8}$$

and, by substituting from (A.10.8) into (A.10.6), we get, after obvious simplifications,

$$r^F_{ji}r^F_{im}r^F_{mj}=1, \tag{A.10.9}$$

which is the condition for three-point forward arbitrage (concerning the same three financial centres) to be non-profitable.

A.10.2 On the Measure of the Approximation Error of the Interest Differential

We mentioned in the text — see Eqs. (10.12) and (10.15) — that the neutrality condition in covered interest arbitrage

$$\frac{r^F - r}{r} = \frac{i_h - i_f}{1 + i_f}, \qquad (A.10.10)$$

is often approximated to

$$\frac{r^F - r}{r} = i_h - i_f. \qquad (A.10.11)$$

A measure of the approximation error is obtained by multiplying both sides of (A.10.10) by $(1+i_f)$ and rewriting this equation as

$$\frac{r^F - r}{r} = i_h - i_f - \frac{r^F - r}{r} i_f, \qquad (A.10.10.1)$$

which differs from (A.10.11) by the quantity $[(r^F - r)/r]/i_f$. This quantity can be considered of the second order as it is the product of two relatively small magnitudes; the approximation error, therefore, can be neglected. This representation of the approximation error, however, is not satisfactory as the unknown variable to be determined appears in the error itself. Let us then consider the power series

$$\frac{1}{1+i_f} = 1 - i_f + (i_f)^2 - (i_f)^3 + (i_f)^4 - (i_f)^5 + \ldots = \sum_{j=0}^{\infty} (-1)^j (i_f)^j, \qquad (A.10.12)$$

which converges, since $i_f < 1$. Therefore, from (A.10.10) we get

$$\begin{aligned}\frac{r^F - r}{r} &= (i_h - i_f)[1 - i_f + (i_f)^2 - (i_f)^3 + (i_f)^4 - (i_f)^5 + \ldots] \\ &= (i_h - i_f) + (i_h - i_f) \sum_{j=1}^{\infty} (-1)^j (i_f)^j \\ &= (i_h - i_f) + (i_h - i_f) \frac{-i_f}{1 + i_f}. \end{aligned} \qquad (A.10.10.2)$$

The quantity $-(i_h - i_f)[i_f/(1+i_f)]$ measures the approximation error independently of the unknown.

A.10.3 Marginal Conditions and Portfolio Selection Theory in Speculative Equilibrium

The purpose of this section is twofold. On the one hand, it aims at giving a rigorous proof of the traditional marginal conditions of equilibrium in speculative activity [see Eq. (10.18) in Sect. 10.4] and on the other at showing the equivalence of these conditions to those deriving from the modern theory of portfolio choice.

A.10.3.1 Proof of the Marginal Conditions

Let us denote by A_u, Q_u, C_u, L_u, I the average values of the variables whose marginal values have been denoted by a_u, q_u, c_u, l_u, i in Sect. 10.4; by x the total amount of the funds and by x_u the amount of funds placed in the u-th asset. We adopt the simplifying assumption that A_u, Q_u, C_u, L_u are functions solely of x_u and not of the amount of funds placed in assets other than the u-th, and that I is a function of x.

The corresponding total values are then $A_u x_u, Q_u x_u, C_u x_u, L_u x_u, Ix$, and so the marginal values are

$$\frac{d(A_u x_u)}{dx_u} = \frac{dA_u}{dx_u} x_u + A_u, \quad \frac{d(Q_u x_u)}{dx_u} = \frac{dQ_u}{dx_u} x_u + Q_u,$$

$$\frac{d(C_u x_u)}{dx_u} = \frac{dC_u}{dx_u} x_u + C_u, \quad \frac{d(L_u x_u)}{dx_u} = \frac{dL_u}{dx_u} x_u + L_u, \quad (A.10.13)$$

$$\frac{d(Ix)}{dx} = \frac{dI}{dx} x + I.$$

Therefore, as the marginal values have been indicated by a_u, q_u, etc., we have

$$a_u = \frac{dA_u}{dx_u} x_u + A_u, \quad q_u = \frac{dQ_u}{dx_u} x_u + Q_u, \quad c_u = \frac{dC_u}{dx_u} x_u + C_u,$$

$$l_u = \frac{dL_u}{dx_u} x_u + L_u, \quad i = \frac{dI}{dx} x + I. \quad (A.10.14)$$

It is self-evident that if the average values were independent even of x_u (that is, $dA_u/dx_u \equiv 0$, etc.), then $a_u = A_u =$ constant, etc. It is likewise evident that at least one term on the left-hand side of Eq. (10.18) in Sect. 10.4 must be variable in function of x_u, otherwise Eq. (10.18) could not hold except by chance. Let us now consider the profit of the operator, given by the expression

$$\sum_{u=1}^{n} (A_u + Q_u - C_u + L_u) x_u - Ix, \quad (A.10.15)$$

which has to be maximized subject to the constraint $\sum_{u=1}^{n} x_u = x$.

It should be noted that x can be considered either as exogenously given or as variable. For greater generality we adopt the latter alternative, assuming that the operator can obtain additional funds at an increasing marginal cost, i.e. $di/dx > 0$.

To solve the constrained maximization problem at hand we form the Lagrangian

$$F = \sum_{u=1}^{n} (A_u + Q_u - C_u + L_u) x_u - Ix - \lambda \left(\sum_{u=1}^{n} x_u - x \right), \quad (A.10.16)$$

where λ is a Lagrange multiplier. The first-order conditions, account being taken of (A.10.14), are

$$a_u + q_u - c_u + l_u - \lambda = 0, \quad u = 1, 2, \ldots, n,$$
$$-i + \lambda = 0, \qquad (A.10.17)$$
$$\sum_{u=1}^{n} x_u - x = 0.$$

From the second equation in (A.10.17) we immediately see that the Lagrange multiplier is identified with the (marginal) interest rate, so that, by substituting this into the first equation of (A.10.17), we obtain Eq. (10.18) in Sect. 10.4.

As regards the second-order conditions, it is possible to demonstrate the following important proposition: *the second-order conditions are satisfied if the marginal net yield of each asset is decreasing as the amount of funds placed in it increases, and the marginal cost of funds is non-decreasing*. To show this, let us consider the bordered Hessian whose leading principal minors (starting with the

$$\mathbf{H} \equiv \begin{bmatrix} 0 & 1 & 1 & 1 & \ldots & 1 & -1 \\ 1 & \varrho_1 & 0 & 0 & \ldots & 0 & 0 \\ 1 & 0 & \varrho_2 & 0 & \ldots & 0 & 0 \\ 1 & 0 & 0 & \varrho_3 & \ldots & 0 & 0 \\ \vdots & \vdots & \vdots & \vdots & \ldots & \vdots & \vdots \\ 1 & 0 & 0 & 0 & \ldots & \varrho_n & 0 \\ -1 & 0 & 0 & 0 & \ldots & 0 & -\dfrac{di}{dx} \end{bmatrix}$$

third-order one) must alternate in sign, beginning with plus (these are the second-order conditions). For notational convenience ϱ_u indicates the derivative of the net yield of the u-th asset, that is

$$\varrho_u \equiv \frac{da_u}{dx_u} + \frac{dq_u}{dx_u} - \frac{dc_u}{dx_u} + \frac{dl_u}{dx_u}, \quad u = 1, 2, \ldots, n.$$

The explicit form of the above conditions is

$$-\varrho_1 - \varrho_2 > 0,$$
$$-\varrho_1 \varrho_2 - \varrho_3(\varrho_1 + \varrho_2) < 0,$$
$$\ldots\ldots\ldots\ldots\ldots \qquad (A.10.18)$$
$$\operatorname{sgn} \det(H) = -\operatorname{sgn}(-1)^{n+2}.$$

It is easy to check that the first two inequalities are satisfied if $\varrho_u < 0$; we must show that also the subsequent inequalities (not written in (A.10.18) for brevity) are satisfied if $\varrho_u < 0$, and that the last inequality is satisfied if $\varrho_u < 0$ and $di/dx \geq 0$.

As regards the former inequalities, we shall use mathematical induction and show that, when $\varrho_u < 0$, if the condition concerning the principal minor of order $s-1$ is satisfied, then the condition concerning the principal minor of order s

($3 < s < n+1$) is also satisfied. Having shown this, and since we have already checked that the condition concerning the first principal minor of the succession ($s=3$) is satisfied, we have proved that all the conditions under consideration are satisfied. The proof is rather lengthy, but only involves elementary properties of determinants.

If we denote by $\det(H_s)$ the principal minor of order s, the condition to be considered is

$$\operatorname{sgn} \det(H_s) = -\operatorname{sgn}(-1)^s, \qquad (A.10.19)$$

which has to be shown to hold when — assuming $\varrho_u < 0$ — the following condition holds

$$\operatorname{sgn} \det(H_{s-1}) = -\operatorname{sgn}(-1)^{s-1} = \operatorname{sgn}(-1)^s. \qquad (A.10.20)$$

We have

$$\det(H_{s-1}) = \begin{vmatrix} 0 & 1 & 1 & \ldots & 1 \\ 1 & \varrho_1 & 0 & \ldots & 0 \\ 1 & 0 & \varrho_2 & \ldots & 0 \\ \multicolumn{5}{c}{\dotfill} \\ 1 & 0 & 0 & \ldots & \varrho_{s-2} \end{vmatrix},$$

$$\det(H_s) = \begin{vmatrix} 0 & 1 & 1 & \ldots & 1 & 1 \\ 1 & \varrho_1 & 0 & \ldots & 0 & 0 \\ 1 & 0 & \varrho_2 & \ldots & 0 & 0 \\ \multicolumn{6}{c}{\dotfill} \\ 1 & 0 & 0 & \ldots & \varrho_{s-2} & 0 \\ 1 & 0 & 0 & \ldots & 0 & \varrho_{s-1} \end{vmatrix}$$

(A.10.21)

If we expand $\det(H_s)$ by the elements of the last column, we have

$$\det(H_s) = (-1)^{s+1} \begin{vmatrix} 1 & \varrho_1 & 0 & \ldots & 0 \\ 1 & 0 & \varrho_2 & \ldots & 0 \\ \multicolumn{5}{c}{\dotfill} \\ 1 & 0 & 0 & \ldots & \varrho_{s-2} \\ 1 & 0 & 0 & \ldots & 0 \end{vmatrix} + \varrho_{s-1} \det(H_{s-1}). \qquad (A.10.22)$$

Consider now the first determinant on the right-hand side of Eq. (A.10.22). It can be written, by $(s-2)$ interchanges of two adjacent colums (for example, interchange the first and second columns, then the (new) second column with the third, etc.) in the form

$$\Delta \equiv \begin{vmatrix} \varrho_1 & 0 & 0 & \ldots & 0 & 1 \\ 0 & \varrho_2 & 0 & \ldots & 0 & 1 \\ \multicolumn{6}{c}{\dotfill} \\ 0 & 0 & 0 & \ldots & \varrho_{s-2} & 1 \\ 0 & 0 & 0 & \ldots & 0 & 1 \end{vmatrix}. \qquad (A.10.23)$$

Since each interchange of two columns implies a change in the sign of the determinant, we have that the first determinant on the right-hand side of (A.10.22) equals $(-1)^{s-2}\Delta$. In turn Δ, being a triangular determinant, equals the product of the elements along the main diagonal, i.e. $\varrho_1\varrho_2...\varrho_{s-2}$, so that (A.10.22) becomes

$$\begin{aligned}\det(H_s) &= (-1)^{s+1}(-1)^{s-2}\varrho_1\varrho_2...\varrho_{s-2}+\varrho_{s-1}\det(H_{s-1})\\ &= (-1)^{2s-2}(-1)\varrho_1\varrho_2...\varrho_{s-2}+\varrho_{s-1}\det(H_{s-1}) \quad (A.10.22.1)\\ &= -\varrho_1\varrho_2...\varrho_{s-2}+\varrho_{s-1}\det(H_{s-1}),\end{aligned}$$

since $(-1)^{2s-2}=+1$, as $2s-2$ is certainly even. Eq. (A.10.19) can therefore be written as

$$\text{sgn}[-\varrho_1\varrho_2...\varrho_{s-2}+\varrho_{s-1}\det(H_{s-1})]=-\text{sgn}(-1)^s. \quad (A.10.19.1)$$

It is self-evident that, if $\varrho_{s-1}<0$ and sgn $\det(H_{s-1})=\text{sgn}(-1)^s$ — see Eq. (A.10.20) — then $\text{sgn}[\varrho_{s-1}\det(H_{s-1})]=-\text{sgn}(-1)^s$. Also, if $\varrho_u<0$, then $\text{sgn}(-\varrho_1\varrho_2...\varrho_{s-2})$ is negative (positive) if $s-2$ is even (odd). But if $s-2$ is even (odd), then s is even (odd) as well, so that $\text{sgn}(-\varrho_1\varrho_2...\varrho_{s-2})=-\text{sgn}(-1)^s$. It follows from all the above that both expressions in square brackets on the right-hand side of Eq. (A.10.19.1) have the same sign as $-\text{sgn}(-1)^s$, so that (A.10.19.1) is satisfied. This completes the first part of the proof of our proposition.

As regards the last inequality in (A.10.18), we first show that

$$\det(H) = -\varrho_1\varrho_2...\varrho_n - \frac{di}{dx}\det(H_{n+1}), \quad (A.10.24)$$

where $\det(H_{n+1})$ denotes the determinant of the matrix obtained by eliminating the last column and row of $\mathbf{H}$. In fact, if we expand $\det(H)$ by the elements of the last column we have

$$\det(H) = (-1)^{n+3}(-1)\begin{vmatrix} 1 & \varrho_1 & 0 & 0 & ... & 0 \\ 1 & 0 & \varrho_2 & 0 & ... & 0 \\ 1 & 0 & 0 & \varrho_3 & ... & 0 \\ \vdots & \vdots & \vdots & \vdots & ... & \vdots \\ 1 & 0 & 0 & 0 & ... & \varrho_n \\ -1 & 0 & 0 & 0 & ... & 0 \end{vmatrix} - \frac{di}{dx}\det(H_{n+1}). \quad (A.10.25)$$

The first determinant on the right-hand side can be written, by n successive interchanges of two adjacent columns, as

$$T = \begin{vmatrix} \varrho_1 & 0 & 0 & ... & 0 & 1 \\ 0 & \varrho_2 & 0 & ... & 0 & 1 \\ 0 & 0 & \varrho_3 & ... & 0 & 1 \\ \vdots & \vdots & \vdots & ... & \vdots & \vdots \\ 0 & 0 & 0 & ... & \varrho_n & 1 \\ 0 & 0 & 0 & ... & 0 & -1 \end{vmatrix}. \quad (A.10.26)$$

Since each interchange of two columns implies a change in the sign of the determinant, it follows that the first determinant on the right-hand side of (A.10.25) equals $(-1)^n T$ which in turns equals $(-1)^n(-\varrho_1\varrho_2...\varrho_n)$ as T is a triangular determinant. Therefore Eq. (A.10.25) can be written in the form

$$\det(H) = (-1)^{n+3}(-1)(-1)^n(-\varrho_1\varrho_2...\varrho_n) - \frac{di}{dx}\det(H_{n+1})$$

$$= (-1)^{2n+4}(-\varrho_1\varrho_2...\varrho_n) - \frac{di}{dx}\det(H_{n+1}), \qquad (A.10.25.1)$$

whence (A.10.24) follows, as $2n+4$ is even.

Consider now the last inequality in (A.10.18), which can be written, account being taken of (A.10.24), as

$$\operatorname{sgn}\left[-\varrho_1\varrho_2...\varrho_n - \frac{di}{dx}\det(H_{n+1})\right] = -\operatorname{sgn}(-1)^{n+2}. \qquad (A.10.27)$$

Thus we must show that (A.10.27) holds if $\varrho_u < 0$ and $di/dx \geq 0$. For this purpose we distinguish two cases.

(i) n is even and so is $n+2$. Then, if $\varrho_u < 0$, we have $-\varrho_1\varrho_2...\varrho_n < 0$. Also, from Eq. (A.10.19), $\operatorname{sgn}\det(H_{n+1}) = -\operatorname{sgn}(-1)^{n+1}$ and so, as $n+1$ is odd, $\operatorname{sgn}\det(H_{n+1})$ is positive. Therefore, $(-di/dx)\det(H_{n+1})$ is negative or zero according as $di/dx \geq 0$. It follows from all the above that $\operatorname{sgn}[...]$ is negative and so (A.10.27) holds as $-\operatorname{sgn}(-1)^{n+2}$ is negative.

(ii) n is odd and so is $n+2$. Then, if $\varrho_u < 0$, we have $-\varrho_1\varrho_2...\varrho_n > 0$. Also, from Eq. (A.10.19), $\operatorname{sgn}\det(H_{n+1}) = -\operatorname{sgn}(-1)^{n+1}$ and so, as $n+1$ is even $\operatorname{sgn}\det(H_{n+1})$ is negative. Therefore, $(-di/dx)\det(H_{n+1})$ is positive or zero according as $di/dx \geq 0$. It follows from all the above that $\operatorname{sgn}[...]$ is positive and so (A.10.27) is verified as $-\operatorname{sgn}(-1)^{n+2}$ is positive.

This completes the proof of our proposition. We may now ask ourselves whether the conditions that it involves can be met. The answer is in the affirmative, as it is plausible that additional funds can be obtained at increasing or, at best, constant (but certainly not decreasing) marginal cost, and that the components a_u, q_u, l_u of the marginal net yield are non-increasing (and at least one decreasing) as x_u increases, and/or that c_u is non-decreasing (or even increasing) as x_u increases. In any case, as the conditions $\varrho_u < 0$, $di/dx \geq 0$ are only sufficient, but not necessary, for the second-order conditions to hold, these may hold even if either or both of the above inequalities do not hold.

A.10.3.2 Marginal Conditions and Portfolio Selection Theory

Speculative equilibrium, involving a problem of choice among different assets under uncertainty, easily lends itself to a treatment in terms of the theory of portfolio selection. According to this theory, originated by Markowitz (1952, 1959; see also Tobin, 1958, and Hicks, 1967b), the first step is to find the set of *efficient* portfolios[28], amongst which the economic agent then selects the *optimum* one. This second step is carried out by maximizing the agent's utility function, which has as its arguments the expected return of the portfolio and its riskiness (measured for example by the variance or by the standard deviation)[29]. As a matter of fact the speculator, who willingly incurs an exchange risk in the expectation of a speculative gain, will give a greater weight to expected return, and a smaller weight to risk, than the average investor, but this is simply a matter of a different utility function, and does not undermine the basic theory. The aim of this section is to show that the traditional formulation of the speculative equilibrium is equivalent to the modern formulation in terms of portfolio choice.

For this purpose it is convenient to use Hicks' formulation of the theory of portfolio selection. This shows (Hicks, 1967b) that the choice made according to this theory can be described in terms of the equalization of the *marginal advantages* of the various assets, where the marginal advantage of an asset is its expected net yield minus a factor determined by the additional uncertainty deriving from the placing of the marginal unit of funds in that asset. Now, if we consider Eqs. (10.18) and (10.19) in Sect. 10.4, and allow for the modifications introduced by Kaldor and Tsiang — see Eqs. (10.20) and (10.10.1) — we can write the following relation

$$(a_1 + q_1 - c_1 - i) - \delta_1 = (a_2 + q_2 - c_2 - i) - \delta_2 = ... =$$
$$= (a_n + q_n - c_n - i) - \delta_n. \quad (A.10.28)$$

The expression

$$M_u = (a_u + q_u - c_u - i) - \delta_u, \quad u = 1, 2, ..., n, \quad (A.10.29)$$

coincides with the marginal advantage of Hicks, since $(a_u + q_u - c_u - i)$ represents the expected net yield and δ_u is a marginal risk coefficient to account for uncertainty (see Sect. 10.4). Equation (A.10.28) does therefore coincide with the result obtained through portfolio selection theory.

One point needs to be clarified. In the risk coefficient (δ_u) of the traditional theory, both *objective* elements (past observed variability of the returns as an index of the future variability, etc.) and *subjective* elements (different individual attitudes towards risk — the coefficient will be different, *ceteris paribus*, for a risk lover and a risk averter, etc.) are present.

The proof of the equivalence of the two formulations can be given more rigorously as follows. Let

$$U = U(E, V), \quad \frac{\partial U}{\partial E} > 0, \quad \frac{\partial U}{\partial V} < 0, \quad (A.10.30)$$

---

[28] A portfolio (that is, a given distribution among the various assets of available funds) is efficient if a higher expected return can be obtained only by taking on more risk (or, conversely, lower risk can be achieved only by giving up expected return). Formally, the set of efficient portfolios is obtained by maximizing expected return for given risk (or minimizing risk for given expected return) under the appropriate constraints.

[29] This implies that the variance (or standard deviation) can be taken as an appropriate measure of risk. Actually, this is true only under certain assumptions (see, for example, Levy and Sarnat, 1972), whose discussion is outside the scope of the present work.

or

$$U = U(E,S), \quad \frac{\partial U}{\partial E} > 0, \quad \frac{\partial U}{\partial S} < 0, \tag{A.10.31}$$

be the utility function, where E represents the expected return (in the sense of mathematical expectation) of the portfolio, V and $S = \sqrt{V}$ the variance and standard deviation respectively. The maximization of this function over the set of efficient portfolios implies (Hicks, 1967b, p. 111) that "the marginal utilities of all investments that are used must be equalized, while those of investments that are not used must be less than this common value". Therefore for each asset j the following magnitudes must be equal

$$U_j = U_E E_j + U_S S_j = \frac{\partial U}{\partial E} \frac{\partial E}{\partial x_j} + \frac{\partial U}{\partial S} \frac{\partial S}{\partial x_j}. \tag{A.10.32}$$

If we divide through by U_E we obtain the formal expression for the marginal advantages M_j:

$$M_j = \frac{U_j}{U_E} = \frac{\partial E}{\partial x_j} - W \frac{\partial S}{\partial x_j}, \tag{A.10.33}$$

where $W = -(\partial U/\partial S)/(\partial U/\partial E)$ is the marginal rate of substitution between E and S.

The optimum condition can, therefore, be also expressed as the equalization of the marginal advantages. If we indicate by μ_j the average (unit) expected yield of the j-th asset, we have

$$\frac{\partial E}{\partial x_j} = \mu_j, \tag{A.10.34}$$

since $E = \sum_{j=1}^{n} \mu_j x_j$ by definition. Further, $\partial S/\partial x_j$ is a function not only of x_j but also of the various amounts of funds invested in the other assets; this is due to the presence of the covariances between the yields of the various assets in the definition of the variance of the portfolio, $V = \sum_{i=1}^{n} \sum_{j=1}^{n} \sigma_{ij} x_i x_j$. If these covariances were zero (i.e., $\sigma_{ij} = 0$ for $i \neq j$), then $\partial S/\partial x_j$ would be a function of x_j only, but this is possible only when the yields of the various assets are independent of one another. In any case, $\partial S/\partial x_j$ reflects what have been called above the objective elements of risk, because the marginal rate of substitution between E and S (which reflects the investor's attitude towards risk) depends on the form of the agent's utility function. As E and S, and therefore $\partial U/\partial S$ and $\partial U/\partial E$, are functions of all x_j's, then W is also, so that we can write

$$W \frac{\partial S}{\partial x_j} = \delta_j \tag{A.10.35}$$

where $\delta_j(x_1, x_2, ..., x_n)$ is a marginal risk coefficient reflecting both objective and subjective factors. Therefore Eq. (A.10.33) can be rewritten, account being taken of (A.10.34) and (A.10.35), as

$$M_j = \mu_j - \delta_j, \tag{A.10.33.1}$$

which must have a common value for all j's. The expected net yield, in turn, can be specified as $a_j + q_j - c_j - i$; it follows that (A.10.33.1) coincides with (A.10.29) and the equalization of the marginal advantages coincides with the traditional condition (A.10.28). This completes the proof of the formal equivalence between the traditional theory and the results of portfolio selection theory. What portfolio theory does is to give a precise derivation of the risk coefficient δ and a method to compute it (at least as far as the objective elements are concerned), which in the traditional theory remained rather vague, but from the formal point of view the final formulations of the two approaches are equivalent[30]. Therefore the formulation of the speculative equilibrium used in the text and consisting in the equalization of expected net marginal yields, account being taken of a risk coefficient, is valid both in the context of the traditional theory and in the context of the theory of portfolio choice.

A.10.4 Expectations, Interest Parity and Market Efficiency

A.10.4.1 Rational Expectations and Market Efficiency

Let us consider an agent who forms his exchange rate expectations according to the rational expectations hypothesis (REH). As is well known, rational expectations, introduced by Muth (1960, 1961), mean that the forecasting agent uses all available information, including the knowledge of the "true" model that determines the evolution of the variable(s) concerned. We recall that expectations formed according to REH have the following properties:

---

[30] To be precise, some differences exist in two respects:
(a) in portfolio theory μ_j is generally assumed constant, whereas in the traditional formulation it is usually assumed to be a decreasing function of x_j.
(b) in the traditional formulation δ_j is usually assumed a function solely of x_j, whilst in portfolio theory the expression that we have interpreted as δ_j depends on all the x_j's. Besides, portfolio theory enables one to quantify $\partial \delta_j / \partial x_j$ which, for the objective part, depends on

$$\frac{\partial S}{\partial x_j} = \frac{1}{2\sqrt{V}} \frac{\partial V}{\partial x_j} = \frac{1}{2\sqrt{V}} \left(2\sigma_{jj} x_j + 2 \sum_{i=1/i \neq j}^{n} \sigma_{ij} x_i \right),$$

and, for the subjective part, on

$$\frac{dW}{dx_j} = -\frac{\left(\frac{\partial^2 U}{\partial S^2} \frac{\partial S}{\partial x_j} + \frac{\partial^2 U}{\partial S \partial E} \frac{\partial E}{\partial x_j} \right) \frac{\partial U}{\partial E} - \frac{\partial U}{\partial S} \left(\frac{\partial^2 U}{\partial E^2} \frac{\partial E}{\partial x_j} + \frac{\partial^2 U}{\partial S \partial E} \frac{\partial S}{\partial x_j} \right)}{\left(\frac{\partial U}{\partial E} \right)^2}.$$

These differences, however, do not impinge on the fact that the condition for speculative equilibrium can in any case be expressed as the equalization of expected net marginal yields, account taken of a risk coefficient.

a) there are no *systematic* forecast errors, as these errors are stochastically distributed with mean zero *(unbiasedness)*. If $_{t-1}\tilde{r}_t$ denotes the expected exchange rate (expectations are formed at time $t-1$ with reference to period t) then we have $_{t-1}\tilde{r}_t - r_t = \epsilon_t$, where $E(\epsilon_t) = 0$ for all t.
b) Forecast errors are *uncorrelated*, i.e. $E(\epsilon_t \epsilon_{t-i}) = 0$ for any integer i.
c) Forecasts errors are not correlated with the past history of the variable being forecasted nor with other variables contained in the information set, I_{t-1}, available at the time of forecast *(orthogonality,* i.e. $E(\epsilon_t | I_{t-1}) = 0)$. This property implies that RE are statistically *efficient,* namely the variance of the forecast error is lower than that of forecasts obtained with any other method (minimum variance property).

Rational expectations are a particularly convenient way of describing expectation formation in an efficient market. This is because REH, like EMH (efficient market hypothesis), presumes that economic agents do not make systematic errors when making their predictions. If we consider expectations formed at time t for period $t+1$ and apply property (a), we have

$$r_{t+1} = {}_t\tilde{r}_{t+1} + \epsilon_{t+1}, \tag{A.10.36}$$

which states that the actual future spot exchange rate corresponds to that which was anticipated by rational economic agents plus a (positive or negative) "well behaved" random error. Here "rational" is taken to mean "using REH", and "well behaved" is taken to mean "independently distributed with mean zero" (properties (b) and (c) above).

Let us next assume that economic agents are risk neutral, so that there is no risk premium (see Sects. 10.7.2 and 10.7.3). As we know (see Eq. (10.39) in the text), in this case EMH implies

$$r_t^F = {}_t\tilde{r}_{t+1}, \tag{A.10.37}$$

where r_t^F is the forward exchange rate quoted at time t (for delivery at time $t+1$). If we substitute equation (A.10.37) into equation (A.10.36) we have

$$r_{t+1} = r_t^F + \epsilon_{t+1}. \tag{A.10.38}$$

This equation states that, so long as agents have RE and there is no risk premium, the forward exchange rate is the best (i.e., minimum variance) unbiased predictor of the future spot exchange rate.

This conclusion does no longer hold if there is a risk premium. Instead of Eq. (10.39) we must now use Eq. (10.41), so that instead of Eq. (A.10.38) we get

$$r_{t+1} = r_t^F + RP_t + \epsilon_{t+1}. \tag{A.10.39}$$

Equation (A.10.39) shows that the use of the forward rate to predict the future spot rate may give rise to systematic forecast errors because of the presence of a risk premium.

The efficiency of the foreign exchange markets has been subject to extensive empirical testing. The result of these tests reject the EMH hypothesis (for a survey see MacDonald and Taylor, 1992, Sect. III). The fact is that what is usually tested is the joint hypothesis of rational expectations and risk neutrality. Hence it is not possible to say which leg of the joint hypothesis is responsible for

A.10.4.2 The Peso Problem

The consequences, on the relationships expressing REH and EMH (see the previous section), of the existence of a positive probability of a drastic event (for example the abandonment of fixed exchange rates) constitute the so called "peso problem". The name derives from the fact that these consequences were first observed in the foreign exchange market for the Mexican peso. In the period from April 1954 to August 1976, the peso/US$ spot exchange rate remained fixed at 0.080 dollars per peso. However, during all this period the forward exchange rate of the peso vis-à-vis the dollar was always smaller than the spot rate prevailing on the day of delivery (which was of course the given fixed spot rate). One possible inerpretation of this evidence is to take it as rejecting REH and/or EMH. Another possibility is to interpret this evidence as reflecting the existence of a risk premium.

On 31 August 1976 the Mexican authorities abandoned the fixed parity, and the peso dropped to around 0.050 dollars per peso. Forward contracts stipulated before 31 August 1976 with a maturity after that date, used a forward exchange rate that turned out to be higher than the post-devaluation spot rate, thus denoting that agents had underestimated the extent of the devaluation. This, again, could be interpreted as rejecting REH and EMH.

It was however shown by Lizondo (1983) that the peso-market evidence is perfectly consistent with both REH and EMH if economic agents hypothesize the existence, also in the fixed-parity period, of a positive probability of a devaluation in forming their expectations. For further studies of the peso paradox see Lewis (1992).

A.10.4.3 The Siegel Paradox

In empirical analyses it is customary to express the forward and spot exchange rates in logarithms. This serves to avoid the Siegel paradox. Siegel (1972) noted that, if the equality between the forward exchange rate and the expected spot rate holds, it must hold on both sides of the foreign exchange. This means that it must also hold for the foreign country. If we use the expectation operator E and recall the consistency conditions (see Sect. 10.2), we have

$$r_t^F = E_t(r_{t+1}) \tag{A.10.40}$$

for the home country, and

$$\frac{1}{r_t^F} = E_t\left(\frac{1}{r_{t+1}}\right) \tag{A.10.41}$$

for the foreign country. However, a well-known theorem in statistics (Jensen's inequality: see, for example, Mood et al, 1974, Sect. 4.5) states that $E(1/x) > 1/E(x)$ for any stochastic variable x. It follows that (A.10.40) and (A.10.41) cannot simultaneously be true. Although it has been demonstrated that Siegel's paradox is irrelevant in empirical work (McCulloch, 1975; see, however, Sinn, 1989, for an opposite view), the conceptual problem remains. This can be avoided if one defines the variables in logarithms. Then

$$\ln r_{t+1}^F = E_t(\ln r_{t+1}) \tag{A.10.42}$$

and

$$\ln\left(\frac{1}{r_{t+1}^F}\right) = E_t\left(\frac{1}{\ln r_{t+1}}\right). \tag{A.10.43}$$

Since $\ln(1/r_{t+1}^F) = -\ln r_{t+1}^F$, and $E_t(1/\ln r_{t+1}) = -E_t(\ln r_{t+1})$, conditions (A.10.42) and (A.10.43) are simultaneously true.

References

The references will be indicated only by name(s) and date. Complete information is contained in the Bibliography at the end of this volume.

Aliber, R.Z. (ed.), 1969
Argy, V., 1981, Part One and Chap. 19
Bell, G., 1973
Brown, B., 1983
Chacholiades, M., 1971
Chacholiades, M., 1978, Chap. 1
Cohen, B., 1969, Chap. 2
Cutilli, B. and G. Gandolfo, 1963
Cutilli, B. and G. Gandolfo, 1972
Cutilli, B. and G. Gandolfo, 1973
Dornbusch, R. and P. Krugman, 1976
Einzig, P., 1966
Fama, E.F., 1970, 1976
Frankel, J.A., 1983
Froot, K.A. and R.H. Thaler, 1990
Grubel, H.G., 1966, Part I
Grubel, H.G., 1977, Chaps. 10–12
Hakkio, C.S., 1981
Halm, G.N., 1965
Hicks, J.R., 1967b
IMF, *Annual Report on Exchange Rate and Exchange Restrictions*.
Kaldor, N., 1939
Keynes, J.M., 1923, Chap. 3, Sect. 4
Keynes, J.M., 1936, Chap. 17, Sect. II
Kindleberger, C.P. and P.H. Lindert, 1978, Chap. 13 and App. G
Levy, H. and M. Sarnat, 1972
Lewis, K.K., 1992

Lizondo, J.S., 1983
MacDonald, R., 1988
MacDonald, R. and M.P. Taylor, 1989, 1990, 1992
Machlup, F., 1970b
Machlup, F., 1972
Markowitz, H., 1952
Markowitz, H., 1959
McCulloch, J.H., 1975
McKinnon, R.I., 1979, Chaps. 2, 4, 5, 7
Meade, J.E., 1951, Chap. XIV.
Meade, J.E., 1964
Mood, A.M., et al., 1974
Morishima, M., 1984, Chap. 4
Mundell, R.A., 1963
Muth, J.F., 1960, 1961
Niehans, J., 1984, Chap. 8
Riehl, H. and R.M. Rodriquez, 1977
Siegel, J.J., 1972
Sinn, H.-W., 1989
Sohmen, E., 1969, Chap. IV
Spraos, J., 1959
Stern, R.M., 1973, Chap. 2
Tobin, J., 1958
Tsiang, S.C., 1958
Tsiang, S.C., 1959
Williamson, J., 1976
Williamson, J. (ed.), 1981
Yeager, L.B., 1976, Chap. 2

11 Balance of Payments and National Accounts

11.1 Balance-of-Payments Accounting and Presentation

11.1.1 Introduction

Before coming to grips with the adjustment processes of the balance of payments, we must have a clear idea of what a balance of payments is and be able to understand the content of the statistical data presented therein. Although the various national presentations look different, all obey a common set of accounting rules and definitions, which can be given a general treatment. Furthermore, where possible, the IMF (International Monetary Fund) publishes the balances of payments of all member countries in a standardized presentation (see the IMF's publications *Balance of Payments Statistics Yearbook* and *International Financial Statistics*) in accordance with the classification scheme of the Fund's *Balance of Payments Manual*. This contains the recommended concepts, rules, definitions, etc., to guide member countries in making their regular reports on the balance of payments, as stipulated in the Fund's Articles of Agreement; at the time of writing the latest edition is the fifth (henceforth referred to as the *Manual*).

Therefore we shall first explain the general principles (in this and the following section) then treat the standard classification scheme. This well enable the student, independently of his or her country of residence, to understand what a balance of payments is and to obtain information on any country's balance of payments through the Fund's publications (these, it should be noted, contain references to the original national sources, to which all those interested in a particular country can turn)[1]. In the appendix to this chapter we shall give a brief description of the balance of payments of the United States, which may interest, besides US students, those from other countries as well, given the obvious importance of this country in the world economy.

In synthesis, the balance of payments of a country is a systematic record of all economic transactions which have taken place during a given period of time between the residents of the reporting country and residents of foreign countries

---

[1] For uniformity presentation the *Yearbook* data are in SDRs (for a precise definition of this composite currency see Sect. 20.1.4). As the exchange rates of any currency in terms of the SDR are also published by the Fund (see *International Financial Statistics*), there is no problem in transforming the data into any currency that one wishes to consider. The national sources usually publish the country's balance of payments in the national currency.

(also called, for brevity, "nonresidents", "foreigners", or "rest of the world"). This record is normally kept in terms of the domestic currency of the compiling country.

This definition needs some clarification, especially as regards the concepts of economic transaction and resident. As regards the period of time, it can be a year, a quarter, or a month, though other periods are in principle possible; note also that, as the balance of payments refers to a given time period, it is a *flow* concept.

(a) The term *economic transaction* means the transfer from one economic agent (individual, business, etc.) to another of an economic value. It includes both real transfers [i.e., transfer of (title to) an economic good or rendering of an economic service] and financial transfers [i.e., transfer of (title to) a financial asset, including the creation of a new one or the cancellation of an existing one]. Furthermore, an economic transaction may involve either a *quid pro quo* (that is, the transferee gives an economic value in return to the transferor: a two-way or *bilateral* transfer) or it may not (a one-way or *unilateral* or *unrequited* transfer). Thus we have five basic types of economic transactions:

1) purchase or sale of goods and services with a financial *quid pro quo* (the latter can be, e.g., a payment in cash, the granting of a credit, etc.): one real and one financial transfer;
2) exchange of goods and services for goods and services (barter): two real transfers;
3) exchange of financial items for financial items (for example purchase of bonds with payment in cash; cancellation of an outstanding debt against the creation of a new one, etc.): two financial transfers;
4) transfer of goods and services without a *quid pro quo* (for example, a gift in kind): one real transfer;
5) transfer of financial items without a *quid pro quo* (for example, a gift of money): one financial transfer.

This classification of economic transactions is obviously valid in general and not only in international economics; what qualifies a transaction as international is that it takes place between a resident and a nonresident (for exceptions to this rule see Sect. 11.1.3, points I and II).

(b) The second concept to be clarified is that of *resident*. To begin with, the concept of resident does *not* coincide with that of citizen, though a considerable degree of overlapping normally exists. In fact, as regards individuals, residents are the persons whose general centre of interest is considered to rest in the given economy, that is, who consume goods and services, participate in production, or engage in other economic activities in the territory of an economy on other than a temporary basis, even if they have a foreign citizenship. On the basis of this definition, the Fund's *Manual* indicates a set of rules to solve possible doubtful cases: for example, migrants are to be considered as residents of the country in which they work, even if they maintain the citizenship of the country of origin; students, tourists, commercial travelers are considered residents of the country of origin provided that their stay abroad is for less than one year; official diplomatic and consular representatives, members of the armed forces abroad are in any case residents of the country of origin; etc.

As regards non-individuals, the general government (central, state, and local governments, etc.), and private non-profit bodies serving individuals, are residents of the relative country; enterprises (either private or public) have more complicated rules. In fact, the international character of many enterprises often makes it necessary to divide a single legal entity (for example a parent company operating in one economy and its unincorporated branches operating in other economies) into two or more separate enterprises, each to be considered as resident of the country where it operates, according to the rules of the Fund's *Manual*.

International organisations, i.e. political, administrative, economic etc., international bodies in which the members are governments (the United Nations, the International Monetary Fund, the World Bank, etc.) are not considered residents of any national economy, not excluding that in which they are located or conduct their affairs. It follows that all economic transactions (for example, sale of goods and services) of a country with the international organizations located in its territory are to be included in that country's balance of payments.

The standard presentation of the balance of payments consists of two sections. Section I is called the *current account:* it includes all real transfers involving a *quid pro quo,* and all unrequited transfers. Section II is called the *capital and financial account:* it shows changes of ownership and other specified changes in an economy's foreign financial assets and liabilities (including changes in the country's international reserves). A classification of the main components of these two sections will be given in Sect. 11.1.3; before that, however, we must examine the basic accounting principles on which the balance of payments rests.

11.1.2 Accounting Principles

(a) The first basic principle is that the balance of payments is kept under standard *double-entry bookkeeping*. Therefore each international transaction of the residents of a country will result in two entries that have exactly equal values but opposite signs: a credit ($+$) and a debit ($-$) entry in that country's balance of payments. The result of this accounting principle is that the total value of debit entries necessarily equals the total value of credit entries (so that the net balance of all the entries is necessarily zero), that is, the balance of payments always balances (the relation of this with the problem of balance-of-payments equilibrium and disequilibrium will be examined in Sect. 11.2).

Naturally, the credit and debit entries are not arbitrary but must follow precise rules. "Under the conventions of the system, a compiling economy records credit entries (i) for real resources denoting exports and (ii) for financial items reflecting reductions in an economy's foreign assets or increases in an economy's foreign liabilities. Conversely, a compiling economy records debit entries (i) for real resources denoting imports and (ii) for financial items reflecting increases in assets or decreases in liabilities. In other words, for assets – whether real or financial – a positive figure (credit) represents a decrease in holdings, and a negative figure (debit) represents an increase. In contrast, for liabilities, a positive figure shows an increase, and a negative figure shows a decrease. Transfers are shown as credits when the entries to which they provide the offsets are debits and as debits when those entries are credits" (from the *Manual*, p. 7).

Experience shows that those who do not have a background in accounting get confused by the convention concerning financial items, as it seems odd that an *increase* in foreign assets owned by the country should give rise to a *debit* $(-)$ entry, etc. Various ways have been devised to prevent this possible confusion; we list the main ones, in the hope that at least one will be to the student's taste.

A first rule of thumb is that all transactions giving rise to a (actual or prospective) payment *from* the rest of the world are to be recorded as *credit* entries, whilst all transactions giving rise to a (actual or prospective) payment *to* the rest of the world are to be recorded as *debit* entries. The (actual or prospective) payment is to be recorded as an offsetting entry (and so as a debit or credit entry, respectively) to the transactions which are its cause, so as to respect double-entry bookkeeping. The obvious corollary of this principle is that an increase in the country's foreign assets (or decrease in liabilities) is a debit entry and that a decrease in the country's assets (or increase in liabilities) is a credit entry.

In fact, suppose that Italy (the compiling country) exports goods to the USA; since the US importer will have to pay for these in some way, this transaction gives rise to a (actual or prospective) payment from the USA to Italy and so it must be recorded as a credit (precisely, as an item of merchandise in the current account). The payment can take various forms: for example, a bank draft in dollars, or the granting of a credit by the Italian exporter to the US importer: in both cases there is an increase in Italy's foreign assets, that must be recorded as a debit (in the capital account) to offset the credit entry.

The convention concerning the recording of financial items implies that a *capital outflow* is a *debit* in the capital account, as it gives rise to an increase in foreign assets, or to a decrease in foreign liabilities, of the country; similarly, a *capital inflow* is a *credit* in the capital account, as it gives rise to an increase in foreign liabilities or a decrease in foreign assets.

Finally, as regards unrequited transfers, which have no economic *quid pro quo*, the offsetting entry is created through the *unrequited transfers* account: thus, for example, a merchandise gift is recorded as an export of goods (credit entry) by the donor country and an offsetting debit entry is made in the unrequited transfers account.

A second rule of thumb is that all economic transactions giving rise to a demand for foreign exchange result in debit entries in original accounts and, conversely, all transactions giving rise to a supply of foreign exchange result in credit entries. Thus an export of goods and services gives rise to a supply of foreign exchange, and is thus a credit entry, whilst an export of capital (capital outflow) gives rise to a demand for foreign exchange (for example by residents to pay for the foreign assets purchased) and so is a debit entry. Similarly, an import of goods and services gives rise to a demand for foreign exchange and is thus a debit entry, whilst an import of capital (capital inflow) gives rise to a supply of foreign exchange (for example by nonresidents to pay for the domestic assets, i.e. the assets of the compiling country, that they purchase). By the same token, the payment of foreign debt (decrease in liabilities) gives rise to a demand for foreign exchange and so is a debit entry, whilst the granting by the rest of the world of a loan (increase in liabilities) gives rise to a supply of foreign currency (the proceeds of the loan) and is thus a credit entry.

This rule is not applicable to gifts in kind made by private agents and governments, for which the same considerations hold as were made above in relation to unrequited transfers.

Third rule of thumb: learn the accounting convention by heart and forget about explanations, as the explanation may be more confusing than the convention itself.

All the better to drive this convention home, we now give very simple numerical examples of the five basic types of economic transactions listed in Sect. 11.1.1, by using the basic tool of double-entry bookkeeping, the T-accounts, which have credit entries on the left-hand side and debit entries on the right-hand side. In these examples, country 1 and country 2 are synthetic expressions to denote generically the relevant economic agents who are residents of country 1 and country 2 respectively. Besides, to be as clear as possible, each transaction will be recorded from the point of view of both countries, and the exchange rate is assumed to be fixed at 1 for simplicity's sake. It is as well to point out that in the real world things are not nearly so clear-cut and simultaneous as they appear from the examples, since they require the gathering and processing of information from several sources (the customs, banks, etc., etc.).

1) Country 1 exports goods for a value of 100 to country 2. The payment is in country 2's currency and is credited to an account that country 1's exporter holds with a bank in country 2 (note that such an account is a foreign asset for country 1 and a foreign liability for country 2).

Country 1

	Current Account				Capital Account	
	Cr	Deb			Cr	Deb
Merchandise (exp)	100		Increase in claims on foreign banks			100

Country 2

	Current Account				Capital Account	
	Cr	Deb			Cr	Deb
Merchandise (imp)		100	Increase in banks' liabilities to foreigners		100	

2) Country 1 supplies oil for a value of 100 to country 2 which, in turn, supplies machinery for an equivalent value to country 1 (barter). In this case only the current account is involved.

11.1 Balance-of-Payments Accounting and Presentation

	Country 1 Current Account			Country 2 Current Account	
	Cr	Deb		Cr	Deb
Merchandise (exp)	100		Merchandise (imp)		100
Merchandise (imp)		100	Merchandise (exp)	100	

3) Country 1 purchases country 2's bonds for a value of 200 in country 2's currency and pays by drawing on a current accunt that country 1 holds with a bank in country 2. Note that bonds are a liability for the issuing country, so that country 2's foreign liabilities increase and country 1's foreign assets increase. As regards the banking account, see under case 1. In this case only the capital account is involved.

	Country 1 Capital Account			Country 2 Capital Account	
	Cr	Deb		Cr	Deb
Increase in foreign bond assets		200	Increase in bond liabilities to abroad	200	
Decrease in claims on foreign banks	200		Decrease in banks' liabilities to foreigners		200

3) Country 1 purchases country 2's bonds for a value of 200 in country 2's currency and pays by drawing on a current account that country 1 holds with a bank in country 2. Note that bonds are a liability for the issuing country, so that country 2's foreign liabilities increase and country 1's foreign assets increase. As regards the banking account, see under case 1. In this case only the capital account is involved.

	Country 1 Current Account			Country 2 Current Account	
	Cr	Deb		Cr	Deb
Merchandise (exp)	10		Merchandise (imp)		10
Unrequited transfers		10	Unrequited transfers	10	

5) Country 1 pays pensions for a value of 20 to country 2 in country 1's currency which accrues to country 2's foreign exchange reserves. Note that this means an increase in foreign assets for country 2 and an increase in foreign liabilities for country 1; *contra* items are reported in the unrequited transfers accounts of the two countries (a debit entry in country 1 to offset the credit entry in its capital account, and a credit entry in country 2 to offset the debit entry in its capital account).

Country 1

Current Account			Capital Account		
	Cr	Deb		Cr	Deb
Unrequired transfers (pensions)		20	Increase in foreign liabilities	20	

Country 2

Current Account			Capital Account		
	Cr	Deb		Cr	Deb
Unrequired transfers (pensions)	20		Increase in foreign reserve assets		20

As a general guide, we indicate the entries that have to be made in the relevant accounts in each of the five typical cases (see Table 11.1).

As we said above, since balance-of-payments accounting is kept according to the principle of double-entry bookkeeping, the balance of payments *always* balances, that is, the total value of credit entries equals the total value of debit entries or, in other words, the net balance of all the entries is zero. In practice this never occurs, either because sometimes the double-entry principle cannot be complied with (for some transactions it is possible to record only one side of it and the other has to be estimated[2]) or because of the inevitable material errors, inconsistencies in the estimates, omissions from the statement, etc. Therefore an item for *(net) errors and omissions* is introduced as an offset to the over or understatement of the recorded components, so that the net balance of all the entries, including the net errors and omissions, is zero.

(b) The second basic principle concerns the *timing of recording*, that is, the time at which transactions are deemed to have taken place. In general, various rules are possible, such as the payments basis (transactions are recorded at the time of the payment), the contract or commitment basis (transactions are recorded at the time of contract), the movement basis (transactions are recorded when the economic value changes ownership). The principle adopted is that suggested by the Fund's *Manual*, namely the *change of ownership* principle. By convention, the time of change of ownership is normally taken to be the time that the parties concerned record the transaction in their books. Rules of thumb have to be applied in the case of transactions that do not actually involve a change of ownership (for example goods made available under financial lease arrangements), for which we refer the reader to the *Manual*. It should be noted that under this principle an

---

[2] Think, for example, of a gift of money from a resident of country 1 (the reporting country) to a resident of country 2 which is deposited in an account that country 2's resident holds with a bank in country 1. The foreign liabilities of country 1 have increased, and this is recorded as a credit. But, as there is no independent information on the gift, it is necessary to make an estimate of these gifts to record as a debit in the unrequited transfers account. A similar problem arises for country 2.

Table 11.1. Entries in the balance of payments accounts in the five typical cases

Basic types of transactions	Number of entries		
	Current account		Capital account
	Goods and services	Unrequited transfers	
1) Exchange of goods and services for financial items	one	none	one
2) Exchange of goods and services for goods and services	two	none	none
3) Exchange of financial items for financial items	none	none	two
4) Real transfer without *quid pro quo*	one	one	none
5) Financial transfer without *quid pro quo*	none	one	one

import of goods with deferred payment gives rise to a debit entry in the current account at the moment of change of ownership of the goods, with a simultaneous credit entry in the capital account for the increase in liabilities (the importer's debt). When the importer settles the debt (possibly in a different period from that covered by the balance of payments in which the import was recorded), there will be two offsetting entries in the capital account: a debit for the decrease in foreign liabilities (the extinction of the debt), and a credit for the decrease in foreign assets or increase in foreign liabilities involved in the payment of the debt.

(c) The third basic principle is that of the *uniformity of valuation* of exports and imports. Commodities must be valued on a consistent basis, and this may give rise to problems if, for example, the exporting country values exports on an f.o.b. (*free on board*) basis, whilst the importing country values the same commodities as imports on a c.i.f. (*cost, insurance, and freight*) basis. The Fund suggests that all exports and imports should be valued f.o.b. to achieve uniformity of valuation. This matter will be taken up again in Sect. 11.1.3.

11.1.3 Standard Components

We shall examine here the main standard components of the two sections (current account and capital account) into which a standard balance of payments is divided.

11.1.3.I Current Account

The current account, as we know, includes goods, services, and unilateral transfers.

A) Goods and Services

A.1) *Exports and Imports of Goods.* These are also called the "visible" items of trade (the "invisible" items being the services). The main recording problem that arises in this connection is that of uniformity of valuation, mentioned in section 11.1.2

Once it was customary to record the value of traded goods at the country's border. This meant that imports were valued *c.i.f.* (that is, including cost, insurance, and freight). whilst exports were valued *f.o.b.* (free on board, that is, including, in addition to the cost of the goods, only the cost of stevedoring or loading the merchandise into the carrier) or *f.a.s.* (free alongside: the difference between f.a.s. and f.o.b. being the cost of stevedoring or loading).

From this two difficulties arose. The first was that the value of world exports was different from the value of world imports (naturally, to calculate these totals a single currency is used), since the latter exceeded the former by an amount determined by insurance and freight. This statistical discrepancy is illogical, as we are dealing with the *same goods*, first as exports, then as imports.

The second and perhaps more serious difficulty is that there was a confusion between visible and invisible items in the balance of payments: insurance and freight, in fact, are services and must be properly reported as such rather than being included in the merchandise item.

The principle of uniformity of valuation of course requires that all goods should be valued in the same way; the rule adopted by the Fund's *Manual* is that they should be valued at the place of uniform valuation, i.e. the customs frontier of the economy from which they are exported, up to and including any loading of the goods on board the carrier at that frontier. That is, merchandise exports *and* imports are to be valued *f.o.b.*

To conclude this item, we shall only mention a few other problems. One is related to the fact that it is possible for an export or import to take place even if *physically* the goods have not left or entered the territory of the country (an example is that of merchandise transactions with an international organization situated in the territory of the reporting country). Another is related to tourists' expenditures: the goods they buy ought in principle to be recorded as exports or imports in the merchandise entry, but for simplicity's sake all tourists' expenditures are recorded as services (see below).

A.2) *Exports and Imports of Services*, also called the "invisible" items of trade. They include both services proper and items classified under this heading for convenience. Insurance and freight charges for goods, passenger transportation, film rentals, banking, fees and royalties for the use of intangible property or rights (patents, trademarks, copyright, etc.), income from labour, etc., are clearly payments for services. As regards labour income, care must be taken to check the residence. The labour income item records wages, salaries, and other compensation that persons earn in an economy other than the one in which they reside by working for a resident of that economy, i.e. — from the point of view of the compiling country — income earned by residents working abroad for nonresidents and income earned by nonresidents working in the domestic country for residents. Therefore, migrants' remittances do *not* belong to this category. Migrants, in fact, are no longer considered as residents of the country of origin, but as residents of the country in which they work, so that any remittance to the country of origin of a migrant cannot be considered as the *quid pro quo* for services of domestic factors abroad (from the point of view of the receiving country), nor as the *quid pro quo* for services of foreign factors (from the point of view of the paying country). These remittances are therefore to be considered as unrequited transfers.

Conceptual doubts may arise in relation to other items. For example, at the beginning of the process of standardization of balance of payments accounting, there was much discussion as to whether payments for interest on investment and for profits should be considered unrequited transfers or payments for services. The second solution was adopted, which is in agreement with the neoclassical tradition for which interest is the return for the service rendered by the capital loaned and profits are the return for the efforts of entrepreneurs[3]. Differently from the previous editions, the fifth edition fo the *Manual* suggests that factor incomes (compensation of employees and investment income) be included in a separate sub-account of the current account. Thus the current account should have three subsections: A. Goods and services; B. Income; C. Current transfers.

Another example of a doubtful case arises in relation to tourist expenditures, which, as we have said above, are all included in the item travel (which also contains similar expenditure by commercial travellers, students abroad for less than a year, etc.); note that the international carriage of travellers is not included here, as it is covered in passenger services.

The examination of the service account allows us to illustrate a possible *exception* to the general rule that the balance of payments of a country records solely transactions between residents and nonresidents. This possible exception concerns shipment (a comprehensive term used for brevity to denote freight, insurance, and other distributive services related to merchandise trade) and depends on the fact that there are various possible methods for estimating these services. One method proposes that the compiling country should enter as credit all shipping services performed by residents, both as to exports and to imports, and as debits all shipping services performed as to imports, both by residents and by nonresidents. It follows that, when an importer of the compiling country purchases a shipment directly from a resident in the same country, this transaction should be entered both as a credit (as a shipment performed by a resident) and as a debit (as a shipment performed on imports). These two entries offset each other, as they should, but the fact remains that a transaction involving two residents has been recorded in the balance of payments.

Although this method is used by some countries and is analogous to the one employed by the UN's system of national accounts in its rest-of-the-world account, the Fund's *Manual* recommends a different method (there is also a third possible method, not examined here), according to which the compiling country enters as credit all shipping services performed by residents on its exports and as debits all shipping services performed by foreigners on its imports. The main reason for suggesting this method is that it eliminates any offsetting flows of services between residents and thus complies with the general rule on balance-of-payments accounting.

---

[3] We may note, incidentally, that this a case in which accounting conventions reflect the dominant economic theory.

B) Unrequited or Unilateral Transfers

These are divided into two groups, according to the nature of the operator: private or official. In the case of the former the main item consists of migrants' remittances; the latter includes voluntary subsidies to defence budgets, government contributions to international organizations for administrative expenses, war reparations, etc. An innovation of the fifth edition of the *Manual* is to include in this account current transfers only. Capital transfers (e.g., transfer of ownership of a fixed asset, forgiveness of a liability by a creditor, etc., of course when no counterpart is received in return) should be included in the capital and financial account, to which we now turn.

11.1.3.II Capital Account

The capital account includes all *changes* in the country's foreign financial assets and liabilities (including reserve assets, on which see below), or, as they are also called, all *capital movements*. In the fifth edition of the *Manual* this is called the 'Capital and financial account' and is divided into: A. Capital account, and B. Financial account. The capital account contains all unilateral capital transfers (see above). The financial account is what was formerly called the capital account. To avoid confusion we shall continue using the old terminology. In general several classification criteria can be used:

1) the nature of the operation, or type of capital: direct investment, portfolio investment, reserves, other capital. The main feature of direct investment is taken to be the fact that the direct investor seeks to have, on a lasting basis, an effective voice in the management of a nonresident enterprise; this gives rise to accounting conventions which will be examined in Sect. 17.3. Portfolio investment covers investment in financial assets (bonds, corporate equities other than direct investment, etc.). On reserves see below. "Other capital" is a residual category.

2) The length of the operation: long-term and short-term capital. The convention adopted is based on the *original* contractual maturity of more than one year (long term) and one year or less (short-term). Assets with no stated maturity (e.g. corporate equities, property rights) are also considered as long-term capital. The initial maturity convention may give rise to problems: for example the purchase of, say, a foreign bond with an original maturity of three years, but only 6 months to maturity when the purchase is made, is nonetheless recorded as a long-term capital movement. The inevitable convention derives from the fact that usually no data are available on the time to maturity of securities when international transactions occur.

3) The nature of the operator: private and official, the latter possibly divided in general government, central monetary institutions (central banks etc.) and other official institutions.

The *Manual* adopts the first criterion, and categorizes between: 1. Direct investment, 2. Portfolio investment, 3. Other investment, 4. Reserve assets. Within these categories further subdivisions are present, which use the other criteria.

"Reserves" is a *functional category* comprising all those assets available for use by the central authorities of a country in meeting balance of payments needs[4]; this availability is not linked in principle to criteria of ownership or nature of the assets. In practice, however, the term reserves is taken to include monetary gold, special drawing rights (SDRs) in the Fund, reserve position in the Fund, foreign exchange and other claims available to the central authorities for the use described above (for example, ECUs – the European Currency Units – under the agreements of the EMS, the European Monetary System). For a more detailed treatment of these items we refer the reader to Sect. 20.1. These are also called *gross official reserves;* if we deduct the central bank's short-term foreign liabilities we obtain *net official reserves.* A notion of gross official reserves in the wide sense is also defined, i.e. gross official reserves plus the central bank's medium and long term foreign assets. Incidentally, note that the flow of interest earned by the central bank on these assets (which increases the stock of reserves) is entered in the services account of the current account. Finally, by deducting all foreign liabilities of the central bank from gross official reserves in the wide sense, we obtain net official reserves in the wide sense.

As regards ownership, the concept of reserves, which requires these assets to be strictly under the central authorities' direct and effective control, usually limits the consideration to foreign claims actually owned by the central authorities. But this is not a necessary condition, as private deposit money banks may sometimes be allowed to hold foreign assets, but may have permission to deal in them only on the terms specified by the authorities and with their express approval. These assets can thus be considered as under the authorities' direct and effective control, so that the (net) foreign asset position of banks can, in such a case, be considered as part of the country's reserves.

An problem related to reserves is "reclassification" or "revaluation", a term which includes both the changes in the value of reserve assets resulting from fluctuations in their price ("valuation changes") and the changes due to "reserve creation", i.e. to allocation of SDRs (on which see Sect. 20.1.4) and to monetization or demonetization of gold (i.e., when the authorities increase their holdings of monetary gold by acquiring commodity gold, or decrease their holdings of monetary gold for nonmonetary purposes, for example by selling it to private agents). Under a system of fixed exchange rates (see Sect. 10.5) valuation changes were a rare event, but under the present system of widespread floating and no official price for gold (this has been abolished: see Sect. 20.1.7) the various reserve components can show frequent valuation changes relative to each other. Therefore the *Manual* suggests that for each type of reserve asset the main entry should refer to changes other than revaluation changes, with supplementary information on the total change (i.e., including revaluation changes), the valuation change and the reserve creation change, if applicable. This information, according to the fifth edition of the *Manual,* should no longer

---

[4] We have already said above that the fact that the balance of payments always balances must not be confused with the "equilibrium" in the balance of payments: see the detailed treatment in Sect. 11.2.

be shown in the balance of payments (as was previously), but in a completely separate account, the international investment position (on which see below).

The examination of the capital account allows us to mention other exceptions to the general rule that the balance of payments includes all and only the transactions between residents and nonresidents[5].

These derive from the (practical) fact that, when a transaction in a foreign asset or liability takes place, it is sometimes impossible for the compiler to know the identities of both parties and thus to ascertain whether the resident-nonresident principle is met. Thus the compiler may not be able to find out whether a nonresident who is reported as having acquired or relinquished a financial claim on a resident did so by transacting with another nonresident or with a resident and, similarly, whether a resident who is reported as having acquired or relinquished a financial claim on a nonresident dealt with another resident or with a nonresident. Since is important that the balance of payments covers all transactions in foreign liabilities and assets, the *Manual*'s recommendation is that the transactions exemplified above should be included in the balance of payments. Thus a transaction between two nonresidents as well as a transaction between two residents may happen to be included in the compiling country's balance of payments.

To conclude this section we point out that, in addition to the balance of payments, there also exists the *balance of indebtedness* (also called by the *Manual* the international investment position). In general, the balance of indebtedness records the outstanding claims of residents on nonresidents and the outstanding claims of nonresidents on residents at a given point in time, such as the end of the year. Therefore this balance is concerned with *stocks,* unlike the balance of payments, which refers to *flows.*

Various balances of indebtedness can be reported according to the claims considered. One is that which considers only the stock of foreign assets and liabilities of the central authorities; another considers the direct investment position, etc.

---

[5] The (possible) exception already met concerns shipping services: see Sect. 11.1.3.1 under A.2. To complete our overview of exceptions, mention should also be made of the cases in which some transactions, though involving a resident and a nonresident, are *omitted* from the balance of payments. One (possible) case concerns free military assistance in kind (military equipment).

11.2 The Meaning of "Surplus", "Deficit", and "Equilibrium" in the Balance of Payments

As we saw in Chap. 1, the examination of balance-of-payments disequilibria and of their adjustments forms the starting point of international monetary theory. It is therefore indispensable to examine carefully the meaning of "equilibrium" and "disequilibrium" in the balance of payments.

We recall from Sect. 11.1.2 that, as the economic transactions between residents and nonresidents are reported under double-entry bookkeeping, the balance of payments always balances. It is therefore a concept of (economic) equilibrium to which one refers when one talks of equilibrium and disequilibrium of the balance of payments. In order to avoid terminological confusion, we shall use the term *equilibrium* to denote economic equilibrium, and *balance* to denote accounting identities. We shall also use the terminology *surplus* and *deficit* to qualify a disequilibrium[6] of the balance of payments, avoiding the terminology "favourable" and "unfavourable" balance of payments (which derives from the Mercantilists), as this terminology implies the identities surplus = good on the one hand, and deficit = evil on the other, which is not necessarily true.

An appropriate definition of deficit and surplus is important for economic analysis and policy, and requires the classification of all the standard components of the balance of payments into two categories. The first includes all those items whose net sum constitutes the surplus (if positive), the deficit (if negative) or indicates equilibrium (if zero); the second includes all the remaining items, whose net sum is necessarily the opposite of the former (since the grand total must, as we know, be zero) and is sometimes said to "finance" or "settle" the imbalance. If we imagine all the standard components being arranged in a column in such a way that all the components included in the first category are listed first, then the balance of payments may be visualized as being separated into the two categories by drawing a horizontal line between the last component of the first category and the first component of the second category (hence the accountants' terminology *to draw the line*). Therefore the transactions whose net sum gives rise to a surplus or deficit (or indicates equilibrium, if zero) are said to be *above the line*, whilst the remaining ones are said to be *below the line*.

---

[6] Some authors even suggest that the term "disequilibrium of the balance of payments" should be avoided entirely, and replaced with "imbalance of payments". See the *Notes on Terminology* in the appendix to Fellner *et al.* (1966, pp. 244–5). For a penetrating analysis of the notion of equilibrium and disequilibrium in economic theory in general and in international economics in paticular, see Machlup (1958, especially section IV). Machlup also distinguishes three concepts of the balance of payments relevant to economic analysis: an *accounting balance*, i.e. a balance of selected debits and credits; a *market balance*, i.e. a balance of supply and demand for foreign exchange; a *programme balance*, i.e. a balance of needs and desires. The meaning of equilibrium and disequilibrium (surplus or deficit) is different for each of the three concepts. While referring the reader to Machlup (1950) for detailed analysis of these questions, we should point out that the concept examined in the text and now usually employed in practice corresponds to the accounting balance in Machlup's terminology.

However, in most treatments the term "balance of payments" is still used both in the sense of the complete accounting statement (treated in the previous section) and in the sense of the net sum of the items included in the first category, hence the usual terminology "balance-of-payments surplus" and "balance-of-payments deficit".

To recapitulate: we shall say that the balance of payments is in *equilibrium* when the net sum of the items *above the line* is zero, in *disequilibrium* when this net sum is different from zero, showing a *surplus* if positive, a *deficit* if negative.

All this is very fine, but how are we to divide the items into the two categories, i.e. how shall we draw the line? This is the crucial point to give an operational content to the concepts we have been talking about.

According to the concept developed by the IMF in 1949—50[7] and by private scholars, the criterion to be adopted is the *purpose* or *motive* of the transaction. The main distinction is that between *compensatory* or *accomodating* transactions and *autonomous* or *non-compensatory* transactions. An autonomous transaction is any transaction undertaken for its own sake, i.e. for motives specific to the transaction itself, and not determined by (or at most only indirectly depending on) the situation of other items of the balance of payments. Compensatory transactions, on the contrary, are those undertaken with the sole or primary purpose of providing financing to the imbalances in other items of the balance of payments. The payments balance to be considered is then the balance of all autonomous transactions, with the balance of all compensatory transactions providing the economic (and accounting) offset. It should be noted that a surplus or deficit implies an excess demand (positive or negative, respectively) for foreign exchange and therefore a pressure on the exchange rate; this excess demand is met by compensatory transactions.

The distinction between autonomous and accomodating transactions, which is plain enough in theory, is by no means easy to translate into practice. Many transactions, of course, do not present difficulties: merchandise trade, shipping services, investment income, labour income and workers' remittances, reparations, portfolio investment, direct investment can be considered autonomous. Sales and purchases of foreign exchange by the central authorities to stabilize the exchange rate are certainly accomodating transactions. But suppose that the central authorities negotiate an international loan: if this serves to provide them with foreign exchange reserves to intervene on the foreign exchange market, then it is a compensatory transaction, but it is not if the loan serves for specific purposes (say a development programme). Both purposes may be present simultaneously. Or consider a bank which increases its foreign liabilities: if this is done for specific purposes (say, interest arbitrage), then it is a non-compensatory transaction; but it is accomodating if it is made at the suggestion of the monetary authorities (moral suasion or other), who wish to obtain a capital inflow to offset a deficit in other parts of the balance of payments. The examples could be multiplied ad lib.

To cut through these problems, the Fund (1949—50) suggested the concept of *compensatory official financing*, defined as "the financing undertaken by the

---

[7] See IMF, 1949, and second edition (1950) of the *Manual*, appendix C. For a criticism of this concept, see Machlup, 1950, Sect. C.

11.2 The Meaning of "Surplus", "Deficit", and "Equilibrium"

monetary authorities to provide exchange to cover a surplus or deficit in the rest of the balance of payments". This included, in addition to the use of reserve assets, all those transactions in which the authorities engage for the specific purpose of making up for a surplus or deficit in the rest of the balance of payments. Notwithstanding an abundant exemplification, this begged the question and introduced a judgmental element on the part of the compiler of the presentation. Besides, this measure may give rise to inconsistencies at the world level inasmuch as the motives for the same transaction may be different for the two parties (thus an international loan may be compensatory from the point of view of the receiving country, autonomous from the point of view of the extending country).

All these problems induced the Fund to drop this concept[8]. The nearest thing to it now in use is the *overall balance*[9] which considers all components except changes in reserve assets to be above the line. The idea behind it is to provide a measure of the residual imbalance that is financed through the use and acquisition of reserves.

Besides the overall balance several other types of balance are also in use. In principle these types are very numerous and range almost continuously from the least inclusive one, the trade balance, to the overall balance. But the typical balances generally considered are few in number (although individual countries may build other types for the examination of some particular aspect of international economic relationships; as regards the USA, see the Appendix). We give a list in increasing order of coverage.

1) *Trade Balance.* As the name indicates, this is the balance between exports and imports of goods. The trade balance in the strict sense or in the broad sense (i.e. taken to include also invisible trade, in which case it is now more usual to speak of balance on goods and services) was that considered by mercantilists and by the traditional theory of the processes of adjustment of the balance of payments (see below, Sect. 11.4).

2) *Balance on Goods and Services.* In addition to visible trade, also invisibles are put above the line. This balance measures the net transfer of real resources between an economy and the rest of the world.

3) *Current (Account) Balance.* This is obtained by adding net unilateral transfers to the balance on goods and services, and represents the transactions that give rise to changes in the economy's stock of foreign financial items.

4) *Balance on Current Account and Long-Term Capital*, also called *Basic Balance.* This includes above the line, besides the items of the current account balance, the flow of long-term capital, and is intended to be a rough indicator of long-

---

[8] As a matter of fact it was no longer suggested after the second edition of the *Manual.* See also the fourth edition, p. 55, and the fifth edition, Appendix V.

[9] To avoid terminological confusion, it should be noted that the term "overall balance" is also used to denote a *category* (rather than a single balance, as we use it here), i.e. a type of balance that places below the line the changes in official reserve assets *and* in certain selected liabilities regarded as being closely related to those reserves. One such balance would be the official reserve transactions (or official settlements) balances (see Sect. A.11.1) once in use in the presentation of the US balance of payments, which places below the line changes in official reserve assets plus changes in all liquid and nonliquid liabilities to foreign official agencies. However, since the choice of which liabilities are to be selected is somewhat arbitrary, we prefer to limit the use of the term overall balance to the definition stated in the text.

term trends in the balance of payments. The idea behind it is that short-term capital flows are temporary and reversible, whilst long-term ones are less volatile and more permanent. This may be true in principle, but in practice serious difficulties arise. One is due to the accounting convention according to which the distinction between long-term and short-term capital is made on the basis of the initial maturity of the claim involved, so that, if an investor buys a foreign bond which had an initial maturity of five years, but now has only a few months to maturity, what is clearly a short-term investment is recorded as a long-term one. Another is related to the fact that all equities are considered long-term items, but many of them are easily marketable and transactions in stocks (e.g. for speculative purposes) can behave very much like short-term flows.

5) *Overall Balance*. All that has to be added to the definition given above is the convention that the net errors and omissions item is included above the line. The obvious reason is that the use and acquisition of reserves is usually known and measured with a high degree of accuracy, so that errors and omissions must pertain to items above the line.

To conclude this section we must examine whether an answer can be given to the question that is said to have been asked by one writer on financial matters: "All I want is one number, with no if's, but's or maybe's". Unfortunately no answer to such a question can be given. The definition of a surplus or deficit is an analytic rather than an accounting problem, and the use of one concept of payments balance or the other cannot be separated from the nature of the problem that one wants to analyze. Therefore *the* payments balance does not exist, and different types may have to be examined on different occasions or even simultaneously on the same occasion.

Similar considerations hold for the notion of balance-of-payments equilibrium. An equilibrium in the overall balance, for example, can occur in various ways: with a simultaneous equilibrium within the main items separately considered (i.e., zero balance in merchandise trade, in invisible trade, in unrequited transfers, in long-term capital movements, in short-term capital movements) or with an imbalance in some items offset by an opposite imbalance in other items (for instance, a deficit in the current account balance offset by a surplus in the capital account balance). The former case, which we may define as *full* equilibrium, is altogether hypothetical, since in reality even the more equilibrated situations belong to the latter. One should also take the time period into account, since a situation may be one of equilibrium, but only in the *short-run* and not in the *long-run*: for example, a situation of continuing deficits in the balance on goods and services offset by continuing short-term capital inflows cannot be maintained in the long-run (see, for example, Sect. 15.5.2.1). The situation might be different if the said deficits were offset by long-term capital inflows, in which case the basic balance would be in equilibrium; the problem of the increase in the stock of long-term foreign liabilities would however remain (see, for example, Sect. 17.3).

It is therefore important always to state clearly which type of balance is being considered when one examines the adjustment processes of the balance of payments.

11.3 The Balance of Payments and National Accounts

In this section we draw from national economic accounting and flow-of-funds analysis some elementary relations among the main macroeconomic (real and financial) aggregates in order to fit the balance of payments into the context of the whole economic system, always keeping within an accounting framework. The reason for giving this treatment in an international economics textbook is not that we are particularly fond of accounting, but that the accounting framework that we propose will render us invaluable services in the course of the examination of the adjustment processes of the balance of payments.

We have built a framework — which, though very much simplified, is sufficient to include the basic elements — in which there are only five sectors and six markets or transaction categories (real resources and financial assets). This framework is *exhaustive*, in the sense that it includes all transactors and transactions. In other words, all transactors are included in one of the sectors and all the transactions they carry out are included in one of the categories. It should also be pointed out that this accounting framework records *flows*, that is movements, or changes, that have occurred during a given time period.

The framework under consideration can be represented schematically in a table (see Table 11.2), where the columns refer to sectors and the rows to markets. Let us begin by clarifying the meaning of the sectors.

The *private sector* includes all transactors who do not belong to any other sector. The adjective "private" must not, therefore, be interpreted as the opposite of "public" in a juridical sense. For example, public enterprises which sell to the public most of the goods or services they produce are included here (unless they are banks). The private sector therefore includes the producing and household sectors.

The *government sector* refers to the *general* government and includes all departments, establishments, and agencies of the country's central, regional, and local governments (excluding the central bank if this is institutionally part of the government and not an independent body).

Table 11.2. A simplified accounting framework for real and financial flows

Market	Sector					
	Private	Government	Banking	Central bank	Rest-of-the-world (Foreign)	Row totals
Goods and services	I-S	G-T	~	~	EXP-IMP	0
Domestic monetary base	ΔH_p	~	ΔH_b	ΔH^c	~	0
Domestic bank deposits	ΔD_p	~	ΔD^b	–	ΔD_f	0
Domestic securities	ΔN_p	ΔN^g	ΔN_b	ΔN_c	ΔN_f	0
Foreign money	ΔR_p	~	ΔR_b	ΔR_c	ΔR^f	0
Foreign securities	ΔF_p	~	ΔF_b	ΔF_c	ΔF^f	0
Column totals	0	0	0	0	0	

The *banking sector* includes commercial banks, savings banks and all financial institutions other than the central bank.

The *central bank* includes, besides the central bank, the exchange stabilization fund, if this exists as an institutionally separate body.

The *rest-of-the-world* sector includes all nonresidents in the sense explained in Sect. 11.1.1.

Let us now turn to an examination of the categories of transactions or markets.

Goods and services includes all transactions on goods and services (production, exchange and transfers) and gives rise to the real market. Then there are the markets concerning national or domestic money, distinguished into *monetary base* (also called high-powered money, primary money, etc.) and *bank deposits*. Generally the *monetary base* is the liability of the central bank and consists of coin, banknotes and the balances which the banks keep with the central bank. As regards *bank deposits*, it is outside the scope of the present work to discuss whether only demand deposits or also time deposits (and other types of deposits or financial assets) are to be considered as money. In any case what is *not* included as money here, comes under the heading of the *national* (or *domestic*) *securities* item, which includes, besides securities proper, any form of marketable debt instrument. As regards *foreign money*, we do not make the distinction between monetary base and bank deposits, since all the foreign sectors (including the central bank and the banking sector) have been consolidated into a single sector (the rest-of-the-world or foreign sector), and for residents foreign exchange in either of its forms (cash or deposits) is foreign money[10]. There are, finally, *foreign securities*, for which similar considerations hold as for domestic ones.

The table can be read along either the rows or the columns: in any case, as this is an accounting presentation, the algebraic sum of the magnitudes in any row is zero, as is the algebraic sum of the magnitudes in each column. It should be noted that the items have an intrinsic sign: see below, footnote 13.

More precisely, the fact that the row totals are zero reflects the circumstance that, as the magnitudes considered represent "excess demands" (positive or negative: a negative excess demand is, of course, an excess supply) by the single sectors for the item which gives the name to the row, the total quantity of it *actually* exchanged is necessarily the same both from the point of view of demand and from the point of view of supply. In other words, the *ex post total amount* demanded and the *ex post total amount* supplied are necessarily equal[11], as they are one and the same thing.

The equality to zero of the column totals reflects the *budget constraint* of each transactor, that is, the fact that total receipts and total outlays must necessarily coincide, where *receipts* and *outlays* are of course taken to include the change in financial liabilities and assets. Thus an accounting link is established between real

---

[10] For simplicity's sake we assume that banks do not accept deposits denominated in currencies other than that issued by the country in which the bank is resident (Euro-deposits or Xeno-deposits: see Sects. 10.5, 19.3, 19.4).

[11] It should be stressed that this is a mere fact of accounting, which must *not* be confused with the equilibrium of the market where the item is being transacted, or equality between *ex ante* magnitudes.

and financial flows, according to which for any transactor the excess of investment over saving coincides with the change in his net liabilities (i.e. the change in liabilities net of the change in assets). Since the budget constraint must hold for each transactor it will hold for their aggregate, i.e. for the sector.

This said, we can go on to a detailed examination of the accounting relationships present in the table, beginning with the rows.

The first row gives the relation

$$(I-S)+(G-T)+(EXP-IMP)=0. \tag{11.1}$$

Note that the tildes ($\sim$) in correspondence to the third and fourth columns are due to the simplifying assumptions that the real transactions of the banking sector and the central bank are negligible, i.e. that these sectors neither consume nor produce goods and (real) services, and thus do not transact in the real market, but only in the financial markets.

In Eq. (11.1), I and S denote the private sector's investment and saving respectively; G and T denote government expenditure and revenue (fiscal receipts net of transfer payments); EXP and IMP indicate exports and imports of goods and services. Therefore, $(I-S)$ is the private sector's excess demand for goods and services, $(G-T)$ the excess demand of the government, $(EXP-IMP)$ the excess demand of the rest of the world.

In the subsequent rows, the simbol Δ denotes the changes (which may be positive or negative); the subscripts and superscripts indicate the holding or issuing sector respectively. Thus, from the second row, we have

$$\Delta H_p + \Delta H_b + \Delta H^c = 0, \tag{11.2}$$

where H denotes the domestic monetary base, issued by the central bank (ΔH^c) and held by the private sector (ΔH_p) and the banking sector (ΔH_b), whilst the tildes in correspondence to the second and fifth columns reflect the simplifying assumptions that the government does not hold or issue monetary base and that the rest of the world does not hold domestic monetary base.

The third row gives

$$\Delta D_p + \Delta D_f + \Delta D^b = 0, \tag{11.3}$$

which incorporates the simplifying assumption that only the private and foreign sectors hold deposits with the banking sector which, of course, issues them. It should be noted the the dash (instead of the tilde) under the fourth column indicates the fact the central bank does not hold deposits with the banking sector and that any deposits with the central bank to be considered as monetary base.

From the fourth row we obtain

$$\Delta N_p + \Delta N^g + \Delta N_b + \Delta N_c + \Delta N_f = 0, \tag{11.4}$$

where the simplifying assumption is that domestic securities are issued solely by the government[12].

---

[12] One might relax this assumption slightly with no change in the results by hypothesizing that any domestic securities issued by other sectors are held solely by the issuing sector, so that they cancel out within the sector.

The fifth row yields

$$\Delta R_p + \Delta R_b + \Delta R_c + \Delta R^f = 0, \tag{11.5}$$

where the government is assumed to hold no foreign money.

Finally from the sixth row we get

$$\Delta F_p + \Delta F_b + \Delta F_c + \Delta F^f = 0, \tag{11.6}$$

where the simplifying assumption is that the government does not hold foreign securities, which of course are issued by the rest of the world.

Let us now consider the *budget constraints* (column totals). The first column gives

$$(I - S) + \Delta H_p + \Delta D_p + \Delta N_p + \Delta R_p + \Delta F_p = 0, \tag{11.7}$$

which is the private sector's budget constraint. An alternative way of writing this is

$$S - I = \Delta H_p + \Delta D_p + \Delta N_p + \Delta R_p + \Delta F_p, \tag{11.7.1}$$

where the excess of saving over investment (if we consider it to be positive) of the private sector is employed by this sector to accumulate monetary base (ΔH_p), deposits (ΔD_p), domestic securities (ΔN_p), foreign money (ΔR_p), and foreign securities (ΔF_p). A third way of writing this constraint is

$$I - S = -\Delta H_p - \Delta D_p - \Delta N_p - \Delta R_p - \Delta F_p, \tag{11.7.2}$$

that is, the excess of investment over saving (if we now assume this excess to be positive) of the private sector is financed by this sector through decumulation (i.e., decrease in the stocks owned) of monetary base ($-\Delta H_p$), deposits ($-\Delta D_p$), domestic securities ($-\Delta N_p$), foreign money ($-\Delta R_p$), and foreign securities ($-\Delta F_p$).

It should be pointed out that it is not necessary for *all* the stocks to increase in the case of (11.7.1) or to decrease in the case of (11.7.2). It is in fact perfectly possible for a divergence between S and I to give rise to changes in only one of the financial stocks, and more complicated intermediate cases are also possible in which some stocks vary in one direction and the others in the opposite direction (though always respecting the budget constraint).

The second column gives the government budget constraint

$$G - T + \Delta N^g = 0, \tag{11.8}$$

that is

$$G - T = -\Delta N^g, \tag{11.8.1}$$

which states that the government budget deficit (excess of expenditure over receipts) is financed by issuing securities (a negative excess demand, that is an excess supply, equal to $-\Delta N^g$). Remember that in such a constraint there are the simplifying assumptions that the government does not issue domestic monetary base and does not hold foreign money or securities. If we dropped these assumptions, it can easily be seen that the government can also meet a budget deficit by issuing monetary base and reducing its stocks of foreign money and securities.

The budget constraint of the banking sector is

$$\Delta H_b + \Delta D^b + \Delta N_b + \Delta R_b + \Delta F_b = 0, \tag{11.9}$$

which expresses the fact that banks — given the simplifying assumption that they do not transact in the real market — record on the credit side a change in the domestic monetary base owned (ΔH_b), a change in foreign money (ΔR_b), and a change in the loans extended by buying domestic (ΔN_b) and foreign (ΔF_b) securities; on the debit side the change in deposits (ΔD^b)[13].

The fourth column yields

$$\Delta H^c + \Delta N_c + \Delta R_c + \Delta F_c = 0, \tag{11.10}$$

which is the budget constraint — always referring to changes — of the central bank, in which the issuing of monetary base (ΔH^c) is a debit item, whilst the acquisition of national (ΔN_c) and foreign (ΔF_c) securities and of foreign exchange (ΔR_c) is a credit item.

Finally, the last column gives the rest-of-the-world's budget constraint:

$$(EXP - IMP) + \Delta D_f + \Delta N_f + \Delta F^f + \Delta R^f = 0, \tag{11.11}$$

that is, using (11.5) and (11.6), and rearranging terms,

$$(EXP - IMP) + \{(\Delta D_f + \Delta N_f) - [(\Delta R_p + \Delta F_p) + (\Delta R_b + \Delta F_b)]\}$$
$$= \Delta R_c + \Delta F_c. \tag{11.11.1}$$

Equation (11.11.1) is simply the expression of the *overall balance* already examined in Sect. 11.2[14]. In fact, $(EXP - IMP)$ is the current account balance[15] and the expression in braces is the autonomous-capital balance, consisting of the change in domestic assets (deposits, ΔD_f, and securities, ΔN_f) owned by non residents plus the change in foreign assets (money, ΔR, and securities, ΔF) owned by residents, who are subdivided into private sector (hence $\Delta R_p + \Delta F_p$) and banking sector (hence $\Delta R_b + \Delta F_b$); note that the minus sign before the square bracket reflects the accounting convention illustrated in Sect. 11.1.2. The

---

[13] To avoid confusion it should be remembered that in a balance sheet the credit items have an intrinsic positive sign whilst the debit items have an intrinsic negative sign, so that: change in assets + change in liabilities = 0, since the two totals are numerically equal but with opposite sign. In other words, an increase in a credit item, say H^b, means $\Delta H^b > 0$ and a decrease in H^b means $\Delta H^b < 0$. Conversely, D^b is a debit item and carries with it an intrinsic negative sign, so that an increase in deposits (D^b numerically greater) means a negative ΔD^b and a decrease in deposits (D^b numerically smaller) means a positive ΔD^b. These observations on the intrinsic negative sign of the debit entries hold, of course, for all the accounting identities considered in the text.

[14] It should be noted that the balance of payments does not conform exactly with the rest-of-the-world account in SNA (the United Nation's *System of National Accounts*, which forms the basis of national economic accounting in most countries). For our purposes, however, we can ignore these differences, as they are of secondary importance with respect to the fact that the agreement on underlying principles makes the balance of payments consistent with the overall framework of SNA. For a detailed comparison of balance-of-payments classification with external transactions in SNA, see the Fund's *Manual*, pp. 10–13 and App. I.

[15] For simplicity's sake, we have neglected unilateral transfers so as to identify the current account balance with the balance on goods and services. Alternatively, we could assume that unilateral transfers are included in the goods and services account or in the capital account as the case may be.

offsetting item is given by the change in official international reserves in the wide sense[16], subdivided into liquid assets (foreign money, ΔR_c) and medium/long term assets (foreign securities, ΔF_c) owned by the central bank.

Having thus completed the examination of the table, we must again emphasize that we are in the presence of a *mere accounting framework, from which it would be logically invalid to draw causal relations automatically*. The better to drive this important point home we shall offer a few examples. If we consider, for instance, Eq. (11.1) and rewrite it in the form

$$IMP - EXP = (I - S) + (G - T), \qquad (11.1.1)$$

we might be induced to believe that the government budget deficit $(G-T)$ "determines" the current account deficit $(IMP-EXP)$, so that the "cause" of increases in this external deficit is to be seen in increases in the budget deficit; conversely, the current account improves if the budget deficit is reduced. All this might well be true, but it is logically illegitimate to derive it from Eq. (11.1.1), which merely states that, *ex post*, we observe from the accounts that the excess of imports over exports equals the algebraic sum of the private sector's excess of investment over saving and the government sector's excess of expenditure over receipts. To continue with the example, we might rewrite (11.1) in yet another form:

$$G - T = (IMP - EXP) + (S - I), \qquad (11.1.2)$$

and be induced to claim that it is the current account deficit which "determines" the budget deficit! Also, if we remember that the private sector's saving equals disposable income (given by national income minus taxes net of transfer payments) minus consumption, i.e. $S = Y_d - C = Y - T - C$, and if we define a new aggregate called "absorption" A as the sum $C + I + G$ (i.e. national expenditure), we can rewrite (11.1) as

$$EXP - IMP = Y - A, \qquad (11.1.3)$$

and might be induced to claim that the current account deficit ($EXP - IMP < 0$) is "determined" by the fact that the country spends more than its income ($A > Y$).

We stress once again that, as the generating relation of (11.1.1), (11.1.2), (11.1.3), is Eq. (11.1), that is an accounting identity, also the derived relations maintain the nature of mere accounting identities with no causal content. In other words, *given an accounting identity, it is logically inadmissible to draw causal relations from it simply by shifting terms from one side to the other of the equality sign*.

We have dwelt on this topic because, as we shall see in future chapters[17], many debates on the theory of the adjustment processes of the balance of payments seem to have been partly due to confusions between accounting identities and causal relations.

---

[16] For this notion see Sect. 11.1.3.II.

[17] For example, when dealing with the absorption approach (Sect. 14.1), which uses (11.1.3); with the monetary approach to the balance of payments (Sect. 15.2), which uses an identity obtained by consolidating the banking sector and the central bank; with the new Cambridge school (Sect. 16.4), which uses (11.1.1) and (11.7.1).

11.4 The International Adjustment Process and Open-Economy Macroeconomics: An Overview

The study of the adjustment processes of the balance of payments is, from the analytical point of view, about 235 years old, if it is to David Hume (1752) that one attributes the merit of having offered the first complete treatment of the classical price-specie-flow mechanism. The adjustment problem is not only of theoretical interest but has also always been of great practical importance, which is confirmed by contemporary events. The importance of this problem manifests itself both when the adjustment processes take place automatically and spontaneously, i.e. in the absence of any specific policy intervention (in which case the use of the term *mechanism* is justified), and when they are brought about by specific policy measures. In fact, independently of the debate on the desirability in general of policy interventions against laissez-faire, an analysis of the spontaneous behaviour of the system is also a necessary preliminary step for the study of the appropriate policy measures.

The balance-of-payments adjustment processes can be classified according to numerous criteria: the exchange-rate regime (fixed or flexible), the role played by money and other financial assets (i.e. whether their presence is essential or otherwise), the partial or general equilibrium nature of the framework considered, etc. All these classifications will be used, but the basic criterion followed in our treatment is first to examine the traditional processes and then more complex or recent models.

By *traditional processes* we mean those based on the variations in the exchange rate (other things — in particular national income — being equal) and those based on the variations in national income (other things — in particular the exchange rate — being equal); the integration between these two processes can also be considered as belonging to traditional theory.

The common feature of the traditional processes is to focus on the current account and to consider balance-of-payments disequilibria as *flow disequilibria*, that is, as disequilibria deriving from imbalances between the main macroeconomic aggregates that have the nature of flows (first of all exports and imports of goods and services, and then — if it is the case — consumption, investment, national income, etc.) and considered as *pure flows*, i.e. not deriving from stock adjustments. It should be noted that in these processes (described in Chaps. 12–14) money is neglected not because it is absent, but because it plays no essential role.

On the other hand, money has an essential role to play in subsequent chapters, both under fixed exchange rates (Chap. 15) and under flexible exchange rates (Chap. 16). In these more complex models *stock disequilibria* will be considered besides flow disequilibria. Stock disequilibra are those deriving from imbalances between the main aggregates which have the nature of stocks (first of all the stock of money and then those of other financial assets), so that the flows which occur derive from the adjustments of stocks. It is interesting to note that the oldest adjustment process, the Humean price-specie-flow mechanism mentioned at the beginning of this section, can be fitted into the stock disequilibria framework, as can the more recent monetary approach to the balance of payments. It should however be pointed out that these two mechanisms consider stock disequilibria *exclusively*; for an attempt at a synthesis in which *both* stocks *and* (pure) flows are given due consideration, one must have recourse to the analysis of the relationships between portfolio equilibrium and macroeconomic equilibrium in an open economy.

As stated in the Preface, we have tried to give a balanced treatment of the various approaches and to provide the valuational elements that will enable the reader to form a personal opinion and to choose one approach without ignoring the others. It is however as well for us to state our personal opinion here. First of all, we believe that the balance of payments cannot be seen as a separate sector but must be fitted into the dynamics of the whole economic system. From this point of view, the theory of balance-of-payments adjustment processes, of exchange-rate determination, etc., is synonymous with *open-economy macroeconomics* (for a general overview, see Kenen, 1985). And since both real and financial variables and both stocks and flows are relevant for such dynamics, we believe that it is not correct to claim in a *general* way that balance-of-payments disequilibria are of a certain type. In our opinion, the "real versus financial disequilibria" and "flow versus stock disequilibria" debates, which have been useful the better to clarify the various points of view on the issue at hand and to make up for the deficiencies in older theories, run the risk — if pursued to the death — of becoming sterile. The reason — we repeat — is that balance-of-payments disequilibria are a complex phenomenon, into which real and financial, stock and flow, disequilibria enter, in an inter-play of relations and feedbacks with all the other parts of the economic system; this complex phenomenon can be coped with, we believe, only by way of an eclectic and not by a dogmatic approach.

As stated at the beginning of this section, in the various chapters concerning the adjustment processes we shall examine both the spontaneous adjustment mechanisms and the main policy interventions aimed at bringing about the adjustment (and possibly at other policy targets).

Given their increasing importance, capital movements, already present in Chaps. 15 and 16, then receive a specific treatment in Chap. 17, together with related issues, such as the transfer problem. Chapter 18 is dedicated to an evaluation of the age-old debate on fixed versus flexible exchange rates and to exchange-rate determination. Chapter 19 examines the theory of monetary integration, including the EMS (European Monetary System) and the prospective European monetary union. The problems of the international monetary system and international financial markets are examined in Chap. 20. The last chapter offers brief comments on the problem of the integration between the pure theory of internation trade and international monetary theory.

In the course of our exposition we shall have recourse to models which can be one-country or two-country ones[18]. With the expression *one-country model* or *small country model* (also called SOE, small open economy) we refer to a model in

---

[18] This distinction is applicable to all international economics and not only to international monetary theory. As a matter of fact, we have used both one-country and two-country models in the pure theory of international trade.

which the rest of the world is taken as exogenous, in the sense that what happens in the country under consideration (call it country 1) is assumed to have a negligible influence — since this country is small relative to the rest of the world — on the rest-of-the-world variables (income, price level, interest rate, etc.). This means that these variables can be taken as *exogenous* in the model. With the expression *two-country model* (or large country model) we refer to a model in which the effect on the rest-of-the-world's variables of country 1's actions cannot be neglected, so that the rest of the world has to be explicitly included in the analysis (as country 2) so that, through the channels of exports and imports of goods and services and of capital movements, the economic events taking place in a country have repercussions on the other country, and vice versa.

At first sight two-country models may seen more realistic, as in the real world inter-country repercussions do come about. It should however be noted that in such models the various countries making up the rest of the world are assumedly aggregated into a single whole (country 2). This gives rise to aggregation problems, which involve — amongst other things — the stability of country 2's behaviour functions (demand for domestic goods, for imports, etc.). Even allowing that these problems can be solved (or at least are not different from those concerning the aggregation of the various regions etc., within a country, from which the country's aggregate behaviour functions are derived), the fact remains that (exception being made for certain countries, such as the USA) country 1 is usually fairly small with respect to the rest of the world, whence the validity, at least as a first approximation, of one-country models. These problems can of course be overcome by the construction of n-country models, which will be examined in the relevant Appendixes, given their degree of mathematical difficulty.

Thus no valid reason exists for denying the logical validity of one-country models. Besides, in some cases the use of two-country models, though enabling us to carry out a more sophisticated analysis, does not yield substantially different results from those obtained by way of one-country models. It is therefore not possible to formulate general criteria for the use of one or the other type of model; what can be said is that to analyze certain problems it is necessary to use two country models, whilst for other problems it is sufficient to use one-country models, at least as a first approximation.

We note, in conclusion, that when two-country (or n-country) models are used, it is often expedient to use the constraint that the sum of the balances of payments (measured in terms of a common unit) of all countries is zero; this is also called an *international consistency condition*. It should however be added that this condition holds true insofar as no reserve creation (on which see Sects. 11.1.3.II and 20.1.4) occurs: as a matter of fact, the sum of the balances of payments of all countries (i.e., the world balance of payments) equals the increase in net world reserves (see Mundell, 1968). Therefore, the reader should bear in mind that, when we use this constraint in the following chapters, we shall implicity be assuming that no reserve creation is taking place.

Appendix

A.11.1 The Presentation of the US Balance of Payments

The main national source of balance-of-payments data in the USA is the monthly *Survey of Current Business* issued by the US Department of Commerce. In Tables A.11.1 and A.11.2 we reproduce the US balance of payments both in a summarized and in a detailed presentation from the December 1985 issue of this periodical. The first thing to note is that in this presentation the items are arranged in a purely accounting framework; the item statistical discrepancy is what has been called net errors and omissions in the text. No emphasis is put on any particular balance: a few of the most common ones are given as memoranda at the bottom of Table A.11.2 (lines 64 onwards). Different presentations have been used in the past, however, and a brief history of the main changes in the presentation of the US balance of payments is now in order.

In the past, in addition to giving the data in an "aseptic" way as they are now given, a series of payments balances were also published, by suitably arranging the data above the line and below the line as explained in the text. This arrangement[19] was made in such a way that each payments balance was obtained by adding the net sum of a certain number of new items to the previous balance. Starting from (1) the merchandise trade balance, this presentation went on to (2) the balance on goods and services, (3) the balance on goods, services and remittances (remittances included all unilateral transfers, except US Government grants), (4) the balance on current account, (5) the balance on current account and long-term capital, (6) the *liquidity balance*, (7) the *official reserve transactions balance*. The first five balances conformed to the concepts explained in the text, and need no further comment. Some comments are called for as regards the last two.

The liquidity balance was introduced about 1955 as a consequence of the concern then existing over the gradually mounting volume of US liabilities to foreigners. The purpose it was intended to serve was to give a broad indicator of potential pressures on the dollar resulting from changes in the US liquidity position. The liquidity balance is obtained by adding the following items to the balance on current account and long-term capital: (i) the changes in US claims against foreigners, and (ii) net errors and omissions. It therefore places the changes in US liquid liabilities to all foreigners (both private and official) and changes in US official reserves below the line. The asymmetric treatment of the changes in liquid claims (included above the line) and in liquid liabilities (included below the line) was justified (see, for example, Lederer, 1963) by arguing that (a) liquid liabilities (i.e. liquid claims by foreigners against the US) pose a potential danger for US official reserves, as foreigners might liquidate their liquid claims, and so the changes in these must be included below the line to give a prudential measure of the ultimate ability of the US monetary authorities to defend the dollar; (b) on the contrary, the US monetary authorities cannot be

---

[19] It should be noted that this arrangement, before being discontinued at the suggestion of the Advisory Committee (see below in the text), varied through time, in the sense that it did not always include all the balances listed here. The most comprehensive arrangement, including all of these balances, began with the June 1971 issue of the *Survey of Current Business*.

Appendix 77

Table A.11.1. Summary of US international transactions – seasonally adjusted (millions of dollars)

Line	Lines in Table A.11.2 in which transactions are included in ()	1992	1992 I	1992 II	1992 III	1992 IV	1993 I	1993 II^r	1993 III^p	Change: 1993 II-III	Jan–Sep 1992	Jan–Sep 1993	Change: 1992–93
1	Exports of goods, services, and income (1)	730,460	182,211	181,454	182,038	184,759	184,071	187,791	187,244	-547	545,703	559,106	13,403
2	Merchandise, excluding military (2)	440,138	108,347	108,306	109,493	113,992	111,530	113,118	111,912	-1,206	326,146	336,560	10,414
3	Services (3)	179,710	44,836	44,507	45,350	45,018	46,463	46,797	46,637	-160	134,693	139,897	5,204
4	Income receipts on investments (11)	110,612	29,028	28,641	27,195	25,749	26,078	27,876	28,695	819	84,864	82,649	-2,215
5	Imports of goods, services, and income (15)	-763,965	-181,507	-191,697	-192,666	-198,098	-198,793	-207,669	-207,668	1	-665,870	-614,130	-48,260
6	Merchandise, excluding military (16)	-536,276	-126,110	-133,107	-137,105	-139,954	-140,839	-147,502	-148,191	-689	-396,322	-436,532	-40,210
7	Services (17)	-123,299	-30,788	-30,856	-30,069	-31,589	-31,839	-32,338	-32,530	-192	-91,713	-96,707	-4,994
8	Income payments on investments (25)	-104,391	-24,609	-27,734	-25,492	-26,555	-26,115	-27,829	-26,947	882	-77,835	-80,891	-3,056
9	Unilateral transfers (29)	-32,895	-7,389	-8,010	-7,147	-10,348	-7,586	-7,294	-7,562	-268	-22,546	-22,442	104
10	U.S. assets abroad, net (increase/capital outflow (-)) (33)	-50,961	-1,029	-8,695	-10,798	-30,438	-12,358	-29,341	-43,961	-14,620	-20,522	-85,660	-65,138
11	U.S. official reserve assets, net (34)	3,901	-1,057	1,464	1,952	1,542	-983	822	-545	-1,367	2,359	-706	-3,065
12	U.S. Government assets, other than official reserve assets, net (39)	-1,609	-275	-293	-305	-737	535	-275	-86	189	-873	174	1,047
13	U.S. private assets, net (43)	-53,253	303	-9,866	-12,445	-31,243	-11,910	-29,888	-43,331	-13,443	-22,008	-85,129	-63,121
14	Foreign assets in the United States, net (increase/capital inflow (+)) (48)	129,579	19,834	44,450	26,450	38,845	25,718	42,380	66,452	24,072	90,734	134,550	43,816
15	Foreign official assets, net (49)	40,684	21,124	21,008	-7,378	5,931	10,929	17,699	19,646	1,947	34,754	48,274	13,520
16	Other foreign assets, net (56)	88,895	-1,290	23,442	33,828	32,914	14,789	24,681	46,806	22,125	55,980	86,276	30,296
17	Allocations of special drawing rights (62)	–	–	–	–	–	–	–	–	–	–	–	–
18	Statistical discrepancy (63)	-12,218	-12,120	-17,502	2,123	15,280	8,948	14,133	5,495	-8,638	-27,499	28,576	56,075
	Memorandum: Balance on current account (70)	-66,400	-6,685	-18,253	-17,775	-23,687	-22,308	-27,172	-27,986	-814	-42,713	-77,466	-34,753

^r Revised.
^p Preliminary.

78   11 Balance of Payments and National Accounts

Table A.11.2. US international transactions (millions of dollars)

Line	(Credits +; debits −)[1]	1992	Not seasonally adjusted							Seasonally adjusted						
			1992			1993				1992				1993		
			II	III	IV	I	II[r]	III[p]		II	III	IV	I	II	III[p]
1	**Exports of goods, services, and income**	**730,460**	**182,880**	**180,212**	**184,892**	**183,832**	**189,162**	**185,656**		**181,454**	**182,038**	**184,759**	**184,071**	**187,791**	**187,244**
2	Merchandise, adjusted, excluding military[2]	440,138	110,864	105,626	114,418	112,023	115,811	108,078		108,306	109,493	113,992	111,530	113,118	111,912
3	Services[3]	179,710	43,436	48,351	44,295	45,171	45,628	49,984		44,507	45,350	45,010	46,463	46,797	46,637
4	Transfers under U.S. military agency sales contracts[4]	11,015	2,744	2,695	2,523	3,058	2,950	2,709		2,744	2,695	2,523	3,058	2,950	2,709
5	Travel	53,861	13,446	15,839	12,448	12,384	14,093	16,886		13,513	13,405	13,460	13,868	14,156	14,172
6	Passenger fares	17,353	4,133	5,165	4,066	4,022	4,404	5,312		4,243	4,327	4,405	4,450	4,536	4,425
7	Other transportation	22,773	5,668	5,788	5,751	5,732	5,839	5,921		5,718	5,696	5,677	5,855	5,894	5,823
8	Royalties and license fees[5]	20,238	4,893	5,026	5,532	4,697	5,095	4,967		5,002	5,252	4,976	4,901	5,225	5,194
9	Other private services[5]	53,601	12,276	13,534	13,825	15,115	12,958	13,998		13,012	13,671	13,826	14,166	13,746	14,123
10	U.S. Government miscellaneous services	869	275	304	151	165	290	191		275	304	151	165	290	191
11	Income receipts on U.S. assets abroad	110,612	28,581	26,235	26,179	26,638	27,723	27,594		28,641	27,195	25,749	26,078	27,876	28,695
12	Direct investment receipts	49,888	13,222	11,500	11,682	13,205	14,336	13,765		13,193	12,455	11,202	12,763	14,405	14,878
13	Other private receipts	53,687	13,828	12,742	12,702	12,043	12,297	12,462		13,828	12,741	12,702	12,043	12,297	12,462
14	U.S. Government receipts	7,038	1,531	1,993	1,795	1,390	1,090	1,368		1,620	1,998	1,845	1,272	1,174	1,355
15	**Imports of goods, services, and income**	**−763,965**	**−191,618**	**−197,030**	**−200,094**	**−191,037**	**−207,817**	**−213,139**		**−191,697**	**−192,666**	**−198,098**	**−198,793**	**−207,669**	**−207,668**
16	Merchandise, adjusted, excluding military[2]	−536,276	−131,671	−136,176	−143,601	−136,194	−146,288	−150,368		−133,107	−137,105	−139,954	−140,839	−147,502	−148,191
17	Services[3]	−123,299	−31,789	−32,784	−30,294	−29,399	−33,272	−35,226		−30,856	−30,069	−31,589	−31,839	−32,338	−32,530
18	Direct defense expenditures	−13,766	−3,471	−3,312	−3,359	−3,203	−3,176	−3,050		−3,471	−3,312	−3,359	−3,203	−3,176	−3,050
19	Travel	−39,872	−10,976	−12,153	−8,687	−8,396	−11,387	−12,538		−9,899	−9,825	−10,140	−10,463	−10,280	−10,226
20	Passenger fares	−10,943	−2,821	−3,118	−2,634	−2,404	−2,895	−3,130		−2,674	−2,722	−2,833	−2,765	−2,749	−2,747
21	Other transportation	−23,454	−5,618	−6,161	−5,953	−5,847	−6,092	−6,335		−5,700	−5,999	−5,945	−5,931	−6,185	−6,168
22	Royalties and license fees[5]	−4,986	−1,078	−1,478	−1,113	−1,071	−1,174	−1,237		−1,101	−1,464	−1,088	−1,088	−1,201	−1,218
23	Other private services[5]	−27,988	−7,195	−5,957	−7,986	−7,884	−7,977	−8,356		−7,380	−6,142	−7,662	−7,795	−8,141	−8,540
24	U.S. Government miscellaneous services	−2,290	−631	−605	−562	−594	−571	−581		−631	−605	−562	−594	−571	−581
25	Income payments on foreign assets in the United States	−104,391	−28,158	−26,070	−26,199	−25,445	−28,257	−27,544		−27,734	−25,492	−26,555	−26,115	−27,829	−26,947
26	Direct investment payments	−1,630	−1,720	−1,259	−655	−795	−3,132	−2,785		−1,296	−681	−1,011	−1,465	−2,704	−2,188
27	Other private payments	−61,582	−16,113	−14,472	−15,204	−14,240	−14,820	−14,173		−16,113	−14,472	−15,204	−14,240	−14,820	−14,173
28	U.S. Government payments	−41,179	−10,325	−10,339	−10,340	−10,410	−10,305	−10,586		−10,325	−10,339	−10,340	−10,410	−10,305	−10,586

Appendix 79

29	Unilateral transfers, net	-32,895	-7,588	-7,043	-10,900	-7,471	-7,022	-7,356	-8,010	-7,147	-10,348	-7,586	-7,294	-7,562
30	U.S. Government grants[4]	-14,688	-3,234	-2,783	-5,883	-3,242	-2,730	-2,970	-3,234	-2,783	-5,883	-3,242	-2,730	-2,970
31	U.S. Government pensions and other transfers	-3,735	-929	-811	-1,348	-679	-954	-725	-1,118	-940	-846	-978	-979	-976
32	Private remittances and other transfers[6]	-14,473	-3,425	-3,448	-3,669	-3,550	-3,338	-3,661	-3,659	-3,424	-3,619	-3,366	-3,585	-3,616
33	**U.S. assets abroad, net (increase/capital outflow (−))**	**-50,961**	**-10,635**	**-12,203**	**-25,987**	**-13,676**	**-31,201**	**-45,497**	**-8,695**	**-10,798**	**-30,438**	**-12,358**	**-29,341**	**-43,961**
34	U.S. official reserve assets, net[7]	3,901	1,464	1,952	1,542	-983	822	-545	1,464	1,952	1,542	-983	822	-545
35	Gold	—	—	—	—	—	—	—	—	—	—	—	—	—
36	Special drawing rights	2,316	-168	-173	2,829	-140	-166	-118	-168	-173	2,829	-140	-166	-118
37	Reserve position in the International Monetary Fund	-2,692	1	-118	-2,685	-228	313	-48	1	-118	-2,685	-228	313	-48
38	Foreign currencies	4,277	1,631	2,243	1,398	-615	675	-378	1,631	2,243	1,398	-615	675	-378
39	U.S. Government assets, other than official reserve assets, net	-1,609	-364	-234	-667	535	-275	-87	-293	-305	-737	535	-275	-86
40	U.S. credits and other long-term assets	-7,140	-1,232	-1,890	-2,470	-940	-727	-1,505	-1,232	-1,890	-2,470	-940	-727	-1,505
41	Repayments on U.S. credits and other long-term assets[8]	5,596	1,002	1,430	1,878	1,807	859	1,988	1,072	1,360	1,808	1,807	859	1,988
42	U.S. foreign currency holdings and U.S. short-term assets, net	-65	-133	225	-75	-332	-407	-569	-133	225	-75	-332	-407	-569
43	U.S. private assets, net	-53,253	-11,735	-13,921	-26,682	-13,228	-31,749	-44,866	-9,866	-12,445	-31,243	-11,910	-29,888	-43,331
44	Direct investment	-34,791	-8,803	-3,504	-7,108	-9,620	-13,411	-7,123	-6,934	-2,028	-11,489	-8,302	-11,550	-5,588
45	Foreign securities	-47,961	-8,276	-13,787	-17,405	-26,889	-26,098	-45,290	-8,276	-13,787	-17,405	-26,889	-24,098	-45,290
46	U.S. claims on unaffiliated foreigners reported by U.S. nonbanking concerns	4,551	1,294	-3,214	1,132	-4,774	443	n.a.	1,294	-3,214	1,132	-4,774	443	n.a.
47	U.S. claims reported by U.S. banks, not included elsewhere	24,948	4,050	6,584	-3,481	28,055	5,317	7,547	4,050	6,584	28,055	5,317	7,547	
48	**Foreign assets in the United States, net (increase/capital inflow (+))**	**129,579**	**45,117**	**27,186**	**38,031**	**25,218**	**43,426**	**67,235**	**44,450**	**26,450**	**38,845**	**25,718**	**42,380**	**66,452**
49	Foreign official assets in the United States, net	40,684	21,008	-7,378	5,931	10,929	17,699	19,646	21,008	-7,378	5,931	10,929	17,699	19,646
50	U.S. Government securities	22,403	12,939	589	-6,505	1,749	6,750	20,353	12,939	589	-6,505	1,749	6,750	20,353
51	U.S. Treasury securities[9]	18,454	11,240	-323	-7,379	1,039	5,668	18,808	11,240	-323	-7,379	1,039	5,668	18,808
52	Other[10]	3,949	1,699	912	874	710	1,082	1,545	1,699	912	874	710	1,082	1,545
53	Other U.S. Government liabilities[11]	2,542	678	864	943	-395	396	1,322	678	864	943	-395	396	1,322
54	U.S. liabilities reported by U.S. banks, not included elsewhere	16,427	7,466	-7,831	11,219	8,171	9,454	-2,213	7,466	-7,831	11,219	8,171	9,454	-2,213
55	Other foreign official assets[12]	-688	-75	-1,000	274	1,404	1,099	184	-75	-1,000	274	1,404	1,099	184
56	Other foreign assets in the United States, net	88,895	24,109	34,565	32,100	14,289	25,727	47,589	23,442	33,828	32,914	14,789	24,681	46,806

Table A.11.2. (continued)

Line	(Credits +; debits −)[1]	1992	Not seasonally adjusted 1992 II	III	IV	1993 I	II[r]	III[p]	Seasonally adjusted 1992 II	III	IV	1993 I	II[r]	III[p]
57	Direct investment	2,378	3,037	1,765	2,278	8,101	11,345	2,658	2,370	1,028	3,092	8,601	10,299	1,875
58	U.S. Treasury securities	36,893	10,168	4,870	21,232	13,599	−623	3,995	10,168	4,870	21,232	13,599	−623	3,995
59	U.S. securities other than U.S. Treasury securities	30,274	10,453	2,730	12,478	9,394	15,025	17,411	10,453	2,730	12,478	9,394	15,025	17,411
60	U.S. liabilities to unaffiliated foreigners reported by U.S. nonbanking concerns	741	979	1,553	−2,717	2,057	1,361	n.a.	979	1,553	−2,717	2,057	1,361	n.a.
61	U.S. liabilities reported by U.S. banks, not included elsewhere	18,609	−528	23,647	−1,171	−18,862	−1,381	23,525	−528	23,647	−1,171	−18,862	−1,381	23,525
62	Allocations of special drawing rights	−	−	−	−	−	−	−	−	−	−	−	−	−
63	Statistical discrepancy (sum of above items with sign reversed)	−12,218	−18,155	8,877	14,058	3,134	13,452	13,100	−17,502	2,123	15,289	8,948	14,133	5,495
63a	Of which seasonal adjustment discrepancy	−	−	−	−	−	−	−	653	−6,754	1,222	5,814	681	−7,605
	Memoranda:													
64	Balance on merchandise trade (lines 2 and 16)	−96,138	−20,807	−32,550	−29,183	−24,171	−30,477	−42,290	−24,801	−27,612	−25,962	−29,309	−34,384	−36,279
65	Balance on services (lines 3 and 17)	56,411	11,647	15,567	14,001	15,773	12,356	14,758	13,651	15,281	13,429	14,624	14,459	14,107
66	Balance on goods and services (lines 64 and 65)	−39,727	−9,161	−16,983	−15,182	−8,398	−18,121	−27,532	−11,150	−12,331	−12,533	−14,685	−19,925	−22,172
67	Balance on investment income (lines 11 and 25)	6,222	422	166	−20	1,193	−534	50	907	1,703	−806	−37	47	1,748
68	Balance on goods, services and income (lines 1 and 15 or lines 66 and 67)[13]	−33,505	−8,738	−16,818	−15,202	−7,205	−18,655	−27,482	−10,243	−10,628	−13,339	−14,722	−19,878	−20,424
69	Unilateral transfers, net (line 29)	−32,895	−7,588	−7,043	−10,900	−7,471	−7,022	−7,356	−8,010	−7,147	−10,348	−7,586	−7,294	−7,562
70	Balance on current account (lines 1, 15, and 29 or lines 68 and 69)[13]	−66,400	−16,327	−23,861	−26,102	−14,676	−25,677	−34,838	−18,253	−17,775	−23,687	−22,308	−27,172	−27,986

[1] Credits, +: Exports of goods, services, and income; unilateral transfers to United States; capital inflows (increase in foreign assets (U.S. liabilities) or decrease in U.S. assets); decrease in U.S. official reserve assets: increase in foreign official assets in the United States.
Debits, −: Imports of goods, services, and income; unilateral transfers to foreigners; capital outflows (decrease in foreign assets (U.S. liabilities) or increase in U.S. assets); increase in U.S. official reserve assets; decrease in foreign official assets in the United States.
[2] Excludes exports of goods under U.S. military agency sales contracts identified in Census export documents, excludes imports of goods under direct defense expenditures identified in Census import documents, and reflects various other adjustments (for valuation, coverage, and timing) of Census statistics to balance of payment basis; see table 2.

3. Includes some goods: Mainly military equipment in line 4; major equipment, other materials, supplies, and petroleum products purchased abroad by U.S. military agencies in line 18; and fuels purchased by airline and steamship operators in lines 7 and 21.

4. Includes transfers of goods and services under U.S. military grant programs.

5. Beginning in 1982, these lines are presented on a gross basis. The definition of exports is revised to exclude U.S. parents' payments to foreign affiliates and to include U.S. affiliates' receipts from foreign parents. The definition of imports is revised to include U.S. parents' payments to foreign affiliates and to exclude U.S. affiliates' receipts from foreign parents.

6. Beginning in 1982, the "other transfers" component includes taxes paid by U.S. private residents to foreign governments and taxes paid by private nonresidents to the U.S. Government.

7. For all areas, amounts outstanding Sept. 30, 1993, were as follows in millions of dollars: Line 34, 75,835; line 35, 11,057; line 36, 9,203; line 37, 12,101; line 38, 43,474. Data are preliminary.

8. Includes sales of foreign obligations to foreigners.

9. Consists of bills, certificates, marketable bonds and notes, and nonmarkable convertible and nonconvertible bonds and notes.

10. Consists of U.S. Treasury and Export-Import Bank obligations, not included elsewhere, and of debt securities of U.S. Government corporations and agencies.

11. Includes, primarily, U.S. Government liabilities with military agency sales contracts and other transactions arranged with or through foreign official agencies; see table 4.

12. Consists of investments in U.S. corporate stocks and in debt securities of private corporations and State and local governments.

13. Conceptually, the sum of lines 69 and 62 is equal to "net foreign investment" in the national income and product accounts (NIPA's). However, the foreign transactions account in the NIPA's (a) includes adjustments to the international transactions accounts for the treatment of gold, (b) includes adjustments for the different geographical treatment of transactions with U.S. territories and Puerto Rico, and (c) includes services furnished without payment by financial pension plans except life insurance carriers and private noninsured pension plans. A reconciliation of the balance on goods and services from the international accounts and the NIPA net exports appears in the "Reconciliation and Other Special Tables" section in this issue of the SURVEY OF CURRENT BUSINESS. A reconciliation of the other foreign transactions in the two sets of accounts appears in table 4.5 of the full set of NIPA tables (published annually in the July issue of the SURVEY).

certain that they can liquidate the US private liquid claims on foreigners and use them to offset the US liquid liabilities, so that the changes in these liquid claims cannot be included below the line but must be placed above it.

The liquidity balance was severely critized on various grounds (for a summary see, for example, the Bernstein *Report*) and an alternative definition, the *net liquidity balance*, was subsequently suggested (and implemented in the June 1971 issue of the *Survey of Current Business*). This differs from the liquidity balance in that changes in liquid claims and in liquid liabilities are treated symmetrically, as both are below the line. In the meantime (1963) the US Government had appointed a committee chaired by E.M. Bernstein to review the US balance-of-payments statistics and presentation. It is interesting to give here the warning issued by this committee (p. 101 of the *Report*): "... No single number can adequately describe the international position of the United States during any given period. The definition of an international surplus or deficit is an analytical problem rather than an accounting problem. The appropriate focus of analysis will change with changing circumstances and with the nature of the particular problem being analyzed. Data must therefore be compiled and presented in a form that facilitates a wide variety of analyses. Furthermore, useful analysis of the international position is rarely possible on the basis of balance of payments data alone; internal developments and policy objectives here and abroad need also to be taken into account".

Nevertheless, the committee recommended the introduction of a new statistic, the *balance on official reserve transactions* or *official settlements balance*, whose purpose was "to measure the gap between the normal supply of and demand for foreign exchange — a gap which the monetary authorities, here and abroad, must fill by adding to or drawing down, their reserve assets if exchange rates are to be held stable" (p. 109 of the *Report*). This balance is measured by changes in US official reserve assets plus changes in liquid and nonliquid liabilities to foreign official agencies.

The official settlements balance is obtained by adding net private capital flows to the net liquidity balance, and was introduced into the official balance-of-payments accounts in the June 1965 issue of the *Survey of Current Business*. Apart from criticism of a general type (for example, it is not always possible effectively to distinguish foreign private ownership of dollar balances in New York from foreign official ownership), the relevance of the official reserve transactions balance was challenged because of changes in the international monetary system. With the advent of (more) flexible exchange rates (see Sects. 10.5.4, and 19.1.5) it was no longer sensible to consider the changes in official reserves and in liabilities in foreign-exchange markets to fulfil the obligation of holding the exchange-rate stable (it should be kept in mind that we are dealing with the United States; this criticism is not relevant for those countries which still follow some form of pegging: see Sect. 10.5.4), Therefore the US government appointed another committee, the Advisory Committee on the Presentation of Balance of Payments Statistics, which issued its Report in June 1976.

This committee, in endorsing the warning issued by the earlier committee (see the quotation above), brought it to its logical conclusion (account being taken of the changed international monetary setting), i.e., that the publication of the data arranged to show a range of net balances should be discontinued, that no overall balance should be published, and that the data themselves should be published in a "neutral" way, but in sufficient detail to permit users to calculate for themselves any of the traditional balances which they continued to find useful, *except* those based on the distinction between liquid and nonliquid assets (in practice, the net liquidity balance). The committee, in fact, felt that such a distinction could not properly be made in practice because of statistical difficulties, so that any balance using this distinction was both fuzzy and misleading.

The committee, however, recommended that two of the traditional partial balances — the balance on goods and services and the current account balance — should continue to be published as memorandum items because of their relationship to other economic accounting systems (see above, Sect. 11.3).

The recommendations of the committee were accepted in full, with the exception that two further partial balances — the merchandise trade and the goods, services and remittances balances — were deemed useful items for inclusion in the memoranda. The new balance-of-payments presentation was implemented immediately, in the same June 1976 issue of the *Survey of Current Business,* where the committee's report was published, and is now in use (with the addition of two further partial balances: the balance on investment income, and the balance on goods, services, and income) as shown above in Tables A.11.1 and A.11.2. The reader interested in knowing the exact content of each of the items can consult the June 1978 issue (Part II) of the *Survey of Current Business,* where each line of the standard table is given a detailed explanation.

The advisability of discontinuing the presentation of various balances, especially as regards the lack of any official overall balance to which reference could be made, gave rise to much debate, and a symposium was published with the opinions of R. M. Stern, C. F. Schwartz, R. Triffin, E. M. Bernstein, and W. Lederer (Stern et al., 1977). Briefly speaking, those who were against the disappearance of an overall balance, such as the official reserve transactions balance, complained that the news media, and also the general public, might give undue attention to the balances that survived (as memoranda items) and accord them a greater significance than these partial measures deserve, and also pointed out the difficulty of communicating the conclusions of the analysis of the country's international transactions to government officials. On the contrary, those who were in favour, whilst recognizing these difficulties, emphasized that the absence of official overall balances reduces the possibility that users of the analysis will accept them as comprehensive appraisals and as single guides in the formulation of policies. Any useful analysis of the international position of a country and of the interrelations between this and the domestic economy requires the evaluation of a spectrum of balances.

Recently, alternative measures of U.S. international transactions on goods and services have been suggested, amongst which a new residency-based measure that "combines the standard balance on trade in goods and services between residents and nonresidents of the United States (cross-border trade) with a measure of the net effect on the U.S. economy of the operations of U.S.-owned companies abroad and of foreign-owned companies in the United States" (Landefeld et al., 1993, p. 50). This measure has been presented in the December

1993 issue of *Survey of Current Business,* and shows striking differences with the standard balance on goods and services. For example, the new measure shows a surplus of $24 billion in the 1991 balance on goods and services, compared with a deficit of $28 billion according to the standard measure.

A.11.2 Illegal Transactions in the Balance of Payments

The presence of restrictions to international transactions — which, it should be noted, may concern both current account transactions (tariffs etc.: see Chap. 5) and capital account transactions (controls on capital movements etc.) — may give rise to a series of illegal activities aimed at avoiding the restrictions. These activities are not limited to "ships in the night" operations (inflows and outflows of goods through illegal places of entry) but also include illegal trade through legal checkpoints or, more generally, illegal transactions through legal channels (such as misinvoicing, fictitious tourist expenditures, etc. etc.). The former type does not, of course, appear in the balance of payments, but the latter does, insofar as it gives rise to inexact entries in the balance of payments and/or to entries in the wrong accounts.

As regards illegal commercial transactions or smuggling, its economic effects have already been examined in Sect. 7.9. The main question posed there was whether tariff evasion increased or decreased welfare, the answer depending on the assumptions made to study the problem. In the present context we are interested in illegal transactions purely from the point of view of accounting, a brief mention of which is in order, since in some countries they are widely practised (and are probably present at a "physiological" level in all countries).

Let us begin by examining merchandise trade. It should be stressed that this channel can be used not only for tariff evasion, but also to evade controls on capital movements, i.e. to permit clandestine capital movements. The main tool employed here is misinvoicing. For example, to evade an import duty, legal imports need to be shown to have a lower value. This can be obtained by underinvoicing, by forging invoices, etc. In the first case the foreign exporter will issue an invoice for a lower value. In the second case the foreign exporter issues a correct invoice but the importer forges it or declares false values at the customs etc. Similarly, to evade an export duty, legal exports need to be shown to have a lower value (for example by underinvoicing exports).

But, as we said, merchandise trade can also serve as a channel for clandestine capital movements, which are usually outward movements. To achieve this, imports will be overinvoiced, or exports underinvoiced. In the former case the foreign exporter, who receives a greater amount than the true value of the goods, will credit the difference to, say, an account that the domestic importer (illegally)[20] holds abroad. In the latter case the foreign importer, who has to pay a lower amount than the true value of the goods, will credit the difference to, say, an account that the domestic exporter (illegally) holds abroad. These differences are

---

[20] "Illegally" is to be understood from the point of view of the regulations of the importer's country; from the point of view of the country which receives the deposit, everything will be perfectly legal. This observation also holds for the illegal deposits mentioned later.

(clandestine) capital movements, which of course are not recorded as such in the capital account, since they are hidden in merchandise trade.

These illegal transactions can sometimes be detected by partner-country trade-data comparison insofar as they show up in discrepancies in the records of the exporting and importing countries (duly adjusted for c.i.f.-f.o.b. valuation), but this is not always the case (if, for example, the foreign partner underinvoices or overinvoices, no discrepancy will arise, whilst it will if the domestic trader fakes etc., a correct invoice issued by the foreign partner).

Clandestine capital movements can also be hidden in other current account items, such as travel, labour income and workers' remittances. As regards travel, purchases of foreign exchange by a resident for legitimate tourism abroad can be fictitious (the purchaser does not actually leave the country and sells the currency on the black market) and, similarly, foreign tourists coming to visit the country may purchase the domestic currency on the black market. This will give rise to an increase in the debit entries and a decrease in the credit entries recorded in the travel item in the current account.

As regards labour income and worker's remittances (for this purpose it is irrelevant whether we are dealing with a service or an unrequited transfer) the best known device is that of *direct compensation* through an illegal organization. Mr. X, a resident of country 1 with heavy controls on capital movements, who wishes to export capital to country 2, pays out a sum of x units of domestic currency to the domestic representative of the organization. Immediately the organization's representative in country 2 deposits the equivalent in country 2's currency into an account that Mr. X (illegally) holds with a bank in country 2 (or buys country 2's bearer securities for Mr. X, etc., etc.); it goes without saying that such an equivalent will be calculated at a much higher exchange rate than the official one applied in country 1 for legal transactions, the difference going to cover the organizations's costs and profit. Now, country 2's representative has obtained the necessary amount of country 2's currency from Mr. Y, a worker who has (temporarily or definitively) come to work in country 2 from country 1, and who wishes to send part of his earnings to his relatives in country 1. Mr. Y can either use the official banking and postal channels (in which case there will be a record in the balance of payments), or give the money to the organization's man in country 2, who offers him perhaps a more favourable exchange rate, or immediate delivery, etc. In fact, country 2's representative only has to instruct country 1's representative to pay out the agreed amount to Mr. Y's relatives.

In conclusion, nothing has materially moved (and, if Mr. X prefers bearer securities bought by country 2's representative, no increase in foreign liabilities will be recorded in country 2's balance of payments), but a clandestine capital outflow from country 1 will have taken place; this will be reflected in lower credit entries in the "labour income" and "migrants' remittances" items.

The ingenuity of persons wishing to undertake illegal international transactions is of course much greater than may appear from the above examples, but as this is not a treatise on the economics of crime we must stop at this point.

References

Advisory Committee on the Presentation of Balance of Payments Statistics, 1976
Bain, A.D., 1973
Bernstein *Report*, see Review Committee etc.
Cohen, B., 1969, Chap. 1
Fellner, W. et al., 1966, 243–254
IMF (International Monetary Fund), 1948, *Balance of Payments Manual,* 1st ed.; 2nd ed. 1950; 3rd ed. 1961; 4th ed. 1977; 5th ed. 1993
IFM, 1949, 4–24
IMF, *Balance of Payments Statistics Yearbook; International Financial Statistics* (monthly)
Johnson, H.G., 1958a
Kenen, P.B., 1985
Kindleberger, C.P., 1969
Landefeld, J.S., et al., 1993
Lederer, W., 1963
Machlup, F., 1950
Machlup, F., 1958
Meade, J.E., 1951, Part I
Mundell, R.A., 1968, Chap. 10
Review Committee for Balance of Payments Statistics, 1965
Stern, R.M., 1973, Chap. 1
Stern, R.M. et al., 1977
United States Department of Commerce-Bureau of Economic Analysis, *Survey of Current Business* (monthly)
Yeager, L.B., 1976, Chap. 3

12 The Role of the Exchange Rate in the Adjustment Process in a Partial Equilibrium Framework

12.1 Introduction

As was clarified in Sect. 11.4, the balance of payments considered here is the balance on goods and services, and its adjustment through exchange-rate changes relies upon the effect of the relative price of domestic and foreign goods[1] (considered as not perfectly homogeneous) on the trade flows with the rest of the world. This relative price, or (international) terms of trade is defined by the ratio

$$\pi = \frac{p_x}{r p_m}, \tag{12.1}$$

where p_x represents export prices[2] (in terms of domestic currency), p_m represents import prices (in terms of a single reference foreign currency), and r is the exchange rate of the country under consideration. The presence of r is necessary owing to the fact that p_x and p_m are absolute prices expressed in different currencies, and must be made homogeneous to permit comparisons. From the point of view of the consumer, π represents the relative price of foreign and domestic goods on which — in accordance with standard consumer's theory — demand will depend. From the point of view of the country as a whole, π represents the amount of imports that can be obtained in exchange for a unit of exports (or the amount of exports required to obtain one unit of imports)[3]. Therefore an *increase* in π is also defined as an improvement in the terms of trade, as it means that a greater amount of imports can be obtained per unit of exports (or, equivalently, that a smaller amount of exports is required per unit of imports).

It should also be noted that it is irrelevant whether π is defined as above or as

$$\pi = \frac{\frac{1}{r} p_x}{p_m}, \tag{12.1.1}$$

---

[1] For brevity we shall henceforth use *goods* in the broad sense (i.e., including services), and, similarly, *trade flows* in the sense of flows of goods and services.
[2] Prices — both export and import prices — will usually be measured by index numbers.
[3] This has the same meaning as the term-of-trade notion defined in the pure theory of international trade. See Part I, *passim*.

since the two formulae are mathematically equivalent. From the economic point of view, it is easy to see that in (12.1) domestic and foreign prices have been made homogeneous by expressing the latter in domestic currency before taking their ratio, whilst in (12.1.1) they have been made homogeneous by expressing the former in foreign currency; the ratio is of course the same. The terms of trade π can therefore serve both the domestic and the foreign consumer for the relevant price-comparison. The domestic consumer, as mentioned above, will compare the price of domestic goods (identical to those exported) with that of imported goods by translating this price into domestic currency terms (in practice this will be done by the importer), for example (if the home country is the USA), US$ 2.5 (price of a certain domestic commodity) with US$ $(0.125 \times FF\ 10) =$ US$ 1.25, i.e. the equivalent in dollars of a French commodity costing ten French francs per unit, given the exchange rate of 0.125. The French consumer will compare the price of the French commodity (FF 10) with that of the US commodity expressed in francs which is $(8 \times 2.5) = 20$, given the exchange rate of 8.

In any case the ratio is 2, that is, one unit of the US commodity exchange for two units of the French commodity considered[4].

The idea behind the adjustment process under consideration is that a change in the relative price of goods, *ceteris paribus*, brings about a change in the demands for the various goods by both domestic and foreign consumers, thus inducing changes in the *flows* of exports and imports which will hopefully adjust a disequilibrium in the payments balance considered.

The terms of trade may vary both because of a change in the prices p_x and p_m expressed in the respective national currencies and because r changes. The analysis with which we are concerned in this chapter focusses on the changes in r and so assumes that p_x and p_m, as well as all other variables that might influence the balance of payments, are constant. It is, therefore, a *partial equilibrium* analysis, in which the *ceteris paribus* clause is imposed when the exchange rate varies[5]. We shall look more closely into this interpretation of the analysis later on.

It is important to observe at this point that the problem of the effects of exchange-rate changes does not vary whether we consider a free movement of the exchange rate in a flexible exchange rate regime or a discretionary or managed movement in an adjustable peg or other limited-flexibility regime (see Sect. 10.5). In the latter case (i.e. the case of a policy-determined change), we are in the presence, in Johnson's (1958a) terminology, of an *expenditure switching*[6] policy, that is of a policy aiming at restoring balance-of-payments equilibrium by effecting a switch of expenditure (by residents and foreigners) between domestic and foreign goods.

---

[4] In practice, if the US terms of trade are $\pi_{US} = (p_{xUS})/(r_{US}p_{mUS})$, the French terms of trade will be $\pi_F = (p_{xF})/(r_F p_{mF})$. Given the arbitrage conditions (see Sect. 10.2), $r_F = (1/r_{US})$, and if we assume for simplicity that $p_{xUS} = p_{mF}$ etc., we have $\pi_{US} = 1/\pi_F$.

[5] This is the received interpretation. See Sect. A.12.1.2 for the case in which prices are allowed to vary (but other variables are not, so that we still are in a context of partial equilibrium). See however Chipman (1978), for an attempt at a reinterpretation of the elasticity approach in the context of a neoclassical general equilibrium model.

[6] By contrast, if we consider a deficit, an *expenditure reducing* policy involves measures inducing a decrease in residents' total expenditure (and thus in that part of it which is directed to foreign goods, i.e. imports) by monetary or fiscal restriction, etc. See Sect. 15.5.1.

Another important preliminary observation is that the problem of the effects on the balance of payments of a variation in the exchange rate is often identified in the traditional literature with that of the effects on the foreign exchange market of the same variation. The same stability conditions are, in fact, stated for both problems, where "stability conditions" refer both to the conditions under which an exchange-rate depreciation improves the balance of payments (thus eliminating a deficit) and to the conditions under which such depreciation reduces the excess demand for foreign currency (thus equilibrating the foreign exchange market). Of course, if a depreciation improves the balance of payments, an appreciation will worsen it (thus eliminating any surplus); and if a depreciation reduces the excess demand, an appreciation increases it (reduces the excess supply, again equilibrating the foreign exchange market).

The underlying (explicit or implicit) assumption to this identification is that the demand for and supply of foreign exchange as a function of the exchange rate derive *exclusively* from merchandise trade. More generally, the identification remains valid if we assume that any demand and supply deriving from other sources are independent of the exchange rate and its variations, and can therefore be considered as exogenous components of the demand and supply schedules. It is clear that by so doing much is lost, as there may be capital flows depending, among other things, on the exchange rate and its variations (for example, speculative flows). It should therefore be stressed that the identification which we are examining (and which will be taken up again later on) is valid only under the assumption discussed.

12.2 Critical Elasticities and the So-Called Marshall-Lerner Condition

To begin with, we observe that the *ceteris paribus* clause enables us to consider exchange-rate variations as the sole cause of changes in export and import flows. A depreciation in the exchange rate at unchanged domestic and foreign prices in the respective currencies, in fact, makes domestic goods cheaper in foreign markets and foreign goods dearer in the domestic market. The opposite is true for an appreciation. Thus we can say, on the basis of conventional demand theory, that exports vary in the same direction as the exchange rate (an increase in the exchange rate, that is a depreciation, stimulates exports and a decrease, that is an appreciation, lowers them) whilst imports vary in the opposite direction to the exchange rate[7].

But this is not sufficient to allow us to state that suitable exchange-rate variations (a depreciation in the case of a deficit, an appreciation in the case of a

---

[7] Strictly speaking, this is true as regards the foreign *demand* for domestic goods (demand for exports) and the domestic *demand* for foreign imports (demand for imports). To be able to identify the demand for exports with exports and the demand for imports with imports, we need the further assumption that the relevant supplies (supply of domestic goods by domestic producers to meet foreign demand, and of foreign goods by foreign producers to meet our demand) are perfectly elastic. The consequences of dropping this assumption will be examined in Sect. A.12.1.2.

surplus) will equilibrate the balance of payments. The balance of payments is, in fact, expressed in monetary terms, and it is not certain that a movement of the *quantities* of exports and imports in the right direction ensures that their *value* also changes in the right direction. The change in receipts and outlays depends on the *elasticities*, as the student knows from microeconomics.

We define the exchange-rate elasticity of exports, η_x, and of imports, η_m, as any price-elasticity, that is as the ratio between the proportional change in quantity and the proportional change in price (here represented by the exchange rate). Thus, letting x and m denote the quantities of exports and imports respectively, we have,

$$\eta_x \equiv \frac{\Delta x/x}{\Delta r/r}, \quad \eta_m \equiv -\frac{\Delta m/m}{\Delta r/r}, \tag{12.2}$$

where Δ as usual denotes a change, and the minus sign before the second fraction serves to make it a positive number (Δm and Δr have, in fact, opposite signs because of what we said at the beginning, so that the fraction by itself is negative).

12.2.1 The Balance of Payments in Domestic Currency

Since each country normally records its balance of payments in terms of domestic currency, we begin by considering the payments balance in domestic currency

$$B = p_x x - r p_m m; \tag{12.3}$$

where the value of imports in terms of foreign currency (p_m, we remember, is expressed in foreign currency) has to be multiplied by the exchange rate to transform it into domestic currency units; as p_x is expressed in terms of domestic currency, the value of exports, $p_x x$, is already in domestic currency units.

To examine the effects of a variation in the exchange rate, let us consider a depreciation by a small amount, say 1% (the case of an appreciation being perfectly symmetrical). Given the definition of elasticity, the quantity of imports increases by η_x%: from Eqs. (12.2) we in fact have

$$\frac{\Delta x}{x} = \eta_x \frac{\Delta r}{r}. \tag{12.4}$$

Since the price p_x is assumed to be unchanged, the value of exports in domestic currency increases by the same percentage as the quantity, i.e. by η_x%. If we apply this percentage increase to the initial value of exports ($p_x x$) we obtain the (nominal) increase in the value of exports, which is

$$\eta_x p_x x / 100. \tag{12.5}$$

As regards imports, their quantity decreases by η_m%, since from Eqs. (12.2) we have

$$\frac{\Delta m}{m} = -\eta_m \frac{\Delta r}{r}. \tag{12.6}$$

Since the foreign price p_m is assumed to be unchanged, the value of imports in *foreign currency* also decreases by $\eta_m\%$. But since the exchange rate has depreciated, by 1%, the domestic-currency price of imports has increased by this same percentage, so that the lower quantity of imports has a higher unit value, and what happens to the total outlay in terms of domestic currency depends on whether $\eta_m\% \gtreqless 1\%$. In the first case, in fact ($\eta_m\% > 1\%$), the value of imports in foreign currency decreases more than proportionally to the increase in the price of foreign currency, so that the former change more than offsets the latter and the value of imports in domestic currency decreases. This, coupled with the increase in the domestic-currency value of exports shown above, certainly improves the balance of payments.

In the latter case ($\eta_m\% < 1\%$) the value of imports in foreign currency decreases less than proportionally to the increase in the price of foreign currency, so that the value of imports in domestic currency increases. In general, the domestic-currency value of imports changes approximately[8] by $(1-\eta_m)\%$, so that — by applying this percentage to the initial value of imports ($rp_m m$) — we obtain the (nominal) increase in the value of imports

$$(1-\eta_m)rp_m m/100. \qquad (12.7)$$

The condition for the balance of payments to improve is obviously that the increase in the value of exports should be greater than the increase in the value of imports, that is

$$\eta_x p_x x > (1-\eta_m)rp_m m, \qquad (12.8)$$

whence, if we divide through by $rp_m m$ and rearrange terms, we get

$$\frac{p_x x}{rp_m m}\eta_x + \eta_m > 1. \qquad (12.9)$$

---

[8] If we denote by $E = rp_m m$ the domestic-currency value of import expenditure and consider changes, we have

$$\Delta E = (r+\Delta r)p_m(m+\Delta m) - rp_m m = p_m m \Delta r + rp_m \Delta m + p_m \Delta r \Delta m.$$

If we neglect the last term, which is of the second order of smalls, and collect terms we get

$$\Delta E = rp_m m\left(\frac{\Delta r}{r} + \frac{\Delta m}{m}\right).$$

If we divide through by $E = rp_m m$ and rearrange terms we get

$$\frac{\Delta E}{E} = \frac{\Delta r}{r}\left(1 + \frac{\Delta m/m}{\Delta r/r}\right).$$

and so, given (12.2),

$$\frac{\Delta E}{E} = (1-\eta_m)\frac{\Delta r}{r},$$

whence it follows that $\Delta E/E = (1-\eta_m)\%$ when $\Delta r/r = 1\%$.

Table 12.1. Exchange-rate depreciation and balance of payments: a numerical example

Exports ($\eta_x=0.3$)			Imports				
Quantity	Value	Change in value	Elasticity	Quantity	Foreign-currency value	Domestic-currency value	Change in dom.-curr. value
1,003	100,300	+300	a) $\eta_m=1.1$	989	989	99,889	−111
			b) $\eta_m=0.8$	992	992	100,192	+192
			c) $\eta_m=0.6$	994	994	100,394	+394

In the particular case in which, as is often assumed for simplicity of expression, the balance of payments is initially in equilibrium (i.e. $p_x x = r p_m m$), inequality (12.9) becomes

$$\eta_x + \eta_m > 1. \tag{12.10}$$

that is, the condition for an exchange-rate depreciation to improve the balance of payments is that the sum of the elasticity of exports and the elasticity of imports should be greater than one. In the general case, however, we must consider inequality (12.9), and it is immediately obvious that, when there is an initial deficit (which is the case in which an exchange-rate depreciation normally comes about, either spontaneously or through discretionary intervention by the monetary authorities), the condition on the elasticities for a balance-of-payments improvement to occur is more stringent. In fact, in (12.9) the fraction multiplying η_x is smaller than one in the case of a deficit ($p_x x < r p_m m$), and the smaller it is, the higher the deficit, so that higher elasticity values are required to satisfy (12.9) than (12.10); in general, condition (12.9) might *not* be satisfied even when (12.10) is.

It should now be noted that the result arrived at, in an admittedly roundabout manner, could have been very easily obtained by straightforward differentiation of Eq. (12.3). But — apart from problems of mathematical competence — we believe that the beginner will be better able to grasp the economic sense of what is going on by following the simple algebra used here than by differentiating Eq. (12.3).

A simple numerical example may help further to clarify the analysis. For simplicity's sake we consider the case of initial payments balance. The data are

$$x=1,000; \; p_x=100; \; m=1,000; \; p_m=1; \; r=100,$$

so that the value of exports equals the value of imports. A 1% depreciation brings the exchange rate to 101. Table 12.1 gives the details of the calculations, assuming an elasticity of exports equal to 0.3 and three alternative values for the elasticity of imports.

As regards exports, given an elasticity of 0.3, the 1% depreciation brings about a quantity increase of 3 and a value increase of 300.

As regards imports, in case (a), with an elasticity of 1.1 the quantity decreases by 11. If we multiply the foreign-currency value (989) by the new exchange rate (101) we get the new domestic-currency value, which shows a decrease of 111. The payments balance improves by $300-(-111)=411$.

In case (b), since the elasticity is lower than one, the domestic-currency value of imports will increase. The increase is 192, approximately equal[9] to $rp_m m(1-\eta_m)\% = 100{,}000(1-0.8)\% = 200$. The balance of payments improves, since the value of imports increases by less than the value of exports (and, in fact, condition (12.10) is fulfilled, since $\eta_x + \eta_m = 1.1 > 1$); the improvement is $300 - 192 = 108$.

In case (c) the domestic-currency value of imports increases by more than the value of exports since the sum of the elasticities is lower than one; the balance of payments deteriorates.

12.2.2 The Balance of Payments in Foreign Currency

Conditions (12.9) and (12.10) have been assumedly obtained with reference to the balance of payments expressed in terms of domestic currency. Various authors, however, suggest the use of the balance of payments in terms of *foreign* currency, as the ultimate aim of the analysis of the effects of an exchange-rate depreciation is to ascertain the conditions under which this depreciation eases the pressure on the country's reserves, i.e. brings about a decrease in the net outlay of foreign exchange (or, better still, brings about an increase in the net receipts of foreign exchange), as foreign exchange, unlike the domestic currency, is the "scarce" asset from the point of view of the country experiencing balance-of-payments difficulties[10]. Other writers object to this view by pointing out that when one wants to study the relations between the balance of payments and the other aggregates of the country under consideration (see Sect. 11.3), it is necessary to consider the domestic currency balance of payments (an objection which is not, however, relevant in the partial equilibrium context in which the present analysis is assumedly carried out). Be that as it may, we shall describe briefly what happens when the foreign-currency balance is considered. Now, if $B = px - rp_m m$ is the domestic-currency balance, then

$$B' = \frac{1}{r}B = \frac{1}{r}px - p_m m \qquad (12.3.1)$$

is the foreign-currency balance. In the case of an initial equilibrium, the condition for a depreciation to improve the balance is the same as before, i.e.

$$\eta_x + \eta_m > 1, \qquad (12.10)$$

whilst in the case of an initial disequilibrium the condition (see Sect. A.12.1.1) becomes

$$\eta_x + \frac{rp_m m}{px}\eta_m > 1. \qquad (12.11)$$

---

[9] It should be stressed that the formulae previously derived are exact for infinitesimal changes only, and become less and less precise (though the direction of change is not altered) as the magnitude of the changes increases. To check this the reader can perform the calculations by assuming alternatively a depreciation of 0.1% and of 10%.

[10] This, of course, does not hold for reserve-currency countries, i.e. for countries whose currency is held as an asset in other countries' reserves.

It is quite clear that, in the presence of an initial deficit, condition (12.11) can more easily occur than condition (12.9) — the elasticities being the same. In the extreme case, it is possible, when there is an initial deficit, that a depreciation will improve the foreign-currency balance and at the same time worsen the domestic-currency balance[11]. It is therefore important, when one deals with depreciation and balance of payments, to specify whether this is expressed in domestic or foreign currency; it goes without saying that when an initial equilibrium situation is considered, condition (12.10) ensures that the payments balance will improve in terms of both domestic and foreign currency.

12.2.3 Partial vs Total Elasticities

Some considerations are now in order as to the meaning to be given to the elasticities appearing in the various formulae derived in the previous sections. As we said in Sect. 12.1, the present analyis of the conditions under which an exchange-rate depreciation improves the payments balance is a partial equilibrium analysis, where all the other variables are assumed constant on the basis of the *ceteris paribus* clause; the elasticities appearing in the conditions examined above are, therefore, *partial* elasticities. In the context of the assumptions made, the analysis is formally correct, but doubts may arise as to the validity of the assumptions themselves. Generally speaking, no partial equilibrium analysis can be considered fully satisfactory, because, by definition, it neglects all elements other than the one being considered. It can, however, be considered as a good (first) approximation, and its results can be accepted as a first approximation, insofar as, in the context examined, the *ceteris paribus* clause does not do too much violence to reality. This requires that the other variables should not indeed undergo appreciable changes and/or that their possible changes have a negligible or at least secondary influence on the problem at hand.

Thus we must inquire whether the *ceteris paribus* clause is admissible in the context under examination. The answer seems to be in the negative. In fact, the change in the payments balance directly determined by the exchange-rate variation influences, among other things, national income and the stock of money. The change in national income feeds back (through the marginal propensity to import) on the balance of payments, modifying the initial results (see Chap. 14); the change in the money stock has important effects which may differ according to the various approaches (these will be examined in due course: see Chaps. 15 and 16), but are not in any case negligible. Also, a depreciation may have an inflationary impact on domestic prices (the vicious circle: see Sect. 18.5), etc., etc. All these effects are indeed important and it does not seem legitimate to assume them away.

---

[11] It is in fact possible that following a depreciation, there will be a decrease in the outlay of foreign exchange (payment for imports) in absolute value greater than the decrease in foreign exchange receipts (from exports), whilst there will be an increase in the outlay of domestic currency (payment for imports) in absolute value greater than the increase in the domestic-currency value of exports. This means that the balance of payments expressed in foreign currency improves whilst that expressed in domestic currency deteriorates.

One way out of this dilemma was sought by redefining the elasticities that appear in the various formulae as *total elasticities*. The adjective total refers to the fact that these elasticities ought to be computed by including in the change in exports and imports not only the partial variation directly determined by the exchange-rate variation, but also the sum of all other indirect variations due to the factors mentioned a moment ago[12]. This can be criticized by observing that, if the elasticities are defined in this way, one falls into a tautology, unless the other effects are independently specified and analyzed. But if this is done, it becomes superfluous to reformulate the results in terms of total elasticities. In other words, the analysis ought to be carried out from the beginning in terms of partial elasticities *and* of the other various relevant behavioural parameters, without trying *ex post* to squeeze the results into the straitjacket of elasticities (albeit total). This more general analysis will be carried out later (in Chap. 14, in the context of the traditional theory, and in Chap. 16, in the context of more recent approaches) because we must first analyze the adjustment mechanisms based solely on income changes (Chap. 13). These mechanisms have, in fact, a twofold relevance. On the one hand they may be seen as the counterpart — always in a partial equilibrium context — to the present analysis based solely on exchange-rate variations, and thus as a step towards the integration of the two mechanisms. On the other hand, they have an importance of their own insofar as they are applicable to an institutional setting in which the exchange rate as well as prices is rigid.

These short notes on the problem of partial versus total elasticities are sufficient to show the futility of the old debate (which went on after the second world war and in the 1950's: for a survey see, for example, Sohmen, 1969, Chap. I, Sect. 3) between *elasticity pessimism* and *elasticity optimism*. In the pessimists' opinion, the elasticities were too low to satisfy the critical condition, so that an exchange rate depreciation, instead of improving the payments balance, would have worsened it. The opposite view was, of course, held by the optimists. And the copious empirical analyses were not able to settle the controversy (for a complete survey of the older empirical studies aimed at estimating these elasticities, see Stern et al., 1976; see also Himarios, 1989). But this is not surprising, because these analyses were based on single equations relating export and import demands to relative prices and possibly to other variables (such as national income) in a partial equilibrium context, thus neglecting the interrelationship among the different variables, which can be evaluated only in a more general setting which requires economy-wide simultaneous econometric models.

12.2.4 A Note on Terminology

Condition (12.10) is generally referred to in the literature as the *Marshall-Lerner condition*. As regards the second author, there is no doubt that the problem examined in this section is the subject of his treatment. He (Lerner, 1944) shows

---

[12] In practice these elasticities could be calculated by observing *ex post* the *total* variations in exports and imports that actually occurred and relating these variations to the given variation in the exchange rate.

that the critical point lies where the sum of the export and import elasticities equals one, and observes that when this sum is lower than one, an exchange-rate depreciation worsens the balance of payments (in this case to obtain an improvement an appreciation would be indicated), whilst a depreciation improves the balance when the sum of the elasticities exceeds one.

Many doubts, on the contrary, exist as regards Marshall. His contributions, in fact, refer to the pure theory of international trade and the conditions that he developed concern the stability of barter international equilibrium analyzed in terms of offer curves (see above, Chap. 3); some authors — we among them — believe that offer curves are not suitable instruments for analyzing the problem of how an exchange-rate variation influences the balance of payments in a monetary economy. Therefore the attribution of the condition under examination to Marshall is not convincing. Besides, if one wishes to make a question of chronological priority, there exists a treatment by Joan Robinson (1937) prior to Lerner's and, if we go further back still in time, we find the contribution of Bickerdicke (1920), who seems to have been the first to give the full and correct formal conditions for an exchange-rate depreciation to improve the balance of payments.

It follows that a historically more correct denomination would be the Bickerdicke condition, or perhaps the Bickerdicke-Robinson(-Lerner) condition. In our opinion, however, it would be simpler to drop any discussion of priority, subjective originality, stimulus to diffusion etc., and refer to the condition under examination as the "critical (sum of the export and import) elasticities condition".

12.3 The Equilibrium Exchange Rate; Multiple Equilibria and Stability

As regards the second problem mentioned in Sect. 12.1 (effects of an exchange-rate variation in the foreign exchange market), given the restrictive assumptions made there, it follows that the demand for foreign exchange (which we denote by D) comes from importers and equals the foreign-exchange value of imports, whilst the supply (S) of foreign exchange is due to exporters and equals the foreign-exchange value of exports[13]. Thus we have

$$D(r) = p_m m(r),$$
$$S(r) = \frac{1}{r} p_x x(r), \qquad (12.12)$$

---

[13] Given the international nature of the foreign exchange market, it should be noted that it makes no difference whether some or all of the transactions are settled in domestic currency. If, for example, domestic importers pay out domestic currency to foreign suppliers, these will sell it in exchange for their own currency, which is a demand for foreign currency from the point of view of the importing country. Similarly, if domestic exporters are paid in domestic currency, this means that foreign importers sell their own currency to purchase the exporters' currency, which is a supply of foreign currency from the point of view of the home country.

where, owing to the *ceteris paribus* clause, imports and exports are functions solely of the exchange rate (note that, as is implicit in our treatment, we are considering exclusively the spot market. The forward market will be introduced in the next section).

The condition of equilibrium in the foreign exchange market is that typical of all markets, i.e. the equality between demand and supply

$$D(r)=S(r), \; D(r)-S(r)=0, \tag{12.13}$$

which determines the equilibrium exchange rate[14]; it goes without saying that this is a partial equilibrium, for the reasons explained in Sect. 12.2. The analogy with any other kind of market whatsoever is obvious: here the "commodity" exchanged is foreign exchange, and the equality between demand and supply determines the equilibrium price i.e. the equilibrium exchange rate (remember that the exchange rate is quoted as the price of foreign currency: see Sect. 10.1).

Let us now observe that by substituting from Eqs. (12.12) into Eq. (12.13) and rearranging terms we get

$$p_x x(r) - r p_m m(r) = 0, \; \frac{1}{r} p_x x(r) - p_m m(r) = 0, \tag{12.13.1}$$

so that the equilibrium in the foreign exchange market coincides with the equilibrium in the balance of payments (no matter whether the latter is expressed in domestic or foreign currency). It can also easily be seen that the presence of an excess demand for foreign exchange is equivalent to a disequilibrium situation in the balance of payments. To be precise, if we define $E(r)=D(r)-S(r)$ and use Eqs. (12.12) we get

$$E(r) \gtreqless 0 \text{ is equivalent to } B \lesseqgtr 0, \; B' \lesseqgtr 0, \tag{12.14}$$

that is, a positive (negative) excess demand for foreign exchange is equivalent to a deficit (surplus) in the balance of payments however expressed. This is of course intuitive given the assumption made at the beginning on the sources of the demand for and supply of foreign exchange.

However, these demand and supply schedules present some peculiarities which need clarification.

12.3.1 Derivation of the Demand and Supply Schedules; Stability

The main peculiarity of demand and supply schedules for foreign exchange is the fact that they are *derived* or *indirect* schedules in the sense that they come from the underlying demand schedules for goods (demand for domestic goods by nonresidents and demand for foreign goods by residents). In other words, in the context we are considering, transactors do not directly demand and supply foreign exchange as such[15], but demand and supply it as a consequence of the underlying demands for goods. From these elementary and apparently irrelevant consider-

---

[14] The problem of the equilibrium exchange rate will be dealt with in a general way in Sect. 18.8.

[15] In a wider context there would also be, of course, a demand and supply of foreign exchange for its own sake (speculation etc.), but this is assumed away as we are considering commercial transactions exclusively.

ations important consequences follow, and precisely that *even if we assume that the underlying demand schedules for goods are perfectly normal, the resulting supply schedules for foreign exchange may show an abnormal behaviour and even give rise to multiple equilibria.*

Let us then take up Eqs. (12.12) again and assume that import and export demands are normal, that is, the demand for imports decreases monotonically as r increases (since the foreign price of imports is assumed constant, an increase in r means an increase in the domestic-currency price of imports), and the demand for exports increases monotonically as r increases (since the domestic price of exports is assumed constant, an increase in r means a decrease in the foreign-currency price of exports). Is this enough for us to be able to state that the demand and supply schedules for foreign exchange are normal, i.e. that the demand for foreign exchange is a monotonically decreasing function of r and the supply of foreign exchange is a monotonically increasing function of r? The answer is partly in the negative.

In fact, as regards the demand for foreign exchange, since it is obtained simply by multiplying the demand for imports by the foreign price of imports p_m, a constant by assumption, the behaviour of the former demand coincides with that of the latter. But the case of the supply of foreign exchange is much more complicated, as it is obtained by multiplying the demand for exports by the factor p_x/r, which varies inversely with r since p_x is a constant. Thus when r increases x increases but p_x/r decreases and their product, namely $S(r)$, can move either way. It can be shown that the direction in which $S(r)$ moves depends on the exchange-rate elasticity of exports. A formal proof will be given in footnote 16; here it is sufficient to recall the relations between elasticity and total revenue (in fact, $S(r)$ is total revenue of foreign exchange from exports). If the elasticity of exports is greater than one, an exchange-rate depreciation of, say, one per cent, causes an increase in the volume of exports greater than one per cent, which thus more than offsets the decrease in the foreign currency price of exports: total receipts of foreign exchange therefore increase. The opposite is true when the elasticity is lower than one.

We must now distinguish two cases and the respective consequences on the foreign exchange market.

(1) The demand for exports has an elasticity everywhere greater than one or everywhere smaller than one. In this case the receipts (and so the supply) of foreign exchange will be either a monotonically increasing function of r (if $\eta_x > 1$) or a monotonically decreasing function of r (if $\eta_x < 1$). In the latter eventuality the decrease in the receipts following a one percent depreciation is measured approximately by $(1/r)p_x x(1-\eta_x)/100$[16].

(2) The demand for exports has an elasticity greater than one in some stretch(es), and smaller than one in other stretch(es). This is a perfectly normal

---

[16] If we compute the total differential of $(1/r)p_x x$ we get

$$d\left(\frac{1}{r}p_x x\right) = \left(-\frac{1}{r^2}p_x x + \frac{1}{r}p_x\frac{dx}{dr}\right)dr = -\frac{1}{r}p_x x\left(1 - \frac{r}{x}\frac{dx}{dr}\right)\frac{dr}{r} = -\frac{1}{r}p_x x(1-\eta_x)/100$$

given the definition of x and letting $dr/r = 0.01$.

12.3 The Equilibrium Exchange Rate; Multiple Equilibria and Stability

case: for example, we remember from elementary microeconomics that a simple linear demand curve has an elasticity greater than one in the upper part, equal to one at the intermediate point, lower than one in the lower part. In this case, foreign exchange receipts (and thus the supply) will increase in some stretch(es) and decrease in other stretch(es).

To examine the consequences on the foreign exchange market of the two cases (and relative subcases) we must first introduce behaviour hypotheses. The hypothesis made here is that the exchange rate tends to depreciate when there is a positive excess demand for foreign exchange and to appreciate in the opposite case. This is an extension to the foreign exchange market (where, as we said above, the good transacted is foreign exchange) of the usual hypothesis concerning the change in the price of a good determined by the forces of demand and supply. We also assume that we are in a regime of freely flexible exchange rates, so that there is no intervention on the part of the monetary authorities to peg the exchange rate (this will be treated below, in Sect. 12.3.3).

To begin with, we shall consider case (1) and its three possible subcases. In the upper three panels of Fig. 12.1 we have drawn the demand curve for foreign exchange, which for reasons already stated is normally decreasing, and various supply curves.

In the lower three panels, derived from the upper three, we have drawn the corresponding curves of *excess demand* for foreign exchange, given by the algebraic difference between demand and supply, $E(r) = D(r) - S(r)$.

In Fig. 12.1a the supply curve is monotonically increasing, on the assumption that $\eta_x > 1$. It can be seen that the equilibrium point is stable, since for values of r lower than r_e there is a positive excess demand for foreign exchange which causes an increase in r: the exchange rate will therefore move towards r_e. When r is higher than r_e the negative excess demand (i.e., excess supply) will cause r to decrease towards r_e.

In Fig. 12.1b the supply curve is monotonically decreasing, on the assumption that $\eta_x < 1$. This curve, however, is less steep (*with respect to the price axis, i.e. to the r axis*) than the demand curve. Now, the slope of the demand curve with respect to the r axis represents the decrease in the foreign exchange outlay as r increases (this decrease is measured by $p_m m_m \eta_m / 100$ for a 1% increase in r)[17] and the slope of the supply curve represents in this case the decrease in foreign exchange receipts as r increases (this decrease is measured, as we have shown above, by $(1/r) p_x x (1 - \eta_x) / 100$). Therefore the decrease in outlay following a depreciation is greater in absolute value than the decrease in receipts, so that a positive excess demand for foreign exchange will gradually be reduced by exchange-rate depreciations. Likewise, exchange-rate appreciations will gradually reduce an excess supply.

The equilibrium point is, therefore, stable in case (b) as well, as can also be seen in the diagram by observing that below (above) r_e there is a positive (negative) excess demand, exactly as in case (a). But there is more to it than that.

---

[17] A 1% depreciation causes a η_m% decrease in import demand and so in foreign exchange outlay, as p_m is constant. By applying this percentage to the initial outlay $p_m m$, we get the decrease in the outlay itself, that is $p_m m_m \eta_m$%.

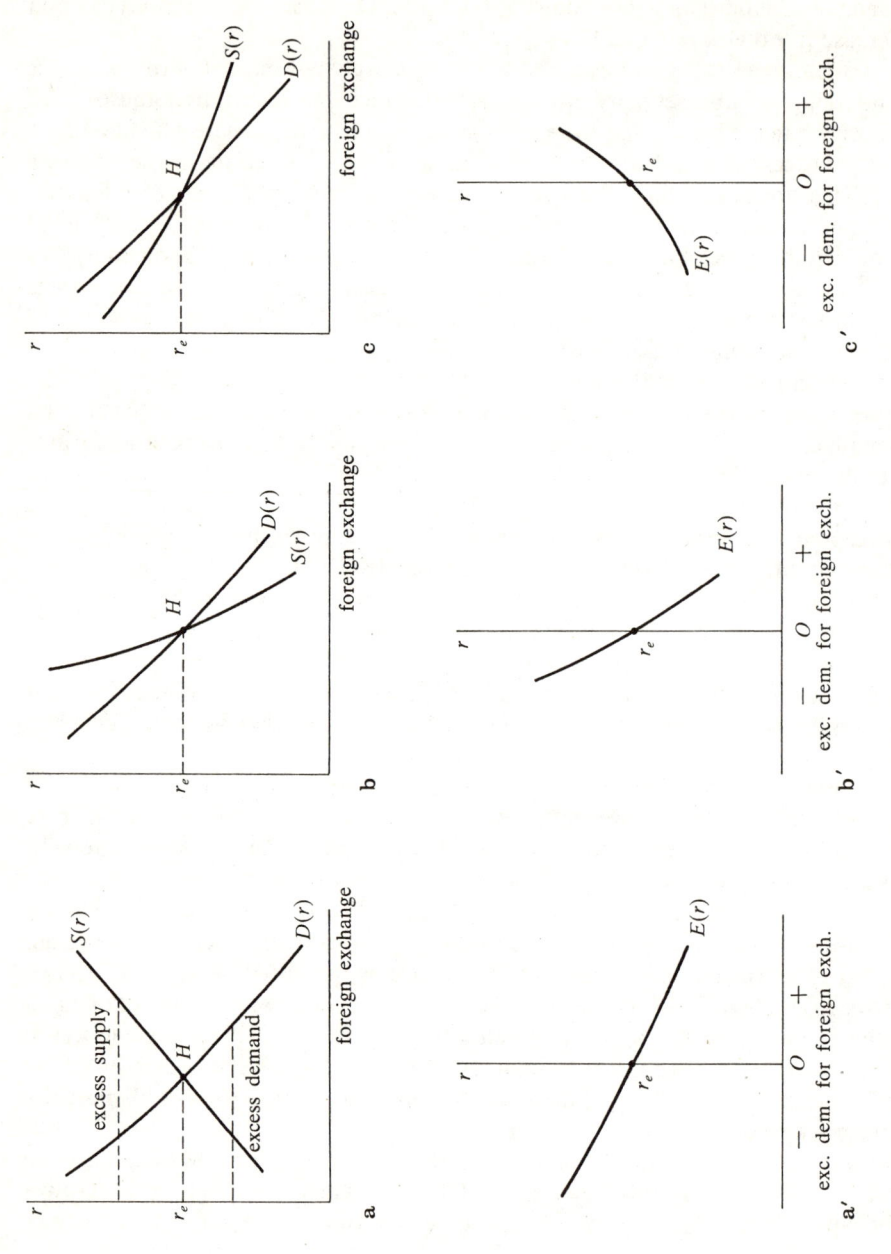

Fig. 12.1. Various forms of the supply curve of foreign exchange and stability

What we have said on outlays and receipts leads us to state that equilibrium is stable because

$$p_m m \eta_m > \frac{1}{r} p_x x (1 - \eta_x),$$

that is

$$\eta_x + \frac{r p_m m}{p_x x} \eta_m > 1. \tag{12.15}$$

It will be noted that condition (12.15) coincides with (12.11) and that, if one considers a situation near to equilibrium, (12.15) becomes

$$\eta_x + \eta_m > 1, \tag{12.16}$$

which coincides with (12.10). All this is by no means casual, as was already noted in Sect. 12.1. More precisely, the condition for the equilibrium in the foreign exchange market to be stable is that an exchange-rate depreciation causes a decrease in the excess demand for foreign exchange and vice versa, that is

$$\frac{\Delta E(r)}{\Delta r} < 0.$$

It is possible to verify the fact that this condition coincides with the condition that an exchange-rate variation brings about a change in the foreign-currency payments balance in the same direction, that is $\Delta B'/\Delta r > 0$. In fact, if we recall the definitions of $E(r)$ and B', we have $E(r) = -B'$, so that

$$\frac{\Delta E(r)}{\Delta r} = -\frac{\Delta B'}{\Delta r}, \tag{12.17}$$

and so when $\Delta B'/\Delta r$ is positive (that is, a depreciation improves the foreign-currency payments balance) then $\Delta E(r)/\Delta r$ will be negative, as was to be demonstrated. This proves that — in the circumstances hypothesized — the conditions concerning the twin problems of balance-of-payments adjustment and of foreign-exchange market stability coincide.

Let us now examine case (c), in which the equilibrium point is unstable. In fact, when $r > r_e$ there is a positive excess demand for foreign exchange, which will cause an exchange-rate depreciation, that is, r will move further away from r_e. Likewise, when $r < r_e$ there is a negative excess demand (excess supply): the consequent exchange-rate appreciation will drive r further away from its equilibrium value. In terms of receipts and outlays, the fact that the absolute value of the slope (referring to the r axis) of S is greater than that of D means that an exchange-rate depreciation brings about a decrease in receipts greater than the decrease in outlay, i.e. $(1/r) p_x x (1 - \eta_x) > p_m m \eta_m$, hence the stability condition (12.15) is not fulfilled.

Those illustrated in Fig. 12.1 are, as it were, the simplest eventualities, corresponding to case (1). More complicated is the situation of case (2), to which we now turn.

12.3.2 Multiple Equilibria

Case (2) can give rise to multiple equilibria, which in general will be alternatively stable and unstable. In Fig. 12.2 we have illustrated just two of the several possible occurrences; for brevity we have only drawn the demand and supply schedules, but not the corresponding excess demand schedules, which the reader who so wishes may derive by way of the same procedure as used in Fig. 12.1.

In Fig. 12.2a there is a case of two equilibrium points, due to the fact that the export demand elasticity is initially higher than one (so that the supply of foreign exchange is increasing, as explained in relation to case (1) above) and then falls below one. It is possible to verify immediately that H_1 is a *stable* equilibrium point, since for r below (above) r_{e1}, demand is higher (lower) than supply, and so r increases (decreases) towards r_{e1}. On the contrary, H_2 is an *unstable* equilibrium point, because for r below (above) r_{e2}, demand is lower (higher) than supply, and so r decreases (increases) away from r_{e2}.

In Fig. 12.2b a case of *three* equilibrium points is illustrated: by the usual reasoning, the reader may verify that H_1 and H_3 are stable equilibrium points whilst H_2 is an unstable one.

Since the considerations on foreign-exchange receipts and outlays previously explained can be applied to each equilibrium point, it follows that stable equilibrium points will be characterized by condition (12.15) [or (12.16), if we consider a neighbourhood of the point], whilst unstable points will be characterized by these conditions not being fulfilled.

It has already been stated in Sect. 12.3.1 that the nature of the supply schedule of foreign exchange makes the presence of multiple equilibria a normal occurrence; the present graphic analysis has shown that stable and unstable equilibria usually[18] alternate.

These considerations were taken by the supporters of freely flexible exchange rates as a starting point to claim that this regime is on the whole stable, in the sense that even if it runs into an unstable equilibrium point, this will not make it wander about unrestrained, as the movement away from the unstable point will necessarily converge to a stable equilibrium point.

But this would be true — the critics object — only if the alternation of unstable and stable equilibrium points were the norm, that is if the norm were a situation like that illustrated in Fig. 12.2b, where the system, when moving away from point H_2, will necessarily converge either to point H_1 or point H_3. But in a case such as that illustrated in Fig. 12.2a, the movement away from the unstable point H_2 will end up at a stable point only if the initial situation (or shift from H_2) is below H_2 (the system converges to H_1), whilst in the opposite case (if the initial situation or shift from H_2 is above H_2), no equilibrium point is found, so that the system becomes unstable.

As the reader can see, this aspect of the fixed-vs-flexible-exchange-rates debate — a debate which will be examined in its entirety in Sect. 18.2 — depends on whether any unstable equilibrium point is surrounded by a stable equilibrium

---

[18] We say "usually" because the extreme case — of $S(r)$ being tangent to $D(r)$ at one point — cannot be excluded: this equilibrium point will be stable on one side, unstable on the other (one-sided stability-instability in Samuelson's terminology).

12.3 The Equilibrium Exchange Rate; Multiple Equilibria and Stability

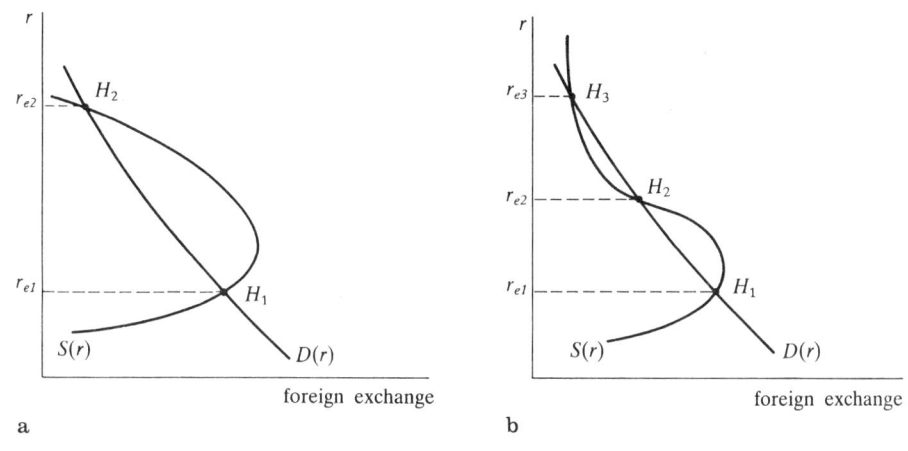

Fig. 12.2. Multiple equilibria and stability

point on either side or not. Notwithstanding subtle arguments for and against (we only mention, amongst others, the controversy between Bhagwati-Johnson (1960, 1961) on the one hand and Sohmen (1961,1969) on the other) we do not believe that it is possible to give a *generally* valid answer, so that from the purely theoretical point of view each faction has good points to make as far as this aspect is concerned.

12.3.3 Monetary Authorities' Intervention to Peg the Exchange Rate

The graphic treatment of Sects. 12.3.1 – 12.3.2 allows a simple exposition of the monetary authorities' intervention in the spot foreign-exchange market to peg the exchange rate at a certain given value (see Sect. 10.5.2). Let us, for example, take up Fig. 12.1a again and assume — see Fig. 12.3 — that the exchange rate has to be pegged at r' whilst the equilibrium value is r_e. In the absence of official intervention, the exchange rate would move towards r_e, driven by the excess supply of foreign exchange. To prevent this from happening, the monetary authorities must absorb, as residual buyers, the excess supply $A'B'$ (providing the market with the corresponding amount of domestic currency). If, on the contrary,

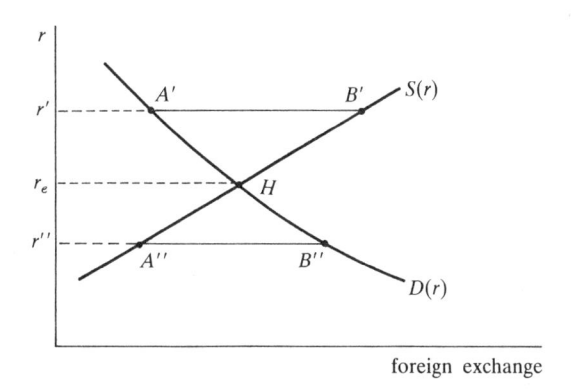

Fig. 12.3. Pegging of the exchange rate and monetary authorities' intervention

the exchange rate were to be pegged at r'', to prevent it from depreciating towards r_e, the monetary authorities would have to meet (as residual sellers) the excess demand, by supplying an amount $A''B''$ of foreign currency to the market.

It should be pointed out that, as the schedules in question represent *flows*, the monetary authorities must go on absorbing $A'B'$, or supplying $A''B''$, of foreign exchange per unit of time. This may well give rise to problems, especially in the case r'', because by continuously giving up foreign exchange the monetary authorities run out of reserves. Therefore, unless automatic mechanisms are at work, other interventions are called for, such as a depreciation of the exchange rate and/or policy measures which — short of exchange control — cause shifts in the $D(r)$ and $S(r)$ schedules so as to eliminate or reduce the excess demand for foreign exchange. These problems (both the automatic mechanisms and the policy interventions) will be dealt with in Chap. 15.

12.4 Interrelations between the Spot and the Forward Exchange Rate

To examine the interrelations between the spot and the forward exchange rate, we must first examine the determination of the equilibrium in the forward exchange market. For this purpose we have to consider the supplies of and demands for forward exchange by the various operators treated in Sect. 10.3 and 10.4, which we are going to take up again and illustrate here by way of diagrams.

12.4.1 The Various Excess Demand Schedules

(a) Covered Interest Arbitrage

We have seen in Sect. 10.3.3 that short-term funds will tend to flow in, remain where they are, or tend to flow out according to inequality (10.14), that we rewrite in the form

$$r^F \lesseqgtr r\frac{1+i_h}{1+i_f}. \qquad (12.18)$$

It is clear that a supply of forward exchange corresponds to an outflow of funds (demand for spot exchange) and vice versa. Therefore, if we denote by E_{AF} the (positive or negative) excess demand for forward exchange and by $r^F_N = r(1+i_h)/(1+i_f)$ the interest-parity forward rate (i.e. that which satisfies the neutrality condition), we have that $E_{AF}=0$ when $r^F = r^F_N$, whilst $E_{AF}>0$ (demand for forward exchange) when $r^F_N > r^F$ and $E_{AF}<0$ (supply of forward exchange) when $r^F_N < r^F$. We must now examine the features of the E_{AF} schedule.

Since it is profitable to move funds (inwards or outwards as the case may be) as long as $r^F \neq r^F_N$ because there is an interest gain with no exchange risk, it might seem obvious *prima facie* to assume an infinite elasticity of these funds in the neighbourhood of the forward exchange rate which satisfies the neutrality condition. If it were so, the traditional theory would be right to identify the neutrality condition with an *equilibrium* condition. In fact, any deviation[19] of the forward exchange rate from r_N^F would set into motion unlimited flows of arbitrage funds, which would prevail over the demands and supplies of other operators (commercial hedgers and speculators) and so would bring the forward exchange rate immediately back to r_N^F. In other words, if the elasticity of arbitrage funds (that is, of the arbitrageurs' excess demand for forward exchange) were indeed infinite, the other components of the total demand and supply in the forward market would be altogether irrelevant for the determination of the forward exchange rate. In this case the neutrality condition would also be the equilibrium condition and interest parity would prevail.

However, various considerations can be made to support the argument that arbitrage funds are not infinitely elastic, with the consequent possibility of the forward rate deviating from r_N^F.

A first consideration, already present in Keynes (1923) and taken up by Spraos (1953) amongst others, is based on the fact that arbitrage funds are in any case a finite amount, so that the forward rate moves towards r_N^F until arbitrageurs run out of funds (or cannot borrow any more).

A second consideration (Tsiang, 1959), is based on the *marginal convenience yield* of funds. In point of fact the availability of arbitrage funds does not abruptly drop to zero at a particular point. It is more likely that arbitrageurs will become more and more reluctant to transfer further amounts of funds in the same direction. The reason is that these funds also have, in addition to their yield in the strict sense (measured by the interest rate) some intangible returns of convenience: these derive from the fact that, for their regular business operations, banks, financial institutions, multinational corporations, etc., must have command over certain amounts of spot liquid funds in every major financial centre (including their own), and forward claims would not serve the purpose (Tsiang, 1959, p. 81). To these considerations we add the fact that forward cover eliminates the exchange risk, but not other kinds of risk (political risk; risk of default of the debtor; etc.). Now, it is presumable that the marginal convenience yield is a decreasing function of the amount of funds placed in any financial centre whilst the marginal non-exchange risk is an increasing function of the same. It follows that by moving funds from one centre to another the marginal convenience yield increases, and the marginal non-exchange risk decreases, in the centre of origin, whilst the opposite occurs in the centre of destination. At a certain point this will offset the profit from the covered interest differential and funds will cease to flow.

Other authors (see, e.g., Kenen, 1965; Grubel, 1966) point out that covered interest arbitrage must be seen in the broader context of optimal portfolio choice

---

[19] More precisely, the deviation should be such as to yield a profit rate above a certain threshold, that is the value below which arbitrageurs do not find it worth their while to move funds from one centre to another. This minimum, also called *arbitrage incentive*, may vary according to the historical period and institutional context. Keynes (1923, p. 28) stated the value of 1/2 per cent per annum; Stern (1973, p. 50) believes that in the postwar period arbitrage was undertaken for as little as 1/10 or 1/32 per cent per annum. At any given moment, however, this threshold is given and so we need not worry about its determination. The presence of this arbitrage incentive causes the AA schedule — see below, Fig. 12.4 — to have a point of discontinuity at zero, as the right-hand branch should start at r_N^F minus incentive, and the left-hand branch at r_N^F plus incentive. Given the smallness of the incentive, we ignore this fact for graphic convenience.

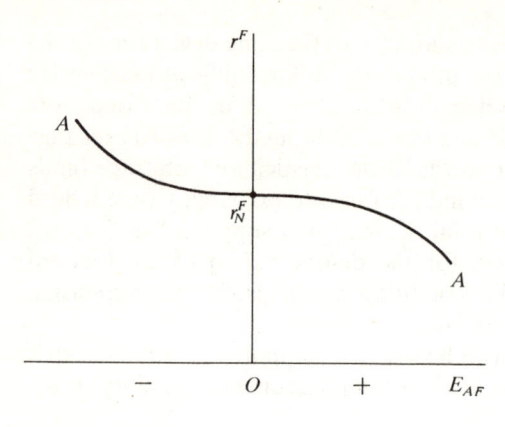

Fig. 12.4. The arbitrageurs' excess demand for forward exchange

by international financial investors. From the theory of portfolio selection (see Sect. A.10.3) it follows that when no foreign assets exist in the agent's portfolio, a small differential return is sufficient to induce heavy purchases, thus making the demand schedule highly elastic at the initial point. However, as the stock of foreign assets in the agent's portfolio increases, higher and higher covered interest differentials will be necessary to induce further additions to that stock, which explains why the schedule becomes more and more rigid (and there is a possibility that it will become perfectly rigid at a certain level of forward commitments).

In graphic terms, all these considerations point to an arbitrageurs' excess demand schedule for forward exchange like that drawn in Fig. 12.4.

(b) Commercial Hedging

We refer to those commercial operators whose export and import contracts are stipulated in foreign exchange and do not contemplate immediate payment. If these operators do not cover the exchange risk, they become (functionally) speculators. We shall consider here only the operators who wish to hedge against the exchange risk. These, as we saw in Sect. 10.3.2, can hedge either through a spot transaction associated with suitable financing (in which case they also act as arbitrageurs[20]) or by having recourse to the forward market. That is, the importer purchases the necessary foreign exchange forward, and the exporter sells the future foreign exchange receipts forward. It is presumable that, in general, the demand for forward exchange (coming from importers) will be — *ceteris paribus* — a decreasing function of the price of forward exchange, i.e. of the forward exchange rate (as this rate increases the profitability of importing will be affected; besides, some importers will reduce the hedging or will not hedge at all, etc., see Grubel, 1966, Chap. 5), and the supply of forward exchange (coming from exporters) will be, for analogous reasons, an increasing function of the forward exchange rate. Thus we get Fig. 12.5, where r_c^F denotes that value of the forward exchange rate which equates the demand for and supply of forward exchange by

---

[20] For example, an importer who hedges a future payment by purchasing foreign exchange spot acts as an arbitrageur, buying the foreign exchange spot and selling it forward, and then as a commercial hedger, by purchasing from himself (in the former capacity) the forward exchange. As we saw in Sect. 10.3.2, the indifference line between covering on the spot or on the forward market is given by the neutrality condition.

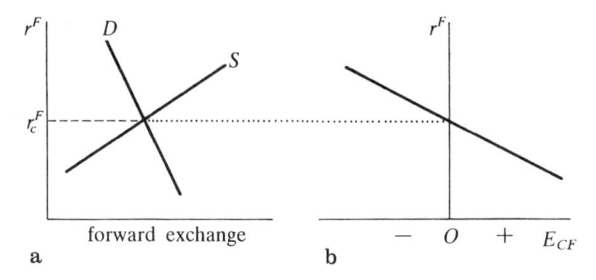

Fig. 12.5. Commercial traders' excess demand for forward exchange

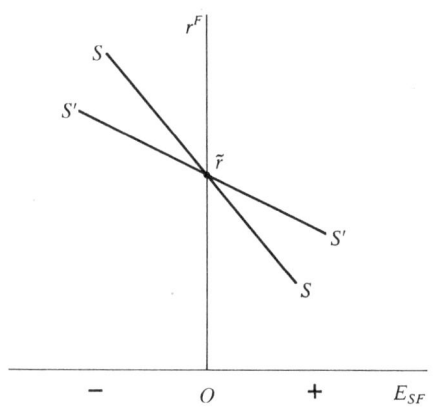

Fig. 12.6. Speculator's excess demand for forward exchange

commercial traders. In Fig. 12.5a we have drawn the demand and supply schedules (assumed to be linear for simplicity's sake) and in Fig. 12.5b the resulting excess demand schedule.

(c) Speculation

Forward speculation derives from the existence of a discrepancy between the current forward exchange rate and the future spot exchange rate expected to exist at the maturity of the forward contract. Speculation in general and forward speculation in particular have been treated in Sect. 10.4.1, so that, on the basis of the speculative equilibrium expressed either traditionally or in terms of portfolio selection[21], we can state that the extent of the speculative position, i.e. of the speculative excess demand for forward exchange, is in absolute value an increasing function of the gap between the current forward rate and the expected future spot rate, and a decreasing function of risk. Given a certain evaluation of risk we get a certain functional relation between the speculative position and the said gap; it is possible, in other words, to subsume the evaluation of risk in this functional form. In Fig. 12.6 we have drawn two alternative schedules of speculators' excess demand for forward exchange, where $\tilde{r}$ is the spot exchange rate expected to exist at the maturity of the forward contract. Both schedules (assumed to be linear for simplicity's sake) cross the vertical axis at $r^F = \tilde{r}$ (no forward speculative position will be opened in this case); schedule SS corresponds to the case in which the

---

[21] See Sects. 10.4.1 and A.10.3. For an explicit formulation of the forward speculator's equilibrium based on portfolio choice theory see, for example, Kenen (1965), Frevert (1967), Feldstein (1968).

evaluation of risk (which includes the speculators' attitude towards risk) is such as to give a higher marginal risk coefficient in the speculators' calculation than schedule $S'S'$.

It is clear that if we take $\tilde{r}$ as exogenous, we can write the speculators' excess demand for forward exchange as a function of r^F only. This procedure, which may be legitimate in the context of a static or uniperiodal equilibrium, is no longer so in a dynamic context (see Sect. A.12.3).

12.4.2 Forward Market Equilibrium and the Spot Rate

We now have all the elements to determine the *equilibrium in the forward exchange market*. Equilibrium means, as usual, the equality between (total) demand and (total) supply, or the equality to zero of the total excess demand, which in turn is the sum of the excess demands examined above.

In graphic terms, we bring together into a single diagram (see Fig. 12.7) the various excess demand schedules from Figs. 12.4, 12.5b and 12.6. Note that for graphic convenience we have also drawn the AA schedule linear; furthermore we have assumed that the excess demand by commercial hedgers is zero at the forward rate which satisfies the neutrality condition, r_N^F.

The equilibrium forward exchange rate is r_E^F, as the algebraic sum of the various excess demands becomes zero at this value. In fact, $OB'' = OB' + OB$ in absolute value; we must remember that OB'' has to be given a positive sign and OB, OB' a negative one.

Now, this representation is perfectly satisfactory in the context of a uniperiodal static equilibrium and it might also be in the context of any model where exchange rates are rigid and expected to remain so, whence $r = \tilde{r} =$ given constant not only within a single period but also over any relevant time interval. Unfortunately the representation in question is less satisfactory in a different exchange-rate regime, where r and/or $\tilde{r}$ vary in time.

When r changes, r_N^F changes as well and so the AA (and possibly the CC) schedule will shift; when $\tilde{r}$ changes the SS schedule will shift. Thus a different value

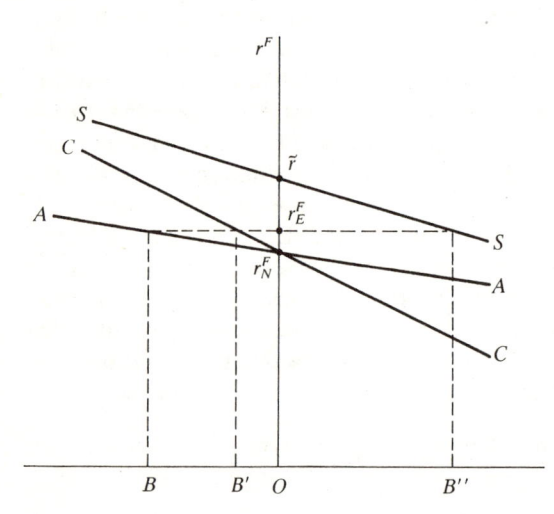

Fig. 12.7. Determination of the equilibrium in the forward market

of r_N^F will be determined at any particular moment; the time path followed by r_N^F can be obtained only by way of a dynamic analysis which should also consider the interrelations between the spot and forward exchange rates, that simultaneously determine these rates. It should be pointed out that, if no such interrelations existed, or, more precisely, if only one-way relations did (from the spot to the forward market but not vice versa), the problem would admit of an easy and immediate solution. In fact, the spot exchange market would determine r (and possibly $\tilde{r}$) independently of r^F; by substituting these values for r and $\tilde{r}$ in the forward market excess demands and by solving the equilibrium equation, one would then determine the forward exchange rate and its time path. However, in a complete model the influence of r^F on r cannot be neglected so that the causation runs both ways and the problem can be solved only by a simultaneous determination of the spot and forward exchange rate in a dynamic context. This will be dealt with in Sect. A.12.3.

12.4.3 The Monetary Authorities' Intervention

We conclude by briefly examining the problem of the monetary authorities' intervention on the forward market. This has been discussed in the literature both as a policy tool alternative to other tools (for example to an intervention on the domestic interest rate) and in relation to the effectiveness of the forward support of a currency undergoing speculative pressures.

As regards the former aspect, it should be recalled from Sect. 10.3.3 that in order to stimulate the inflow of (arbitrage) funds the authorities should act so as to make the inequality

$$r^F < r \frac{1+i_h}{1+i_f}, \qquad (12.19)$$

hold. It follows that, if we consider r and i_f as exogenous, the alternative to an increase in i_h is a reduction in r^F. Therefore, if the monetary authorities want to attract capital, for example to offset a current account deficit, instead of manoeuvering i_h (this manoeuvre will be dealt with in Sect. 15.5 at some length) they can try to cause a decrease in r^F by selling foreign exchange forward. For an extensive analysis of this aspect (which also involves the interactions between the forward exchange market and the national financial markets), we refer the reader to Herring and Marston (1977); see also Eaton and Turnovsky (1984), where the monetary authorities' intervention on the forward market for stabilizing income is examined.

As regards the latter aspect, it is a moot question whether official support of the forward exchange rate of a currency undergoing speculative (spot) attack in a devaluative direction is appropriate or not. This official support consists in the monetary authorities selling foreign exchange forward so as to prevent r^F from increasing too much. We shall give a brief summary of the main arguments for and against.

On the one hand, to begin with, one must make the observation that the official support tends to favour the inflow (or put a brake on the outflow) of covered interest arbitrage funds and thus brings an immediate benefit to the authorities' reserves subject to the speculative drain. Secondly, the official support, especially if very strong and resolute, helps to restore confidence in the currency under attack and so may ease the speculative pressure. Finally, in the absence of the support, the cost of forward cover to commercial traders might become prohibitive, with the consequence of inducing these operators to omit hedging and to become speculators.

On the other hand, the critics observe in the first place that, if the monetary authorities do not succeed in overcoming the speculative attack and the spot exchange rate depreciates[22], the forward support will cause them heavy additional losses, since when the forward contracts mature they have to procure the foreign exchange spot at a higher price. Secondly, the support decreases the speculators' risk: in fact, if the forward discount is very high, though smaller than the expected depreciation (i.e., $\tilde{r} > r^F > r$), the speculators, by opening a forward speculative position, run the risk of heavy losses if the spot exchange rate does not depreciate when the forward contract matures (they will in fact have to pay out the difference $r^F - r$ per unit of foreign currency: see Sect. 10.4.1). By supporting the forward rate, the difference $r^F - r$ is reduced and so is the risk of speculators, who will intensify their activity.

It is not easy to strike a balance between the opposite views, partly because the appropriateness of official support may depend on circumstances. In this respect we believe that the opinion of Fleming and Mundell (1964) and of Grubel (1966) is sensible. These authors hold the view that if the speculative attack is caused by a temporary loss of confidence in a currency which is basically sound (in the sense that in the long run the current exchange rate could be maintained without depreciation), then the official support of the forward exchange is advisable and effective. If, on the contrary, the monetary authorities themselves believe that the current spot rate cannot be maintained in the long run because of an irreversible fundamental disequilibrium in the balance of payments, then the support in question is a costly way of putting off the inevitable.

We must however add that if we want to examine more adequately the problems barely touched upon here, we cannot restrict the analysis to the foreign exchange market, but we must consider the interrelations between this market and the other real and financial markets (Casprini, 1976), which will be dealt with in Chap. 16.

On the immediate and delayed effects of the official support of the forward exchange see also Levin (1970), Yeager (1976, Chap. 14), McCormick (1977), Tseng (1993).

Appendix

A.12.1 The Critical Elasticities Condition

We shall first examine the simple case in which the supplies are perfectly elastic and then the general case.

---

[22] This includes both the case in which a higher official parity is declared in an adjustable peg system, in which case the term "devaluation" is used, and the case in which the authorities discontinue their support of the spot rate and let it depreciate in a managed float system.

A.12.1.1 The Simple Case

The condition for a variation in the exchange rate to make the payments balance move in the same direction is obtained by differentiating B with respect to r and ascertaining the conditions for $dB/dr > 0$. Given the definition of B we have

$$\frac{dB}{dr} = \frac{d[p_x x - r p_m m]}{dr} = p_x \frac{dx}{dr} - p_m m - r p_m \frac{dm}{dr}$$

$$= p_m m \left(\frac{p_x}{p_m m} \frac{dx}{dr} - 1 - \frac{r}{m} \frac{dm}{dr} \right). \tag{A.12.1}$$

If we multiply and divide the first term in parentheses by rx we obtain

$$\frac{dB}{dr} = p_m m \left(\frac{p_x x}{r p_m m} \frac{r}{x} \frac{dx}{dr} - 1 - \frac{r}{m} \frac{dm}{dr} \right)$$

$$= p_m m \left(\frac{p_x x}{r p_m m} \eta_x - 1 + \eta_m \right), \tag{A.12.2}$$

where

$$\eta_x \equiv \frac{dx}{x} \bigg/ \frac{dr}{r} \equiv \frac{r}{x} \frac{dx}{dr}, \quad \eta_m \equiv -\frac{dm}{m} \bigg/ \frac{dr}{r} \equiv -\frac{r}{m} \frac{dm}{dr}. \tag{A.12.3}$$

Since $p_m m > 0$, dB/dr will be positive if and only if

$$\frac{p_x x}{r p_m m} \eta_x - 1 + \eta_m > 0, \tag{A.12.4}$$

whence condition (12.9) immediately follows.

Let us now consider the balance of payments expressed in terms of foreign currency, $B' = (1/r) B$. We have

$$\frac{dB'}{dr} = \frac{d[(1/r) p_x x - p_m m]}{dr}$$

$$= -\frac{1}{r^2} p_x x + \frac{1}{r} p_x \frac{dx}{dr} - p_m \frac{dm}{dr}$$

$$= \frac{p_x x}{r^2} \left(-1 + \frac{r}{x} \frac{dx}{dr} - \frac{r^2 p_m}{p_x x} \frac{dm}{dr} \right). \tag{A.12.5}$$

If we multiply and divide the last term in parentheses by m, we get

$$\frac{dB'}{dr} = \frac{p_x x}{r^2} \left(-1 + \frac{r}{x} \frac{dx}{dr} - \frac{r p_m m}{p_x x} \frac{r}{m} \frac{dm}{dr} \right)$$

$$= \frac{p_x x}{r^2} \left(-1 + \eta_x + \frac{r p_m m}{p_x x} \eta_m \right), \tag{A.12.6}$$

where the elasticities are defined as above. Since $(p_x x/r^2) > 0$, dB'/dr will be positive if and only if

$$-1 + \eta_x + \frac{rp_m m}{p_x x} \eta_m > 0, \tag{A.12.7}$$

whence condition (12.11) immediately follows.

Condition (A.12.4) can be rewritten as

$$\frac{rp_m m}{p_x x} \eta_m + \eta_x > \frac{rp_m m}{p_x x}. \tag{A.12.4.1}$$

The necessary and sufficient condition for the foreign-currency balance to move in the right direction and the domestic-currency balance to move in the wrong direction at the same time, is that (A.12.7) occurs whilst (A.12.4) does *not*, that is

$$\frac{rp_m m}{p_x x} > \frac{rp_m m}{p_x x} \eta_m + \eta_x > 1, \tag{A.12.8}$$

where the left-hand side of this inequality means that (A.12.4.1) is *not* satisfied and the right-hand side that (A.12.7) *is* satisfied. It can be seen immediately that the double inequality (A.12.8) can occur only when there is a balance-of-payments deficit.

Likewise we can find the necessary and sufficient condition for the domestic-currency balance to move in the right direction and the foreign-currency balance to move in the wrong direction at the same time. It turns out to be

$$\frac{p_x x}{rp_m m} > \eta_m + \frac{p_x x}{rp_m m} \eta_x > 1, \tag{A.12.9}$$

which can be verified only when there is a balance-of-payments surplus.

The simple analysis carried out in the text and in the present section *considers only the demand elasticities*: demand for foreign goods by the home country (demand for imports) and demand for domestic goods by the rest of the world (demand for exports). This analysis is therefore based on the assumption that the respective supply elasticities are infinite, so that supply adjusts to demand with no price adjustment. In other words, producers supply any quantity of goods demanded without changing the supply price (expressed in terms of their own currency), as is shown by the fact that p_m and p_x are assumedly constant. It is not, of course, necessary that this should be true everywhere, as it is sufficient that it holds in the range within which the demand changes (triggered by the exchange-rate changes) fall. From this point of view the assumption seems plausible in the context of economies with less than full employment, where it is not infrequent that increases in demand — especially if coming from abroad — are met at the going price; besides, the downward rigidity of prices justifies the fact that decreases in demand do not usually cause a fall in selling prices.

This explains why the problem of the effects of an exchange-rate variation is usually dealt with by way of the simple analysis. However, both for theoretical completeness and because supply effects cannot be neglected, we deal with the general case in Sect. A.12.1.3.

A.12.1.2 The General Case

In general, supply will be an increasing function of the price (expressed in the supplier's currency) of the commodity exchanged; the equilibrium between demand and supply determines both the quantity exchanged and the price, which is thus no longer a datum. Let us begin by considering the exports of the home country, and let $S_x = S_x(p_x)$ be the supply of exports, an increasing function of their domestic-currency price p_x; the demand for exports by the foreign buyers will be $D_x = D_x\left(\frac{1}{r}p_x\right)$, a decreasing function of the price expressed in foreign currency $\left(\frac{1}{r}p_x\right.$, neglecting transport costs, etc.$\left.\right)$. Thus we have the system

$$S_x = S_x(p_x),$$
$$D_x = D_x\left(\frac{1}{r}p_x\right), \quad \text{(A.12.10)}$$
$$S_x = D_x,$$

whose solution — in correspondence to any given exchange rate r — determines the equilibrium price p_x and the equilibrium quantity, which we denote by $x = S_x = D_x$. In equilibrium we thus have the system

$$x - S_x(p_x) = 0,$$
$$x - D_x\left(\frac{1}{r}p_x\right) = 0, \quad \text{(A.12.10.1)}$$

which is a system of two implicit functions in the three variables x, p_x, r. By using the implicit function theorem (we assume that the required condition on the Jacobian occurs) we can express x and p_x as differentiable functions of r and then compute the derivatives dx/dr and dp_x/dr by the method of comparative statics (see, for example, Gandolfo, 1980, Part III, Chap. 1). Thus, by differentiating (A.12.10.1) with respect to r, we have

$$\frac{dx}{dr} - \frac{dS_x}{dp_x}\frac{dp_x}{dr} = 0,$$
$$\frac{dx}{dr} - \frac{dD_x}{d[(1/r)p_x]}\frac{d[(1/r)p_x]}{dr} = 0. \quad \text{(A.12.11)}$$

Since $d\left(\frac{1}{r}p_x\right)/dr = -(1/r^2)p_x + (1/r)dp_x/dr$, after rearranging terms we have

$$\frac{dx}{dr} - \frac{dS_x}{dp_x}\frac{dp_x}{dr} = 0,$$
$$\frac{dx}{dr} - \frac{1}{r}\frac{dD_x}{d[(1/r)p_x]}\frac{dp_x}{dr} = -\frac{1}{r^2}\frac{dD_x}{d[(1/r)p_x]}p_x, \quad \text{(A.12.11.1)}$$

whose solution yields the required derivatives dx/dr, dp_x/dr. These turn out to be

$$\frac{dx}{dr} = \frac{-\dfrac{dD_x}{d[(1/r)p_x]} p_x \dfrac{dS_x}{dp_x}}{\dfrac{dS_x}{dp_x} - \dfrac{1}{r}\dfrac{dD_x}{d[(1/r)p_x]}}, \quad \frac{dp_x}{dr} = \frac{-\dfrac{dD_x}{d[(1/r)p_x]} p_x}{\dfrac{dS_x}{dp_x} - \dfrac{1}{r}\dfrac{dD_x}{d[(1/r)p_x]}}. \quad (A.12.12)$$

We now define the elasticities of the demand for and supply of exports

$$\eta_x \equiv -\frac{dD_x}{d[(1/r)p_x]} \frac{(1/r)p_x}{D_x}, \quad \varepsilon_x \equiv \frac{dS_x}{dp_x} \frac{p_x}{S_x}, \quad (A.12.13)$$

and manipulate Eq. (A.12.12) so as to express the derivatives in terms of elasticities. Beginning with dx/dr and multiplying numerator and denominator by the same quantity $p_x/x = p_x/S_x = p_x/D_x$ (remember that we are considering the equilibrium point) we get

$$\frac{dx}{dr} = \frac{-\dfrac{dD_x}{d[(1/r)p_x]} p_x \dfrac{dS_x}{dp_x}\dfrac{p_x}{S_x}}{\dfrac{dS_x}{dp_x}\dfrac{p_x}{S_x} - \dfrac{dD_x}{d[(1/r)p_x]}\dfrac{(1/r)p_x}{D_x}} = \frac{-\dfrac{dD_x}{d[(1/r)p_x]} p_x \varepsilon_x}{\varepsilon_x + \eta_x}. \quad (A.12.14)$$

If we multiply and divide the numerator by the same quantity $D_x/(1/r)$ we get

$$\frac{dx}{dr} = \frac{-\dfrac{D_x}{1/r}\dfrac{dD_x}{d[(1/r)p_x]}\dfrac{(1/r)p_x}{D_x}\varepsilon_x}{\varepsilon_x + \eta_x} = \frac{x\eta_x \varepsilon_x}{\varepsilon_x + \eta_x}, \quad (A.12.14.1)$$

where in the last passage we have used the fact that $D_x = x$ and introduced the assumption that the exchange rate equals one in the initial situation (this does not involve any loss of generality as it simply implies a suitable definition of the units of measurement).

As regards dp_x/dr, by a similar procedure (multiply numerator and denominator by $x/p_x = S_x/p_x = D_x/p_x$, then multiply and divide the numerator by $1/r$) and assuming $r = 1$ initially, we obtain

$$\frac{dp_x}{dr} = \frac{p_x \eta_x}{\varepsilon_x + \eta_x}. \quad (A.12.14.2)$$

Let us now consider the imported commodity and let $S_m = S_m(p_m)$ be its supply as a function of its price p_m in foreign currency (the currency of the producing country), and $D_m = D_m(rp_m)$ its demand by the importing country as a function of its domestic-currency price (rp_m). Thus we have the system

$$S_m = S_m(p_m),$$
$$D_m = D_m(rp_m), \quad (A.12.15)$$
$$S_m = D_m,$$

whose solution determines – at any given value of r – the equilibrium price (p_m) and the equilibrium quantity which we denote by $m = S_m = D_m$. If we consider the system of implicit functions

$$m - S_m(p_m) = 0,$$
$$m - D_m(rp_m) = 0,$$
(A.12.15.1)

and use the comparative static method as explained in relation to (A.12.10.1) above, we get

$$\frac{dm}{dr} - \frac{dS_m}{dp_m}\frac{dp_m}{dr} = 0,$$

$$\frac{dm}{dr} - \frac{dD_m}{d(rp_m)}\left(p_m + r\frac{dp_m}{dr}\right) = 0,$$
(A.12.16)

that is

$$\frac{dm}{dr} - \frac{dS_m}{dp_m}\frac{dp_m}{dr} = 0,$$

$$\frac{dm}{dr} - \frac{dD_m}{d(rp_m)} r \frac{dp_m}{dr} = \frac{dD_m}{d(rp_m)} p_m,$$
(A.12.16.1)

whose solution yields

$$\frac{dm}{dr} = \frac{\dfrac{dS_m}{dp_m}\dfrac{dD_m}{d(rp_m)} p_m}{\dfrac{dS_m}{dp_m} - \dfrac{dD_m}{d(rp_m)} r}, \quad \frac{dp_m}{dr} = \frac{\dfrac{dD_m}{d(rp_m)} p_m}{\dfrac{dS_m}{dp_m} - \dfrac{dD_m}{d(rp_m)} r}.$$
(A.12.17)

We now define the import demand and supply elasticities

$$\eta_m \equiv -\frac{dD_m}{d(rp_m)}\frac{rp_m}{D_m}, \quad \varepsilon_m \equiv \frac{dS_m}{dp_m}\frac{p_m}{S_m},$$
(A.12.18)

and manipulate Eqs. (A.12.17) to express them in terms of elasticities. Beginning with dm/dr we multiply numerator and denominator by the same quantity p_m/m, then multiply and divide the numerator by r/D_m; thus we arrive at

$$\frac{dm}{dr} = \frac{\dfrac{p_m}{S_m}\dfrac{dS_m}{dp_m}\dfrac{dD_m}{d(rp_m)}\dfrac{rp_m}{D_m}\dfrac{D_m}{r}}{\dfrac{p_m}{S_m}\dfrac{dS_m}{dp_m} - \dfrac{dD_m}{d(rp_m)}\dfrac{rp_m}{D_m}} = \frac{-m\varepsilon_m \eta_m}{\varepsilon_m + \eta_m},$$
(A.12.19)

where in the last passage we have used Eqs. (A.12.18) and set $r = 1$ in the initial situation.

By a similar procecure we get

$$\frac{dp_m}{dr} = \frac{\dfrac{1}{r}\dfrac{rp_m}{D_m}\dfrac{dD_m}{d(rp_m)} p_m}{\dfrac{p_m}{S_m}\dfrac{dS_m}{dp_m} - \dfrac{dD_m}{d(rp_m)}\dfrac{rp_m}{D_m}} = \frac{-p_m\eta_m}{\varepsilon_m + \eta_m}, \qquad (A.12.20)$$

where in the last passage we have again used Eqs. (A.12.18) and set $r=1$.

We thus have all the elements to examine the effects on the balance of payments of an exchange-rate variation in the general case. To begin with, we consider the balance of payments in domestic currency $B = p_x x - rp_m m$ and differentiate it totally with respect to r, remembering that also p_x and p_m are functions of r as shown above. Thus we have

$$\frac{dB}{dr} = \frac{dp_x}{dr}x + p_x\frac{dx}{dr} - p_m m - r\frac{dp_m}{dr}m - rp_m\frac{dm}{dr}. \qquad (A.12.21)$$

If we now subsitute expressions (A.12.14.1), (A.12.14.2), (A.12.19) and (A.12.20) into (A.12.21), we get

$$\frac{dB}{dr} = p_x x \frac{\eta_x}{\varepsilon_x + \eta_x} + p_x x \frac{\eta_x \varepsilon_x}{\varepsilon_x + \eta_x} - p_m m + rp_m m \frac{\eta_m}{\varepsilon_m + \eta_m} + rp_m m \frac{\varepsilon_m \eta_m}{\varepsilon_m + \eta_m}, \qquad (A.12.21.1)$$

whence, by collecting terms (as we set $r=1$, we have $rp_m m = p_m m$)

$$\frac{dB}{dr} = rp_m m \left[\frac{p_x x}{rp_m m}\frac{\eta_x(1+\varepsilon_x)}{\varepsilon_x + \eta_x} + \frac{\eta_m(1+\varepsilon_m)}{\varepsilon_m + \eta_m} - 1\right]. \qquad (A.12.21.2)$$

The condition for $dB/dr > 0$ is thus

$$\frac{p_x x}{rp_m m}\frac{\eta_x(1+\varepsilon_x)}{\varepsilon_x + \eta_x} + \frac{\eta_m(1+\varepsilon_m)}{\varepsilon_m + \eta_m} - 1 > 0. \qquad (A.12.22)$$

When we assume $B=0$ initially, then condition (A.12.22) can be rewritten by simple manipulations as

$$\frac{\eta_x\eta_m(\varepsilon_x + \varepsilon_m + 1) + \varepsilon_m\varepsilon_x(\eta_x + \eta_m - 1)}{(\varepsilon_x + \eta_x)(\varepsilon_m + \eta_m)} > 0. \qquad (A.12.22.1)$$

Conditions (A.12.22) and (A.12.22.1) are the two forms usually found in the literature, apart from notational differences.

When ε_m and ε_x tend to infinity, by evaluating the limit of (A.12.22) we get

$$\frac{p_x x}{rp_m m}\eta_x + \eta_m - 1 > 0, \qquad (A.12.23)$$

which is the condition holding in the simple case as shown in (A.12.4).

It is important to stress that the consideration of the supply elasticities makes the situation more favourable, in the sense that the balance of payments may move in the right direction even if the sum of the demand elasticities is smaller than one. In fact, if we consider (A.12.22.1), we see that the fraction may be positive even if $\eta_x+\eta_m<1$, provided that the supplies are sufficiently rigid: in the extreme case, for $\varepsilon_x=\varepsilon_m=0$ (absolutely rigid supplies) the condition is *always* satisfied no matter how small the demand elasticities are (but neither can be zero). In this case, in fact, the quantities exported and imported cannot deviate from the given supplies and all the adjustment falls on prices. If we consider, for example, a depreciation, we see that, on the one hand, the increase in the demand for exports is checked by an increase in p_x: as the supply is perfectly rigid, the excess demand causes an increase in p_x up to the point where the demand falls back to its initial amount. This means that $(1/r)p_x$ must go back to its initial value for $D_x=D_x\left(\frac{1}{r}p_x\right)$ to remain the same, hence the percentage increase in p_x is exactly equal to the percentage increase in r and the domestic-currency receipts from exports increase by the same percentage as the depreciation.

On the other hand, the decrease in the demand for imports induced by the depreciation will — since the foreign supply is perfectly rigid — cause a decrease in the foreign price p_m such as to bring the demand back to its initial level. This decrease must be such that rp_m goes back to its initial value for $D_m=D_m(rp_m)$ to remain the same. This means that the outlay for imports will return to its initial value, and so — as the receipts from exports have increased — the balance of payments must necessarily improve.

Similar observations hold for the more general condition (A.12.22), which for $\varepsilon_x=\varepsilon_m=0$ and η_x,η_m however small but positive, certainly occurs.

We now turn to the foreign-currency balance, $B'=(1/r)p_xx-p_mm$; total differentiation with respect to r gives

$$\frac{dB'}{dr}=-\frac{1}{r^2}p_xx+\frac{1}{r}\frac{dp_x}{dr}x+\frac{1}{r}p_x\frac{dx}{dr}-\frac{dp_m}{dr}m-p_m\frac{dm}{dr}, \qquad (A.12.24)$$

which, after substitution of (A.12.14.1), (A.12.14.2), (A.12.19) and (A.12.20) into it, becomes

$$\frac{dB'}{dr}=\frac{1}{r}p_xx\left[-1+\frac{\eta_x(1+\varepsilon_x)}{\varepsilon_x+\eta_x}+\frac{rp_mm}{p_xx}\frac{\eta_m(1+\varepsilon_m)}{\varepsilon_m+\eta_m}\right]. \qquad (A.12.24.1)$$

The condition for $dB'/dr>0$ thus is

$$\frac{\eta_x(1+\varepsilon_x)}{\varepsilon_x+\eta_x}+\frac{rp_mm}{p_xx}\frac{\eta_m(1+\varepsilon_m)}{\varepsilon_m+\eta_m}-1>0. \qquad (A.12.25)$$

When an initial situation of equilibrium ($B'=0$) is assumed, condition (A.12.25) can be reduced to (A.12.22.1) as well.

Finally, if we evaluate the limit (for $\varepsilon_x,\varepsilon_m$ tending to infinity) of the expression on the left-hand side of (A.12.25), we get

$$\eta_x+\frac{rp_mm}{p_xx}\eta_m>1, \qquad (A.12.26)$$

which coincides with (A.12.4.1).

A.12.1.3 Effects on the Terms of Trade

We conclude this section by examining the effects of an exchange-rate variation on the terms of trade $\pi = p_x/rp_m$. It is obvious that when p_x and p_m are constant (this corresponds to the simple case examined in Sect. A.12.1.1), π varies in the opposite direction to r. In the general case, by totally differentiating π with respect to r, using Eqs. (A.12.14.2) and (A.12.20), and (where convenient) the fact that $r=1$ in the initial situation, we have

$$\frac{d\pi}{dr} = \frac{\frac{dp_x}{dr}rp_m - \left(p_m + r\frac{dp_m}{dr}\right)p_x}{r^2 p_m^2} = \frac{1}{rp_m}\frac{p_x\eta_x}{\varepsilon_x+\eta_x} - \frac{1}{rp_m}\left(p_x - \frac{rp_x}{rp_m}\frac{p_m\eta_m}{\varepsilon_m+\eta_m}\right)$$

$$= \frac{p_x}{rp_m}\left(\frac{\eta_x}{\varepsilon_x+\eta_x} - 1 + \frac{\eta_m}{\varepsilon_m+\eta_m}\right), \tag{A.12.27}$$

whence, by simple manipulations,

$$\frac{d\pi}{dr} = \pi \frac{\eta_x\eta_m - \varepsilon_x\varepsilon_m}{(\varepsilon_x+\eta_x)(\varepsilon_m+\eta_m)}, \tag{A.12.28}$$

so that $d\pi/dr \gtreqless 0$ according as $\eta_x\eta_m - \varepsilon_x\varepsilon_m \gtreqless 0$. We remember that an increase in π is usually classified as an improvement: an increase in π, in fact, means that with a given amount of exports we obtain a greater amount of imports, or that less exports are required to obtain the same amount of imports. Thus, we can conclude that an exchange-rate depreciation will improve the terms of trade if the product of the demand elasticities is greater than the product of the supply elasticities. This will always be the case if at least one of the supply elasticities is zero, provided that both demand elasticities, no matter how small, are positive. On the contrary, when $\varepsilon_x, \varepsilon_m$ go to infinity, the terms of trade will necessarily worsen.

A.12.2 The Stability of the Foreign Exchange Market

The coincidence — in the assumed situation (i.e. that the supply and demand for foreign exchange come exclusively from transactions in goods and services) — between the conditions for an exchange-rate variation to make the balance of payments move in the same direction, and the stability conditions in the foreign exchange market can be shown as follows.

The dynamic assumption according to which the exchange rate depreciates (appreciates) when there is a positive (negative) excess demand for foreign exchange gives rise to the differential equation

$$\frac{dr}{dt} = \Phi[E(r)], \tag{A.12.29}$$

where Φ is a sign-preserving function and $\Phi'[0] \equiv k > 0$. If we linearize the Φ function at the equilibrium point we get

$$\frac{dr}{dt} = kE(r), \tag{A.12.29.1}$$

where k can be interpreted as an adjustment speed. Since, in the assumed situation, $E(r) = -B'(r)$, we have

$$\frac{dr}{dt} = -kB'(r). \qquad (A.12.29.2)$$

To examine the local stability it is sufficient to linearize $B'(r)$ at the equilibrium point[23], thus obtaining

$$\frac{d\tilde{r}}{dt} = -k\frac{dB'}{dr}\tilde{r}, \qquad (A.12.30)$$

where $\tilde{r} = r - r_e$ denotes the deviations from equilibrium and dB'/dr is evaluated at r_e. The solution to this simple differential equation is

$$\tilde{r}(t) = Ae^{-k(dB'/dr)t}, \qquad (A.12.31)$$

where A depends on the initial deviation from equilibrium. The necessary and sufficient stability condition is

$$-k\frac{dB'}{dr} < 0, \qquad (A.12.32)$$

that is, as $k > 0$,

$$\frac{dB'}{dr} > 0, \qquad (A.12.32.1)$$

which proves the stated coincidence.

A.12.3 A Framework for the Simultaneous Determination of the Spot and Forward Exchange Rate

In any market, equilibrium is reached when the algebraic sum of all operators' excess demands is zero. We must, then, formally express these excess demands as described in Sect. 10.4; we begin by considering the *spot market*.

A first category of transactors consists in non speculators. By definition, their supplies of and demands for foreign exchange are influenced by the current and not by the expected exchange rate. Thus, by assuming a linear relation for simplicity, we can write

$$E_{n_t} = a_1 r_t + A \cos \omega t, \quad a_1 < 0, \quad A > 0, \qquad (A.12.33)$$

where E_{nt} is non-speculators' excess demand at time t and $A \cos \omega t$ represents exogenous factors, for example seasonal influences, acting on both the demand and the supply. More complicated functions could be used, but we wish to simplify to the utmost to convey the basic idea. In (A.12.33) the stability condition examined in the previous section is assumed to be satisfied: in fact, $dE_{nt}/dr = a_1 < 0$.

---

[23] In the case of multiple equilibria the linearization will have to be performed at each equilibrium separately; it will then be possible to ascertain the stable or unstable nature of each point.

A second category consists in (covered interest) arbitrageurs. From what was explained in Sect. 10.3 and 10.4 it follows that an excess demand for spot exchange corresponds to an excess demand for forward exchange, but with its sign reversed. Thus we have, in general[24]

$$E_{A_t} = -jE_{AF_t}, \qquad (A.12.34)$$

where E_{A_t} denotes the arbitrageurs' excess demand for forward exchange and j is a coefficient depending on the interest rate[25].

Speculators make up the third category. The considerations made in Sect. 10.4.1 enable us to state that their excess demand is an increasing function of the discrepancy between the expected and the current spot exchange rate: the greater this discrepancy (and so the expected profit) the greater the speculative position (for a detailed examination of this, see, for example, Cutilli and Gandolfo, 1973, pp. 35–40). Thus we have (a linear relation is used for simplicity's sake)

$$E_{s_t} = k(\tilde{r}_t - r_t), \quad k > 0, \qquad (A.12.35)$$

where $\tilde{r}_t$ is the spot exchange rate expected to hold in the future (expectations are, of course, formed at time t).

As regards the *forward market*, we recall that covered interest arbitrageurs demand (supply) forward exchange when the conditions exist for profitably placing short-term liquid funds at home (abroad), so that their excess demand for forward exchange can be taken as an increasing function of the discrepancy

---

[24] Strictly speaking we should also add the excess demand for spot exchange coming from the liquidation of forward contracts stipulated at time $t-\tau$ and maturing at time t. It is however easy to show that, if the forward market is in equilibrium at each instant, that is, if the following relation holds

$$E_{AF_t} + E_{CF_t} + E_{SF_t} = 0, \qquad (a)$$

which, as we shall see, expresses forward market equilibrium, then the excess demand under consideration (denoted by E_{Lt}) is zero. In fact

$$E_{L_t} = E_{AF_{t-\tau}} + E_{CF_{t-\tau}} + E_{SF_{t-\tau}};$$

now, since (a) holds at each instant, and so also at $t-\tau$, we have

$$E_{AF_{t-\tau}} + E_{CF_{t-\tau}} + E_{SF_{t-\tau}} = 0, \text{ that is, } E_{L_t} = 0.$$

[25] Let us assume, for example, that condition (10.14) holds with the $>$ sign and let X be the amount of foreign exchange that arbitrageurs wish to place in the foreign centre. Thus we have a demand, i.e. a positive excess demand (or a non-supply of spot foreign exchange, if the funds are already abroad; the non-supply can be considered as a negative excess supply i.e. a positive excess demand) for spot exchange equal to X. At the same time the arbitrageurs sell forward not only the capital but also the interest accrued on it (the non-consideration of the interest accrued induced some authors erroneously to set E_{A_t} and E_{AF_t} equal in absolute value), that is to say there is a supply (negative excess demand) of forward exchange equal to $(1+i_f)X$. Therefore, as $E_{A_t} = X$, $E_{AF_t} = -(1+i_f)X$, it follows that $E_{AF_t} = -(1+i_f)E_{A_t}$, i.e.

$$E_{A_t} = -\frac{1}{1+i_f} E_{AF_t}.$$

between the forward rate satisfying the neutrality condition and the current forward rate:

$$E_{AF_t}=j_1(r^F_{N_t}-r^F_t)=j_1\left(\frac{1+i_h}{1+i_f}r_t-r^F_t\right),\ j_1>0. \quad (A.12.36)$$

The excess demand of commercial traders hedging in the forward market is, as clarified in the text, a decreasing function of the forward exchange rate, that is

$$E_{CF_t}=j_2+j_3\cos\omega t+j_4 r^F_t,\ j_2>0, j_3>0, j_4<0, \quad (A.12.37)$$

where the introduction of the term $j_3\cos\omega t$ is due to the fact that it seems legitimate to assume that the exogenous factors exert their influence not only on the part of trade settled spot — see Eq. (A.12.33) — but also on the part of it settled forward.

The forward speculators' excess demand, as clarified in Sect. 10.4.1, is to be considered as an increasing function of the discrepancy between the expected spot rate and the current forward rate, that is, to a linear approximation,

$$E_{SF_t}=j_5(\tilde{r}_t-r^F_t),\ j_5>0. \quad (A.12.38)$$

The simultaneous determination of the spot and forward exchange rate is obtained by solving the system

$$\begin{aligned}E_{n_t}+E_{A_t}+E_{S_t}&=0,\\ E_{AF_t}+E_{CF_t}+E_{SF_t}&=0.\end{aligned} \quad (A.12.39)$$

It can be readily verified that the solution of this system does not present any difficulty if $\tilde{r}_t$ is assumed to be an exogenous datum. But this assumption cannot be seriously maintained. Expectations can be formed in various ways but will certainly include elements based on the behaviour of endogenous variables (in our simplified model, current and past values of both the spot and the forward rate), so that it is not possible to solve the system if $\tilde{r}_t$ is not specified. But as there is no universally accepted way of specifying $\tilde{r}_t$[26], it is clear that different results will be obtained with different specifications, as shown, for example, in Cutilli and Gandolfo (1973, pp. 104–119). On the simultaneous determination of the spot and forward exchange rate see also Black (1973) and McCormick (1977).

---

[26] Various authors share the opinion that, in the context of an efficient foreign exchange market (which in order to form expectations uses all the available information: for the definition see, for example, Fama, 1970, 1976; see also Casprini, 1984), the forward exchange rate ought to be an unbiased predictor of the future spot rate; thus the expected spot rate can be fairly well approximated by the current forward rate. However, the empirical evidence does not seem to support this opinion (see, for example, Frenkel and Mussa, 1980; Dooley and Shafer, 1983, Stein et al., 1983; Bailey et al., 1984; Casprini, 1984; Hsieh, 1984) and also from the theoretical point of view, objections are not lacking (see, e.g., Kindleberger, 1980, pp. 134–6, and Stein et al., 1983).

References

Argy, V., 1981, Chap. 19
Argy, V. and K.W. Clements, 1982
Bailey, R.W., R.T. Baillie and P.C. McMahon, 1984
Balogh, T. and P.P. Streeten, 1951
Bhagwati, J.N. and H.G. Johnson, 1960
Bhagwati, J.N. and H.G. Johnson, 1961
Bickerdicke, C.F., 1920
Black, S.W., 1973
Casprini, F., 1976
Casprini, F., 1984
Chacholiades, M., 1978, Chaps. 3–6
Chipman, J.S., 1978
Cutilli, B. and G. Gandolfo, 1963
Cutilli, B. and G. Gandolfo, 1972
Cutilli, B. and G. Gandolfo, 1973
Dooley, M.P. and J.R. Shafer, 1983
Dornbusch, R., 1975
Eaton, J. and S.J. Turnovsky, 1984
Einzig, P., 1961
Fama, E.F., 1970
Fama, E., 1976, Chap.5
Feldstein, M.S., 1968
Fleming, J.M. and R.A. Mundell, 1964
Frenkel, J.A. and M.L. Mussa, 1980
Frevert, P., 1967
Gandolfo, G., 1980
Grubel, H.G., 1966, Part I
Herring, R.J. and R.C. Marston, 1977, Chap. 3
Himarios, D., 1989
Hirschman, A.O., 1949
Hsieh, D.A., 1984
Johnson, H.G., 1958a
Kenen, P.B., 1965
Keynes, J.M., 1923, Chap. 3, Sect. 4
Kindleberger, C.P., 1980
Lerner, A.P., 1944, 377–379
Levich, R.M., 1978
Levin, J.H., 1970, Chap. V
Machlup, F., 1939
McCormick, F., 1977
McKinnon, R.I., 1979, Chap. 5
Metzler, L.A., 1949
Morishima, M., 1984, Chap. 4
Niehans, J., 1984, Chap. 4
Robinson, J., 1937
Sohmen, E., 1961
Sohmen, E., 1966
Sohmen, E., 1969, Chap. 1
Spraos, J., 1953
Stein, J.L., M. Rzepczynski and R. Selvaggio, 1983
Stern, R.M., 1973, Chaps. 2,3,5
Stern, R.M., J. Francis and B. Schumacher, 1976
Stuvel, G., 1951
Tseng, K.K., 1993
Tsiang, S.C., 1959
Yeager, L.B., 1976, Chaps. 8 and 14

13 The Role of Income Changes in the Adjustment Process

13.1 Introduction

The extension of the theory of the multiplier to an open economy[1] gave rise, in the years 1938−41, to a heated debate on whether the introduction of the foreign sector implied a modification in the multiplicand only, or also in the multiplier. Without entering into details (for a summing-up see Polak, 1947, and Gandolfo, 1970), it is interesting to note that it was this debate which made it possible to arrive at the now well-known general principle that changes in the autonomous components of aggregate demand must be included in the multiplicand, whereas the influence of the induced components (those depending on income) is manifested in a modification of the multiplier. Now, if imports are a function of national income, it follows that the marginal propensity to import should be accounted for in the multiplier, which will be different from that in the closed economy.

This principle goes beyond the field of international economics and is applicable to any problem susceptible to multiplier analysis. In our context, however, the principle is propaedeutic to the following treatment, which is meant both to give a general analysis of the open economy multiplier and to relate this analysis to that of balance-of-payments adjustment.

We first examine the small country case, that is the multiplier with no foreign repercussions, which implies that exports are entirely exogenous. In fact, the small country assumption means that what happens in the country under consideration has no appreciable effect on the rest-of-the-world variables (and, in particular, that changes in the country's imports − which are the rest-of-the-world exports − have no appreciable effect on the rest-of-the-world income and therefore on its imports); consequently, in the model, these variables can be considered as exogenous. We then analyze a two-country model, in which foreign repercussions are present; the general n-country model will be treated in the Appendix. The restrictive assumptions common to all such models are the usual ones: underemployed resources, rigidity of all prices (including the exchange rate and the rate of interest), absence of capital movements (so that balance of payments is synonymous with balance on goods and services), and all exports are made out of

---

[1] It should however be pointed out that the first formulation of the foreign trade multiplier, which is attributed to Harrod (1933), actually predated the Keynesian theory of the multiplier by three years.

current production. For simplicity of exposition, we assume linear functions; the case of general functions will be treated in the Appendix.

13.2 The Multiplier without Foreign Repercussions and the Balance of Payments

13.2.1 The Basic Model

The model used is the standard Keynesian textbook model with the inclusion of the foreign sector; the equations are as follows:

$$C = C_0 + by, \qquad 0 < b < 1, \qquad (13.1)$$

$$I = I_0 + hy, \qquad 0 < h < 1, \qquad (13.2)$$

$$m = m_0 + \mu y, \qquad 0 < \mu < 1, \qquad (13.3)$$

$$x = x_0, \qquad (13.4)$$

$$y = C + I + x - m. \qquad (13.5)$$

The equations represent, in this order: the consumption function (C_0 is the autonomous component, b is the marginal propensity to consume, and y is national income), the investment function (the autonomous component is I_0, and h is the marginal propensity to invest), the import function (m_0 is the autonomous component, and μ is the marginal propensity to import), the export function (the absence of foreign repercussions, as we said above, is reflected in the fact that exports are entirely exogenous), the determination of national income. The meaning of Eq. (13.5) is simple: in an open economy, the total demand for domestic output is no longer $C + I$, but $C + I - m + x$ which is composed of $C + I - m$ (aggregate demand for domestic output by residents) and of x (demand for domestic output by nonresidents). Actually, in $C + I$ both home and foreign goods and services are now included, and the demand for foreign goods and services by residents in our simplified model is m: therefore, by subtracting m from $C + I$ we obtain the demand for domestic output by residents.

Government expenditure is not explicitly included in Eq. (13.5) both because it can be considered as present in the autonomous components of the appropriate expenditure functions and because its inclusion as an additive term G in the r.h.s. of Eq. (13.5) — as is usually done — may be a source of potential error. In fact, the often used equation

$$y = C + I + x - m + G, \qquad (13.5a)$$

may convey the impression that any increase in government expenditure is income generating. This is not true, because government expenditure on foreign goods and services is not income generating: in this case, the increase in G is matched by an (exogenous) increase in m. The use of (13.5a) tends to obscure this fact; the use of (13.5), on the contrary, draws our attention to the fact that government

13.2 The Multiplier without Foreign Repercussions and the Balance of Payments

expenditure, if present, should be appropriately included in C_0, I_0, m_0 as the case may be[2]. It goes without saying that the use of Eq. (13.5a) is not incorrect, provided that one bears in mind that the part (if any) of G which is used to purchase foreign goods and services must also be counted in m_0.

Equation (13.5) can be written in several alternative forms. For example, if we shift C and m to the left-hand side and remember that $y - C$ is, by definition, saving (S), we have

$$S + m = I + x, \tag{13.5.1}$$

which is the extension to an open economy of the well-known $S = I$ condition. From (13.5.1) we obtain

$$S - I = x - m, \tag{13.5.1'}$$

$$I - S = m - x, \tag{13.5.1''}$$

that is, the excess of exports over imports is equal to the excess of saving over investment, viz the excess of imports over exports is equal to the excess of investment over saving. See Sect. 11.3, Eq. (11.1.1), where G and T are explicitly present.

Equations (13.1) – (13.5) form a complete system by means of which the foreign multiplier can be analyzed. Since, however, we are interested in balance of payments adjustment, we add the equation which defines the balance of payments B[3]

$$B = x - m. \tag{13.6}$$

The problem which interests us consists in ascertaining whether, and to what extent, balance of payments disequilibria can be corrected by income changes. Suppose, for example, that a situation of equilibrium is altered by an increase in exports, so that B shifts to a surplus situation. What are the (automatic) corrective forces that tend to re-equilibrate the balance of payments? The answer is simple: via the multiplier the increase in exports brings about an increase in income, which in turn determines an induced increase in imports via the marginal propensity to import. This increase in imports tends to offset the initial increase in exports, and we must ascertain whether the former matches the latter exactly (so that the balance of payments returns to an equilibrium situation) or not. In the second case the situation usually depicted is that the balance of payments will show a surplus, although smaller than the initial increase in exports: in other words, the induced change in imports will not be sufficient to re-equilibrate the balance of payments. However, we shall see presently that the contrary case (that is, when induced imports increase more than the initial increase in exports) as well as the borderline case cannot be excluded on *a priori grounds*.

The case of an exogenous increase in imports is harder to examine. It might seem that this increase would cause, via the multiplier, a decrease in income and

---

[2] Taxation (T) is not considered for simplicity's sake, but it could easily be introduced.
[3] Since prices and the exchange rate are rigid, they can be set to one.

thus an induced decrease in imports, which tends to offset the initial autonomous increase. Things are not so simple as that however. In fact, we must check whether or not the autonomous increase in imports is accompanied by a simultaneous autonomous decrease in the demand for home output by residents. If the answer is yes, this will indeed cause a decrease in income etc. If not (which means that the autonomous increase in imports is matched by an autonomous decrease in saving), no depressive effect on income takes place and no adjustment via induced imports occurs. Intermediate cases are of course possible.

To analyze these and similar problems rigorously the first step is to find the formula for the multiplier. If we substitute from Eqs. (13.1) – (13.4) into Eq. (13.5), solve for y and then consider the variations (denoted by Δ), we get

$$\Delta y = \frac{1}{1-b-h+\mu} (\Delta C_0 + \Delta I_0 - \Delta m_0 + \Delta x_0). \tag{13.7}$$

Note that if we assume no induced investment, the multiplier is reduced to the familiar formula $1/(s+\mu)$, where $s \equiv 1-b$ is the marginal propensity to save. Also observe that, as we said in Sect. 13.1, the autonomous components are included in the multiplicand (where Δm_0 appears) whereas the coefficients concerning the induced components enter into the multiplier (where μ is included). This multiplier is smaller than that for the closed economy — of course we must assume that b and h remain the same — because of the additional leakage due to imports.

For the solution (13.7) to be economically meaningful the condition

$$1-b-h+\mu > 0, \tag{13.8}$$

must hold, whence

$$b+h < 1+\mu, \tag{13.8.1}$$

or

$$b+h-\mu < 1. \tag{13.8.2}$$

It can be shown (see Sect. A.13.1.1) that the necessary and sufficient condition for the dynamic stability of the model is the same as (13.8): therefore, results for dynamic stability and meaningful comparative statics go hand in hand, as is often the case (Samuelson's correspondence principle).

Condition (13.8.1) means that the *marginal propensity to spend*, $(b+h)$, must be smaller than one plus the marginal propensity to import. Condition (13.8.2) means that the marginal propensity to spend on *domestic* output by residents, $(b+h-\mu)$, must be smaller than one. To clarify the meaning of $b+h-\mu$, consider a unit increment in income, which causes an increment in the induced components of the various expenditure functions. The increment in consumption and investment is $b+h$ and contains both national and foreign goods. The part pertaining to the latter is thus a part of the total increment $b+h$, and coincides with μ. Algebraically, let the subscripts d and f denote domestic and foreign goods (and services) respectively; then $b \equiv b_d + b_f$, $h \equiv h_d + h_f$, and in our simplified model $b_f + h_f = \mu$. Therefore $b+h-\mu = b_d + h_d$ measures the marginal propensity to spend on domestic output by residents.

13.2.2 Balance-of-Payments Adjustment in the Case of an Exogenous Increase in Exports

Let us now consider the balance of payments. By substituting from Eqs. (13.3) and (13.4) into Eq. (13.6) and considering the variations we have

$$\Delta B = \Delta x_0 - \Delta m_0 - \mu \Delta y, \tag{13.9}$$

which states that the change in the balance of payments is equal to the exogenous change in exports minus the change in imports, the latter being partly exogenous (Δm_0) and partly induced ($\mu \Delta y$, where Δy is given by the multiplier formula (13.7) found above). Here we have all that is needed to analyze the balance-of-payments adjustment problem.

Consider first the case of an exogenous increase in exports. By assumption, no other exogenous change occurs, so that $\Delta C_0 = \Delta I_0 = \Delta m_0 = 0$, and the equations of change become

$$\Delta B = \Delta x_0 - \mu \Delta y, \quad \Delta y = \frac{1}{1-b-h+\mu} \Delta x_0,$$

whence

$$\Delta B = \Delta x_0 - \mu \frac{\Delta x_0}{1-b-h+\mu},$$

i.e.

$$\Delta B = \frac{1-b-h}{1-b-h+\mu} \Delta x_0, \tag{13.9.1}$$

which expresses the final change in the balance of payments. The reader will note that the simple mathematical procedure followed is nothing more than the algebraic transposition of the verbal reasoning made above; but it enables us to find the precise conditions under which the adjustment is incomplete, complete, or more than complete. These conditions are easily derived from (13.9.1). If the marginal propensity to spend is smaller than one, $b+h<1$, then $1-b-h>0$ and so $\Delta B > 0$; furthermore, since $1-b-h<1-b-h+\mu$, the fraction in the right-hand-side of (13.9.1) is smaller than one, whence $\Delta B < \Delta x_0$. The conclusion is that adjustment is incomplete: the induced increase in imports is not great enough to match the initial exogenous increase in exports, so that the balance of payments will show a surplus ($\Delta B > 0$), although smaller than the initial one ($\Delta B < \Delta x_0$). Figure 13.1 gives a graphic representation of the situation. The graphic counterpart of the assumption $b+h<1$ is the fact that the S schedule crosses the I schedule from below, namely: slope of $I <$ slope of S, that is $h < 1 - b$. The stability condition is satisfied since slope of $S+m = 1-b+\mu >$ slope of $I+x = h$.

The initial equilibrium point is E, which corresponds to an income of OA. Exports are represented by the vertical distance between the $I+x$ and the I schedules, and imports by the vertical distance between the $S+m$ and the S schedules. Therefore, in line with our assumptions, in E we have balance-of-payments equilibrium as well, since exports $= BE =$ imports [note that in B we have $S = I$, so that, according to Eq. (13.5.1), it must be $m = x$]. Consider now an

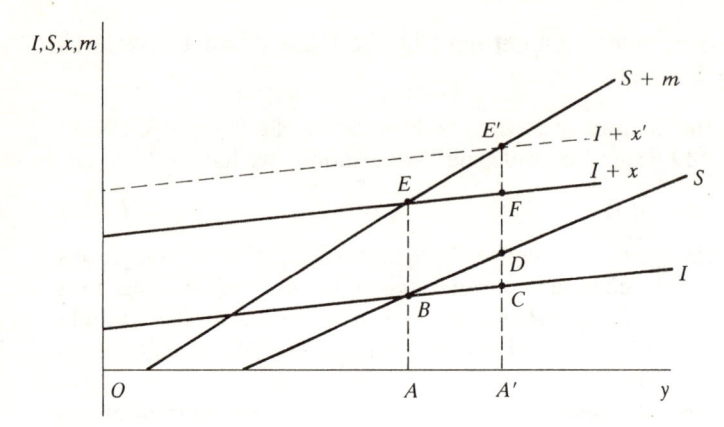

128   13 The Role of Income Changes in the Adjustment Process

Fig. 13.1. The multiplier without foreign repercussions and the balance of payments

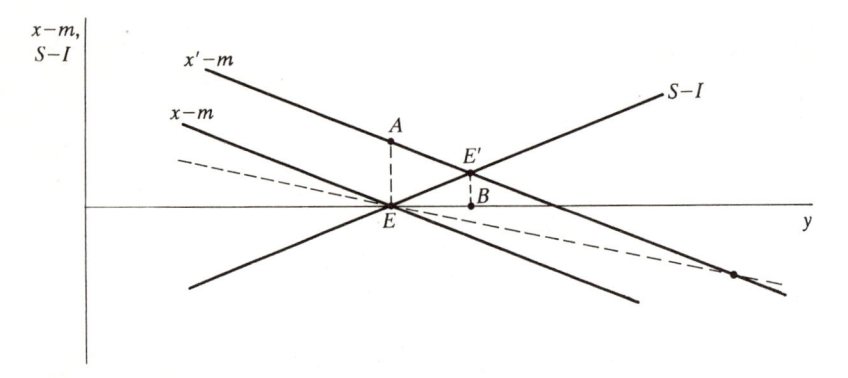

Fig. 13.2. The balance of payments and national income: exogenous increase in exports

exogenous increase in exports from x_0 to $x' = x_0 + \Delta x_0$, so that the $I + x$ schedule shifts vertically to $I + x'$; the new equilibrium point is E', to which an income of OA' corresponds. At this level of income, imports are DE' whereas exports are CE': the balance-of-payments surplus is CD. Note that $CD < FE'$: since FE' is a measure of the exogenous increase in exports, a partial adjustment has taken place. Note also that CD measures the excess of saving over investment, as expressed by Eq. (13.5.1′).

An alternative graphic representation is given in Fig. 13.2. In fact, Fig. 13.1 is well suited for illustrating national income movements, but it fails to show very clearly and immediately the effects on the balance of payments. If we consider Eq. (13.5.1′) we can draw the $(x - m)$ schedule — that is, the balance-of-payments schedule — and the $(S - I)$ schedule, both as functions of y; equilibrium will obtain at the intersection of these schedules. In Fig. 13.2, the $(x - m)$ schedule is downward sloping because we are subtracting an ever greater amount of imports from an exogenously given amount of exports $(x - m = x_0 - m_0 - \mu y)$. The positive intercept reflects the assumption that the autonomous component of imports is smaller than exports; this assumption is necessary to ensure that it is in principle possible to reach balance-of-payments equilibrium at a positive level of income. The $(S-I)$ schedule is increasing, on the assumption that the marginal propensity to spend is smaller than one $[S-I=(1-b-h)y-(C_0+I_0)]$. The fact that the two schedules intersect at a point lying on the y axis reflects the assumption, already made above, that in the initial situation the balance of payments is in equilibrium. An increase in exports shifts the $(x-m)$ schedule to $(x'-m)$; the new intersection occurs at E' where the balance of payments shows a surplus BE'. This is smaller than the initial increase in exports, measured by the vertical distance between $(x'-m)$ and $(x-m)$, for example AE.

As we said above, the case of underadjustment examined so far is not the only one possible. From Eq. (13.9.1) we see that adjustment is complete ($\Delta B=0$) when $1-b-h=0$, that is when the marginal propensity to spend equals one. In this borderline case the induced increase in imports exactly offsets the initial exogenous increase in exports. But the case of *overadjustment* is also possible: when the marginal propensity to spend is greater than one, then $1-b-h<0$, and $\Delta B<0$, that is, the induced increase in imports is greater than the initial exogenous increase in exports. From the economic point of view it is easy to understand why this is so: the greater the marginal propensity to spend, the greater — *ceteris paribus* — the multiplier; this means a higher income increase given the exogenous increase in exports, and finally, a greater increase in induced imports. In terms of Fig. 13.2, the case under consideration implies that the $(S-I)$ schedule is downward sloping (as shown by the broken line); the slope, however, must be smaller in absolute value than the slope of the $(x-m)$ schedule for stability to obtain: in fact, from Eq. (13.8.1) we get $(b+h-1)<\mu$. Therefore, overadjustment cannot be ruled out on the basis of considerations of stability. It is true that if the country is stable in isolation, $b+h<1$ and underadjustment only can occur. But since we are dealing with an open economy, what matters is that it is stable *qua* open economy, and to impose on it the condition that it should also be stable in isolation seems unwarranted. Thus, on theoretical grounds we must accept the possibility of overadjustment (as well as the borderline case of exact adjustment), and the assertion that the multiplier is incapable of restoring equilibrium in the balance of payments is wrong.

13.2.3 Balance-of-Payments Adjustment in the Case of an Exogenous Increase in Imports

Let us now consider the case of an exogenous increase in imports. As we said in Sect. 13.2.1, the problem is complicated by the fact that we must check what happens to the autonomous component of residents' expenditure on domestic output, which is included — together with their autonomous expenditure on foreign output — in C_0 and I_0. The commonly followed procedure of considering a Δm_0 while keeping C_0 and I_0 constant, implicitly assumes that the increase in the exogenous expenditure on foreign output is accompanied by a simultaneous decrease of the same amount in the exogenous expenditure by residents on domestic output. This is a very restrictive assumption, because it implies that domestic and foreign output are perfect substitutes. At the opposite extreme is the assumption that Δm_0 leaves the exogenous expenditure on domestic output

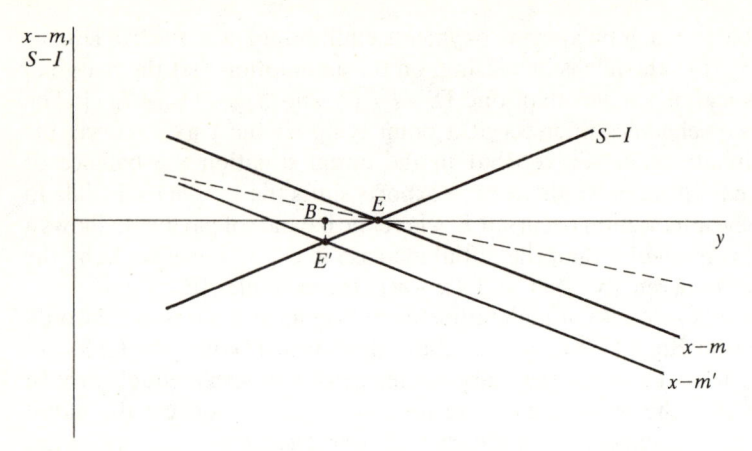

Fig. 13.3. The balance of payments and national income: exogenous increase in imports, case (i)

unaffected (i.e., Δm_0 entirely derives from an exogenous decrease in savings), which means that $C_0 + I_0$ increases by the same amount as m_0. Intermediate cases are of course possible, and they will be examined in Sect. A.13.1.1; here we limit ourselves to an examination of the two extremes.

(i) When only m_0 varies, Eqs. (13.7) and (13.9) become

$$\Delta y = -\frac{1}{1-b-h+\mu}\Delta m_0, \quad \Delta B = -\Delta m_0 - \mu \Delta y,$$

whence

$$\Delta B = \frac{b+h-1}{1-b-h+\mu}\Delta m_0. \tag{13.9.2}$$

Since $1-b-h+\mu > 0$ by the stability condition, underadjustment, exact adjustment, overadjustment will take place according as $b+h \lesseqgtr 1$. Therefore, if the marginal propensity to spend is smaller than one, the induced decrease in imports following the decrease in income caused by the initial exogenous increase in imports is not enough to restore balance of payments equilibrium completely. In the opposite case the balance of payments will go into surplus. These shifts are illustrated in Fig. 13.3, where the exogenous increase in imports is represented by a shift of the $(x-m)$ schedule to $(x-m')$. The same remarks made above concerning the marginal propensity to spend hold here too.

(ii) When the exogenous increase in imports is not accompanied by any reduction in exogenous expenditure on domestic output by residents, we have $\Delta m_0 = \Delta C_0 + \Delta I_0$. From Eq. (13.7) we see that there is no effect on income. Therefore, no adjustment is possible through induced changes in imports, and the balance of payments deteriorates by the full amount of the exogenous increase in imports, $\Delta B = -\Delta m_0$. In terms of Fig. 13.4, the downward shift of the $(x-m)$ schedule is accompanied by an identical downward shift of the $(S-I)$ schedule, so that the value of y does not change and the balance of payments shows a deficit $EE' = \Delta m_0$.

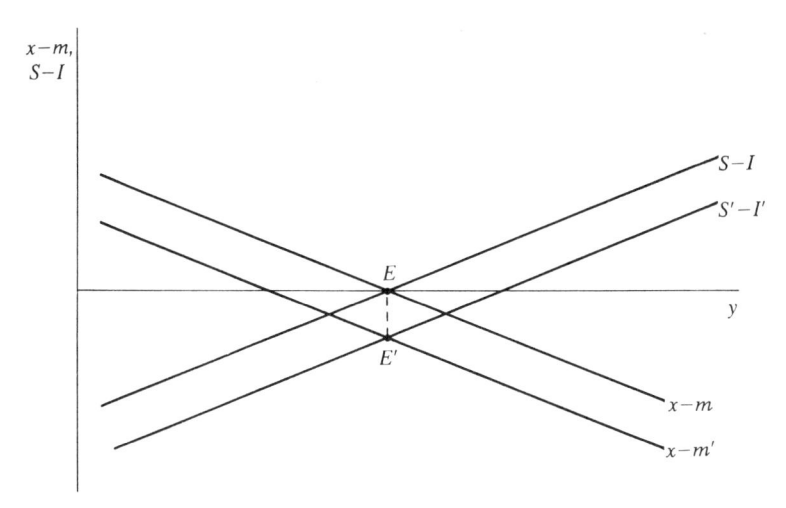

Fig. 13.4. The balance of payments and national income: exogenous increase in imports, case (ii)

By means of the same procedure illustrated so far we can examine the effects on the balance of payments of all other kinds of shifts in the exogenous components. But this can be left as an exercise for the reader, and we now turn to the multiplier with foreign repercussions.

13.3 Foreign Repercussions

13.3.1 A Simplified Two-Country Model

Several important feedbacks are neglected by assuming no foreign repercussions. In fact, the imports of the country under consideration (henceforth referred to as country 1) are the exports of one or more other countries and so enter into their income determination; similarly the exports of country 1 are the imports of one or more other countries. Thus, for example, an increase in income in country 1 causes — through the increase in this country's imports, which means an increase in the exports of one or more other countries — an increase in their income and therefore in their imports. All or part of these will be directed to country 1, which will experience an increase in exports and so in income, a consequent increase in imports, and so on, with a chain of repercussions whose final result (assuming that the process converges) will certainly be different from that obtaining if no such repercussions occurred.

A complete analysis of the problem of repercussions would require a n-country model, which will be treated in Sect. A.13.7 because it requires the knowledge of some advanced mathematical tools. A simplified treatment can be given if we assume that the world is composed of two countries only, country 1 and the rest of the world (henceforth called country 2). In Fig. 13.5a we illustrate the initial situation of country 1, where an exogenous increase in investment from I to I' occurs. The new equilibrium point is E', to which an income of OA' corresponds.

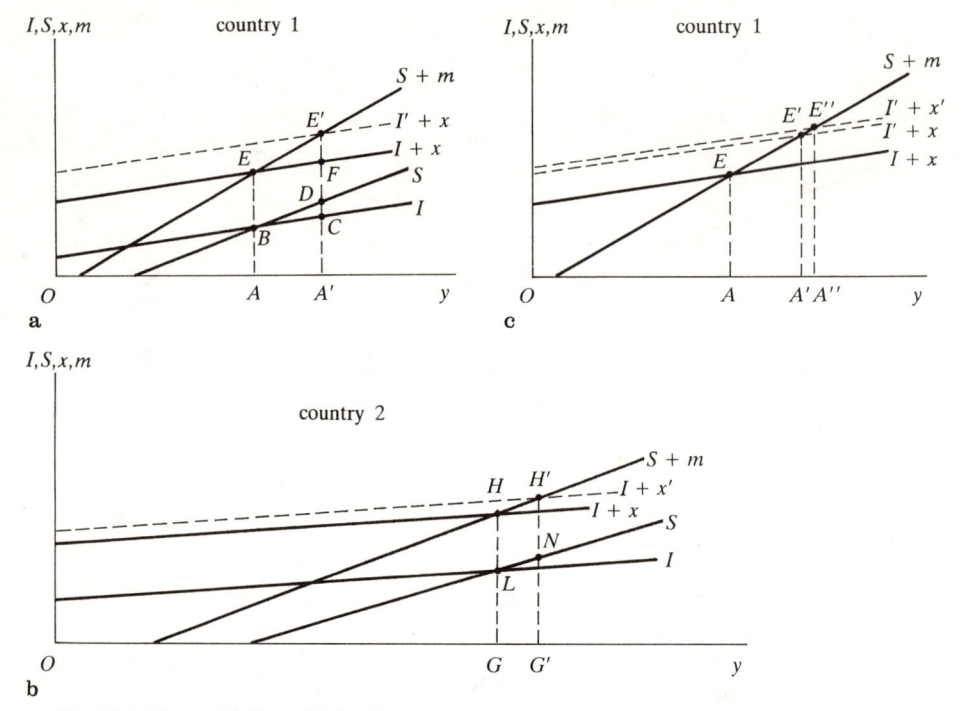

Fig. 13.5. The multiplier with foreign repercussions

The new level of imports is $E'D$, and since it was EB initially, the difference $E'D - EB$ measures the *increase* in imports. This increase is an increase in the exports of country 2, and gives rise to a shift of the $I+x$ schedule to $I+x'$ in Fig. 13.5b. In country 2 the new equilibrium point is then H' and the income increase is GG'. As a consequence the imports of country 2 increase from HL to $H'N$. This increase is drawn as an increase in the exports of country 1 in Fig. 13.5c, where equilibrium shifts to E'' and income to OA''. We have a further increase in country's 1 imports, thus in country's 2 exports, and so on. If certain stability conditions are satisfied (see Sect. A.13.2.2), the process converges to a final equilibrium point where all repercussions are concluded.

13.3.2 An Alternative Graphic Representation and Stability Analysis

An alternative graphic representation, based on R. Robinson (1952), is available. Consider first the following model, which is an obvious extension of the model described in Sect. 13.2:

Country 1

$C_1 = C_{01} + b_1 y_1,$
$I_1 = I_{01} + h_1 y_1,$
$m_1 = m_{01} + \mu_1 y_1,$
$x_1 = m_2,$
$y_1 = C_1 + I_1 + x_1 - m_1,$

Country 2

$C_2 = C_{02} + b_2 y_2,$
$I_2 = I_{02} + h_2 y_2,$
$m_2 = m_{02} + \mu_2 y_2,$
$x_2 = m_1$
$y_2 = C_2 + I_2 + x_2 - m_2,$

where the symbols have their usual meaning and the subscripts 1 and 2 refer to country 1 and country 2. It should be pointed out that the equations which express the equality between the exports of one country and the imports of the other can be seen under a twofold aspect. First, they hold as definitional equations, because in our two-country world the exports of one country coincide with the imports of the other and vice versa. Secondly, they can be considered as demand and supply equilibrium conditions under the assumption that the supply of exports of each country is perfectly elastic in the relevant interval. This means that each country is willing to export (supply side) any amount of its output being demanded as imports by the other country (demand side), which is consistent with the assumption of underemployed economies etc., made at the beginning (Sect. 13.1).

If we substitute C, I, m, x from the first four equations of each set into the fifth and rearrange terms, we obtain

$$y_1 = (b_1 + h_1 - \mu_1) y_1 + \mu_2 y_2 + (C_{01} + I_{01} + m_{02} - m_{01}),$$
$$y_2 = (b_2 + h_2 - \mu_2) y_2 + \mu_1 y_1 + (C_{02} + I_{02} + m_{01} - m_{02}),$$
(13.10)

that is

$$(1 - b_1 - h_1 + \mu_1) y_1 - \mu_2 y_2 = C_{01} + I_{01} + m_{02} - m_{01},$$
$$-\mu_1 y_1 + (1 - b_2 - h_2 + \mu_2) y_2 = C_{02} + I_{02} + m_{01} - m_{02},$$
(13.10.1)

which can be written as

$$y_1 = \frac{\mu_2}{1 - b_1 - h_1 + \mu_1} y_2 + \frac{C_{01} + I_{01} + m_{02} - m_{01}}{1 - b_1 - h_1 + \mu_1},$$

$$y_2 = \frac{\mu_1}{1 - b_2 - h_2 + \mu_2} y_1 + \frac{C_{02} + I_{02} + m_{01} - m_{02}}{1 - b_2 - h_2 + \mu_2}.$$
(13.10.2)

The first equation expresses the (equilibrium) income level in country 1 as a linear function of the income level in country 2, and similarly the second equation expresses y_2 as a linear function of y_1. These functions are drawn in Fig. 13.6 and have the following properties:

(i) They are both increasing because (see Sect. A.13.2.2) stability requires that $1 - b_i - h_i + \mu_i > 0$, $i = 1, 2$;

(ii) since $C_{01} + I_{01} + m_{02} - m_{01}$ and $C_{02} + I_{02} + m_{01} - m_{02}$ can be safely assumed to be positive[4], they also have a positive intercept on the axis where the respective dependent variable is represented (remember that the first equation in (13.10.2) expresses y_1 in terms of y_2; if we prefer, we can solve it for y_2 in terms of y_1 and get

$$y_2 = \frac{1 - b_1 - h_1 + \mu_1}{\mu_2} y_1 - \frac{C_{01} + I_{01} + m_{02} - m_{01}}{\mu_2},$$

which means a negative intercept on the y_2 axis);

---
[4] As we saw above, m_{0i} is part of $C_{0i} + I_{0i}$.

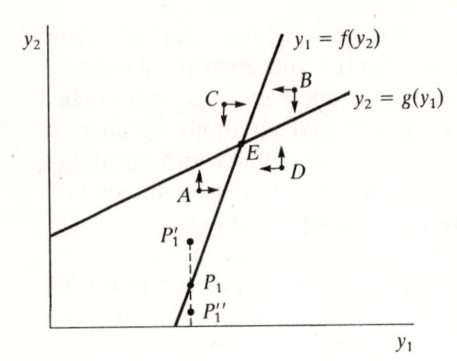

Fig. 13.6. The multiplier with foreign repercussions: alternative representation and stability analysis

(iii) the slope of the $y_1 = f(y_2)$ schedule is greater than the slope of the $y_2 = g(y_1)$ schedule when both slopes are referred to the y_1 axis (that is, $\dfrac{1-b_1-h_1+\mu_1}{\mu_2} > \dfrac{\mu_1}{1-b_2-h_2+\mu_2}$, which follows from the stability conditions derived in the Appendix);

(iv) each schedule can be considered to be composed of the sum of four constituent elements which are: (a) the sum of autonomous consumption and investment of domestic output; (b) expenditure (by residents on domestic output) induced by the income generated — via multiplier — by component (a); (c) earnings from exports; (d) expenditure (by residents on domestic output) induced by the income generated — via multiplier — by component (c). In fact, if we consider for example y_2, we can rewrite the second equation in (13.10.1) as

$$y_2 = (C_{02} + I_{02} - m_{02})$$
$$+ (b_2 + h_2 - \mu_2) \frac{1}{1 - b_2 - h_2 + \mu_2} (C_{02} + I_{02} - m_{02}) + (m_{01} + \mu_1 y_1)$$
$$+ (b_2 + h_2 - \mu_2) \frac{1}{1 - b_2 - h_2 + \mu_2} (m_{01} + \mu_1 y_1), \qquad (13.10.3)$$

where the four terms on the r.h.s. correspond to the four components listed above, and could be represented in Fig. 13.6 as a series of "slabs" stacked one upon the other.

The intersection of the two curves determines, of course, the pair of equilibrium values of incomes that will satisfy *both* equations, and is therefore the simultaneous equilibrium of our two-country world.

Let us now examine the stability of equilibrium by means of the graphic technique of arrow diagrams.

We will first consider the $y_1 = f(y_2)$ schedule and show that at all points above and to the left of it there is a situation of excess demand, whereas at all points below and to the right of it there is a situation of excess supply. Examine for example points P_1, P'_1, P''_1. Point P_1 lies on the $y_1 = f(y_2)$ schedule and so at an equilibrium point for country 1, where aggregate supply and aggregate demand are equal. Point P'_1 corresponds to a situation in which y_1 is the same as at P_1 but y_2 is greater. This means that aggregate supply (y_1) is the same but aggregate demand is greater because a greater value of y_2 means a greater value of country's 1 exports, and other things are equal. Therefore at P'_1, excess demand for country's 1 output obtains. As regards point P''_1, here y_1 is the same as at P_1 but y_2 is smaller. Consequently, to the same aggregate supply there corresponds a lower aggregate demand, because, other things being equal, country 1's exports are lower. Therefore at P''_1 there is insufficient demand (excess supply) for country 1's output.

By a similar argument it can be shown that at all points to the right (left) of the $y_2 = g(y_1)$ schedule there is a situation of excess demand (supply).

We now introduce the familiar dynamic behaviour assumption according to which in any country the level of national income (output) varies in relation to excess demand, that is, it tends to increase if aggregate demand exceeds aggregate supply, and in the opposite case, to decrease. On the basis of this dynamic behaviour all disequilibrium points tend to converge towards the equilibrium point E. A point like A, for example, lies above the $y_1 = f(y_2)$ schedule and to the right of the $y_2 = g(y_1)$ schedule. Therefore, according to what we have shown above, there is excess demand for country's 1 output, which tends to increase (the horizontal arrow originating from A points to the right) as well as excess demand for country 2's output, which tends to increase (the vertical arrow originating from A points upwards). Thus point A tends to move in a direction included between the two arrows and converges towards the equilibrium point E. Similar arguments can be made with respect to points such as B, C, and D; the usual caveat applies, namely that only a rigorous mathematical analysis can confirm the results of this intuitive graphic treatment (see Sect. A.13.2.2, where we also show that the convergence towards equilibrium is monotonic).

13.3.3 Multipliers and Balance-of-Payments Adjustment

Changes in the exogenous elements $C_{0i}, I_{0i}, m_{0i}, i = 1, 2$, shift one or both schedules in parallel, and the new equilibrium will be determined by their new intersection. For our purposes, however, we need explicit expressions for the multipliers. These can be obtained by solving system (13.10.1), thus expressing y_1 and y_2 in terms of the various propensities and of the exogenous variables, and then by considering the variations. The result is

$$\Delta y_1 = \frac{(1-b_2-h_2)(\Delta C_{01}+\Delta I_{01}+\Delta m_{02}-\Delta m_{01})+\mu_2(\Delta C_{01}+\Delta I_{01}+\Delta C_{02}+\Delta I_{02})}{(1-b_1-h_1+\mu_1)(1-b_2-h_2+\mu_2)-\mu_1\mu_2},$$

$$\Delta y_2 = \frac{(1-b_1-h_1)(\Delta C_{02}+\Delta I_{02}+\Delta m_{01}-\Delta m_{02})+\mu_1(\Delta C_{01}+\Delta I_{01}+\Delta C_{02}+\Delta I_{02})}{(1-b_1-h_1+\mu_1)(1-b_2-h_2+\mu_2)-\mu_1\mu_2}.$$

(13.11)

All existing multipliers and their properties can be derived from these expressions by considering the appropriate exogenous changes. This taxonomic exercise can be easily carried out by any reader who has a mind to do so; the problems on which we wish to concentrate our attention are:

1) the relationships between the closed economy multiplier, the open economy multiplier without repercussions, and the open economy multiplier with repercussions;
2) the adjustment of the balance of payments in the presence of foreign repercussions.

As regards point (1), the usual conclusion is that the multiplier with foreign repercussions, though lower than the closed economy multiplier, is greater than the open economy multiplier without repercussions (if we assume that b and h remain the same). This sounds economically plausible. The multiplier without foreign repercussions is certainly smaller than the closed economy one, because of the additional leakage due to imports (see Eq. (13.7) in Sect. 13.2). Now, foreign repercussions make it possible to recover part of this leakage, which returns in the form of increased exports: therefore, the multiplier with repercussions is greater than the multiplier without repercussions, though always smaller than that of the closed economy because only part of the leakage can be recovered. It turns out that this proposition is indeed true provided that the stability conditions are satisfied in all conceivable cases (that is, the countries are stable in isolation, stable when they are open but repercussions are ignored, and stable when repercussions are considered); the proof involves some algebra which is best dealt with in Sect. A.13.3.3.

As regards point (2), it must be remembered that the sum of the balances of payments (measured in terms of a common unit) of all countries is zero; it is therefore sufficient to consider one country, say country 1, since $\Delta B_2 = -\Delta B_1$. By definition,

$$B_1 = x_1 - m_1 = m_2 - m_1 = (m_{02} - m_{01}) + \mu_2 y_2 - \mu_1 y_1, \quad (13.12)$$

whence

$$\Delta B_1 = \Delta m_{02} - \Delta m_{01} + \mu_2 \Delta y_2 - \mu_1 \Delta y_1, \quad (13.12.1)$$

where Δy_1 and Δy_2 are given by Eqs. (13.11). A variety of situations can be considered; we shall limit ourselves to the case in which there is an exogenous increase in the exports of country 1. To avoid possible mistakes, it must be remembered that such an increase is the same as an exogenous increase in country 2's imports: therefore, the problem necessarily arises of determining what happens to the exogenous expenditure by country 2's residents on country 2's output. This problem is the same as that met in the simpler case of the multiplier without foreign repercussions. As an example we examine the situation in which the residents of country 2 demand more foreign goods without changing their autonomous spending on domestic goods, so that $\Delta C_{02} + \Delta I_{02} = \Delta m_{02}$ as explained in Sect. 13.2. Since $\Delta C_{01}, \Delta I_{01}$, and Δm_{01}, are zero by assumption, the multipliers (13.11) become

$$\Delta y_1 = \frac{1-b_2-h_2+\mu_2}{(1-b_1-h_1+\mu_1)(1-b_2-h_2+\mu_2)-\mu_1\mu_2}\Delta m_{02},$$

(13.11.1)

$$\Delta y_2 = \frac{\mu_1}{(1-b_1-h_1+\mu_1)(1-b_2-h_2+\mu_2)-\mu_1\mu_2}\Delta m_{02}.$$

Incidentally, note that income increases not only in country 1, which is intuitively obvious, but also in country 2, due to foreign repercussions.

From (13.12.1) and (13.11.1) we obtain

$$\Delta B_1 = \frac{(1-b_1-h_1)(1-b_2-h_2+\mu_2)}{(1-b_1-h_1+\mu_1)(1-b_2-h_2+\mu_2)-\mu_1\mu_2}\Delta m_{02}. \qquad (13.13)$$

Since $(1-b_2-h_2+\mu_2)$ as well as the denominator of the fraction must be positive for stability, the sign of the fraction depends on the sign of $(1-b_1-h_1)$. We can therefore conclude that an exogenous increase in country 1's exports eventually improves its balance of payments (although by less than the initial surplus) when the country's marginal propensity to spend is smaller than one. In other words, the (final) induced increase in imports, account being taken of all the repercussions, does not match the items on the credit side, which are the initial exogenous increase in exports plus the (final) induced increase in exports due to the increase in country 2's income. However, if country 1's marginal propensity to spend is greater than one, its balance of payments will deteriorate, and will not change in the borderline case $b_1+h_1=1$. These results are qualitatively the same as those obtained by using the multiplier without repercussions, and we refer the reader to the comments made in Sect. 13.2.2. We only add that, although the marginal propensity to spend of *one* country may be greater than 1 (but, of course, smaller than 1 plus the marginal propensity to import) without impairing stability, the marginal propensities to spend *cannot* be greater than 1 *in both* countries. In other words, if *all* countries are unstable in isolation, the world is unstable. This limitation must be kept in mind when exercising oneself in the taxonomy of multipliers with foreign repercussions.

13.4 Intermediate Goods and the Multiplier

13.4.1 Introductory Remarks

In the equation for determining income in an open economy, which for convenience is rewritten here

$$y = C + I + x - m, \qquad (13.5)$$

the symbol y represents national income (product), the calculation of which is carried out on the side of value added, where (as is well known from national economic accounting) intermediate goods are not included. But the total imports of goods and services m also include intermediate goods, and account must be taken of this fact when the various multipliers are calculated (Miyazawa, 1960). The formulae examined in the previous sections are obviously still valid if it is assumed that domestic production does not require imported intermediate goods. On the other hand, in the case where there are also imports of intermediate goods present, these formulae remain valid *only* if the content of intermediate goods in the various categories of final goods (consumer, investment and export) which make up the national product is the same. Otherwise they must be modified[5].

In order to clarify this point we must distinguish total imports m into imports of final goods m^F and imports of intermediate goods m^R, where obviously $m^F + m^R = m$. Imports of final goods can be related directly to income by way of the import function

$$m^F = m_0^F + \mu^F y, \qquad (13.14)$$

while, as far as imports of intermediate goods are concerned, it is necessary first of all to establish the requirements of intermediate goods per unit of the national product. Let us assume that this requirement is a constant independently of the type of good. Let us also assume that a constant quota of this requirement consists of imported intermediate goods. We can then write

$$m^R = \mu^R y, \ 0 < \mu^R < 1, \qquad (13.15)$$

where μ^R is the marginal propensity (assumed to coincide with the average) to import intermediate goods. The total import function thus becomes

$$m = m^F + m^R = m_0^F + (\mu^F + \mu^R) y = m_0^F + \mu y, \qquad (13.16)$$

where μ is the total marginal propensity to import. It can be seen at once that (13.16) coincides with (13.3) in Sect. 13.2.1 (except for the qualification that the autonomous component consists entirely of final goods), so that the rest of the treatment and in particular the formulae for multipliers remain unchanged.

13.4.2 Different Requirements of Intermediate Goods

Let us now examine the case in which the requirement of intermediate goods differs according to the type of good produced. Imports of intermediate goods are now related to the various components of final demand which are satisfied by domestic production, on the basis of coefficients which express the requirements of imported intermediate goods. In what follows we simplify by assuming that investment is entirely exogenous and we also assume that all exports consist of domestically produced goods (in other words, we exclude the case of simple reexport — that is without any transformation — of imported final goods). We thus have

$$m^R = \lambda_c C_d + \lambda_I I_d + \lambda_x x, \ 0 < \lambda_c < 1, \ 0 < \lambda_I < 1, \ 0 < \lambda_x < 1, \qquad (13.17)$$

---

[5] The proof by Metzler (1973a, but written in 1963 independently of Miyazawa's work) that imported raw materials do not change the results in any essential respect (he was applying the multiplier analysis to the transfer problem, on which see Sect. 17.4), was based on the implicit assumption of identical requirements of intermediate goods. The same assumption is implicit in Meade's analysis of the role of raw materials in multiplier analysis (Meade, 1948, pp. 497–498).

13.4 Intermediate Goods and the Multiplier

where the λ's are the coefficients mentioned above and C_d, I_d, indicate consumer and investment goods produced domestically. As we know, C and I contain both domestic and foreign goods, that is

$$C = C_d + C_f, \quad I = I_d + I_f, \tag{13.18}$$

and, in our simplified model, the part of consumption and investment goods coming from abroad coincides with the imports of final goods, so that the equation for the determination of income can be re-written as

$$y = C + I + x - m = C_d + C_f + I_d + I_f + x - m^F - m^R$$
$$= C_d + I_d + x - m^R. \tag{13.19}$$

Given Eq. (13.17), we have

$$y = (1 - \lambda_c) C_d + (1 - \lambda_I) I_d + (1 - \lambda_x) x, \tag{13.19.1}$$

and given the assumptions made on the various functions, it follows that

$$y = (1 - \lambda_c)(C_{0d} + b_d y) + (1 - \lambda_I) I_{0d} + (1 - \lambda_x) x_0, \tag{13.20}$$

where

$$b_d = b - b_f \tag{13.21}$$

is, as we know, the marginal propensity to consume domestically produced goods, equal to the difference between the total marginal propensity to consume (b), and the marginal propensity to consume foreign goods (b_f, which we can indentify, in our simplified model, with the marginal propensity to import final goods, μ^F).

From (13.20) we immediately obtain the multiplier by solving for y and considering the variations

$$\Delta y = \frac{1}{1 - b_d(1 - \lambda_d)} [(1 - \lambda_c) \Delta C_{0d} + (1 - \lambda_I) \Delta I_{0d} + (1 - \lambda_x) \Delta x_0]. \tag{13.22}$$

First, note that the multiplier is now different according to the exogenous variation which occurs, given the presence of various coefficients $[(1 - \lambda_c)$ etc.] applied to the different variations. The traditional multiplier, instead, is the same whatever the exogenous variation may be and is[6]

$$\frac{1}{1 - b + \mu}. \tag{13.23}$$

13.4.3 Identical Requirements of Intermediate Goods

It is now possible to demonstrate that the multiplier (13.22) coincides with the traditional multiplier (13.23) *if and only if* the content of imported intermediate goods in the various categories of final goods produced domestically is the same.

---

[6] Equation (13.23) is obtained immediately from (13.7) by putting $h = 0$ given the assumption of entirely autonomous investment.

As this content is expressed by $\lambda_c, \lambda_I, \lambda_x$, we now assume that these coefficients are equal, that is

$$\lambda_c = \lambda_I = \lambda_x = \lambda, \qquad (13.24)$$

where λ is their common value[7]. Then (13.22) is reduced to

$$\Delta y = \frac{1-\lambda}{1-b_d(1-\lambda)} (\Delta C_{0d} + \Delta I_{0d} + \Delta x_0), \qquad (13.22.1)$$

and therefore the multiplier (equal for all the exogenous variations), which we denote by k, is

$$k = \frac{1-\lambda}{1-b_d(1-\lambda)}. \qquad (13.22.2)$$

It remains to be demonstrated that the multiplier (13.22.2) coincides with the traditional multiplier (13.23). If we divide the numerator and the denominator of (13.22.2) by $(1-\lambda)$, we have

$$k = \frac{1}{\dfrac{1}{1-\lambda} - b_d}. \qquad (13.22.3)$$

Since, as can be ascertained by direct substitution,

$$\frac{1}{1-\lambda} = 1 + \frac{\lambda}{1-\lambda},$$

Eq. (13.22.3) becomes

$$k = \frac{1}{1 - b_d + \dfrac{\lambda}{1-\lambda}}. \qquad (13.22.4)$$

By adding and subtracting $b_f = \mu^F$ [see (13.21)] we have

$$k = \frac{1}{1 - b + \mu^F + \dfrac{\lambda}{1-\lambda}}. \qquad (13.22.5)$$

The last passage consists in demonstrating that $\lambda/(1-\lambda)$ is nothing other than the marginal propensity to import intermediate goods, μ^R. In fact, if we take (13.17) into consideration, then, given (13.24), we have

$$m^R = \lambda(C_d + I_d + x),$$

and as it follows from (13.19), given (13.24), that $C_d + I_d + x = y + m^R$, we get

$$m^R = \lambda(y + m^R),$$

---

[7] It will be clear to the reader that we are demonstrating the sufficiency of this condition (the "if" part of the proposition); the necessity (the "only if" part) is implicit in the fact that (13.22) differs from (13.23) when the various λ's are different.

from which

$$m^R = \frac{\lambda}{1-\lambda} y, \qquad (13.25)$$

which expresses the imports of intermediate goods as a function of income. Therefore $\lambda/(1-\lambda) = \mu^R$, as also can be seen from (13.15), which had been obtained by introducing at the very beginning the assumption that the requirement of imported intermediate goods should be independent of the type of good produced.

Thus, by substituting in (13.22.5) and remembering that $\mu^F + \mu^R = \mu$, we finally have

$$k = \frac{1}{1-b+\mu}, \qquad (13.22.6)$$

which completes the demonstration.

The treatment can also be extended to the case in which account is taken of international repercussions, for the examination of which we refer the reader to Kennedy and Thirlwall (1980) and Thirlwall (1980)[8].

13.4.4 Some Empirical Results

We can now ask what empirical relevance there is in the theoretical considerations so far made. As the textbook treatments of the multiplier in an open economy are almost entirely of the traditional type (in that they ignore the problems examined in this section), if the coefficients expressing the requirements of imported intermediate goods (and therefore the multipliers) were significantly different, one would have to conclude that these treatments give an erroneous view of the functioning of the multiplier in an open economy.

Empirical studies have been carried out by Kennedy and Thirlwall (1980) for the United Kingdom (using the 1971 input-output table for that country) and by Milana (1984) for Italy (using the 1975 Italian input-output table). In Table 13.1 we have given the maximum and minimum values of the various coefficients (which concern inventories and public expenditure respectively), their average value and also the relative multipliers.

Qualitatively, the results in both countries are similar, as the lowest coefficient (and therefore the highest multiplier) for requirements of intermediate imports is that of public expenditure, while the highest coefficient (hence the lowest multiplier) is that of inventories[9]. The coefficient for total autonomous expendi-

---

[8] It should be pointed out that, while Miyazawa's analysis explicitly refers to the question of imported intermediate goods, Kennedy and Thirlwall's refers generically to the import content of the various components of total expenditure (consumption, etc.). The latter, therefore, can also be interpreted in the sense that it simply makes explicit the fact that all the components of total national expenditure consist (in different proportions) of final imported goods and final domestically produced goods, without taking intermediate goods into consideration.

[9] In our treatment we have not taken inventories into consideration, but they can easily be included as a further autonomous component. As far as public expenditure is concerned, see Sect. 13.2.1.

Table 13.1. Coefficients of imports of intermediate goods and open economy multipliers

Expenditure	United Kingdom		Italy	
	Coefficient of imports of intermediate goods (λ)	Multiplier	Coefficient of imports of intermediate goods (λ)	Multiplier
Inventories	0.245	2.21	0.238	1.726
Public expenditure	0.087	2.68	0.058	2.156
Total autonomous expenditure	0.174	2.44	0.153	1.920

ture incorporates the assumption of equality of the various λ coefficients and therefore the relative multiplier coincides with the traditional one, as clarified above in relation to Eq. (13.22).

Within each country the coefficients are in effect numerically different and seem therefore to support the thesis of those who maintain that the traditional formulation of the multiplier is inexact. However, it should be pointed out that the calculations have been made under the assumption that there are no stochastic disturbances[10], so that it is not possible to determine confidence intervals for the various coefficients and multipliers. It is therefore not even possible to establish whether the numerical differences found are statistically significant or not. We must therefore conclude that further studies are necessary and desirable, before we can reach definite conclusions about this subject.

Appendix

A.13.1 The Multiplier without Foreign Repercussions

A.13.1.1 Basic Results

Consider the following model

$$C = C(y, \alpha_C), \quad 0 < \partial C/\partial y < 1, \quad \partial C/\partial \alpha_C > 0,$$
$$I = I(y, \alpha_I), \quad 0 < \partial I/\partial y < 1, \quad \partial I/\partial \alpha_I > 0,$$
$$m = m(y, \alpha_m), \quad 0 < \partial m/\partial y < 1, \quad \partial m/\partial \alpha_m > 0, \quad \text{(A.13.1)}$$
$$x = \alpha_x,$$
$$y - C - I - x + m = 0,$$

where the α's are shift parameters which can be interpreted as the exogenous components of the various expenditure functions. No loss of generality is involved

---

[10] This is explicitly recognised by Milana, while Kennedy and Thirlwall are silent on the matter.

if we assume that $\partial C/\partial \alpha_C$, $\partial I/\partial \alpha_I$, $\partial m/\partial \alpha_m$ are all equal to one. The model written in the text can be considered as a suitable linear approximation to system (A.13.1), with $b \equiv \partial C/\partial y$ etc.

By means of the implicit function theorem, y can be expressed as a differentiable function of the α's (provided that the condition $1 - \partial C/\partial y - \partial I/\partial y + \partial m/\partial y \neq 0$ is satisfied), and consequently, exercises of comparative statics can be carried out. If we differentiate the last equation in (A.13.1) with respect to the relevant parameters, bearing in mind that y is a function of the α's, we obtain the multiplier formula

$$\frac{\partial y}{\partial \alpha_C} = \frac{\partial y}{\partial \alpha_I} = \frac{\partial y}{\partial \alpha_x} = -\frac{\partial y}{\partial \alpha_m} = \frac{1}{1-b-h+\mu}, \qquad (A.13.2)$$

and so

$$dy = \frac{1}{1-b-h+\mu}(d\alpha_C + d\alpha_I + d\alpha_x - d\alpha_m), \qquad (A.13.3)$$

where b, h, μ denote $\partial C/\partial y$, $\partial I/\partial y$, $\partial m/\partial y$ evaluated at the equilibrium point.

The correspondence principle enables us to determine the sign of the denominator of the fraction and so to obtain determinate comparative statics results. The usual dynamic behaviour assumption is that producers react to excess demand by making adjustments in output: if aggregate demand exceeds (falls short of) current output, the latter will be increased (decreased); this mechanism operates independently of the origin of excess demand. Formally,

$$\frac{dy}{dt} = f[(C+I+x-m)-y], \qquad (A.13.4)$$

where f is a sign-preserving function and $f'[0] > 0$. In order to examine local stability, we take a linear approximation at the equilibrium point and obtain

$$\frac{d\bar{y}}{dt} = k(b+h-\mu-1)\bar{y}, \qquad (A.13.4.1)$$

where $\bar{y}$ denotes the deviations from equilibrium, k is $f'[0]$ and can be interpreted as a speed of adjustment, and b, h, μ are $\partial C/\partial y$, $\partial I/\partial y$, $\partial m/\partial y$ evaluated at the equilibrium point. The stability condition derived from the solution of the differential equation (A.13.4.1) is

$$k(b+h-\mu-1) < 0,$$

that is

$$1-b-h+\mu > 0, \qquad (A.13.5)$$

which ensures that the multiplier is positive, and has been discussed in Sect. 13.2.1.

Going back to the multiplier (A.13.3), we introduce a coefficient q, $0 \leq q \leq 1$, which measures the relationship between the change in the autonomous expenditure by residents on domestic output and the change in their autonomous expenditure on foreign output (imports). Letting h and f denote home and foreign output respectively, we have

$$d\alpha_C = d\alpha_{Ch} + d\alpha_{Cf}, \quad d\alpha_I = d\alpha_{Ih} + d\alpha_{If}, \quad d\alpha_{Cf} + d\alpha_{If} = d\alpha_m, \quad (A.13.6)$$

and assuming for the sake of simplicity the q is the same for both consumption and investment expenditure, we have

$$d\alpha_{Ch} = -q d\alpha_{Cf}, \quad d\alpha_{Ih} = -q d\alpha_{If}. \quad (A.13.7)$$

From Eqs. (A.13.6) and (A.13.7) we obtain

$$d\alpha_C + d\alpha_I - d\alpha_m = -q d\alpha_m, \quad (A.13.8)$$

and so the multiplier formula (A.13.3) becomes

$$dy = \frac{1}{1-b-h+\mu}(d\alpha_x - q d\alpha_m). \quad (A.13.3.1)$$

According to some authors, it is not sufficient simply to subtract the proportion of imports in autonomous expenditure from the multiplicand, for the multiplier also should be changed. This can be carried out by making imports a function of aggregate demand $(C+I)$ or of C and I separately (with different import coefficients) instead of y, namely

$$m = m(C, I, \alpha_m), \quad 0 < \partial m/\partial C < 1, \quad 0 < \partial m/\partial I < 1, \quad \partial m/\partial \alpha_m > 0, \quad \partial m/\partial C \neq \partial m/\partial I.$$

If we substitute this import function in the place of the third equation in system (A.13.1) we get a new model, that the reader can easily examine as an exercise. On this point, see Meade (1948), Kennedy and Thirlwall (1979, 1980), Thirlwall (1980, pp. 57 ff.), Sect. 13.4, and Miyazawa (1960).

A.13.1.2 The Balance of Payments

Consider now the balance of payments, $B = x - m$, and differentiate it totally, obtaining

$$dB = d\alpha_x - d\alpha_m - \mu dy, \quad (A.13.9)$$

where dy is given by (A.13.3) or (A.13.3.1) as the case may be. When exports change, we have

$$dB = \frac{1-b-h}{1-b-h+\mu} d\alpha_x, \quad (A.13.10)$$

and when imports change exogenously the result, account being taken of (A.13.3.1), is

$$dB = \frac{b+h-1-\mu(1-q)}{1-b-h+\mu} d\alpha_m. \quad (A.13.11)$$

The cases discussed in Sect. 13.2.3 correspond to the extreme cases $q=1$ (domestic and foreign output are perfect substitutes) and $q=0$ (autonomous expenditure by residents on domestic output is not influenced at all by their autonomous expenditure on foreign output). Formula (A.13.11) makes it possible to examine also all intermediate cases.

We can add a further refinement to our analysis, not discussed in the text, if we relax the assumption that all expenditures on exports are income-creating. Following Holzman and Zellner (1958), we suppose that only a proportion β of (the change in) exports is income-creating, $0<\beta\leq 1$. The effect on national income and on the balance of payments of an autonomous change in exports is given by the formulae

$$dy = \frac{\beta}{1-b-h+\mu}d\alpha_x, \quad dB = \frac{1-b-h+\mu(1-\beta)}{1-b-h+\mu}d\alpha_x, \qquad (A.13.12)$$

which of course reduce to the previous ones when $\beta=1$. Note that, when $\beta<1$, the effect on the balance of payments is greater than when $\beta=1$, for $1-b-h+\mu(1-\beta)>1-b-h$. In fact, when $\beta<1$ the multiplier is smaller, the induced increase in income is smaller, and the induced increase in imports is smaller.

Suppose now that imports and exports change exogenously by the same amount, say $d\alpha$, so that $d\alpha_x=d\alpha_m=d\alpha$. We have

$$dy = \frac{\beta-q}{1-b-h+\mu}d\alpha, \quad dB = \frac{\mu(q-\beta)}{1-b-h+\mu}d\alpha. \qquad (A.13.13)$$

If one considers as normal the case in which both β and q are equal to one (this, in fact, is the case often implicitly presented in textbooks), the conclusion is that the "balanced trade multiplier" is zero and that the balance of payments does not change. The general expressions (A.13.13) give the outcome in all possible cases.

Finally, let us consider the problem of the *import content of exports*. For many nations it is true that exports contain a significant amount of imports; in this case, any change in exports will be accompanied by a change in imports, and if we call γ the parameter which measures the import content of exports, to any $d\alpha_x$ a $d\alpha_m=\gamma d\alpha_x$ will correspond. The consequences are easily found, for it is enough to put $(1-\gamma)d\alpha_x$ in the place of $d\alpha_x$ wherever the latter appears in the relevant formulae. This will not change the results qualitatively so long as $0<\gamma<1$, a reasonable assumption. On the specific problem of imported intermediate goods see Sect. 13.4.

A.13.2 The Multiplier with Foreign Repercussions

A.13.2.1 The Basic Model

Consider the following model

Country 1

$$\begin{aligned}
&C_1 = C_1(y_1, \alpha_{1C}), && 0 < \partial C_1/\partial y_1 < 1, && \partial C_1/\partial \alpha_{1C} > 0, \\
&I_1 = I_1(y_1, \alpha_{1I}), && 0 < \partial I_1/\partial y_1 < 1, && \partial I_1/\partial \alpha_{1I} > 0, \\
&m_1 = m_1(y_1, \alpha_{1m}), && 0 < \partial m_1/\partial y_1 < 1, && \partial m_1/\partial \alpha_{1m} > 0, \\
&x_1 = m_2, \\
&y_1 - C_1 - I_1 - x_1 + m_1 = 0.
\end{aligned}$$

Country 2

$$C_2 = C_2(y_2, \alpha_{2C}), \quad 0 < \partial C_2/\partial y_2 < 1, \quad \partial C_2/\partial \alpha_{2C} > 0,$$
$$I_2 = I_2(y_2, \alpha_{2I}), \quad 0 < \partial I_2/\partial y_2 < 1, \quad \partial I_2/\partial \alpha_{2I} > 0,$$
$$m_2 = m_2(y_2, \alpha_{2m}), \quad 0 < \partial m_2/\partial y_2 < 1, \quad \partial m_2/\partial \alpha_{2m} > 0,$$
$$x_2 = m_1,$$
$$y_2 - C_2 - I_2 - x_2 + m_2 = 0. \tag{A.13.12}$$

which is an obvious extension of the model in Sect. A.13.1. Without loss of generality we can assume that in both countries all the partial derivatives of the expenditure functions with respect to the shift parameters are equal to one. The model written in Sect. 13.3.2 can be considered as a suitable linear approximation to system (A.13.12).

By substituting, for each country, C,I,m,x, from the first four equations into the fifth we have the system of implicit functions

$$y_1 - C_1(y_1, \alpha_{1C}) - I_1(y_1, \alpha_{1I}) - m_2(y_2, \alpha_{2m}) + m_1(y_1, \alpha_{1m}) = 0,$$
$$\tag{A.13.13}$$
$$y_2 - C_2(y_2, \alpha_{2C}) - I_2(y_2, \alpha_{2I}) - m_1(y_1, \alpha_{1m}) + m_2(y_2, \alpha_{2m}) = 0.$$

According to the general implicit function theorem (Gandolfo, 1980, Part III, Chap. 1), if the Jacobian matrix **J** of these functions with respect to y_1, y_2 is non singular at the equilibrium point, that is if

$$|\mathbf{J}| \equiv \begin{vmatrix} 1 - b_1 - h_1 + \mu_1 & -\mu_2 \\ -\mu_1 & 1 - b_2 - h_2 + \mu_2 \end{vmatrix}$$
$$= (1 - b_1 - h_1 + \mu_1)(1 - b_2 - h_2 + \mu_2) - \mu_1 \mu_2 \neq 0, \tag{A.13.14}$$

where b_i, h_i, μ_i are $\partial C_i/\partial y_i$, $\partial I_i/\partial y_i$, $\partial m_i/\partial y_i$, $i=1,2$, evaluated at the equilibrium point, then we can express y_1 and y_2 as differentiable functions of the α's in the neighbourhood of the equilibrium point:

$$y_1 = y_1(\alpha_{1C}, \alpha_{1I}, \alpha_{1m}, \alpha_{2C}, \alpha_{2I}, \alpha_{2m}),$$
$$\tag{A.13.15}$$
$$y_2 = y_2(\alpha_{1C}, \alpha_{1I}, \alpha_{1m}, \alpha_{2C}, \alpha_{2I}, \alpha_{2m}),$$

and, consequently, we can carry out exercises in comparative statics by differentiating (A.13.13), account being taken of (A.13.15). Consider for example a change in the exogenous component of consumption in country 1, α_{1C}. We obtain

$$(1 - b_1 - h_1 + \mu_1) \frac{\partial y_1}{\partial \alpha_{1C}} - \mu_2 \frac{\partial y_2}{\partial \alpha_{1C}} = 1,$$
$$\tag{A.13.16}$$
$$-\mu_1 \frac{\partial y_1}{\partial \alpha_{1C}} + (1 - b_2 - h_2 + \mu_2) \frac{\partial y_2}{\partial \alpha_{1C}} = 0,$$

whence

$$\frac{\partial y_1}{\partial \alpha_{1C}} = \frac{1 - b_2 - h_2 + \mu_2}{|\mathbf{J}|}, \quad \frac{\partial y_2}{\partial \alpha_{1C}} = \frac{\mu_1}{|\mathbf{J}|}. \tag{A.13.17}$$

By the same procedure it can be shown that

$$\frac{\partial y_1}{\partial \alpha_{1I}} = \frac{\partial y_1}{\partial \alpha_{1C}}, \frac{\partial y_2}{\partial \alpha_{1I}} = \frac{\partial y_2}{\partial \alpha_{1C}}, \tag{A.13.18}$$

and that

$$\frac{\partial y_1}{\partial \alpha_{1m}} = -\frac{\partial y_1}{\partial \alpha_{2m}} = -\frac{1-b_2-h_2}{|J|}, \frac{\partial y_2}{\partial \alpha_{1m}} = -\frac{\partial y_2}{\partial \alpha_{2m}} = \frac{1-b_1-h_1}{|J|},$$

$$\frac{\partial y_1}{\partial \alpha_{2C}} = \frac{\partial y_1}{\partial \alpha_{2I}} = \frac{\mu_2}{|J|}, \frac{\partial y_2}{\partial \alpha_{2C}} = \frac{\partial y_2}{\partial \alpha_{2I}} = \frac{1-b_1-h_1+\mu_1}{|J|}.$$
(A.13.19)

All these multipliers can be condensed in the total differentials

$$dy_1 = \frac{(1-b_2-h_2)(d\alpha_{1C}+d\alpha_{1I}+d\alpha_{2m}-d\alpha_{1m})+\mu_2(d\alpha_{1C}+d\alpha_{1I}+d\alpha_{2C}+d\alpha_{2I})}{|J|},$$

(A.13.20)

$$dy_2 = \frac{(1-b_1-h_1)(d\alpha_{2C}+d\alpha_{2I}+d\alpha_{1m}-d\alpha_{2m})+\mu_1(d\alpha_{1C}+d\alpha_{1I}+d\alpha_{2C}+d\alpha_{2I})}{|J|}.$$

The sign of $|J|$ can be determined by means of Samuelson's correspondence principle (Gandolfo, 1980, Part III, Chap. 1, §4), which requires the results of stability analysis.

A.13.2.2 Stability Analysis

If we make the usual assumption that in each country the level of national output varies in relation to excess demand, and, more precisely, that it tends to increase (decrease) if aggregate demand exceeds (falls short of) current output, we obtain the following system of differential equations

$$\frac{dy_1}{dt} = f_1[(C_1+I_1+x_1-m_1)-y_1],$$

(A.13.21)

$$\frac{dy_2}{dt} = f_2[(C_2+I_2+x_2-m_2)-y_2],$$

where f_1 and f_2 are sign-preserving functions, and $f'_1[0] \equiv k_1 > 0, f'_2[0] \equiv k_2 > 0$. The study of local stability leads to the analysis of the linear approximation to (A.13.21) at the equilibrium point, that is of the linear differential system

$$\frac{d\bar{y}_1}{dt} = k_1[(b_1+h_1-\mu_1-1)\bar{y}_1+\mu_2\bar{y}_2],$$

(A.13.21.1)

$$\frac{d\bar{y}_2}{dt} = k_2[\mu_1\bar{y}_1+(b_2+h_2-\mu_2-1)\bar{y}_2].$$

The characteristic equation of this system is

$$\lambda^2 + [k_1(1-b_1-h_1+\mu_1) + k_2(1-b_2-h_2+\mu_2)]\lambda$$
$$+ k_1 k_2[(1-b_1-h_1+\mu_1)(1-b_2-h_2+\mu_2) - \mu_1\mu_2] \quad \text{(A.13.22)}$$

and the necessary and sufficient stability conditions are

$$k_1(1-b_1-h_1+\mu_1) + k_2(1-b_2-h_2+\mu_2) > 0,$$
$$(1-b_1-h_1+\mu_1)(1-b_2-h_2+\mu_2) - \mu_1\mu_2 > 0, \quad \text{(A.13.23)}$$

from the second of which it follows immediately that $|J|>0$. Furthermore, this same condition implies that $(1-b_1-h_1+\mu_1)(1-b_2-h_2+\mu_2)$ is a positive quantity, namely that $(1-b_1-h_1+\mu_1)$ and $(1-b_2-h_2+\mu_2)$ have the same sign. This, together with the first condition in (A.13.23), implies that this sign is positive. Therefore we can also write the stability conditions as

$$1-b_i-h_i+\mu_i > 0, \quad i=1,2,$$
$$(1-b_1-h_1+\mu_1)(1-b_2-h_2+\mu_2) - \mu_1\mu_2 > 0. \quad \text{(A.13.23.1)}$$

These conditions enable us to determine the sign of almost all the multipliers (A.13.17), (A.13.18), (A.13.19); only the multipliers which depend on the sign of $1-b_i-h_i$ remain indeterminate, because the stability conditions do not require both $(1-b_1-h_1)$ and $(1-b_2-h_2)$ to be positive. However, they cannot be both negative. In fact, the second condition in (A.13.23) can also be written as

$$(1-b_1-h_1)(1-b_2-h_2+\mu_2) + \mu_1(1-b_2-h_2) > 0, \quad \text{(A.13.24)}$$

and, since $(1-b_2-h_2+\mu_2)$ must be positive, $(1-b_1-h_1)$ and $(1-b_2-h_2)$ cannot be both negative: at least one must be positive. It can also be easily checked that if both $(1-b_1-h_1)$ and $(1-b_2-h_2)$ are positive, then the stability conditions are satisfied.

All these results concerning stability can be conveniently listed together with their economic meaning (on the assumption that the relevant marginal propensities remain the same in the various cases):

(1) a necessary (but not sufficient) stability condition is that $1-b_i-h_i+\mu_i > 0$, $i=1,2$, namely that in both countries the foreign multiplier without repercussions is stable;
(2) a sufficient (but not necessary) stability condition is that $1-b_i-h_i > 0$, $i=1,2$, namely that both countries are stable in isolation (i.e., the closed economy multiplier is stable in each country);
(3) a sufficient *instability* condition is that $1-b_i-h_i < 0$, $i=1,2$, namely if both countries are unstable in isolation then the multiplier with repercussions is unstable;
(4) if one of the quantities $(1-b_1-h_1)$, $(1-b_2-h_2)$ is positive and the other negative, the model may be stable or unstable according to the magnitude of μ_1 and μ_2, namely if one country is stable in isolation and the other is unstable in isolation, the multiplier with repercussions may be either stable or unstable.

Appendix

The $y_1 = f(y_2)$ and $y_2 = g(y_1)$ schedules drawn in Fig. 13.6 satisfy the stability conditions. Their slopes, both referring to the y_1 axis, are $(1-b_1-h_1+\mu_1)/\mu_2$ and $\mu_1/(1-b_2-h_2+\mu_2)$, and so the first condition in (A.13.23.1) means that these schedules are increasing. The second condition in (A.13.23.1) can be written as $(1-b_1-h_1+\mu_1)/\mu_2 > \mu_1/(1-b_2-h_2+\mu_2)$, and this means that the $y_1 = f(y_2)$ schedule has a greater slope than the $y_2 = g(y_1)$ schedule with respect to the y_1 axis. Therefore the intuitive graphical analysis of stability carried out in the text is warranted by the rigorous derivation of the stability conditions. Finally, if we compute the discriminant of the characteristic equation (A.13.22) and rearrange terms, we get

$$[k_1(1-b_1-h_1+\mu_1)+k_2(1-b_2-h_2+\mu_2)]^2$$
$$-4k_1k_2(1-b_1-h_1+\mu_1)(1-b_2-h_2+\mu_2)$$
$$+4k_1k_2\mu_1\mu_2 = [k_1(1-b_1-h_1+\mu_1)-k_2(1-b_2-h_2+\mu_2)]^2$$
$$+4k_1k_2\mu_1\mu_2 > 0. \quad (A.13.25)$$

Therefore, both roots are real and the approach to equilibrium is monotonic.

A.13.2.3 The Various Multipliers: A Comparison

We now examine the relationship between the multipliers in a closed economy, in an open economy without foreign repercussions, and in an open economy with foreign repercussions. As a standard of comparison we take an increase in the autonomous component of domestic expenditure on domestic output in country 1, and consider the double inequality

$$\frac{1}{1-b_1-h_1+\mu_1} < \frac{1-b_2-h_2+\mu_2}{|J|} < \frac{1}{1-b_1-h_1}. \quad (A.13.26)$$

If the stability conditions for an open economy are satisfied, we can multiply through by $(1-b_1-h_1+\mu_1) > 0$ and obtain

$$1 < \frac{(1-b_1-h_1+\mu_1)(1-b_2-h_2+\mu_2)}{(1-b_1-h_1+\mu_1)(1-b_2-h_2+\mu_2)-\mu_1\mu_2} < \frac{1-b_1-h_1+\mu_1}{1-b_1-h_1}. \quad (A.13.26.1)$$

The left part of this inequality is certainly satisfied, because the denominator of the central fraction is smaller than the numerator. As regards the right part, it is also satisfied if $1-b_i-h_i > 0$ (both countries are stable in isolation): this can be checked by multiplying through by the positive quantity $|J|(1-b_1-h_1)$, which gives

$$(1-b_1-h_1+\mu_1)(1-b_2-h_2+\mu_2)(1-b_1-h_1) < (1-b_1-h_1+\mu_1)|J|,$$

whence

$$0 < \mu_1(1-b_2-h_2), \quad (A.13.26.2)$$

which is satisfied under our assumptions. But since stability of *both* countries in isolation is not required for stability of the world economy, a situation in which $1-b_2-h_2 < 0$ is admissible, in which case (A.13.26.2) will not be satisfied and the multiplier with foreign repercussions will be greater than the closed economy multiplier in country 1. The magnitude of b_2+h_2 is also crucial to determine whether country 1's multiplier is greater when an increase in its exogenous domestic expenditure occurs or when the increase occurs in country 2's exogenous expenditure. In fact, from (A.13.17), (A.13.18), and (A.13.19) it follows that $\partial y_1/\partial \alpha_{1C} \gtreqless \partial y_1/\partial \alpha_{2C}$ and $\partial y_1/\partial \alpha_{1I} \gtreqless \partial y_1/\partial \alpha_{2I}$ according as $1-b_2-h_2 \gtreqless 0$.

A.13.2.4 The Balance of Payments

We now consider the balance of payments of country 1, $B_1 = x_1 - m_1 = m_2 - m_1$ and differentiate it totally, obtaining

$$dB_1 = d\alpha_{2m} - d\alpha_{1m} + \mu_2 dy_2 - \mu_1 dy_1, \qquad (A.13.27)$$

where dy_1 and dy_2 are given by the multiplier formulae (A.13.20). As an example we will examine the case in which country 2 exogenously increases the demand for country 1's products, *ceteris paribus* (namely, no offsetting change occurs in country 2's exogenous demand for its own products[11]). The result is

$$dB_1 = \frac{(1-b_1-h_1)(1-b_2-h_2+\mu_2)}{|J|} d\alpha_{2m}, \qquad (A.13.28)$$

and so $dB_1 \gtreqless 0$ according as $(1-b_1-h_1) \gtreqless 0$, a result which has already been commented on in Sect. 13.3.3. All we need add is that, if $(1-b_1-h_1)>0$, the fraction on the r.h.s. of (A.13.28) is smaller than one, so that $dB_1 < d\alpha_{2m}$.

A.13.3 Foreign Repercussions in a *n*-Country Model

A.13.3.1 The General Model

The general model is composed of n sets of equations of the form

$$C_i = C_i(y_i, \alpha_{iC}), \quad 0 < \partial C_i/\partial y_i < 1, \quad \partial C_i/\partial \alpha_{iC} > 0,$$

$$I_i = I_i(y_i, \alpha_{iI}), \quad 0 < \partial I_i/\partial y_i < 1, \quad \partial I_i/\partial \alpha_{iI} > 0,$$

$$m_i = m_i(y_i, \alpha_{im}), \quad 0 < \partial m_i/\partial y_i < 1, \quad \partial m_i/\partial \alpha_{im} > 0, \qquad (A.13.29)$$

$$m_i \equiv \sum_{j=1/j \neq i}^{n} m_{ji}(y_i, \alpha_{jim}), \quad 0 \leq \partial m_{ji}/\partial y_i < 1, \quad \sum_{j=1/j \neq i}^{n} \frac{\partial m_{ji}}{\partial y_i} \equiv \frac{\partial m_i}{\partial y_i},$$

$$\partial m_{ji}/\partial \alpha_{jim} \geq 0, \quad \sum_{j=1/j \neq i}^{n} \frac{\partial m_{ji}}{\partial \alpha_{jim}} = \frac{\partial m_i}{\partial \alpha_{im}},$$

$$x_i = \sum_{k=1/k \neq 1}^{n} m_{ik}(y_k, \alpha_{ikm}),$$

$$y_i - C_i - I_i - x_i + m_i = 0.$$

The fourth and fifth equations in (A.13.29) need some clarification. In a n-country world, the $m_i(y_i, \alpha_{im})$ function shows how *total* imports of country i are related to national income, y_i, of the importing country, but we must also know the countries of origin of these imports. As Metzler (1950) made clear, we can

---

[11] The general case can be analyzed, as we did in the treatment of the multiplier without foreign repercussions, by introducing suitable parameters q_1 and q_2.

think of the total import function of the ith country as composed of a number of subfunctions each showing how much the ith country imports from the jth country at any given level of y_i. By $m_{ji}=m_{ji}(y_i,\alpha_{jim})$ we denote the imports of the ith country from the jth country, expressed as a function of income in the ith country, so that the fourth equation in (A.13.29) follows by definition. In the real world, some of the m_{ji} functions may be zero, because each country does not necessarily import from all other countries, but this does not present any difficulty. The relationships between the partial derivatives of the subfunctions and the partial derivatives of the total import function follow from the fact that we have an identity.

As regards the exports of country i, they are the sum of what all the other countries import from it, and can be obtained by summing over all countries the subfunctions which express the imports of the kth country from the ith country. This gives the fifth equation in (A.13.29).

Straightforward substitutions yield the following set of n implicit functions:

$$y_i - C_i(y_i,\alpha_{iC}) - I_i(y_i,\alpha_{iI}) - \sum_{k=1/k\neq i}^{n} m_{ik}(y_k,\alpha_{ikm}) + m_i(y_i,\alpha_{im}) = 0,$$

$$i=1,2,...,m. \quad (A.13.30)$$

The Jacobian matrix of these functions with respect to the y_i is

$$\mathbf{J} \equiv \begin{bmatrix} 1-b_1-h_1+\mu_1 & -\mu_{12} & \cdots & -\mu_{1n} \\ -\mu_{21} & 1-b_2-h_2+\mu_2 & \cdots & -\mu_{2n} \\ \cdot & \cdot & & \cdot \\ -\mu_{n1} & -\mu_{n2} & \cdots & 1-b_n-h_n+\mu_n \end{bmatrix} \quad (A.13.31)$$

where μ_{ji} is $\partial m_{ji}/\partial y_i$ evaluated at the equilibrium point, and the other symbols have the usual meanings. By using the implicit function theorem already recalled in Sect. A.13.2, if $\mathbf{J}$ is non-singular at the equilibrium point we can express the y_i as differentiable functions of all the parameters (the α's). Without loss of generality we can assume as before that the various partial derivatives of the expenditure functions with respect to the parameters ($\partial C_i/\partial \alpha_{iC}$ etc.) are equal to one, so that total differentiation of (A.13.20) yields

$$\mathbf{J}d\mathbf{y} = d\boldsymbol{\alpha}, \quad (A.13.32)$$

where $\mathbf{J}$ is the matrix (A.13.31) and $d\mathbf{y}$, $d\boldsymbol{\alpha}$ are the column vectors

$$d\mathbf{y} \equiv \begin{bmatrix} dy_1 \\ dy_2 \\ \cdots \\ dy_n \end{bmatrix}, \quad d\boldsymbol{\alpha} \equiv \begin{bmatrix} d\alpha_{1C}+d\alpha_{1I}-d\alpha_{1m}+\sum_{k=2}^{n}\frac{\partial m_{1k}}{\partial \alpha_{1km}}d\alpha_{1km} \\ d\alpha_{2C}+d\alpha_{2I}-d\alpha_{2m}+\sum_{k=1\atop k\neq 2}^{n}\frac{\partial m_{2k}}{\partial \alpha_{2km}}d\alpha_{2km} \\ \cdots \\ d\alpha_{nC}+d\alpha_{nI}-d\alpha_{nm}+\sum_{k=1}^{n-1}\frac{\partial m_{nk}}{\partial \alpha_{nkm}}d\alpha_{nkm} \end{bmatrix}. \quad (A.13.33)$$

Therefore, the solution of (A.13.32), which is

$$dy = J^{-1} d\alpha, \qquad (A.13.34)$$

summarizes all possible multipliers in a n-country framework. Since the non-singularity of the Jacobian lies at the basis of our analysis, J^{-1} exists; but to obtain determinate comparative static results we must use the correspondence principle as before.

A.13.3.2 Stability Analysis

The usual dynamic behaviour assumption (in each country, output varies according to excess demand) gives rise to the following system of differential equations

$$\frac{dy_i}{dt} = f_i[(C_i + I_i + x_i - m_i) - y_i], \quad i = 1, 2, \ldots, n, \qquad (A.13.35)$$

where f_i are sign-preserving functions, and $f'_i[0] \equiv k_i > 0$. To study local stability we perform a linear approximation at the equilibrium point, which reduces (A.13.35) to the linear differential system with constant coefficients

$$\frac{d\bar{y}}{dt} = k[-J]\bar{y}, \qquad (A.13.36)$$

where $\bar{y}$ is the vector of the deviations and k is the diagonal matrix of the speeds of adjustment k_i. We assume for the moment that $k_i = 1$ for all i; we shall show afterwards that this does not involve any loss of generality. The matrix $[-J]$ is a Metzlerian matrix, that is a matrix with non-negative off-diagonal elements. In this case, necessary and sufficient stability conditions (Gandolfo, 1980, Part II, Chap. 8, §2) are that the leading principal minors of the matrix $[-J]$ alternate in sign, beginning with minus:

$$b_1 + h_1 - \mu_1 - 1 < 0, \quad \begin{vmatrix} b_1 + h_1 - \mu_1 - 1 & \mu_{12} \\ \mu_{21} & b_2 + h_2 - \mu_2 - 1 \end{vmatrix} > 0, \ldots,$$

$$\operatorname{sgn} \det(-J) = \operatorname{sgn}(-1)^n. \qquad (A.13.37)$$

This implies that each country's foreign multiplier without repercussions must be stable ($1 - b_i - h_i + \mu_i > 0$) and that all subsets of $2, 3, \ldots, n-1$ countries must give rise to stable foreign multipliers with repercussions. The approach to equilibrium will not be necessarily monotonic (whereas in the two-country model it was); a very special case of monotonic movement occurs when the partial marginal propensity of country i to import from country j is equal to the partial marginal propensity of country j to import from country i. In this case $\mu_{ij} = \mu_{ji}$ and the characteristic roots of $[-J]$ are all real because it is a symmetric matrix.

Other interesting results concerning stability can be obtained if we consider only sufficient or only necessary stability conditions. A sufficient stability condition is that the matrix $[-J]$ has a dominant negative diagonal (Gandolfo, 1980, pp. 276–7), namely

$$b_i + h_i - \mu_i - 1 < 0,$$

$$|b_i + h_i - \mu_i - 1| > \sum_{j=1/j \neq i}^{n} \mu_{ji}, \text{ from which } 1 - b_i - h_i > 0. \qquad (A.13.38)$$

Since $1-b_i-h_i>0$ is the stability condition for the closed economy multiplier, we conclude that the n-country model is stable *if* each country is stable in isolation, namely if the marginal propensity to spend is smaller than one in all countries. Conversely, it can be shown that the n-country model is unstable if each country is unstable in isolation: in other words, $b_i+h_i>1$ for all i is a sufficient *instability* condition. We must distinguish two cases. The first is when, for at least one i, b_i+h_i is not only greater than one but also greater than $1+\mu_i$. In this case at least one of the necessary and sufficient conditions stated above is violated and therefore the model is unstable. The second case occurs when $1<b_i+h_i<1+\mu_i$ for all i. Noting that $[-\mathbf{J}]$ is a non-negative matrix, it follows from a theorem on such matrices that min $S_i \leq \lambda_M \leq$ max S_i (Gantmacher, 1959, p. 82), where the real number λ_M is the dominant root of the matrix and S_i are the column sums of the matrix. Now, $S_i = b_i + h_i - \mu_i - 1 + \sum_{j=1/j \neq i}^{n} \mu_{ji} = b_i + h_i - 1$; therefore, λ_M is positive if $b_i+h_i-1>0$ for all i, which proves instability. Of course, if $b_i+h_i-1>0$ for some i, and <0 for some other i, the model may be stable or unstable. In other words, if only some countries are unstable in isolation, the world may still be stable.

We have assumed above that all the speeds of adjustment are equal to one, stating that this does not involve any loss of generality. In fact, the results on D-stability (Gandolfo, 1980, p. 278) enable us to conclude that if the matrix $[-\mathbf{J}]$ satisfies conditions (A.13.37) or (A.13.38), also the matrix $\mathbf{k}[-\mathbf{J}]$ is stable for any positive diagonal matrix $\mathbf{k}$.

A.13.3.3 Comparative Statics. A Comparison between the Various Multipliers

Let us now come to the problem of comparative statics. If $[-\mathbf{J}]$ satisfies conditions (A.13.37) — note that if it satisfies conditions (A.13.38) it will also satisfy conditions (A.13.37), although the converse is not true (Gandolfo, 1980, p. 277) — it follows from elementary rules on determinants that the matrix $\mathbf{J}$ will have leading principal minors which are all positive, namely

$$1-b_1-h_1+\mu_1>0, \quad \begin{vmatrix} 1-b_1-h_1+\mu_1 & -\mu_{12} \\ -\mu_{21} & 1-b_2-h_2+\mu_2 \end{vmatrix} > 0, ..., |\mathbf{J}|>0. \tag{A.13.39}$$

Conditions (A.13.39) are nothing more nor less than the well-known Hawkins-Simon conditions, which ensure that system (A.13.32) has a non-negative solution corresponding to any non-negative $d\alpha$, namely $\mathbf{J}^{-1}$ is a non-negative matrix. This result can be strengthened if we assume that each country imports directly or indirectly from all other countries (we say that a country i imports indirectly from another country j when country i imports directly from country j_1, which in turn imports directly from country j_2 etc. which in turn imports directly from country j). Under this assumption, which seems reasonable, and remembering that $b_i+h_i-\mu_i>0$ because μ_i is part of b_i+h_i, the matrix

$$\mathbf{A} = \begin{bmatrix} b_1+h_1-\mu_1 & \mu_{12} & \cdots & \mu_{1n} \\ \mu_{21} & b_2+h_2-\mu_2 & \cdots & \mu_{2n} \\ \vdots & \vdots & & \vdots \\ \mu_{n1} & \mu_{n2} & \cdots & b_n+h_n-\mu_n \end{bmatrix}$$

is a non-negative *indecomposable* matrix; noting that $\mathbf{J} \equiv [\mathbf{I} - \mathbf{A}]$, it follows from the properties of such matrices (Gandolfo, 1980, p. 303 fn) that conditions (A.13.39) are necessary and sufficient for $\mathbf{J}^{-1}$ to have only positive elements, $\mathbf{J}^{-1} > 0$. In this case system (A.13.32) has a positive solution corresponding to any non-negative $d\alpha$. Let us note for future reference that, since $\mathbf{J}^{-1} = [\text{adj } \mathbf{J}]/|\mathbf{J}|$, and $|\mathbf{J}| > 0$ from (A.13.39), $\mathbf{J}^{-1} > 0$ implies $[\text{adj } \mathbf{J}] > 0$, that is

$$|\mathbf{J}_{rs}| > 0, \quad r,s = 1,2,\ldots,n, \tag{A.13.40}$$

where $|\mathbf{J}_{rs}|$ is the cofactor of the element (r,s) in $\mathbf{J}$.

The relationships between the closed economy multiplier and the open economy multipliers with and without repercussions shown in the 2-country model remain valid in the general model under consideration, as was proved by Metzler (1950). Consider for example an exogenous increase in investment expenditure on domestic goods in country 1, $d\alpha_{1I} > 0$. Let us examine the inequality

$$\frac{1}{1 - b_1 - h_2 + \mu_1} < \frac{dy_1}{d\alpha_{1I}} < \frac{1}{1 - b_1 - h_1}, \tag{A.13.41}$$

where $dy_1/d\alpha_{1I}$ is the multiplier with foreign repercussions derived from the solution of system (A.13.32), which turns out to be

$$\frac{dy_1}{d\alpha_{1I}} = \frac{|\mathbf{J}_{11}|}{|\mathbf{J}|}. \tag{A.13.42}$$

Now add all other rows to the first row of $|\mathbf{J}|$ and expand according to the elements of this new row. The result is

$$|\mathbf{J}| = (1 - b_1 - h_1)|\mathbf{J}_{11}| + (1 - b_2 - h_2)|\mathbf{J}_{12}| + \ldots + (1 - b_n - h_n)|\mathbf{J}_{1n}|, \tag{A.13.43}$$

where $|\mathbf{J}_{1k}|$, $k = 1,2,3,\ldots,n$, is the cofactor of the element $(1,k)$ in $|\mathbf{J}|$. If we substitute (A.13.43) in (A.13.42) and divide both numerator and denominator by $|\mathbf{J}_{11}|$, we obtain

$$\frac{dy_1}{d\alpha_{1I}} = \frac{1}{(1 - b_1 - h_1) + \{[(1 - b_2 - h_2)|\mathbf{J}_{12}| + \ldots + (1 - b_n - h_n)|\mathbf{J}_{1n}|]/|\mathbf{J}_{11}|\}}. \tag{A.13.42.1}$$

Now, $|\mathbf{J}_{1k}| > 0$ according to (A.13.40); therefore, if the marginal propensity to spend is smaller than one in all countries, the denominator in (A.13.42.1) will be greater than $(1 - b_1 - h_1)$. This proves the right-hand part of inequality (A.13.41) under the assumption that all countries are stable in isolation.

The left-hand part of inequality (A.13.41) can be proved by expanding $|\mathbf{J}|$ according to the elements of its first column and then dividing both numerator and denominator of (A.13.42) by $|\mathbf{J}_{11}|$, which gives

$$\frac{dy_1}{d\alpha_{1I}} = \frac{1}{(1 - b_1 - h_1 + \mu_1) - \{[\mu_{21}|\mathbf{J}_{21}| + \ldots + \mu_{n1}|\mathbf{J}_{n1}|]/|\mathbf{J}_{11}|\}}. \tag{A.13.42.2}$$

Since $|\mathbf{J}_{k1}|>0$ from (A.13.40), the denominator in (A.13.42.2) is smaller than $(1-b_1-h_1+\mu_1)$, and this is the proof of inequality in the left-hand part of (A.13.41). In conclusion, provided that the necessary and sufficient stability conditions are satisfied, the multiplier with foreign repercussions is always greater than the corresponding multiplier without foreign repercussions, and it is certainly smaller than the closed economy multiplier under the additional (sufficient) assumption that the marginal propensity to spend is smaller than one in all countries.

It can also be shown that, if the marginal propensity to spend is smaller than one in all countries, the i-th country multiplier is greater when the increase in exogenous investment occurs in country i than when it occurs in any other country j, namely $dy_i/d\alpha_{iI} > dy_i/d\alpha_{jI}, j \neq i$. Consider for example country 1: the expression for $dy_1/d\alpha_{1I}$ is given by (A.13.42), and the expression for, say, $dy_1/d\alpha_{2I}$ is

$$\frac{dy_1}{d\alpha_{2I}} = \frac{|\mathbf{J}_{21}|}{|\mathbf{J}|}, \qquad (A.13.42.3)$$

so that $dy_1/d\alpha_{1I} > dy_1/d\alpha_{2I}$ is equivalent to $|\mathbf{J}_{11}|-|\mathbf{J}_{21}|>0$.

We have

$$|\mathbf{J}_{11}|-|\mathbf{J}_{21}|$$

$$= \begin{vmatrix} 1-b_2-h_2+\mu_2-\mu_{12} & -\mu_{23}-\mu_{13} & \cdots & -\mu_{2n}-\mu_{1n} \\ -\mu_{32} & 1-b_3-h_3+\mu_3 & \cdots & -\mu_{3n} \\ \cdot & \cdot & & \cdot \\ -\mu_{n2} & -\mu_{n3} & \cdots & 1-b_n-h_n+\mu_n \end{vmatrix}$$

$$= \det(\mathbf{I}-\mathbf{B}),$$

where

$$\mathbf{B} \equiv \begin{bmatrix} b_2+h_2-\mu_2+\mu_{12} & \mu_{23}+\mu_{13} & \cdots & \mu_{2n}+\mu_{1n} \\ \mu_{32} & b_3+h_3+\mu_3 & \cdots & \mu_{3n} \\ \cdot & \cdot & & \cdot \\ \mu_{n2} & \mu_{n3} & \cdots & b_n+h_n-\mu_n \end{bmatrix}$$

Now, $\mathbf{B}$ is a non-negative matrix; its columns sums are equal to b_j+h_j, $j=2,...,n$ and so are all less than one *if* $b_j+h_j<1$. Therefore it follows from the theorem already used above that the dominant root of $\mathbf{B}$ is smaller than 1. Consequently (Gantmacher, 1959, p. 85), $\det(\mathbf{I}-\mathbf{B})$ is positive. The same method of proof can be used for any difference $|\mathbf{J}_{11}|-|\mathbf{J}_{k1}|$, $k=3,...,n$.

A.13.3.4 The Balance of Payments

We now turn to balance-of-payments adjustment. Since $B_i = x_i - m_i$, and $x_i - m_i = y_i - C_i - I_i$ from the national income equation, it is convenient to use the relation

$$B_i = y_i - C_i - I_i, \qquad (A.13.43)$$

which relates each country's balance of payments to the income of that country alone. Total differentiation of (A.13.43) yields

$$dB_i = (1 - b_i - h_i) dy_i - d\alpha_{iC} - d\alpha_{iI}, \qquad (A.13.44)$$

from which the effects of an exogenous increase in a country's expenditure can be determined. Take for example an increase in α_{1I}, *ceteris paribus*. We have

$$\frac{dB_1}{d\alpha_{1I}} = (1 - b_1 - h_1) \frac{dy_1}{d\alpha_{1I}} - 1,$$

$$\frac{dB_k}{d\alpha_{1I}} = (1 - b_k - h_k) \frac{dy_k}{d\alpha_{1I}}, \quad k = 2, \ldots, n, \qquad (A.13.44.1)$$

where the $dy_i/d\alpha_{1I}$, $i = 1, 2, \ldots, n$, are given by our previous analysis, so that we know that they are all positive. The effect on the balance of payments depends as usual on the magnitude of the marginal propensity to spend. If we assume that this propensity is smaller than one in all countries, then the right-hand part of inequality (A.13.41) holds, and so (A.13.44.1) gives

$$-1 < \frac{dB_1}{d\alpha_{1I}} < 0, \qquad \frac{dB_k}{d\alpha_{1I}} > 0. \qquad (A.13.44.2)$$

Therefore, an increase in exogenous investment in a country moves the balance of payments against that country and in favour of all the other countries. This needs not be true any longer if we drop the assumption concerning the marginal propensity to spend. We know from our dynamic analysis that stability is compatible with one or more (but not all) marginal propensities to spend being greater than one. An extreme situation is therefore conceivable in which $1 - b_1 - h_1 > 0$, $1 - b_k - h_k < 0$, $k = 2, \ldots, n$. In this case all the other countries will suffer a worsening of their balance of payments and, consequently, country 1's balance of payments will improve. Intermediate situations in which $1 - b_1 - h_1 > 0$ and $1 - b_k - h_k \lessgtr 0$ for different k's are possible. Then some of these countries will suffer a deterioration in their balances of payments, while others will find an improvement; the result on country 1's balance of payments will depend on whether the sum of the deteriorations is greater or smaller in absolute value than the sum of the improvements[12]. Note also that if $1 - b_1 - h_1 < 0$ the balance of payments of country 1 necessarily deteriorates.

A.13.4 Concluding Remarks. The Empirical Relevance of the Foreign Multiplier

We would like to point out that the *n*-country model gives results which are much the same as those obtained in the two-country model (as regards both the dynamics and the comparative statics). This the reader can easily verify by comparing Sects. A.13.2 and A.13.3. The fact that there is a large measure of

---

[12] It goes without saying that the analysis is based on the usual assumption that the balances of payments of the various countries are expressed in terms of a common unit of measurement, so that the condition $\sum_{i=1}^{n} B_i = 0$ holds.

agreement between the two-country and the *n*-country model is encouraging, and it makes it possible for the textbook writer to illustrate foreign repercussions by means of the simpler model. This, of course, does not mean that we should not bother with the general theory, if only because we are able to ascertain the agreement between the simple and the general theory *after* examining the latter fully; for further remarks see Metzler (1950, last section), Johnson (1956b), Mundell (1965).

It should also be noted that the formal treatment of the dynamics of the various models has been made here — as throughout this book — in terms of differential equations. However, since the dynamic multiplier mechanism is often presented in terms of difference equations, we would like to reassure the reader that in this case the results of the two analytical approaches are the same, as can be verified by reference to the treatment in terms of difference equations contained in Gandolfo (1980, pp. 40–41 and pp. 146–151).

As regards the empirical relevance of multiplier analysis, it might seem that this mechanism — which, together with the elasticity approach, forms the core of the traditional theory (see Chap. 14) — must nowadays be considered, by itself, not only to be theoretically obsolete (the new approaches are treated in Chaps. 15 ff.)[13] but also of little help in analyzing actual problems, such as fiscal-policy transmission. In fact, the effects of fiscal policy on incomes in a multiple-country world are analyzed by using linked econometric models of the countries concerned and simulating the change in fiscal policy (for a recent survey of this approach see Helliwell and Padmore, 1985). The complexity of these models might lead one to think that no hope exists for the poor old foreign multiplier, so why bother studying it in such depth. Well, Deardoff and Stern (1979) share the opposite view, namely that (p. 416) "the linked econometric models, *as a group*, do not appreciably add to our knowledge about fiscal-policy transmission beyond what is suggest by our calculations using a simple and relatively naive model": meaning that based on the foreign multiplier! In fact, these authors have compared the results obtained from simulations of several linked econometric models (Project LINK; DEMOS; COMET; etc.: for a description see Sect. II of their paper) with those calculated using the naive multiplier, for the year 1973, and they found that most results obtained by these calculations fell between the simulation extremes. This exercise has been repeated by Ferrara (1984) and by Rotondi (1989), who, additionally, take account of international repercussions in the multiplier (which were neglected by Deardoff and Stern), with reference to the years 1978 and 1979: they obtain similarly good results. See also Helliwell and Padmore (1985, Sect. 3).

Of course, as Deardoff and Stern note, the comparison of fiscal-policy multipliers leaves open the question whether the linked models can provide useful information on other issues. In our opinion the results of these exercises are not to be seen from a negative view-point (i.e., as a symptom of the limited contributions of the linked multi-country models to our understanding of the problem at hand) but rather from a positive one, that is as an indication of the usefulness of the foreign multiplier (at least to obtain a first, rough idea of fiscal-policy transmission).

---

[13] See, however, McCombie (1985, and references therein) for a recent revival of the foreign trade multiplier in relation to export-led growth (on which see Sect. 17.5.1).

References

Black, J., 1957
Chacholiades, M., 1978, Chap. 10 and Appendix
Deardoff, A.V. and R.M. Stern, 1979
Dornbusch, R., 1980, Chap. 3 and Appendix
Ferrara, L., 1984
Gandolfo, G., 1970, Appendix I to Chap. III
Gandolfo, G., 1980, Part I, Chap. 3, Sect. 2 and Chap. 9, Sect. 1; Part II, Chap. 8; Part III, Chap. 1, Sects. 1,2,4
Gantmacher, F.R., 1959, Chap. III, Sects. 1 – 3
Goodwin, R.M., 1980
Harrod, R.F., 1933, Chap. VI
Hawkins, D. and H.A. Simon, 1949
Helliwell, J.F. and T. Padmore, 1985
Holzman, F.D. and A. Zellner, 1958
Johnson, H.G., 1956b
Kennedy, C. and A.P. Thirlwall, 1979
Kennedy, C. and A.P. Thirlwall, 1980
Keynes, J.M., 1936, Chap. 10, Sect. III
Kindleberger, C.P., 1973, Chap. 20 and Appendix H
Machlup, F., 1943
McCombie, J.S.L., 1985
Meade, J.E., 1948
Meade, J.E., 1951, Parts I and II, Note to Parts II and III, and *Mathematical Supplement*
Metzler, L.A., 1942
Metzler, L.A., 1950
Metzler, L.A., 1973a
Milana, C., 1984
Miyazawa, K., 1960
Mundell, R.A., 1965
Polak, J.J., 1947
Robinson, R., 1952
Rotondi, Z., 1989
Stern, R.M., 1973, Chap. 7 and Appendix
Thirlwall, A.P., 1980, 57–65

14 The Absorption Approach and Interactions between Exchange Rate and Income in the Adjustment Process

14.1 The Absorption Approach

In the previous chapters we have examined the role of the exchange-rate variations (Chap. 12) and of income changes (Chap. 13) in the adjustment process of the balance of payments. An obvious step forward to be taken while remaining in the context of the traditional theory, is to attempt an integration between the two mechanisms in a broader framework in which the adjustment can come from both exchange rate and income simultaneously. In our opinion, the *absorption approach* suggested by Alexander (1952) also belongs to this framework, since after an initial debate in which it was presented as a new approach, alternative to the elasticity approach, the final synthesis suggested by Alexander himself (1959) can easily be fitted into this framework. Other attempts at integrating the two mechanism do of course exist and will be treated in Sect. 14.3.

We recall from Sect. 12.2.3 that the study of the effects of an exchange-rate depreciation on the balance of payments based on elasticity analysis, raises the problem of the meaning to be given to the elasticities. If these are interpreted as *partial* elasticities, then the analysis is seriously incomplete, as it neglects all the other direct and indirect effects of the exchange-rate variation on the other variables and from these on the balance of payments and on the exchange rate. If, on the contrary, the elasticities are interpreted as *total* ones, then one commits a tautology, since total elasticities can be defined only *ex post*. As we said in Sect. 12.2.3, a total elasticity has no operational content because of the way in which it is defined. Let us consider an exchange-rate variation, so that imports and exports vary: their variation has effects on national income and other variables as well, which in turn feed back on imports and exports and so on and so forth. If we assume that this process converges, we can determine the overall variations in imports and exports, thus defining, *ex post*, the total elasticities of exports and imports. It should then be clear that "...the statement that the effect of a devaluation depends on the elasticities boils down to the statement that it depends on how the economic system behaves" (Alexander, 1952, p. 360 of the 1968 reprint).

These observations formed the starting point for Alexander (1952) to suggest the novel *absorption approach* as a superior substitute for the traditional elasticity one.

If we denote national income (product) by y, total aggregate demand (for both consumption and investment) or *absorption* by A, the payments balance (on

Table 14.1. Effects of a devaluation according to the absorption approach

Effects upon and via income $[(1-c)\Delta y]$	Direct effects on absorption (d)
Idle-resources effect Terms-of-trade effect	Cash-balance effect Income-redistribution effect Money-illusion effect Three other direct absorption effects

goods and services) by B, we have the basic accounting identity (see Section 11.3)

$$y = A + B, \tag{14.1}$$

and so

$$B = y - A, \tag{14.2}$$

whence, considering the variations,

$$\Delta B = \Delta y - \Delta A. \tag{14.3}$$

Equation (14.3) shows that for a devaluation to improve the balance of payments it must either cause a decrease in absorption at unchanged income, or an increase in income at unchanged absorption or (better still) both effects, or suitable combinations of changes in the two variables (for instance, both income and absorption may increase, provided that the latter increases by less, etc.). No elasticities are involved. Equation (14.3) is an accounting identity, and, to give it a "causal" interpretation, we must ask three questions: (i) how does the devaluation affect income; (ii) how does a change in income affect absorption; (iii) how does the devaluation directly (i.e. at any given level of income) affect absorption. For this purpose we first recall from Chap. 13 that consumption and investment are functions of income, so that we can write the functional relation

$$\Delta A = c\Delta y - d, \tag{14.4}$$

where c is the sum of the marginal propensity to consume and the marginal propensity to invest, and d denotes the direct effect of the devaluation on absorption. By self-evident substitutions we get

$$\Delta B = (1-c)\Delta y + d. \tag{14.5}$$

Question (i) bears on Δy, question (ii) on the magnitude of c, question (iii) on d. Table 14.1, taken from Machlup (1955), summarizes the various effects.

A synthetic exposition of the various effects (for details see Alexander, 1952; Machlup, 1955) is:

Idle-resources effect: if there are unemployed resources, the increase in exports following the devaluation brings about an increase in income via the foreign multiplier.

Terms-of-trade effect: the devaluation causes a deterioration in the terms of trade (see Chap. 12) and hence a reduction in the country's real income.

Thus the two effects upon income are in opposite directions, so that Δy may have either sign and the answer to question (i) is ambiguous. As regards question (ii), Alexander is inclined to believe that c is greater than one, hence $(1-c)$ is negative, so that — as regards effects (i) and (ii) — a devaluation will improve the balance of payments if its net effect on income is negative. Let us now turn to the direct effects on absorption.

Cash-balance effect: the devaluation causes an increase in the domestic price of imports and hence in the general price level. This brings about a decrease in the real value of wealth held in monetary form (cash balances): the public will try to build up their cash balances (to restore the real value of these) both by reducing absorption and by selling bonds. The sale of bonds causes a decrease in their price, i.e. an increase in the interest rate, which further reduces absorption.

Income-redistribution effect: the increase in prices (see above) caused by the devaluation may bring about a redistribution of income (for example from fixed-income recipients to the rest of the economy) and this influences absorption provided that the different groups of income recipients have different marginal propensities to spend.

Money-illusion effect: assuming that prices and money income increase in the same proportion, real income does not change, but if people do not realize this because they are subject to money illusion, they will change their absorption (the direction of change depends on the type of money illusion).

The *three other direct effects* concern the expectation of further price increases (so that people may buy goods in advance to avoid paying higher prices in the future); the discouragement to investment caused by the increased price of imported investment goods; the discouragement to expenditure on foreign goods in general, caused by their increased price.

14.2 Elasticities versus Absorption: Controversy and Synthesis

The absorption approach, which attacked the conventional elasticity formulae as poor and misleading tools, gave rise to a heated debate in the 1950s. Amongst the supporters of the elasticity approach, Machlup (1955) points out that it is not correct to neglect the relative price of imports and exports (and so the elasticities) to concentrate on absorption and income. These prices, for example, have a crucial importance in the determination of the terms-of-trade effect and may also enter into the determination of the value of the marginal propensity to spend. Besides, Machlup in turn accuses the rival approach of implicit theorizing based upon purely definitional tautologies such as (14.2) and (14.3) above; these accounting definitions do not allow one to state that B depends on y and A in a causal sense (any more than y depends on B and A, etc.: see Sect. 11.3). To evaluate the absorption approach, it is necessary to introduce additional hypotheses on the direction of causation; now, the hypotheses made by this approach (see the previous section) can be represented by the following scheme (unbroken-line arrows):

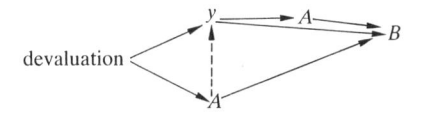

that is, in words: the devaluation affects y; y affects A; the devaluation affects A directly; the net changes in y and A determine the change in B. But this is not the whole story. If, in fact, the devaluation affects A directly, these autonomous changes in A will influence y, as shown by the broken-line arrow. If, for example, the net sum of the direct effects of the devaluation on absorption (see above, Table 14.1) is negative, this can be treated as an exogenous decrease in the autonomous components of expenditure which may cause — via the multiplier (see Chap. 13) — a decrease in income; this will tend to offset the idle-resources effect etc., with a chain of further effects, neglected by the absorption approach.

Several attempts at reconciliation of the two approaches by various authors followed the initial debate, and Alexander himself put an end to it by giving his own synthesis of elasticities and absorption approaches (Alexander, 1959). This synthesis consists in treating the effect of the devaluation on the balance of payments, as determined by the traditional elasticity approach (in which the elasticities are taken as partial ones), as an *initial effect*, to which a multiplier is applied in order to obtain the changes in the national incomes of the two countries concerned (the devaluing country and the rest of the world) and hence the induced changes in the home country's imports and exports; these last changes concur with the initial change (the initial effect of the devaluation) to determine the *final* (total) effect on the balance of payments. It can be shown that the multiplier in question is nothing more than the standard foreign multiplier with repercussions in which the usual propensities (to consume, to import, etc.: see Sect. 13.3) are present. It should in fact be noted that to consider — as Alexander does — the initial effect of the devaluation as a multiplicand, is equivalent to considering the effects of an exogenous change in the autonomous components of the balance of payments in a context of rigid exchange rates in which no exchange-rate variation has occurred. This will be clear if one thinks that in the synthesis in question the devaluation — as said above — has the *sole* effect of determining the *multiplicand* to which the *same multiplier* that would be applied to an autonomous change in the balance of payments at unchanged exchange rate, is to be applied to obtain the final effect of the devaluation. We can thus write the fundamental relation of this synthesis as

Final effect of the devaluation on the balance of payments	=	initial effect (determined solely by the elasticities)	×	multiplier (determined by the propensities)

More precisely, let E_h be the initial effect of the devaluation on the balance of payments of country 1 (the devaluing country) determined by the devaluation; since we are considering an occasional exchange rate variation (which is assumed to determine E_h instantaneously), after it the exchange rate remains fixed at the new level, so that in Alexander's analysis the further effects on the economic system take place exactly as under a regime of fixed exchange rates with the foreign multiplier operating. If we use the symbology in Chap. 13, we can identify E_h with $\Delta m_{02} - \Delta m_{01}$[1]. In fact, in the context of the present analysis, the effects of a

---

[1] It is understood that these variations are expressed in country 1's currency at the new and constant exchange rate. Likewise, the subsequent variables (income and balance of payments) that we shall meet are evaluated at the new and constant exchange rate.

devaluation on country 1's exports (i.e. country 2's imports) and imports, is expressed as a change in those components of the two countries' import functions which are autonomous — with respect to income, of course. It would of course be possible to express $(\Delta m_{02}-\Delta m_{01})$ as a function of the elasticities (see Sect. A.14.1) but, without complicating the analysis, it is sufficient to observe that $(\Delta m_{02}-\Delta m_{01})>0$ if the suitable critical elasticities condition (see Sect. 12.2) holds, as in this case the devaluation has a positive initial effect on the payments balance. We also assume, following Alexander, that the initial exogenous change in the two countries' aggregate spending and national income equals the initial change in the respective balance of payments, which is $\Delta m_{02}-\Delta m_{01}$ in country 1 and $\Delta m_{01}-\Delta m_{02}$ in country 2 (as is usual in multiplier analysis, the new fixed exchange rate is taken to be one). This means that the autonomous components in C and I do *not* change; this, in turn, is equivalent to assuming, as we know from Sect. 13.2, that the autonomous component of the residents' demand for domestic goods changes by the same absolute amount, but in the opposite direction, as the change in the autonomous component of the residents' demand for foreign goods (demand for imports) which in our case is due to the devaluation and so is indeed autonomous with respect to income. Thus we have, by letting $\Delta C_{0i}=\Delta I_{0i}=0, i=1,2$, in the foreign multiplier formulae (13.11), the result

$$\Delta y_1 = \frac{(1-b_2-h_2)\cdot(\Delta m_{02}-\Delta m_{01})}{D}, \qquad (14.6)$$

$$\Delta y_2 = \frac{(1-b_1-h_1)\cdot(\Delta m_{01}-\Delta m_{02})}{D}, \qquad (14.7)$$

where D denotes the denominator in Eqs. (13.11). If we consider country 1's balance of payments and remember Eq. (13.12.1), we have

$$\Delta B_1 = (\Delta m_{02}-\Delta m_{01})+\mu_2\Delta y_2-\mu_1\Delta y_1. \qquad (14.8)$$

By substituting Eqs. (14.6) and (14.7) into Eq. (14.8) and simplifying we finally obtain

$$\Delta B_1 = \frac{(1-b_1-h_1)\cdot(1-b_2-h_2)}{D}(\Delta m_{02}-\Delta m_{01}), \qquad (14.9)$$

which is the formula suggested in Alexander's synthesis (apart from notational differences) and which clearly shows that the final effect of the devaluation is obtained by applying the multiplier to the initial effect $(\Delta m_{02}-\Delta m_{01})$.

This synthesis is disappointing, as was noted by Tsiang (1961), because it merely operates the superimposition of a multiplier upon the elasticities solution of the effect of a devaluation. Also, this superimposition is imprecise, because the multiplier effect of the initial variation in the balance of payments will cause additional variations in relative prices and so further substitution between domestic and foreign goods, etc. Therefore the multiplier itself should again involve the relevant elasticities that are in the multiplicand, but this is not true in Alexander's synthesis. A satisfactory synthesis should be made in the context of a model in which the interactions of changes in prices and income are taken into consideration simultaneously. Attempts in this direction had already been made *before* the beginning of the absorption versus-elasticity controversy (see Sect. 14.3). "If the controversy between the relative-prices and aggregate-spending approaches merely leads to a synthesis which had already been worked out before the controversy, what then has been gained by the debate?" (Tsiang, 1961, p. 390 of the 1968 reprint).

We share the opinion of Tsiang (1961) and Johnson (1958a) who believe that, if anything has been gained by the debate, it is the highlighting of the importance of monetary factors in the analysis of the adjustment process of payments imbalances, and of the wrongness of considering the balance of payments as a sector on its own, since this balance must be examined in the context of the dynamics of the whole economic system.

14.3 A Dynamic Model of Interaction between Exchange Rate and Income in the Adjustment Process

Attempts at integration, into a unified theory, of the balance-of-payments adjustment mechanism based on income and the multiplier, and of the traditional mechanism based on relative prices and elasticities, were undertaken in 1950 by various authors independently and simultaneously, a sure sign of the theoretical exigency of such an integration. These first attempts were followed by others and also the absorption-versus-elasticities controversy and synthesis can be seen in the context of an analysis of the effects of income and exchange-rate changes on the balance of payments, as shown at the end of the Sect. 14.2.

Among these early attempts, which contain the germs of the more general theory of internal and external macroeconomic equilibrium (treated in Chaps. 15 and 16), we shall examine that of Laursen and Metzler (1950); one of the reasons of this choice[2] is that their model will serve us subsequently for other purposes (see Sect. 16.4).

14.3.1 The Basic Model

The Laursen and Metzler model will be examined here in a simplified version (for the original general version see Sect. A.14.4) so that it can be analyzed graphically.

The model can be reduced to two equations, one expressing the determination of national income in an open economy and the other expressing balance-of-payments equilibrium. As regards the former, instead of the usual equation (also adopted by Laursen and Metzler)

national income (output) = consumption + investment − imports + exports, (I)

we use the equivalent relation

national income (output) = demand for domestic output by residents + demand for domestic output by nonresidents (exports). (II)

---
[2] Two other attempts worthy of mention are those of Harberger (1950) and Stolper (1950). However, the first contains no dynamic analysis and the second contains a less sophisticated analysis than Laursen and Metzler's. Another important contribution is that of Tsiang (1961).

14.3 A Dynamic Model of Interaction

It can easily be seen that Eq. (II) coincides with Eq. (I) if we remember (see Sect. 13.2.1) that by subtracting the demand for imports from the aggregate demand for all goods (as usual by goods we mean both goods and services) we obtain the residents' (aggregate) demand for domestically produced goods (domestic output). In fact, as shown in Sect. 13.2.1, the aggregate demand $C+I$ includes both domestic and foreign goods, and in our simplified model the latter coincide with imports. Therefore

demand for domestic output by residents = consumption + investment − imports. (III)

The reason for using (II) instead of (I) is that it allows for an easier presentation of the model; we also remember from Sect. 13.2.1, that from Eq. (III) we get the following relation between the various propensities

marginal propensity to demand (to spend on) domestic output by residents = marginal propensity to consume + marginal propensity to invest − marginal propensity to import, (IV)

where the propensities on the right-hand side are defined in the traditional way. To simplify the terminology we shall call *domestic demand* (*expenditure*) the demand for domestic output by residents, and marginal propensity to domestic demand (expenditure) that defined in Eq. (IV). We must emphasize that it is a terminological convention valid in the context of the present volume, since "domestic demand" is also used in the literature with different meanings.

The second equation of the model expresses the equilibrium in the balance of payments (in the sense of balance on goods and services).

This said, we can write the basic equations of the model, which remains Keynesian in spirit, in the sense that underemployment prevails and prices are taken to be rigid; these are

$$y = d(y,r) + x(r), \quad (14.10)$$

$$x(r) - rm(y,r) = 0, \quad (14.11)$$

where in addition to the usual symbols d appears, which denotes domestic demand. We observe that, given the rigidity of prices, we have set both export and import prices (expressed in the respective domestic currencies) at one, which entails no loss of generality and allows us to eliminate symbols representing mere constants (p and p_m).

Exports and imports are functions of the exchange rate; for the same reasons explained in Sect. 12.1, a change in r makes exports change in the same direction as r and imports in the opposite direction. Imports also depend on national income in a positive manner.

As regards domestic demand, it is obviously a function of national income and also depends on the exchange rate. A variation in the exchange rate, in fact, causes a variation in the relative price of domestic and foreign goods (given their prices in the respective domestic currencies) and so a substitution between domestic and foreign (imported) goods in aggregate national expenditure. Therefore an exchange-rate variation causes a variation of domestic demand in the same direction: for example, a depreciation brings about an increase in domestic demand with a concomitant decrease in imports. It is important to stress that these two variations are *not* necessarily equal in absolute value, a point which — amongst others — underlies the debate on the insulating properties of flexible exchange rates and which will be taken up again in Sect. 16.4. Equation (14.10) is the formal counterpart of (II); the left-hand side of Eq. (14.11) expresses the payments balance, which in equilibrium is zero.

We note that there are two equations and two unknowns (or endogenous variables): income and the exchange rate. In principle, it is therefore possible simultaneously to determine the level of income and the exchange rate which ensure the contemporaneous equilibrium in the goods market (real equilibrium) and in the balance of payments. For an intuitive analysis of the model it is expedient to present it graphically.

14.3.2 A Graphic Representation

Let us begin by considering the real equilibrium as determined by relation (II) or Eq. (14.10). Since domestic demand is a function of income and the exchange rate, and exports are a function of the exchange rate, it is possible to show in a diagram the locus of all the combinations of income and the exchange rate which ensure the equality expressed by Eq. (14.10). We thus get a positively sloped curve (for simplicity's sake we have assumed that it is a straight line) in the (r,y) plane. In fact, greater values of domestic demand correspond to greater values of income but, as we assume that the marginal propensity to domestic demand is lower than one[3], the increase in domestic demand does not entirely absorb the increase in income. It is therefore necessary for the exchange rate to increase, thus causing both an additional increase in domestic demand and an increase in exports so as to absorb the residual and maintain the equality (14.10). This is the RR schedule in Fig. 14.1.

Besides being increasing, the RR schedule has the property that at all points below (above) it there is a positive (negative) excess demand for goods, where this excess demand is measured by the difference between the total (domestic + foreign) demand for domestic output and the output itself (or national income). With reference to Fig. 14.1, consider any point above the RR schedule, for example A'. At A' income is higher than at A (which is a point of real equilibrium) and therefore, as the exchange rate is the same at both A and A', at A' domestic demand will be higher than at A. But since the marginal propensity to domestic demand is assumedly lower than one, the higher domestic demand will not absorb the higher output entirely, at unchanged exchange rate. Therefore at A' there will be an excess supply (negative excess demand). It can be similarly shown that at any point below the RR schedule (for example, A'') there is a positive excess demand.

---

[3] This is a very plausible assumption if we bear (IV) in mind. In fact, even if the sum of the marginal propensity to consume and the marginal propensity to invest happened to be greater than one, it is likely that by subtracting the marginal propensity to import, the result would be a number smaller than one. See also Sect. 13.2.1.

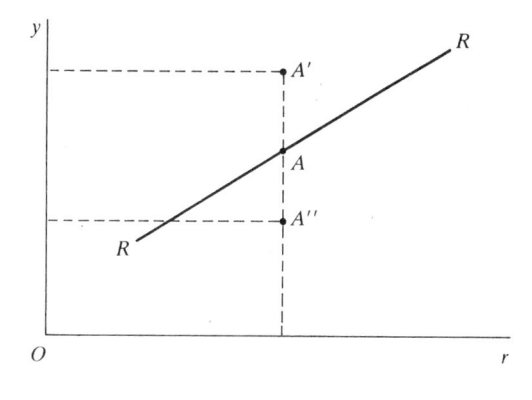

Fig. 14.1. Flexible exchange rates and the level of income: the real-equilibrium schedule

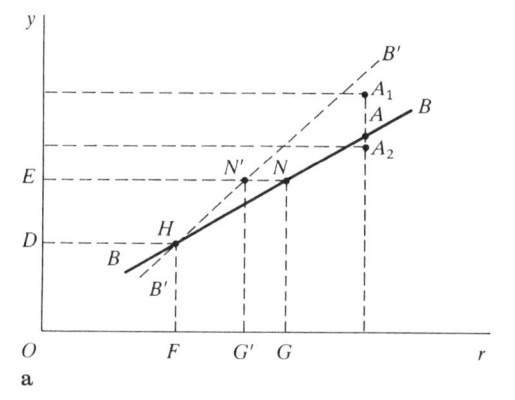

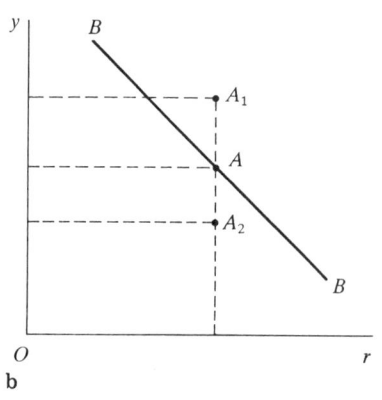

Fig. 14.2. Flexible exchange rates and the level of income: the balance-of-payments schedule

Let us now consider the locus of all the combinations of income and the exchange rate which ensure balance-of-payments equilibrium. This locus is a curve (the *BB* schedule in Fig. 14.2, represented as a straight line for simplicity) in the (r,y) plane, which will be positively or negatively sloped according as the critical elasticities condition occurs or not. As we know from Sect. 12.2, if the sum of the export and import elasticities is greater than one, the balance of payments changes in the same direction as the exchange rate, that is, *ceteris paribus*, an increase in r (a depreciation) improves the balance of payments and vice versa. If we examine Fig. 14.2a, we see that a higher income means higher imports and so a deterioration in the balance of payments, which can be offset by a higher exchange rate as the critical elasticities condition occurs.

If, on the contrary, the critical elasticities condition does not occur, the balance of payments varies in the opposite direction to the exchange rate, so that — see Fig. 14.2b — if income increases (hence also imports), a lower exchange rate is called for to offset the deterioration in the payments balance. In this case we get a decreasing *BB* schedule.

If we now go back to Fig. 14.2a, we see that the higher the sum of the elasticities, the higher the slope of the balance-of-payments equilibrium line: in $B'B'$, for example, this sum is greater than that underlying the *BB* schedule (both sums are of course higher than one for what was said above). In fact, the higher the sum of the elasticities, the higher the effect on the balance of payments of an exchange-rate variation, so that this variation will have to be smaller to offset the same balance-of-payments change due to an income change. If we take H as example of an initial payments equilibrium point, and if we consider income OE instead of OD, we see that along the BB schedule the corresponding exchange rate will have to be OG so as to maintain balance-of-payments equilibrium (point N). We also see that along the $B'B'$ schedule — where the sum of the elasticities is assumedly higher — the exchange rate corresponding to income OE will have to be OG' so as to maintain balance-of-payments equilibrium (point N'). With respect to the initial value of the exchange rate, OG' denotes a smaller depreciation than OG.

Finally observe that at any point above (below) the BB schedule — irrespectively of its slope — the balance of payments shows a deficit (surplus). In fact, if we consider a point A_1 above the BB schedule — note that what we are saying holds for both Fig. 14.2a and b — we see that this point, at unchanged exchange rate, corresponds to a higher income than the equilibrium point A does. Since higher income means higher imports, and the exchange rate is the same, at A_1 the balance of payments will be in deficit if it was in equilibrium at A. It can be similarly shown that at A_2 the balance of payments shows a surplus.

If we now draw schedules RR and BB in the *same diagram*, their intersection will determine the point at which real equilibrium and balance-of-payments equilibrium will *simultaneously* obtain; the coordinates of this point will give us the equilibrium values of income and the exchange rate. This is done in Fig. 14.3 below, which also serves to examine the problem of the *stability* of equilibrium, to which we now turn.

14.3.3 Stability and Comparative Statics

To examine the dynamic stability of the equilibrium point we must first examine the forces acting on income and on the exchange rate when either of these variables is outside equilibrium, and then investigate whether, and under what conditions, these forces cause the deviating variable(s) to converge to the equilibrium point.

For this purpose, the dynamic behaviour assumptions usually made are the following:

(a) national income (output) varies in relation to the excess demand for goods and, precisely, it increases if total demand exceeds output (positive excess demand), decreases in the opposite case. This is the usual assumption made in the context of a model of the Keynesian type with underemployment and rigid prices and, in fact, it is the same as that already adopted in the course of the dynamic analysis of the multiplier (see Sects. 13.3.2, A.13.1.1, etc.).

(b) the exchange rate, that is the price of foreign exchange, increases (decreases) if there is a positive (negative) excess demand for foreign exchange in the foreign exchange market. This is the usual assumption already examined in Sect. 12.3.1, where it was also shown that — since in our simplified context the supply of foreign exchange comes from exporters and the demand for it from

14.3 A Dynamic Model of Interaction 169

importers — this assumption is equivalent to saying that the exchange rate depreciates (appreciates) if there is a balance-of-payments deficit (surplus).

This said, it is possible to give a simple graphic representation of the dynamic behaviour of the system and of the stability conditions. It should be emphasized that the intuitive study of stability by way of arrows (see below) is to be taken as a simple expository device and not as giving a rigorous proof (for which see Sect. A.14.2). The procedure is fairly simple. The intersection between the *BB* and *RR* schedules subdivides the space of the first quadrant into four sub-spaces or zones in each of which, on the basis of what was shown above (Sect. 14.3.2), it will be possible to give a precise sign to the excess demand for goods and to the balance of payments; these will then indicate the direction of movement of income and the exchange rate in accordance with assumptions (a) and (b) above.

Consider for example Fig. 14.3a, which depicts an unstable equilibrium point. We begin with point A_1. As this point lies below the *RR* and above the *BB* schedule, it implies a positive excess demand for goods (denoted by $ED>0$ in the diagram) and a balance-of-payments deficit ($B<0$ in the diagram). Therefore, as a consequence of the dynamic behaviour assumptions made above, income tends to increase, as shown by the vertical arrow (income is measured on the vertical axis) drawn from A_1 and pointing upwards, and the exchange rate tends to depreciate (i.e. to increase), as shown by the horizontal arrow (the exchange rate is measured on the horizontal axis) drawn from A_1 and pointing to the right. Point A_1 will therefore tend to move in a direction included between the two arrows and so will move farther and farther away from the equilibrium point E. This reasoning holds for any point lying in the same zone as A_1, i.e. below the *RR* and above the *BB* schedule, so that any initial point lying there will diverge from equilibrium.

With similar reasoning applied to the other three zones of Fig. 14.3a we can find the suitable arrows — see for example points A_2, A_3, A_4 — and conclude that in any case the system will move away from the equilibrium point[4], which is therefore unstable.

We can now ask the reason for this instability: in graphic terms, it is due to the position of the *BB* relative to the *RR* schedule, namely — if we remember what has been said above on the decreasing *BB* schedule — the cause of instability is to be seen in the fact that the critical elasticities condition does not occur. So far, there is nothing new with respect to the traditional elasticity approach, which tells us that equilibrium is unstable when the critical elasticities condition does not occur (see Sects. 12.2 and 12.3). But there is more to it than that: the novelty of the present analysis lies in the fact that the equilibrium point may be unstable even if the critical elasticities condition is fulfilled. In precise terms, this condition is only *necessary but not sufficient* for the stability of equilibrium.

To understand this important fact let us have a look at panels b and c of Fig. 14.3. In Fig. 14.3b the *BB* is an increasing schedule, but — as can be seen from an inspection of the arrows (which have been drawn following the same procedure

---

[4] Doubts might arise in relation to points lying in the zones where A_2 and A_4 lie, but it can be proved (see Sect. A.14.2) that the equilibrium is indeed unstable. Similar observations hold in relation to Fig. 14.3b.

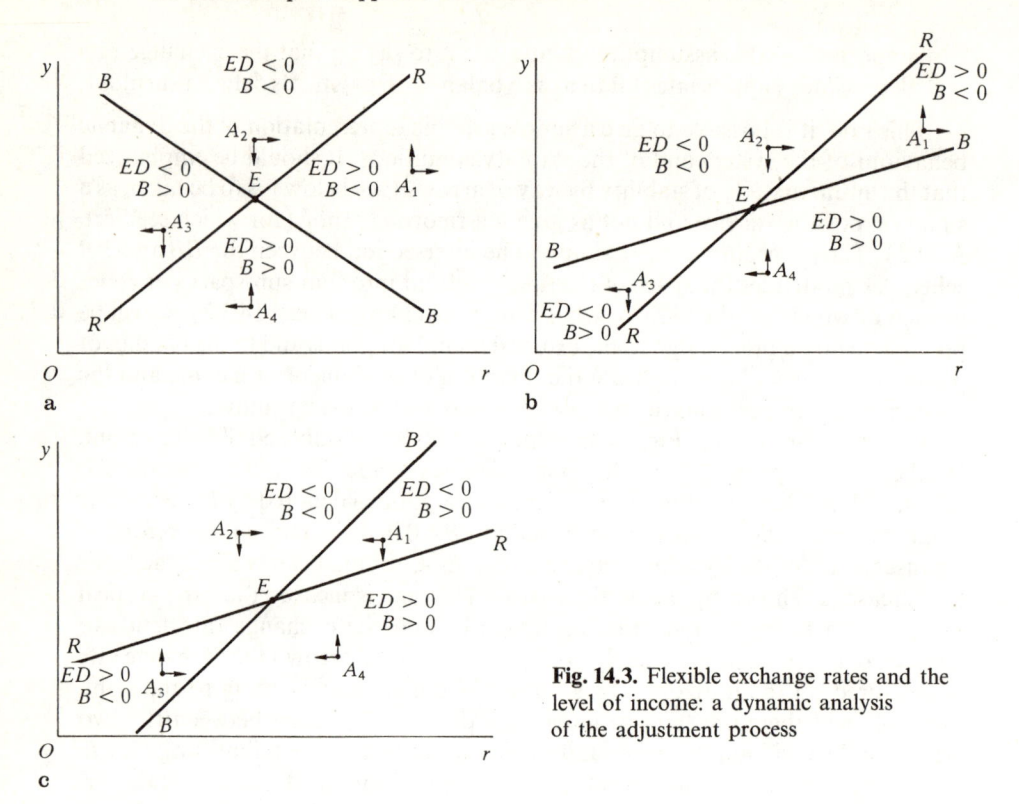

Fig. 14.3. Flexible exchange rates and the level of income: a dynamic analysis of the adjustment process

explained in relation to panel a of the figure — the points outside equilibrium tend to move away from it rather than converge to it: the equilibrium point is again unstable. In Fig. 14.3c, on the contrary, the equilibrium point is stable, as can be seen from the arrows: compare, for example, point A_1 in panel c with point A_1 in panel b.

It can readily be seen from Fig. 14.3 that in panel b the BB schedule, though increasing, cuts the RR schedule from above, i.e. it is above (below) it to the left (right) of the intersection point. In panel c, on the contrary, the increasing BB schedule cuts the RR schedule from below. This different position of the BB schedule depends on the fact that *the BB has a higher (lower) slope than the RR schedule in Fig. 14.3c and b respectively*: we also see that BB in c has a higher slope than BB in b. If we remember what has been said in Sect. 14.3.2 on the slope of the BB schedule, we see that *the sum of the elasticities is greater in c than in b*: in other words, *for stability to obtain, it does not suffice that the sum of the elasticities is greater than one, but this sum must be greater than a critical value greater than one.*

As a matter of fact, as will be demonstrated in Sect. A.14.2, the stability condition is

$$\eta_x + \eta_m > 1 + \frac{rm_y(d_r + x_r)}{m(1 - d_y)}, \qquad (14.12)$$

where, in addition to the symbols already defined, we find m_y (marginal propensity to import), d_y (marginal propensity to domestic demand), d_r (effect

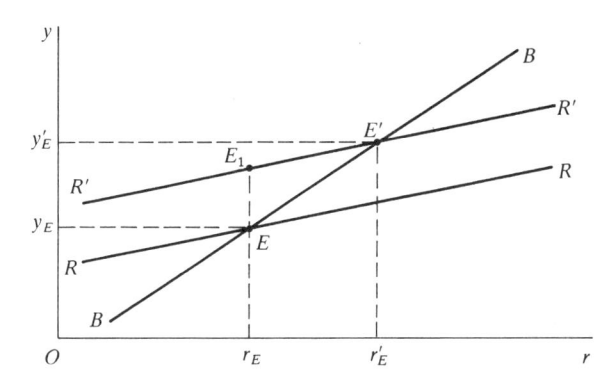

Fig. 14.4. Flexible exchange rates and the level of income: effects of an exogenous increase in domestic demand

of an exchange-rate variation on domestic demand), and x_r (effect of an exchange-rate variation on exports). Given the assumptions (in particular, $d_y < 1$), the fraction on the right-hand side of (14.12) is positive, so that the whole right-hand side, which represents the critical value of the sum of the elasticities, is greater than one. Note also that the higher is the slope of the RR schedule the higher will this fraction be (see Sect. A.14.2).

Leaving aside diagrams and formulae, the economic reason for this result is intuitive. Let us assume, for example, that the balance of payments is in deficit. The exchange rate depreciates and, assuming that the traditional critical elasticities condition occurs, the deficit is reduced. However, the depreciation increases total demand for domestic output (domestic demand and exports, in fact, both increase); this causes an increase in income and so imports increase, thus opposing the initial favourable effect of the depreciation on the balance of payments: this effect must therefore be more intense than it had to be in the absence of income effects, i.e. the sum of the elasticities must be higher than in the traditional case.

Let us now look at the analysis of multiplier effects in the present model; for example, we take the case of an exogenous increase in domestic demand and, naturally, consider a situation of stable equilibrium. With reference to Fig. 14.4, the RR schedule shifts upwards because income will be higher at any given exchange rate as total demand is higher. The reason why we have considered a stable equilibrium is self-evident: the passage from the old (E) to the new (E') equilibrium point, in fact, can take place only if stability prevails; the study of the comparative static properties of unstable equilibria is, therefore, uninteresting in the context of the analysis of the spontaneous behaviour of the system, as it is useless to find out the position of the new equilibrium if the system cannot approach it.

At E' income is clearly higher than at E; the increase in income can be expressed in terms of the exogenous increase in domestic demand to which a sort of multiplier is applied. In the formula for this multiplier [see Eq. (A.14.12) in Sect. A.14.3] not only are the propensities present but also the elasticities, as they should be (see the end of Sect. 14.2).

As regards the exchange rate, this has increased (a depreciation). This is an obvious result, as the higher income implies higher imports, and so a balance-of-payments deficit, which requires a depreciation to be eliminated. It is however important to note that the depreciation stimulates exports, and so the final result is a higher income increase than under fixed exchange rates for the same exogenous increase in domestic demand (point E_1 in Fig. 14.4, where of course the balance of payments is in deficit).

The reader who so wishes can use the same procedure illustrated above to examine the effects of other exogenous variations.

14.3.4 The *J*-Curve

It is important to point out that the stability condition (14.12), if satisfied, also ensures that the balance of payments will improve when the exchange rate is officially devalued in a regime of fixed exchange rates (such as the adjustable peg: see Sect. 10.5.2) or is manoeuvred in the direction for a depreciation in a managed float regime[5]. It should however be stressed that the improvement manifests itself in the *new* equilibrium position that the system will reach *after* all the adjustments have worked themselves out; this does not exclude the eventuality that — in the context of less restrictive assumptions than those adopted here — the balance of payments may deteriorate *in the course of the adjustment process* because of effects of the exchange-rate devaluation on domestic prices and income and of other effects. All these effects may in fact cause — immediately after the devaluation — a *temporary* balance-of-payments deterioration (which is often referred to as the "perverse" effect of the devaluation) before the final improvement. This phenomenon is also called in the literature the *J-curve*, to denote the time path of the payments balance, which initially decreases (deteriorates) and subsequently increases (improves) to a level higher than the one prior to devaluation, thus resembling a *J* slanted to the right in a diagram in which time is measured on the horizontal axis and the balance of payments on the vertical one.

This terminology was introduced after the 1967 devaluation of the pound sterling (see NIESR, 1968, p. 11), which was followed by a trade deficit which lasted until 1970. Several studies attempted to explain this phenomenon by distinguishing various periods following the devaluation in which the effects of the devaluation itself take place. These are, in the terminology of Magee (1973), the *currency-contract period*, the *pass-through period*, and the *quantity-adjustment period*.

The *currency-contract period* is defined as that short period of time immediately following the exchange-rate variation in which the contracts stipulated before the variation mature. It is clear that during this period both prices and quantities are predetermined, so that — if we consider a devaluation undertaken to correct a deficit — what happens to the payments balance in domestic currency depends on the currency in which the import and export contracts were stipulated. Although from the purely taxonomic viewpoint a case in which import contracts were stipulated in domestic currency and export contracts in foreign currency cannot be excluded (in which case the domestic-currency payments balance

---

[5] Naturally one must take account of the fact that in these cases the exchange-rate variation is (wholly or in part) the consequence of a decision of the monetary authorities, whilst in the context so far examined this variation is determined by the market in a regime of freely flexible exchange rates.

necessarily improves), normally both the export and import contracts stipulated before the devaluation are expressed in foreign currency. In fact, in the expectation of a possible devaluation, both domestic and foreign exporters will try to avoid an exchange-rate loss by stipulating contracts in foreign currency. Now, as a consequence of the devaluation, the domestic-currency value of both imports and exports will increase by the same percentage as the devaluation, so that — as the pre-devaluation value of the former was assumedly higher than that of the latter — the deficit will increase (a perverse effect).

The *pass-through period* is defined as that short period of time following the exchange-rate variation in which prices can change (as they refer to contracts agreed upon after the exchange rate has varied), but quantities remain unchanged due to rigidities in the demand for and/or supply of imports and exports. Consider, for example, the case of a devaluation with a demand for imports by residents of the devaluing country and a demand for the devaluing country's exports by the rest of the world which are both inelastic in the short-run. The domestic-currency price of imports increases as a consequence of the devaluation but the demand does not change, so that the outlay for imports increases. The foreign-currency price of exports decreases as a consequence of the devaluation (by the same percentage as the devaluation, if we assume that domestic exporters, given the domestic currency price, change the foreign-currency price in accordance with the devaluation), but the demand does not change, so that the foreign-currency receipts will decrease and their domestic-currency value will not change. Therefore the domestic-currency balance deteriorates (again a perverse effect).

Of course these perverse effects are not inevitable — only possible: for a complete classification of the possible effects of a devaluation during the currency-contract period and the pass-through period see Magee (1973, Tables 1 and 2).

Finally, we come to the *quantity-adjustment period*, in which both quantities and prices can change. Now, if the suitable conditions on the elasticities are fulfilled, the balance of payments ought to improve. This is undoubtedly true from the viewpoint of comparative statics, but from the dynamic point of view it may happen that quantities do not adjust as quickly as prices, owing to reaction lags, frictions etc., so that — even if the stability conditions occur — the balance of payments may again deteriorate before improving towards the new equilibrium point. The analysis of the dynamic process of transition from the old to the new equilibrium with different speeds of adjustment of the variables concerned is by no means an easy matter, and we refer the reader to Sect. A.14.3.

On the empirical evidence concerning the J curve see Rose and Yellen (1989) and Wood (1991).

Appendix

A.14.1 Alexander's Synthesis

As explained in the text, the synthesis between the elasticity approach and the absorption approach suggested by Alexander (1959) consists in treating the initial effect of a devaluation on the balance of payments (determined by the elasticities) as a multiplicand to which a multiplier (determined by the propensities) is applied to obtain the final result; this multiplier turns out to be the same as that valid for any exogenous change in the autonomous components of imports and exports. This is not immediately evident but can be shown in the following way. The formula suggested by Alexander is

$$dB_h = \frac{H_1 H_2}{1 - F_1 F_2} E_h, \qquad (A.14.1)$$

where

$dB_h =$ final change in country 1's balance of payments (the devaluing country) in domestic currency;

$E_h =$ initial change in country 1's balance of payments determined by the elasticity formula (see Sect. A.12.1);

$H_i =$ ratio of the marginal propensity to hoard to the sum of this propensity and the marginal propensity to import in country i ($i = 1,2$);

$F_i =$ ratio of the marginal propensity to import to the sum of this propensity and the marginal propensity to hoard in country i.

The marginal propensity to hoard equals one minus the marginal propensity to spend, which in turn equals the sum of the marginal propensity to consume and the marginal propensity to invest. Therefore, in our symbology, we can write the following equivalences

$$H_i = \frac{1 - b_i - h_i}{1 - b_i - h_i + \mu_i}, \quad F_i = \frac{\mu_i}{1 - b_i - h_i + \mu_i}. \qquad (A.14.2)$$

By substituting Eqs. (A.14.2) into Eq. (A.14.1) and multiplying both numerator and denominator by $(1 - b_1 - h_1 + \mu_1)(1 - b_2 - h_2 + \mu_2)$ we obtain

$$dB_h = \frac{(1 - b_1 - h_1)(1 - b_2 - h_2)}{(1 - b_1 - h_1 + \mu_1)(1 - b_2 - h_2 + \mu_2) - \mu_1 \mu_2} E_h. \qquad (A.14.3)$$

Since, given the assumptions made, E_h can be identified with $(\Delta m_{02} - \Delta m_{01})$, it can immediately be seen that Alexander's formula coincides with Eq. (14.9) examined in the text.

A.14.2 A Simplified Version of the Laursen and Metzler Model

The model that we present is simplified because it considers one country only (for the original two-country model see Sect. A.14.4). Its equations, commented on in Sect. 14.3.1, are

$$\begin{aligned} y - d(y,r) - x(r) &= 0, & 0 < d_y < 1,\ d_r > 0,\ x_r > 0, \\ x(r) - rm(y,r) &= 0, & 0 < m_y < 1,\ m_r < 0. \end{aligned} \qquad (A.14.4)$$

A.14.2.1 The *RR* and *BB* Schedules

By using the implicit-function differentiation rule we can calculate the derivative dy/dr with reference to both equations in (A.14.4), thus obtaining the slopes of the *RR* and *BB* schedules respectively. Thus we have

$$\left(\frac{dy}{dr}\right)_{RR} = \frac{d_r + x_r}{1 - d_y},$$

$$\left(\frac{dy}{dr}\right)_{BB} = \frac{x_r - m - rm_r}{rm_y}.$$

(A.14.5)

The slope of the *BB* schedule can also be written, after obvious passages, in the form

$$\left(\frac{dy}{dr}\right)_{BB} = \frac{m\left(\eta_m + \frac{x}{mr}\eta_x - 1\right)}{rm_y},$$

(A.14.5.1)

where $\eta_x \equiv x_r(r/x)$, $\eta_m \equiv -m_r(r/m)$ are the elasticities of exports and imports with respect to the exchange rate. It can be seen from the first equation in (A.14.5) that $(dy/dr)_{RR} > 0$ given the assumptions concerning the various derivatives. As regards the *BB* schedule, it follows from Eq. (A.14.5.1) that $(dy/dr)_{BB} \gtreqless 0$ according as $\eta_m + (x/mr)\eta_x - 1 \gtreqless 0$; besides, the greater the sum of the two elasticities *ceteris paribus*, the greater will be this derivative.

If we consider a neighbourhood of the equilibrium point, where the payments balance is in equilibrium and so $x = mr$, Eq. (A.14.5.1) becomes

$$\left(\frac{dy}{dr}\right)_{BB} = \frac{m(\eta_m + \eta_x - 1)}{rm_y}.$$

(A.14.5.2)

As regards the points off the *RR* and *BB* schedules, if we define the functions

$$ED = [d(y,r) + x(r)] - y,$$
$$B = x(r) - rm(y,r),$$

(A.14.4.1)

we see that the *RR* and *BB* schedules are determined by $ED = 0$, $B = 0$ respectively. We now compute

$$\frac{\partial ED}{\partial y} = d_y - 1 < 0,$$

$$\frac{\partial B}{\partial y} = -rm_y < 0,$$

(A.14.4.2)

from wich it follows that $ED \lesseqgtr 0$ according as y is higher (lower) than the value for which $ED = 0$ at any given r, and that $B \gtreqless 0$ according as y is lower (higher) than the value for which $B = 0$ at any given r.

A.14.2.2 The Dynamics of the System

To examine the stability of the equilibrium point, let us consider the following differential equation system, which is the formal expression of the dynamic behaviour assumed in Sect. 14.3.3:

$$\frac{dy}{dt} = f_1[d(y,r) + x(r) - y],$$
$$\frac{dr}{dt} = f_2[rm(y,r) - x(r)],$$
(A.14.6)

where f_1 and f_2 are sign-preserving functions, and $f'_1[0] \equiv k_1 > 0$, $f'_2[0] \equiv k_2 > 0$. The study of local stability involves the analysis of the linear approximation to system (A.14.6) at the equilibrium point, that is, of the system

$$\frac{d\bar{y}}{dt} = k_1[(d_y - 1)\bar{y} + (d_r + x_r)\bar{r}],$$
$$\frac{d\bar{r}}{dt} = k_2[rm_y \bar{y} - (x_r - m - rm_r)\bar{r}],$$
(A.14.7)

where a bar over a variable denotes as usual the deviations from equilibrium. The dynamic path of the system depends on the roots of the characteristic equation

$$\lambda^2 + [k_1(1-d_y) + k_2(x_r - m - rm_r)]\lambda$$
$$+ k_1 k_2[(1-d_y)(x_r - m - rm_r) - rm_y(d_r + x_r)] = 0.$$
(A.14.8)

Necessary and sufficient stability conditions are

$$k_1(1-d_y) + k_2(x_r - m - rm_r) > 0,$$
$$(1-d_y)(x_r - m - rm_r) - rm_y(d_r + x_r) > 0.$$
(A.14.9)

The first inequality, together with the second, implies $1 - d_y > 0$, which was assumed from the beginning. The second can be rewritten in the form

$$\eta_m + \eta_x > 1 + \frac{rm_y(d_r + x_r)}{m(1-d_y)},$$
(A.14.9.1)

where we have used the fact that $x = mr$, since the system has been linearized at the equilibrium point. Condition (A.14.9.1) is (14.12) of the text. It can easily be shown that the graphic counterpart of (A.14.9.1) is that the BB schedule has a higher slope than the RR schedule in the neighbourhood of the equilibrium point: in fact, the inequality under examination can be rewritten, after simple passages, in the form

$$\frac{m(\eta_m + \eta_x - 1)}{rm_y} > \frac{d_r + x_r}{1 - d_y},$$
(A.14.9.2)

which, given Eqs. (A.14.5) and (A.14.5.2), is equivalent to $(dy/dr)_{BB} > (dy/dr)_{RR}$.

To better relate this mathematical analysis to the results shown graphically in Fig. 14.3, we must discover the nature of the singular point E. We first compute the discriminant of Eq. (A.14.8), which turns out to be

$$\Delta = [k_1(1-d_y) - k_2(x_r - m - rm_r)]^2 + 4rm_y(d_r + x_r), \quad (A.14.8.1)$$

and is obviously positive. Therefore (see, for example, Gandolfo, 1980, pp. 435–440) the equilibrium point will be either a *stable node* (if the stability condition is satisfied) or a *saddle point*, if the stability condition is not satisfied. When the singular point is a saddle point, the movement along the integral curves is always away from equilibrium, *except for* the motion along one of the two asymptotes. Therefore, if the initial point happens by sheer chance to lie along the stable asymptote — which, in Fig. 14.3a and b, passes through point E in a northwest to south-east direction — it will converge to equilibrium; any other point will diverge. This resolves any doubts that the mere inspection of the arrows in Fig. 14.3a and b might leave.

A.14.2.3 Comparative Statics

To examine the effects of an exogenous increase in domestic demand, we introduce a parameter α representing this increase in Eqs. (A.14.4):

$$\begin{aligned} y - d(y,r) - x(r) - \alpha &= 0, \\ x(r) - rm(y,r) &= 0, \end{aligned} \quad (A.14.4.3)$$

If the Jacobian of Eqs. (A.14.4.3) with respect to y and r is different from zero in the neighbourhood of the equilibrium point, that is if

$$|\mathbf{J}| = \begin{vmatrix} 1-d_y & -(d_r+x_r) \\ -rm_y & x_r - m - rm_r \end{vmatrix} = (1-d_y)(x_r - m - rm_r) - rm_y(d_r + x_r) \neq 0, \quad (A.14.10)$$

then we can express y and r as continously differentiable functions of α in the neighbourhood of the equilibrium point, i.e. $y = y(\alpha)$, $r = r(\alpha)$. Now, $|\mathbf{J}|$ is certainly different from zero if the equilibrium is stable – see (A.14.9) – and so we can calculate the derivatives $dy/d\alpha$, $dr/d\alpha$ by the method of comparative statics. From Eqs. (A.14.4.3) we get

$$\begin{aligned} (1-d_y)\frac{dy}{d\alpha} - (d_r+x_r)\frac{dr}{d\alpha} &= 1, \\ -rm_y\frac{dy}{d\alpha} + (x_r - m - rm_r)\frac{dr}{d\alpha} &= 0, \end{aligned} \quad (A.14.11)$$

whence, by solving

$$\frac{dy}{d\alpha} = \frac{(x_r - m - rm_r)}{|\mathbf{J}|}, \quad (A.14.12)$$

$$\frac{dr}{d\alpha} = \frac{rm_y}{|\mathbf{J}|}. \quad (A.14.13)$$

Since $|J|>0$ owing to the stability conditions and since the numerator of the fraction which gives $dy/d\alpha$ is also positive by the same conditions, the multiplier $dy/d\alpha$, which is that discussed in Sect. 14.3.3, is certainly positive. Since $dr/d\alpha$ is positive as well, the exchange rate is higher (a depreciation) in the new equilibrium.

We now show that the multiplier $dy/d\alpha$ is greater than the multiplier under fixed exchange rates. The latter is given by Eq. (A.13.3) that is, in the symbology of the present chapter, by $1/(1-d_y)$. If we consider Eq. (A.14.12) and rewrite it in the form

$$\frac{dy}{d\alpha} = \frac{1}{(1-d_y)-rm_y(d_r+x_r)/(x_r-m-rm_r)}. \qquad (A.14.12.1)$$

we can see that this fraction is greater than $1/(1-d_y)$. In fact, the denominator — which is positive on account of the stability conditions — is certainly smaller than $(1-d_y)$, since $rm_y(d_r+x_r)>0$ (given the assumptions on the signs of the various derivatives) and $x_r-m-rm_r>0$ by the stability conditions. This proves the assertion.

A.14.3 The J-curve

The perverse effects of a devaluation, which may occur in the short period, notwithstanding the occurrence of the critical elasticities condition (see Sect. A.12.1) or of the more general condition (A.14.9.1) discussed above, can ultimately be seen as a consequence of *adjustment lags* of various types acting on both quantities and prices. The purpose of this section is to give a truly dynamic treatment of the problem in the context of the model explained in section A.14.2, duly modified and integrated to account for adjustment lags. Let us rewrite the model with an explicit consideration of import and export prices, i.e.

$$\begin{aligned} y &= d(y,r) + x(r), \\ B &= p_x x(r) - p_{hm} m(y,r), \end{aligned} \qquad (A.14.14)$$

where $p_{hm} \equiv rp_m$ is the domestic-currency price of imports (their foreign-currency price being p_m). Since we are, by assumption, in the context of a fixed but adjustable exchange-rate regime (adjustable peg), r has to be considered as a parameter and not as an endogenous variable. Given r, system (A.14.14) determines the values of y and B. By using the method of comparative statics we can calculate dB/dr, which turns out to be

$$\begin{aligned} \frac{dB}{dr} &= p_x x_r - p_m m - rp_m \left(m_y \frac{d_r + x_r}{1-d_y} + m_r \right) \\ &= x_r - m - rm_r - \frac{rm_y(d_r + x_r)}{1-d_y}, \end{aligned} \qquad (A.14.15)$$

where we have assumed that not only the international price of imports but also the domestic-currency price of exports remain unchanged as a consequence of the devaluation[6]. If we assume that the stability conditions (A.14.9.1) occur, it follows that $dB/dr > 0$. Therefore the balance of payments will certainly improve in the final position.

Let us now introduce the adjustment lags by way of suitable *partial adjustment equations*:

$$\frac{dp_{hm}}{dt} = \alpha_1 [(r_0 + dr)p_m - p_{hm}], \qquad \alpha_1 > 0,$$

$$\frac{dx}{dt} = \alpha_2 [(x_0 + x_r dr) - x], \qquad \alpha_2 > 0, \qquad \text{(A.14.16)}$$

$$\frac{dm}{dt} = \alpha_3 \left[\left(m_0 + m_y \frac{d_r + x_r}{1 - d_y} + m_r dr \right) - m \right], \qquad \alpha_3 > 0,$$

where, given the assumptions[7], α_2 and α_3 are much lower than α_1, because prices adjust much more rapidly than quantities, so that the mean time-lag of the latter is much higher than that of the former.

The first equation in (A.14.16) expresses the fact that — given a devaluation dr — the domestic-currency price of imports, p_{hm}, adjusts with a mean time-lag $1/\alpha_1$ to the value corresponding to the new exchange rate (which is $r_0 + dr$, r_0 being the given initial exchange rate) applied to the given international price p_m. The second equation expresses the fact that the quantity of exports adjusts with a mean time-lag $1/\alpha_2$ to the value corresponding to the new exchange rate: this value is $x_0 + dx = x_0 + x_r dr$, where x_0 is the initial quantity. The third equation expresses the fact that the quantity of imports adjusts with a mean time-lag $1/\alpha_3$ to the value corresponding to the new exchange rate: this value is $m_0 + dm = m_0 + m_y dy + m_r dr$ where m_0 is the initial quantity; from the first equation in (A.14.14) we then have $dy = [(d_r + x_r)/(1 - d_y)] dr^8$. System (A.14.16) is diagonal and has the explicit solution

$$p_{hm}(t) = A_1 e^{-\alpha_1 t} + (r_0 + dr) p_m,$$

$$x(t) = A_2 e^{-\alpha_2 t} + (x_0 + x_r dr), \qquad \text{(A.14.17)}$$

$$m(t) = A_3 e^{-\alpha_3 t} + \left(m_0 + m_y \frac{x_r + d_r}{1 - d_y} dr + m_r dr \right),$$

where the arbitrary constant A_1, A_2, A_3 can be determined by means of the initial conditions. Thus we get

$$A_1 = -p_m dr, \quad A_2 = -x_r dr, \quad A_3 = -m_y \frac{x_r + d_r}{1 - d_y} dr - m_r dr. \qquad \text{(A.14.18)}$$

---

[6] Since p_m and p_x have been assumed constant, they may be conventionally set at one. For an analysis in which p_x changes as a consequence of the devaluation see, for example, Casprini (1977).

[7] We are considering the various periods as dynamically related through mean time-lags. On partial adjustment equations and mean time-lags see, for example, Gandolfo, 1981, Sect. 1.2.

[8] This implies the simplifying assumption that the income determination equation holds instantaneously. Greater generality would be achieved by introducing an adjustment lag on income as well, but this would complicate the analysis without substantially altering the results.

180   14 The Absorption Approach and Interactions

For notational convenience we define

$$r_0 + dr \equiv r_n, \quad x_0 + x_r dr \equiv x_n, \quad m_0 + m_y \frac{x_r + d_r}{1 - d_y} dr + m_r dr \equiv m_n. \tag{A.14.19}$$

If we now substitute Eqs. (A.14.17) in the second equation of (A.14.14) we immediately obtain the time path of the balance of payments

$$B(t) = A_2 e^{-\alpha_2 t} + x_n - (A_1 e^{-\alpha_1 t} + r_n p_m)(A_3 e^{-\alpha_3 t} + m_n). \tag{A.14.20}$$

From this equation we see that, as t tends to infinity, $B(t)$ converges to the value $B_n = x_n - r_n p_m m_n$ that is the value $B_0 + dB$, where $dB = (dB/dr) dr$ is equal, as it must be, to the value which can be derived from Eq. (A.14.15). Since we have already assumed above that $dB > 0$, it follows that $B_n > B_0$. Thus, when the adjustment process has worked itself out, the balance of payments will certainly improve, because the limit to which $B(t)$ converges is $B_n > B_0$. But what happens in the meantime? To answer this question we can use Eq. (A.14.20) to calculate the derivative

$$\frac{dB}{dt} = -\alpha_2 A_2 e^{-\alpha_2 t} + \alpha_1 A_1 e^{-\alpha_1 t}(A_3 e^{-\alpha_3 t} + m_n)$$
$$+ \alpha_3 A_3 e^{-\alpha_3 t}(A_1 e^{-\alpha_1 t} + r_n p_m), \tag{A.14.21}$$

and see whether $dB/dt \gtreqless 0$. If dB/dt is always positive, the balance of payments will improve from the beginning, whilst if $dB/dt < 0$ for "small" t, the balance of payments will initially deteriorate before improving (even if initially $dB/dt < 0$, it will have to be positive subsequently, given the assumption that $B_n > B_0$). Now, for sufficiently small t, the exponential functions in (A.14.21) are approximately equal to one, so that

$$\left(\frac{dB}{dt}\right)_{t \cong 0} \cong -\alpha_2 A_2 + \alpha_1 A_1 (A_3 + m_n) + \alpha_3 A_3 (A_1 + r_n p_m). \tag{A.14.22}$$

By using the definitions of A_i, m_n, r_n given in Eqs. (A.14.18) and (A.14.19), we get

$$\left(\frac{dB}{dt}\right)_{t \cong 0} \cong \left[\alpha_2 x_r - \alpha_1 p_m m_0 - \alpha_3 \left(m_y \frac{x_r + d_r}{1 - d_y} + m_r\right) r_0 p_m\right] dr, \tag{A.14.22.1}$$

whose sign is determined by the expression in square brackets. If the adjustment speeds α_i were approximately equal, the expression under consideration would be positive owing to the assumed positivity of (A.14.15)[9]. But since we have assumed that α_1 is much greater than α_2 and α_3, it is quite possible that the negative term $-\alpha_1 p_m m_0$ prevails (note that the term containing α_3 has an ambiguous sign), so that expression (A.14.22.1) may well turn out to be negative.

In conclusion, we can say that the result depends essentially on the adjustment lags of prices and quantities. If these lags are similar, then the balance of payments will presumably improve from the beginning provided that the conditions for its

---

[9] We must bear in mind that the magnitudes appearing on the right-hand side of Eq. (A.14.15) are evaluated at the initial point, so that $m = m_0$ etc.

final improvement are fulfilled. If, on the contrary, prices adjust much more rapidly than quantities, then — even if the conditions for a final improvement are fulfilled — the balance of payments will initially deteriorate before improving. Therefore, if one believes that the mean time-lag of quantities is much higher than that of prices, then the *J*-curve will have to be considered, as it were, a physiological event in the context of the model under consideration.

A.14.4 The Original Two-Country Version of the Laursen and Metzler Model[10]

A.14.4.1 The Basic Model

Let Y be national money income; assuming that the prices of domestic goods and services are constant (we can then, without loss of generality, put the price level equal to 1), variations in Y measure variations in the physical output. The subscripts 1 and 2 refer to country 1 (e.g., the home country) and country 2 (e.g., the rest of the world), in a two-country world.

Imports M are measured in local currency (i.e. the currency of the importing country), and are assumed to depend on national income and on the relative price of imports with respect to home goods; given the assumption that in each country the price level of home goods is constant, this relative price is measured by the exchange rate. The exchange rate r is defined as the number of units of the currency of country 1 for one unit of the currency of country 2; of course, from the point of view of the other country, the exchange rate is $1/r$. Now, an increase in national income has a positive effect on imports, whereas the effect of a variation in the exchange rate is uncertain, since it depends on the elasticity of the demand for imports (remember that we are dealing not with physical quantities, but with expenditure on imported goods).

For brevity, aggregate national expenditure (consumption plus investment) is indicated as ω. The marginal propensity to spend (the marginal propensity to consume plus the marginal propensity to invest) is, of course, positive, and is assumed to be less than 1.

Another variable which influences ω is the relative price r of imports. This is an important point and must be discussed further.

Total expenditure ω includes both expenditure on domestic and on foreign goods. Now, if we did not take account of r as an argument on which ω depends, we would implicitly assume that when the price of imports changes, the consequent change in the expenditure on imports is exactly offset by a change of equal absolute amount, and in the opposite direction, in the expenditure on domestic goods, so that the total expenditure ω remains the same. This sounds rather unrealistic, so that an effect of r on ω must be introduced. It remains to determine the nature of this effect. Let us consider a fall in the relative price of imports. Since the prices of domestic goods have been assumed constant, this fall means a fall in the absolute price of imports. This, of course, increases the real income corresponding to any given level of money income. Now, the short-run

---

[10] The treatment of this section draws heavily on Gandolfo (1980, pp. 327–334 and 391–393).

consumption function is non-proportional, so that the average propensity to consume decreases as real income increases, and vice versa. From this it follows that "as import prices fall and the real income corresponding to a given money income increases, the amount spent on goods and services out of a given money income will fall. The argument is applicable in reverse, of course, to a rise of import prices. In short, our basic premise is that, other things being the same, the expenditure schedule of any given country rises when import prices rise and falls when import prices fall" (Laursen and Metzler, 1950, p. 286)[11].

We can express all this formally as follows:

$$\omega_1 = \omega_1(Y_1, r), \qquad 0 < \frac{\partial \omega_1}{\partial Y_1} < 1, \qquad \frac{\partial \omega_1}{\partial r} > 0,$$

$$\omega_2 = \omega_2\left(Y_2, \frac{1}{r}\right), \qquad 0 < \frac{\partial \omega_2}{\partial Y_2} < 1, \qquad \frac{\partial \omega_2}{\partial (1/r)} > 0,$$

$$M_1 = M_1(Y_1, r), \qquad 0 < \frac{\partial M_1}{\partial Y_1} < 1, \qquad \frac{\partial M_1}{\partial r}?$$

$$M_2 = M_2\left(Y_2, \frac{1}{r}\right), \qquad 0 < \frac{\partial M_2}{\partial Y_2} < 1, \qquad \frac{\partial M_2}{\partial (1/r)}?$$

The static model consists in the following equations

$$Y_1 = \omega_1(Y_1, r) + rM_2\left(Y_2, \frac{1}{r}\right) - M_1(Y_1, r),$$

$$Y_2 = \omega_2\left(Y_2, \frac{1}{r}\right) + \frac{1}{r}M_1(Y_1, r) - M_2\left(Y_2, \frac{1}{r}\right), \qquad (A.14.23)$$

$$B_2 = \frac{1}{r}M_1(Y_1, r) - M_2\left(Y_2, \frac{1}{r}\right),$$

The first and second equations express the national income determination in the two countries (remember that exports of country 1 are the imports of country 2 and vice versa; exports must be multiplied by the exchange rate to convert them into local currency). The third equation defines the balance of payments of country 2, expressed in country 2's currency; there is no need of a separate equation for the balance of payments of country 1, since in our two-country world the balance of payments of country 1 equals minus the balance of payments of country 2 multiplied by r.

The above model is indeterminate, since there are three equations and four unknowns (Y_1, Y_2, r, B_2). Thus we can use the degree of freedom to impose the

---

[11] This effect was independently stated also by Harberger (1950), who however, was using a static model. For recent theoretical studies of this effect see Svensson and Razin (1983) and Persson and Svensson (1985). The empirical evidence has been examined by Deardoff and Stern (1978a) and Obstfeld (1982).

Appendix 183

condition that the balance of payments is in equilibrium, i.e. $B_2 = 0$, so that we have

$$Y_1 = \omega_1(Y_1, r),$$

$$Y_2 = \omega_2\left(Y_2, \frac{1}{r}\right), \qquad (A.14.24)$$

$$\frac{1}{r} M_1(Y_1, r) - M_2\left(Y_2, \frac{1}{r}\right) = 0,$$

which determine the equilibrium point Y_1^e, Y_2^e, r^e.

A.14.4.2 Stability

Let us now consider the adjustment process. The behaviour assumptions are the usual ones, i.e.

(1) The level of national income (output) varies in relation to excess demand, and, more precisely, it tends to increase if aggregate demand exceeds aggregate supply (i.e. the level of current output), and to decrease in the opposite case. This behaviour assumption is commonly considered valid in the context of a model with rigid prices and less than full employment. It must be noted that, since we are examining disequilibrium situations, the excess demands must be computed using (A.14.23) and not (A.14.24) as the latter equations refer only to the equilibrium situation. Thus excess demand in country 1 is

$$[\omega_1(Y_1, r) + r M_2(Y_2, 1/r) - M_1(Y_1, r)] - Y_1,$$

and similarly for country 2.

(2) The rate of exchange, which is the price of the foreign currency, tends to increase (decrease) if in the foreign exchange market there is a positive (negative) excess demand for the foreign currency. We assume that the dominant currency, which is used in international transactions, is the currency of country 2. Thus the relevant price is r; the demand for such currency emanates from the import demand of country 1 and so is $(1/r)M_1$, the supply emanates from export revenue and so is M_2.

The above assumptions can be formally expressed by the following system of differential equations

$$\frac{dY_1}{dt} = k_1 \left[\omega_1(Y_1, r) + r M_2\left(Y_2, \frac{1}{r}\right) - M_1(Y_1, r) - Y_1 \right],$$

$$\frac{dY_2}{dt} = k_2 \left[\omega_2\left(Y_2, \frac{1}{r}\right) + \frac{1}{r} M_1(Y_1, r) - M_2\left(Y_2, \frac{1}{r}\right) - Y_2 \right], \qquad (A.14.25)$$

$$\frac{dr}{dt} = k_3 \left[\frac{1}{r} M_1(Y_1, r) - M_2\left(Y_2, \frac{1}{r}\right) \right],$$

where k_1, k_2, k_3 are positive constants. The linearization of this system and the study of the stability conditions involve lengthy and tedious manipulations, for which we refer the reader to Gandolfo (1980, pp. 330–3). The interesting thing is that all the stability conditions boil down to the crucial inequality

$$\eta_1 + \eta_2 > 1 + \frac{1}{M_1}\left(\frac{m_1 s_1}{1-w_1} + \frac{m_2 s_2}{1-w_2}\right), \quad (A.14.26)$$

where $m_i \equiv \partial M_i/\partial Y_i$, $s_1 \equiv \partial \omega_1/\partial r$, $s_2 \equiv \partial \omega_2/\partial(1/r)$, $w_i \equiv \partial w_i/\partial Y_i$, and η_1, η_2 are the price elasticities of the import demands of the two countries. The result found in the simple one-country model is therefore confirmed in the context of this more general two-country model.

A.14.4.3 Comparative Statics

Let us introduce a parameter α_1 representing an exogenous increase in country 1's aggregate demand. Thus we have

$$Y_1 = \omega_1(Y_1, r) + \alpha_1,$$

$$Y_2 = \omega_2\left(Y_2, \frac{1}{r}\right), \quad (A.14.27)$$

$$\frac{1}{r} M_1(Y_1, r) = M_2\left(Y_2, \frac{1}{r}\right).$$

On the assumption that the suitable conditions concerning the Jacobian are verified, there exist the differentiable functions

$$Y_1 = Y_1(\alpha_1),$$
$$Y_2 = Y_2(\alpha_1), \quad (A.14.28)$$
$$r = r(\alpha_1).$$

The multiplier we are interested in is given by the derivative $dY_1/d\alpha_1$; as a by-product we shall also obtain the derivatives $dY_2/d\alpha_1$ and $dr/d\alpha_1$. Differentiating totally Eqs. (A.14.27) with respect to α_1 — account being taken of Eqs. (A.14.28) —, setting $r=1$ in the initial equilibrium situation (this involves only a change in units of measurement) and rearranging terms, we obtain

$$(1-w_1)\frac{dY_1}{d\alpha_1} - s_1\frac{dr}{d\alpha_1} = 1,$$

$$(1-w_2)\frac{dY_2}{d\alpha_1} + s_2\frac{dr}{d\alpha_1} = 0, \quad (A.14.29)$$

$$-m_1\frac{dY_1}{d\alpha_1} + m_2\frac{dY_2}{d\alpha_1} + M_1(\eta_1+\eta_2-1)\frac{dr}{d\alpha_1} = 0,$$

where the symbols have been defined above. The solution of this system is

$$\frac{dY_1}{d\alpha_1} = \frac{(1-w_2)M_1(\eta_1+\eta_2-1)-m_2s_2}{\Delta},$$

$$\frac{dY_2}{d\alpha_1} = \frac{-m_1s_2}{\Delta}, \qquad (A.14.30)$$

$$\frac{dr}{d\alpha_1} = \frac{m_1(1-w_2)}{\Delta},$$

where

$$\Delta \equiv \begin{vmatrix} 1-w_1 & 0 & -s_1 \\ 0 & 1-w_2 & s_2 \\ -m_1 & m_2 & M_1(\eta_1+\eta_2-1) \end{vmatrix}$$

$$= (1-w_1)(1-w_2)M_1(\eta_1+\eta_2-1) - s_1m_1(1-w_2) - s_2m_2(1-w_1). \qquad (A.14.31)$$

The sign of Δ is indeterminate, since expression (A.14.31) contains both positive and negative terms and also a term whose sign is not known *a priori*, i.e. $(\eta_1+\eta_2-1)$. However, from the dynamic analysis we know that a necessary (and in this case also sufficient) stability condition is that $\Delta>0$: see condition (A.14.26). Moreover, $\Delta>0$ implies that

$$(1-w_2)M_1(\eta_1+\eta_2-1)-m_2s_2>0,$$

as can easily be seen from the fact that $\Delta>0$ can be rewritten as

$$(1-w_2)M_1(\eta_1+\eta_2-1)-m_2s_2>s_1m_1\frac{1-w_2}{1-w_1},$$

where the right-hand side is a positive quantity as $0<w_i<1$. Thus we may conclude that $dY_1/d\alpha_1>0$, $dr/d\alpha_1>0$, $dY_2/d\alpha_1<0$.

The fact that, notwithstanding the full flexibility of the exchange rate, a change in income in country 1 brings about a change in income in country 2, is sufficient to show the falsity of the opinion which attributes an insulating property to flexible exchange rates. The fact is that, although the exchange rate adjusts so as to eliminate any effect of the trade balance, keeping it at a zero level, the variations in the exchange rate, however, have a direct effect on aggregate expenditure $C+I$. It follows that $Y=C+I+x-M$ cannot remain constant, although $x-M=0$. This is the essence of Laursen's and Metzler's argument. The conclusion reached above on the signs of $dY_1/d\alpha_1$ and of $dr/d\alpha_1$ are no surprise: an increase in autonomous expenditure in country 1, account being taken of all the repercussions, brings about an increase in national income and thus an increase in imports; the consequent deficit in country 1's balance of payments is corrected by a devaluation, that is an increase in r. But the result on the sign of $dY_2/d\alpha_1$ may be somewhat surprising: a boom in one country causes a recession in the other country. However, this result will become intuitively clear if we remember that an increase in r — that is, an *appreciation* in country 2's currency — brings about a *fall* in the aggregate expenditure schedule of country 2, whose national income must therefore decrease, as the balance of trade is in equilibrium.

The problem of the insulating power of flexible exchange rates will be taken up again in Sect. 16.4.

References

Alexander, S.S., 1952
Alexander, S.S., 1959
Casprini, F., 1977
Deardoff, A.V. and R.M. Stern, 1978a
Dornbusch, R., 1980, Chap. 4
Gandolfo, G., 1980, 326–335
Gandolfo, G., 1981, Chap. 1, Sect. 1.2
Harberger, A.C., 1950
Johnson, H.G., 1956 (especially, Sect. III of the 1958 reprint)
Johnson, H.G., 1958a
Laursen, S. and L.A. Metzler, 1950
Machlup, F., 1955
Machlup, F., 1956
Magee, S.P., 1973
Masera, R.S., 1974
Niehans, J., 1984, Chap. 4, Sect. 3; Chap. 5
NIESR, 1968
Obstfeld, M., 1982
Persson, T. and L.E.O. Svensson, 1985
Rose, A.K. and J.L. Yellen, 1989
Scitovsky, T., 1969, Chap. XIII, Sect. A and Appendix
Stern, R.M., 1973, Chap. 7
Stolper, W.F., 1950
Svensson, L.E.O. and A. Razin, 1983
Swan, A.P., 1955
Thirlwall, A.P., 1959
Tsiang, S.C., 1961
Wood, G., 1991

15 Money and Other Assets in the Adjustment Process under Fixed Exchange Rates

15.1 Introduction

As mentioned in Sect. 11.4, we propose in the present chapter to begin the examination of the processes of adjustment of the balance of payments in which money plays an essential part and in which stock disequilibria are taken into consideration. The prototype of the processes in which money-stock disequilibria regulate the whole is the classical model of gold flows (flows which derive precisely from the adjustment of stocks) that goes back to Hume (1752), to which — with a jump of more than two hundred years — the proponents of the monetary approach to the balance of payments declare their allegiance.

On the other hand, the introduction of money and the rate of interest into the traditional Keynesian model — which comes about by extending the well-known IS-LM model of a closed economy to an open one — does not alter the view of the disequilibria in the balance of payments as flow disequilibria and its adjustments as flow adjustments. The role of the money market is in fact to determine the interest rate on which depend, among other things, the capital movements, understood as pure flows and not as flows that derive from the adjustments of stocks.

It is however possible to go beyond the various views by way of the analysis of the relationships between portfolio equilibrium and macroeconomic equilibrium in an open economy.

During the course of our treatment of this subject, in addition to the questions of spontaneous adjustment mechanisms, we shall tackle those connected with policy interventions which aim to achieve internal equilibrium (full employment) as well as external equilibrium (equilibrium in the balance of payments).

15.2 The Classical (Humean) Price-Specie-Flow Mechanism

15.2.1 Introductory Remarks

The first complete formulation of the classical theory of the mechanism for the adjustment of the balance of payments based on the flows of money (gold) is commonly associated with the name of David Hume (1752), although the most important elements that go to make up the theory itself had been established by earlier writers. The theory can be summed up as follows: a surplus in the balance of payments causes an inflow of gold into a country, that is to say — as there is a strict connection between gold reserves and the amount of money — it causes an increase in prices (the quantity theory of money is assumed to be valid). This increase tends on the one hand to reduce exports, as the goods of the country in question become relatively more expensive on the international market, and on the other, it stimulates imports, as foreign goods become relatively cheaper. There is thus a gradual reduction in the balance-of-payments surplus. An analogous piece of reasoning is used to explain the adjustment in the case of a deficit: there is an outflow of gold which causes a reduction in the stock of money and a reduction in domestic prices, with a consequent stimulation of exports and a reduction of imports, which thus leads to a gradual elimination of the deficit itself.

Leaving aside the question of whether the conclusion arrived at, as to the automatic adjustment of the balance of payments, is valid or not, even if we accept all the hypotheses on which this reasoning is based (the gold standard, the validity of the quantity theory of money, etc.), there still remain problems that have to be faced. The first is that, in the theory examined, balance of payments is taken to mean trade balance.

The second question is strictly connected with the mechanism already described (in effect it is neither more nor less than a different way of looking at the same thing). It consists in the problem of the *optimum distribution of specie*. As the level of prices in each country, under the gold standard, and under the assumption that the quantity theory of money is valid, depends on the quantity of gold that exists in the country and as the balance of payments of a country can be in equilibrium only when the levels of domestic and foreign prices, on which both imports and exports depend, are in fact such as to ensure this equilibrium, then it follows that the equilibrium under consideration corresponds to a very precise distribution (in fact known as the *optimum* distribution), among all countries, of the total amount of gold available in the world. If this balanced distribution is altered in any way, then upsets in the levels of prices will follow, with payments imbalances and therefore flows of gold which, by way of the mechanism described above, will automatically re-establish the balance.

The description of these mechanisms is clearly stated in Hume's work, where he uses an example which is well worth quoting. In order to understand the spirit of this example it is necessary briefly to put Hume's work in economics into proper perspective. His essays in economics consist of a series of critical comments on the economic thought of his age, so that there is very little in these writings which is not discussed in a polemical frame of reference. Practically all the essays take the form of a debate in which Hume attempts to expound and rectify what he considers to be the main errors in the economic thought of his times. The object of his essay "Of the Balance of Trade" (1752) is precisely a confutation of the doctrine of the mercantilists, who advocated a balance of payments permanently in surplus so as to obtain a continual inflow of gold into the country and who, when faced with a deficit, pointed to the danger that the outflow of gold from the country would — in the absence of any restrictions — end up by draining away England's entire gold supply.

After some historical comments, Hume takes his cue from certain writings of the mercantilist, Joshua Gee, who twenty years earlier had (in Hume's words) caused a panic in the country. Gee's writings claimed to demonstrate — Hume continues — that "the balance was against them for so considerable a sum as must leave them without a single shilling in five or six years. But luckily, twenty years have since elapsed, with an expensive foreign war; yet is it commonly supposed, that money is still more plentiful among us than in any former period" (p. 26 of the 1969 reprint).

After making some points, Hume declares his aim to be that of formulating a general argument which will demonstrate that it is impossible for the event feared by Gee to occur. At this point Hume produces the example mentioned above. Let us suppose that suddenly four-fifths of all the money that exists in England were destroyed. Market prices and wages would fall in proportion, no other country would be able to meet the competition of the British on the international market and in a short time Britain would recover the money that had been destroyed. This would eliminate the British superiority, because prices would once again rise and further inflows of gold would be halted. By the same token, if we suppose that the money existing in England were suddenly increased fivefold, then wages and the prices of goods would rise to such high levels that no country would be able to afford British goods, while foreign goods would become so relatively cheap as to cause an increase in imports and thus an exit of money, until a new equilibrium was reached.

The same forces which cause the situation to be re-established after such exceptional happenings as those in the above hypothesis would, Hume continues, prevent a permanent disequilibrium from coming about also in the ordinary course of events.

The third observation concerns the fact that Hume identified another cause that contributes to the adjustment, namely the fluctuation of the rate of exchange between those values which, to use a more recent terminology, are known as gold points (which are calculated by adding or subtracting from the mint parity — which is determined by the ratio between the gold content of the two currencies — cost of transport, insurance, etc., of gold between the two markets: cfr. Sect. 10.5.1). However, it must be noticed that these fluctuations may be sufficient only in the presence of slight disturbances, while in the case of larger ones it is necessary to rely on the mechanism previously described. This opinion — which is undoubtedly correct — must also have been Hume's, who mentions these fluctuations only in a note, while the text is dedicated to the explanation of the mechanism based on the flow of gold.

The distinction between the two mechanisms was later explained more clearly by other classical economists. For example, John Stuart Mill distinguished between small-size accidental disturbances which can be corrected by fluctuations in the exchange rate between the two gold points, without movement of gold, and disturbances that derive from causes concerning the price levels, which can only be corrected by the movement of gold in accordance with the now well-known mechanism.

In the rest of our treatment of this subject we shall concentrate our attention only on the mechanism based on flows of gold, which forms the core of the adjustment of the balance of payments under the conditions hypothesized.

Hume's theory was accepted by later writers. Schumpeter wrote (1954, p. 367): "In fact it is not far from the truth to say that Hume's theory, including his overemphasis on price movements as the vehicle of adjustments, remained substantially unchallenged until the twenties of this century." We shall therefore refer to the classical theory as explained up to this point.

15.2.2 A Simple Model of the Classical Theory

A rigorous examination of the classical adjustment mechanism is carried out here through the construction of a model[1] (Gandolfo, 1966) in which the classical hypotheses are incorporated, then by studying its characteristics and above all its dynamic behaviour. Besides the existence of the gold standard and the validity of the quantity theory of money, these hypotheses are as follows:

(1) That there exists a situation of free trade with no interference on the part of the public authorities or of monopolistic agents.

(2) Productive activity is given and is constant. The hypothesis of a constant level of productive activity is necessary so that given variations in the money supply are translated unequivocally, velocity of circulation being constant, into given variations in the level of prices. It should be remembered that, according to the classical writers, this constant level is that of full employment.

(3) Given that, on the basis of the gold standard, the rate of exchange is fixed, it may be supposed, without any loss of generality (in fact an appropriate choice of units of measurement is sufficient), that it is equal to one. Furthermore it is assumed that international payments are made in gold.

(4) Variations in the money supply can occur only as a result of surpluses or deficits in the balance of payments. Note that, in the case of paper currency, circulation must be of the type with a 100% gold reserve or with a fixed fractional gold reserve. While in the first case, as with the circulation of gold, the variations in the quantity of money are equal to the imbalances in international payments (which, as we have seen, are made in gold), in the second case the variations themselves are a multiple of the same surplus or deficit. This does not substantially alter the following analysis.

(5) For the sake of simplicity, cost of transport, insurance, etc., are neglected.

The above-mentioned hypotheses are all, with the exception only of those introduced in order to simplify matters, either explicitly or implicitly present in the classical adjustment model described at the outset. However, it seemed useful to state them explicitly, both for greater clarity and to avoid having to refer back to them during the course of the examination of the model, which we shall now consider. So as not to complicate matters, only one country is taken into consideration and no explicit account is taken of the rest of the world: it is, then, in the terminology of Sect. 11.4, a one-country model. The construction of the model includes two successive phases which, naturally, are interdependent: one phase is

---

[1] For an alternative model, which emphasizes capital flows and banking policy as the main factors in the adjustment process, see Dornbusch and Frenkel (1984). Another view is held by Niehans (1984, pp. 44 ff.), who believes that the decisive element is the reaction of commodity demand to excess cash balances, much like the mechanism championed by the monetary approach to the balance of payments (see Sect. 15.3.1).

15.2 The Classical (Humean) Price-Specie-Flow Mechanism

related to the situation of equilibrium and the other to the mechanism of adjustment in the case of disequilibrium. The model can be expressed by the following system of equations:

$$MV = py, \qquad (15.1)$$

where M indicates the money supply, V the velocity of circulation, p the general level of prices and y the level of productive activity; V and y are considered to be constant, i.e. (15.1) expresses the quantity theory of money. We now pass to exports (x) and imports (m) in physical terms, which depend on the level of prices:

$$x = x(p), \qquad (15.2)$$

$$m = m(p), \qquad (15.3)$$

where $x(p)$ is a decreasing function of p (if p increases exports decrease and vice versa), while $m(p)$ is an increasing function of p, (if p increases imports increase and vice versa); it goes without saying that in this case, the imperfect substitutability between national and foreign goods is assumed, as in Sect. 12.1. Finally we have the equation

$$B = px(p) - p_m m(p) = 0, \qquad (15.4)$$

which expresses the balance-of-payments equilibrium. The value of exports is in fact equal to the product of the quantity of exports times their price, which given the assumptions made above, coincides with the domestic price. Similarly, by multiplying the quantity of imports by their price, indicated by p_m, we obtain the value of imports. Note that in this model p_m equals the international price of the goods imported and is an exogenous datum, given the hypothesis of the one-country model[2].

Before going any further, it will be as well to observe that the model can be interpreted in two different ways (without that meaning any difference in the results). One way is to take it as a macroeconomic model, in which case y must be given the meaning of real national income, while py, obviously, is the corresponding money income. The other way to interpret the model is to consider a country that produces only one good in a given quantity y and exports a part of it (x) and uses the other part domestically ($y-x$), and imports another good (m). The above-mentioned goods can naturally be composite goods, that is "baskets" in which the various goods (produced domestically and imported respectively) enter in fixed and constant proportions. The second interpretation seems to be more rigorously logical, even if less realistic. This discussion into the degree of rigour of more or less aggregated macroeconomic models — which is proceeding actively in other branches of the science of economics — cannot be entered into here, so we shall leave the question of the two interpretations open. On the other hand, as we have already seen, the acceptance of one or the other interpretation does not change the conclusions to be reached with regard to the problem of adjustment under examination.

---

[2] This is the same as assuming that the country is small enough for the flows of gold into and out of it to have no appreciable influence on the level of prices in the rest of the world.

Returning to the system expressed by Eqs. (15.1) – (15.4), it is determined, because there are four equations to determine the values of equilibrium of the four unknowns M,x,m,p, which will be indicated by M^e,x^e,m^e,p^e. Note that *the value of equilibrium of M is an unknown*, determined by the system: in fact the system cannot be in equilibrium if the quantity of money is not such as to furnish a value of p which is precisely the one which ensures equilibrium of the balance of payments. This confirms what has already been said above with regard to the connection between the equilibrium in the balance of payments and the optimum distribution of gold among the various countries.

We now come to the mechanism of adjustment proper. If the balance of payments is not in equilibrium, there will be flows of gold which will set the process already described into motion. Formally, the basic hypothesis of this process can be described by the following equation:

$$\Delta M = px(p) - p_m m(p), \tag{15.5}$$

which expresses the fact that the variation in the quantity of money is equal, in absolute value and sign, to the payments imbalance.

It is possible to give a simple graphic representation of the dynamic behaviour of the system. In Fig. 15.1a, we represent the function which defines the payments imbalance. For simplicity's sake, this function is assumed to be linear. In other words, the straight line is the graphic equivalent of $B = px(p) - p_m m(p)$. This straight line intersects the horizontal axis in correspondence with the price p^e: that is to say at the point where the condition (15.4) occurs ($B=0$), and so p^e is the price level which assures equilibrium in the balance of payments. In Fig. 15.1b is the representation of Eq. (15.1), which is linear by definition. The equilibrium value of the quantity of money is M^e, which in fact gives rise to the price level p^e: note that the p^e in part b of the graph coincides with the one in part a.

Let us now suppose that the system is in disequilibrium, for example at p', which corresponds to M' in b and that there is a deficit in the balance of payments measured by the segment $p'A'$ in a. In this case there is an outflow of gold exactly equal to $p'A'$, so that the quantity of money is reduced to M'': the segment $M'M''$ in b is equal to segment $p'A'$ in a. The movement from A' to A'' in consequence of, and in equal measure to, the deficit $p'A'$, can be considered approximately the equivalent of Eq. (15.5). As a result of the reduction in the quantity of money, prices are reduced to p'' as can be seen in b. By transferring p'' to part a it will be seen that the deficit is now $p''A''$: in other words, the balance of payments is still in deficit, but for a smaller amount than before. There will be a fresh outflow of gold $p''A'' = M''M'''$, prices drop still further to p''' and so on, with a tendency to reach equilibrium. The arrows in the diagram indicate the direction in which the different variables move: all tend towards equilibrium.

With similar reasoning, it can be seen that, other things being equal, there is also a tendency towards equilibrium whenever p' is to the left of p^e: the reader might like to ascertain, as an exercise, that the surplus causes an increase in the quantity of money and therefore in prices, which reduces the surplus, etc.

So far we have been examining the case of *stability*. The case of instability occurs when B is increasing rather than decreasing in the neighbourhood of p^e. In

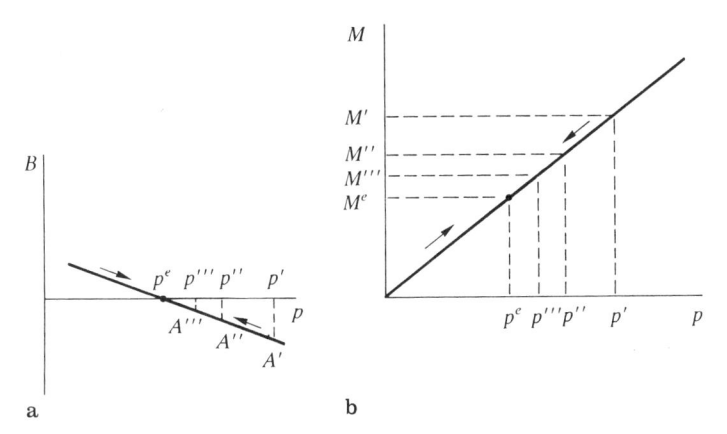

15.2 The Classical (Humean) Price-Specie-Flow Mechanism

Fig. 15.1. Graphic representation of the classical theory of the adjustment mechanism of the balance of payments

this situation, as can easily be established graphically with an appropriate modification to Fig. 15.1a, that is, by drawing an increasing instead of a decreasing line, each disequilibrium tends to get worse. We have thus reached a first important conclusion, namely that the automatic adjustment mechanism does not necessarily work in the direction wanted: it occurs, that is, only if certain conditions are fulfilled.

These conditions can be expressed in the diagram by the decreasing slope of B in Fig. 15.1a. We must now ask ourselves what the economic meaning of this slope is and what hypotheses need to be made for it to occur. From a simple examination of the graph, we can clearly see that the decreasing slope of the line B means that *a variation in the level of prices causes the balance of payments to vary in the opposite direction*, and, more accurately, a reduction (increase) in this level improves (or worsens, respectively) the balance itself. This does not occur of necessity, because it depends essentially on the elasticity of exports and imports with respect to prices. It is in fact true that, for instance, a reduction of p causes exports to increase and imports to fall, but, while the value of imports (that is $p_m m$) is reduced as the price p_m has, by hypothesis, remained unvaried, the value of exports (that is, px) can, in principle, either increase or decrease. When it increases there is undoubtedly an improvement in the balance of payments, while in the case in which it decreases the balance can either improve or deteriorate, according to whether the reduction in the value of imports is greater or less in absolute terms than the reduction in the value of exports. As we said above, the result depends on the price elasticity of imports and exports, defined as usual as the ratio between the proportional variation in the quantity and the proportional variation in the price:

$$\eta_m \equiv \frac{\Delta m/m}{\Delta p/p}, \quad \eta_x \equiv -\frac{\Delta x/x}{\Delta p/p}, \qquad (15.6)$$

where the minus sign before the fraction in the expression for η_x serves to make η_x a positive value (Δx and Δp, for reasons already given, have in fact opposite signs).

Let us now consider the case of a reduction in price[3], for example of one per cent. On the basis of (15.6), we have $\Delta m/m = \eta_m(\Delta p/p)$ and therefore imports are reduced by $\eta_m\%$. As p_m is constant by hypothesis, the value of imports also decreases by $\eta_m\%$. If we apply this percentage to the initial value of the imports we have the absolute value of the reduction in outlay for imports, which is thus $\eta_m p_m m/100$.

As regards exports, as $\Delta x/x = -\eta_x(\Delta p/p)$, the one per cent reduction in the price causes exports to rise by $\eta_x\%$, and therefore, given the well-known relationship between elasticity and total revenue, the value of exports will increase if $\eta_x > 1$, and decrease if $\eta_x < 1$.

In the first case the balance of payments will certainly improve, while in the second case, if it is to improve, the reduction in the value of imports must exceed the reduction in the value of exports. Now, when $\eta_x < 1$, the reduction in the revenue from exports, following a 1% reduction in price, is approximately $(1 - \eta_x)\%$[4] and, if we apply this percentage to the initial value of exports, we obtain the absolute value of the reduction in revenue for exports, which is therefore $(1 - \eta_x)px/100$. Thus the condition needed for the balance of payments to improve is that

$$\eta_m p_m m > (1 - \eta_x) px, \tag{15.7}$$

that is, with simple passages,

$$\frac{p_m m}{px} \eta_m + \eta_x > 1. \tag{15.8}$$

In the case in which the initial situation is in equilibrium, that is, $p_m m = px$, (15.8) becomes

$$\eta_m + \eta_x > 1, \tag{15.8.1}$$

that is, the sum of the elasticities of imports and exports must be greater than one.

It is easy to see that, if the balance of payments is initially in deficit, the coefficient of η_m is greater than one ($p_m m > px$) and therefore, with the same value

---

[3] The case of an increase in price is entirely symmetrical.

[4] We shall indicate the value of exports with $R = px$. If p varies and passes to $p + \Delta p$, the new value is $(p + \Delta p) \cdot (x + \Delta x)$, since as a consequence of the variation in p, x also varies, passing to $x + \Delta x$. Thus the variation in value, ΔR, is given by $\Delta R = (p + \Delta p)(x + \Delta x) - px = x\Delta p + p\Delta x + \Delta p \Delta x$. If we neglect the expression $\Delta p \Delta x$, as it is product of two small variations (which explains that "approximately" in the text), then by dividing both members by $R = px$, we have

$$\frac{\Delta R}{R} = \frac{\Delta p}{p} + \frac{\Delta x}{x} = \frac{\Delta p}{p}\left(1 + \frac{p}{\Delta p}\frac{\Delta x}{x}\right).$$

Now, as can easily be seen from the definition, $\frac{p}{\Delta p}\frac{\Delta x}{x} = -\eta_x$ and therefore

$$\frac{\Delta R}{R} = \frac{\Delta p}{p}(1 - \eta_x),$$

from which, given that $\Delta p/p = -1\%$, we obtain $\Delta R/R = -(1 - \eta_x)\%$, that is, a percentage reduction of $(1 - \eta_x)\%$, which is the result stated in the text.

of the elasticities, (15.8) is more easily satisfied than (15.8.1). Conversely, if the balance of payments is initially in surplus, the coefficient of η_m is smaller than one, and so, with the same values of the elasticities, it is more difficult to satisfy (15.8) than (15.8.1).

15.2.3 Concluding Remarks

We have thus reached the conclusion that Hume's adjustment mechanism is not, even if we accept all the basic hypotheses, such as to always ensure the adjustment towards equilibrium: for such an adjustment to come about, it is in fact necessary, that the elasticities should satisfy condition (15.8) which we define as a condition of "critical elasticities". This condition is similar to the one we have already met in Sect. 12.2 when dealing with the effects of a variation in the exchange rate. And in fact, in the context examined, the case of a variation in the exchange rate at constant price levels is equivalent to the case of a variation in price levels with a fixed exchange rate. This confirms the observation already made in Sect. 12.1, with regard to the effects of a variation in the terms of trade $\pi = p_x/rp_m$. In fact, once we accept that the key variable which acts upon the demands for imports and exports is the relative price of the goods, π, it becomes irrelevant that π varies because the prices (expressed in the respective national currencies) vary while the exchange rate r is given or because r varies while the prices themselves are given. It is therefore not surprising that the conditions concerning the elasticities are formally the same[5]. However, it is necessary at this point to introduce some important qualifications.

In the first place, the analysis of the effects of a variation in the exchange rate on the balance of payments is a partial equilibrium analysis, as explained in Sect. 12.1, whereas the one examined in the present section is a general equilibrium analysis, in which money, prices and quantities interact. The assumption that y is constant (see above) should not be deceptive: national income is in fact not treated as a constant within the ambit of a *ceteris paribus* clause, but is given at the level of full employment, thanks to the operation of those spontaneous forces which, according to the classical economists[6], keep the "real" system in full employment. These forces are of an exclusively real nature, in that money is a veil, which serves only to determine the absolute level of prices. It is therefore this dichotomy which makes it possible for us to examine the monetary part of the model with a given y, as we have done.

In the second place, bearing in mind the distinction between flow and stock disequilibria (Sect. 11.4), we must note that the analysis of the effects of a variation in the exchange rate on the balance of payments refers to *flow disequilibria* (cfr. Sect. 12.1), while the analysis in the present section refers to *stock disequilibria*. It is likewise true that in this case the balance-of-payments disequilibrium also shows itself — and it could not be otherwise — in a divergence

---

[5] One must not be deceived by the fact that in one case the elasticities have been defined with respect to the exchange rate and in the other with respect to the price. In general, elasticities are defined with respect to π and therefore with respect to the rate of exchange, when prices are constant, and with respect to prices when the rate of exchange is constant.

[6] The term "classical" is used here in Keynes' sense.

between the value of imports and that of exports, but this divergence between the flows is ultimately due to a stock disequilibrium: as we have seen, the balance-of-payments disequilibrium is determined, ultimately, by an inexact distribution of the stock of money (gold) existing in the world, that is to say, a divergence, in each country, between the existing and the optimum stock. It is in this sense that we have talked, in the present context, about a stock disequilibrium. This in substance is the meaning of the idea of "optimum distribution of specie (gold)."

It is from these considerations that the supporters of the monetary approach to the balance of payments took their cue. We shall turn to an examination of this approach in Sect. 15.3.

15.3 The Monetary Approach to the Balance of Payments

15.3.1 The Basic Propositions and Implications

With a leap of over two hundred years, the supporters of the monetary approach to the problem of the balance of payments (which was born during the sixties and widely diffused during the following decade) claim their allegiance to Hume. This claim is justified only in part: it is correct insofar as it finds the final cause of the balance-of-payments disequilibria in a divergence between the quantity of money in existence and the optimum or desired quantity (to be defined in due course). It is incorrect insofar as it expresses the adjustment mechanism, as based on a *direct* effect of money-stock disequilibria on the expenditure functions (demand for goods and services) without any intervention of relative prices (which, on the contrary, it keeps constant at a level determined by purchasing power parity, as we shall see later): we have in fact seen that for Hume the adjustment mechanism acted precisely through changes in relative prices[7].

We shall however leave these problems to historians of economic thought and we shall deal with the monetary approach to the balance of payments[8] (MABP) and try to grasp the main points from the numerous works written by its founders (Johnson, Mundell, Frenkel, etc.).

---

[7] It is as well to warn the reader that certain classical writers admitted the existence of a direct influence of "purchasing power" (identified with the amount of specie in circulation) on imports, by means of which, they believed, it would be possible to re-establish the balance-of-payments equilibrium without movements in prices necessarily intervening. Painstaking research into what the classical economists had to say concerning this influence was carried out by Viner, 1937, to whom we refer the reader. Cfr. also Gandolfo (1966), where it is demonstrated — on the basis of the correspondence between Hume and Oswald — that Hume was indeed aware of the possible existence of a direct influence of purchasing power on imports, but that he deliberately ignored this, as he wanted to stress the play of the movements in prices. Therefore — as Samuelson (1980) also observes — to father the monetary approach to the balance of payments on Hume is in this respect erroneous. For an opposite view see Niehans (1984, pp. 44 ff.) who holds that "... the mechanism has been misnamed: it is indeed a specie-flow mechanism, but prices do not play a crucial role in it. The decisive element is the reaction of commodity demand to excess cash balances" (p. 45).

[8] Although the MABP incorporates some of the ideas of monetarism (for example, that the demand for money is a stable function of few macroeconomic variables) it is not identified — according to its supporters — with monetarism itself. Cfr. Frenkel and Johnson (1976, p. 24).

15.3 The Monetary Approach to the Balance of Payments

The MABP can be summed up in a few basic propositions, from which certain implications for economic policy can be derived. The principal propositions are the following.

Proposition I

The balance of payments is essentially a monetary phenomenon and must therefore be analyzed in terms of adjustment of money stocks. More precisely, the balance-of-payments disequilibria reflect stock disequilibria on the money market (excess demand or supply) and must therefore be analyzed in terms of adjustment of these stocks towards their respective desired levels (it is in fact the disequilibria in stocks which generate adjustment flows). It follows that the demand for money (assumed to be a stable function of few macroeconomic variables) and the supply of money represent the theoretical relations on which the analysis of the balance of payments must be concentrated.

In order to understand fully the meaning of this proposition, we shall begin by examining the initial statement.

That the balance of payments is essentially a monetary phenomenon is obvious (if we take this statement in the trivial sense that the balance of payments has, by its very nature, to do with monetary magnitudes) and a necessary consequence of the accounting relationship examined in Chap. 11. In particular, considering the matrix of real and financial flows illustrated in Sect. 11.3, aggregating the banking sector (commercial and other banks plus the central bank), defining the money stock M as the sum of the monetary base (net of that held by the banks) and bank deposits, by shifting the liability elements to the right[9], we obtain the accounting identity

$$\Delta R + \Delta Q = \Delta M, \tag{15.9}$$

where ΔQ represents the variation of all other assets (excluding international reserves, R) in the consolidated banking sector[10]. From (15.9) it follows that

$$\Delta R = \Delta M - \Delta Q. \tag{15.9.1}$$

---

[9] In carrying out this shift, it is necessary to take into account the instrinsic negative sign of the liability items: cfr. Chap. 11, note 13.

[10] If we consider Table 11.2, and aggregate the columns "Banking" and "Central Bank", we get the budget constraint

$$(\Delta H_b + \Delta H^c) + \Delta D^b + (\Delta N_b + \Delta N_c) + (\Delta R_b + \Delta R_c) + (\Delta F_b + \Delta F_c) = 0,$$

from which, rearranging terms,

$$(\Delta R_c + \Delta F_c) + (\Delta R_b + \Delta F_b + \Delta N_c) = -\Delta D^b - (\Delta H_b + \Delta H^c).$$

Let us now observe that from the second row of Table 11.2 we have

$$-(\Delta H_b + \Delta H^c) = \Delta H_p,$$

and from the third we get

$$-\Delta D^b = \Delta D_p + \Delta D_f.$$

Therefore, if we define

$$\Delta R = \Delta R_c + \Delta F_c,$$
$$\Delta Q = \Delta R_b + \Delta N_b + \Delta F_b + \Delta N_c,$$
$$\Delta M = \Delta D_p + \Delta D_f + \Delta H_p,$$

we obtain Eq. (15.9.1).

Now, as the variation in international reserves is nothing but the overall balance of payments, as already seen in (11.11.1), which in turn coincides on the basis of (15.9.1) with the difference between the variation in the stock of money and the variation in the other financial assets, it is obvious that the balance of payments is a monetary phenomenon. But — and this is the point already stressed in Sect. 11.3 — as it is a question of a mere accounting identity, it is quite incorrect to obtain from it any causal relationships, *sic et simpliciter*. We could in fact say, still on the basis of the accounting identities, that the balance of payments (or more precisely the current account) is a real phenomenon, because, on the bais of (11.1.3), we have

$$EXP - IMP = Y - A,$$

where Y is disposable income and A the absorption.

Thus, in order to derive operational consequences from the statement that the balance of payments is a monetary phenomenon, it is necessary to go beyond the identity (15.9.1) and introduce behaviour hypotheses, and this in fact constitutes the aim of the second part of the proposition under examination.

More precisely, the basic idea is that any monetary disequilibria produce an effect on the aggregate expenditure for goods and services (absorption) in the sense that an excess supply of money causes — *ceteris paribus* — absorption to be greater than income and, conversely, an excess demand for money causes absorption to be smaller than income itself[11]. The connection between the demand for money and the other macroeconomic variables is in turn immediate, given the hypothesis that it is a stable function of few of these variables; it is therefore easy, if the existing money stock is known, to determine the excess demand or supply of money.

On the other hand, the divergence between income and absorption which is created in this way, is necessarily translated into an increase or decrease in the stock of assets owned by the public: in fact, this divergence is the equivalent of one between saving and investment and therefore, given the balance constraint of the private sector (cfr. Sect. 11.3), it is translated into a variation in the stock of assets held by this sector. If, for the sake of simplicity, we introduce the hypothesis that the only asset is money, a variation in the money stock comes about, which in turn, given (15.9.1), coincides with the overall balance of payments.

Ultimately what has happened, through this sequence of effects (for which we shall give a model below) is that an excess demand or supply of money, by causing an excess or deficiency of absorption with respect to national income (product), has been unloaded onto the balance of payments: an excess of absorption means a balance-of-payments deficit (the only way of absorbing more than one produces is to receive from foreign countries more than one supplies to them) and a deficiency in absorption means a balance-of-payments surplus. In other words, if the public has an excess supply of money it gets rid of it by increasing absorption and, ultimately, by passing this excess on to foreign countries in exchange for goods and services (balance-of-payments deficit). If on the other hand the public desires more money than it has in stock, it procures it by reducing absorption and,

---

[11] It is necessary at this point to warn the reader that so far we have not made any distinction between money in nominal terms (M) and money in real terms (M/p), given the hypothesis of a constant price level. It is however important to stress that, in a context of variable prices, what is important is money in real terms.

ultimately, it passes goods and services on to foreign countries in exchange for money (balance-of-payments surplus).

What is implicit in our reasoning is the hypothesis that the level of prices is a datum (otherwise the variations in absorption with respect to income could generate variations in price) and in fact this is what, among other things, the next proposition, No. II, refers to.

Proposition II

There exists an efficient world market for goods, services and assets and that implies, as far as goods are concerned (as usual, goods refers to both goods and services), that the goods themselves must have the same price everywhere (law of one price), naturally account being taken of the rate of exchange (which, it must be remembered, is, by hypothesis, fixed) and therefore that the levels of prices must be connected — if we ignore the cost of transport — by the relationship

$$p = r p_f, \tag{15.10}$$

where p_f is the foreign price level expressed in foreign currency, p is the domestic price level in domestic currency, and r is the exchange rate. Equation (15.10), which is also called the equation of *purchasing power parity*[12], has the effect that, given r and p_f, p will be fixed[13].

Proposition III

Production is given at the level of full employment. This proposition is self-explanatory[14]. From this point of view the strict relationship with the classical theory examined in Sect. 15.2 is clear.

The main policy implications are the following:

Implication I. In a regime of fixed exchange rates, monetary policy does not control the country's money supply. This implication comes directly from the propositions given above and particularly Proposition I. In fact, if the monetary authorities try to create a different money supply from that desired by the public, the sole result will be to generate a balance-of-payments disequilibrium, onto which, as we have seen, the divergence between the existing money stock and the demand for money will be unloaded.

Implication II. The process of adjustment of the balance of payments is automatic and the best thing that the monetary authorities can do is to abstain from all intervention. This implication also derives immediately from the propositions given above and particularly from Proposition I. The balance-of-payments disequilibria are in fact monetary symptoms of money-stock disequilibria which correct themselves in time, if the automatic mechanism of variation in the money stock is allowed to work. If, let us say, there is a balance-of-payments deficit (which is a symptom of an excess supply of money), this deficit will automatically

---

[12] We shall deal more fully with the purchasing power parity later, among other things so as to examine the reasons for deviations from it, in Sect. 18.5.1.

[13] This is under the hypothesis of a one-country model. It is also possible to extend the analysis to two countries and to determine both p and p_f, but the results of the analysis do not change substantially. Cfr. Sect. A.15.2.2.

[14] This leads us to believe that the MABP is a long-term theory, in which it is assumed that production tends towards the level of full employment thanks to price and wage adjustments.

cause a reduction in the stock of money — cfr. (15.9.1), where (as we assumed above) ΔQ is zero — and therefore a movement of this stock towards its desired value. When it reaches this, the deficit in the balance of payments will disappear. It may happen, however, in a fixed exchange regime other than the gold standard, that in the course of this adjustment the stock of international reserves of the country will show signs of exhaustion before equilibrium is reached. In this and only this case, a policy intervention is advisable, which in any case should consist of a monetary restriction (so as to reduce the money supply more rapidly towards its desired value) and not of a devaluation in the exchange rate or any other measure, which are inadvisable palliatives, with purely transitory effects.

15.3.2 A Simple Model

It is possible to give a simple model for the MABP in the basic version so far illustrated. We must remember in the following discussion that the level of prices is considered to be constant.

The first behavioural equation expresses the fact that excess or deficiency of absorption with respect to income varies in relation to the divergence between money supply (M) and demand (L)

$$A = py + \alpha(M-L), \quad 0 < \alpha < 1. \tag{15.11}$$

The parameter α is a coefficient which denotes the intensity of the effect on absorption of a divergence between M and L.

The second behavioural equation expresses the demand for money which is a stable function of income:

$$L = kpy. \tag{15.12}$$

Equation (15.12) can be interpreted as a simple version of the quantity theory of money; alternatively, one can take parameter k (equal to the reciprocal of the velocity of circulation of money) as a function of the interest rate (in which case the demand for money becomes a function of this variable). However, given Proposition II, i is a datum [15] and therefore L becomes in point of fact a function of income only.

We then have an accounting equation, which expresses the fact that — if we assume that money is the sole asset in existence — the excess of income over expenditure coincides with an increase in the money stock held by the public (monetary base in the hands of the public plus bank deposits) and vice versa, as can be seen from the matrix of real and financial flows illustrated in Sect. 11.3 [16].

The equation under examination is thus

$$\Delta M = py - A. \tag{15.13}$$

---

[15] The hypothesis of efficient markets (Proposition II) in fact implies that the national interest rate cannot diverge from the value which ensures the condition of interest parity (cfr. Sect. 10.3). Therefore, as the rate of exchange (spot and forward) and the foreign interest rate are given, the national interest rate is fixed.

[16] Formally (15.13) is obtained from the accounting identities (11.7), (11.2), (11.3), by putting $\Delta N_p = \Delta F_p = 0$, taking account of the intrinsic signs, remembering that $S - I = Y - A$ (for simplicity, it is assumed that the public sector is absent) where $Y = py$ and taking into account the definition of M as the sum of the monetary base in the hands of the public and bank deposits.

15.3 The Monetary Approach to the Balance of Payments

Given the hypothesis that the only existing asset is money, the accounting identity (15.9.1) becomes

$$\Delta R = \Delta M. \tag{15.14}$$

Finally, we have the equation

$$y = \bar{y}, \tag{15.15}$$

which expresses Proposition III ($\bar{y}$ indicates the level of full employment income expressed in real terms).

By substituting (15.11) into (15.13) and then into (15.14), we have

$$\Delta R = \alpha (L - M), \tag{15.16}$$

which expresses the circumstance that the variation in reserves (coinciding with the balance of payments) depends, through coefficient α, on the divergence between the demand and supply of money. Given (15.12) and (15.15), we can also write

$$\Delta R = \alpha (kp\bar{y} - M), \tag{15.16.1}$$

where $kp\bar{y}$ is the desired stock of money. The self-correcting nature of the disequilibria can be clearly seen from (15.16.1) and (15.14): if the existing money stock is excessive, that is $M > kp\bar{y}$, ΔR is negative and therefore so is ΔM, thus M decreases and moves towards its equilibrium value $kp\bar{y}$. If the existing stock of money is inadequate, that is if $M < kp\bar{y}$, ΔR is positive and therefore so too is ΔM, so that M increases towards its equilibrium value.

It is possible to give a simple graphic representation of this model. Figure 15.2a represents Eq. (15.11), where we have substituted (15.13) and (15.15), then reordered the terms. This is an increasing straight line with a slope α, which intersects the line $py = p\bar{y}$ (parallel to the axis of the abscissae) at the point of equilibrium E: in fact, only when M is at the desired level $kp\bar{y}$, does absorption coincide with income and there are no variations either in the money stock or in international reserves ($\Delta M = \Delta R = 0$). The variation in international reserves expressed by (15.16.1) is plotted in Fig. 15.2b.

Considering, for example, the non-equilibrium point Q_0, where the existing money stock is excessive, Fig. 15.2a shows that absorption exceeds income by the amount $Q'_0 Q''_0$, giving rise to a balance-of-payments deficit of the same amount (segment $Q_0 Q'''_0$ in Fig. 15.2b has the same length as segment $Q'_0 Q''_0$ in part a of the figure) and to a reduction in the money stock of the same amount. This reduction is deducted from Q_0, giving rise to the new point Q_1 (the segment $Q_0 Q_1$ has the same length as $Q'_0 Q''_0$) and so on. The movement clearly converges towards the point of equilibrium E, where the excess supply of money disappears and the balance-of-payments deficit is annulled.

Following exactly the same reasoning, which we leave as an excercise for the reader, it is possible to demonstrate that the economic system tends towards E also when we start from a point to the left of $kp\bar{y}$.

The diagram we have discussed also makes it easy for us to examine the *effects of a devaluation* in the exchange rate. In fig. 15.3, we have reproduced Fig. 15.2. Supposing that we start off in a position of equilibrium (point E), let us now consider a devaluation. Given (15.10), the level of prices will increase by the same

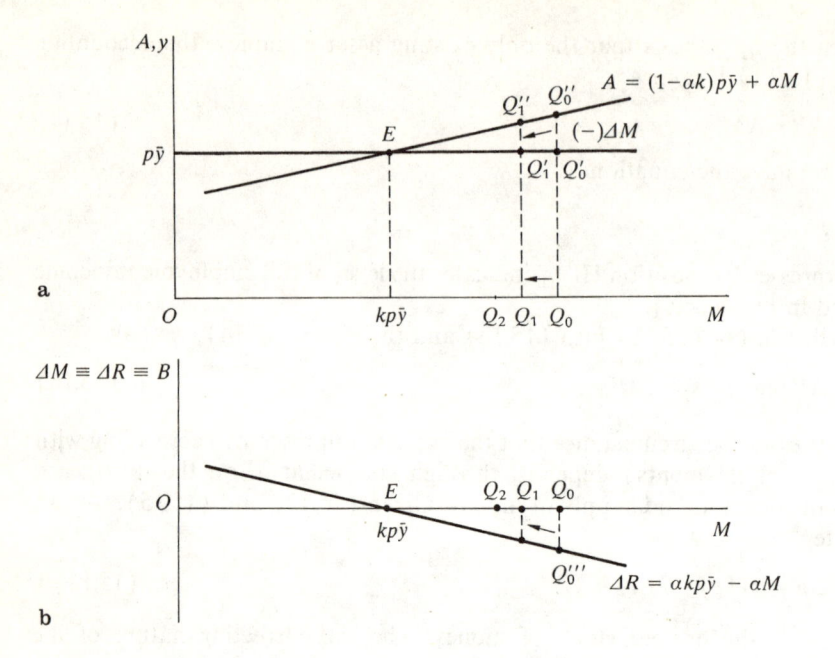

Fig. 15.2. A diagram of the adjustment mechanism according to the MABP

percentage as the devaluation, say from p to p'. Consequently, the various lines move upwards to the position of the dotted lines. We can see at once from Fig. 15.3b that in correspondence with initial point E (which is no longer an equilibrium point: the new point of equilibrium is E'), there is a *surplus* equal to HE (equal to $E'_0 E_0$ in Fig. 15.3a). It would seem, therefore, in contradiction to what we said above, that devaluation can bring about an *improvement* in the balance of payments. However this effect is *transitory*: in part a of the figure it can be seen that, through the increase in the money stock generated by the surplus, the economic system moves towards the new position of equilibrium E'. In the course of this movement the surplus gradually dwindles until it disappears altogether.

Beyond the analysis through the diagram, what is the cause of this sharp difference in results compared to the traditional approach? We must bear in mind that, according to the traditional approach, if the critical elasticities condition occurs (or the more restrictive condition that must come about when account is also taken of the income effect: cfr. Sect. 14.3), then a devaluation will cause a lasting improvement[17] in the balance of payments. The fact is that the logical frame of reference is entirely different. In the traditional approach, a devaluation causes variations in relative prices and therefore induces substitution effects and also (where contemplated) effects on income. Nothing of this can happen in the MABP, given the assumption of purchasing power parity (Proposition II) and of full employment (Proposition III). What happens in the MABP frame of

---

[17] Account should be taken of the fact that in the traditional approach, based on flows, the improvement due to devaluation is *itself* a flow which is maintained in time, naturally other things being equal. See, however, Niehans (1984, Sect. 4.3), who maintains that this interpretation of the elasticity approach is incorrect.

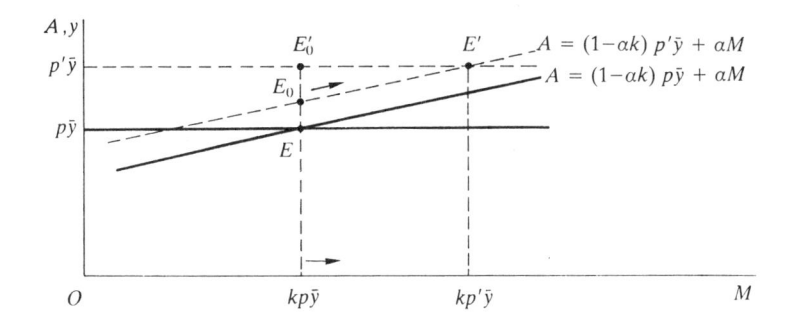

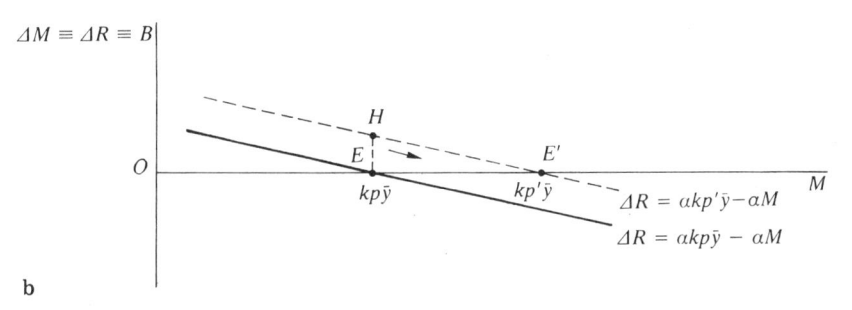

15.3 The Monetary Approach to the Balance of Payments

Fig. 15.3. Effects of a devaluation according to the MABP

reference is that a devaluation, by causing the price level to rise, generates an increase in the desired money supply. As the existing supply is what it is, and therefore insufficient, the mechanism already described (reduction in absorption, concomitant balance-of-payments surplus i.e. increases in international reserves and the money supply) is set into motion; when the desired money supply is reached, the adjustment comes to an end and the balance-of-payments surplus thus disappears.

On the other hand, the fact that this must be the case according to the MABP is obvious: the flows deriving from stock disequilibria — unlike pure flows — are necessarily transitory, insofar as they are destined to disappear once the stocks have reached their desired levels. It is important to note that the argument could be conducted in terms of real magnitudes without thereby causing a change in the results. The demand for money in real terms, $L/p = k\bar{y}$, is given. The supply of money in real terms, M/p, varies inversely with the price-level. The increase in p, by causing the real value of the money stock to diminish, causes an excess demand for money and thus the mechanism for the reduction in absorption is set into motion[18], etc., which produces an increase in the nominal stock of money. This increase continues to the point where the real value of the money stock has returned to the initial level of equilibrium (that is, when M has increased in the same proportion as p). It can be seen that, in the long term, the real variables do not change, insofar as the variations in one of the nominal variables (e.g. in the level of prices just examined) set automatic adjustment mechanisms of other

---

[18] The absorption in real terms is $A/p = \bar{y} + \alpha(M/p - L/p)$.

nominal variables into motion and these re-establish the equilibrium value of the real variables[19].

15.3.3 Concluding Remarks

The demolishing effect of the MABP on the traditional theory of the adjustment processes is obvious: not only are standard measures, like devaluation, ineffective, but even the most sophisticated macroeconomic policies (which we shall deal with in Sect. 15.5) have to be discarded. It is enough to leave the system to its own devices (Implication II) for everything to be adjusted automatically.

It is not surprising therefore that the MABP has given rise to a large number of criticisms, which we shall try to sum up briefly.

The first and most obvious one is directed at Proposition III. That full employment is not the norm, but, if anything, a rare exception is a fact. Furthermore the automatic tendency towards full employment equilibrium in the long term is still a moot question and it does not seem permissible simply to assume that it exists.

Acceptance of this criticism is ultimately tantamount to admitting that the claim of MABP to relegate the whole of Keynesian and post-Keynesian macroeconomics to the wastepaper basket is wrong. As soon as the variability of income below full employment level is admitted, and differentiated expenditure functions between consumption and investment are introduced, then the MABP theses are no longer necessarily valid.

A second criticism is internal to the logical structure of the MABP itself. The statement that the imbalances in international payments coincide with the excess demand for money is in fact true only under the assumption that the excess demand for bonds is nil, as can be clearly seen from (15.9.1). It is possible to get around the problem by supposing that money is the only asset in existence, but it is clear that the models must be made to conform to reality and not the opposite. When there are bonds, it is quite possible to have a balance-of-payments disequilibrium without one on the money market, as can be seen once again from (15.9.1). The existence of a plurality of assets lies at the basis of the more recent *portfolio approach* to the balance of payments, which will be dealt with in Sect. 15.6.

For further criticism and investigation, we refer the reader to Hahn (1977), Miller (1978), Thirlwall (1980) and Rabin and Yeager (1982).

For ourselves, while we do not subscribe to the theories of the MABP, we do believe that it should be given due acknowledgement for one fundamental merit: that of having directed attention to the fact that in the case of balance-of-payments disequilibria and the related adjustment processes, stock equilibria and disequilibria must be taken into account. Naturally, this must not be accepted in the sense — typical of the cruder versions of the MABP — that *only* stock equilibria and disequilibria count, but that they *also* count in addition to pure flow equilibria and disequilibria. But if this is the case, then nothing new under the sun. As long ago as 1954 Clower and Bushaw had drawn attention, with rigorous

---

[19] As can be seen from the expression in the previous note, the equilibrium value of absorption in real terms is given and is equal to $\bar{y}$.

scholarship, to the fact that there was a need for economic theory in general to consider stocks and flows simultaneously, and had shown that a theory based only on flows or one based solely on stocks was inherently incomplete and could lead to inexact conclusions.

15.4 Macroeconomic Equilibrium in a Standard Keynesian-type Open Model

15.4.1 Introductory Remarks: The Mundell-Fleming model

By "macroeconomic equilibrium in an open model" we mean a situation in which real, monetary, and balance-of-payments equilibria are to be found simultaneously, all in a standard Keynesian-type model. Substantially it is the extension, to an open economy, of the analysis based on the *IS* and *LM* schedules[20]. This extension was carried out by Mundell and Fleming in the early 1960s, and is called the Mundell-Fleming model (see Frenkel and Razin, 1987), although the two authors wrote independently. The study of macroeconomic equilibrium, in an open model and in a Keynesian context, was first carried out in the economic literature essentially, if not exclusively, with regard for real equilibrium, by way of an analysis based on the international multiplier. From this analysis, certain effects on the balance of payments emerge, as it were, as a by-product, which we have analyzed in Chap. 13. This analysis is not however complete, in that it does not take into consideration the influence of the interest rate on real equilibrium and, furthermore, it completely ignores monetary equilibrium. In this section we shall make a more complete analysis of the problem of macroeconomic equilibrium in an open economy with a fixed exchange regime. To this end we shall use a one-country model, in which the rate of exchange and prices are considered to be fixed.

The model can be reduced to three equations, one which expresses the determination of national income in an open economy (equilibrium in the goods market or real equilibrium), one which expresses the balance-of-payments equilibrium (external balance) and the third which expresses the equilibrium in the money market (monetary equilibrium).

As far as real equilibrium is concerned, we shall make use of the alternative formulation, already explained in Sect. 14.3 [see Eq. (II) there].

Naturally, the variables on which domestic demand[21] and exports depend, are subject to change. In particular, exports are now exogenous by hypothesis (as the

---

[20] As is well-known, the graphic apparatus *IS* − *LM* was devised by Hicks (1937) to provide an interpretation of Keynes' theory. Much discussion has occurred and still goes on as to how far this apparatus is a faithful interpretation of Keynes' thought (it is sufficient to refer the reader to Hicks' own lucid essays on the subject, 1967c and 1981), but this is not the place to enter into these doctrinaire controversies. However, it is as well at this point to recall that if this approach can be given a logical consistency with reference to a closed economy (where the stock of wealth is taken to be constant), its transposition to an open economy creates problems, which will be tackled in Sect. 15.6.

[21] It should be remembered that by "domestic demand (or expenditure)" we mean aggregate demand for domestic output by residents, and by "marginal propensity to domestic demand (or expenditure)" the marginal propensity of residents to spend on domestic output. Furthermore, by goods we mean both goods and services.

rate of exchange is fixed), while domestic demand depends on the interest rate and on income. With regard to the dependence on income, there are no particular observations to be made (one should simply remember the assumption that the marginal propensity to domestic expenditure is less than one). As far as the interest rate is concerned, a variation in it causes domestic demand to vary in the opposite direction: an increase in the interest rate in fact has a depressive influence on total demand (via a reduction in investment and presumably also consumption) and therefore on the part of it which is directed towards national goods, while the opposite applies for a drop in the interest rate itself. We thus have the equation for real equilibrium

$$y = d(y,i) + x_0, \tag{15.17}$$

where i denotes the interest rate.

As far as the balance of payments is concerned, this now includes not only imports and exports of goods, but also capital movements, which obviously are not compensatory. Exports, as we have seen, are exogenous, while imports are a function of income and of the interest rate. Dependence on the rate of interest, which at first sight might seem strange, is obvious if we remember that the interest rate influences total demand in the way just explained and therefore also the part of it which is directed towards foreign goods, that is, imports. The introduction of the interest rate as an explanatory variable in the domestic demand function thus necessarily implies its introduction as an explanatory variable into the import function with the same qualitative effects (even if, obviously, these are quantitatively different). As for the movement of capital, its imbalance (inflows less outflows) is expressed as an increasing function of the interest differential. It is in fact clear that the greater the domestic interest rate with respect to the foreign rate, the greater, *ceteris paribus*, will be the incentive to capital inflows and the less to outflows. The capital movements under examination are substantially short-term movements for covered interest arbitrage (cfr. Sect. 10.3.3; note that, as this is a one-country model, the foreign interest rate is exogenous, so that the movement of capital is, ultimately, a function of the domestic interest rate)[22]. We can therefore write the following equation for the equilibrium in the balance of payments[23]

$$x_0 - m(y,i) + K(i) = 0, \tag{15.18}$$

where $K(i)$ indicates the surplus or deficit in the capital account. Let us note, in passing, that the condition that the overall balance of payments is in equilibrium is equivalent to the condition that the stock of international reserves is stationary, as shown in Sect. 11.3.

Finally we have the usual equation for monetary equilibrium

$$M = L(y,i), \tag{15.19}$$

where M indicates the money stock and L the demand for money.

---

[22] Naturally, given the context of fixed exchange rates (spot and forward) in which this model operates.

[23] Given the hypothesis of fixed exchange rates and prices, a suitable choice can be made of the units of measurement so that real and nominal magnitudes coincide. This is true also in relation to the following equation for monetary equilibrium.

15.4.2 Graphic Representation of the Equilibrium Conditions

Given that, as we have seen, the real equilibrium is determined by the equality

income = domestic expenditure + exports,

and given that domestic expenditure is by assumption a function of the interest rate and of income while exports are to be considered exogenous, it is possible to show graphically all the combinations of the interest rate and income which ensure the above-mentioned equality.

In this way we obtain a curve (which as usual for simplicity we shall assume to be linear: this is also true for curves, which we shall come across later) which corresponds, in an open economy, to the *IS* schedule for a closed economy and which we shall call *RR*.

The characteristic of this curve, which as we have just seen, is a locus of equilibrium points, is that it is downward sloping. In fact, if income is higher, domestic expenditure is likewise higher, but by a smaller amount (as the marginal propensity to domestic expenditure is less than one). It is therefore necessary to have a lower value for the rate of interest, so that there will be a further increase in domestic expenditure, to maintain the equality: income = domestic expenditure + exports.

Furthermore, the *RR* curve has the property that at all points above it there will be a negative excess demand, while at all points below it the excess demand for goods will be positive.

Consider in fact any point A' above the *RR* curve. Here the rate of interest is greater than at point A, while income is the same. Point A is a point of real equilibrium, being on the *RR* schedule. If, income being equal, the rate of interest

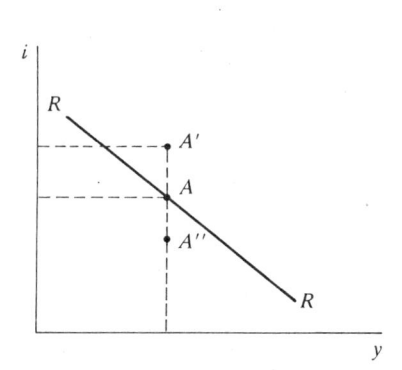

Fig. 15.4. Macroeconomic equilibrium under fixed exchange rates: the real-equilibrium schedule

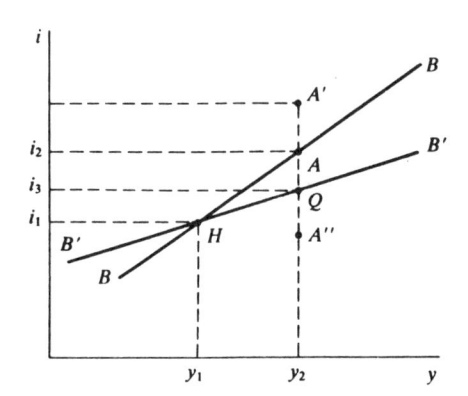

Fig. 15.5. Macroeconomic equilibrium under fixed exchange rates: the external balance schedule

is greater, domestic demand will be less, so that at A' there will be negative excess demand (excess supply). In the same way, it can be demonstrated that at A'' there is positive excess demand.

Equilibrium of the balance of payments occurs, as explained in Sect. 15.4.1, when the algebraic sum of the imbalance between exports and imports and the imbalance in capital movements is nil. As exports have been assumed exogenous and imports a function of income and the interest rate, and the imbalance in capital movements as a function of the interest rate, it is possible to show in a diagram all the combinations of the interest rate and of income which ensure balance-of-payments equilibrium, thus obtaining the *BB* schedule.

This schedule is upward sloping: in fact, as exports are given, greater imports correspond to greater income and therefore it is necessary to have a higher interest rate (which tends on the one hand to put a brake on the increase in imports and on the other to improve the capital account) in order to maintain balance-of-payments equilibrium. We observe that the slope of *BB* depends, *ceteris paribus*, on the responsiveness of capital flows to the interest rate, i.e. on the degree of international capital mobility. The higher the mobility of capital, the flatter the *BB* schedule. In Fig. 15.5, the degree of capital mobility underlying schedule $B'B'$ is higher than that underlying schedule *BB*. In fact, if consider for example the external equilibrium point H, a higher income (for example, y_2 instedad of y_1) will mean a balance-of-payments deficit. This requires – as we have just seen – a higher value of the interest rate to maintain external equilibrium. Now, the more reactive capital flows to the interest rate, the lower the required interest rate increase. Given y_2, the interest rate will have to be i_2 in the case of *BB*, and only i_3 in the case of $B'B'$.

Furthermore, the *BB* schedule has the property that at all points above it there is a surplus in the balance of payments, while at all points below it there is a deficit. In fact, consider any point A' above the line *BB*. At A', while income is the same, the interest rate is greater than at A, where the balance of payments is in equilibrium. Thus, as imports are a decreasing function of the interest rate and as the capital account balance is an increasing function of the rate itself, at A' imports will be lower and the capital account balance will be higher – *ceteris paribus* – than at A, so that if at A the balance of payments is in equilibrium, at A' there must be a surplus.

In the same way, it is possible to show that at all points below *BB* (see, for example, point A'') there will be a balance-of-payments deficit.

Finally, it is important to take note of another property of the *BB* schedule. As $K(i)$, the capital account balance, is an increasing function of the interest rate, it will be in surplus for "high" values of i (generally for $i > i_f$), in deficit for "low" values of i ($i < i_f$) and zero for $i = i_f$. On the other hand, the current account will show a surplus for "low" values of y, for those values, that is, which give rise to lower imports at the given exogenous exports, a deficit for "high" values of y and zero for the value of y at which imports equal exports[24]. There will exist, therefore, only one combination of i and y that gives rise to a *full* equilibrium in the balance of payments, taking "full" equilibrium to mean a situation in which *both* the

---

[24] As imports also depend on i, this value will be calculated by holding i at the value i_f.

15.4 Macroeconomic Equilibrium in a Standard Keynesian-type Open Model

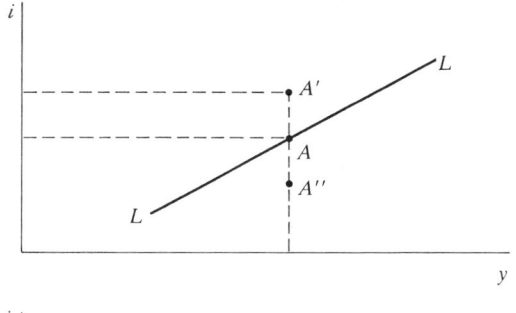

Fig. 15.6. Macroeconomic equilibrium under fixed exchange rates: the monetary equilibrium schedule

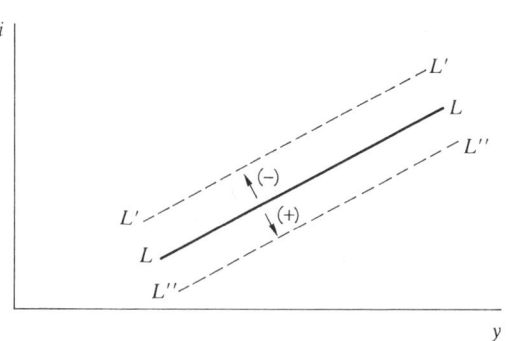

Fig. 15.7. Variations in the quantity of money and shifts in the LL schedule

current account balance *and* the capital account balance are nil. Let us assume that this combination is the one which occurs at point H in Fig. 15.5. It follows from what we have seen above that at all points along BB to the right of H there will be a deficit in the current account, exactly matched by net capital inflows (so that the overall balance of payments will be in equilibrium), and that, on the other hand, at all points along BB to the left of H, equilibrium in the balance of payments will come about with a surplus in the current account matched by an equal net outflow of capital. These considerations will be useful when one wishes to take into account not only the overall balance of payments, but also its structure.

Finally, we still have to examine the monetary equilibrium schedule. Given that the demand for money is an (increasing) function of income and a (decreasing) function of the interest rate, there will be a locus of the combinations of these two variables which make the total demand for money equal to the supply, which is represented by the familiar schedule, LL in Fig. 15.6.

The LL curve is increasing; in fact, given a certain supply of money, if income is higher the demand for money will also be higher: in consequence, it is necessary to have a higher value for the interest rate, so as to reduce the demand for money itself, to maintain the equality between demand and supply. Furthermore the LL schedule has the property that, at all points above it, there is negative excess demand for money; while at all points below it, there is positive excess demand. Consider for example any point above LL, for example, A'; there the rate of interest is higher, income being equal, than at point A on LL. At A', therefore, there is a lower demand for money than at A. Since at A the demand for money equals the supply and given that at A' the demand for money is lower than at A, it follows that at A' the demand for money is less than the supply. In the same way, it is possible to show that at any point below the LL schedule (for example at A'') the demand for money is greater than the supply.

The LL schedule undergoes shifts as the supply of money varies and, to be precise, it moves to the left (for example to $L'L'$ in Fig. 15.7) if the supply of money is reduced, and to the right (for example to $L''L''$) if the supply of money increases.

In fact, to each given value of income must correspond a lower rate of interest, if the money supply is higher, so that the greater demand for money will absorb the greater supply so as to maintain equilibrium between demand and supply of money; in consequence, LL must shift downwards and to the right. Similarly, it is possible to demonstrate that LL shifts upwards and to the left if the supply of money is reduced. Thus there is a very precise position for the LL schedule for each level of money supply in the diagram.

15.4.3 Simultaneous Real, Monetary and External Equilibrium; Stability

The three schedules RR, BB, and LL so far examined separately, can now be brought together in a single diagram. Consider first of all the RR and BB schedules (Fig. 15.8). They intersect at a point E, where real equilibrium and balance-of-payments equilibrium are established simultaneously with values y_E for income and i_E for the interest rate. Now consider schedule LL. There are two possibilities (Fig. 15.9):

(a) if the quantity of money is considered as given, it is altogether exceptional for the corresponding LL schedule to pass through point E. And if the LL schedule does not pass through E, it follows that monetary equilibrium does not correspond to real and balance-of-payments equilibrium;

(b) if, on the other hand, the quantity of money is considered to be variable, then, in principle, it is always possible to find a value for the quantity of money itself, so that the corresponding LL schedule will also pass through point E. In this case — cfr. Fig. 15.9b — we have the simultaneous occurence of real equilibrium, balance of payments equilibrium and monetary equilibrium.

But, one might ask, do any forces exist which tend to cause the necessary shifts in the LL schedule. The answer to this question cannot be given in isolation, but requires a general analysis of the dynamics of the disequilibria in the system, that is, of the behaviour of the system itself when one or more of the equilibrium conditions are not satisfied. For precisely this purpose it is necessary to make certain assumptions regarding the dynamic behaviour of the relevant variables: money supply, income and interest rate. The assumptions are as follows:

(a) the money supply varies in relationship to the surplus or deficit in the balance of payments and, to be exact, it increases (diminishes) if there is a surplus (deficit). This assumption — which is identical to the one made in the analysis of the classical theory of the adjustment mechanism of the balance of payments in Sect. 15.2 and in the MABP in Sect. 15.3 — implies that the monetary authorities do not intervene to offset the variations in the quantity

15.4 Macroeconomic Equilibrium in a Standard Keynesian-type Open Model

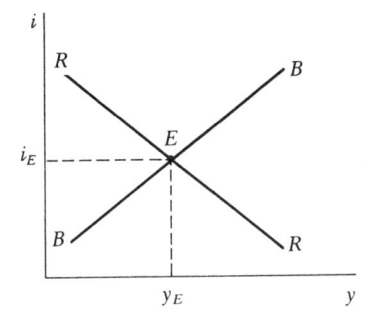

Fig. 15.8. Determination of real and balance-of-payments equilibrium

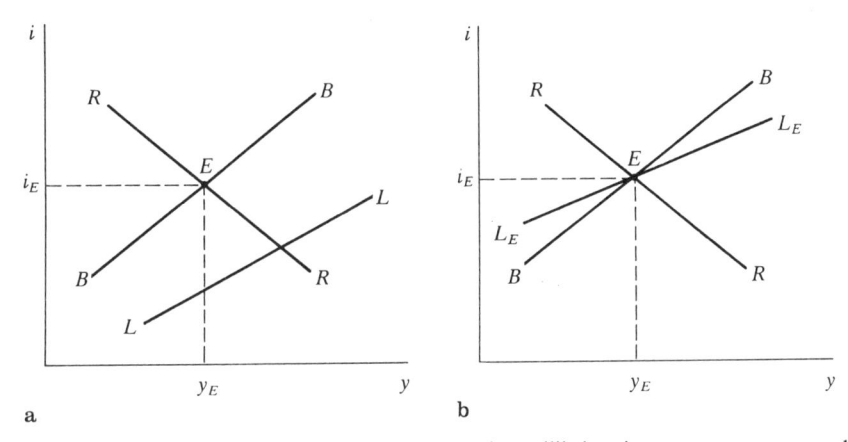

Fig. 15.9. Determination of general macroeconomic equilibrium in an open economy under fixed exchange rates

of money determined by disequilibria in the balance of payments[25]. This might give rise to some doubts about the plausibility of the hypothesis itself. In fact, if it is acceptable in a national and international monetary system that is based on the pure gold standard, it appears to be far less acceptable in the present-day institutional context, where the monetary authorities of a country are unlikely to allow the quantity of money to vary freely in relation to the state of the balance of payments. It is as well to warn the reader here that the hypothesis in question will be dropped in Sect. 15.5, which is dedicated to the analysis of monetary and fiscal policy in an open economy.

---

[25] In the absence of sterilization operations on the part of the monetary authorities, the variation in the quantity of money is determined by the surplus or deficit in the balance of payments, whatever the actual exchange rate regime. On the foreign exchange market, in fact, when foreign currency is demanded, national currency is given up (which reduces the quantity of the latter in circulation) and when foreign currency is supplied national currency is obtained (which increases the quantity of the latter in circulation). If these counteracting operations do not match exactly, their imbalance, in other words in the balance of payments, constitutes — apart from technical details which we do not need to go into here — the net variation in the quantity of national currency in circulation. If the monetary authorities wish to offset this variation, they can act upon the domestic component of the money supply, for example by varying the required-reserve ratio or by way of open market operations. In terms of accounting identities, given (15.9), the monetary authorities can act upon ΔQ, so that $\Delta R + \Delta Q = 0$. For further details see Sect. 11.3.

However, the validity of the analysis carried out in the present section lies in the opportunity it offers to analyse what might be termed the spontaneous behaviour of the system before coming to grips with the problems connected with the use of monetary and fiscal policies to produce external and internal equilibrium in the system itself.

(b) Income varies in relation to the excess demand for goods and, to be exact, it increases (decreases) according to whether this excess demand is positive (negative). This is the same assumption made on more than one occasion (cfr., for example, Sects. 14.3 and A.13.1)

(c) The rate of interest varies in relation to the excess demand for money and, more precisely, it increases (decreases) if this excess demand is positive (negative). This is a plausible hypothesis within the context of an analysis of the spontaneous behaviour of the system. In fact, if the interest rate is, in a broad sense, the price of liquidity, an excess demand for liquidity causes an increase on the market in this price and vice versa. The mechanism, commonly described in textbooks, is the following: an excess demand for money − that is, a scarcity of liquidity − induces holders of bonds to offer them in exchange for money: this causes a fall in the price of bonds, and thus an increase in the interest rate (which is inversely related to the price of bonds).

Having made these behavioural hypotheses, it will be seen that the system is stable and will therefore tend to eliminate disequilibria, that is to say, it will tend to reach the point of simultaneous real, monetary and balance-of-payments equilibrium, *if the marginal propensity to domestic expenditure is less than one* (as already previously assumed) and *if in addition the marginal propensity to import is below a certain critical value*. It is as well to point out that the condition concerning the marginal propensity to domestic expenditure is only a sufficient condition and not a necessary one, so that the simultaneous equilibrium may still be stable even if the above-mentioned condition is not satisfied. Note the difference from the result obtained in the analysis based only on the international multiplier (cfr. Sect. 13.2), where the condition under examination besides being sufficient, is also necessary, so that if it does not occur there will inevitably be instability. The reason for this difference lies substantially in the fact that the introduction of the variability in the interest rate and the related effects confers a greater flexibility on the system. The general, necessary and sufficient conditions for stability are analyzed in Sect. A.15.3.2.

A simple case of disequilibrium and the related adjustment process can be analysed intuitively on the basis of Fig. 15.10. Assume, for example, that the system is initially at point A. At that point there is real and monetary equilibrium, but not equilibrium of the balance of payments: more exactly, as point A lies below the BB schedule, there is a deficit. Point A is thus as it were a partial or temporary point of equilibrium. It is necessary here to distinguish two possible cases: if the monetary authorities were to intervene in order to sterilize the payments imbalances, the money supply would remain constant and the economic system would remain at A; naturally, a reduction in the stock of international reserves would correspond to the continued balance-of-payments deficit (except

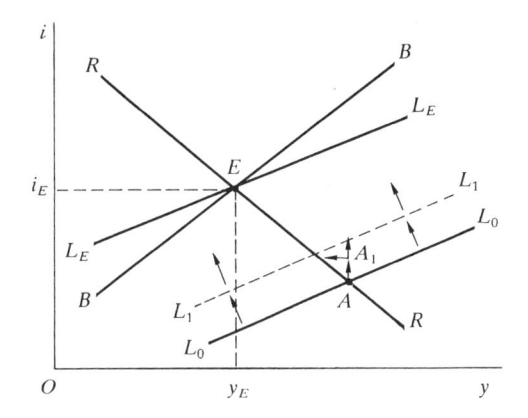

15.4 Macroeconomic Equilibrium in a Standard Keynesian-type Open Model 213

Fig. 15.10. General macroeconomic equilibrium in an open economy under fixed exchange rates: dynamic analysis of the adjustment process

in the case of a country with a reserve currency). However, we have assumed — hypothesis (a) — that an intervention of this kind would not take place, so that the supply of money diminishes and the LL schedule moves upwards and to the left, for example from $L_0 L_0$ to $L_1 L_1$. Then at A there is a (positive) excess demand for money, so that — hypothesis (c) — the interest rate increases. The increase in the interest rate causes a fall in the demand for goods and thus a (negative) excess demand in the real market, which is confirmed by the fact that point A_1, which is reached from A following the increase in i (vertical arrow from A towards A_1), is above RR. Given, as we said, that at A_1 there is negative excess demand on the real market, by hypothesis (b) income falls (horizontal arrow from A_1 towards the left). At A_1, on the other hand, we are still below BB and therefore there is still a deficit in the balance of payments; consequently the money supply falls still further and LL continues to shift upwards and to the left, so that at A_1 a situation of positive excess demand for money remains, with a further tendency for the interest rate to increase (vertical arrow rising above A_1). We thus have a situation in which y and i approach their respective equilibrium values and also a shift of LL towards the position $L_E L_E$. Note that a graphical analysis of stability cannot be made simply with a scheme with two arrows of the kind adopted in Sect. 14.3 (cfr. Fig. 14.3). In that diagram, in fact, the schedules which represent the various equilibria *do not move*; in our case on the contrary the disequilibrium also causes a shift of one of the schedules (that of monetary equilibrium). In effect, in our model, there are three variables which adjust themselves: income, interest rate and the quantity of money, so that the two-dimensional graph of this adjustment is necessarily inadequate, differently from the case in which there are only two variables to be adjusted.

We can now ask ourselves what the economic meaning of the conditions of stability might be. As far as concerns the condition that the marginal propensity to domestic expenditure is less than one, the meaning is the usual one: an increase in income, due to a positive excess demand, causes a further increase in domestic demand, but the process is certainly convergent, if the increases in demand are below the increases in income, that is to say, if the marginal propensity to domestic expenditure is less than one. In the opposite case, the process could be divergent, unless other conditions of stability intervene.

With regard to the condition that concerns the marginal propensity to import, the meaning is as follows: if this propensity is too great, it may happen, in the course of the adjustment process, that the reduction in imports (induced by the reduction in y and the increase in i) is such as to bring the balance of payments into surplus (that is to say, point E is passed). An adjustment in the opposite direction is then set into motion: the money supply increases, the rate of interest drops, domestic demand, income and imports all increase (both because y has increased and i decreased). And if the marginal propensity to import is too high, then it may be that the increase in imports is such as to produce a new deficit in the balance of payments. At this point, a new process comes into being, working in the opposite direction and so on, with continual fluctuations around the point of equilibrium which each time may take the system further away from equilibrium itself. In effect, as is shown in Sect. A.15.3.2, the condition that the marginal propensity to import should be less than a critical value serves precisely to exclude the possibility that divergent fluctuations take place. Note that, while it is possible to discover from the graph whether the marginal propensity to domestic expenditure is less than one (a negative slope in RR), it is not, on the other hand, possible to ascertain whether the condition related to the marginal propensity to import is satisfied or not, as this condition has no counterpart in the graph in terms of slope and positions of the various schedules (all that one can say is that the slope of the BB schedule must not rise above a certain maximum, but this cannot be determined unless the magnitudes of all parameters that appear in the model are known).

15.4.3.1 Observations and Qualifications

It is important to note at this point that the adjustment process described in the previous section is, like that of Hume and the MABP, an *automatic* process, also in this case set off ultimately by movements in the money stock generated by the balance-of-payments disequilibria. But it is equally important to note that the cause of the disequilibria is very different, as is the operation of the adjustment mechanism. In the present case the disequilibria are flow disequilibria: in the example given, the balance of payments is in deficit because the initial values of income (which is a flow) and the interest rate (which is not a flow, but is a point variable, that is, a variable measured at a given moment in time) bring about *flows* of goods, services and capital[26], so that payments exceed revenues vis-à-vis the rest of the world. This is a perfectly legitimate way of looking at the deficit, which refers back to Eq. (11.11.1), which is just as true as (15.9.1), which is at the basis of the MABP. The operation of the adjustment mechanism is likewise different, as it does not act through a direct effect of the excess demand for money on absorption (as postulated by the MABP), but through an effect of this excess demand on the interest rate and through this on the flows of expenditure and movements of capital. This reflects the different view-point of the MABP and the traditional approach.

---

[26] Implicit in this affirmation is the hypothesis that the movements of capital are pure flows. The abandonment of this hypothesis will be examined later in the text. Cfr. also Johnson (1958a).

15.4 Macroeconomic Equilibrium in a Standard Keynesian-type Open Model

Another important point to note is the substantially short-term nature of the traditional analysis. In fact, it is very unlikely that the point of equilibrium E in Fig. 15.10 will coincide with the point of *full* equilibrium of the balance of payments (point H, for which see Fig. 15.5). Normally point E will be to the right or to the left of point H. Assuming, by way of example, that it is to the right, then this means that at E there will be a deficit in the current account matched by an inflow of capital. This is perfectly normal and acceptable in the short term, but in the long one it will be necessary to take into account certain considerations which till now have been ignored. As we are here dealing with *flows*, the continuance of the situation of equilibrium E means that, other things being equal, there will be a constant inflow of capital *per unit of time*. This in turn means that the stock of debt to foreign countries is continually growing and so, given i, the burden of interest payments to the rest of the world will also continue to grow. We know (see Sect. 11.1.1) that these payments go into the services account (under the item "investment income") and therefore feed the deficit in the current account beyond that accounted for in Fig. 15.10. The only way to avoid this problem is to suppose that the owners of the foreign capital that has flowed in should not repatriate the interest due to them, but should capitalize it, leaving it to increment their capital, given the advantage of the favourable interest differential. In the opposite case, in fact, the payment abroad for investment income would cause the form and the position of the BB schedule to change. As far as the *form* is concerned, let us consider a given moment in time, in which therefore the stock of debt to foreign countries is given. A variation in i thus causes the burden of interest payments on this debt to vary in the same direction[27]. From this follows the possibility that by increasing i beyond a certain limit, the burden of interest payments will exceed the inflow of new capital, in which case the BB schedule will become backward-sloping: in fact, increases in i beyond a certain critical limit (i_c) will on the whole cause a *worsening* in the balance of payments, hence the need for lower values of y to reduce m.

The BB schedule *may* therefore[28] assume the form described in Fig. 15.11, in which case there will be two points of intersection[29] with the RR schedule: points E and E'. With the reasoning followed above it can be ascertained that point E is a stable equilibrium (it has in fact the same properties as E in Fig. 15.19), while point E' is an unstable equilibrium: any shift from E' sets into motion forces which cause further movement away. In fact, a downward shift from E' sets off the forces

---

[27] This implies the hypothesis that the new rate of interest will be applied to old debts as well as new ones. This is an entirely plausible assumption, in that the movements of capital considered are short-term ones and so are not incorporated in fixed-income securities (in which case the coupon remains unchanged and the variations in i have repercussions on the market value of the securities), but in other financial instruments, for example, bank deposits (in which case the new interest rate starts to run immediately on the entire amount of the capital deposited) or in bonds with variable coupons. Intermediate cases are of course possible, but these have been ignored for the sake of simplicity.

[28] The accent is put on *may* to emphasize yet again that we are talking about a possibility: in fact, if the movements of capital are very elastic with respect to i, the burden of interest payments will always remain below the inflow of new capital and BB will have its normal upward slope.

[29] We leave aside any particular cases, such as the absence of intersection, the tangency, etc., of the RR with the BB schedule.

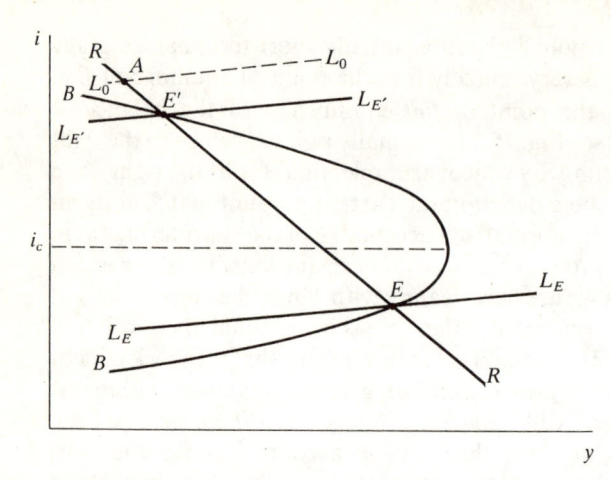

Fig. 15.11. The burden of interest payments and the *BB* schedule

of attraction towards point *E* already described. An upward shift, for example to *A*, generates further upward movements. At *A* in fact there is a balance-of-payments deficit: note that in the upper branch of the *BB* curve, the opposite of the rule encountered in Fig. 15.5 is valid (though the rule remains valid for the lower branch), because now greater values of *i* have an unfavourable effect on the balance of payments. The deficit causes a reduction in *M* and therefore a shift of *LL* from L_0L_0 upwards and to the left, and so on; so that point *A* tends to move further and further away from *E'*.

But there is more to it even than this. In fact, let us consider the *position* of the *BB* curve and, so as to simplify to the maximum, let us assume that the eventuality described in Fig. 15.11 does not come about, so that the *BB* curve has a normal upward slope. Now, over time, the stock of debt increases and thus the interest payments abroad also increase. This means — with reference to Fig. 15.10 — that *BB* shifts upwards and to the left, as at each given interest rate the growing deficit due to these interest payments can only be offset by lower imports and therefore smaller *y*. It follows that point *E* in Fig. 15.10 would shift gradually to the left along the *RR* schedule and the entire economic system would follow a trajectory of ever-increasing values of *i* accompanied by ever-decreasing values of *y*, which would clearly produce a situation that would be intolerable in the long term.

But the situation in which the interest is not repatriated, discussed above, cannot be calmly accepted in the long term either. Growing foreign debt, in fact, exposes the country to the risk of insolvency if foreign investors decide to withdraw their funds (interest and capital) or even if they merely cease to allow *new* funds to flow in. This last eventuality is only too likely if it is believed, on the basis of the theory of portfolio choice, that capital flows induced by a *given* differential in interest are *limited*.

This is the same as considering that the flows under discussion are not pure flows, but ones deriving from stock adjustments. If they were pure flows, in fact, they would remain constant in time as long as a given interest differential held, other things being equal. In the opposite case, as at each given constellation of yields there corresponds an optimum distribution of the stock of funds between various assets in the various countries, once the holders of funds have realized this

15.4 Macroeconomic Equilibrium in a Standard Keynesian-type Open Model   217

optimum distribution, the movements of capital cease, even if the interest differential remains[30]. The movements could be reactivated only as a result of an *increment* in the differential, that is, an increase in i, as, by hypothesis, i_f is given. In this case the situation already described previously (increasing values of i and decreasing ones for y) presents itself again in a different form.

From all that has been said above, the nature of *short-term equilibrium* of point E is clarified (in accordance with the model of a closed economy from which the basic scheme derives).

15.4.4 Comparative Statics

The shifting of the point of equilibrium — and hence the variations in income and interest rate — in consequence of exogenous variations can be analyzed graphically by examining the shifts of the various schedules RR, BB, LL. As an example we shall examine the effects of an exogenous increase in domestic expenditure, an exogenous increase in exports and a devaluation of the exchange rate in a regime of fixed but adjustable exchange rates[31].

An *exogenous increase in domestic expenditure* (with the import function remaining the same) causes the RR schedule to shift to the right, to $R'R'$ (cfr. Fig. 15.12), because, if aggregate demand increases, production must increase at each given level of the interest rate. From Fig. 15.12 it can be seen that at the new point of equilibrium E', both income and the interest rate are higher. The increase in income is due to the multiplier process; but, as this increase causes an increase in imports, the balance of payments, initially in equilibrium, goes into deficit, hence the need for an increase in the interest rate, in order to get the balance of payments back into equilibrium. It goes without saying that this increase in the interest rate tends to put a brake on the increase in income. In fact, as can be seen from the figure, the increase in income from y_E to $y_{E'}$ is less than it would have been if the interest rate had remained unchanged (abscissa of point P); in other words, the multiplier is less than that met with in the analysis carried out in Sect. 13.2. In consequence of the shift of the point of equilibrium, the LL schedule must shift to $L'L'$: there is, that is to say, a decrease in the quantity of money. Note that the consequences can also be the opposite; in fact if the LL schedule had initially been in the position indicated in Fig. 15.13, it would have had to shift to the right, which indicates an increase in the quantity of money.

The reason for all this is intuitive: as at E' both income and the interest rate are greater than at E, the demand for money on the one hand tends to increase and on the other to decrease, so that the total demand for money (and therefore, in equilibrium, the supply) can either increase or decrease according to the relative intensity of the two variations.

Consider now an *exogenous increase in exports*. In this case also there is a shift to the right of the RR schedule: in fact, aggregate demand increases in the case

---

[30] The reason is that the optimum distribution never consists — apart from exceptional cases — in placing the entire stock of funds in a single country even if the yield there is higher (the principle of diversification).

[31] Note that we shall in any case consider the *traditional* situation and leave aside the problems examined at the end of Sect. 15.4.3.1 that derive from payment of interest abroad.

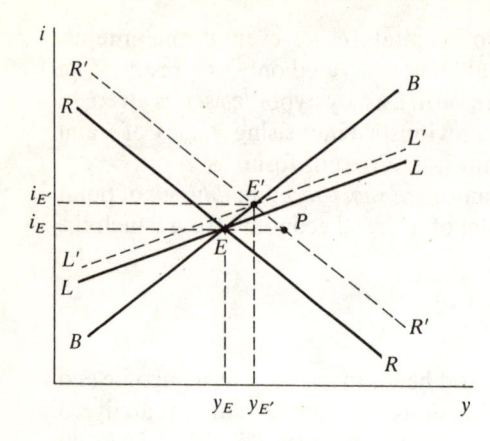

Fig. 15.12. Effects of an exogenous variation of domestic expenditure (case 1)

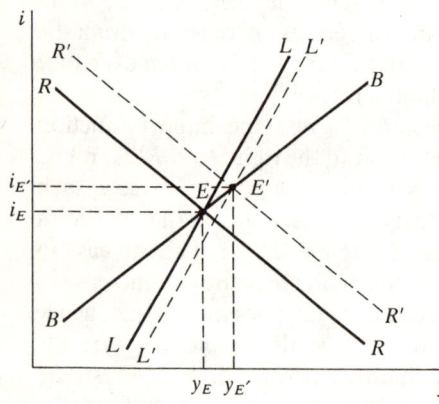

Fig. 15.13. Effects of an exogenous variation of domestic expenditure (case 2)

both of an exogenous increase in domestic demand and of an exogenous increase in exports. But, in addition, given the increase in exports, the BB schedule shifts to the right (see Fig. 15.14): in fact, at each given level of the interest rate income can be greater, given that the consequent increase in imports is compensated by the exogenous increase in exports. At the new point of equilibrium E'' income is greater; in Fig. 15.14, it can also be seen that at E'' the increase in income is greater than it would be (with a similar shift in the RR schedule) in the case of an exogenous increase in domestic expenditure (point E'): this is due to the shift in BB.

The variation in the interest rate can now be in any direction. In fact, in the face of an increase in imports (as a consequence of the increase in income), there is now an increase in exports, so that the effect on the balance of payments can be of any kind, according to whether the increase in imports is greater or less than the initial exogenous increase in exports: consequently, the variations in the interest rate required to put the balance of payments once more into equilibrium can be either in one direction or the other. Figure 15.14 represents the case in which the interest rate increases; in the opposite case the two schedules $R'R'$ and $B'B'$ would be such as to intersect at a point which, though still to the right of E, would be below rather than above E. However, note that, even in the most unfavourable case, in which there is a worsening in the balance of payments, this will certainly be

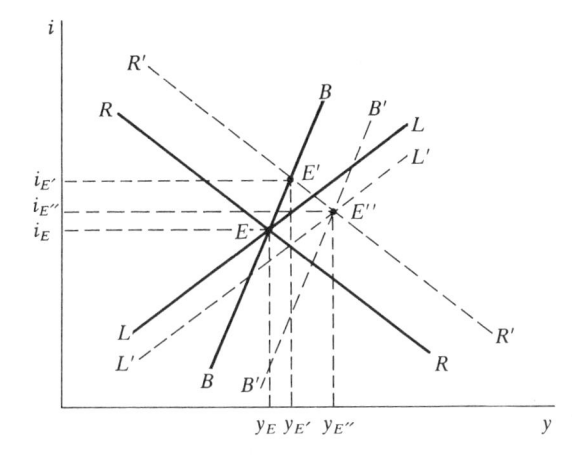

15.4 Macroeconomic Equilibrium in a Standard Keynesian-type Open Model

Fig. 15.14. Effects of an exogenous variation in exports

less than would have occurred in the case of an exogenous increase in domestic expenditure (see above), so that any increase in the interest rate required to bring the balance of payments back into equilibrium is less than in the above-mentioned case; consequently, the braking effect on domestic expenditure is less and the final increase in income is more, as stated above.

As far as the variation in the quantity of money is concerned, there are two possibilities. If, at the new point of equilibrium, the interest rate is higher, then — following the same reasoning as before — there can be either an increase or a decrease in the quantity of money (Fig. 15.14 shows, by way of example, the case in which LL must shift to the right). If, on the other hand, at the new point of equilibrium, the interest rate is lower, then there is no doubt that the quantity of money must increase. In fact, the greater income and the lower interest rate involve a greater demand for money, and therefore the supply of money must also increase to maintain monetary equilibrium.

The same graphic analysis adopted to examine the consequences of an exogenous variation in exports can be applied to examine the consequences of a (*once-and-for-all*) *devaluation* of the exchange rate in an adjustable peg regime[32]. In fact the devaluation causes an increase in exports[33], so that the RR schedule shifts to the right as already observed. Assuming that the condition of the critical elasticities is satisfied, the devaluation causes an improvement in the balance of payments and thus a shift to the right of the BB curve, for the same reasons shown above with regard to the exogenous increase in exports. Therefore, once again, we have the same shifts as those described in Fig. 15.14.

---

[32] In the reasoning which follows the simplifying hypothesis that devaluation will have no influence on the general price level is implicit. We shall return to the devaluation-price relationships in Sect. 18.5. Here we shall limit ourselves to the observation that, if it is admitted that devaluation causes an increase in the general level of prices, the LL schedule also shifts (upwards and to the left) because — with the same real income (and interest rate) — the nominal demand for money increases. This still does not alter the final result. At any rate, given our hypothesis, it is obvious that in the context under study devaluation acts in the same way as any other event that causes an exogenous increase in exports.

[33] Devaluation furthermore causes an increase in domestic expenditure (cfr. Sect. 14.3), which reinforces the shift of the RR schedule to the right.

In all the cases examined, the shifts in income from y_E to $y_{E'}$ or $y_{E''}$ are the result of the product of the exogenous increase in domestic expenditure or exports for the appropriate international multipliers. The explicit formulae for these multipliers (which differ, as mentioned above, from the common international multiplier deduced from an analysis that takes account exclusively of real equilibrium) will be presented in Sect. A.15.3.3. What interests us here above all is to note that the restoration of real equilibrium corresponds likewise to a restoration of balance-of-payments equilibrium (besides monetary equilibrium). Therefore, a once-and-for-all devaluation has only transitory effects on the balance of payments: a result analogous — even if for different reasons — to that found in the MABP (see Sect. 15.3.2).

Note that the process of transition from the old equilibrium E to the new one E' (or E'') is assured by the same dynamic conditions examined in Sect. 15.4.3. In fact, once the various schedules have shifted, the new point of equilibrium is no longer E (which now becomes a disequilibrium point) but E' or E'', towards which the system is driven by the dynamic forces previously described.

We shall conclude with an examination of the effects of a variation in the money supply. For this purpose we can refer to Fig. 15.10, supposing that we are starting from point E. An increase in the money supply causes the LL schedule to shift to the right from $L_E L_E$, for example, to $L_0 L_0$. At this point the adjustment mechanism already described with reference to the same figure, is set in motion, so that LL returns to $L_E L_E$. Note how the final result of the monetary manoeuvre is analogous — even if for different reasons — to that found in the MABP (cfr. Implication I in Sect. 15.3): this manoeuvre, in fact, has no lasting effect on the real magnitudes of the system.

15.5 Monetary and Fiscal Policy for External and Internal Balance. The Assignment Problem. The Coordination Problem

15.5.1 Introductory Remarks

In a regime of fixed exchange rates, the problem of achieving and maintaining simultaneous external and internal balance — where *internal balance* is taken to mean real equilibrium with full employment[34] and external balance to mean balance-of-payments equilibrium — may seem in certain cases to be insoluble (in the so-called *dilemma cases*, as for example that of a balance-of-payments deficit accompanied by a situation of underemployment; we shall go more fully into these questions shortly). From the point of view of the general theory of economic policy, however, the conflict between internal and external equilibrium might seem strange, because even if exchange controls and other restrictions are excluded, two instruments of economic policy — fiscal and monetary policy — are still available to achieve the two targets, so that Tinbergen's principle — at the

---

[34] When one wishes to indicate a situation in which the excess demand on the goods market is zero, then the term *real equilibrium* is used — as was done in the previous sections — while *internal equilibrium (balance)* is taken to mean something more, namely, the case in which real equilibrium occurs at an income level that corresponds to full employment.

15.5 Monetary and Fiscal Policy for External and Internal Balance

heart of the traditional theory of economic policy[35] — is satisfied. According to this theory, in order to achieve a plurality of independent targets, the number of independent instruments should not be less than the number of targets themselves. It is necessary to emphasize the fact that the instruments must be *independent*, in that, if two or more instruments act in the same way on the same variables, they constitute to all intents and purposes a single instrument. Now, in the theory developed during the fifties, monetary and fiscal policies were considered *equivalent* means of influencing only aggregate demand (and thus the level of income and imports). If imports and income move in the same direction, it follows from this equivalence that only in certain cases will there not be conflict between the internal and external targets.

Take first of all the case in which there is underemployment and a balance-of-payments surplus; in this case the line to follow is an expansionary (fiscal and monetary) policy, which will cause income to increase and the balance of payments to worsen (seeing that there will be an increase in imports induced by the increase in income).

Now consider the case in which there is excess aggregate demand with respect to full employment income accompanied by a balance-of-payments deficit. The line to follow, in this case, is also clear: a restrictive policy must be adopted, which will reduce the excess aggregate demand, and at the same time improve the balance of payments by way of a reduction in imports connected to the restriction in total demand.

On the other hand, if there is a situation in which there is under-employment and a deficit in the balance of payments, or a situation in which there is excess demand with respect to full employment income and a balance-of-payments surplus, then there appears to be a conflict between internal and external equilibrium. In the first situation, in fact, internal equilibrium requires an expansionary policy, while external equilibrium requires a restrictive one; in the second situation internal equilibrium requires a restrictive policy, while external equilibrium requires an expansionary one. These are the *dilemma cases* already mentioned. The first situation is undoubtedly the more difficult. In fact, a surplus in the balance of payments may, at worst, be tolerated indefinitely, insofar as it translates itself into an accumulation of international reserves as a counterpart to national currency (which can be issued in unlimited amounts; naturally to avoid undesirable domestic effects of increases in the quantity of money, the monetary authorities will, if necessary, have to offset the increase in the quantity of money due to the foreign channel by a reduction through other domestic channels).

---

[35] It must be emphasized that this is a principle which is valid within the ambit of the static theory of economic policy, which still constitutes a point of reference for scholars of this discipline. It is however as well to inform the reader that according to recent developments of "control theory" applied to the instruments-targets problem, in a dynamic context, the Tinbergen principle is no longer generally valid. For further information on the matter, see Petit (1985), and references therein. It is also important to point out that, after the traditional instruments-(fixed) targets approach, an optimizing approach to economic policy has been developing. This approach involves the maximization of a social welfare function (or of a preference function of the policy-maker) subject to the constraint of the model representing the structure of the economy. In order to avoid further burdening of the present chapter, we postpone the presentation of some considerations on this approach until the end of Sect. A.19.1.3.

Conversely, a deficit in the balance of payments cannot be tolerated for long and it is necessary to find a remedy before international reserves drop to zero or below the minimum considered acceptable. In the context studied here, therefore, all that remains to be done is to give up the internal target and adopt a restrictive policy, thus eliminating the balance-of-payments deficit at the expense of employment.

The argument has been carried on up to this point on the assumption made at the beginning, that monetary and fiscal policies have the same effect on the same variables. In reality they do not, because monetary policy also has an effect on capital movements by way of variation in the interest rate, while fiscal policy does not have this effect. Therefore, apart from the exceptional case in which capital movements are completely insensitive to variations in the interest rate, or the equally exceptional case of perfect capital mobility[36], the two instruments *cannot* be considered equivalent: the possibility therefore once more arises of obtaining both internal and external equilibrium by means of an appropriate combination of fiscal and monetary policies.

15.5.2 Internal and External Balance and the Assignment Problem

Once it has been ascertained that fiscal and monetary policies are distinct instruments, the possibility of obtaining internal and external equilibrium by way of an appropriate use of these two instruments can be studied with a simple graphic analysis, by using the *RR* and *BB* schedules, on which see the previous section[37]. The only thing to note is that the position of *RR* now depends on government expenditure (for simplicity, fiscal policy is identified with the management of government expenditure and monetary policy with that of the interest rate), so that the schedule shifts to the right if government expenditure increases and to the left if it decreases. Take for example the case in which the system is initially at point *E*, at which there is external, but not internal, equilibrium. The objectives are to boost income from y_E to y_F, while maintaining the balance-of-payments equilibrium; that is, to take the system from *E* to E_F; this requires an increase in government expenditure such that the *RR* schedule moves to the position $R_F R_F$ and an increase in the interest rate from i_E to i_F. It is important

---

[36] In this case (also referred to as infinite elasticity of capital movements with respect to the interest differential) the domestic interest rate cannot move away from the foreign interest rate (in fact the slightest difference would set unlimited quantities of capital into motion, which would annul the difference itself) and monetary policy is paralyzed; for further considerations on this case, cfr. Sect. 16.3.1. The normal case, on which the treatment in the text is based, is that of imperfect mobility of capital (that is to say, capital movements are sensitive to interest differentials, but are not infinitely elastic).

[37] The *BB* schedule in the form assumed in Sect. 15.4.2 implies the hypothesis of normal capital mobility. In fact, in the case of insensitivity of these movements to the interest rate the *BB* schedule would become much steeper, in that the sole effect of the interest rate on the balance of payments would be the direct one of this rate on imports. Then, if this effect were negligible, the *BB* schedule would become a vertical line parallel to the *i* axis with an intercept on the *y* axis equal to the only value of income which determines a value for imports equal to the sum of the value of (exogenous) exports plus the capital movement balance (now also exogenous). It is clear that in this case it is impossible to achieve the two objectives at the same time: in fact we are back at the simple multiplier analysis dealt with in Chap. 13. For the case of perfect mobility of capital, already mentioned in Footnote 36, see Sect. 16.3.1.

15.5 Monetary and Fiscal Policy for External and Internal Balance

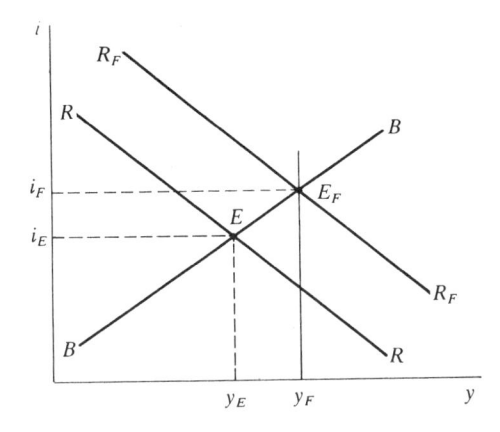

Fig. 15.15. Internal and external balance and monetary and fiscal policy under fixed exchange rates

to note that we have not indicated the LL schedule in Fig. 15.15. We are assuming that the interest rate is the instrument of monetary policy. It follows that the monetary authorities control the money supply so that it is always such that the appropriate value of the interest rate will occur (hence a "given" monetary policy is not a policy that keeps the money supply constant, but a policy which keeps the interest rate constant). This makes any explicit consideration of monetary equilibrium superfluous. Our assumption on monetary policy is made for analytical convenience, as it enables us to eliminate one equation so as to simplify the treatment. The results of our analysis continue to hold also in the case in which one adopts the standard definition of monetary policy (see Sect. A.15.4.1).

Having ascertained the possibility of achieving external and internal equilibrium simultaneously, it is necessary to solve the so-called *assignment problem*, that is of assigning instruments to targets or, more precisely, of assigning each given instrument to the achievement of one single target. This is a problem which arises when there is decentralization of economic policy decisions and/or when the policy-maker has incomplete information. It is essentially a dynamic problem: from the static point of view, in fact, by solving the system of targets-instruments equations, one obtains those sets of values to be attributed simultaneously to each of the various instruments so as to achieve the various targets. In statics there is thus no sense in talking of "assigning" each instrument to one or the other target. Now in the case in which all instruments and economic policy decisions are centralized in a single authority, in theory, this authority could immediately make the instruments assume the appropriate values for the achievement of the targets. But whenever the instruments are in the hands of distinct authorities which are more or less independent of each other, the problem arises of how (that is, in relation to which target) should each of them manage the respective instrument. This gives rise to the problem of pairing off instruments with objectives. It is however important to note that this problem also arises in the previous case (with centralized decision-making) whenever the numerical values of the various parameters (propensities, etc.) *are not known with sufficient accuracy* (imperfect information: this is the more realistic case) so that the policy-maker must try to approach the targets by way of successive approximations and therefore must know on the basis of which indicators it must move the instrumental variables at its disposal. At the very least, the theoretical solution to the assignment problem puts these authorities in a position to cause the system to move towards the targets without any precise numerical information as to the magnitude of the various parameters, but only knowing their signs.

The solution to the assignment problem can be found by applying Mundell's principle (also called the *principle of effective market classification*) according to which each instrument must be used in relation to the objective upon which it has relatively more influence (Mundell, 1962). The reason is that, otherwise, it may happen that it will not be possible to achieve equilibrium, as we shall see shortly.

Now, it can be argued that monetary policy has a relatively greater effect on external equilibrium. In fact, let us examine a monetary and a fiscal intervention with the same quantitative effects on aggregate demand and therefore on income. They have likewise an effect on the balance of payments, which is greater in the case of monetary policy, because it acts not only on current transactions (by way of variations induced on imports by variations in income — which is an identical effect to that which can be obtained by way of fiscal policy —), but it also acts upon capital movements by way of variations in the interest rate.

It follows from all this that monetary policy must be associated with the external target, while fiscal policy must be associated with the internal target; otherwise, as we said, it may be impossible to reach the situation of external and internal balance. A much simplified example may serve to clarify these statements.

Consider a situation in which income is 100 units below the full employment level and there is a balance-of-payments deficit of ten. An increase of 100 in income, obtained by way of fiscal policy, causes, for example, an increase of 20 in imports (assuming there is a marginal propensity to import of 0.20) so that the balance-of-payments deficit rises to 30. A restrictive monetary policy is now set into motion, which causes, let us say, a decrease in income of 50, with a consequent reduction in imports of 10; this policy also causes an improvement in the capital movements balance of, say, 15. The net result of the two policies is that an increase in income of 50 is obtained, and a reduction in the balance-of-payments deficit from 10 to 5. If we continue in this way, it is possible, through successive adjustments, to reach a point at which the two targets are simultaneously achieved.

Now consider the same initial situation and pair the instruments and targets in the opposite way to that just examined. An expansionary monetary policy which causes an increase in income of 100 also causes, alongside it, an increase of 20 in imports, a worsening in the capital balance of, let's say, 10; consequently, the balance-of-payments deficit passes from 10 to 40. Now, in order to reduce this deficit, or even simply to bring it down to the initial level of 10, by means of fiscal policy, it is necessary for the fiscal policy adopted to cause a restriction in income of 150 (hence a reduction in imports of 30) which is greater than the initial expansion. The net result is that income is reduced while the balance of payments remains unaltered. The process clearly moves further away from equilibrium.

It is also possible to provide an intuitive graphic analysis of the problem of pairing off instruments and targets by the use of an arrow diagram (see Fig. 15.16)[38]. Let us again look at the case already analyzed statically in Fig. 15.15. If fiscal policy is associated with internal equilibrium, government expenditure

---

[38] For an alternative graphic representation, based on a diagram on the axes of which the two instruments are measured, cfr. Mundell (1962).

15.5 Monetary and Fiscal Policy for External and Internal Balance

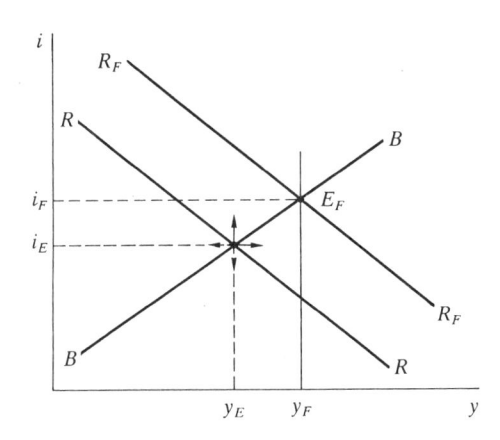

Fig. 15.16. Internal and external balance and monetary and fiscal policy under fixed exchange rates: the assignment problem

increases and the RR schedule tends to shift to the right (unbroken horizontal arrow) and, at the same time, if the monetary policy is associated with external equilibrium, it intervenes by causing the interest rate to increase (unbroken vertical arrow) because the increase in income, caused by the fiscal policy, has led, on account of the increase in imports, to a deficit in the balance of payments (which was initially in equilibrium). It can be seen therefore that the system, by moving in a direction between the two arrows, tends towards the point of equilibrium E_F.

With a similar piece of reasoning applied to the case in which fiscal policy is associated with external equilibrium and monetary policy with internal equilibrium, the broken-line arrows are obtained, which point in the opposite direction to that in which equilibrium is found.

15.5.2.1 Observations and Qualifications

What has been said so far illustrates in simplified form the problem of achieving simultaneous internal and external equilibrium and its solution; for a more rigorous analysis see Sect. A.15.4. Here we wish instead to review the various objections which have been raised to the theory so far described, that is, the possibility of achieving internal and external balance by way of an appropriate combination of monetary and fiscal policy.

(1) The first observation that one can make is that capital movements induced by manoeuvring the interest rate are short-term movements, which take the place of movements of reserves and of compensatory official financing. They are thus appropriate for correcting temporary and reversible disequilibria in the balance of payments, but not fundamental disequilibria. The manoeuvre in question can therefore cope with conjunctural disequilibria, but not structural ones, which must be cured by different means.

(2) When there is a serious and chronic deficit in the balance of payments, it is probable that even a drastic increase in the rate of interest will have no favourable effect on capital movements, as operators expect a devaluation in the exchange rate and shift their capital to other currencies, notwithstanding the increase in the rate of interest. However, this criticism is valid only in the case when one tries, as it were, to close the stable door after the horse has

bolted, that is, in the case in which the policy-maker intervenes by adopting a combination of monetary and fiscal policies when the situation has already become serious. In fact, this kind of combination should be an *habitual* policy, used constantly, precisely with the aim of *preventing* the situation from coming about in which the policy becomes ineffective. A necessary condition for prevention in this way, even if not sufficient in itself, is that the policy-maker has a wealth of information and acts with great speed and timeliness of intervention.

(3) As we have already observed in Sect. 15.4.3.1, it is to be presumed that capital flows induced by a *given* difference between domestic and foreign interest rates will be *limited*. This is a consequence of the general principle of capital stock adjustment. In fact, to each given difference between the rates of interest, there corresponds a certain stock of financial capital which investors wish to place; if the existing stock (that is, the stock they have already placed) is different, there will be a capital flow — spread out over a certain period of time — to bring the stock already in existence up to the level desired. Once the adjustment process is completed, the flows cease. In order to start them off again it is necessary for the difference between the rates of interest to vary, so that the desired stock will be made to diverge once again from that in existence, and so on and so forth. From all this the following conclusions can be drawn: if the disequilibrium in the current account persists over time, then it is necessary to continue to broaden the difference between the interest rates to keep the equilibrating flows of capital in existence; but it may not turn out to be possible to broaden the difference beyond a certain limit.

(4) According to some writers (for example, Johnson, 1965) the capital flows are also sensitive to the level of income, on account of the profitability expected from investment in shares, which would be positively connected to the level of income. If one admits this sensitivity, the comparative advantage of the monetary over the fiscal policy with regard to the balance of payments is no longer certain. Note that this objection is not directed so much at the theory in general, but rather at the instrument-target assignment mentioned above, which could be turned upside down if this sensitivity is taken into consideration.

(5) As we have already said in Sect. 15.4.3.1, increasing interest rates put an increasing load on interest payments (these payments have not been considered in the previous treatment). At a certain point, these payments could more than offset the advantage of increased inflows of foreign capital. In other words, the sum of the capital movements balance plus the interest payments could react *negatively* to an increase in the domestic interest rate. In this case, of course, the correct assignment is uncertain *a priori* (this objection, like the previous one, is directed at Mundell's assignment and not at the general theory).

(6) Finally, in order to achieve the desired simultaneous equilibrium, it may happen that the instruments have to assume values which are *politically and institutionally unacceptable* (for example, unacceptable levels of fiscal pressure or unacceptably high values for the interest rate). If, let us suppose,

the domestic demand is very sensitive to monetary restrictions while capital movements are relatively insensitive to the rate of interest, then in a situation of underemployment and balance-of-payments deficit, it would be necessary to introduce a very considerable increase in the interest rate to attract sufficient capital and a no less considerable increase in public expenditure to compensate for the depressive effect of the increase in the interest rate and to bring income up to full employment. These exceptional increases could turn out to be politically and institutionally unacceptable, as we said, consequently making it impossible to achieve simultaneous internal and external equilibrium. Naturally these are considerations which may or may not be relevant according to the values assumed by the various parameters in each given concrete case.

These critical observations make it permissible at least to doubt that the appropriate combination of monetary and fiscal policies is a panacea, even though it cannot be denied that it has some validity as a short-term expedient. If this is the case, there seems to be no other way out than the introduction of another instrument, such as flexibility of exchange rates (not necessarily free and complete, but even controlled and limited), with regard to which we shall have occasion to discuss exhaustively in the coming chapters. For further considerations of the problem of monetary and fiscal policy in an open economy under a regime of fixed interest rates, see von Neumann Whitman (1970), Casprini (1973), Tsiang (1975) and Gandolfo (1980).

15.5.3 The Policy Coordination Problem across Countries

The problem of internal and external equilibrium and that connected with the assignment of instruments to targets have been tackled, to use the terminology of Sect. 11.4, within the context of a one-country model. As soon as we pass from this simplified model to a two-country model, the problem becomes more complicated and, in particular, there arises the problem of *redundancy* and the more complex one of *coordination*.

The redundancy problem refers to the fact that, if at the one-country level there is equality between the number of instruments and the number of targets (including balance-of-payments equilibrium), at the international level it necessarily happens that there is one more instrument than there are targets. This derives from the fact that the sum of the imbalances in international payments of all countries (expressed in a common unit of measure) is by definition zero, so that if $n-1$ countries have a balance of payments in equilibrium then the nth, without having to do anything about it, will have its own balance of payments in equilibrium. This country thus has a degree of freedom insofar as it may take no notice of its balance of payments and use the instrument thus freed for other purposes. As any country may in theory be the nth, it is necessary to establish which of the n countries will enjoy this privilege (the so-called nth country problem), which cannot be done solely within the ambit of economics; alternatively an additional target can be established by common accord.

Within the context of a two-country model the problem is easy to represent. There are four instruments (government expenditure, and interest rate[39] of both countries) and the targets are reduced from four (equilibrium in the balance of payments and full employment in both countries) to three, because balance-of-payments equilibrium of one country necessarily implies balance-of-payments equilibrium of the other. As it would be arbitrary to attribute to one country rather than the other the exploitation of the degree of freedom, we can assume that one other objective is the presence of a *zero balance in capital movements*, that is, *full* equilibrium of the balance of payments, thus also resolving the problem of its composition.

This is a plausible hypothesis, insofar as it makes it possible to eliminate all those problems that derive from the presence of an equilibrium in the overall balance of payments but with disequilibria in the capital movements account (a growing burden for the payment of interest etc.: cfr. Sects. 15.4.3.1 and 15.5.2.1).

Equipped with this additional hypothesis, we can pass on to deal with the *problem of coordination* of economic policies. We must note at once that we are not speaking here of "coordination" in the vague (or obvious) sense in which the term is sometimes used (that is that the various countries must not be following conflicting objectives and policies), but in the technical sense in which the term is used by Cooper (1969). More precisely, we speak of "coordination":

(a) when a country, instead of adjusting each instrument in relation to one single target, adjusts it by taking all its own objectives into account (internal coordination);
(b) when each country manages each instrument not only as under (a), but also taking into account the targets of the rest of the world (international coordination or "full coordination" in Cooper's terminology).

The coordination problem can be summed up in the question of whether domestic and/or international coordination represent an improvement on the simple instrument-target pairing-off situation described above. The improvement will be measured, following Cooper, in terms of greater speed of convergence of the system to the point of equilibrium (that is, to the given values of the targets), naturally given the same initial situation. Cooper showed, through numerical examples, that coordination in effect gives rise to more rapid convergence. However, it is possible to go beyond numerical examples and to obtain more general results with an analysis in which:

(1) we do not assume a predetermined mode for associating each instrument with the additional objectives (by additional objectives we mean all those targets different from the "principal" one, to which each instrument is assigned according to the rule of simple pairing), in the sense that the way in which a given instrument must react to a given additional target is not specified (apart from the linear form), but is determined so as to contribute positively to the velocity of convergence;
(2) we shall not base our work on examples and numerical simulations, but will avail ourselves of more powerful analytical methods.

---

[39] Always on the hypothesis of normal capital mobility; hence the two countries can have different rates of interest.

15.5 Monetary and Fiscal Policy for External and Internal Balance

We must now specify the criteria on the basis of which the instruments are managed. They are the following:

(a) *Simple Pairing*. The fiscal policy is directed towards the internal target and monetary policy towards the external target in the way already seen in Sect. 15.5.2, that is:

(a_1) Government expenditure is increased (reduced) if national income is less than (more than) the full employment level;

(a_2) The interest rate is increased (reduced) if there is a deficit (surplus) in the balance of payments.

(b) *Internal Coordination*. Monetary policy and fiscal policy are directed at both objectives, namely:

(b_1) Besides being adjusted as in (a_1), government expenditure is also adjusted in relation to the external target, in a way to be determined;

(b_2) Besides being adjusted as in (a_2), the interest rate is also adjusted in relation to the internal target, in a way to be determined.

(c) *International Coordination*. In each country, monetary and fiscal policies are managed not only in relation to the targets of the country itself, but also in relation to the other country's targets, that is, in both countries:

(c_1) Besides being adjusted as in (b_1), government expenditure is also adjusted in relation to the internal target of the other country, in a way to be determined[40];

(c_2) Besides being adjusted as in (b_2), the interest rate is also adjusted in relation to the internal target of the other country, in a way to be determined.

The examination of this problem requires an analysis which is extremely complex from a mathematical view-point (see Sect. A.15.5). Here we shall limit ourselves to a discussion of the main results of the analysis: internal and international coordination (the latter more than the former), in effect bring an improvement, provided that certain rules are followed regarding the association of each instrument with the additional targets. If these rules are not followed, coordination may cause a deterioration rather than an improvement in the situation. These rules are not immutable, but can vary according to the position of the system with respect to the position of the equilibrium point. In other words, the type of additional associations cannot be fixed once and for all, as the associations in simple pairing can, but may require changes in accordance with the above-mentioned position. Consequently the straightforward nature and lack of ambiguity of the simple assignment are lost and the chances of errors in economic policy increase. The policy-maker must therefore make an assessment of whether the gain in terms of rapidity of approach to the targets is such that it more than compensates for the above mentioned disadvantages.

For an alternative approach to the policy-coordination problem see Sect. 20.7.

---

[40] Since each country, by taking account of its own external target, also takes account of the other country's external target, it is unnecessary to introduce here the external target of the other country. The same observation holds in relation to (c_2).

15.6 Portfolio Equilibrium in an Open Economy

15.6.1 Introduction

We have already mentioned (Sects. 15.4.3.1 and 15.5.1) the problems which arise when capital movements are no longer considered to be pure flows, but ones which derive from stock adjustments. The formulation of these adjustments comes within the framework of the Tobin-Markowitz theory of portfolio equilibrium, extended to an open economy by McKinnon and Oates (1966), McKinnon (1969), Branson (1968, 1974) and numerous other scholars.

The extension of the theory of portfolio equilibrium to international capital movements can be effected in two principal ways. The first is to see the problem as one of partial equilibrium, that is, by examining how the holders of wealth divide up their wealth among the various national and international assets in a context in which national income, current transactions in the balance of payments, etc., are given by hypothesis, that is to say, are exogenous variables. This problem will be dealt with in Sect. 15.6.2.

The second way is to insert the portfolio analysis of capital movements into the framework of macroeconomic equilibrium, in which therefore national income, current transactions, etc., are endogenous variables. One thus obtains a more general and more satisfactory model (which can be considered an evolution of the one in Sect. 15.4), but which is also more complicated, because alongside flow equilibria and disequilibria, it is necessary to consider stock equilibria and disequilibria and also the interrelations between stocks and flows over the short and long terms. We shall deal with these matters in Sect. 15.6.3.

15.6.2 Asset Stock Adjustment in a Partial Equilibrium Framework

The central idea of the Tobin-Markowitz theory of portfolio equilibrium[41] is that the holders of financial wealth (which is a magnitude with the nature of a stock) divide their wealth among the various assets[42] on the basis of the yield and risk of the assets themselves. Let us suppose therefore that the holders of wealth have a choice between national money, and national and foreign bonds; if we indicate total wealth by W, considered exogenous, and the three components just mentioned by L, N and F, we have first of all the balance constraint:

$$L+N+F=W, \quad \frac{L}{W}+\frac{N}{W}+\frac{F}{W}=1. \tag{15.20}$$

---

[41] We have already mentioned this theory in the Appendix to Chap. 10. For further information, cfr. Markowitz (1959) and Tobin (1969).

[42] In general the wealth holder's portfolio can also contain real goods (for example, fixed capital) or securities that represent them (shares). For simplicity we ignore this component and only take account of the main purely financial assets; another simplifying hypothesis is that private residents cannot hold foreign currencies (for the "currency substitution" models, in which, in theory, private residents also can freely hold foreign currencies, see Sect. A.18.3.4).

15.6 Portfolio Equilibrium in an Open Economy

The three fractions are determined, as we said, on the basis of the yield and risk, account also being taken of income[43]; supposing for the sake of simplicity that the risk element does not undergo any variations, we have the functions

$$\frac{L}{W} = h(i_h, i_f, y), \quad \frac{N}{W} = g(i_h, i_f, y), \quad \frac{F}{W} = f(i_h, i_f, y), \quad (15.21)$$

where i_h and i_f indicate as usual the home and foreign interest rates respectively. The three functions (15.21) are not independent of each other insofar as once two of them are known the third is also determined given the balance constraint (15.20).

It is then assumed that these functions have certain plausible properties. First of all, the fraction of wealth held in the form of money is a decreasing function of the yields of both national and foreign bonds: an increase in the interest rates i_h and i_f has, other things being equal, a depressive effect on the demand for money and, obviously, an expansionary effect on the demand for bonds (see below). Also, h is an increasing function of y and this means that, on the whole, the demand for bonds is a decreasing function of y.

The fraction of wealth held in the form of domestic bonds, on account of what has just been said, is an increasing function of i_h; it is, furthermore, a decreasing function of i_f insofar as an increase in the foreign interest rate will induce the holders of wealth to prefer foreign bonds, *ceteris paribus*. Similarly the fraction of wealth held in the form of foreign bonds is an increasing function of i_f and a decreasing function of i_h. Finally the fraction of wealth held totally in the form of bonds, $(N+F)/W$, is — for the reasons given above — a decreasing function of y.

We could at this point introduce similar equations for the rest of the world, but so as to simplify the analysis we shall make the assumption of a small country and thus use a one-country model[44]. This implies that the foreign interest rate is exogenous and that the variations in the demand for foreign bonds on the part of residents do not influence the foreign market for these bonds, so that the (foreign) supply of foreign bonds to residents is perfectly elastic. Another implication of the small-country hypothesis is that non-residents have no interest in holding bonds from this country, so that capital flows are due to the fact that residents buy foreign bonds (capital outflow) or sell them (capital inflow).

Having made this assumption, we now pass to the description of the asset market equilibrium and introduce, alongside the demand functions for the various assets, the respective supply functions, which we shall indicate by M for money and N^S for domestic bonds; for foreign bonds no symbol is needed as the hypothesis that their supply is perfectly elastic has the effect that the supply is always equal to the demand on the part of residents. The equilibrium under consideration is described as usual by the condition that supply and demand are equal, that is[45]

$$M = h(i_h, i_f, y)W, \quad N^S = g(i_h, i_f, y)W, \quad F = f(i_h, i_f, y)W. \quad (15.22)$$

---

[43] Among other things, this accounts for the transactions demand for money.
[44] It has been demonstrated that, within the framework under consideration, the results of a two-country model would not be substantially different: see, e.g., De Grauwe (1983, Sect. 10.13).
[45] The demand functions expressed as levels, rather than as fractions, are immediately obtained from (15.21), if we multiply through by W: for example, $L = h(i_h, i_f, y)W$, etc.

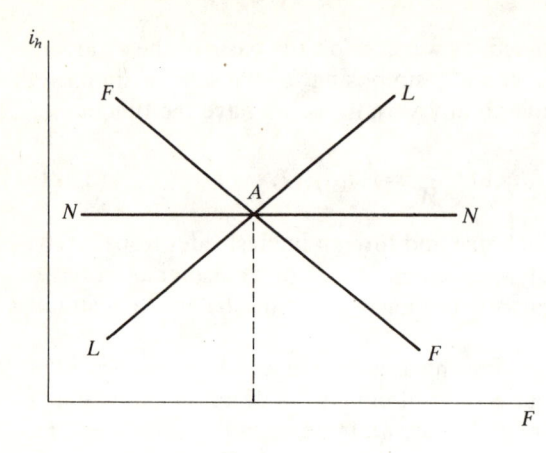

Fig. 15.17. Determination of portfolio equilibrium in an open economy

It is easy to demonstrate that only two of (15.22) are independent and therefore that, when any two of these three equations are satisfied, the third is necessarily also satisfied. This is a reflection of the general rule (also called Walras' law) according to which, when n markets are connected by a balance constraint, if any $n-1$ of them are in equilibrium, then the nth is necessarily in equilibrium. In the case under consideration, let us begin by observing that the *given* stock of wealth W is the same seen from both the demand and the supply sides, namely

$$M + N^S + F = W. \tag{15.20.1}$$

From Eqs. (15.20) and (15.21), we obtain

$$h(i_h,i_f,y)W + g(i_h,i_f,y)W + f(i_h,i_f,y)W = W, \tag{15.23}$$

and so, if we subtract (15.23) from (15.20.1), we obtain

$$[M - h(i_h,i_f,y)W] + [N^S - g(i_h,i_f,y)W] + [F - f(i_h,i_f,y)W] = 0, \tag{15.22.1}$$

which is the formal statement of Walras' law. From Eq. (15.22.1) we see that, if any two of the expressions in square brackets are zero (namely, if any two of Eqs. (15.22) are satisfied), the third is also.

Equations (15.22) therefore provide us with two independent equations which, together with (15.20.1) make it possible to determine the three unknowns, which were the home interest rate (i_h), the stock of foreign bonds held by residents (F), and the stock of domestic money (M): the equilibrium values of these three variables will thus result from the solution of the problem of portfolio equilibrium, while the stock of domestic bonds (N^S) is given as are i_f, y and W.

The system being examined can be represented graphically. In Fig. 15.17, taken from De Grauwe (1983, Chap. 10), we have shown three schedules, LL, NN and FF, derived from Eqs. (15.22). The LL schedule represents the combinations of i_h and F which keep the money market in equilibrium, given, of course, the

15.6 Portfolio Equilibrium in an Open Economy   233

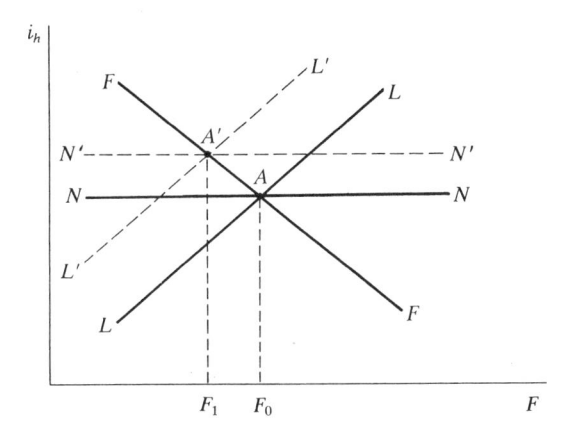

Fig. 15.18. Monetary policy, portfolio equilibrium and capital movements

exogenous variables. It is upward sloping on account of the following considerations. An increase in the stock of foreign securities held by residents implies – *ceteris paribus* (and so given N) – a decrease in the money stock (because residents give up domestic money to the central bank in exchange for foreign money to buy the foreign securities). Thus in order to maintain monetary equilibrium, domestic money demand must be correspondingly reduced, which requires an increase in i_h.

The NN schedule represents the combinations of i_h and F which ensure equilibrium in the domestic bond market. It is a horizontal line because, whatever the amount of foreign bonds held by residents, variations in this amount give rise to variations of equal absolute value in the stock of money[46], but in the opposite direction, so that W does not change. Hence the demand for domestic bonds does not vary and consequently, as its supply is given, i_h cannot vary.

Finally, the FF schedule represents the combinations of i_h and F which keep the demand for foreign bonds on the part of residents equal to the supply (which, remember, is perfectly elastic). It has a negative slope because an increase in i_h by generating, as we have said, a reduction in the residents' demand for foreign bonds, generates an equal reduction in the stock of these bonds held by residents themselves.

The three schedules necessarily intersect at the same point A, thanks to Walras' law, mentioned above. In economic terms, given the stock of domestic bonds N^S and the other exogenous variables, the equilibrium in the market for these bonds determines i_h. Consequently the demand for money is determined and thus the stock of foreign bonds to which it corresponds, given the balance constraint, a stock of money exactly equal to the demand for money itself.

What interests us particularly in all this analysis is to examine what happens to capital movements as a consequence of monetary policy, which, by acting on the national interest rate, generates a portfolio reallocation. In this context, monetary policy influences the interest rate indirectly, by acting on the stock of money. This action can come about in various ways, for example by way of open market

---

[46] The mechanism is the same as that described above with regard to LL. An increase (decrease) in F means that residents give up to (acquire from) the central bank national money in exchange for foreign currency. Note that F is already expressed in terms of national currency at the given and fixed rate of exchange.

operations, in which the central bank trades national bonds for money[47]. Let us suppose then that the monetary authorities increase the supply of domestic bonds, N^S. We can now begin an examination of the shifts in the various schedules. NN shifts in parallel upwards to position $N'N'$: in fact, a greater value of i_h is needed in order to have a greater value of the demand for bonds so as to absorb the greater supply. In concomitance, LL shifts upwards to the left, because, as a consequence of the aquisition of new bonds, the stock of money is reduced. The FF schedule remains where it was, because none of the exogenous variables[48] present in it has shifted.

The new point of equilibrium is obviously A' to which there corresponds a stock of foreign bonds (F_1) *less* than that (F_0) which occurred in correspondence to the previous point of equilibrium A. The reduction in the stock of foreign bonds from F_0 to F_1 obviously involves an *inflow* of capital, but when this stock has reached the new position of equilibrium, these capital movements will cease, and can begin again only in the case of a further increase in i_h. This provides a rigorous demonstration of what was already said in Sects. 15.4.3.1 and 15.5.2.1.

We shall conclude with a mention of the dynamic process which takes the system from A to A'. The supply of new domestic bonds on the part of the monetary authorities creates an excess supply of bonds with respect to the previous situation of equilibrium, so that the price falls: thus i_h, which is inversely related to the price of bonds, increases until the demand for bonds increases to a sufficient extent to absorb the greater supply. As the bonds are sold by the monetary authorities in exchange for money, the stock of money is reduced; besides, as i_h has increased, the demand for money falls so that monetary equilibrium is maintained. Finally, as the demand for foreign bonds is in inverse relationship to i_h, the increase in the latter leads to a reduction in F of which we have already spoken. As the quantities being demanded and supplied have the nature of *stocks* and as the total in existence (wealth W) is given[49], once the new equilibrium stocks have been reached, the adjustment flows will cease, including the capital movements, as already stated.

15.6.3 Portfolio Equilibrium and Macroeconomic Equilibrium

15.6.3.1 Introductory Remarks

When, within a macroeconomic equilibrium framework, one proceeds to the integration of stocks and flows, it is necessary to take a series of problems into account (usually neglected in analyses based solely on flows), among which

(a) the way the budget deficit is financed. It is in fact clear that, to the extent in which it is financed by issuing bonds, the stock of these increases, possibly

---

[47] These operations obviously leave the total wealth W unaltered. Other operations on the other hand — for example the financing of the government's deficit by the printing of money — cause variations in W. However, the results do not change quantitatively. Cfr., for example, De Grauwe (1983, Sect. 10.5).

[48] From (15.22) it can be seen that the exogenous variables in FF are W, i_f and y; in NN they are W, i_f, y, N^S (the last of which has increased); in LL they are W, i_f, y and M (the last of which has decreased).

[49] It is clear that if W went on increasing in time, then there could be a continuous flow of capital.

causing modifications in financial wealth and in portfolio equilibrium. Similar observations hold as regards the financing by printing money.
(b) The presence in private disposable income (on which private expenditure depends) of the flow of interest on bonds (both domestic and foreign) owned by residents.
(c) The payment of interest on government bonds constitutes a component of government expenditure, which must be explicitly taken into account. Besides — as we have already seen in Sects. 15.4.3.1 and 15.5.2.1 — the interest on the part of those government bonds owned by nonresidents is counted in the balance of payments, as is the interest received by residents on the foreign bonds that they own.

15.6.3.2 A Simple Model

In the following treatment, we shall adopt certain simplifying hypotheses, which will allow us to make the exposition less complex, without losing sight of the central points. First of all there is the assumption — common to the whole of the present chapter — of fixed exchange rates and rigid prices, by which nominal and real magnitudes coincide. Let us assume then that there are only two assets, money and securities. We now make the small country assumption and the assumption of *perfect capital mobility* with perfect asset substitutability[50]: this means not only that capital is freely mobile, but also that domestic and foreign securities are homogeneous[51], so that the national interest rate is exogenous (equal to the given foreign interest rate). Finally — with reference to the matrix of real and financial flows shown in Sect. 11.3 — we shall consolidate the sectors of public administration and banking (which in turn includes the central bank and the commercial banks) into a single sector which for brevity we shall call the public sector. This public sector, then, can finance any excess of expenditure over receipts both by issuing bonds and by printing money.

The consideration of the payment of interest by the public sector on securities which it has issued makes it necessary to divide total public expenditure, G, into two components: one of course consisting of the payment of this interest, iN^g, and the other of the purchase of goods and services which we shall call G_R. According to a first thesis, the discretionary variable of current public expenditure is therefore G_R, the variable which the government fixes exogenously. According to another thesis, the policy-maker fixes the total expenditure G exogenously, and so the amount of expenditure for goods and services G_R becomes an endogenous variable, as it is determined by difference once interest payments have been accounted for. Finally — as others observe — there are all the intermediate possibilities, which occur when the policy-maker in determining G_R takes account with a certain weight (represented by a parameter between zero and one) of the

---

[50] Perfect capital mobility is often taken to imply perfect asset substitutability automatically (as, for example, is implicit in Mundell, 1968, Chap. 18). See Sect. 10.7.6.
[51] This homogeneity does not mean that, in the portfolios of residents and nonresidents alike, there cannot be both domestic and foreign securities: as there can be different subjective evaluations on the part of both residents and nonresidents which, as we already know, concur, together with objective elements, in determining portfolio equilibrium.

payment of interest. Following O'Connell (1984), we shall now introduce an auxiliary variable Z, which represents the discretionary variable of economic policy[52] and is made up of the sum of the expenditure for goods and services and of the fraction k of interest payments:

$$Z = G_R + kiN^g, \quad 0 \leq k \leq 1, \tag{15.24}$$

while the actual total public expenditure is, as stated above,

$$G = G_R + iN^g. \tag{15.25}$$

We see at once that, for $k=0$, we have $Z=G_R$ (the first of the theses illustrated above), while for $k=1$ we have $Z=G$ (the second thesis); for $0<k<1$ there are all the intermediate cases. By substituting from (15.24) into (15.25), we have

$$G = Z + (1-k)iN^g. \tag{15.26}$$

Fiscal revenue is assumed, for simplicity, to be proportional to personal income in accordance with a constant rate, u. Personal income is given by the sum of the domestic product Y and residents' income from interest on both domestic and foreign securities held by them. The stock of domestic securities[53] N^g is held in part by residents (N_p) and in part by non-residents (N_f, where[54] $N_p + N_f = N^g$); residents also hold a stock of foreign securities F_p. Personal income is therefore $Y + i(N_p + F_p)$. From the above it follows that the public sector budget deficit, which we indicate by g[55], is

$$g = G - u(Y + iN_p + iF_p) = Z + (1-k)iN^g - u(Y + iN_p + iF_p), \tag{15.27}$$

where in the second passage we have used (15.26).

We now move on to the balance of payments, which we divide into current account (CA) and capital movements (K). The current account includes, besides imports and exports of goods and services, interest payments on domestic securities held by nonresidents and income from interest on foreign securities held by residents (item: "investment income" in the balance of payments: see Sect. 11.1.3[56]). In symbols

$$CA = x_0 - m[(1-u)(Y + iN_p + iF_p), W] - i(N^g - N_p) + iF_p, \tag{15.28}$$

where exports are as usual assumed to be exogenous, while imports are a function not only of disposable income (with a positive marginal propensity to import, but

---

[52] The two extreme theses are already present in Christ (1979); the introduction of the parameter k makes a simple generalizations possible.

[53] These are assumed to be perpetuities, as are foreign bonds.

[54] As we have consolidated the sector of the public administration, the central and commercial banks, any public securities held by the latter two of these sectors to meet issues by the first sector cancel out.

[55] It is assumed that interest on government bonds is subject to taxation. The introduction of tax-exemption would tend to complicate the treatment without substantially changing the results.

[56] As we know, unilateral transfers are also present in the current account. On account of their exogenous nature we can ignore them (for example by assuming that they have a nil balance) without altering the results of the analysis substantially.

less than one), but also of the stock of private wealth W, so as to account for a possible wealth effect[57] on total private expenditure (thus on the part of it which is directed to foreign goods). Wealth is defined as the sum of the stock of money M and the stock of domestic[58] and foreign securities held by residents:

$$W = M + N_p + F_p. \tag{15.29}$$

Capital movements are given by the *flow* of securities, that is by the *variation* in the stock of domestic securities held by non-residents net of the *variation* in the stock of foreign securities held by residents; remembering the recording rules for capital movements, we have

$$K = \Delta(N^g - N_p) - \Delta F_p = \Delta N^g - \Delta N_p - \Delta F_p. \tag{15.30}$$

The overall balance is, obviously,

$$B = CA + K. \tag{15.31}$$

The equation for the determination of income in an open economy is, as usual,

$$Y = d[(1-u)(Y + iN_p + iF_p), W] + x_0 + (Z - kiN^g), \tag{15.32}$$

where domestic demand d is a function of disposable income and wealth (see above) and $Z - kiN^g$ is G_R — cfr. (15.24) — that is the government expenditure for goods and services. The marginal propensity to domestic expenditure is as usual assumed to be positive, but less than one.

We then have the equation for monetary equilibrium

$$M = L(Y, W), \tag{15.33}$$

where the demand for money is an increasing function of income and of the stock of wealth (this derives from the portfolio equilibrium discussed in Sect. 15.6.2)[59]. The interest rate, being given and constant, has been omitted for brevity.

It is now necessary to stress an important point. While in a static context the stocks of assets are considered given, in a dynamic context they vary and this variation is due to the balance of payments and the budget deficit. This can be seen from the matrix of real and financial flows explained in Sect. 11.3 (duly consolidated according to the assumptions made at the beginning of the present section), but it can also be simply explained within the framework of the present model. The public sector finances its own deficit either by issuing securities or by printing money; a part of the variation in the money supply is therefore due to the financing of the public deficit, to which a part of the new issue of securities is also due (variations in the stock of securities). The money stock also varies, as we

---

[57] The wealth effect — which we have already dealt with in another regard in Sect. 14.1 — is too well known to need clarification here. See any macroeconomics text.

[58] We do not wish to enter here into the controversy on whether domestic (government) bonds can be considered net wealth and the related "Ricardian equivalence theorem" (see, for example, Tobin, 1980, Chap. III, and references therein); we shall simply assume — here and in the following chapters — that they are to be included in W.

[59] As only two assets exist (remember the assumption of homogeneity between domestic and foreign securities), the balance constraint makes it possible to omit the function of demand for securities.

know, in consequence of disequilibria in the balance of payments (variations in the stock of international reserves), which the monetary authorities can however sterilize in part or in their entirety; in the model before us this sterilization occurs through open market operations, that is, by a sale of government bonds to residents (in order to sterilize a balance-of-payments surplus) and a purchase from them (to sterilize a deficit). Another part of the variation in the stock of domestic securities is therefore due to these sterilization operations.

We can therefore state the relationships

$$\Delta M = sB + hg,$$
$$\Delta N^g = (1-s)B + (1-h)g, \quad 0 \leq s \leq 1, \quad 0 \leq h \leq 1, \tag{15.34}$$

where s represents the unsterilized fraction of the international payments imbalance and h the fraction of the public deficit financed by the printing of money. The meaning of (15.34) corresponds to what we have just said. In fact, given a payments imbalance B, a fraction $(1-s)B$ is sterilized by means of open market operations, while the remaining fraction sB gives rise to a change in the money supply. The latter also varies to finance a fraction h of the public deficit g, the remaining part of which, $(1-h)g$, is financed by the issue of bonds.

The model is now fully described and its solution and analysis can be carried out in successive phases. By following a now well-tried methodology for the analysis of stock-flow models, we shall distinguish between a *momentary or short-run* and a *long-run equilibrium*[60].

15.6.3.3 Momentary and Long-Run Equilibrium

At any given moment in time, in addition to intrinsically exogenous variables, there are certain stock variables that result from past flows, which can therefore also be dealt with as exogenous variables in finding out the solution to the model; this solution therefore determines a momentary equilibrium. With the passing of time, however, the stocks just referred to vary as a result of flows and thus become endogenous variables, whose equilibrium values must therefore be determined together with those of the other endogenous variables in the solution for the long-run equilibrium.

With reference to the model we are examining, we shall begin with the observation that at a given moment in time, in which the money supply and the stock of domestic securities are given, Eqs. (15.32), (15.33) and (15.29) constitute a short-term sub-system, which determines the momentary-equilibrium values of the domestic product Y, of the total stock of securities (domestic and foreign) held by residents $(N_p + F_p)$, and wealth W, as a function of the other magnitudes (x_0, Z, i, M, N^g): the first two are in the nature of pure flows, i is a "point" variable, i.e. a variable measured at a point in time, and the last two are stocks). Note that, while x_0, Z and i are *intrinsically exogenous* variables in the model, M and N^g are exogenous simply because we are considering an instant in time: in fact, with the passing of time these magnitudes will vary endogenously on the basis of the relationships (15.34).

---

[60] This terminology was introduced with regard to capital accumulation and growth models (see Gandolfo, 1980, pp. 483 ff.). The concepts expressed by this terminology, however, have general validity in the presence of stock-flow models where the stocks vary in time as a result of flows.

We now turn to the examination of long-run equilibrium, in which all the stocks must be in equilibrium. Stock equilibrium of the private sector means that wealth W must be constant in time. Thus, given definition (15.29), it is necessary for both money-supply M and the total stock of securities held by the private sector (N_p+F_p) to be stationary. Given (15.33), the fact that M and W are constant implies that Y must also be constant.

Furthermore, in private sector stock equilibrium, private "saving" is zero, using saving to mean the *unspent* part of disposable income (the spent part including both consumer and investment goods, both domestic and foreign). Alternatively, if saving is defined as that part of disposable income that is *not consumed*, then, in the equilibrium under study, there is equality between saving and investment[61]. This in turn implies — as a result of Eq. (11.1) — that the sum of the budget deficit and current account balance[62] is zero:

$$g+CA=0. \tag{15.35}$$

At this point we must ask ourselves whether, in addition to this condition, it is necessary for g and CA (in addition to the overall balance of payments B) to be separately zero. This requires an explicit consideration of the other conditions of long-run equilibrium, which we shall make by distinguishing the case in which the parameter k is positive from the one in which $k=0$.

When $k>0$, the condition for a stationary Y, already discussed above, implies, as can be seen from (15.32), that the stock of domestic bonds N^g will remain constant, that is $\Delta N^g=0$. As $\Delta M=0$ insofar as M must also be constant, as stated above, from Eq. (15.34) we have the conditions

$$sB+hg=0, \quad (1-s)B+(1-h)g=0. \tag{15.34.1}$$

If $s \neq h$, then these conditions can be simultaneously satisfied if and only if

$$B=0, \quad g=0, \tag{15.36}$$

which, together with (15.35), implies

$$CA=0. \tag{15.37}$$

Therefore, if the unsterilized fraction of the international payments imbalance is different from the fraction of the public deficit financed by the printing of

---

[61] In the opposite case, in fact, the stock of assets of the private sector would vary (cfr. (11.7.1) in Chap. 11), contrary to the condition that stocks should be stationary. Note that, if the constancy of the stock of physical capital is also considered among the conditions of stationarity, the investment in question will be that of replacement only.

[62] Remember that the variables EXP and IMP, present in the matrix of real and financial flows, include both goods and services; in the services, interest payments and receipts are included (item: investment income), which we have shown separately from all the other items (included in x_0 and m) for clarity of exposition. The same equation (15.35) can be arrived at within the framework of the model under examination starting from the relationship $(1-u)(Y+iN_p+iF_p)=d+m$, which expresses the condition that disposable income is entirely spent (on domestic goods d and foreign goods m), and by making the appropriate substitutions in Eqs. (15.27), (15.28) and (15.32).

money[63], then in the long-run equilibrium, the budget must be in equilibrium and there must be *full* equilibrium of the balance of payments because not only the overall balance, but also the current account and the capital account balances, taken separately, must be zero.

If, on the other hand, $s=h$, then from (15.34.1) it only follows that

$$B+g=0, \qquad (15.38)$$

which together with (15.35) implies

$$B=CA, \qquad (15.39)$$

and so, given (15.31),

$$K=0. \qquad (15.40)$$

Long-run equilibrium now only requires the capital movements balance to be zero, while the budget and the overall balance of payments (in this case coinciding with the current account balance) do not have to be in equilibrium. However, if we introduce a further condition into the analysis, that is, that the stock of international reserves R is stationary, then it is clear that long-run equilibrium requires the overall balance of payments (and therefore the budget) to be in equilibrium, because, as $\Delta R = B$, the stock of reserves will be stationary only if $B=0$.

Let us now consider the case $k=0$. The first observation is that interest payments on public debt disappear from the public expenditure term in the equation for the determination of the domestic product (15.32), which now becomes

$$Y = d[(1-u)(Y+iN_p+iF_p), W] + x_0 + G_R. \qquad (15.32.1)$$

Besides, letting $k=0$ in (15.24) and (15.27), the equation which expresses the public sector deficit becomes

$$g = G_R + iN^g - u(Y+iN_p+iF_p). \qquad (15.27.1)$$

The condition of private sector stock equilibrium (15.35), by using (15.27.1) and (15.28) becomes

$$G_R - u(Y+iN_p+iF_p) \\ + x_0 - m[(1-u)(Y+iN_p+iF_p), W] + iN_p + iF_p = 0. \qquad (15.41)$$

This condition now, like (15.32.1), is independent of N^g. Thus the condition of a stationary Y does *not* imply the constancy of the stock of domestic bonds, in other words the short-run model is independent of the outstanding stock of domestic bonds. Equation (15.41), together with the temporary equilibrium model, now consisting of Eqs. (15.32.1), (15.29) and (15.33), determines the long-run equilibrium values of Y, $(N_p+F_p), W, M$.

---

[63] We can assume that this is the normal case as there does not seem to be any economic reason why these two fractions have to be equal.

The stationary nature of M makes it possible to obtain the "equilibrium" balance of payments (in the sense of the balance of payments compatible with long-run equilibrium) from the first of Eqs. (15.34)

$$B = -\frac{h}{s}g, \tag{15.42}$$

which is in general different from zero; if, as is normal, we assume that the budget is in deficit ($g>0$) then $B<0$. Note also that, as N^g is not now necessarily constant, K can also be different from zero. Naturally if we impose the additional condition of stationary international reserves in the long-run, then it should be that $B=0$, which can occur in general when $g=0$ (balanced budget).

Apart from this obvious case, it can be seen from (15.42) that $B=0$ also when $h=0$, that is when the public deficit is financed entirely by issuing new securities. The implication of this is that, as the (domestic and foreign) stock of bonds held by residents is determined, the entire amount of the new bonds issued is absorbed by nonresidents, as can be seen from (15.30), where $K = \Delta N^g$. The overall balance of payments is therefore in equilibrium, with a deficit on current account, matched by an equivalent surplus on capital account. Naturally — as the balance $x_0 - m$ is given, because the variables which influence m are given — there will be an increasing deficit on current account and a concomitantly increasing budget deficit, which reflects the increasing interest payments.

The overall balance of payments will tend towards zero also when $h>s$. From (15.42) it can be seen that if we start from a budget deficit, the balance of payments will have a greater deficit in absolute value. And as the fraction of the budget deficit that is financed by issuing securities $(1-h)$ is smaller than the fraction of the deficit in the balance of payments which is sterilized by way of open market operations $(1-s)$, the stock of securities outstanding is reduced. Interest payments are reduced and therefore, *ceteris paribus*, the current account and the deficit in the balance of payments tend towards zero.

We conclude with the observation that we have not yet talked about the problem of full employment: it is however easy to see that, as in any case the solution of the model expresses the equilibrium values of the endogenous variables in terms of the exogenous ones, including the policy variable Z, it is in principle possible to fix Z so that the resulting equilibrium value of Y coincides with that which corresponds to full employment Y_F. What happens to the balance of payments can then be determined by applying the analysis carried out above.

Appendix

A.15.1 A Formal Interpretation of the Classical Theory

Given the definition of the balance of payments,

$$B = px(p) - p_m m(p), \tag{A.15.1}$$

the condition by which a variation of p will cause the balance of payments to vary in the opposite direction is obtained by differentiating B with respect to p and putting $dB/dp<0$. We have

$$\frac{dB}{dp} = \frac{d[px - p_m m]}{dp} = p\frac{dx}{dp} + x - p_m\frac{dm}{dp} = x\left(\frac{p}{x}\frac{dx}{dp} + 1 - \frac{p_m}{x}\frac{dm}{dp}\right). \quad (A.15.2)$$

We now multiply and divide the last term in brackets by p/m, obtaining

$$\frac{dB}{dp} = x\left(\frac{p}{x}\frac{dx}{dp} + 1 - \frac{p_m m}{px}\frac{p}{m}\frac{dm}{dp}\right) = x\left(-\eta_x + 1 - \frac{p_m m}{px}\eta_m\right), \quad (A.15.2.1)$$

where

$$\eta_x \equiv -\frac{dx/x}{dp/p} \equiv -\frac{dx}{dp}\frac{p}{x}, \quad \eta_m \equiv \frac{dm/m}{dp/p} \equiv \frac{dm}{dp}\frac{p}{m}. \quad (A.15.3)$$

As $x > 0$, then $dB/dp < 0$ if and only if

$$-\eta_x + 1 - \frac{p_m m}{px}\eta_m < 0, \quad (A.15.4)$$

from which, reordering the terms, we obtain inequality (15.8) of the text.

In the text we used the fact that the value of exports varies by a percentage equal to that of the variation of price multiplied by $(1-\eta_x)$.

Putting $R = px$, we have

$$dR = xdp + pdx = xdp\left(1 + \frac{p}{x}\frac{dx}{dp}\right) = xdp(1-\eta_x), \quad (A.15.5)$$

and therefore, by dividing both sides by $R = px$, we have in fact

$$\frac{dR}{R} = \frac{dp}{p}(1-\eta_x). \quad (A.15.5.1)$$

We now come to the dynamic analysis. The assumption that the variation in the money supply coincides with the international payments imbalance, expressed in terms of differential equations rather than discrete variations as in the text, gives rise to the equation

$$\frac{dM}{dt} = px(p) - p_m m(p), \quad (A.15.6)$$

which — taking into account that from (15.1) we have $dM/dt = (y/V)dp/dt$ — becomes

$$\frac{dp}{dt} = \frac{V}{y}[px(p) - p_m m(p)]. \quad (A.15.7)$$

This is a differential equation of the first order; in order to examine its local stability, we linearize and consider the deviations from the equilibrium (indicated with a dash over the variable), thus obtaining

$$\frac{d\bar{p}}{dt} = \frac{V}{y}\left(x + p\frac{dx}{dp} - p_m\frac{dm}{dp}\right)\bar{p}, \quad (A.15.8)$$

where all the derivatives are calculated at the point of equilibrium. Indicating the expression in brackets with γ, the solution is

$$\bar{p}(t) = \bar{p}_0 e^{(V/y)\gamma t}, \tag{A.15.9}$$

where $\bar{p}_0$ indicates the initial deviation. A necessary and sufficient stability condition is that $\gamma < 0$. We note at once that γ coincides with dB/dp obtained above; from this it follows that the condition for dynamic stability is also $\eta_m + \eta_x > 1$ (seeing that we linearize at the point of equilibrium we have $p_m m = px$) and that there is dynamic stability if $dB/dp < 0$, that is, if B in Fig. 15.1a is decreasing. We also observe that, the greater the sum of the elasticities, the greater in absolute value is γ and therefore the more rapid the convergence towards equilibrium. The elasticities, therefore, influence not only the stability but also the velocity of adjustment.

The model we have presented is based on the small country hypothesis by which p_m can be considered as given. However, the results do not change substantially if a two-country model is considered: cfr. Gandolfo (1966). For further studies in the formalization of the classical theory of the balance of payments, cfr. Gandolfo (1980, pp. 535–540) and Samuelson (1980).

A.15.2 The Monetary Approach to the Balance of Payments

A.15.2.1 A Simple Model

If we express the model shown in the text in terms of differential equations, then from (15.16.1) and (15.14), we have the equation[64]

$$\frac{dM}{dt} = \alpha(kp\bar{y} - M), \tag{A.15.10}$$

the solution of which is

$$M(t) = (M_0 - M^e)e^{-\alpha t} + M^e, \tag{A.15.11}$$

where $M^e = kp\bar{y}$ represents the equilibrium money supply and M_0 the initial stock (so that $M_0 - M^e$ is the initial deviation). As α is a positive coefficient, it can be seen from (A.15.11) that $M(t)$ converges towards M^e so that the equilibrium is stable. The movements of the balance of payments can easily be obtained from the definitional relationship $B = dR/dt = dM/dt$, by which, taking account of (A.15.10) and (A.15.11), we have

$$B(t) = -\alpha(M_0 - M^e)e^{-\alpha t}, \tag{A.15.12}$$

from which it can be seen that $B(t)$ necessarily tends towards zero.

We mentioned in the text with regard to Proposition II, that, while it is possible within the context of a one-country model to consider p as given according to the relationship $p = rp_f$, in the context of a two-country model price levels are also determined endogenously.

---

[64] To avoid confusion, it should be noted that in this section — unlike the other ones in this Appendix — a dash over a variable denotes that it is given (and not a deviation from the equilibrium). This is for the sake of conformity with the notation used in the text.

A.15.2.2 A Two-Country Model

The two-country model has the same equations for each country as described in the text. So alongside (A.15.10), we have the analogous equation for the rest of the world

$$\frac{dM_f}{dt} = \alpha_f(k_f p_f \bar{y}_f - M_f). \tag{A.15.13}$$

As p and p_f are now unknowns, it is necessary to introduce two other equations. One is the already mentioned purchasing power parity relation, which is given here for convenience

$$p = r p_f. \tag{A.15.14}$$

The other is obtained from the assumption that the world money stock is a given constant[65]

$$M + r M_f = \bar{M}_w, \tag{A.15.15}$$

where the magnitudes are made homogeneous (which it is necessary to do in order to add them together) by expressing them in terms of the currency of the first country.

When both countries are in equilibrium, $M = kp\bar{y}$ and $M_f = k_f p_f \bar{y}_f$ and therefore, by substituting in (A.15.15) and taking account of (15.14), we have

$$kp\bar{y} + rk_f \frac{1}{r} p \bar{y}_f = \bar{M}_w. \tag{A.15.16}$$

By solving we obtain the equilibrium price levels

$$p^e = \frac{\bar{M}_w}{k\bar{y} + k_f \bar{y}_f}, \quad p_f^e = \frac{\frac{1}{r}\bar{M}_w}{k\bar{y} + k_f \bar{y}_f}, \tag{A.15.17}$$

given which, we can determine the optimum or equilibrium distribution of the world money supply

$$M^e = \frac{k\bar{M}_w}{k\bar{y} + k_f \bar{y}_f} \bar{y}, \quad M_f^e = \frac{\frac{1}{r} k_f \bar{M}_w}{k\bar{y} + k_f \bar{y}_f} \bar{y}_f. \tag{A.15.18}$$

We now come to the adjustment process. This is complicated in that, when the system is in disequilibrium, prices also vary. To find the law of price variation we begin by observing that, as world money supply is given, a variation in the money supply of one of the two countries in one direction will correspond to a variation in the money supply of the other country in the opposite direction. Formally, if we differentiate both sides of (A.15.15), we have

$$\frac{dM}{dt} + r\frac{dM_f}{dt} = 0. \tag{A.15.19}$$

---

[65] In a gold standard regime this given stock is obviously fixed by the amount of gold in the world.

Substituting the values of dM/dt and dM_f/dt, [for which see (A.15.10) and (A.15.13)], in this equation we have

$$\alpha(kp\bar{y}-M)+\alpha_f(k_f rp_f\bar{y}_f - rM_f)=0, \qquad (A.15.20)$$

from which, taking into account (A.15.14) and solving, we have

$$p=\frac{\alpha M+\alpha_f rM_f}{\alpha k\bar{y}+\alpha_f k_f\bar{y}_f}, \quad p_f=\frac{\alpha\frac{1}{r}M+\alpha_f M_f}{\alpha k\bar{y}+\alpha_f k_f\bar{y}_f}, \qquad (A.15.21)$$

which determine price levels out of equilibrium[66]. These levels are therefore determined by the division of the world money stock between the two countries. Differentiating (A.15.21) with respect to time, we have the movement of prices in time

$$\frac{dp}{dt}=\frac{\alpha}{D}\frac{dM}{dt}+\frac{\alpha_f r}{D}\frac{dM_f}{dt}, \quad \frac{dp_f}{dt}=\frac{\alpha\frac{1}{r}}{D}\frac{dM}{dt}+\frac{\alpha_f}{D}\frac{dM_f}{dt}, \qquad (A.15.22)$$

where D denotes the expression in the denominator of Eqs. (A.15.21). From now on, as $p=rp_f$ and $dp/dt=rdp_f/dt$, we shall limit ourselves to the consideration of the price level of the home country. The first of Eqs. (A.15.22) can be written as

$$\frac{dp}{dt}=\frac{\alpha_f}{D}\left(\frac{\alpha}{\alpha_f}\frac{dM}{dt}+r\frac{dM_f}{dt}\right), \qquad (A.15.23)$$

from which, by using (A.15.19) and collecting the terms, we have

$$\frac{dp}{dt}=\frac{\alpha-\alpha_f}{D}\frac{dM}{dt}. \qquad (A.15.24)$$

The price level, then, varies in the same direction or in the opposite direction to that in which the national money supply moves, according to $\alpha \gtrless \alpha_f$, that is, according to whether the national speed of adjustment of absorption to monetary disequilibria is greater or less than the foreign one. We shall return to this point later; for the moment we shall examine the behaviour of the money stock. Given (A.15.15) and (A.15.19), it is sufficient to examine the differential equation (A.15.10), which – taking (A.15.21) into account – can be written as

$$\frac{dM}{dt}=\alpha\left(\frac{k\bar{y}\alpha}{D}M+\frac{k\bar{y}\alpha_f}{D}rM_f-M\right). \qquad (A.15.10.1)$$

If we substitute $rM_f=\bar{M}_w-M$ from Eq. (A.15.15) and rearrange terms, we get

$$\frac{dM}{dt}=\alpha\left(\frac{\alpha_f k\bar{y}}{D}\bar{M}_w+\frac{k\bar{y}\alpha-k\bar{y}\alpha_f-D}{D}M\right)$$

$$=\alpha\left(\frac{\alpha_f k\bar{y}}{D}\bar{M}_w-\frac{\alpha_f(k\bar{y}+k_f\bar{y}_f)}{D}M\right)=\alpha\frac{\alpha_f(k\bar{y}+k_f\bar{y}_f)}{D}(M^e-M). \qquad (A.15.10.2)$$

---

[66] It can be seen at once that in equilibrium, as $M=kp\bar{y}$ and $M_f=k_f p_f\bar{y}_f$, Eqs. (A.15.21) are reduced to identities.

From this differential equation, in which the price movements are also included, it can be seen that when M is below (above) its equilibrium value M^e given by (A.15.18), then $dM/dt \gtreqless 0$ and thus M increases (decreases), converging towards its equilibrium value. In fact the general solution of (A.15.10.2) is

$$M(t) = (M_0 - M^e)e^{-\alpha Ht} + M^e. \tag{A.15.10.3}$$

where H indicates the multiplying fraction of $(M^e - M)$ in (A.15.10.2). As $H > 0$, the equilibrium is stable.

Given (A.15.15), if M tends towards its equilibrium value, M_f also tends towards equilibrium; consequently — given (A.15.21) and (A.15.17) — p and p_f also tend towards their respective equilibrium levels.

It is interesting to observe that when $\alpha = \alpha_f$, that is to say, when the adjustment speeds are equal, we have — on the basis of (A.15.24) — $dp/dt = 0$, that is, prices do not vary. This is due to the fact that, in this case, the *world* demand does not vary, insofar as the greater absorption of one country is exactly compensated by the lesser absorption of the other. In fact, with equal adjustment velocities, the redistribution of money through the balance of payments would leave *world* expenditure unaltered and therefore, at world level, there would be no excess demand and thus no effect on prices. Instead, when the national adjustment velocity exceeds that of the rest of the world ($\alpha > \alpha_f$), then to a surplus in the home country balance of payments (and therefore a deficit in the rest of the world) there will correspond, instant by instant, an increase in world expenditure and therefore — as the world product is given — an excess demand, which in turn will cause the increase in prices. Conversely, if $\alpha_f > \alpha$, then the contraction in expenditure of the rest of the world would more than compensate for the increase in the home country and there would thus be a world excess supply and a reduction in prices.

The fact that the adjustment equation arrived at above can be interpreted in terms of world excess demand can be demonstrated as follows. Remembering that, as explained in the text,

$$\begin{aligned} A &= p\bar{y} + \alpha(M - kp\bar{y}), \\ A_f &= p_f\bar{y}_f + \alpha_f(M_f - k_f p_f \bar{y}_f), \end{aligned} \tag{A.15.25}$$

we get

$$\frac{dM}{dt} = \alpha(M - kp\bar{y}) = A - p\bar{y},$$

$$\frac{dM_f}{dt} = \alpha_f(M_f - k_f p_f \bar{y}_f) = A_f - p_f \bar{y}_f.$$

Substituting in (A.15.23), we have

$$\begin{aligned} \frac{dp}{dt} &= \frac{\alpha_f}{D}\left[\frac{\alpha}{\alpha_f}(A - p\bar{y}) + r(A_f - p_f \bar{y}_f)\right] \\ &= \frac{1}{D}[\alpha(A - p\bar{y}) + \alpha_f r(A_f - p_f \bar{y}_f)]. \end{aligned} \tag{A.15.27}$$

The variation in prices depends on the excess demand in the two countries. It is necessary to bear in mind that, on the basis of Walras' law, the sum of the nominal excess demand of both countries is zero[67]

$$(A - p\bar{y}) + r(A_f - p_f \bar{y}_f) = 0, \tag{A.15.28}$$

where naturally the nominal excess demand of each country is expressed in a common unit of measurement, in this case the currency of the home country. This at once explains that, when $\alpha = \alpha_f$, the level of prices does not vary: in that case, in fact, the expression in square brackets in (A.15.27) is cancelled out. On the other hand, when $\alpha > \alpha_f$, any positive excess demand in the home country is less than compensated for by the negative excess demand in the rest of the world[68], so that the expression in square brackets in (A.15.27) remains positive and $dp/dt > 0$. The opposite happens when $\alpha < \alpha_f$.

A.15.2.3 The Effects of a Devaluation

We conclude by examining the effects of a devaluation, distinguishing the impact effects from the long-run effects. The impact effect is an improvement in the balance of payments of the country which devalues (and, obviously, a worsening of the balance of payments of the other country) as already illustrated in the text. Formally this can be demonstrated in the following way. Let us assume that we are starting from an equilibrium situation, in which therefore there is no money supply movement and the balance of payments is in equilibrium. Now let us consider a devaluation on the part of the home country. The equilibrium is altered and the impact effect on price levels is obtained by differentiating (A.15.21) with respect to r:

$$\frac{dp}{dr} = \frac{\alpha_f M_f}{D} > 0, \quad \frac{dp_f}{dr} = -\frac{\frac{1}{r^2} \alpha M}{D} < 0, \tag{A.15.29}$$

from which it can be seen that p increases and p_f decreases. Therefore the demand for money increases in the home country and decreases in the rest of the world, so that in correspondence to existing money supply there is excess demand for money in the home country and excess supply in the other. It follows that, given (A.15.10) and (A.15.13), we get $dM/dt > 0$ (and therefore $B > 0$) and $dM_f/dt < 0$ (and thus $B_f < 0$).

The long-run effect is the disappearance of every surplus and deficit in the balance of payments: in fact, the dynamic mechanism described above causes M and M_f to coincide eventually with their new equilibrium values. Once these are reached, the money flows cease so that the surplus of the home country and the deficit of the rest of the world are eliminated.

We have thus demonstrated the transitory nature of the effects of a devaluation. It is however interesting to observe that there *is* an improvement

---

[67] The fact that Walras' law holds can easily be seen thanks to the constraint (A.15.19). In fact, by substituting from (A.15.26) in (A.15.19) we obtain (A.15.28).

[68] The magnitudes $(A - p\bar{y})$ and $r(A_f - p_f \bar{y}_f)$ are of opposite signs and equal in absolute value on the basis of (A.15.28), but as the former is multiplied by a greater positive coefficient than that which multiplies the latter, it is the former which prevails.

(though of a transitory nature) in the balance of payments without any condition being placed on the elasticities. Indeed, these do not even appear in the analysis. This is due to the fact that, in the model we are examining, there is no substitution effect between domestic and foreign goods, a fact which, on the contrary, as we saw in Sect. 15.2, was at the basis of Hume's theory. It is possible to introduce an exchange rate effect into the MABP (in which case the elasticities come into play once again, on which the stability of the adjustment mechanism comes to depend); the reader who is interested in this exercise can consult, for example, Dornbusch (1980, Chap. 7, Sect. III). See also Niehans (1984, Sect. 4.4) for an interesting parallelism between the monetary approach and the elasticity approach.

A.15.3 Macroeconomic Equilibrium in a Standard Keynesian-Type Open Model

A.15.3.1 The Slopes of the Various Schedules

Given the three equilibrium equations

$$d(y,i) + x_0 - y = 0, \quad 0 < d_y < 1, \quad d_i < 0,$$
$$x_0 - m(y,i) + K(i) = 0, \quad 0 < m_y < 1, \quad m_i < 0, \quad K_i > 0, \quad (A.15.30)$$
$$L(y,i) - M = 0, \quad L_y > 0, \quad L_i < 0,$$

if we apply the rule for the differentiation of implicit functions to each one of them, we can calculate the derivatives of the schedules RR, BB and LL, which are

$$\left(\frac{di}{dy}\right)_{RR} = \frac{1-d_y}{d_i} < 0,$$

$$\left(\frac{di}{dy}\right)_{BB} = \frac{m_y}{K_i - m_i} > 0, \qquad (A.15.31)$$

$$\left(\frac{di}{dy}\right)_{LL} = -\frac{L_y}{L_i} > 0.$$

As far as points outside the schedules are concerned, consider, for example, the real equilibrium. Once the excess demand for goods function is defined

$$ED_G = d(y,i) + x_0 - y, \qquad (A.15.30.1)$$

one can calculate the partial derivative

$$\frac{\partial ED_G}{\partial i} = d_i < 0, \qquad (A.15.30.2)$$

from which it can be seen that for every given y, values of i above or below those which give rise to $ED_G = 0$ (points along the RR schedule) imply $ED_G \lessgtr 0$. One can proceed in the same way for the other two schedules.

Finally, we shall examine the shifts of *LL*. Taking *M* as a parameter, the third of Eqs. (A.15.10)) defines an implicit function in three variables of the type

$$h(M,y,i) = 0. \tag{A.15.30.3}$$

On the basis of the implicit-function rule, we can calculate

$$\frac{\partial i}{\partial M} = -\frac{h_M}{h_i} = \frac{1}{L_i} < 0, \tag{A.15.30.4}$$

from which it can be seen that for every given *y*, to greater (smaller) values of *M* there correspond smaller (greater) values of *i*, from which the downward (upward) shift of *LL* follows.

A.15.3.2 The Study of Dynamic Stability

The dynamic behaviour assumptions in Sect. 15.4.3 give rise to the following system of differential equations

$$\frac{dM}{dt} = a[x_0 - m(y,i) + K(i)], \quad a > 0,$$

$$\frac{dy}{dt} = k_1[d(y,i) + x_0 - y)], \quad k_1 > 0, \tag{A.15.32}$$

$$\frac{di}{dt} = k_2[L(y,i) - M], \quad k_2 > 0,$$

from which, by linearizing at the point of equilibrium, by indicating, as usual, the deviations from equilibrium with a dash above the variable and by putting, for simplicity, $a=1$, $k_1=1$, $k_2=1$, we have

$$\frac{d\bar{M}}{dt} = -m_y \bar{y} + (K_i - m_i)\bar{i},$$

$$\frac{d\bar{y}}{dt} = (d_y - 1)\bar{y} + d_i \bar{i}, \tag{A.15.32.1}$$

$$\frac{d\bar{i}}{dt} = -\bar{M} + L_y \bar{y} + L_i \bar{i}.$$

Stability depends on the roots of the characteristic equation

$$\begin{vmatrix} 0-\lambda & -m_y & (K_i - m_i) \\ 0 & (d_y-1)-\lambda & d_i \\ -1 & L_y & L_i-\lambda \end{vmatrix}$$

$$= \lambda^3 + (1-d_y-L_i)\lambda^2 + [K_i - m_i - L_y d_i - L_i(1-d_y)]\lambda$$
$$+ [(1-d_y)(K_i - m_i) - m_y d_i] = 0. \tag{A.15.33}$$

Necessary and sufficient stability conditions are (cfr. Gandolfo, 1980)

$$d_y < 1 - L_i,$$

$$d_y < 1 + \frac{K_i - m_i - d_i L_y}{-L_i},$$

$$d_y < 1 - \frac{m_y d_i}{K_i - m_i},$$

$$m_y < \frac{L_i(K_i - m_i) + (1 - d_y - L_i)[-L_y d_i - L_i(1 - d_y)]}{-d_i}.$$
(A.15.34)

Taking account of the signs of the various derivatives, it can at once be observed that $d_y < 1$ is a sufficient (even if not a necessary) condition for the first three inequalities to be satisfied. Furthermore, if $d_y < 1$, the right-hand side of the last inequality is certainly positive, so that this inequality admits positive values of m_y.

Not that the first three inequalities are necessary and sufficient for each real root of the characteristic equation to be negative and therefore exclude monotonic (but not oscillatory) instability; the fourth inequality, on the other hand, is necessary and sufficient, together with the previous ones, for the complex roots to have a negative real part, and therefore, as stated in the text, it excludes oscillatory instability.

We now come to the form and position of BB when interest payments on the stock of debts to foreigners are considered. The equation for the equilibrium of the balance of payments becomes

$$x_0 - m(y, i) - i \int_0^t K(i) d\tau + K(i) = 0.$$
(A.15.35)

In the current period (t is given) the integral $\int_0^t K(i) d\tau$ is a given constant, which we indicate with γ. By applying the implicit-function rule to (A.15.35) we have

$$\left(\frac{di}{dy}\right)_{BB} = \frac{m_y}{K_i - m_i - \gamma}.$$
(A.15.36)

If the sensitivity of capital movements to the rate of interest (represented by K_i) is sufficiently great, then the denominator of (A.15.36) remains positive and BB has the normal positive slope. In the opposite case, BB will have a negative slope. There is however a third possibility: it is in fact to be presumed that K_i will decrease as i increases, because successive equal increases in i lead to progressively smaller inflows of capital (it is in fact a kind of "decreasing responsiveness principle", due, for example, to increasing risks). What can then occur is the presence of some critical value of i — say i_c — such that

$$K_i - m_i - \gamma \gtreqless 0 \quad \text{for} \quad i \lesseqgtr i_c.$$
(A.15.37)

In this case it can be seen at once from (A.15.36) that

$$\left(\frac{di}{dy}\right)_{BB} \gtreqless 0 \quad \text{for } i \lesseqgtr i_c \text{ and } \lim_{i \to i_c} \left(\frac{di}{dy}\right)_{BB} = \infty,$$

so that BB, initially increasing, bends backwards when i reaches $i = i_c$, as described in Fig. 15.11.

Let us now consider the shifts of BB with the passing of time. Equation (A.15.35) can be considered as an implicit function in the *three* variables, i, y, t, say

$$\Phi(i, y, t) = 0, \tag{A.15.39}$$

so that the shifts of BB as time goes on can be determined by calculating, for example, the partial derivative

$$\frac{\partial y}{\partial t} = -\frac{\Phi_t}{\Phi_y}, \tag{A.15.40}$$

which tells us how y must move in correspondence to each given i, so as to maintain the balance of payments in equilibrium as t varies. By applying formula (A.15.40) to (A.15.35), account being taken of the rules for the differentiation of an integral with respect to a parameter (cfr., for example, Courant, 1962), we have

$$\frac{\partial y}{\partial t} = \frac{iK(i)}{-m_y} < 0, \tag{A.15.41}$$

from which it follows the shift to the left of BB.

A.15.3.3 Comparative Statics

In order to study the consequences on the equilibrium of an exogenous variation of domestic expenditure or of exports, we introduce parameters α, β. If we denote by α the parameter whose increase (decrease) represents an exogenous increase (decrease) in *domestic expenditure* and if we introduce it into the equilibrium equations, we have, by differentiating these with respect to α[69] and rearranging terms,

$$\begin{aligned}
(1 - d_y)\frac{\partial y}{\partial \alpha} - d_i \frac{\partial i}{\partial \alpha} &= 1, \\
m_y \frac{\partial y}{\partial \alpha} + (m_i - K_i)\frac{\partial i}{\partial \alpha} &= 0, \\
L_y \frac{\partial y}{\partial \alpha} + L_i \frac{\partial i}{\partial \alpha} - \frac{\partial M}{\partial \alpha} &= 0.
\end{aligned} \tag{A.15.42}$$

---

[69] The Jacobian of the system coincides with D — see below, Eq. (A.15.44) — and so it is positive. Therefore the implicit-function theorem is satisfied and these exercises in comparative statics are legitimate. The same is true with regard to β and to r (see below).

The solution of this system gives the values for the unknowns $\frac{\partial y}{\partial \alpha}, \frac{\partial i}{\partial \alpha}, \frac{\partial M}{\partial \alpha}$, which turn out to be

$$\frac{\partial y}{\partial \alpha} = \frac{K_i - m_i}{D},$$

$$\frac{\partial i}{\partial \alpha} = \frac{m_y}{D}, \qquad (A.15.43)$$

$$\frac{\partial M}{\partial \alpha} = \frac{m_y L_i + (K_i - m_i) L_y}{D},$$

where

$$D \equiv (1 - d_y)(K_i - m_i) - m_y d_i, \qquad (A.15.44)$$

is the value of the determinant of the system. Given the third inequality in (A.15.34), D is positive. Once this has been ascertained, we immediately find that $\partial y/\partial \alpha > 0$, $\partial i/\partial \alpha > 0$, while the sign of $\partial M/\partial \alpha$ remains uncertain.

More precisely, we have $\frac{\partial M}{\partial \alpha} \gtreqless 0$ according as $m_y L_i + (K_i - m_i) L_y \gtreqless 0$ namely according as

$$-\frac{L_y}{L_i} \gtreqless \frac{m_y}{K_i - m_i}. \qquad (A.15.45)$$

Remembering Eqs. (A.15.31), we then have $\partial M/\partial \alpha \gtreqless 0$ according to whether the slope of LL is greater or less than that of BB (see Figs. 15.12 and 15.13).

Using β to indicate the parameter whose increase (decrease) represents an exogenous increase (decrease) of *exports*, introducing it into the equilibrium relationships and differentiating with respect to β, we have

$$(1 - d_y) \frac{\partial y}{\partial \beta} - d_i \frac{\partial i}{\partial \beta} = 1,$$

$$m_y \frac{\partial y}{\partial \beta} + (m_i - K_i) \frac{\partial i}{\partial \beta} = 1, \qquad (A.15.46)$$

$$L_y \frac{\partial y}{\partial \beta} + L_i \frac{\partial i}{\partial \beta} - \frac{\partial M}{\partial \beta} = 0,$$

the solution of which is

$$\frac{\partial y}{\partial \beta} = \frac{K_i - m_i - d_i}{D},$$

$$\frac{\partial i}{\partial \beta} = \frac{m_y - (1 - d_y)}{D}, \qquad (A.15.47)$$

$$\frac{\partial M}{\partial \beta} = \frac{L_i[m_y - (1 - d_y)] + L_y(K_i - m_i - d_i)}{D},$$

where D is the same as before. It immediately follows that $\partial y/\partial\beta>0$, while the signs of $\partial i/\partial\beta$ and of $\partial M/\partial\beta$ remain uncertain. As far as $\partial i/\partial\beta$ is concerned, we have $\partial i/\partial\beta \gtreqless 0$ according as $m_y \gtreqless 1-d_y$; this inequality can be satisfied either way[70]. As far as the sign of $\partial M/\partial\beta$ is concerned, as $\partial M/\partial\beta = L_i(\partial i/\partial\beta) + L_y(\partial y/\partial\beta)$, we get $\partial M/\partial\beta > 0$ unequivocally if $\partial i/\partial\beta < 0$, while if $\partial i/\partial\beta > 0$ the sign of $\partial M/\partial\beta$ would remain uncertain.

The expressions given above for $\partial y/\partial\alpha$ and for $\partial y/\partial\beta$ substantially represent international multipliers in that they furnish, respectively, the effect on equilibrium income of a marginal exogenous variation of domestic expenditure or of exports. In this regard it is interesting to look more closely at some points.

First of all, note that the multiplier effect of an exogenous increase in exports is greater than the multiplier effect of an equal increase in domestic expenditure; in fact, we have

$$\frac{K_i - m_i - d_i}{D} > \frac{K_i - m_i}{D}. \tag{A.15.48}$$

This result is worthy of note, as in traditional multiplier theory the two effects are identical.

Another result worthy of attention is that, if we examine an exogenous variation of domestic expenditure, the multiplier obtained from the present analysis is less than the traditional multiplier. In fact, the latter is $1/(1-d_y)$ and, given that $1-d_y>0$,

$$\frac{K_i - m_i}{D} < \frac{1}{1-d_y}. \tag{A.15.49}$$

is certainly true.

Finally, let us consider an *exogenous variation in the exchange rate* in a regime of adjustable peg. For this purpose, it is necessary to introduce the rate of exchange into the various equations *considering it as a parameter*:

$$y = x(r) + d(y,i,r), \quad dx/dr > 0, \quad \partial d/\partial r > 0,$$
$$x(r) - rm(y,i,r) + K(i) = 0, \quad \partial m/\partial r < 0, \tag{A.15.50}$$
$$M = L(y,i).$$

Implicit in the second of Eqs. (A.15.50) is the simplifying assumption that a once-and-for-all variation in the exchange rate does not influence the balance on capital account. Differentiating Eqs. (A.15.50) with respect to the parameter r, we

---

[70] This indeterminacy can be eliminated if it is supposed that the *total* marginal propensity to spend of residents (that is, for both domestic goods and foreign goods) is less than one. In fact, in this case, $d_y + m_y < 1$ and therefore $\partial i/\partial\beta < 0$. However, as we have already seen in Sect. 13.2, the total marginal propensity to spend, which must be less than one in a closed economy, can also be greater than one in an open economy.

have

$$(1-d_y)\frac{\partial y}{\partial r} - d_i\frac{\partial i}{\partial r} = \frac{dx}{dr} + \frac{\partial d}{\partial r},$$

$$m_y\frac{\partial y}{\partial r} + (m_i - K_i)\frac{\partial i}{\partial r} = \frac{dx}{dr} - m - r\frac{\partial m}{\partial r}, \quad (A.15.51)$$

$$L_y\frac{\partial y}{\partial r} + L_i\frac{\partial i}{\partial r} - \frac{\partial M}{\partial r} = 0.$$

Note that the sign of the right-hand term of the second equation depends on the elasticities, because

$$\frac{dx}{dr} - m - r\frac{\partial m}{\partial r} = m\left(\frac{x}{rm}\frac{r}{x}\frac{dx}{dr} - 1 - \frac{r}{m}\frac{\partial m}{\partial r}\right) = m\left(\frac{x}{rm}\eta_x + \eta_m - 1\right). \quad (A.15.52)$$

This expression will be positive if the condition of critical elasticities (12.9) is satisfied. We shall assume that this is the case and for brevity we shall call the entire expression examined η.

Thus, solving system (A.15.51), we have

$$\frac{\partial y}{\partial r} = \frac{(dx/dr + \partial d/\partial r)(K_i - m_i) - \eta d_i}{D},$$

$$\frac{\partial i}{\partial r} = \frac{(dx/dr + \partial d/\partial r)m_y - \eta(1 - d_y)}{D}, \quad (A.15.53)$$

$$\frac{\partial M}{\partial r} = L_i\frac{\partial i}{\partial r} + L_y\frac{\partial y}{\partial r},$$

where D is the usual determinant. It can be seen at once that $\partial y/\partial r > 0$, while the sign of $\partial i/\partial r$ (and therefore of $\partial M/\partial r$) is uncertain. Note the similarity of the results of Eqs. (A.15.53) to those of Eqs. (A.15.47), as is indeed obvious for reasons explained in the text. The value of $\partial y/\partial r$ also substantially represents an international multiplier, insofar as it gives the effect on equilibrium income of an exogenous variation in exports and imports: the variation of the parameter r, in fact, causes variations in exports and imports which can to all intents and purposes be considered exogenous variations in the context of the model examined.

A.15.4 Monetary and Fiscal Policy and Internal and External Balance
A.15.4.1 The Static Model

Let us consider the system[71]

$$y - [d(y,i) + x_0 + G] = 0,$$
$$B - [x_0 - m(y,i) + K(i)] = 0, \quad (A.15.54)$$

---

[71] As we have expressed the equation for the determination of income in terms of the demand for domestic goods (on the part of residents and non-residents), G is to be taken as (that part of) public expenditure directed at domestic goods.

which includes four variables, of which two are objectives (y and B) and two instruments (G and i). On the basis of the implicit-function theorem, it is possible to express two of the variables in terms of the other two, provided the appropriate Jacobian is different from zero; if we wish to express G and i as functions of y and B, it is necessary to consider the Jacobian of Eqs. (A.15.54) with respect to G and i:

$$J = \begin{vmatrix} -1 & -d_i \\ 0 & m_i - K_i \end{vmatrix} = K_i - m_i. \qquad (A.15.55)$$

The fact that $J \neq 0$ ensures the absence of functional dependence, and is the mathematical equivalent of the possibility of solving the initial system so as to be able to determine the values of the instruments corresponding to prefixed values of the targets. In fact, once condition $J \neq 0$ is satisfied, the following single-valued functions will exist

$$G = G(y,B), \quad i = i(y,B), \qquad (A.15.56)$$

by which, given that $y = y_F$, $B = 0$, it is possible to determine the corresponding values of G and i.

From the economic point of view, condition $J \neq 0$ amounts to saying that a direct effect exists of the rate of interest on the balance of payments, $(K_i - m_i)$.

Let us now examine the relative effectiveness of the various instruments on the various targets. By differentiating[72] Eqs. (A.15.54) we get

$$\frac{\partial y}{\partial G} = \frac{1}{1-d_y}, \quad \frac{\partial y}{\partial i} = \frac{d_i}{1-d_y},$$

$$\frac{\partial B}{\partial G} = -m_y \frac{\partial y}{\partial G}, \quad \frac{\partial B}{\partial i} = -m_y \frac{\partial y}{\partial i} + (K_i - m_i), \qquad (A.15.57)$$

from which

$$\frac{\partial B/\partial i}{\partial y/\partial i} = -m_y + \frac{(K_i - m_i)(1-d_y)}{d_i},$$

$$\frac{\partial B/\partial G}{\partial y/\partial G} = -m_y. \qquad (A.15.58)$$

As the expression $(K_i - m_i)(1-d_y)/d_i$ is negative, given the signs of the various derivatives, and considering the absolute values of the expressions (A.15.58), we have

$$\frac{|\partial B/\partial i|}{|\partial y/\partial i|} > \frac{|\partial B/\partial G|}{|\partial y/\partial G|}; \quad \frac{|\partial y/\partial G|}{|\partial B/\partial G|} > \frac{|\partial y/\partial i|}{|\partial B/\partial i|}.$$

---

[72] This differentiation implies that the opposite operation to that just described in the text is carried out, that is to say that y and B are expressed as functions of G and i. This requires the Jacobian of Eqs. (A.15.54) with respect to y and B to be different from zero; this condition certainly occurs because this Jacobian turns out to be

$$\begin{vmatrix} 1-d_y & 0 \\ m_y & 1 \end{vmatrix} = 1 - d_y.$$

This means that monetary policy has a relative greater influence on the balance of payments than has fiscal policy and that fiscal policy has a relatively greater influence on income than has monetary policy.

In the traditional case in which the instrument of monetary policy is taken to be the money supply, system (A.15.54) has to be integrated by the monetary-equilibrium equation, $L(y,i)-M=0$. Thus we get a system of three equations in five unknowns, of which two are exogenous (the instruments G and M) and three (y,B,i) are endogenous (two of these are the targets y and B). The reader can check that both the Jacobian of these equations with respect to G,M,i and the Jacobian with respect to y,B,i are different from zero. It is then possible to calculate the partial derivatives $\partial y/\partial M$, $\partial B/\partial M$; $\partial y/\partial G$, $\partial B/\partial G$. From these expressions it turns out that inequalities (A.15.59) continue to hold.

A.15.4.2 The Assignment Problem

We now come to the problem of the assignment of instruments to targets. The pairing-off of fiscal policy-internal equilibrium and monetary policy-external equilibrium gives rise to the following system of differential equations

$$\frac{dG}{dt}=v_1(y_F-y), \qquad v_1>0,$$

$$\frac{di}{dt}=v_2[m(y,i)-x_0-K(i)], \qquad v_2>0, \qquad (A.15.60)$$

$$\frac{dy}{dt}=v_3[d(y,i)+x_0+G-y], \qquad v_3>0.$$

The first two equations are the formal counterpart of the adjustment rules described in the text: government expenditure increases (decreases) if income is lower (higher) than the full employment level and the interest rate increases (decreases) if there is a deficit (surplus) in the balance of payments. The third equation describes the usual process of adjustment of national income in response to excess demand in a context of rigid prices; the constants v_1,v_2,v_3 indicate the adjustment velocities.

Expanding in Taylor's series at the point of equilibrium and neglecting non-linear terms, we have

$$\frac{d\mathbf{z}}{dt}=\mathbf{A}\mathbf{z}, \qquad (A.15.61)$$

where $\mathbf{z}$ is the column vector of the deviations $\{\bar{G},\bar{i},\bar{y},\}$ and

$$\mathbf{A}\equiv\begin{bmatrix} 0 & 0 & -v_1 \\ 0 & v_2(m_i-K_i) & v_2 m_y \\ v_3 & v_3 d_i & v_3(d_y-1) \end{bmatrix} \qquad (A.15.62)$$

is the matrix of the system of differential equations. Indicating the characteristic roots by λ and expanding the characteristic equation, we have

$$\lambda^3 + [v_2(K_i - m_i) + v_3(1 - d_y)]\lambda^2 + [v_2 v_3(K_i - m_i)(1 - d_y)$$
$$- v_2 v_3 m_y d_i + v_1 v_3]\lambda + v_1 v_2 v_3 (K_i - m_i) = 0, \qquad (A.15.63)$$

and the necessary and sufficient conditions of stability are (Gandolfo, 1980, pp. 249–50)

$$v_2(K_i - m_i) + v_3(1 - d_y) > 0,$$

$$v_2 v_3 (K_i - m_i)(1 - d_y) - v_2 v_3 m_y d_i + v_1 v_3 > 0,$$

$$v_1 v_2 v_3 (K_i - m_i) > 0,$$

$$[v_2(K_i - m_i) + v_3(1 - d_y)][v_2 v_3(K_i - m_i)(1 - d_y) \qquad (A.15.64)$$
$$- v_2 v_3 m_y d_i + v_1 v_3] - v_1 v_2 v_3 (K_i - m_i)$$
$$= [v_2(K_i - m_i) + v_3(1 - d_y)][v_2 v_3(K_i - m_i)(1 - d_y)$$
$$- v_2 v_3 m_y d_i] + v_1 v_3^2 (1 - d_y) > 0.$$

It is easy to see that, given the signs of the various derivatives and as, by assumption, $d_y < 1$, all these conditions are satisfied.

Let us now consider the assignment of monetary policy to internal equilibrium and fiscal policy to external equilibrium, which gives rise to the following system of differential equations:

$$\frac{dG}{dt} = k_1[x_0 - m(y,i) + K(i)], \quad k_1 > 0,$$

$$\frac{di}{dt} = k_2[y - y_F], \quad k_2 > 0, \qquad (A.15.65)$$

$$\frac{dy}{dt} = k_3[d(y,i) + x_0 + G - y], \quad k_3 > 0,$$

from which, by linearizing,

$$\frac{d\mathbf{z}}{dt} = \mathbf{A}_1 \mathbf{z}, \qquad (A.15.66)$$

where, as before, **z** indicates the vector of the deviations and

$$\mathbf{A}_1 \equiv \begin{bmatrix} 0 & k_1(K_i - m_i) & -k_1 m_y \\ 0 & 0 & k_2 \\ k_3 & k_3 d_i & k_3(d_y - 1) \end{bmatrix}$$

is the matrix of the system of differential equations. If we expand the characteristic equation, we have

$$\lambda^3 + k_3(1 - d_y)\lambda^2 + (k_1 k_3 m_y + k_2 k_3 d_i)\lambda - k_1 k_2 k_3 (K_i - m_i) = 0. \qquad (A.15.68)$$

One can see immediately that, as the constant term is negative, one of the stability conditions is violated and thus the assignment in question gives rise to a movement that diverges from equilibrium.

A.15.5 The Problem of Coordination

A.15.5.1 The Basic Model

Indicating with a prime the variables concerning country 1 and with a double prime those relative to country 2, we have the model

$$\begin{aligned}
&y' = d' + x' + G', &&y'' = d'' + x'' + G'', \\
&B' = x' + K' - m', &&B'' = -B', \\
&d' = d'(y', i'), &&d'' = d''(y'', i''), \\
&m' = m'(y', i'), &&m'' = m''(y'', i''), \\
&K' = K_0 + K'(i' - i''), &&K'' = -K', \\
&x' = m'', &&x'' = m',
\end{aligned} \qquad (A.15.69)$$

which is an obvious extension to the two-country case of the one-country model previously used. We can therefore limit ourselves to observing that, alongside the capital movements induced by the interest differential (which must now be introduced explicitly) we have considered the exogenous capital movements K_0 and that, as the exchange rate is fixed by hypothesis, we have assumed it to be equal to one without any loss of generality.

Let us begin by dealing with the dynamics of the simple pairing, which will serve as a comparison. This gives rise to the following system of differential equations

$$\begin{aligned}
\frac{dG'}{dt} &= v_{11}(y'_F - y'), \\
\frac{dy'}{dt} &= b_1[d'(y', i') + m''(y'', i'') + G' - y'], \\
\frac{di'}{dt} &= v_{22}[m'(y', i') - m''(y'', i'') - K'(i' - i'') - K_0], \\
\frac{dG''}{dt} &= v_{33}(y''_F - y''), \\
\frac{dy''}{dt} &= b_2[d''(y'', i'') + m'(y', i') + G'' - y''], \\
\frac{di''}{dt} &= v_{42}[m''(y'', i'') - m'(y', i') + K'(i' - i'') + K_0],
\end{aligned} \qquad (A.15.70)$$

where the v's and b's are positive constants[73]. After linearization, this system becomes:

$$\frac{d\mathbf{u}}{dt} = \mathbf{Fu}, \qquad (A.15.71)$$

---

[73] We have used a different symbol for the adjustment speed of income, because it is not under the control of the policy-maker unlike the adjustment speeds of instruments, which are policy parameters.

where **u** is the column vector of the deviations $\{\bar{G}'(t), \bar{y}'(t), \bar{i}'(t), \bar{G}''(t), \bar{y}''(t), \bar{i}''(t)\}$, and

$$F = \begin{bmatrix} 0 & -v_{11} & 0 & 0 & 0 & 0 \\ b_1 & -b_1(1-d_y') & b_1 d_1' & 0 & b_1 m_y'' & b_1 m_i'' \\ 0 & v_{22} m_y' & -v_{22}(K'_{i'-i''}-m_i') & 0 & -v_{22} m_y'' & -v_{22}(m_i''-K'_{i'-i''}) \\ 0 & 0 & 0 & 0 & -v_{33} & 0 \\ 0 & b_2 m_y' & b_2 m_i' & b_2 & -b_2(1-d_y'') & b_2 d_i'' \\ 0 & -v_{42} m_y' & v_{42}(K'_{i'-i''}-m_i') & 0 & v_{42} m_y'' & v_{42}(m_i''-K'_{i'-i''}) \end{bmatrix}$$

(A.15.72)

In the case of international coordination we have the system

$$\frac{dG'}{dt} = v_{11}(y'_F - y') + v_{12}[m''(y'',i'') - m'(y',i') + K'(i'-i'') + K_0] + v_{13}(y''_F - y''),$$

$$\frac{dy'}{dt} = b_1[d'(y',i') + m''(y'',i'') + G' - y'],$$

$$\frac{di'}{dt} = v_{21}(y' - y'_F) + v_{22}[m'(y',i') - m''(y'',i'') - K'(i'-i'') - K_0] + v_{23}(y'' - y''_F),$$

$$\frac{dG''}{dt} = v_{31}(y'_F - y') + v_{32}[m'(y',i') - m''(y'',i'') - K'(i'-i'') - K_0] + v_{33}(y''_F - y''),$$ (A.15.73)

$$\frac{dy''}{dt} = b_2[d''(y'',i'') + m'(y',i') + G'' - y''],$$

$$\frac{di''}{dt} = v_{41}(y' - y'_F) + v_{42}[m''(y'',i'') - m'(y',i') + K'(i'-i'') + K_0] + v_{43}(y'' - y''_F),$$

where $v_{12}, v_{13}, v_{21}, v_{23}, v_{31}, v_{32}, v_{41}, v_{43}$ are parameters which for the moment are left indeterminate. After linearization, system (A.15.73) gives[74]:

$$\frac{d\mathbf{s}}{dt} = \mathbf{Hs} \qquad (A.15.74)$$

where

$$H \equiv \begin{bmatrix} 0 & -(v_{11}+v_{12}m_y') & v_{12}(K'_{i'-i''}-m_i') & 0 & v_{12}m_y''-v_{13} & v_{12}(m_i''-K'_{i'-i''}) \\ b_1 & -b_1(1-d_y') & b_1 d_i' & 0 & b_1 m_y'' & b_1 m_i'' \\ 0 & v_{21}+v_{22}m_y' & -v_{22}(K'_{i'-i''}-m_i') & 0 & -v_{22}m_y''+v_{23} & -v_{22}(m_i''-K'_{i'-i''}) \\ 0 & -v_{31}+v_{32}m_y' & -v_{32}(K'_{i'-i''}-m_i') & 0 & -v_{33}-v_{32}m_y'' & -v_{32}(m_i''-K'_{i'-i''}) \\ 0 & b_2 m_y' & b_2 m_i' & b_2 & -b_2(1-d_y'') & b_2 d_i'' \\ 0 & v_{41}-v_{42}m_y' & v_{42}(K'_{i'-i''}-m_i') & 0 & v_{42}m_y''+v_{43} & v_{42}(m_i''-K'_{i'-i''}) \end{bmatrix}.$$

(A.15.75)

---

[74] We use a different symbol for the deviations ($\mathbf{s}$ instead of $\mathbf{u}$) because the functions $\bar{G}'(t)$, $\bar{y}'(t), \bar{i}'(t), \bar{G}''(t), \bar{y}''(t), \bar{i}''(t)$, obtained by solving system (A.15.74) are in principle different from those obtained by solving system (A.15.71). The same observation is valid with regard to system (A.15.79).

It can easily be seen that
$$H \equiv F + M, \tag{A.15.76}$$
where

$$M \equiv \begin{bmatrix} 0 & -v_{12}m'_y & v_{12}(K'_{i'-i''}-m'_i) & 0 & v_{12}m''_y - v_{23} & v_{12}(m''_i - K'_{i'-i''}) \\ 0 & 0 & 0 & 0 & 0 & 0 \\ 0 & v_{21} & 0 & 0 & v_{23} & 0 \\ 0 & -v_{31}+v_{32}m'_y & -v_{32}(K'_{i'-i''}-m'_i) & 0 & -v_{32}m''_y & -v_{32}(m''_i - K'_{i'-i''}) \\ 0 & 0 & 0 & 0 & 0 & 0 \\ 0 & v_{41} & 0 & 0 & v_{43} & 0 \end{bmatrix}.$$

$$\tag{A.15.77}$$

A.15.5.2 International Coordination Compared to Simple Pairing

According to the criterion adopted, international coordination brings an improvement compared to simple pairing, if the solution of system (A.15.74) converges more rapidly to the equilibrium point than the solution of (A.15.71). This in turn depends on the characteristic roots of H in relation to those of F. So it might seem that it is not possible to arrive at general conclusions, seeing that in order to determine and compare these characteristic roots, it is necessary to base the work on numerical examples. To overcome this, we suggest a general procedure by means of which the rates of convergence can be compared without the characteristic roots of the matrices concerned being explicitly known. It seems to us that the method we adopt is conceptually fairly simple. It consists in an examination of the *distance* of the point $\{\bar{G}'(t), \bar{y}'(t), \bar{i}'(t), \bar{G}''(t), \bar{y}''(t), \bar{i}''(t)\}$, from the origin (the latter indicating the point of equilibrium); if this distance decreases more rapidly in one system than in another (given, naturally, the same starting point), then the first system approaches equilibrium more rapidly than the other[75]. It is well known that there are various measurements of the distance[76], but we believe that in our case the most appropriate one is the Euclidean norm, seeing that it measures the length of the vector which we are dealing with (u or s). For simplicity we shall utilize the square of this norm[77]. By indicating with $D(t)$ the distance and with the appropriate subscript (u or s) the vector considered, we have (the prime denotes transposition):

$$D_u(t) = u'u \tag{A.15.78}$$

for system (A.15.71), and

$$D_s(t) = s's \tag{A.15.78.1}$$

for system (A.15.74). Thus,

$$\frac{dD_u}{dt} = \frac{du'}{dt}u + u'\frac{du}{dt}. \tag{A.15.79}$$

---

[75] The reader should note that this idea is substantially a variant of the second method of Liapunov.

[76] For a discussion of this concept, cfr., for example, Gandolfo (1980, pp. 399–400).

[77] This does not imply any variation in the results; in effect the square of the Euclidean norm is itself a distance.

It is easy to ascertain that $\frac{d\mathbf{u}'}{dt}\mathbf{u} = \mathbf{u}'\frac{d\mathbf{u}}{dt}$, so that

$$\frac{dD_u}{dt} = 2\mathbf{u}'\frac{d\mathbf{u}}{dt}. \quad (A.15.80)$$

Similarly,

$$\frac{dD_s}{dt} = 2\mathbf{s}'\frac{d\mathbf{s}}{dt}. \quad (A.15.81.1)$$

According to what we have said above, the convergence speed is greater in the system whose dD/dt is smaller[78] for any $t>0$ (remember that for $t=0$ the distance is the same, seeing that by hypothesis both systems start from the same initial situation). Now, from Eqs. (A.15.80), (A.15.81), (A.15.71) and (A.15.74), we have

$$\frac{dD_u}{dt} = 2\mathbf{u}'\mathbf{Fu} \text{ for the simple pairing,} \quad (A.15.82)$$

$$\frac{dD_s}{dt} = 2\mathbf{s}'\mathbf{Hs} \text{ for international coordination.} \quad (A.15.83)$$

Given (A.15.76), (A.15.83) can be rewritten as

$$\frac{dD_s}{dt} = 2\mathbf{s}'\mathbf{Fs} + 2\mathbf{s}'\mathbf{Ms}, \quad (A.15.84)$$

and so the necessary and sufficient condition for dD_s/dt to be less than dD_u/dt is that

$$\mathbf{s}'\mathbf{Fs} + \mathbf{s}'\mathbf{Ms} - \mathbf{u}'\mathbf{Fu} < 0 \text{ for any } t \geq 0. \quad (A.15.85)$$

For $t=0$, as we are comparing systems with the same initial position, $\mathbf{u} = \mathbf{s}$ and therefore (A.15.85) is reduced to $\mathbf{s}'\mathbf{Ms} > 0$. By multiplying, we obtain

$$\begin{aligned}\mathbf{s}'\mathbf{Ms} = &-v_{12}m'_y s_1 s_2 + v_{12}(K'_{i'-i''} - m'_i) s_1 s_3 \\ &+ (v_{12}m''_y - v_{13}) s_1 s_5 + v_{12}(m''_i - K'_{i'-i''}) s_1 s_6 \\ &+ v_{21} s_2 s_3 + v_{23} s_3 s_5 + (v_{32}m'_y - v_{31}) s_2 s_4 \\ &- v_{32}(K'_{i'-i''} - m'_i) s_3 s_4 - v_{32}m''_y s_4 s_5 \\ &- v_{32}(m''_i - K'_{i'-i''}) s_4 s_6 + v_{41} s_2 s_6 + v_{43} s_5 s_6 < 0, \end{aligned} \quad (A.15.85.1)$$

where s_i indicates the i-th component of the vector $\mathbf{s}$ [i.e. $s_1 = \bar{G}'(t)$, etc.].

We can now determine the signs, till now indeterminate, of the v coefficients, so that, given the signs of the products $s_i s_j$, the inequality (A.15.85.1) is satisfied. If,

---

[78] This can be considered as a general method to compare the degree of stability of two systems. Note that if both dD/dt are positive, the system with the smaller dD/dt will diverge more slowly, while if both are negative, the system with the smaller one (that is, the greater in absolute value) will converge more rapidly. In both these cases it can be said that the system which has the smaller dD/dt is the more stable, including in "the more stable" also "less unstable".

for instance $s_1<0, s_2<0, s_3<0, s_4<0, s_5<0, s_6>0$ (for example, underemployment and external deficit in country 1; underemployment and naturally an external surplus in country 2), the pattern of the signs is as follows: $v_{12}?, v_{13}>0, v_{21}<0, v_{23}<0, v_{31}>0, v_{32}?, v_{41}>0, v_{43}>0$. The symbol ? means that no sign can be given *a priori* to the coefficient, as, whatever the sign attributed to it, the coefficient itself gives rise both to negative terms and positive ones in (A.15.85.1). Thus, the best *a priori* decision is to attribute a zero value to the uncertain-effect coefficients, that is, eliminate the additional associations which they represent.

Once the signs of the coefficients have been determined, we can see the implications from the system (A.15.73), that is, the rules which govern the linking of each instrument with the additional targets.

Considering, for example, $v_{13}>0$, it follows from the first equation of system (A.15.73) that, other things being equal, in the situations in which it is necessary to give a positive sign to v_{13}, government expenditure in country 1 must be increased (decreased) if national income in country 2 is less (more) than the full employment level.

For $t>0$, **s** and **u** will be different and so it is necessary to examine the general condition (A.15.85). The sign of the difference $\mathbf{s'Fs} - \mathbf{u'Fu}$ is not known, but it is easy to see that, in principle, it is always possible to choose the coefficients $v_{12}, v_{13}, v_{21}, v_{23}, v_{31}, v_{41}, v_{43}$ so that the resulting value of $\mathbf{s'Ms}$ satisfies the condition (A.15.85)[79]. However this means that it is *not* possible, as it is in the case of simple pairing, to establish a definitive rule. At any given moment in time, policy makers must ascertain the situation, compare it with the situation that would arise at the same moment in time in the case of simple pairing (that is, assess $\mathbf{s'Fs} - \mathbf{u'Fu}$) and determine the appropriate values of v_{12}, v_{13}, etc., (which may or may not be equal to the previous values). In this process an error may have the undesirable result of slowing down the approach to equilibrium (that is, the left-hand side of (A.15.85) turns out to be positive) and can even cause a divergence from equilibrium (that is, dD/dt comes out positive).

A.15.5.3 International Coordination Compared to Internal Coordination

Finally, it can be demonstrated that, in the two-country model under consideration, international coordination leads to an improvement also with respect to internal coordination. In fact, by formulating the differential equation system relative to internal coordination and linearizing, we obtain

$$\frac{d\mathbf{h}}{dt} = \mathbf{Nh}, \qquad (A.15.86)$$

where matrix **N** is related to matrix **H** — defined in (A.15.75) — by the relationship

$$\mathbf{N} + \mathbf{Q} \equiv \mathbf{H}, \qquad (A.15.87)$$

---

[79] Given **s** and **u**, $\mathbf{s'Fs}$ and $\mathbf{u'Fu}$ are determined. v_{12}, v_{13} etc., can therefore be chosen so that $\mathbf{s'Ms} < \mathbf{u'Fu} - \mathbf{s'Fs}$. Note that infinite combinations of v_{12}, v_{13} etc. exist, which satisfy this inequality; note also, however, that it is no longer sufficient to determine the signs, as the absolute values of v_{12}, v_{13}, etc., come into play.

where

$$\mathbf{Q} \equiv \begin{bmatrix} 0 & 0 & 0 & 0 & -v_{13} & 0 \\ 0 & 0 & 0 & 0 & 0 & 0 \\ 0 & 0 & 0 & 0 & v_{23} & 0 \\ 0 & -v_{31} & 0 & 0 & 0 & 0 \\ 0 & 0 & 0 & 0 & 0 & 0 \\ 0 & v_{41} & 0 & 0 & 0 & 0 \end{bmatrix}. \tag{A.15.88}$$

By applying the distance method, we find that international coordination brings about an improvement with respect to internal coordination[80] if and only if

$$\mathbf{s'Ns} + \mathbf{s'Qs} - \mathbf{h'Nh} < 0. \tag{A.15.89}$$

The reader can check the fact that in principle it is possible to choose values of $v_{13}, v_{23} v_{31}$, and v_{41}, so that the resulting value of $\mathbf{s'Qs}$ satisfies (A.15.89). Naturally, here too the same observations are valid as applied to (A.15.85).

A.15.6 Portfolio Equilibrium in an Open Economy

A.15.6.1 The Case of Partial Equilibrium

On account of the balance constraint (15.20) in Sect. 15.6.2, the demand functions (15.21) are related by the constraint

$$h(i_h, i_f, y) + g(i_h, i_f, y) + f(i_h, i_f, y) = 1, \tag{A.15.90}$$

from which it follows that the sum of the partial derivatives of the three functions with respect to each variable must be zero, that is,

$$\frac{\partial h}{\partial i_h} + \frac{\partial g}{\partial i_h} + \frac{\partial f}{\partial i_h} = 0, \quad \frac{\partial h}{\partial i_f} + \frac{\partial g}{\partial i_f} + \frac{\partial f}{\partial i_f} = 0, \quad \frac{\partial h}{\partial y} + \underbrace{\frac{\partial g}{\partial y} + \frac{\partial f}{\partial y}}_{(-)} = 0. \tag{A.15.91}$$
$$(-)\ (+)\ (-) \quad\quad (-)\ (-)\ (+) \quad\quad (+)$$

Thus, once two partial derivatives are known the third is determined. Under the various partial derivatives we have placed the signs that derive from hypotheses made in the text. The partial derivatives $\partial g/\partial y$ and $\partial f/\partial y$ individually have uncertain signs, but their sum must necessarily be negative.

Given the hypothesized signs of the above-mentioned derivatives, the slopes of the schedules LL, NN, FF, are immediately evident.

Let us now consider the system of equilibrium conditions (15.22) of which, as we know, only two are independent. By choosing the second and third[81] we have

---

[80] It is also possible to demonstrate that internal coordination leads to an improvement with respect to simple pairing, but with the usual *caveat* of the rules to be followed. Cfr. Gandolfo (1974).

[81] As it is arbitrary which of the three equations to eliminate, the choice can be made on the basis of convenience, so as to be consistent with the graphic representation in the text.

the system

$$N^S - g(i_h, i_f, y) W = 0,$$
$$F - f(i_h, i_f, y) W = 0. \tag{A.15.92}$$

On the basis of the implicit function theorem, it is possible to express the two variables F, i_h as differentiable functions of all other variables (N^S, i_f, y) if the Jacobian of (A.15.92) with respect to F, i_h is different from zero, that is

$$\begin{vmatrix} 0 & -\dfrac{\partial g}{\partial i_h} W \\ 1 & -\dfrac{\partial f}{\partial i_h} W \end{vmatrix} = \dfrac{\partial g}{\partial i_h} W \neq 0, \tag{A.15.93}$$

a condition which certainly occurs. We can thus calculate the partial derivatives: $\partial F/\partial N^S$, $\partial i_h/\partial N^S$, which give us the effect of a variation of N^S on the equilibrium values of F and i_h. By differentiating (A.15.92) we have

$$1 - \dfrac{\partial g}{\partial i_h} \dfrac{\partial i_h}{\partial N^S} W = 0,$$
$$\dfrac{\partial F}{\partial N^S} - \dfrac{\partial f}{\partial i_h} \dfrac{\partial i_h}{\partial N^S} W = 0, \tag{A.15.94}$$

from which

$$\dfrac{\partial F}{\partial N^S} = \dfrac{\partial f/\partial i_h}{\partial g/\partial i_h} < 0, \quad \dfrac{\partial i_h}{\partial N^S} = \dfrac{1}{(\partial g/\partial i_h) W} > 0. \tag{A.15.94.1}$$

As can be seen, the signs are unequivocally determined thanks to the assumptions on the signs of various partial derivatives for which see (A.15.91).

Lastly, we come to dynamic stability. The hypothesis that i_h moves in response to the excess supply of domestic securities gives rise to the following differential equation:

$$\dfrac{di_h}{dt} = v[N^S - g(i_h, i_f, y) W], \quad v > 0. \tag{A.15.95}$$

As far as F is concerned, alternative hypotheses are possible. The simplest one, is that the quantity of foreign securities held is always instantly equal to the desired quantity, that is, to the quantity desumed from the demand function. This means that the relationship $F = f(i_h, i_f, y) W$ always occurs at every instant of time. In this case, (A.15.95) determines the path of i_h over time and, by substituting it in the demand function for foreign securities, the path of F is obtained.

The second, more general, hypothesis is that, on account of delays, frictions, etc. of various types, the quantity of foreign securities held cannot be instantly equal to the desired quantity, but moves towards it according to a partial adjustment mechanism of the type

$$\dfrac{dF}{dt} = \alpha[f(i_h, i_f, y) W - F], \tag{A.15.96}$$

where $\alpha > 0$ denotes the adjustment speed: the reciprocal of α represents the mean time-lag, i.e. the time necessary for about 63% of the discrepancy between the current and the desired value to be eliminated by movements of F [82]. Equations (A.15.95) and (A.15.96) constitute a system of two differential equations which, after linearizing about the equilibrium point, becomes

$$\frac{d\bar{i}_h}{dt} = -v\frac{\partial g}{\partial i_h}W\bar{i}_h, \quad \frac{d\bar{F}}{dt} = \alpha\frac{\partial f}{\partial i_h}W\bar{i}_h - \alpha\bar{F}, \qquad (A.15.97)$$

where a dash above the variable as usual indicates the deviations from equilibrium. The characteristic equation of this system is

$$\lambda^2 + \left(v\frac{\partial g}{\partial i_h} + \alpha\right)\lambda + \alpha v\frac{\partial g}{\partial i_h} = 0. \qquad (A.15.98)$$

As the necessary and sufficient stability conditions

$$v\frac{\partial g}{\partial i_h} + \alpha > 0, \quad \alpha v\frac{\partial g}{\partial i_h} > 0, \qquad (A.15.99)$$

certainly occur, because $\alpha, v, \partial g/\partial i_h$ are all positive, the equilibrium is stable[83].

We conclude by observing that, once the path of F has been determined, the path of M will be determined by the constraint (15.20.1), according to which

$$\frac{dM}{dt} + \frac{dF}{dt} = 0. \qquad (A.15.100)$$

A.15.6.2 Portfolio and Macroeconomic Equilibrium

We shall now pass to the examination of the model for the integration between portfolio and macroeconomic equilibrium, which for convenience is given here[84]

$$Y - d[(1-u)(Y + iN_p + iF_p), W] - x_0 - (Z - kiN^g) = 0,$$
$$0 < d_y < 1, \; d_W > 0,$$

$$M - L(Y, W) = 0, \; L_y > 0, \; 0 < L_W < 1,$$

$$W - (M + N_p + F_p) = 0,$$

$$\frac{dM}{dt} = sB + hg,$$

$$\frac{dN^g}{dt} = (1-s)B + (1-h)g, \qquad (A.15.101)$$

$$g = Z + (1-k)iN^g - u(Y + iN_p + iF_p),$$

$$CA = x_0 - m[(1-u)(Y + iN_p + iF_p), W] - i(N^g - N_p) + iF_p,$$
$$0 < m_y < 1, \; m_y < d_y,$$

$$B = CA + \frac{dN^g}{dt} - \left(\frac{dN_p}{dt} + \frac{dF_p}{dt}\right).$$

---

[82] On partial adjustment equations and concepts of mean time-lags in general cfr. Gandolfo (1981, Sect. 1.2).

[83] It is easy to see that in the previous case also, in which the only differential equation is (A.15.95), equilibrium is stable.

[84] Note that, for formal convenience, we have replaced the discrete variations (indicated by the symbol Δ in the text) by derivates with respect to time.

Note that the hypothesis $0 < L_W < 1$ means that only a part of the increase in wealth goes to increase the demand for money, in line with the theory of portfolio choice, and that the hypothesis $m_y < d_y$ indicates that, given an increase in disposable income, residents increase the demand for domestic goods to a greater degree than the demand for imported goods. The other partial derivatives can be interpreted immediately.

The first three equations make it possible to determine the momentary equilibrium and to express the endogenous variables Y, $(N_p + F_p)$, W as functions of the other variables considered as exogenous (x_0, Z, i, M, N^g) provided always that (implicit-function theorem) the Jacobian of these equations is different from zero with respect to the endogenous variables. This Jacobian is

$$J \equiv \begin{vmatrix} 1 - d_y(1-u) & -d_y(1-u)i & -d_W \\ -L_y & 0 & -L_W \\ 0 & -1 & 1 \end{vmatrix} = -[1 - d_y(1-u)]L_W - L_y d_W - L_y d_y(1-u)i,$$

(A.15.102)

which is negative, given the hypotheses made regarding the various partial derivatives.

The following differentiable functions thus exist

$$Y = Y(x_0, Z, i, M, N^g),$$
$$N_p + F_p = V(x_0, Z, i, M, N^g), \qquad (A.15.103)$$
$$W = W(x_0, Z, i, M, N^g).$$

A.15.6.2.1 The Dynamics of the Long-Run Equilibrium

The examination of the dynamic stability of long-run equilibrium is more complex: this requires the combination of equations which define the mechanisms of the movement of stock variables (the fourth and fifth equations) with the remaining equations in the model. If we suppose that the momentary equilibrium equations are valid at any instant[85], we can differentiate the functions (A.15.103) with respect to time; what interests us is the derivative of the second function, which expresses the stock of (national and foreign) securities held by the private sector. Therefore, supposing the intrinsic exogenous variables x_0, Z and i to be constants, we have

$$\frac{dN_p}{dt} + \frac{dF_p}{dt} = \frac{\partial V}{\partial M}\frac{dM}{dt} + \frac{\partial V}{\partial N^g}\frac{dN^g}{dt}, \qquad (A.15.104)$$

where the partial derivatives $\partial V/\partial M$ and $\partial V/\partial N^g$ can be calculated by using the implicit function rule. If we differentiate the first three equations in (A.15.101)

---

[85] This implies the hypothesis that the system moves in the long-run through a succession of momentary equilibria. More generally, it would be possible to analyze a situation in which there is also short-term disequilibrium, by assuming appropriate dynamic adjustment mechanisms for the variables Y, $(N_p + F_p)$, W. However, this would give rise to a system of five differential equations, the formal analysis of which would be excessively complex.

with respect to M, taking account of (A.15.103), we get

$$[1-d_y(1-u)]\frac{\partial Y}{\partial M} - d_y(1-u)i\frac{\partial V}{\partial M} - d_W\frac{\partial W}{\partial M} = 0,$$

$$-L_y\frac{\partial Y}{\partial M} - L_W\frac{\partial W}{\partial M} = -1, \qquad (A.15.105)$$

$$-\frac{\partial V}{\partial M} + \frac{\partial W}{\partial M} = 1,$$

from which:

$$\frac{\partial Y}{\partial M} = \frac{d_y(1-u)i(L_W-1)-d_W}{J},$$

$$\frac{\partial V}{\partial M} = \frac{[1-d_y(1-u)](L_W-1)+L_y d_W}{J}, \qquad (A.15.106)$$

$$\frac{\partial W}{\partial M} = \frac{-[1-d_y(1-u)]-L_y d_y(1-u)i}{J},$$

where J is given by (A.15.102). It is easy to see that $\partial Y/\partial M > 0$, $\partial W/\partial M > 0$, while $\partial V/\partial M$ has an uncertain sign.

Similarly,

$$\frac{\partial Y}{\partial N^g} = \frac{kiL_W}{J},$$

$$\frac{\partial V}{\partial N^g} = \frac{-L_y ki}{J}, \qquad (A.15.107)$$

$$\frac{\partial W}{\partial N^g} = \frac{-L_y ki}{J},$$

where $\partial Y/\partial N^g < 0$, $\partial V/\partial N^g = \partial W/\partial N^g > 0$, as it is easy to establish. It should be noted that (A.15.106) and (A.15.107) can be considered, from the short-run point of view, as *comparative statics* results.

Now, by substituting (A.15.104) into the balance of payments equation, we have

$$B = CA + \frac{dN^g}{dt} - \frac{\partial V}{\partial M}\frac{dM}{dt} - \frac{\partial V}{\partial N^g}\frac{dN^g}{dt}, \qquad (A.15.108)$$

which when substituted in the equations that determine the behaviour of the money supply and domestic securities, that is, in the third and fourth equations of

(A.15.101), gives

$$\frac{dM}{dt} = sCA + s\frac{dN^g}{dt} - s\frac{\partial V}{\partial M}\frac{dM}{dt} - s\frac{\partial V}{\partial N^g}\frac{dN^g}{dt} + hg,$$

(A.15.109)

$$\frac{dN^g}{dt} = (1-s)CA + (1-s)\frac{dN^g}{dt} - (1-s)\frac{\partial V}{\partial M}\frac{dM}{dt}$$

$$- (1-s)\frac{\partial V}{\partial N^g}\frac{dN^g}{dt} + (1-h)g.$$

By collecting and reordering the terms, we have

$$\left(1 + s\frac{\partial V}{\partial M}\right)\frac{dM}{dt} - s\left(1 - \frac{\partial V}{\partial N^g}\right)\frac{dN^g}{dt} = sCA - hg,$$

(A.15.110)

$$(1-s)\frac{\partial V}{\partial M}\frac{dM}{dt} + \left[s + (1-s)\frac{\partial V}{\partial N^g}\right]\frac{dN^g}{dt} = (1-s)CA + (1-h)g.$$

This is a first-order system of differential equations, which can be transformed into the normal form through well-known procedures (Gandolfo, 1980, note to page 281), that is, expressing $\frac{dM}{dt}$ and $\frac{dN^g}{dt}$ in terms of CA and g. The system obtained is

$$\frac{dM}{dt} = \frac{1}{D}\left\{sCA + \left[s + \frac{\partial V}{\partial N^g}(h-s)\right]g\right\},$$

(A.15.111)

$$\frac{dN^g}{dt} = \frac{1}{D}\left\{(1-s)CA + \left[(1-h) + (s-h)\frac{\partial V}{\partial M}\right]g\right\},$$

where

$$D \equiv \frac{\partial V}{\partial N^g}(1-s) + s\left(1 + \frac{\partial V}{\partial M}\right).$$

(A.15.111.1)

It can be established from (A.15.106), account being taken of (A.15.102), that $1 + \partial V/\partial M$ is a positive quantity, so that $D > 0$.

A.15.6.2.2 The Stability Conditions

In order to examine the local stability of system (A.15.111) a linearization is carried out around the point of long-run equilibrium. In order to determine this linearization correctly, it must be born in mind that CA and g are ultimately functions of M and N^g, account being taken of (A.15.103). Therefore, by indicating the deviations from equilibrium as usual with a dash over the variable, we have

$$\frac{d\bar{M}}{dt} = \frac{1}{D}\left\{s\frac{\partial CA}{\partial M} + \left[s + \frac{\partial V}{\partial N^g}(h-s)\right]\frac{\partial g}{\partial M}\right\}\bar{M}$$

$$+ \frac{1}{D}\left\{s\frac{\partial CA}{\partial N^g} + \left[s + \frac{\partial V}{\partial N^g}(h-s)\right]\frac{\partial g}{\partial N^g}\right\}\bar{N}^g,$$

(A.15.112)

$$\frac{d\bar{N}^g}{dt} = \frac{1}{D}\left\{(1-s)\frac{\partial CA}{\partial M} + \left[(1-h) + (s-h)\frac{\partial V}{\partial M}\right]\frac{\partial g}{\partial M}\right\}\bar{M}$$

$$+ \frac{1}{D}\left\{(1-s)\frac{\partial CA}{\partial N^g} + \left[(1-h) + (s-h)\frac{\partial V}{\partial M}\right]\frac{\partial g}{\partial N^g}\right\}\bar{N}^g,$$

where the derivatives $\partial CA/\partial M$ etc., are understood to be calculated at the equilibrium point.

The characteristic equation of this system turns out to be

$$\lambda^2 - \frac{1}{D}\left[(h-s)\left(\frac{\partial V}{\partial N^g}\frac{\partial g}{\partial M} - \frac{\partial V}{\partial M}\frac{\partial g}{\partial N^g}\right) + s\left(\frac{\partial CA}{\partial M} + \frac{\partial g}{\partial M}\right)\right.$$

$$\left. + (1-s)\frac{\partial CA}{\partial N^g} + (1-h)\frac{\partial g}{\partial N^g}\right]\lambda + \frac{1}{D^2}\left(\left\{s\frac{\partial CA}{\partial M}\right.\right.$$

$$+ \left[s + \frac{\partial V}{\partial N^g}(h-s)\right]\frac{\partial g}{\partial M}\right\}\left\{(1-s)\frac{\partial CA}{\partial N^g}$$

$$+ \left[(1-h) + (s-h)\frac{\partial V}{\partial M}\right]\frac{\partial g}{\partial N^g}\right\} - \left\{(1-s)\frac{\partial CA}{\partial M}\right.$$

$$+ \left[(1-h) + (s-h)\frac{\partial V}{\partial M}\right]\frac{\partial g}{\partial M}\right\}\left\{s\frac{\partial CA}{\partial N^g}\right.$$

$$\left.\left. + \left[s + \frac{\partial V}{\partial N^g}(h-s)\right]\frac{\partial g}{\partial N^g}\right\}\right) = 0.$$

(A.15.113)

The necessary and sufficient stability conditions are

$$(h-s)\left(\frac{\partial V}{\partial N^g}\frac{\partial g}{\partial M} - \frac{\partial V}{\partial M}\frac{\partial g}{\partial N^g}\right) + s\left(\frac{\partial CA}{\partial M} + \frac{\partial g}{\partial M}\right)$$

$$+ (1-s)\frac{\partial CA}{\partial N^g} + (1-h)\frac{\partial g}{\partial N^g} < 0,$$

(A.15.114)

$$\left\{s\frac{\partial CA}{\partial M}+\left[s+\frac{\partial V}{\partial N^g}(h-s)\right]\frac{\partial g}{\partial M}\right\}\left\{(1-s)\frac{\partial CA}{\partial N^g}\right.$$

$$+\left[(1-h)+(s-h)\frac{\partial V}{\partial M}\right]\frac{\partial g}{\partial N^g}\right\}-\left\{(1-s)\frac{\partial CA}{\partial M}\right.$$

$$+\left[(1-h)+(s-h)\frac{\partial V}{\partial M}\right]\frac{\partial g}{\partial M}\right\}\left\{s\frac{\partial CA}{\partial N^g}\right.$$

$$\left.+\left[s+\frac{\partial V}{\partial N^g}(h-s)\right]\frac{\partial g}{\partial N^g}\right\}>0. \tag{A.15.115}$$

In order to check whether these conditions are satisfied, a preliminary is to calculate the derivatives $\partial CA/\partial M$ etc. By differentiating the expressions which give CA and g, account being taken of Eqs. (A.15.103), we have

$$\frac{\partial CA}{\partial M}=-m_y(1-u)\frac{\partial Y}{\partial M}-m_y(1-u)i\frac{\partial V}{\partial M}-m_W\frac{\partial W}{\partial M}+i\frac{\partial V}{\partial M},$$

$$\frac{\partial CA}{\partial N^g}=-m_y(1-u)\frac{\partial Y}{\partial N^g}-m_y(1-u)i\frac{\partial V}{\partial N^g}-m_W\frac{\partial W}{\partial N^g}-i+i\frac{\partial V}{\partial N^g},$$

$$\frac{\partial g}{\partial M}=-u\frac{\partial Y}{\partial M}-ui\frac{\partial V}{\partial M},$$

$$\frac{\partial g}{\partial N^g}=(1-k)i-u\frac{\partial Y}{\partial N^g}-ui\frac{\partial V}{\partial N^g}, \tag{A.15.116}$$

where $\partial Y/\partial M$ etc., and $\partial Y/\partial N^g$ etc., are given by (A.15.106) and (A.15.107). Thus by substituting from these into Eqs. (A.15.116), we have

$$\frac{\partial CA}{\partial M}=-m_y(1-u)$$

$$\times\frac{[d_y(1-u)i(L_W-1)-d_W]+i[1-d_y(1-u)](L_y-1)+iL_yd_W}{J}$$

$$+\frac{i[1-d_y(1-u)](L_W-1)\quad iL_yd_W}{J}$$

$$+\frac{m_W[1-d_y(1-u)]+m_WL_yd_y(1-u)i}{J}$$

$$=J^{-1}\{m_y(1-u)d_W-m_y(1-u)i(L_W-1)$$

$$-m_y(1-u)iL_yd_W+i(L_W-1)-d_y(1-u)i(L_W-1)$$

$$+iL_yd_W+m_W-m_Wd_y(1-u)+m_WL_yd_y(1-u)i\}$$

$$=J^{-1}\{i(L_W-1)[1-(1-u)(m_y+d_y)]$$

$$+d_WiL_y[1-m_y(1-u)]+d_Wm_y(1-u)$$

$$+m_W[1-d_y(1-u)+L_yd_y(1-u)i]\}, \tag{A.15.117}$$

$$\frac{\partial CA}{\partial N^g} = -m_y(1-u)\frac{kiL_W}{J} + m_y(1-u)i\frac{L_y ki}{J} + m_W\frac{L_y ki}{J} - i - i\frac{L_y ki}{J}$$

$$= m_y(1-u)ki\frac{iL_y - L_W}{J} + (m_W - i)\frac{L_y ki}{J} - i,$$

$$\frac{\partial g}{\partial M} = -u\frac{d_y(1-u)i(L_W-1) - d_W}{J} - ui\frac{[1-d_y(1-u)](L_W-1) + L_y d_W}{J}$$

$$= \frac{u[d_W(1-iL_y) - i(L_W-1)]}{J},$$

$$\frac{\partial g}{\partial N^g} = (1-k)i - u\frac{kiL_W}{J} + ui\frac{L_y ki}{J} = (1-k)i - \frac{u(1-i)ki}{J}(L_W - L_y).$$

Let us now begin to examine the extreme cases, which occur when $s=h=1$ (there is no sterilization of the deficits or surpluses in the balance of payments and the whole of the budget deficit is financed by printing money) and when $s=h=0$ (complete sterilization of the disequilibrium in the balance of payments, and financing of the whole of the budget deficit through the issue of securities).

As can be seen from (A.15.101), when $s=h=1$, the system is reduced to a single differential equation relating to dM/dt and the stability condition becomes

$$\frac{\partial CA}{\partial M} + \frac{\partial g}{\partial M} < 0. \qquad (A.15.118)$$

By substituting from (A.15.117) and simplifying, we have

$$J^{-1}\{i(1-L_W)[(1-u)(m_y+d_y)]$$
$$+ ud_W(1-iL_y) + d_W iL_y[1 - m_y(1-u)] + d_W m_y(1-u)$$
$$+ m_W[1 - d_y(1-u) + L_y d_y(1-u)i]\} < 0. \qquad (A.15.118.1)$$

Given the assumptions made on the signs of the various partial derivatives, the expression in braces is positive and therefore, as $J<0$, the stability condition is satisfied. Note that the system is stable irrespective of any assumptions regarding parameter k, which in fact does not appear in (A.15.118.1).

When $s=h=0$, the system is reduced to a single differential equation relating to dN^g/dt and the stability condition becomes

$$\frac{\partial CA}{\partial N^g} + \frac{\partial g}{\partial N^g} < 0. \qquad (A.15.119)$$

By substituting from (A.15.117) and rearranging terms we have

$$J^{-1}ki\{(iL_y - L_W)[m_y(1-u) + u] + L_y(m_W - i)\} - ki < 0. \qquad (A.15.119.1)$$

It will be seen at once that this condition cannot be satisfied when $k=0$. If, on the other hand, $k>0$, for (A.15.119.1) to occur, it is sufficient (even if not necessary) that

$$iL_y > L_W, \quad m_W > i. \qquad (A.15.119.2)$$

We conclude with the observation that in all intermediate cases between the two extremes examined, it will be necessary to refer to the general conditions (A.15.114) and (A.15.115), after substituting into them from (A.15.106), (A.15.107) and (A.15.117); the stability will also depend on the relative magnitude of h and s, besides the various partial derivatives.

References

Allen, P.R. and P.B. Kenen, 1980
Angell, J.W., 1926
Aoki, M., 1981, Part Two
Argy, V., 1981, Part Two
Branson, W.H., 1974
Branson, W., 1976
Bruce, N. and D. Purvis, 1985
Brunner, K. and A.H. Meltzer, 1976
Buiter, W.H. and R.C. Marston (eds.), 1985
Casprini, F., 1973
Chacholiades, M., 1978, Part III
Christ, C.F., 1979
Clower, R.W. and D.W. Bushaw, 1954
Cooper, R.N., 1969
Cooper, R.N., 1985
Courant, R., 1962, Chap. IV, Sect. 2
De Grauwe, P., 1983
Dornbusch, R., 1980
Dornbusch, R. and J.A. Frenkel, 1984
Fleming, J.M., 1962
Floyd, J.E., 1985, Chaps. 4–7
Frenkel, J.A. and H.G. Johnson (eds.), 1976
Frenkel, J.A., T. Gylfason and J.F. Helliwell, 1980
Frenkel, J.A. and M.L. Mussa, 1985, Sects. 1-3
Frenkel, J.A. and A. Razin, 1987
Gandolfo, G., 1966
Gandolfo, G., 1974
Gandolfo, G., 1980, Part II, Chap. 9, Sect. 6
Gandolfo, G., 1981, Chap. 1, Sect. 1.2
Grubel, H.G., 1968
Hahn, F.H., 1977
Hicks, J.R., 1937
Hicks, J.R., 1967
Hicks, J.R., 1981
Hume, D., 1752
Johnson, H.G., 1958a
Johnson, H.G., 1965
Johnson, H.G., 1977a
Johnson, H.G., 1977b
Jonson, P.D. and H.I. Kierzkowski, 1975
Kreinin, M. and L. Officer, 1978
Laffer, A.B. and M.A. Miles, 1982, Chaps. 11 and 12
Marston, R.C., 1985
Markowitz, H., 1959
McKinnon, R.I., 1969
McKinnon, R.I. and W.E. Oates, 1966
Miller, N.C., 1978
Mundell, R.A., 1962
Mundell, R.A., 1968, Parts II and III
Mundell, R.A., 1971
Myhrman, J., 1976
Niehans, J., 1984, Chaps. 2–4 (Sects. 4.3 and 4.4), 7,10
Nyberg, L. and S. Viotti, 1979
O'Connell, J., 1984
Oudiz, G. and J. Sachs, 1984
Petit, M.L., 1985
Polak, J.J., 1957
Prais, S.J., 1961
Putnam, B.H. and D.S. Wilford (eds.), 1978
Rabin, A.A. and L.B. Yeager, 1982
Rogoff, K., 1985
Samuelson, P.A., 1980
Schumpeter, J.A., 1954
Shone, R., 1980
Stern, R.M., 1973, Chap. 10
Swoboda, A.K., 1976
Takayama, A., 1978
Thirlwall, A.P., 1980, Chap. 5
Tobin, J., 1969
Tobin, J., 1980
Tsiang, S.C., 1975
Various Authors, 1977
Viner, J., 1937
von Neumann Whitman, M., 1970
von Neumann Whitman, M., 1975
Willet, T.D. and F. Forte, 1969

16 Money and Other Assets in the Adjustment Process under Flexible Exchange Rates

16.1 Introduction

The consideration of exchange-rate flexibility (pure or managed) in a context in which money plays an essential role will first be made in the framework of the standard Keynesian-type model described in Sect. 15.4, which, as we know, considers the problem from the point of view of *flow* disequilibria and their adjustment. In this framework we shall also examine the problem of achieving internal and external equilibrium (i.e., full employment and balance-of-payments equilibrium), and the age-old question of the insulating power of flexible exchange rates and the transmission of perturbations in various exchange-rate regimes.

The traditional assignment of the exchange rate to external equilibrium and of fiscal policy to internal equilibrium was disputed and turned upside down by the so-called new Cambridge school of economic policy. This school, on the basis of a model in which it is the stock of financial assets desired by the private sector which determines this sector's expenditure-saving decisions, suggests in fact the opposite assignment (fiscal policy to external equilibrium and the exchange rate or other instruments to internal equilibrium).

To proceed beyond the various views and move towards a more general framework in which both stocks and flows are adequately accounted for, it will be necessary — as in the case of fixed exchange rates — to analyze the relations between portfolio equilibrium and macroeconomic equilibrium in an open economy under flexible exchange rates.

16.2 The Critical Elasticities Condition is neither Necessary nor Sufficient

We have already examined (Chap. 14) some attempts at integrating the balance-of-payments adjustment mechanism based on the foreign multiplier and the traditional elasticity approach to obtain a unified theory. Those attempts, however, did not consider monetary equilibrium or the influence of the interest rate on capital movements (in point of fact the balance of payments considered there is the balance on goods and services only). In this section we shall examine the problem by way of an analysis which, besides being explicitly dynamic, takes monetary factors into account in an essential way, though remaining in the framework of the standard Keynesian-type model; alternative models will be presented in Sects. 16.5 and 16.6. This model has the same basic features as that described in Sect. 15.4 (to which we refer the reader), with the addition of the flexibility of the exchange rate. Thus we shall talk of macroeconomic equilibrium to denote a situation in which real, balance-of-payments, and monetary equilibrium simultaneously occur. To simplify to the utmost we shall also keep the assumption of rigidity in the price level of both the country concerned and the rest of the world; this assumption will be dropped in the more general analysis of Sect. 16.6.

16.2.1 The Basic Model

The equilibrium relations mentioned above give rise to the following equations

$$y = d(y,r,i) + x(r), \tag{16.1}$$

$$x(r) - rm(y,r,i) + K(i) = 0, \tag{16.2}$$

$$M^* = L(y,i). \tag{16.3}$$

The first equation expresses real equilibrium, with the addition of the exchange rate as an explanatory variable [see Eq. (14.10) in Sect. 14.3 and Eq. (15.17) in Sect. 15.4]. The second equation expresses balance-of-payments equilibrium [see Eq. (14.11) in Sect. 14.3 and Eq. (15.18) in Sect. 15.4], whilst the third expresses monetary equilibrium [see Eq. (15.19) in Sect. 15.4]. The money supply is indicated with an asterisk because, unlike under fixed exchange rates, it must now be considered as given *in a static context*. In fact, whilst under fixed exchange rates the basic three-equation system would be overdetermined if M were considered given, as there would be only two unknowns (y and i: this is case (a) of Sect. 15.4.3, represented in Fig. 15.9a), now — under flexible exchange rates — there are three basic unknowns (y,i,r), so that the system would be underdetermined if M were considered as an unknown. On the contrary, *in a dynamic context* it is possible to consider M as an endogenous variable as well (see below).

Unfortunately it is not possible to give a simple graphic representation like that used in Sect. 15.4. As a matter of fact, if we take up the RR and BB schedules again (see Sect. 15.4.3), we see that a different position of these schedules in the (y,i) plane corresponds to each different exchange rate. In fact, as regards RR, greater (lower) values of d and x correspond to higher (lower) values of r, so that at any given y the interest rate i will have to be higher (lower) to keep total demand at the same value as before. This means that the position of the RR schedule will be found further to the right (left) as the exchange rate is higher (lower), as we have already seen in Sect. 15.4.4. As regards BB, if for simplicity's sake we assume that the critical elasticities condition is satisfied, we find that higher (lower) values of r imply a balance-of-payments surplus (deficit); hence at any given i, higher (lower) values of y are required, so that the higher (lower) value of m offsets the surplus (deficit) exactly. This means that the position of the BB schedule will be found more to the right (left) as the exchange rate is higher

16.2 The Critical Elasticities Condition is neither Necessary nor Sufficient 275

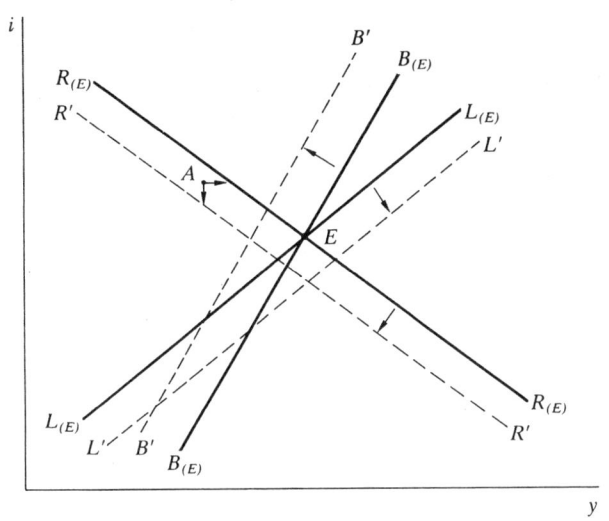

Fig. 16.1. Macroeconomic equilibrium under flexible exchange rates: the dynamics of the adjustment process

(lower), as we have already seen in Sect. 15.4.4. The LL schedule does not shift as it does not depend directly on the exchange rate.

Therefore the BB and RR schedules will shift continuously as r moves, and insofar as balance-of-payments disequilibria occur, the money supply will change and the LL schedule will shift as well, as shown in Sect. 15.4. To visualize the complications of the problem, let us assume we know the equilibrium value of r from the mathematical solution of system (16.1) – (16.3), let it be r_E. We then draw the RR and BB schedules corresponding to r_E (denoted by $R_{(E)}R_{(E)}$ and $B_{(E)}B_{(E)}$ in Fig. 16.1); the intersection of these determines the equilibrium values of y and i, which are of course the same as those obtained from the mathematical solution of the system. To examine the dynamics of the adjustment process let us assume that the system is initially in equilibrium (point E) and that an accidental disturbance brings it to point A. We must now introduce suitable dynamic behaviour assumptions, which are:

(a) Income varies in relation to the excess demand for goods and, to be exact, it increases (decreases) according to whether this excess demand is positive (negative).
(b) The rate of interest varies in relation to the excess demand for money and, more precisely, it increases (decreases) if this excess demand is positive (negative).
(c) The exchange rate varies in relation to the payments imbalance and, to be precise, it increases (decreases) if there is a deficit (surplus).
(d) As regards the money supply, we must distinguish two cases. In the first, the exchange-rate variations described in (c) cannot *instantaneously* maintain the balance of payments in equilibrium. This means that there will be balance-of-payments disequilibria, which will cause changes in the money supply, with

consequent shifts in the *LL* schedule. This is what we meant when we said that in a dynamic context it is possible to consider also M as a variable. In the second case, the exchange-rate variations do instead *instantaneously* maintain the balance of payments in equilibrium. This means that there is no effect of the balance of payments on the money supply, which remains constant (insofar as there are no other causes of variation); hence, the *LL* schedule does not shift.

Assumptions (a), (b), (d) (second case) are the same as those adopted in Sect. 15.4.3, to which we refer the reader. As regards assumption (c), it coincides with that adopted in Sect. 14.3.3, which the reader is referred to. We only add that this assumption can be considered valid not only in the context of freely flexible exchange rates (in which case the cause of exchange-rate variations is to be seen in market forces set into motion by the excess demand for foreign exchange), but also in the context of a managed float if we assume that the monetary authorities manage the exchange rate in relation to balance-of-payments disequilibria. The difference will consist in the speed of adjustment of the exchange rate: very high in the case of a free float, slower in the case of a managed float (as the monetary authorities may deem it advisable to prevent drastic jumps in the exchange rate and so intervene to moderate its movements: more on this at the end of Sect. 18.4.2).

Let us now go back to point A in the diagram and examine what happens in relation to the original schedules. Since the exchange rate is for the moment given at r_E, we can apply to the $R_{(E)}R_{(E)}$ and $B_{(E)}B_{(E)}$ schedules the same reasoning shown in Sect. 15.4.2; it follows that, as A is below the real-equilibrium schedule and above the external-equilibrium schedule, there will be a positive excess demand for goods and a balance-of-payments surplus. The following effects will then come about at the same time:

(1) the money stock (assumption (d), first case) increases due to the external surplus, the *LL* schedule shifts downwards, and the excess supply of money causes a decrease in the interest rate (downwards-pointing arrow from A);
(2) the excess demand for goods induces increases in y (rightwards-pointing arrow from A);
(3) the external surplus brings about an exchange-rate appreciation, so that the *RR* and *BB* schedules shift from the initial equilibrium position to a new position, for example to $R'R'$ and $B'B'$.

Thus we have, besides the movement of point A, movements of the *RR, BB, LL* schedules, which may give rise to changes in the signs of the excess demands, etc., so that it is not possible to ascertain the final result of all these movements by way of a graphic analysis. The situation is less complex it we adopt the second case of assumption (d), so that the *LL* schedule does not shift. In any case it is indispensable to rely on a mathematical analysis (see Sect. A.16.1).

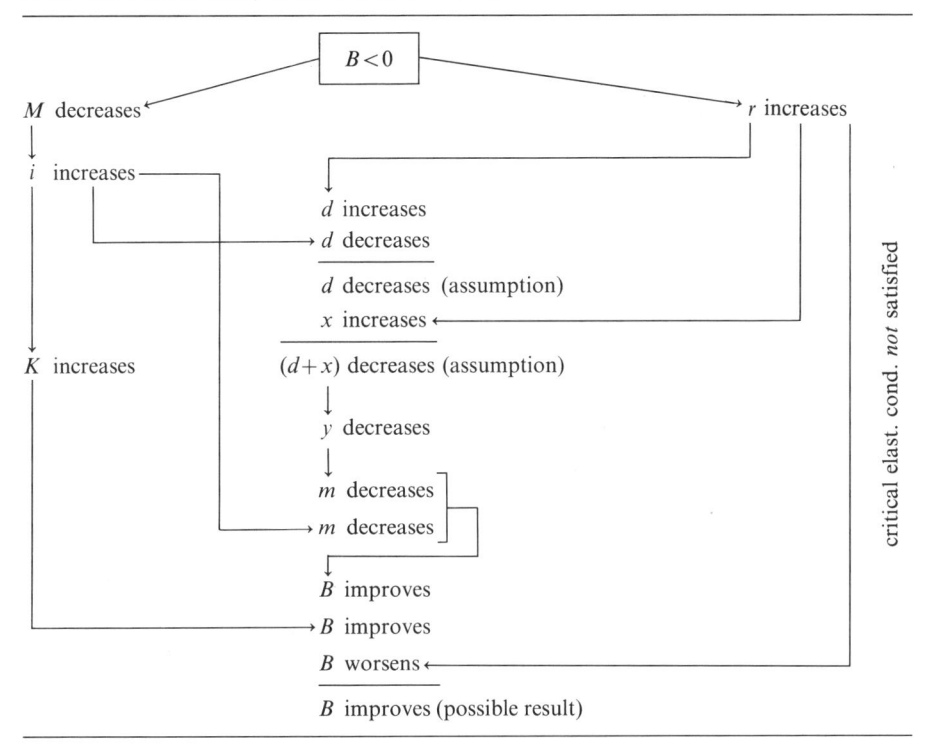

Table 16.1. Non-necessity of the critical elasticities condition

```
                        ┌─────────┐
                    ┌───│  B < 0  │───┐
                    │   └─────────┘   │
              M decreases          r increases
                    │                 │
              i increases             │
                    │   ┌─────────────┘
                    │   ↓
                    │   d increases
                    │ → d decreases
                    │
                    │   d decreases (assumption)
                    │   x increases ←──────────────┐
                    │                              │
              K increases   (d+x) decreases (assumption)
                                    │
                                    ↓
                                y decreases
                                    │
                                    ↓
                                m decreases ┐
                              → m decreases ┘
                                    │
                                    ↓
                                B improves
                              → B improves
                                B worsens ←─────────┘
                                B improves (possible result)
```

(right margin: *critical elast. cond. not satisfied*)

16.2.2 Non-Necessity and Non-Sufficiency of the Critical Elasticities Condition

The most important result of the above mentioned analysis is that *the critical elasticities condition is, in general, neither necessary nor sufficient for the dynamic stability of equilibrium.* This contradicts both the results of the traditional elasticity approach (according to which the critical elasticities condition is both necessary and sufficient: see Sect. 12.2) and the results of the first attempts at integration between the elasticity approach and the multiplier mechanism (according to which the condition, though not sufficient, is necessary: see Sect. 14.3). The reason for this contrast lies in the fact that in the present model the effects of interest-rate variations on the other variables are included as essentials. The Tables 16.1 and 16.2 may be helpful to illustrate the matter in the form of flow charts.

Let us begin by showing the non-necessity; for this purpose we assume that there is a deficit in the balance of payments. This (see Table 16.1) causes an exchange-rate depreciation and a decrease in the supply of money, which in turn brings about an increase in the rate of interest. As regards the direct effect of the depreciation on the balance of payments, this will be negative since we assume that the critical elasticities condition is *not* satisfied. As regards the influence of the

Table 16.2. Non-sufficiency of the critical elasticities condition

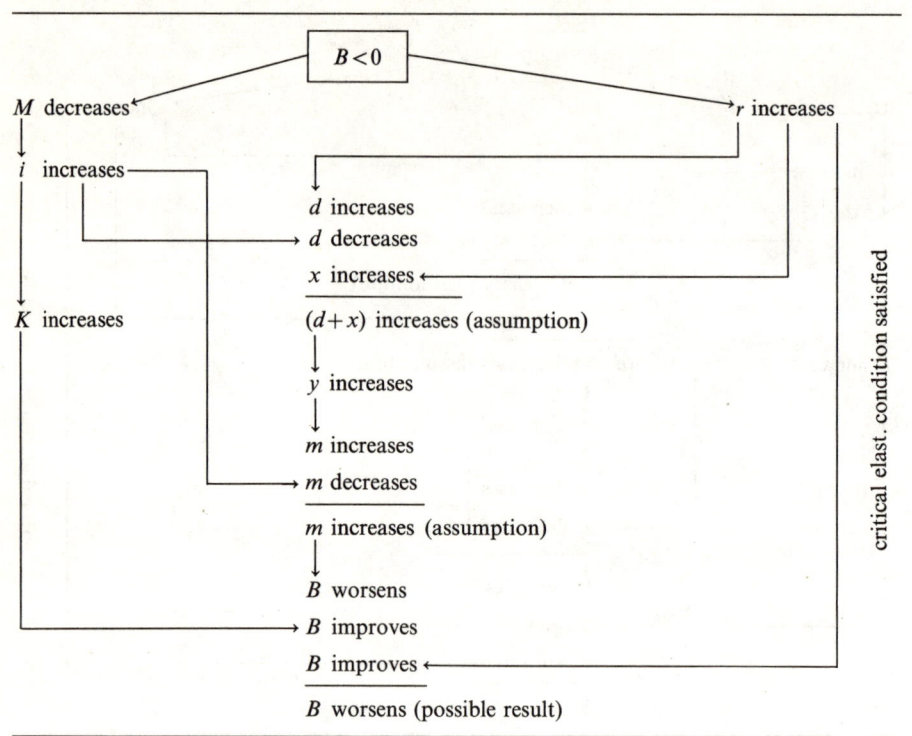

```
                              ┌─── B < 0 ───┐
   M decreases ←──────────────┘             └──────────→ r increases
   ↓                                                           │
   i increases ──────────┐                                     │
   ↓                     │   d increases                       │
                         │ → d decreases                       │
                         │   x increases ←─────────────────────┤
   K increases           │                                     │   critical elast. condition satisfied
   ↓                     │   (d+x) increases (assumption)      │
   ↓                     │   ↓                                 │
                         │   y increases                       │
                         │   ↓                                 │
                         │   m increases                       │
                         │ → m decreases                       │
                         │                                     │
                         │   m increases (assumption)          │
                         │   ↓                                 │
                         │   B worsens                         │
                         │ → B improves                        │
                             B improves ←───────────────────────

                             B worsens (possible result)
```

interest rate, various direct and indirect effects can be distinguished. The direct effects are due to the fact that the increase in the interest rate improves the capital movements balance and tends to depress imports (the latter effect operates in the same sense as the exchange-rate depreciation). The indirect effect is due to the fact that the increase in the rate of interest tends to depress domestic demand and so to oppose the expansionary effects of the exchange rate on both this demand and exports; these expansionary effects would cause a positive excess demand and so an increase in income (which in turn would bring about an increase in imports). If this restrictive effect of the interest rate is sufficiently strong, aggregate demand $(d+x)$ decreases, thus income and imports decrease.

Three contrasting effects ultimately determine the variation in the balance of payments: one unfavourable (due to the fact that the exchange-rate depreciation causes the balance of payments to deteriorate because the critical elasticities condition does not occur); two favourable (due to the direct and indirect effects of the interest rate). If the favourable effects are sufficiently strong, the net result is an improvement in the balance of payments although the critical elasticities condition does not occur. This condition, therefore, is not necessary.

It is likewise possible to show that the condition in question is not sufficient (see Table 16.2): in this case the direct and indirect effects of the interest rate are not sufficiently strong. To be precise, notwithstanding the restrictive effect of the increase of i on domestic demand, aggregate demand increases, income increases and so do imports: if this (unfavourable) effect is sufficiently strong, it may prevail on the favourable effects (reduction in imports due to the increase in i, improvement in the capital account due to the increase in i, improvement in the current account due to the depreciation), thus giving rise to a worsening in the balance of payments notwithstanding the occurrence of the critical elasticities condition. This condition, therefore, is not sufficient.

All the above is nothing more than an approximate description of the various effects; for a rigorous treatment see Sect. A.16.1.

We must now observe that the model employed is subject to the same type of criticism as its fixed exchange rates analogue (see Sect. 15.4.3.1) as regards capital flows, the burden of interest payments, etc., which will be dealt with in Sect. 16.6. In the meantime we shall continue using it to explain the traditional analysis of the problem of economic policy under flexible exchange rates and of the problem of the insulating power of flexible exchange rates.

16.3 Monetary and Fiscal Policy for Internal and External Balance in the Standard Keynesian Macroeconomic Model, and the Choice of Instruments

As was shown in Sect. 15.5, under fixed exchange rates both fiscal and monetary policy are engaged in achieving and maintaining internal (i.e., full employment) and external (i.e., balance of payments) equilibrium. Conversely, under freely flexible exchange rates external equilibrium is taken care of by the exchange rate (provided that the suitable stability conditions occur), so that a single instrument is in principle sufficient to achieve internal equilibrium. The other instrument is thus left free, to be used, if desired, to achieve another target. The problem that now has to be solved is one of choice, namely, which of the two traditional instruments (fiscal and monetary policy) is it preferable to use to achieve internal equilibrium? A host of studies were carried out in the sixties and early seventies with the aim of examining and comparing the effectiveness of these two instruments under fixed and under flexible exchange rates (for surveys see, e.g., von Neumann Whitman, 1970; Casprini, 1973; Shinkai, 1975). From these studies it turned out that in certain cases both policies are more effective under flexible than under fixed exchange rates, whilst in other cases solely monetary policy is definitely more effective, the comparative effectiveness of fiscal policy being uncertain. A crucial role is played by capital mobility, as we shall see in Sect. 16.3.1.

16.3.1 Perfect Capital Mobility

In the case of perfect capital mobility it was shown by Mundell (1963; see also Shinkai, 1975) that fiscal policy becomes completely ineffective under flexible exchange rates. This result is symmetric to that of the complete ineffectiveness of monetary policy under fixed exchange rates (and, of course, perfect capital

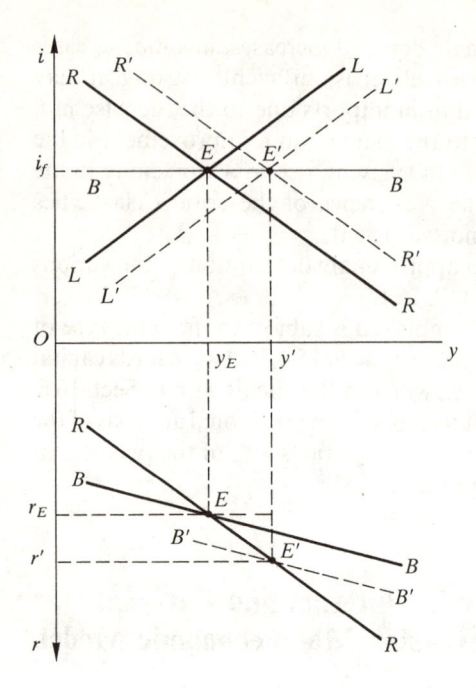

Fig. 16.2. Perfect capital mobility and monetary policy

mobility) which was mentioned in Sect. 15.5.1. We now give a treatment of the two cases, along the lines of Mundell (1963). Let us consider Fig. 16.2, in the upper half of which we have drawn the *RR*, *BB*, *LL* schedules corresponding to the equilibrium value (r_E) of the exchange rate. This panel is similar to Fig. 16.1, except for the fact that the *BB* schedule has been drawn parallel to the *y* axis with an ordinate equal to i_f, to denote that the domestic interest rate cannot deviate from the given foreign interest rate (i_f) owing to the assumption of perfect capital mobility[1].

In the lower half we have drawn the *RR* and *BB* schedules corresponding to the given value of the interest rate, with *y* and *r* variable. This panel is similar to Fig. 14.3c, rotated clockwise by 90°. Note that, as the interest rate is given, the capital movements balance is given and so Eqs. (16.1) and (16.2) yield relations between *y* and *r* altogether similar to Eqs. (14.10) and (14.11)[2], to which we refer the reader. We only point out that for simplicity's sake we have considered solely the case in which the *RR* and *BB* schedules satisfy the stability condition, namely a case similar to that described in Fig. 14.3c.

Let us now consider an expansionary monetary policy: the *LL* schedule shifts rightwards to *L'L'* and the excess supply of money puts a downward pressure on the domestic interest rate. As soon as this tends to decrease below i_f, a capital outflow

---

[1] Mundell implicitly assumed perfect capital mobility to imply perfect asset substitutability, hence the identity between the domestic and the foreign interest rate when no exchange-rate expectations are considered. For some purposes, however, it will be useful to distinguish between perfect capital mobility and perfect asset substitutability: see, for example, Sect. 18.5.3.1. See also Sect. 10.7.6.
[2] The given value of *K* can, in fact, be considered as an exogenous component in (14.11).

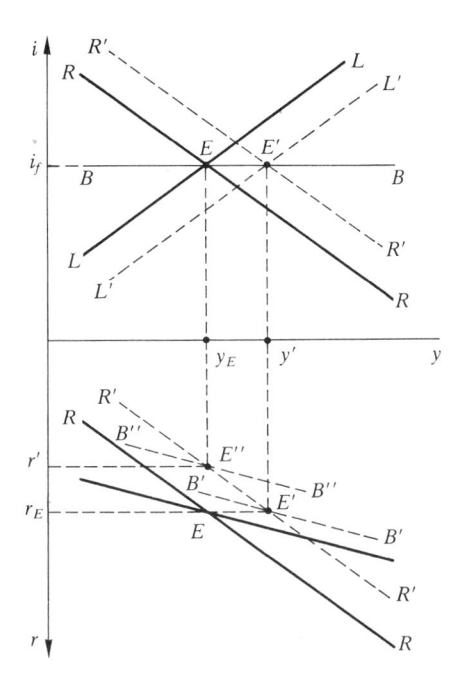

Fig. 16.3. Perfect capital mobility and fiscal policy

takes place which brings about a deficit in the balance of payments. Thus the *BB* schedule in the lower panel shifts downwards to *B'B'*: in fact, the deterioration in the capital account requires that a higher exchange rate (i.e. a depreciation) corresponds to any given income for external balance to be restored.

At this point we must distinguish between fixed and flexible exchange rates. Under fixed exchange rates the rate remains at r_E and so the balance-of-payments deficit causes a decrease in the money stock which pushes the monetary-equilibrium schedule back to the initial position, i.e. from *L'L'* to *LL*. Any attempt at an expansionary monetary policy gives rise to a loss of international reserves with no effect on national income: monetary policy is completely ineffective.

On the contrary, under flexible exchange rates the rate depreciates as a consequence of the balance-of-payments deficit, increasing from r_E to r'; the exchange-rate depreciation also causes a shift in the *RR* schedule (upper panel of the diagram) to the right (see Sect. 15.4.4) to the position *R'R'*. A new equilibrium is thus established at *E'* where income is higher (and the exchange rate is also higher): monetary policy has achieved its aim.

The same kind of diagram can be used to examine the effects of fiscal policy. An expansionary fiscal policy shifts the *RR* schedule to *R'R'* in both panels of Fig. 16.3. If the exchange rate is fixed at r_E, the increase in income causes an increase in the demand for money which, as the supply is given, exerts an upward pressure on the domestic interest rate. As soon as this tends to increase above i_f, a capital inflow takes place which causes *BB* to shift to *B'B'* in the lower panel and brings about an increase in the money supply (*LL* shifts to *L'L'*). The new equilibrium is established at *E'*, where income is higher: fiscal policy has achieved its aim.

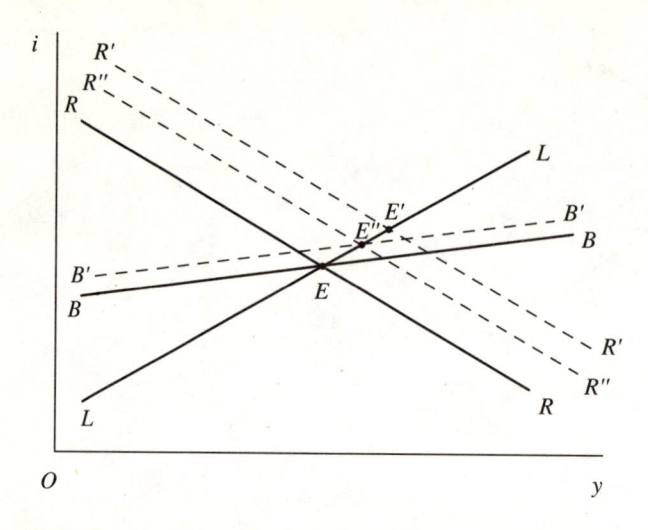

Fig. 16.4. Imperfect capital mobility and fiscal policy: first case

Conversely, under flexible exchange rates the money supply remains constant (the implicit assumption is that we are in the second case of assumption (d) in Sect. 16.2.1), and the upward pressure on the domestic interest rate is greater: there is, in fact, no increase in the money supply since the exchange rate moves to maintain external equilibrium. The increased capital inflow (the BB schedule in the lower panel shifts to $B''B''$) causes an exchange-rate appreciation which nullifies the effects of the expansionary fiscal policy (the real-equilibrium schedule in the upper panel shifts back from $R'R'$ to RR). Income falls back to y_E: fiscal policy is completely ineffective.

16.3.2 The Normal Case

The interesting results reached in the previous section are however limited by the restrictive assumptions of perfect capital mobility and constant price level. Thus, as we did in Chap. 15 in the case of fixed exchange rates, we have to examine what happens under flexible exchange rates when capital has a normal mobility (the case of a price level varying as the exchange rate varies will be dealt with in Sect. (16.6). The main outcome of the analysis is that not only does monetary policy maintain its full effectiveness, but also fiscal policy regains part of its effectiveness[3], with results which are however different according to the degree of capital mobility. By analogy with the case of perfect capital mobility we adopt the second case of assumption (d) in Sect. 16.2.1, and assume that the stability condition described in Sect. 14.3 holds.

In the case in which capital mobility, though not perfect, is very high, we have the graphic representation of Fig. 16.4.

---

[3] For an extension of this result in the context of a more general model, see Sect. 16.6.3.

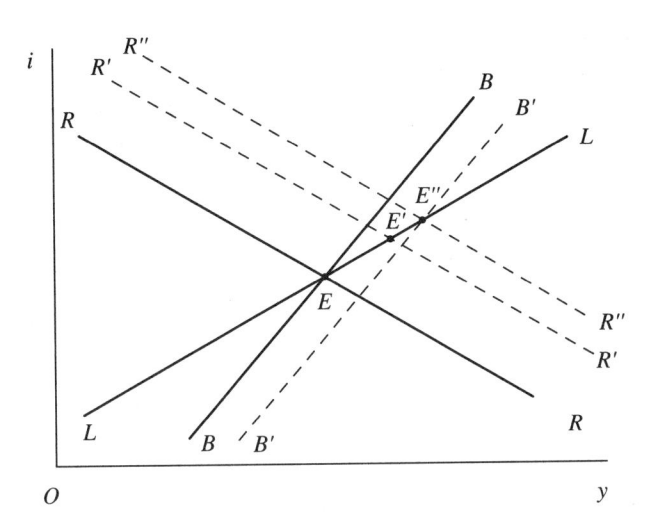

16.3 Monetary and Fiscal Policy for Internal and External Balance

Fig. 16.5. Imperfect capital mobility and fiscal policy: second case

The high capital mobility gives rise to a position of the *BB* schedule that, though not parallel to the *y* axis, is very flat, in any case flatter than the *LL* schedule[4]. An expansionary fiscal policy causes the *RR* schedule to shift rightwards, to $R'R'$, which intersects the *LL* schedule in E', where both the interest rate and income are higher. As a consequence of the high capital mobility, the capital inflow caused by the increase in the interest rate will more than offset the current account deterioration induced by the income increase. This can be seen from the fact that E' lies above the *BB* schedule, thus denoting a surplus. The surplus causes an immediate appreciation in the exchange rate, which causes the *BB* schedule to shift upwards (to $B'B'$) and the $R'R'$ schedule leftwards, to $R''R''$.

Due to this shift in the *BB* schedule, the restrictive effect of the exchange-rate appreciation on the real-equilibrium schedule will not be such as to completely offset the initial expansion: the new equilibrium E'', though being to the left of E', denotes an income increase all the same. Thus, while it remains true that the exchange-rate appreciation contrasts the effectiveness of fiscal policy as in the case of perfect capital mobility, this appreciation does no longer nullify the effects of fiscal policy.

Let us now examine the case of a relatively low capital mobility, in which the *BB* schedule is steep, in any case steeper than the *LL* schedule.

In Fig. 16.5 we see that a fiscal expansion causes a deficit in the balance of payments, as the low capital inflow induced by the interest-rate increase does not offset the current-account deficit (point E' is now below the *BB* schedule). As a consequence the exchange rate depreciates. This reinforces the initial expansion, causing a further rightward shift of the *RR* schedule, to $R''R''$. At the same time the exchange-rate depreciation makes the *BB* schedule shift to the right, to $B'B'$.

---

[4] On the relationship between the slope of the *BB* schedule and capital mobilty, see Sect. 15.4.2.

In the final situation E'', there will therefore be an income increase accompanied by an exchange-rate depreciation. It is clear that, the initial fiscal expansion being equal, the final effect on income will be higher than in the previous case.

We can similarly examine the effects of monetary policy, whose effects are in any case unequivocal. A monetary expansion (the LL schedule shifts to the right) initially causes an interest-rate decrease and an income increase. Both changes cause a balance-of-payments deficit and hence an exchange-rate depreciation, which will make the RR schedule shift to the right. The BB schedule will also shift to the right. In the new equilibrium we shall in any case observe an exchange-rate depreciation and an income increase. The reader may check as an exercise that these results are valid independently of the degree of capital mobility.

16.4 The Alleged Insulating Power of Flexible Exchange Rates and the International Propagation of Disturbances

16.4.1 The Alleged Insulating Power

If the suitable stability conditions are verified, a regime of freely flexible exchange rates maintains equilibrium in the balance of payments. Therefore — since balance-of-payments disequilibria are the way through which foreign economic perturbations influence the domestic economy and vice versa — it might at first sight seem that the regime under consideration has the power of insulating the domestic economy completely from what happens in the rest of the world (for the origins of this thesis see Laursen and Metzler, 1950, who were among the first to criticize it effectively). A simple version of this claim can be given by considering the national income equation

$$y = C + I + x - m, \qquad (16.4)$$

and assuming that flexible exchange rates maintain the balance on goods and services in continuous equilibrium, so that

$$x - m = 0, \qquad (16.5)$$

whence

$$y = C + I, \qquad (16.6)$$

which coincides with the equation valid for a closed economy. Hence the conclusion of the complete insulating power of flexible echange rates.

This conclusion, however, is incorrect for three reasons.

The first is self-evident: given for example a disturbance which causes a payments imbalance, the adjustment is not instantaneous, i.e. a certain period of time may have to elapse before the exchange-rate variations restore balance-of-payments equilibrium. And this period of time may be sufficiently long for the balance-of-payments disequilibrium to influence the domestic economy.

But even if one were prepared to accept that no lags exist so that adjustment is instantaneous and the balance of payments is in continuous equilibrium, there is a second reason, set forth as long ago as 1950 by Laursen and Metzler[5]. The variations in the exchange rate have an effect on the *composition* of aggregate demand ($C+I$), insofar as they bring about variations in the relative price of domestic and foreign (imported) goods and so phenomena of substitution between the two categories of goods. The alleged complete insulating power is based on the implicit assumption that these phenomena *only alter the composition of aggregate demand, but leave the total unchanged*, namely that any change in the expenditure on imported goods is exactly offset by a change in the opposite direction in the residents' expenditure on domestic goods. Only in this case does national income remain unaffected. In fact, if we consider Eq. (16.6), we must bear in mind that in C and I, *both domestic and foreign (imported) goods* are present, hence the necessity of the offsetting changes mentioned above for ($C+I$), and so y, to remain the same. But it seems unlikely that these changes do exactly offset each other, and in any case it does not seem correct to assume this to be the general case.

The third reason is related to the fact that in Eq. (16.5) the balance on goods and services is considered, with the exclusion of capital movements. But external equilibrium must be seen in relation to the overall balance of payments. In other words, in a world in which capital flows are present in an essential way (these were assumed away for simplicity's sake by Laursen and Metzler, 1950), a freely flexible exchange rate will maintain equilibrium in the *overall* balance of payments, as expressed by Eq. (16.2). This equilibrium — leaving aside long-run considerations concerning the increase in the stock of foreign assets or liabilities — may well take place with a non-zero balance on goods and services, offset by a non-zero balance on capital account in the opposite direction. It seems likely that this would be the normal situation, as it is not presumable that a *full* equilibrium in the balance of payments could be maintained even with freely flexible exchange rates. Therefore, if the normal situation is one in which $x-m \neq 0$, the basis itself for the alleged insulating power of freely flexible exchange rates disappears.

16.4.2 The Propagation of Disturbances in a Simple Model

The question examined in the previous section leads naturally to the analysis of the international propagation of disturbances under fixed and flexible exchange rates. If, in fact, flexible exchange rates do not have the alleged insulating power, it follows that the cyclical disturbances occuring in a country will be transmitted to the rest of the world and vice versa. However, one might believe that the propagation of the *same* disturbance is lower under flexible exchange rates than it is under fixed ones, which amounts to believing that flexible exchange rates, though not having a *full* insulating power, possess such power to a limited extent, i.e. have the power of attenuating the propagation of disturbances with respect to fixed exchange rates.

---

[5] Another author who independently examined the effect of the variations in the exchange rate on the level of aggregate expenditure is Harberger (1950). For recent theoretical studies of this effect, see Svensson and Razin (1983) and Persson and Svensson (1985). The empirical evidence is examined in Deardoff and Stern (1978a) and in Obstfeld (1982).

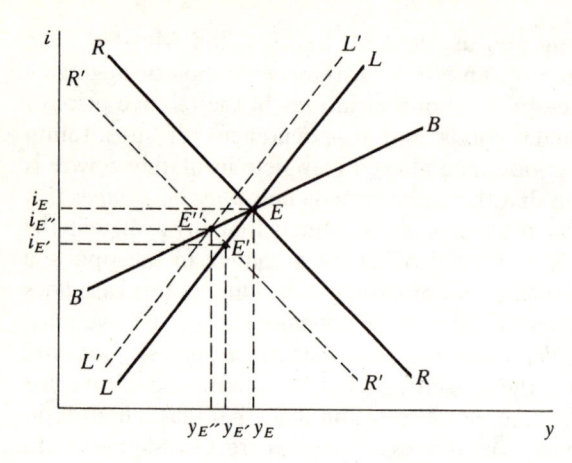

Fig. 16.6. International transmission of perturbations under fixed exchange rates

But even this opinion is not generally valid, since the attenuating power depends essentially on the interest-sensitivity of capital movements in relation to the interest-sensitivity of money demand. The fundamental result that we are going to show is that if the former sensitivity is relatively high, the propagation of disturbances may be *greater* under flexible exchange rates than under fixed ones.

Following Modigliani and Askari (1973) and Gandolfo (1975), let us take for example an exogenous decrease in investment at home, that is a depressive domestic disturbance. Income decreases and so do imports, so that the balance of payments improves. If we assume for the moment that the money supply remains unchanged, the decrease in the (transactions) demand for money due to the decrease in income gives rise to an excess supply of money which — in accordance with the usual behaviour assumption — brings about a decrease in the interest rate. This decrease stimulates capital outflows (or reduces capital inflows), so that the balance of payments worsens. If capital movements are very sensitive to the interest rate, the balance of payments ultimately worsens, as the deterioration in the capital account will more than offset the improvement in the current account due to the decrease in imports. At this point we must distinguish the two exchange-rate regimes.

Under *fixed exchange rates*, in the country under consideration (call it country 1), there will be an increase in the interest rate as a consequence of the decrease in the money supply (this decrease will be automatic if the monetary authorities, as shown in Sect. 15.4.3, allow the restrictive effects on the money supply of the balance-of-payments deficit to come into being, i.e. do not sterilize the deficit). The increase in the rate of interest will cause a further reduction in investment and hence in income, which will be the greater, the greater is the interest-sensitivity of capital movements[6]. If we look at Fig. 16.6, we see that the exogenous decrease in investment shifts the RR schedule downwards to $R'R'$; if M is unchanged the

---

[6] In fact, the more interest-sensitive the capital movements are, the greater is the capital outflow determined by the initial decrease in the interest rate, and so the greater is the successive increase in the interest rate to restore balance-of-payments equilibrium. In turn, the greater is the increase in the interest rate, the greater is the fall in investment and hence in income.

system moves to E', where the balance of payments is in deficit, since point E' is below the BB schedule: note that this occurrence depends on the relatively low slope of BB with respect to LL (this, in turn, depends on the relatively high interest-sensitivity of K with respect to the interest-sensitivity of L). In the opposite case, in fact, BB would have a steeper slope than LL, point E' would lie above BB, and the balance of payments would be in surplus, so that the reasoning made above would be invalidated.

To restore the simultaneous real, external, and monetary equilibrium, the LL schedule must shift to $L'L'$ (a decrease in the money supply); the final equilibrium point is E'', where income is lower than at E' and the interest rate is nearer to its initial value.

Under *flexible exchange rates* the money supply can be left unchanged as the deterioration in the balance of payments causes an exchange-rate depreciation which, if the stability conditions occur, restores equilibrium in the balance of payments, and at the same time supports income. This support comes about at the expense of the rest of the world, which will undergo a decrease in its net exports (exports minus imports). Thus country 1 will have to bear a smaller decrease in income than under fixed exchange rates, whilst *the rest of the world will bear a greater negative effect*: the propagation of the disturbance originating in country 1 has been more intense under flexible exchange rates than under fixed ones.

It should again be stressed that the result depends essentially on the interest-sensitivity of capital movements. Besides, even if this hypothesis occurs, the conclusions may change if a two-country model is used, because of the presence of international repercussions (neglected in the above analysis).

16.4.3 The Propagation of Disturbances in a Two-Country Model

When international repercussions are taken into account, the analysis becomes much more difficult. Let us consider, as in the previous case, an exogenous decrease in investment in country 1. This country's income decreases and so do its imports. However, it is no longer certain that country 1's balance of payments improves: in fact, country 2's income has decreased (through the foreign multiplier with repercussions) as a consequence of the exogenous decrease in country 1's investment, so that country 2's imports (which are country 1's exports) decrease as well. Thus both imports and exports of country 1 decrease, so that the initial impact on this country's balance of payments can be in either direction. To keep the present case on a comparable basis with the case of absence of repercussions, we assume that the impact under consideration is positive (country 1's balance of payments improves)[7]. If we again assume that for the

---

[7] As we show in the Appendix [see Eq. (A.16.35) in Sect. A.16.3], the condition for this to occur is that the sum of the marginal propensity to consume and the marginal propensity to invest should be smaller than one. Since there are no theoretical reasons (as shown in Sect. 13.3.2, the stability condition for the multiplier with foreign repercussions is that this sum should be smaller than one plus the marginal propensity to import), nor empirical ones (at the usual levels, the confidence interval for the sum in question goes from values lower than one to values higher than one), for the sum under consideration to be smaller than one, we must acknowledge that the assumption has been made for convenience.

moment the money supply remains unchanged in both countries, the decrease in their incomes will cause a decrease in their interest rates. The effect on capital flows is also indeterminate: these flows, in fact, depend on the interest rate *differential*, which may have moved in either direction following the interest-rate decrease in both countries. Still with the aim of keeping the present case on a comparable basis with the case of no repercussions, we make the further assumption that the interest differential moves against country 1, so that additional capital flows from this country to country 2. If the interest-sensitivity of these flows is sufficiently great, country 1's balance of payments worsens, because the capital outflow more than offsets the improvement in the current account due to the import decrease. Thus we are in the same situation as when repercussions were absent, and at this point we distinguish, as before, between the two exchange-rate regimes.

Under *fixed exchange rates*, in country 1 the money supply will have to decrease so that the interest rate increases and checks capital outflows; this decrease will take place automatically if the country does not sterilize the balance-of-payments deficit. Similarly in country 2, the surplus country, the money supply will increase with a consequent decrease in the interest rate[8]. In country 1 the increase in the interest rate will cause a further fall in investment and so in income. In country 2, on the contrary, the decrease in the interest rate will bring about an increase in investment and so in income, which will tend to offset the initial decrease: it is not however possible to give an unambiguous answer, since the final result is indeterminate (see Sect. A.16.3).

The money supply can on the contrary remain constant under *flexible exchange rates*, as the exchange-rate variations restore balance-of-payments equilibrium, provided of course that the suitable stability conditions occur. Country 1's exchange rate depreciates and this, besides restoring balance-of-payments equilibrium, supports this country's income. This however is not sufficient for us to state that country 1's income will decrease by less than under fixed exchange rates: it is in fact necessary to ascertain what happens in country 2. The appreciation of country 2's exchange rate will have a negative effect on that country's income and so on its imports, which are country 1's exports: therefore there will be a negative effect on country 1's income. The initial negative effect of the exchange-rate appreciation on country 2's income is however not sufficient for us to state that this country's income will *ultimately* decrease, as one must account for other effects, amongst which those of the interest rate. These effects (which operate in both countries) depend on the fact that the rate of interest, as the money supply is constant, changes in the same direction as income, thus tending to offset the changes in income itself: for example, if income increases, the concomitant increase in the interest rate tends to depress investment and so income. It is not possible to follow this intricate set of interrelations verbally; what

---

[8] This implicitly assumes that the burden of adjustment is shared by all countries, so that not only the deficit country but also the surplus one act so as to eliminate the respective external disequilibrium. Alternatively one might assume that all monetary authorities follow the rules of the game, i.e. do not sterilize payments imbalances so that the money supply automatically increases (decreases) in the surplus (deficit) country. On the problem of the cooperation between deficit and surplus countries to eliminate external disequilibria see, for example, Martinengo (1978).

has been said is however sufficient to convey the point that the final result is ambiguous. Therefore it is not possible to state any precise result concerning the comparison of the two countries' income changes under fixed and flexible exchange rates.

The proposition that the international transmission of disturbances is lower under fixed exchange rates than under flexible ones, provided that the interest-rate sensitivity of capital movements is sufficiently high, is thus true only in a one-country model in which foreign repercussions are neglected. In a two-country model, where these repercussions are explicitly taken into account, that proposition is no longer true or, more precisely, its validity cannot be ascertained on *a priori* grounds. In fact — notwithstanding the fact that in addition to the assumption concerning the interest sensitivity of capital movements other assumptions have been introduced[9], so as to put the model in the same initial situation as that obtaining in the no-repercussions case — it has been impossible to arrive at unambiguous results. Since the international propagation of disturbances is by its very nature a problem for the study of which a two-country model seems more suitable, we must conclude that this problem is not susceptible to a *general* unambiguous solution.

Our analysis has been carried out in the context of a traditional model; for further considerations on the insulating power of flexible exchange rates and on the international propagation of disturbances under various exchange-rate regimes see, for example, Mussa (1979), Goldstein (1980, pp. 48–54), Witte (1983), Lawrence (1984), Marston (1985, Sects. 6.1–6.2), Pitchford (1985).

16.5 The New Cambridge School of Economic Policy

16.5.1 Introductory Remarks

To examine this topic, we must start from a situation in which the exchange rate is flexible but managed, that is, the exchange rate does not freely and automatically move in relation to the excess demand for foreign exchange, but is considered as a policy tool, which is manoeuvred by the authorities to pursue the policy objectives. Now, according to the traditional theory or "old school", the exchange rate ought to be assigned to external equilibrium, and fiscal policy to internal equilibrium: this is the solution that we have examined, though in a slightly different context, in Sect. 16.3 (monetary policy can be used as a tool to achieve another objective or as an additional tool to back fiscal policy). This derives from the general principle examined in Sect. 15.5.2 according to which each instrument should be assigned to the achievement of the target upon which it has the greatest relative effectiveness; since the exchange rate is traditionally believed to have relatively more influence on the balance of payments, the usual assignment follows.

---

[9] These assumptions are firstly that the initial impact on country 1's current account of an exogenous decrease in this country's investment is positive and secondly that the interest differential initially moves against country 1: see above. As already mentioned, these assumptions are made for convenience, as there is no reason why they should occur for certain. If they are dropped, the results become still more indeterminate.

The "new school", on the contrary, claims that it is fiscal policy that has relatively more influence on the balance of payments: its suggestion is, therefore, to assign fiscal policy to external and the exchange rate to internal equilibrium (but, as we shall see, there also are different versions of the new school).

The formation of the thought of the new school has had a rather complicated development, at least from an outsider's point of view. The debate on its theoretical framework has, in fact, taken place in a disorderly manner, as it began in the British newspaper "The Times" in 1973–1974 (articles by Cripps and Godley, Kahn and Posner, Neild, etc.), was continued in "The Economist" (27 April 1974) and in the context of an investigation by a Committee of the House of Commons on public expenditure (1974), and then landed in specialized economics journals (for the references see Vines, 1976, and McCallum and Vines, 1981).

16.5.2 The Basic Model

To understand the position of the new school it is convenient to start from the accounting framework explained in Sect. 11.3. If we consider the budget constraint of the private sector — Eq. (11.7.1) — and consolidate all the net financial assets of this sector in a single stock that we denote by V_p, we get

$$S - I = \Delta V_p, \tag{16.7}$$

where ΔV_p is the algebraic sum of all the terms on the right-hand side of Eq. (11.7.1). Since the private sector's saving is equal to disposable income minus consumption, $S = Y_d - C$, if we call A_p the total current expenditure by the private sector ($A_p = C + I$), we get

$$Y_d - A_p = \Delta V_p, \tag{16.8}$$

which states that the excess of disposable income over private current expenditure equals the change in the private sector's stock of financial assets, also called the *net acquisition of financial assets* (NAFA) or the *financial surplus* of the private sector; it goes without saying that this magnitude may be either positive or negative.

If we consider the market for goods and services, we have the constraint (11.1) which, since $S - I = Y_d - A_p$ by definition of A_p, can be rewritten as

$$(IMP - EXP) = (A_p - Y_d) + (G - T). \tag{16.9}$$

Up to now we are in the context of accounting identities, from which, as we know (see Sect. 11.3) it would be incorrect to deduce causal relations. Of this fact the new school – which starts from Eqs. (16.7)–(16.9) – is well aware, so that at this point it introduces behaviour assumptions which, together with the accounting identities, enable it to give a precise vision of the functioning of the economy and to arrive at the policy suggestions stated above.

16.5 The New Cambridge School of Economic Policy

The first behaviour assumption concerns the functional dependence of private expenditure on disposable income. This relationship is *not*, as in traditional Keynesian models, a relationship directly and originally existing between flows (the flow of expenditure and the flow of income). On the contrary, it is a relationship deriving from an adjustment of stocks. We know that, in the orthodox Keynesian scheme, the private sector decides the flow of expenditure corresponding to any given flow of income on the basis of the propensity to consume. Saving has a residual nature, as it is the part of income not spent. In the approach under consideration, on the contrary, the private sector *first* decides how much to save, and consumption has a residual nature: it is the part of income not saved. The saving decision, in turn, is due to a stock adjustment. More precisely, if we consider Eqs. (16.7) and (16.8), the private sector decides $S-I$, and hence $Y_d - A_p$, on the basis of the *desired* value of ΔV_p, let us call it ΔV_p^*. This last does, in turn, depend on the desire of the private sector to bring its stock of financial assets from the current to the desired value (V_p^*). For the sake of simplicity it is assumed that the private sector is always in equilibrium[10], namely that it is able to realize its plans fully and instantaneously. This means that

$$\Delta V_p = \Delta V_p^* = (V_p^* - V_p). \tag{16.10}$$

If we take the budget constraint (16.8) and the behaviour assumption (16.10) into account, we can write the private sector's expenditure function as

$$A_p = Y_d + (V_p^* - V_p). \tag{16.11}$$

In brief, the behaviour assumption is that the private sector, wishing to hold a certain stock of net financial assets, regulates its expenditure, given its disposable income, so as to achieve the suitable (positive or negative) financial surplus to keep the actual stock of net financial assets equal to the desired one. The vision of the functioning of the economy has induced some authors (see, for example, McCallum and Vines, 1981) to claim that the new school is much nearer to the MABP (see Sect. 15.3: Eq. (16.11) is very similar to Eq. (15.11) with $\alpha = 1$) than to the old school (the traditional Keynesian model), because, like the MABP, it stresses stock adjustments. The difference would consist only in the fact that, whilst the MABP emphasizes the money market, the new school emphasizes the commodity market, as expressed by Eq. (16.9) and as we shall further show presently.

The new school further assumes that the private sector has a fairly stable desired stock of financial assets, which it is not willing to modify appreciably in response to changes in disposable income. This means that, once V_p has been brought to its desired level V_p^*, there will be no incentive to accumulate or decumulate financial assets, hence $A_p = Y_p$, as we get from (16.11) when $V_p^* = V_p$. Thus we have, considering Eq. (16.9),

$$IMP - EXP = G - T. \tag{16.9.1}$$

---

[10] The consideration of situations of disequilibrium, and of the relative adjustment mechanisms of actual to desired stocks, does not change the substance of the argument, though making it more complicated formally. See McCallum and Vines (1981).

Eq. (16.9.1), it should be noted, is *no longer* an identity. It is true that it has been derived from identity (16.9), but by using the private sector's behaviour assumption explained above. Thus it can legitimately be used to find out causal relationships. Of course we cannot yet claim that $(G-T)$ determines $(IMP-EXP)$ or the other way round without further behaviour assumptions, but these do not present any particularly novel feature. Let us assume that we start from a situation in which there is a budget deficit and a deficit in the balance on goods and services, which are equal on the basis of Eq. (16.9.1). Now, suppose there is an increase in G which causes an increase in income (via the multiplier) and hence in imports (IMP). Let us also assume that T is a lump-sum tax (the results do not change with T variable as income varies: see Sect. A.16.4), hence $\Delta T=0$. By applying the formula of the simple multiplier – see Chap. 13, Eq. (13.7) – we get $\Delta y=[1/(1-b-h+\mu)]\Delta G$, and so $\Delta IMP=\mu\Delta y=[\mu/(1-b-h+\mu)]\Delta G$. Since exports are assumed to be exogenous, the variation in $EXP-IMP$ will coincide with ΔIMP.

Now, $A_p=Y_p$ (see above) means that the marginal propensity to spend equals one (i.e., in the symbology of Chap. 13, $b+h=1$), hence $\Delta IMP=\mu\Delta y=[\mu/\mu]\Delta G=\Delta G$. This proves that the (additional) deficit in the balance on goods and services is exactly equal to the increase in the budget deficit. The opposite will, of course, be true in the case of a decrease in G. Thus we have obtained a relationship that clearly goes from the budget deficit to the deficit in the balance on goods and services, and in this sense we can say that $(G-T)$ "determines" $(IMP-EXP)$.

Thus we have shown that fiscal policy influences the balance on goods and services in the ratio of one to one. To complete the policy assignment under examination we must show that exchange-rate variations have a negligible effect on the balance on goods and services and an appreciable effect on income. The latter effect is known: an exchange-rate devaluation, for example, stimulates exports (and the demand for domestic goods by residents as well), so that national income increases. As regards the balance on goods and services, the assumption of the new school is that the values of the elasticities and the marginal propensity to import are such that the improvement (via elasticities) due to the direct effect of the devaluation on EXP and IMP is exactly offset by the deterioration (via marginal propensity to import) indirectly due to the devaluation itself by way of its effect on income.

This said, the application of the assignment principle immediately leads one to assign fiscal policy to external balance and the exchange rate to internal equilibrium.

16.5.3 Observations and Qualifications; Other Versions

The assignment derived above depends essentially on two assumptions: that of the stability of the private sector's expenditure function (with a marginal propensity practically equal to one) and that of the negligible effect of an exchange-rate variation on the balance on goods and services. From the theoretical point of view it is the first assumption which has given rise to most objections. The authors who declare their allegiance to Keynes point out that it is not legitimate to aggregate consumption and investment expenditure into a single aggregate expenditure function, as we are dealing with expenditure decisions taken by functionally distinct agents on the basis of very different variables; besides, the instability of private investment is one of the features most emphasized by Keynes (1936, Chap. 22).

A different kind of criticism is directed at the advisability of using the exchange-rate devaluation to promote domestic expansion. This is a beggar-my-neighbour policy, as the stimulus to exports and the brake on imports in the devaluing country implies the stimulus to imports and the brake on exports in the rest of the world, which thus undergoes a depressionary disturbance. The policy under consideration, then, might possibly be successful only if the rest of the world is willing to accept this negative effect. In the contrary case, the rest of the world may well decide to follow the same policy and devalue in its turn, thus giving rise to a chain of competitive devaluations of the type experienced in the thirties, and international trade would run the risk of again approaching what it was at the time, namely "a desperate expedient to maintain employment at home by forcing sales on foreign markets and restricting purchases" (Keynes, 1936, Chap. 24, pp. 382–3 of the reprint).

Leaving aside this type of criticism, we must concentrate on an extremely important point. It is in fact possible to show mathematically (see Sect. A.16.4) that the equilibrium is stable with both the traditional assignment and the assignment suggested by the new school: in other words, it is possible to reach the equilibrium point by manoeuvring the instruments either way. That is, we are in the presence of a lucky case in which either assignment is valid, although the speed and the path (oscillatory or monotonic) to equilibrium may differ in the two assignments. This fortunate occurrence is due to the fact that it is possible to make the model stable in any case, by suitably choosing the intensity of the policy interventions.

This result, in our opinion, eliminates any reason for controversy between *this version* of the new school and the traditional school. We have stressed *this version* because there are at least other two versions, derivable from the writings of the founders of the new school, though not so sharply distinct as we present them here for didactic purposes.

Now, a *second version* rejects the idea — on which the version so far explained is based — of assigning fiscal policy to external balance and exchange-rate management to internal balance, and holds that it is necessary to use both instruments to achieve both targets. This statement needs to be gone into a bit further.

As we have already explained in Sects. 15.5.1 and 15.5.2, to achieve n independent targets one needs (at least) n independent instruments, and, by solving the relevant model, one can determine the values that each of the n instruments will have to take on as a function of all the given targets. In this sense it is generally true (namely in any traditional *static* framework of policy analysis) that all instruments depend on all targets.

From the *dynamic* point of view the problem arises (for the reasons explained in Sect. 15.5.2) of *how to move the instruments through time*, so as to make them reach the respective equilibrium values, that is, those values in correspondence to which the desired values of the targets are achieved. Thus to assign an instrument to a target does not mean denying that all instruments affect all targets, but only aims to give a practical and operational solution to the problem of linking the *movement* of each single instrument to a particular single indicator, which, according to the assignment principle, is a particular target.

This version of the new school, therefore, seems on the one hand to be a truism (all instruments affect all targets) and on the other seems not to solve the dynamic assignment problem, which should be dealt with — if one wished to relate all instruments to all targets also dynamically — in the context of the *coordination problem* examined in Sect. 15.5.3.

Let us now come to the *third version* of the new school, which advocates protectionist measures (tariffs, quotas, etc.: see Chap. 5), instead of exchange-rate devaluations, to promote domestic expansion.

This version starts from the opinion that an exchange-rate devaluation has only transitory effects on income, which rapidly disappear. The reason is — so the argument runs — that the devaluation causes — through its effects on the prices of imported inputs and on wages — an increase in domestic prices[11] which completely offsets the initial favourable effects of the devaluation on exports and on the demand of domestic goods by residents. In fact, given that these effects depend on the relative price of domestic and foreign goods, and given that foreign prices in foreign currency are exogenous, if domestic prices increase by the same percentage as the devaluation, then relative prices do not change and income is not affected.

Thus another instrument is required to achieve the desired effects on the level of activity, which in this version of the new school is a protectionist policy. By curbing imports and causing domestic demand to shift in favour of domestic goods, this policy will have obvious expansionary effects on income, and beneficial side-effects on the current balance.

This version — in addition to the general criticism against protectionist measures (inflationary effect due to the increase in domestic prices caused by the tariff or quota; inefficient allocation of resources, etc.: see Chap. 5), which, however, has to be seen in the light of the theory of second best (see Sect. 5.6.6) — has been subjected to the same criticism made above against devaluation: retaliation by other countries etc., so that international trade might again become "a desperate expedient, etc.".

Finally it should be observed that, as regards the external balance, the new school only considers the balance on goods and services. If one takes the overall balance and so capital movements, it is no longer at all certain that fiscal policy

---

[11] The devaluation-inflation relations will be examined in detail in Sect. 18.4. Here we simply observe that, if domestic prices are determined by applying a markup on production costs, and if wages (which are a component of production costs) are indexed to prices, then an exchange-rate devaluation causes: a) an increase in production costs (due to the increase in the prices of imported intermediate goods) and so in prices; b) the price increase gives rise to an increase in wages (due to the indexation mechanism) and so in production costs, hence a new price increase, etc. The (arbitrary) assumption is that, when this process has worked itself out, the price increase will be percentually equal to the devaluation.

16.6 Portfolio and Macroeconomic Equilibrium in an Open Economy

16.6.1 Introductory Remarks

The problems arising from the introduction of a plurality of financial assets and from the integration between stocks and flows have already been mentioned in general in Sects. 15.6.1 and 15.6.3.1, to which we refer the reader. Here we propose to come to grips with the same problems when exchange rates are flexible and macroeconomic equilibrium is taken into account[12].

Exchange-rate flexibility does however introduce an additional problem with respect to those stressed in Sect. 15.6.3, a problem which was usually neglected in the traditional analyses of macroeconomic equilibrium under flexible exchange rates. These analyses are based on models like the one examined in Sect. 16.2, in which the assumption of rigid prices is maintained, being carried over from the fixed exchange rates models. Amongst other consequences this assumption implies the absence of the exchange rate from the monetary equilibrium equation (16.3): the exchange rate, in fact, would be present in that equation insofar as it influenced the price level which, then, could no longer be assumed constant and ought to be explicitly introduced in the equation under consideration[13] as well as in the other equations of the model, as we shall see presently.

Now, there are valid theoretical reasons — supported by empirical evidence (see, for example, Deardoff and Stern, 1978b) — for believing that exchange-rate changes influence the price level. If we consider, for example, a depreciation, this will cause an increase in the domestic-currency price of final foreign imported goods and so, even if the price of domestic goods is assumed constant, an increase in the general price-index. If, in addition, we consider imported intermediate inputs, a depreciation (as we mentioned at the end of Sect. 16.5.3) can also cause an increase in the price of domestic goods, insofar as these are set by applying a markup on production costs. To avoid complicating an already difficult treatment we shall neglect the second effect (for which see Sect. 18.5) and concentrate on the first. Thus we have

$$p = p_h^\alpha (rp_f)^{1-\alpha}, \quad 0 < \alpha < 1, \tag{16.12}$$

where α and $(1-\alpha)$ are the given weights of commodities in the general price-index p. These commodities are domestically produced (with a price p_h) and foreign imported (with a foreign-currency price p_f). Since p_f is assumed constant,

---

[12] Thus we omit the study of portfolio equilibrium in a partial equilibrium context only, for which we refer the reader, for example, to Branson (1979). See also Branson and Henderson (1985).
[13] Remember that the price level enters in Eq. (16.3) in the form $M^* = pL(y,i)$ or $M^*/p = L(y,i)$; given the assumption of constancy of p, it is set at one for brevity. For the introduction of the variability of p as a function of r in the traditional Mundell-Fleming model, see, for example, Lai and Chen (1984) and references therein.

it can be set at one, so that

$$p = p_h^\alpha r^{1-\alpha}. \tag{16.12.1}$$

By the same token the terms of trade turn out to be

$$\pi = \frac{p_h}{r}. \tag{16.13}$$

As soon as one introduces the variability of the price level, the *expectations* on its future value come into play, for example to determine the real interest rate (given by the difference between the nominal interest rate and the expected proportional rate of change in the price level), which, together with other variables, is an argument in the aggregate demand function. The topic of expectations is difficult and enormously far-reaching; here we shall only consider two extreme cases: *static expectations* and *rational expectations* or *perfect foresight*. The former consist in the belief that no change will occur in the variable under consideration; the latter in forecasting the variable exactly, so that — in a deterministic context — the expected change coincides with the one that actually occurs[14]. If we denote the change of a variable by putting a dot over it and the expectation by putting a tilde, we have

$$\frac{\tilde{\dot{p}}}{p} = \begin{cases} 0, \\ \dfrac{\dot{p}}{p}, \end{cases} \tag{16.14}$$

in the case of static and rational expectations respectively; the expected changes are expressed as a proportion of the current actual value because, as mentioned above, we are interested in the expected *proportional* change. It should be noted that the case of static expectations is practically equivalent to eliminating expectations wherever they appear and so coincides with the traditional analysis where expectations are not taken into account.

The exchange-rate flexibility suggests the presence of expectations concerning the changes in this variable, which we shall again limit to the two extreme cases:

$$\frac{\tilde{\dot{r}}}{r} = \begin{cases} 0, \\ \dfrac{\dot{r}}{r}. \end{cases} \tag{16.15}$$

Expectations on the exchange rate require a new form of the relation between the domestic and the foreign interest rate in the case of a small country with perfect capital mobility and perfect substitutability between domestic-currency and foreign-currency financial assets (these are the same assumptions already employed in the fixed exchange rate model treated in Sect. 15.6.3; see also Sect. 16.3.1). In fact, the domestic interest rate i is no longer equal to the given foreign

---

[14] There is more to it than that however and, in general, there may be a difference between perfect foresight and rational expectations. But we shall neglect these complications.

interest rate i_f, but is related to it by the equation

$$i = i_f + \tilde{r}/r, \tag{16.16}$$

where i and i_f refer to the same period of time as $\tilde{r}$. This equation is the interest rate parity condition (10.32) explained in Sect. 10.7.2.

16.6.2 The Basic Model

After clarifying these preliminary problems, we go on to the exposition of a model (due to Branson and Buiter, 1983) which enables us, under flexible exchange rates, to deal with the same problems as in Sect. 15.6.3 under fixed exchange rates. We shall however adopt further simplifying assumptions with respect to the framework used there, namely:

(a) we do not introduce the auxiliary variable Z, but consider only the actual overall government expenditure G, given by government expenditure on goods and services[15] plus interest payments on public debt.
(b) we assume that domestic assets are held solely by residents, so that $N^g = N_p$ (for brevity we shall omit both the superscript and the subscript and use the symbol N only).
(c) we do not introduce a taxation function linking fiscal receipts to income, but we assume them to be a discretionary policy variable like G_R; if we call these receipts (in real terms) T, they will be pT in nominal terms.

Thus the budget deficit is

$$g = G - pT - ri_f R = p_h G_R + iN - pT - ri_f R. \tag{16.18}$$

With respect to the definition given in Chap. 15 – see Eq. (15.27) –, besides the explicit presence of the price level p, we note the additional term (on the side of receipts) $ri_f R$, where R denotes the stock of official foreign exchange reserves. The assumption behind this term is that the central bank (remember that it is consolidated together with the government etc. in a single sector, the public sector) holds all the international reserves in the form of interest-bearing foreign assets (at the given interest rate i_f).

Let us now consider the balance of payments, divided as usual into current account (CA) and capital movements (K). As we know, the former includes the flow of interest on net foreign assets (denominated in foreign currency) held by both private and public residents[16]. All the other items of the current account are lumped together under "exports" and "imports". Exports (in real terms) are a function of the terms of trade π; imports (in real terms) are a function of the terms of trade and of private aggregate expenditure or absorption (instead of income) in real terms. The idea is that imports, as part of aggregate expenditure,

---

[15] As usual we assume that government expenditure in real terms (G_R) is entirely directed to domestically produced output.
[16] It should be pointed out that, in general, interest on net foreign assets held by the official authorities is also reported in the "investment income" item of the current account.

are related directly to it and so indirectly to income, which is one of the arguments in the absorption function. Thus, if we denote *net exports* (that is exports less imports) by x and absorption by a, we have $x = x(\pi, a)$, where it is assumed (i) that the effect of an increase in π on x is negative and vice versa [this implies the assumption that the critical elasticities condition — see Sect. 12.3 — occurs: we must remember that an exchange-rate appreciation causes an increase in π and vice versa, on the basis of Eq. (16.13)] and (ii) that the effect of an increase in a on x is negative (and vice versa), included between zero and minus one (this amounts to assuming a positive and smaller-than-one marginal propensity to import with respect to absorption).

Since x is expressed in real terms and, more precisely, in terms of domestic output[17], if we multiply it by p_h we obtain its monetary value.

As regards the flow of interest income, since foreigners do not hold domestic government bonds (all foreign lending or borrowing is done in foreign currency-denominated bonds), it will equal $ri_f(F_p + R)$, where F_p is the stock of net foreign assets privately held[18] (for brevity we shall henceforth omit the subscript p) and R the stock of official foreign-exchange reserves. Thus we have

$$CA = p_h x(\pi, a) + ri_f(F + R). \tag{16.19}$$

Private capital movements (K) are a flow equal to the *change* in the stock of net foreign assets held by the private sector, that is, if we express these flows in domestic-currency terms and remember the recording rules explained in Sect. 11.1,

$$K = -r\dot{F} \tag{16.20}$$

where, according to the convention introduced in Sect. 16.6.1, the dot indicates the change. Therefore the overall payments balance, equal in turn to the change in official international reserves (expressed in terms of domestic currency) is

$$r\dot{R} = p_h x(\pi, a) + ri_f(F + R) - r\dot{F}. \tag{16.21}$$

The equation for the determination of domestic production q is, as usual,

$$q = a\left(y_d, i - \frac{\tilde{p}}{p}, \frac{W}{p}\right) + x(\pi, a) + G_R, \tag{16.22}$$

where a is absorption in real terms, a function of real disposable income (with a marginal propensity to absorb that is smaller than one), the real interest rate (with an inverse relationship), and real private financial wealth (with a positive relationship). We must now define real disposable income. The variability in the price level discussed in Sect. 16.6.1 makes it necessary first to define *nominal disposable income*, which can then be deflated by p to get real disposable income. Nominal disposable income equals the value of domestic output ($p_h q$) plus

---

[17] Inherently exports consist of domestic output. Imports m consist of foreign goods, which have a monetary value rm in domestic currency; if we divide this by p_h we express them in terms of domestic output. See Sect. A.16.5.

[18] Note that, since we are talking of the stock of *net* foreign assets (assets minus liabilities), in general this stock can be either positive or negative.

interest received by residents on both national (iN) and (net) foreign assets (ri_fF) minus taxes (pT). In real terms we have

$$y_d = \frac{p_h}{p}q + \frac{iN}{p} + \frac{ri_fF}{p} - T. \qquad (16.23)$$

We then have the monetary equilibrium equation

$$\frac{M}{p} = L\left(i, q, \frac{W}{p}\right), \qquad (16.24)$$

where money demand in real terms is a decreasing function of the rate of interest, and an increasing function of both domestic production (taken as an index of transactions) and real financial wealth (this derives from the portfolio equilibrium discussed in Sect. 15.6.2)[19]. Wealth is defined as the sum of the stock of money M and the stock of domestic and (net) foreign bonds held by residents[20]; the latter must, of course, be multiplied by the exchange rate to express it in domestic-currency terms:

$$W = M + N + rF. \qquad (16.25)$$

If we divide W by the general price-level we get real financial wealth, W/p.

It is now necessary to introduce — as we did in Sect. 15.6.3, in particular Eq. (15.34) — the ways of financing the budget deficit, and the sources of money creation. The further simplifying assumptions introduced by Branson and Buiter (1983) are the following. Firstly, the government always balances its budget by *endogenous* changes in taxes. In other words, given the other variables entering into g, the level of T is always set by the government so as to make $g = 0$. In terms of comparative-static analysis this means that, when we consider fiscal policy, we shall obtain balanced-budget multipliers[21]. Thus, from Eq. (16.18), we have

$$p_h G_R + iN - pT - ri_f R = 0. \qquad (16.26)$$

The second simplifying assumption is that the government does not carry out *continuative* open market operations (it can carry out these operations but only occasionally) and does not sterilize payments imbalances. Together with the previous assumption, this implies that the stock of national bonds does not change (except occasionally) and that the change in the stock of money coincides with the balance of payments, namely

$$\dot{N} = 0, \qquad (16.27)$$

$$\dot{M} = r\dot{R}. \qquad (16.28)$$

---

[19] Since there are only two financial assets (money and bonds: remember the assumption of perfect substitutability between national and foreign bonds), the budget constraint allows us to omit the demand-for-bonds function and so to avoid the problems related to the specification of this function.

[20] This implies that the stock of physical capital is ignored. This is a simplifying assumption, common to this type of model, which also allows us to ignore the subdivision of absorption between consumption and investment.

[21] The balanced-budget multiplier is an elementary concept in standard macroeconomic and public finance theory, which will be put to use in this more general model.

It goes without saying that in the case of perfectly flexible exchange rates and instantaneous adjustment, the balance of payments in always zero, so that

$$\dot{R}=0, \text{ hence } \dot{M}=0. \tag{16.28.1}$$

Having described the model, we now pass to the examination of its solution and properties according to the type of expectations.

16.6.3 Static Expectations

In the case of static expectations we have $\tilde{r}=0$ and $\tilde{p}=0$. As usual (see Sect. 15.6.3), we distinguish between *short-run* or *momentary equilibrium* and *long-run equilibrium* and begin by examining the former.

At a given point in time, the stocks (money, national and foreign bonds, wealth, international reserves)[22] are given; the domestic interest rate is given [by Eq. (16.16) and the assumption of static expectations, it equals the given foreign interest rate] and government expenditure is also given, as it is an exogenous variable.

Since the price level depends on the exchange rate, it is possible to reduce the short run model to two equations only, which determine the short run endogenous variables r[23] and q, i.e. the exchange rate and domestic production. A simple interpretation in terms of RR and LL schedules can then be given (see Fig. 16.7).

The real equilibrium schedule RR has been drawn after finding the equilibrium value (r_E) of the exchange rate through the mathematical solution of the model (this is the same device that we used in relation to Fig. 16.1). This schedule is the graphic counterpart to Eq. (16.22) for r given at r_E. In fact, given r_E, p (and so π) is given; besides, as W is given, the argument W/p in the absorption function is given. Since G_R, N and R are also given, Eq. (16.26) determines the taxation level T. It follows that, in Eq. (16.23), disposable income varies only as q varies and so, since the marginal propensity to absorb is smaller than one, absorption increases by less than q. It should be noted that, since this propensity is defined with respect to y_d, this result is based on the implicit assumption that y_d varies approximately by the same amount as q, which in turn implies that the ratio p_h/p in (16.23) does not differ greatly from one. This will always be the case if we set $r=p_h=p=1$ in the initial equilibrium situation, which involves no loss of generality[24].

---

[22] The stocks of money, national bonds and international reserves are in any case given owing to the assumptions included in Eqs. (16.28.1) and (16.27). The stock of foreign bonds can, on the contrary, vary through time, so that it is an exogenous variable only because we are considering a given point in time.

[23] From this point of view the model can also be seen as a model for the determination of the exchange rate (a similar observation can be made in relation to the successive analysis of long-run equilibrium and to the case of rational expectations). This, it should be stressed, holds in all models where the exchange rate is flexible and is determined as an endogenous variable. We shall deal with the problem of the equilibrium exchange rate in Sect. 18.5.

[24] When the equilibrium is displaced and a variation in r occurs (see below, in the text), the term p_h/p — which equals $\pi^{1-\alpha}$ by way of (16.12.1) and (16.13) — will become greater or smaller according as r appreciates or depreciates. In the latter case the result is strenghtened, since when q increases y_d will increase by less; in the former, y_d will increase by more than q and so one cannot exclude the possibility that a may increase by more than q. Even in this case, however, since an

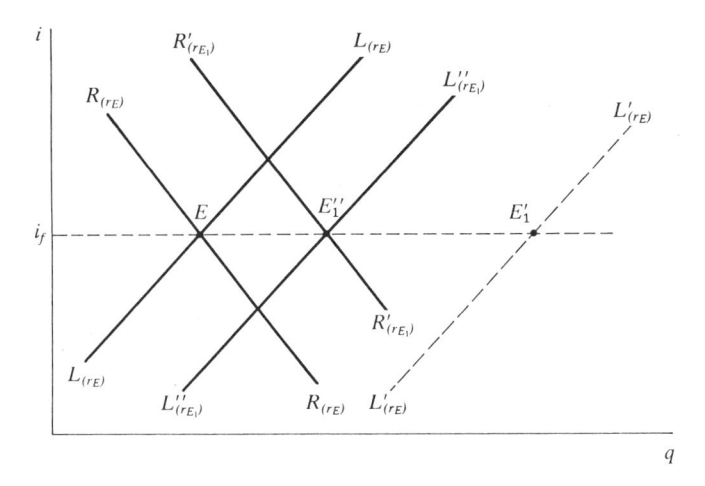

16.6 Portfolio and Macroeconomic Equilibrium in an Open Economy

Fig. 16.7. Static expectations: short-run equilibrium and economic policy

The increase in absorption due to the increase in q also causes a deterioration in the x balance (but by less than the increase in a); therefore, the sum $(a+x)$ increases by less than q. Thus a decrease in i is required for a to increase sufficiently and absorb the increase in q entirely (when a increases x decreases, but by less, since the marginal propensity to import is smaller than one). This shows that the RR schedule is downward sloping.

As regards the LL schedule, it is the graphic counterpart of Eq. (16.24): since, as we explained above, p and W are given, it has the usual positive slope.

It should be noted that the RR and LL schedules cross in correspondence to the foreign interest rate i_f from which — due to the assumptions of perfect capital mobility and static expectations — the domestic interest rate cannot deviate. For this same reason the broken line parallel to the q axis at a distance i_f can be interpreted, as before (see Fig. 16.2), as the BB schedule.

Let us now consider the effects of monetary and fiscal policy.

An expansionary monetary policy, namely — in this context — an increase in the stock of money, for example through a purchase of national bonds by the public sector from the private sector[25], shifts LL to the right, for example to $L'L'$. The excess supply of money puts a downward pressure on the domestic interest rate, which is however brought back to i_f by the incipient capital outflow. Through its effect on the balance of payments, this incipient outflow causes the exchange rate to depreciate, for example from r_E to r_{E1}: this causes a rightward shift in the RR schedule (not shown). Now, in the traditional analysis (see above,

---

increase in a causes a decrease in the x balance, it is likely that the sum $(a+x)$ will increase by less than q (a result which is necessarily true when a increases by less than q). In formal terms, by differentiating $(a+x)$ with respect to q, the condition for this sum to increase by less than q turns out to be $\pi^{1-\alpha}a_y(1+x_a) < 1$, where $0 < a_y < 1$ and $-1 < x_a < 0$ by assumption. This condition is related to the term Ω_3 in Eqs. (A.16.61), Sect. A.16.5.2.1.

[25] We have assumed above that the public sector does not perform *continuative* open market operations. This does not prevent it from performing a *once-and-for-all* operation of this kind.

Sect. 16.3.1), this shift would cause the RR schedule to cross $L'L'$ at E'_1. However, in the present model, the depreciation in the exchange rate causes an *increase in the price level* and so a *decrease in the real stock of money*, so that the monetary equilibrium schedule shifts back from $L'L'$ to the left, though not by so much as to return to the initial position. There is a smaller shift in the real-equilibrium schedule than that envisaged by the traditional analysis, because part of the effect of the exchange-rate depreciation is removed by the increase in p.

The new equilibrium point will thus be found at an intermediate point between E and E'_1, for example at E''_1: domestic production has increased, but by less than was believed by the traditional analysis.

Another result of the traditional analysis is that of the absolute *ineffectiveness of fiscal policy* under flexible exchange rates, when perfect capital mobility obtains. This was shown in Sect. 16.3.1; we can now see that it is *no longer valid* if the link between the general price level and the exchange rate is accounted for.

An increase in government expenditure G_R causes a rightward shift in the RR schedule at unchanged exchange rate, and so an increase in income which, as the supply of money is given, brings about an excess demand for money and so an upward pressure on the domestic interest rate. But this rate is kept at i_f by the incipient capital inflow; by giving rise to a balance-of-payments surplus, this inflow also causes an exchange-rate appreciation which makes the RR schedule shift to the left. According to the traditional theory this shift continues until RR returns to the initial position: this is inevitable because LL has stayed put. In the present model, on the contrary, the exchange-rate appreciation, by causing a *decrease* in the price level[26], makes the real money stock *increase* so that the LL schedule shifts to the right. To put it differently, the decrease in the price level has generated money in real terms, thus enabling the unchanged nominal stock to satisfy at least in part the increased real demand for money (due to the increase in output). Fiscal policy, as we can see, regains its effectiveness.

Let us now come to *long-run equilibrium*.

Since, as we have already seen, the stock of money, the stock of national bonds and the stock of international reserves are constant by assumption, the public sector's stock equilibrium is ensured. The private sector's stock equilibrium, which implies a constant stock of wealth, is ensured if the stock of privately held net foreign assets is constant; this, in turn, means — account being taken of Eq. (16.20) — that the capital movements balance is zero:

$$K = 0. \qquad (16.29)$$

It follows that, since the overall balance of payments is in equilibrium, the current account balance must also be in equilibrium:

$$CA = 0. \qquad (16.30)$$

Long run equilibrium thus implies a *full* equilibrium in the balance of payments.

---

[26] This implicitly assumes, as does Eq. (16.12), downward (and not only upward) price flexibility.

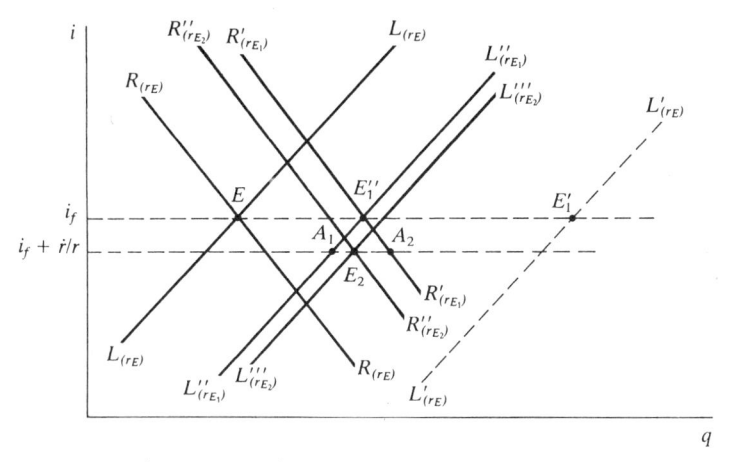

Fig. 16.8. Rational expectations: short-run equilibrium and economic policy

The constancy of all stocks enables us to determine — as we did for the short run equilibrium — the equilibrium values of the exchange rate and domestic production (which are thus constant) and, hence, all the remaining variables.

The analysis of the effects of monetary and fiscal policy in the long run requires a laborious mathematical analysis, for which we refer the reader to Sect. A.16.5.1.2.

16.6.4 Rational Expectations and Overshooting

The analysis of the model with rational expectations is more complicated, owing to the presence of the terms $\tilde{r}/r$ and $\tilde{p}/p$ in the various functions. As an example, we examine the *short-run effects* of an expansionary monetary policy. In Fig. 16.8, we have reproduced Fig. 16.7 so as to have a standard of comparison: as we know from Sect. 16.6.3, a monetary expansion ultimately causes a depreciation in the exchange rate and a shift of the LL and RR schedules to the position $L''L''$ and $R'R'$ respectively, so that the equilibrium point shifts from E to E''_1. Now, it is possible to show (see below, Fig. 16.10) that, when expectations are rational, the exchange-rate depreciation in the *new* equilibrium will be *less* than that occurring under static expectations, so that ultimately the exchange rate will show an *appreciation* with respect to the case of static expectations. Since this appreciation is exactly anticipated, the domestic interest rate will equal $i_f + \dot{r}/r$, where $\dot{r} < 0$ given the appreciation with respect to the value of r underlying point E''_1. Thus the LL and RR schedules will cross along a straight line parallel to the horizontal axis at a height $i_f + \dot{r}/r$. Since, as we said, the exchange rate shows an appreciation with respect to that obtaining under static expectations (even if it does not go all the way back to its initial value r_E), the real-equilibrium schedule shifts from $R'R'$ to the left, for example to $R''R''$, and the monetary-equilibrium schedule shifts from $L''L''$ to the right, for example to $L'''L'''$; the symbol r_{E2} denotes the new equilibrium exchange rate, lower than r_{E1} but higher than r_E. The intersection between the two schedules will in any case occur at a point included between A_1 and A_2, but we do not know whether to the left or to the right of E''_1: in Fig. 16.8 we have determined the new equilibrium point E_2 to the left of E''_1 (so that domestic product q

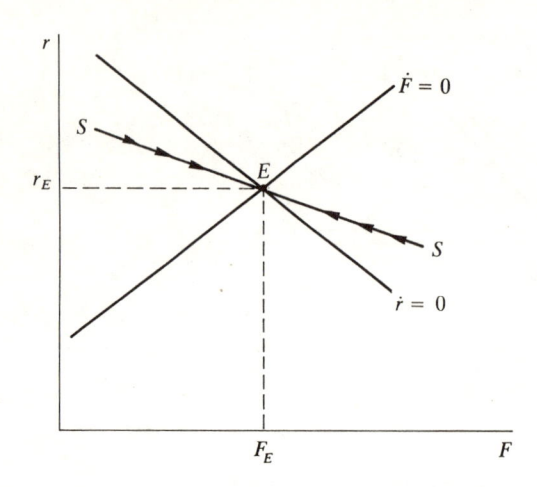

Fig. 16.9. Rational expectations and long-run equilibrium

increases by less than under static expectations), but we could have equally well determined it to the right of E''_1.

Long run equilibrium implies a constant value of the stocks and so of the exchange rate: in fact, only with a constant value of the exchange rate (and hence of the price level), will the stocks in real terms also remain constant. This equilibrium can be described in terms of Fig. 16.9, where the schedule $\dot{r}=0$ denotes all the combinations of r and F such that the exchange rate is constant; similarly, the $\dot{F}=0$ schedule denotes all the combinations of r and F such that the stock of net foreign assets is constant (for the slope of the two schedules see Sect. A.16.5.3). The long-run equilibrium point is E, where the two schedules cross.

The dynamics of the system is very complex and here we limit ourselves to observing that there exists only one trajectory, denoted by the line SS, along which the movement of the system converges to the equilibrium point (which is in the nature of a *saddle point*: see Sect. A.16.5.3); any point outside SS will move farther and farther away from E.

Rational expectations are however such as to bring any (non-equilibrium) initial point not lying on SS onto this line with a discrete jump, as described in Fig. 16.10. Whilst F (see the analysis of the short-run equilibrium) is predetermined at every instant, r on the contrary is free to make discontinuous jumps as a consequence of unanticipated events or *news*. Unanticipated policy changes which cause the schedules to shift and determine a new point of equilibrium also cause the exchange rate to jump immediately onto the stable trajectory in discrete fashion (and then follow it and move smoothly towards the new long-run equilibrium point). This is the implication of rational expectations and an efficient foreign-exchange market.

In Fig. 16.10 we have considered the case of an unanticipated monetary expansion which, in the long-run equilibrium, causes an increase in both r and F (see Sect. A.16.5.3); the two schedules shift and determine the new equilibrium point E'. For simplicity's sake, we have drawn only the new schedule along which the exchange rate is constant ($\dot{r}'=0$) and the new convergent trajectory ($S'S'$). The system was initially at the previous equilibrium point E, which is now no

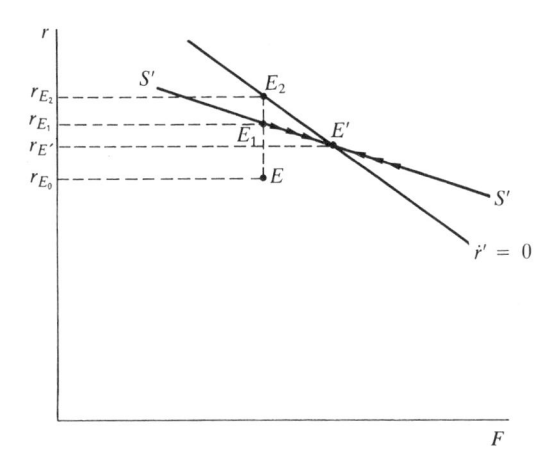

Fig. 16.10. Rational expectations, "news", and overshooting

longer an equilibrium point, owing to the shifts in the schedules. Given, as we said, the stock F, the exchange rate jumps to point E_1 on the $S'S'$ line: as can be seen, at E_1 the exchange rate is *higher* than that corresponding to the new long-run equilibrium; after the jump, r *appreciates* smoothly towards $r_{E'}$, a value higher than r_{E_0} but lower than r_{E_1}. This is the phenomenon known as *overshooting*, since the exchange rate initially depreciates by more than required, and then appreciates.

It should be noted that, also in the case of static expectations, the exchange rate depreciates initially, but since with these expectations it moves by definition along the constant-exchange-rate schedule, the initial jump will be from E to E_2, with a *greater* depreciation than in the case of rational expectations. This confirms what we said in relation to Fig. 16.8; the reason is that, with rational expectations, speculators are aware of the future exchange rate appreciation, which increases the demand for money and reduces the extent of the initial depreciation.

For further elaboration on the Branson and Buiter model see Kawai (1985).

Appendix

A.16.1 The Critical Elasticities Condition is neither Necessary nor Sufficient

Given the model explained in Sect. 16.2, the dynamic behaviour assumptions made there give rise to the following differential equation system

$$\frac{dM}{dt} = a[x(r) + K(i) - rm(y,r,i)], \qquad a > 0,$$

$$\frac{dy}{dt} = k_1[d(y,r,i) + x(r) - y], \qquad k_1 > 0,$$

$$\frac{di}{dt} = k_2[L(y,i) - M], \qquad k_2 > 0,$$

$$\frac{dr}{dt} = k_3[rm(y,r,i) - x(r) - K(i)], \qquad k_3 > 0,$$

(A.16.1)

where a, k_1, k_2, k_3 are positive constants which for simplicity will be taken as equal to one. It can be noted immediately that $dM/dt = -dr/dt$, whence $M(t) + r(t) = $ (arbitrary) constant. Thus it is possible to set $\bar{M} = -\bar{r}$ in a neighbourhood of the equilibrium point, where a bar over the variable denotes the deviations from equilibrium.

If we linearize the system at the equilibrium point, account being taken of the relation between M and r, and set $r = 1$ at the initial situation, we get

$$\frac{d\bar{y}}{dt} = (d_y - 1)\bar{y} + d_i\bar{i} + (x_r + d_r)\bar{r},$$

$$\frac{d\bar{i}}{dt} = L_y\bar{y} + L_i\bar{i} + \bar{r}, \qquad (A.16.2)$$

$$\frac{d\bar{r}}{dt} = m_y\bar{y} - (K_i - m_i)\bar{i} - m\left(\frac{x}{m}\eta_x + \eta_m - 1\right)\bar{r},$$

where

$$\eta_x \equiv (dx/dr)(r/x), \quad \eta_m \equiv -(\partial m/\partial r)(r/m). \qquad (A.16.2.1)$$

The characteristic equation of the system is

$$\begin{vmatrix} (d_y - 1) - \lambda & d_i & (x_r + d_r) \\ L_y & L_i - \lambda & 1 \\ m_y & -(K_i - m_i) & -m\left(\frac{x}{m}\eta_x + \eta_m - 1\right) - \lambda \end{vmatrix} = 0, \qquad (A.16.2.2)$$

whence

$$\lambda^3 + \left[m\left(\frac{x}{m}\eta_x + \eta_m - 1\right) - (d_y - 1) - L_i\right]\lambda^2$$

$$+ \left[-m_y(x_r + d_r) + K_i - m_i - m\left(\frac{x}{m}\eta_x + \eta_m - 1\right)(d_y - 1 + L_i)\right.$$

$$+ (d_y - 1)L_i - d_iL_y\right]\lambda + \left\{m\left(\frac{x}{m}\eta_x + \eta_m - 1\right)\left[(d_y - 1)L_i - d_iL_y\right]\right.$$

$$+ L_y(K_i - m_i)(x_r + d_r) + L_im_y(x_r + d_r)$$

$$- (d_y - 1)(K_i - m_i) - d_im_y\right\} = 0. \qquad (A.16.3)$$

If we assume that $d_y < 1$, we have the following necessary and sufficient stability conditions (see, for example, Gandolfo, 1980, pp. 248ff.)

$$\frac{x}{m}\eta_x + \eta_m > 1 + \frac{d_iL_y + m_i - K_i + m_y(x_r + d_r) + (1 - d_y)L_i}{m(1 - d_y - L_i)},$$

$$\frac{x}{m}\eta_x + \eta_m > 1$$

$$+ \frac{-L_y(K_i - m_i)(x_r + d_r) - L_im_y(x_r + d_r) + (d_y - 1)(K_i - m_i) + d_im_y}{m[L_i(d_y - 1) - d_iL_y]},$$

$$\begin{cases} \dfrac{x}{m}\eta_x+\eta_m>1+\dfrac{1}{m}\varrho_2, \\ \dfrac{x}{m}\eta_x+\eta_m<1+\dfrac{1}{m}\varrho_1, \end{cases} \quad (A.16.4)$$

where ϱ_1, ϱ_2 are the roots of the equation[27]

$$(1-d_y-L_i)\varrho^2+[-m_y(x_r+d_r)+(K_i-m_i)+(d_y-1+L_i)^2]\varrho \\ +[-(1-d_y)m_y(x_r+d_r)+(d_y-1)d_iL_y-L_i(K_i-m_i)+L_id_iL_y \\ -(d_y-1)^2L_i-L_i^2(d_y-1)-L_y(K_i-m_i)(x_r+d_r)+d_im_y]=0. \quad (A.16.5)$$

If we remember the signs of the various derivatives, we can state what follows on the various inequalities.

First inequality: the fraction on the right-hand side has a positive denominator whilst the numerator can, in general, have either sign. Therefore the whole right-hand side can, in general, be either greater or smaller than one.

Second inequality: same conclusion.

Third inequality: in the equation whose solution yields ϱ_1 and ϱ_2, the coefficient of ϱ^2 is positive whilst the coefficient of ϱ and the constant term have an ambiguous sign. Therefore the roots ϱ_1, ϱ_2 can be *any* and, consequently, the right-hand sides of the double inequality can have, in general, any value.

From all this it follows that no general validity can be given to the statement that for stability to obtain, the sum of the elasticities must exceed a precise critical value (equal to one according to the simple critical elasticities condition treated in Sect. 12.2, higher that one according to the more complex condition treated in Sect. 14.3). The critical value, can, in fact, be *any*, and it is impossible to establish *a priori* whether it is greater or smaller than one, as it depends on the values that the various derivatives take on in each specific case.

A.16.2 On the Choice of Policy Instruments

A.16.2.1 Fiscal Policy

In the case in which fiscal policy is used to achieve internal balance, the dynamic model explained in Sect. 16.3.1 gives rise to the following differential equation system

$$\begin{aligned} \dfrac{dr}{dt} &= v_1[rm(y,r,i)-x(r)-K(i)], \\ \dfrac{dG}{dt} &= v_2[y_F-y], \\ \dfrac{dy}{dt} &= v_3[d(y,r,i)+x(r)+G-y], \end{aligned} \quad (A.16.6)$$

---

[27] If we consider the condition according to which the product of the coefficient of λ^2 by the coefficient of λ, minus the constant term, must be a positive quantity, we get a second-degree inequality in $m[(x/m)\eta_x+\eta_m-1]$. Now, the elementary theory of second-degree inequalities tells us that this inequality will be satisfied for values of $m[(x/m)\eta_x+\eta_m-1]$ *outside* the interval between the two roots of (A.16.5), whence the double inequality in (A.16.4). It should be noted that if the roots were complex, the stability condition under consideration would be satisfied for all values of the elasticities; in this case only the first two inequalities in (A.16.4) matter.

where v_1, v_2, v_3 are positive constants representing the adjustment speeds. The first two equations are the formal counterpart to assumptions (i) and (ii) in the text; the third equation expresses the usual adjustment mechanism of income to excess demand.

By linearizing the system at the equilibrium point, then setting the equilibrium exchange rate at one (this involves no loss of generality), remembering that i is constant by assumption (see the text), and denoting with a bar over the variable its deviations from equilibrium, we have the system

$$\frac{d\bar{r}}{dt} = v_1 m \left(1 - \eta_m - \frac{x}{m} \eta_x \right) \bar{r} + v_1 m_y \bar{y},$$

$$\frac{d\bar{G}}{dt} = -v_2 \bar{y}, \qquad (A.16.7)$$

$$\frac{d\bar{y}}{dt} = v_3 (d_r + x_r) \bar{r} + v_3 \bar{G} + v_3 (d_y - 1) \bar{y},$$

Its characteristic equation is

$$\begin{vmatrix} v_1 m \left(1 - \eta_m - \frac{x}{m} \eta_x \right) - \lambda & 0 & v_1 m_y \\ 0 & 0 - \lambda & -v_2 \\ v_3 (d_r + x_r) & v_3 & v_3 (d_y - 1) - \lambda \end{vmatrix} = 0, \qquad (A.16.7.1)$$

whence

$$\lambda^3 + \left[v_3 (1 - d_y) + v_1 m \left(\eta_m + \frac{x}{m} \eta_x - 1 \right) \right] \lambda^2$$

$$+ [v_1 v_3 (1 - d_y) m \left(\eta_m + \frac{x}{m} \eta_x - 1 \right) - v_1 v_3 m_y (d_r + x_r) \qquad (A.16.8)$$

$$+ v_2 v_3] \lambda + v_1 v_2 v_3 m \left(\eta_m + \frac{x}{m} \eta_x - 1 \right) = 0.$$

The necessary and sufficient stability conditions are

$$v_3 (1 - d_y) + v_1 m \left(\eta_m + \frac{x}{m} \eta_x - 1 \right) > 0,$$

$$v_1 v_3 (1 - d_y) m \left(\eta_m + \frac{x}{m} \eta_x - 1 \right) - v_1 v_3 m_y (d_r + x_r) + v_2 v_3 > 0,$$

$$v_1 v_2 v_3 m \left(\eta_m + \frac{x}{m} \eta_x - 1 \right) > 0, \qquad (A.16.9)$$

$$\left[v_3 (1 - d_y) + v_1 m \left(\eta_m + \frac{x}{m} \eta_x - 1 \right) \right] \left[v_1 v_3 (1 - d_y) m \left(\eta_m + \frac{x}{m} \eta_x - 1 \right) \right.$$

$$\left. - v_1 v_3 m_y (d_r + x_r) + v_2 v_3 \right] - v_1 v_2 v_3 m \left(\eta_m + \frac{x}{m} \eta_x - 1 \right) > 0.$$

The third inequality is satisfied if and only if

$$\eta_m + \frac{x}{m}\eta_x > 1. \qquad (A.16.9.1)$$

Since $(1-d_y) > 0$ by assumption, the first inequality is certainly satisfied if the third is. As regards the second and fourth ones, it can easily be checked that, provided (A.16.9.1) is fulfilled, these can be satisfied by choosing a suitable value of v_2. In principle, this is always possible, as v_2 represents the intensity of intervention of the authorities who manage fiscal policy. Thus the crucial condition turns out to be (A.16.9.1).

A.16.2.2 Monetary Policy

In the case in which monetary policy is used to achieve internal equilibrium, we have the following differential equation system

$$\frac{dr}{dt} = c_1[rm(y,r,i) - x(r) - K(i)],$$

$$\frac{di}{dt} = c_2[y - y_F], \qquad (A.16.10)$$

$$\frac{dy}{dt} = c_3[d(y,r,i) + x(r) + G - y],$$

where c_1, c_2, c_3 are positive constants representing adjustment speeds. The first two equations are the formal counterpart to the behaviour assumptions (i) and (ii) in Sect. 16.3.1, and the third one expresses the usual adjustment mechanism of income. If we linearize the system at the equilibrium point, set $r=1$ at equilibrium and remember that G is constant by assumption, we have

$$\frac{d\bar{r}}{dt} = c_1 m \left(1 - \eta_m - \frac{x}{m}\eta_x\right)\bar{r} + c_1(m_i - K_i)\bar{i} + c_1 m_y \bar{y},$$

$$\frac{d\bar{i}}{dt} = c_2 \bar{y}, \qquad (A.16.11)$$

$$\frac{d\bar{y}}{dt} = c_3(d_r + x_r)\bar{r} + c_3 d_i \bar{i} + c_3(d_y - 1)\bar{y}.$$

The characteristic equation of this system is

$$\begin{vmatrix} c_1 m\left(1 - \eta_m - \frac{x}{m}\eta_x\right) - \lambda & c_1(m_i - K_i) & c_1 m_y \\ 0 & 0 - \lambda & c_2 \\ c_3(d_r + x_r) & c_3 d_i & c_3(d_y - 1) - \lambda \end{vmatrix} = 0, \quad (A.16.11.1)$$

whence

$$\lambda^3 + \left[c_3(1-d_y) + c_1 m\left(\eta_m + \frac{x}{m}\eta_x - 1\right)\right]\lambda^2$$

$$+ [c_1 c_3(1-d_y) m\left(\eta_m + \frac{x}{m}\eta_x - 1\right) - c_2 c_3 d_i$$

$$- c_1 c_3 m_y(d_r + x_r)]\lambda$$

$$+ c_1 c_2 c_3 \left[(d_r + x_r)(K_i - m_i) - d_i m\left(\eta_m + \frac{x}{m}\eta_x - 1\right)\right] = 0. \quad (A.16.12)$$

The necessary and sufficient stability conditions are

$$c_3(1-d_y) + c_1 m\left(\eta_m + \frac{x}{m}\eta_x - 1\right) > 0,$$

$$c_1 c_3(1-d_y) m\left(\eta_m + \frac{x}{m}\eta_x - 1\right) - c_2 c_3 d_i - c_1 c_3 m_y(d_r + x_r) > 0,$$

$$(d_r + x_r)(K_i - m_i) - d_i m\left(\eta_m + \frac{x}{m}\eta_x - 1\right) > 0,$$

$$\left[c_3(1-d_y) + c_1 m\left(\eta_m + \frac{x}{m}\eta_x - 1\right)\right]$$

$$\times \left[c_1 c_3(1-d_y) m\left(\eta_m + \frac{x}{m}\eta_x - 1\right) - c_2 c_3 d_i - c_1 c_3 m_y(d_r + x_r)\right]$$

$$- c_1 c_2 c_3 \left[(d_r + x_r)(K_i - m_i) - d_i m\left(\eta_m + \frac{x}{m}\eta_x - 1\right)\right] > 0.$$

$$(A.16.13)$$

The fourth inequality can be written as a second-degree inequality in $[\eta_m + (x/m)\eta_x - 1]$ and will be satisfied for

$$\eta_m + \frac{x}{m}\eta_x < 1 + \varrho_1; \quad \eta_m + \frac{x}{m}\eta_x > 1 + \varrho_2, \quad (A.16.13.1)$$

where ϱ_1, ϱ_2 are the roots of the equation

$$c_1^2(1-d_y) m^2 \varrho^2 + c_1 m [c_3(1-d_y)^2$$

$$- c_1 m_y(d_r + x_r)]\varrho - [c_1 c_3 m_y(1-d_y)(d_r + x_r)$$

$$+ c_2 c_3 d_i(1-d_y) + c_1 c_2(d_r + x_r)(K_i - m_i)] = 0. \quad (A.16.14)$$

If we take the assumed signs of the various derivatives into account, we find that the coefficient of ϱ^2 is positive whilst the coefficient of ϱ and the constant term have ambiguous signs, as they contain both negative and positive elements. It is however possible to eliminate this ambiguity without needing to know the numerical values of all the elements. It is sufficient, in fact, to observe that c_1 is the adjustment speed of the exchange rate to balance-of-payments disequilibria, which is presumably much greater than the adjustment speed of production to excess demand. If this is so, the coefficient of ϱ and the constant term are both likely to be negative. Consequently, by the rule of signs, we find that $\varrho_1 < 0, \varrho_2 > 0$, so that the quantity $1 + \varrho_1$ is lower than one, whilst $1 + \varrho_2$ is greater than one. It follows that the first inequality in (A.16.13.1) must be discarded, as it might turn out to be incompatible with the fulfilment of the first three inequalities in (A.16.13). The second inequality in (A.16.13.1), on the contrary, is admissible, and its occurrence implies the occurrence of the first and third inequality in (A.16.13); the second one will also be satisfied by choosing a suitable magnitude of the policy parameter c_2. Thus the crucial condition turns out to be

$$\eta_m + \frac{x}{m}\eta_x > 1 + \varrho_2, \qquad (A.16.13.2)$$

which is clearly more restrictive than (A.16.19.1).

It should now be pointed out that the conclusion as to the superiority of fiscal policy (superiority understood in the sense of less restrictive dynamic stability conditions) is not generally shared. Some writers, in fact (see, for example, Chacholiades, 1978, Sect. A.17.3), use a model like the one used here, but nevertheless hold the view that the crucial dynamic stability condition is the *same* whether fiscal or monetary policy is used. This different view is, however, based on a simplifying assumption set forth by these writers (see especially Chacholiades *loc. cit.*) to render the mathematical treatment less complex: this assumption is that the elasticity of the demand for imports is greater than 1 plus the marginal propensity to import. Since under this assumption the stability conditions do occur whichever instrument is used for internal equilibrium (Chacholiades, 1978, p. 404), it follows that the choice is irrelevant. But it is precisely when this assumption does not occur — and we cannot be so optimistic as to accept it, since numerous empirical studies fail to support the idea that the elasticity of imports is so high — that the need arises to ascertain which of the two instruments implies less restrictive stability conditions.

A second observation is that the Laursen and Metzler effect (see Sect. 14.3), namely the effect of the exchange rate on the level of national expenditure, has a crucial role in our conclusions. It can, in fact, be shown that if this effect is eliminated, the stability conditions (even without introducing Chacholiades' simplifying assumption) turn out to be the same in both cases (Gandolfo, 1980, pp. 346–349).

A.16.3 On the Alleged Insulating Power of Flexible Exchange Rates and the Propagation of Disturbances

A.16.3.1 The One-Country Model

The absence of the insulating power of flexible exchange rates (even in the absence of capital movements) has already been demonstrated in Sect. A.14.4, to which we refer the reader. The introduction of capital movements does strengthen the conclusions, as shown in Sect. 16.4.1 and as it also turns out from the following analysis of the propagation of disturbances.

To examine the propagation of disturbances under fixed and flexible exchange rates, we begin with a one-country model, by introducing a parameter α whose increase (decrease) represents an exogenous increase (decrease) in domestic demand. Thus under fixed exchange rates we have the model[28]

$$y = d(y,i) + x_0 + \alpha, \qquad 0 < d_y < 1, \qquad d_i < 0,$$
$$B = x_0 - m(y) + K(i) = 0, \qquad 0 < m_y < 1, \qquad K_i > 0, \qquad (A.16.15)$$
$$M = L(y,i). \qquad L_y > 0, \qquad L_i < 0.$$

Under flexible exchange rates in its stead we have the model

$$y = d(y,i,r) + x(r) + \alpha, \qquad d_r > 0, \quad x_r > 0,$$
$$B = x(r) - rm(y,r) + K(i) = 0, \qquad m_r < 0, \qquad (A.16.16)$$
$$M = L(y,i),$$

where we have indicated only the signs of the derivatives with respect to r, as the others are the same as in (A.16.15).

Following the reasoning in Sect. 16.4.2, let us begin by determining the critical value of the interest-rate sensitivity of capital movements. The initial effect of a change in α on income is

$$\frac{dy}{d\alpha} = \frac{1}{1-d_y} > 0, \qquad (A.16.17)$$

where $1/(1-d_y)$ is the multiplier. By differentiating the monetary-equilibrium equation (holding M constant), we get the consequent change in i:

$$\frac{di}{d\alpha} = -\frac{L_y}{L_i}\frac{dy}{d\alpha} = -\frac{L_y}{L_i}\frac{1}{1-d_y} > 0, \qquad (A.16.18)$$

so that the impact effect (at unchanged M and r) on the balance of payments is

$$\frac{dB}{d\alpha} = -m_y\frac{dy}{d\alpha} + K_i\frac{di}{d\alpha} = \frac{-1}{1-d_y}\left(m_y + K_i\frac{L_y}{L_i}\right). \qquad (A.16.19)$$

---

[28] This is the same model as was used in Sects. 15.4 and A.15.3, with the only difference that here we omit the direct effect of the interest rate on imports; an analogous simplification has been introduced into the flexible exchange-rate model and in the following models with repercussions, Sect. A.16.3.2. This simplification does not alter the results of the analysis in any essential way.

For $dB/d\alpha$ to be positive (a decrease in exogenous expenditure causes a deterioration in the balance of payments, as described in the text) the condition is

$$-m_y - K_i \frac{L_y}{L_i} > 0, \qquad (A.16.20)$$

that is

$$K_i L_y + m_y L_i > 0, \qquad (A.16.20')$$

whence

$$K_i > -m_y \frac{L_i}{L_y}, \qquad (A.16.20.1)$$

whose right-hand side represents the critical value of K_i. Since the slope of the BB schedule is $(di/dy)_{BB} = (m_y/K_i)$ and that of the LL schedule is $(di/dy)_{LL} = -(L_y/L_i)$, it immediately follows from inequality (A.16.20.1) that $(di/dy)_{BB} < (di/dy)_{LL}$.

Let us now calculate the final changes (that is those obtaining when all the adjustments described in the text have occurred) in the relevant variables. By applying the method of comparative statics to system (A.16.15) we get the system

$$(1-d_y)\frac{dy}{d\alpha} - d_i \frac{di}{d\alpha} = 1,$$

$$-m_y \frac{dy}{d\alpha} + K_i \frac{di}{d\alpha} = 0, \qquad (A.16.15.1)$$

$$L_y \frac{dy}{d\alpha} + L_i \frac{di}{d\alpha} - \frac{dM}{d\alpha} = 0,$$

whence

$$\left(\frac{dy}{d\alpha}\right)_{FIX} = \frac{1}{(1-d_y) - m_y d_i/K_i} > 0,$$

$$\left(\frac{di}{d\alpha}\right)_{FIX} = \frac{m_y}{(1-d_y)K_i - m_y d_i} > 0, \qquad (A.16.21)$$

$$\left(\frac{dM}{d\alpha}\right)_{FIX} = \frac{L_y K_i + L_i m_y}{(1-d_y)K_i - m_y d_i} > 0,$$

where the signs derive from the assumptions made initially on the various derivatives and from (A.16.20), and confirm what was stated in Sect. 16.4.2.

Similarly, from system (A.16.16) we obtain the system

$$(1-d_y)\frac{dy}{d\alpha} - d_i \frac{di}{d\alpha} - (d_r + x_r)\frac{dr}{d\alpha} = 1,$$

$$-m_y \frac{dy}{d\alpha} + K_i \frac{di}{d\alpha} + m\left(\frac{x}{rm}\eta_x + \eta_m - 1\right)\frac{dr}{d\alpha} = 0, \qquad (A.16.16.1)$$

$$L_y \frac{dy}{d\alpha} + L_i \frac{di}{d\alpha} = 0.$$

Note that the last equation derives from the assumption, made in the text, that, unlike the case of fixed exchange rates, the stock of money is unchanged. By solving system (A.16.16.1) we get

$$\left(\frac{dy}{d\alpha}\right)_{FLEX} = \frac{1}{(1-d_y) + \frac{L_y}{L_i}d_i - \frac{(d_r+x_r)(m_y L_i + L_y K_i)}{L_i m[(x/rm)\eta_x + \eta_m - 1]}} > 0, \quad (A.16.22)$$

$$\left(\frac{dr}{d\alpha}\right)_{FLEX} = \frac{-(m_y L_i + K_i L_y)}{(d_r+x_r)(m_y L_i + K_i L_y) - m\left(\frac{x}{rm}\eta_x + \eta_m - 1\right)[(1-d_y)L_i + d_i L_y]} < 0,$$

where the signs derive from the assumptions made initially on the various derivatives, from (A.16.20) and from the assumption that the critical elasticities condition is fulfilled, that is $(x/rm)\eta_x + \eta_m > 1$. For brevity we omit the expression for $di/d\alpha$, as this is not relevant for the comparison that interests us.

The first proposition to be shown is incorporated in the inequality[29]

$$\left(\frac{dy}{d\alpha}\right)_{FLEX} < \left(\frac{dy}{d\alpha}\right)_{FIX}, \quad (A.16.23)$$

that is, by substituting in it the expressions found above and simplifying,

$$-d_i \frac{L_i m_y + K_i L_y}{K_i L_i} < -\frac{(d_r+x_r)(m_y L_i + L_y K_i)}{L_i m\left(\frac{x}{rm}\eta_x + \eta_m - 1\right)}, \quad (A.16.23.1)$$

which is certainly fulfilled because, given the assumptions made and, in particular, given (A.16.20'), the left-hand side is negative and the right-hand one is positive. Thus the proposition is valid, given the assumption on the interest-rate sensitivity of capital flows.

The second proposition to be shown concerns the extent of the propagation of the disturbance in the two exchange-rate regimes, which is measured by the extent of the variation in the balance on goods and services (*BGS*) of the country under consideration. In fact, since the channel of transmission is *BGS* (as we explained in the text), it follows that the greater in absolute value is its variation (in the rest of the world there will be an identical variation but with the opposite sign), the higher is the propagation of the disturbance. It should be noted that we are in a one-country model, where no account is taken of repercussions, so that the income change in the rest of the world will be given by its multiplier applied to the change in its net exports.

---

[29] To avoid confusion, remember that what was stated in the text is equivalent to saying that, for $d\alpha < 0$, $(dy)_{FIX} < (dy)_{FLEX}$ since the decrease in income is greater in absolute value under fixed exchange rates. Thus, as $dy = (dy/d\alpha)d\alpha$, for $d\alpha < 0$ inequality (A.16.23) follows.

We calculate the differentials

$$\left(\frac{dBGS}{d\alpha}\right)_{FIX} d\alpha = -m_y \left(\frac{dy}{d\alpha}\right)_{FIX} d\alpha,$$

$$\left(\frac{dBGS}{d\alpha}\right)_{FLEX} d\alpha = \left[-m_y \left(\frac{dy}{d\alpha}\right)_{FLEX} \right.$$
$$\left. + m\left(\frac{x}{rm}\eta_x + \eta_m - 1\right)\left(\frac{dr}{d\alpha}\right)_{FLEX}\right] d\alpha.$$

(A.16.24)

Since, as we said, the change in the rest-of-the-world's balance on goods and services is equal in absolute value but with opposite sign (this holds also under flexible exchange rates, owing to the simplifying assumption that $r=1$ initially) and since $d\alpha < 0$, it can easily be seen that the condition for the depressive disturbance under consideration to be propagated more intensely under flexible exchange rates is

$$m_y\left(\frac{dy}{d\alpha}\right)_{FLEX} - m\left(\frac{x}{rm}\eta_x + \eta_m - 1\right)\left(\frac{dr}{d\alpha}\right)_{FLEX} > m_y\left(\frac{dy}{d\alpha}\right)_{FIX}. \quad (A.16.25)$$

By substituting from (A.16.21) and (A.16.22), we find that (A.16.25) holds, given the assumption made in the text (Sect. 16.4.2) that an exchange-rate depreciation improves the balance of payments (this implies that condition (A.14.9.1) holds).

A.16.3.2 The Two-Country Model

To examine the propagation of disturbances when foreign repercussions are present, a two-country model is necessary. We first consider the following model under fixed exchange rates

$$y_1 = d_1(y_1, i_1) + m_2(y_2) + \alpha,$$
$$y_2 = d_2(y_2, i_2) + m_1(y_1),$$
$$M_1 = L_1(y_1, i_1),$$
$$M_2 = L_2(y_2, i_2),$$
$$B_1 = m_2(y_2) - m_1(y_1) + K(i_1 - i_2) = 0,$$
$$M_1 + M_2 = Q,$$

(A.16.26)

with $\quad 0 < d_{1y} < 1, \quad d_{1i} < 0, \quad\quad 0 < m_{2y} < 1,$
$\quad\quad\quad 0 < d_{2y} < 1, \quad d_{2i} < 0, \quad\quad 0 < m_{1y} < 1,$
$\quad\quad\quad L_{1y} > 0, \quad\quad L_{1i} < 0,$
$\quad\quad\quad L_{2y} > 0, \quad\quad L_{2i} < 0,$
$\quad\quad\quad K_i \equiv dK/d(i_1 - i_2) > 0,$

(A.16.26.1)

where the subscripts 1 and 2 refer to the two countries and the assumptions on the various derivatives etc., are the same as in model (A.16.15). The last equation in (A.16.26) is necessary to close the model and reflects the assumption made in Sect. 16.4.3 that both countries follow the rules of the game.

The model under flexible exchange rates is

$$y_1 = d_1(y_1, i_1, r) + m_2(y_2, r) + \alpha, \quad d_{1r} > 0, m_{2r} > 0,$$
$$y_2 = d_2(y_2, i_2, r) + m_1(y_1, r), \quad d_{2r} < 0, m_{1r} < 0,$$
$$M_1 = L_1(y_1, i_1), \quad (A.16.27)$$
$$M_2 = L_2(y_2, i_2),$$
$$B_1 = m_2(y_2, r) - r m_1(y_1, r) + K(i_1 - i_2) = 0,$$

where we have given the signs of only those derivatives not appearing in (A.16.26). Note that an increase in r means a depreciation in country 1's exchange rate and an appreciation in that of country 2, whence the opposite signs of m_{1r} and m_{2r}; a similar observation holds for d_{1r} and d_{2r}.

Following the reasoning given in Sect. 16.4.3, the impact effect of a change in α on the two countries' income levels is

$$\frac{dy_1}{d\alpha} = \frac{1 - d_{2y}}{(1 - d_{1y})(1 - d_{2y}) - m_{1y}m_{2y}} > 0, \quad (A.16.28)$$

$$\frac{dy_2}{d\alpha} = \frac{m_{1y}}{(1 - d_{1y})(1 - d_{2y}) - m_{1y}m_{2y}} > 0, \quad (A.16.29)$$

where the fractions on the right-hand sides are the known foreign multipliers with repercussions (the positivity of the denominator derives from the dynamic stability conditions). If we differentiate the monetary-equilibrium equations (with M_1 and M_2 held constant) we obtain the consequent changes in i_1, i_2:

$$\frac{di_1}{d\alpha} = -\frac{L_{1y}}{L_{1i}} \frac{dy_1}{d\alpha}, \quad (A.16.30)$$

$$\frac{di_2}{d\alpha} = -\frac{L_{2y}}{L_{2i}} \frac{dy_2}{d\alpha}. \quad (A.16.31)$$

The initial change in country 1's balance on goods and services is

$$m_{2y} \frac{dy_2}{d\alpha} - m_{1y} \frac{dy_1}{d\alpha}, \quad (A.16.32)$$

that is, if we substitute Eqs. (A.16.28) and (A.16.29) into it and collect terms,

$$\frac{-m_{1y}(1 - d_{2y} - m_{2y})}{(1 - d_{1y})(1 - d_{2y}) - m_{1y}m_{2y}}. \quad (A.16.33)$$

This expression must be negative in conformity with the assumption that the balance on goods and services improves if α decreases; the condition for negativity is

$$1 - d_{2y} - m_{2y} > 0. \tag{A.16.34}$$

Since, by definition, d_{2y} equals: marg. prop. to consume + marg. prop. to invest − marg. prop. to import, (A.16.34) is equivalent to

$$\text{marg. prop. to consume + marg. prop. to invest} < 1, \tag{A.16.35}$$

as stated in the text.

The assumption made in the text, that the interest differential initially moves against country 1, means that

$$\frac{d(i_1 - i_2)}{d\alpha} = \frac{di_1}{d\alpha} - \frac{di_2}{d\alpha} > 0, \tag{A.16.36}$$

that is, if we substitute Eqs. (A.16.30) and (A.16.31) into it, account being taken of Eqs. (A.16.30) and (A.16.31), and simplify,

$$m_{1y}\frac{L_{2y}}{L_{2i}} - \frac{L_{1y}}{L_{1i}}(1 - d_{2y}) > 0. \tag{A.16.37}$$

Finally, the assumption that the impact effect of a decrease in α on country 1's balance of payments is negative means that

$$\frac{dB_1}{d\alpha} = m_{2y}\frac{dy_2}{d\alpha} - m_{1y}\frac{dy_1}{d\alpha} + K_i\left(\frac{di_1}{d\alpha} - \frac{di_2}{d\alpha}\right) > 0, \tag{A.16.38}$$

that is, if we substitute Eqs. (A.16.28) − (A.16.31) into it and simplify,

$$-m_{1y}(1 - d_{2y} - m_{2y}) + K_i\left[m_{1y}\frac{L_{2y}}{L_{2i}} - \frac{L_{1y}}{L_{1i}}(1 - d_{2y})\right] > 0, \tag{A.16.38.1}$$

whence

$$K_i > \frac{m_{1y}(1 - d_{2y} - m_{2y})}{m_{1y}\frac{L_{2y}}{L_{2i}} - \frac{L_{1y}}{L_{1i}}(1 - d_{2y})}. \tag{A.16.38.2}$$

The fraction on the right-hand side represents the critical value of K_i, which is the equivalent, in this model, of the right-hand side of (A.16.20.1) in the one-country model.

To compute the final changes, that is, those holding when all the adjustments mentioned in the text have occurred, the method of comparative statics is, as usual, employed. After long and tedious manipulations (for lack of space we refer the reader to Gandolfo, 1975) we find that[30]

---

[30] It should be noted that the model with repercussions allows us to determine $dy_1/d\alpha$ and $dy_2/d\alpha$ simultaneously, so that we do not need the two-stage or indirect procedure that was used to determine the change in the rest-of-the-world's income in the one-country model.

$$\left(\frac{dy_1}{d\alpha}\right)_{FIX}>0, \left(\frac{dy_2}{d\alpha}\right)_{FIX}\gtreqless 0; \left(\frac{dy_1}{d\alpha}\right)_{FLEX}\gtreqless 0, \left(\frac{dy_2}{d\alpha}\right)_{FLEX}\gtreqless 0, \tag{A.16.39}$$

from which it follows, as stated in the text, that it is impossible — despite having made all the hypotheses required for an equal impact effect both with and without repercussions — to ascertain on *a priori* grounds under which exchange-rate regime the propagation of disturbances is greater.

A.16.4 The New Cambridge School

A.16.4.1 The Basic Model

To examine the statements of the new school, we must build a model which formally incorporates the assumptions which that school makes and which have been explained in Sect. 16.5.2. For this purpose it is sufficient, in our opinion, to start from a traditional model (with taxation explicitly present) in which the private sector's specific behaviour assumption is introduced. Thus we have, from the static point of view, the model:

$$\begin{aligned} B &= x(r) - rm(y-T,r), \\ rm(y-T,r) - x(r) &= G - T, \end{aligned} \tag{A.16.40}$$

where $T=T(y)$ denotes tax receipts as a function of income, and $(y-T)$ is disposable income. The first equation defines the balance of payments (in the restricted sense of balance on goods and services); the second is the equation for the determination of income and *incorporates the assumption of equality between the private sector's absorption and disposable income*: it is the equivalent of Eq. (16.8.1).

If we rewrite system (A.16.40) in the form

$$\begin{aligned} B - x(r) + rm(y-T,r) &= 0, \\ rm(y-T,r) - x(r) - G + T &= 0, \end{aligned} \tag{A.16.40.1}$$

we have a system of two implicit functions in four variables, two of which are targets (y and B) and two are instruments (G and r). The implicit function theorem tells us that it is possible to express two variables in terms of the other two provided that the relevant Jacobian is different from zero. If we wish to express G and r as functions of y and B we must consider the Jacobian of Eqs. (A.16.40.1) with respect to G and r, which is

$$J = \begin{vmatrix} 0 & -\eta \\ -1 & \eta \end{vmatrix} = -\eta, \tag{A.16.41}$$

where for notational simplicity we have used η to denote the often-encountered elasticity expression, that is (having set $r=1$ at the initial point)

$$\eta \equiv \frac{\partial B}{\partial r} \equiv m\left(\frac{x}{m}\eta_x + \eta_m - 1\right). \tag{A.16.41.1}$$

Since both the old and the new school (in the latter's initial version[31]) admit that an exchange-rate variation has an effect on the balance on goods and services, η will be different from zero and so $J \neq 0$. Thus the single valued functions

$$G = G(y, B), \quad r = r(y, B), \tag{A.16.42}$$

will exist, whence — given the desired value of y (for example $y = y_F$) and B (for example $B = 0$) — we can uniquely determine the corresponding values of G and r. Equations (A.16.42) express the known fact that from the static point of view, and provided that the target-instrument system is solvable, each instrument is a function of all targets. This confirms what we said in Sect. 16.5.3 that the *second version* of the new school does not assert anything new.

To examine the assignment problem, we could calculate the relative effectiveness of the instruments on the targets, but it is more convenient to cope with the problem directly from the dynamic point of view.

The traditional assignment gives rise to the following differential equation system

$$\frac{dr}{dt} = v_1 [rm(y - T, r) - x(r)], \qquad v_1 > 0,$$

$$\frac{dG}{dt} = v_2 [y_F - y], \qquad v_2 > 0, \tag{A.16.43}$$

$$\frac{dy}{dt} = v_3 [G - T + x(r) - rm(y - T, r)], \qquad v_3 > 0.$$

In the first two equations we have set $B = 0$ and $y = y_F$ as targets, but any other fixed value would do just as well. The third equation expresses the usual adjustment mechanism of income to excess demand, but with the incorporation of the new school's assumption. In fact, in an open economy, aggregate demand for domestic output is

$$A_p + x(r) - rm(y - T, r) + G, \tag{A.16.44}$$

and so the excess demand for current output is

$$[A_p + x(r) - rm(y - T, r) + G] - y; \tag{A.16.44.1}$$

and if we now introduce the new school's assumption $A_p = y - T$[32] and write the adjustment equation for y we get the third equation in system (A.16.43).

If we linearize this system at the equilibrium point and use bars over the variables to denote deviations from equilibrium, we get

---

[31] As regards what in Sect. 16.5.3 we called the "third version" of the new school, see Sect. A.16.4.4.

[32] It should be pointed out that results do not change if we formulate the assumption in the form that the private sector's financial surplus is small and stable, namely that private expenditure differs from disposable income by a small and *given* amount. In fact, this constant disappears in the linearization.

$$\frac{d\bar{r}}{dt} = -v_1\eta\bar{r} + v_1 m_{yd}(1-\tau)\bar{y},$$

$$\frac{d\bar{G}}{dt} = -v_2\bar{y} \qquad (A.16.45)$$

$$\frac{d\bar{y}}{dt} = v_3\eta\bar{r} + v_3\bar{G} - v_3[m_{yd}(1-\tau) + \tau]\bar{y},$$

where

$$\tau \equiv \frac{dT}{dy}, \qquad (A.16.45.1)$$

denotes the marginal tax rate; m_{yd} denotes the marginal propensity to imports referred to disposable income.

The characteristic equation of system (A.16.45) is

$$\begin{vmatrix} -v_1\eta - \lambda & 0 & v_1 m_{yd}(1-\tau) \\ 0 & 0 - \lambda & -v_2 \\ v_3\eta & v_3 & -v_3[m_{yd}(1-\tau) + \tau] - \lambda \end{vmatrix} = 0, \qquad (A.16.45.2)$$

that is

$$\lambda^3 + [v_1\eta + v_3\tau + v_3 m_{yd}(1-\tau)]\lambda^2$$
$$+ (v_2 v_3 + v_1 v_3 \eta\tau)\lambda + v_1 v_2 v_3 \eta = 0. \qquad (A.16.46)$$

The necessary and sufficient stability conditions are

$$v_1\eta + v_3\tau + v_3 m_{yd}(1-\tau) > 0,$$
$$v_2 v_3 + v_1 v_3 \eta\tau > 0,$$
$$v_1 v_2 v_3 \eta > 0, \qquad (A.16.47)$$
$$(v_2 v_3 + v_1 v_3 \eta\tau)[v_1\eta + v_3\tau + v_3 m_{yd}(1-\tau)] - v_1^2 v_2 v_3 \eta$$
$$= v_1 v_3 \tau\eta^2 + v_1 v_3 \tau[v_3\tau + v_3 m_{yd}(1-\tau)]\eta$$
$$+ v_2 v_3[v_3\tau + v_3 m_{yd}(1-\tau)] > 0.$$

The third inequality is satisfied if and only if

$$\eta > 0, \qquad (A.16.47.1)$$

which, when it occurs, ensures that all the other inequalities are also fulfilled (remember that $0 < \tau < 1$).

Thus the crucial condition is (A.16.47.1), namely the usual critical elasticities condition.

We now pass to the *new school's* assignment. We obtain the differential equation system

$$\frac{dr}{dt} = c_1[y_F - y], \qquad c_1 > 0,$$

$$\frac{dG}{dt} = c_2[x(r) - rm(y - T,r)], \qquad c_2 > 0, \qquad (A.16.48)$$

$$\frac{dy}{dt} = c_3[G - T + x(r) - rm(y - T,r)], \qquad c_3 > 0.$$

By linearizing at the equilibrium point, we get

$$\frac{d\bar{r}}{dt} = -c_1 \bar{y},$$

$$\frac{d\bar{G}}{dt} = c_2 \eta \bar{r} - c_2 m_{yd}(1-\tau)\bar{y}, \qquad (A.16.48.1)$$

$$\frac{d\bar{y}}{dt} = c_3 \eta \bar{r} + c_3 \bar{G} - c_3[m_{yd}(1-\tau) + \tau]\bar{y},$$

which has the characteristic equation

$$\begin{vmatrix} 0-\lambda & 0 & -c_1 \\ c_2\eta & 0-\lambda & -c_2 m_{yd}(1-\tau) \\ c_3\eta & c_3 & -c_3[m_{yd}(1-\tau)+\tau]-\lambda \end{vmatrix} = 0, \qquad (A.16.48.2)$$

that is,

$$\lambda^3 + c_3[m_{yd}(1-\tau)+\tau]\lambda^2$$
$$+ [c_1 c_3 \eta + c_2 c_3 m_{yd}(1-\tau)]\lambda + c_1 c_2 c_3 \eta = 0. \qquad (A.16.49)$$

The necessary and sufficient stability conditions are

$$c_3[m_{yd}(1-\tau)+\tau] > 0,$$
$$c_1 c_3 \eta + c_2 c_3 m_{yd}(1-\tau) > 0,$$
$$c_1 c_2 c_3 \eta > 0, \qquad (A.16.50)$$
$$c_3[m_{yd}(1-\tau)+\tau][c_1 c_3 \eta + c_2 c_3 m_{yd}(1-\tau))] - c_1 c_2 c_3 \eta$$
$$= c_1[c_3 m_{yd}(1-\tau) + c_3\tau - c_2]\eta$$
$$- c_2[c_3 m_{yd}(1-\tau) + c_3\tau]m_{yd}(1-\tau) > 0.$$

The third inequality is satisfied if and only if

$$\eta > 0, \qquad (A.16.50.1)$$

whose occurrence ensures that all the other inequalities also occur (as regards the fourth one, it is sufficient to make a suitable choice of the policy parameters, in particular of c_2).

Thus we have arrived at the result that the stability condition is the same with both assignments as stated in Sect. 16.5.2.

A.16.4.2 An Extension

Hitherto we have assumed that the private sector is able to keep its current expenditure continuously equal to its desired value (which coincides with disposable income, except for a possible small constant). This is a fairly plausible assumption, but some writers of the new school have claimed that private expenditure adjusts to its desired value after a time-lag.

From the formal point of view this amounts to considering the partial adjustment equation

$$\frac{dA_p}{dt} = u(\hat{A}_p - A_p), \quad \hat{A}_p = y - T, \quad (A.16.51)$$

which expresses the fact that private expenditure adjusts to its desired value $\hat{A}_p$ with a mean time-lag $1/u$ (see Gandolfo, 1981)[33]. As a consequence, the income-adjustment equation must be modified by considering the excess demand in the form (A.16.44.1), as now it is no longer possible to set $A_p = y - T$. This equation will thus be

$$\frac{dy}{dt} = k[A_p + x(r) - rm(y - T, r) + G - y], \quad k > 0. \quad (A.16.52)$$

Equations (A.16.51) and (A.16.52), together with the two equations which express the adjustment of r and G (obviously different according to whether the old or the new school is considered), give rise to a system of four differential equations.

Although the study of a system of four differential equations is by no means an easy task, it is possible to reach the same conclusion as in the simpler case treated in Sect. A.16.4.3.

Since the expressions which express the adjustment of r and g are the same as in the simpler model treated previously, we can use the linearizations of these equations — see the first two equations in systems (A.16.45) and (A.16.48.1). If we then linearize Eqs. (A.16.51) and (A.16.52), we obtain[34], as regards the traditional assignment, the system

$$\frac{d\bar{r}}{dt} = -v_1 \eta \bar{r} + v_1 m_{yd}(1-\tau)\bar{y},$$

$$\frac{d\bar{G}}{dt} = -v_2 \bar{y},$$

$$\frac{d\bar{y}}{dt} = k\eta\bar{r} + k\bar{G} - k[m_{yd}(1-\tau) + 1]\bar{y} + kA_p, \quad (A.16.53)$$

$$\frac{d\bar{A}_p}{dt} = u(1-\tau)\bar{y} - u\bar{A}_p.$$

---

[33] We can assume that u is relatively great, as the adjustment lag in private expenditure is presumably lower than that in the other variables.

[34] To avoid unnecessary complications we shall assume that the adjustment speeds of A_p and y, being independent of the assignment of instruments to targets, are the same in the two systems.

Similarly we obtain, for the new school, the system

$$\frac{d\bar{r}}{dt} = c_1 \bar{y},$$

$$\frac{d\bar{G}}{dt} = c_2 \eta \bar{r} - c_2 m_{yd}(1-\tau) \bar{y},$$

$$\frac{d\bar{y}}{dt} = k\eta \bar{r} + k\bar{G} - k[m_{yd}(1-\tau)+1]\bar{y} + k\bar{A}_p,$$
(A.16.54)

$$\frac{d\bar{A}_p}{dt} = u(1-\tau)\bar{y} - u\bar{A}_p.$$

For the old school, we then get the characteristic equation

$$\begin{vmatrix} -v_1\eta - \lambda & 0 & v_1 m_{yd}(1-\tau) & 0 \\ 0 & 0-\lambda & -v_2 & 0 \\ k\eta & k & -k[m_{yd}(1-\tau)+1]-\lambda & k \\ 0 & 0 & u(1-\tau) & -u-\lambda \end{vmatrix} = 0, \quad (A.16.53.1)$$

that is

$$\lambda^4 + \{v_1\eta + u + k[m_{yd}(1-\tau)+1]\}\lambda^3 + \{v_1\eta k + uk[m_{yd}(1-\tau)+1]\}\lambda^2$$
$$+ (v_1\eta ku + v_1 v_2 \eta k + v_2 ku)\lambda + v_1 v_2 ku\eta = 0. \quad (A.16.55)$$

The characteristic equation of the new school's system is

$$\begin{vmatrix} 0-\lambda & 0 & -c_1 & 0 \\ c_2\eta & 0-\lambda & -c_2 m_{yd}(1-\tau) & 0 \\ k\eta & k & -k[m_{yd}(1-\tau)+1]-\lambda & k \\ 0 & 0 & u(1-\tau) & -u-\lambda \end{vmatrix} = 0, \quad (A.16.54.1)$$

i.e.

$$\lambda^4 + \{u + k[m_{yd}(1-\tau)+1]\}\lambda^3 + \{ku[1-(1-m_{yd})(1-\tau)]$$
$$+ c_1 k m_{yd}(1-\tau) + c_1 k\eta\}\lambda^2$$
$$+ [c_1 k m_{yd}(1-\tau) + c_1 uk\eta + c_1 c_2 k\eta]\lambda + c_1 c_2 ku\eta = 0. \quad (A.16.56)$$

If we denote by a_1, a_2, a_3, a_4 the coefficients of a fourth-degree polynomial of the type under consideration (α_1 = coefficient of λ^3,..., α_4 = constant term), the necessary and sufficient stability conditions are (see Gandolfo, 1980, pp. 248–50):

$$a_i > 0, \ i=1,...,4,$$
$$a_1 a_2 a_3 - a_1^2 - a_3^2 > 0. \quad (A.16.57)$$

It can easily be verified in relation to both (A.16.55) and (A.16.56) that the fourth inequality in (A.16.57), namely $a_4 > 0$, is satisfied if and only if

$$\eta > 0, \tag{A.16.58}$$

which is the usual critical elasticities condition. When (A.16.58) occurs the first three inequalities in (A.16.57) will also occur.

The fifth inequality is more difficult to handle, but without embarking on a full discussion of it, we can point out that it can be reduced — in relation to both (A.16.55) and (A.16.56) — to a third-degree inequality in u, where the coefficient of u^3 is in any case positive owing to (A.16.58). Thus the fifth stability condition is certainly satisfied, with *both* assignments, for sufficiently high values of u, i.e. for sufficiently short mean time-lags[35].

We can then conclude that the stability conditions for both assignments are qualitatively the same.

Let us now come to the *third version* of the new school. This needs no particular formal treatment, because as soon as one assumes that variations in the exchange-rate have no effect (insofar as they are completely offset by ensuing equiproportional price changes), one excludes this variable from the set of instruments.

A.16.5 Portfolio and Macroeconomic Equilibrium

A.16.5.1 The Basic Model

The model explained in Sect. 16.6.2 is reproduced here for convenience of the reader:

$$p = p_h^\alpha r^{1-\alpha},$$
$$\pi = p_h/r,$$
$$\tilde{p}/p = \begin{cases} 0 \\ \dot{p}/p, \end{cases}$$
$$\tilde{r}/r = \begin{cases} 0 \\ \dot{r}/r, \end{cases}$$
$$i = i_f + \tilde{r}/r,$$
$$G = p_h G_R + iN,$$
$$g = p_h G_R + iN - pT - ri_f R,$$
$$CA = p_h x(\pi, a) + ri_f(F + R),$$
$$x_\pi < 0, \quad -1 < x_a < 0,$$
$$r\dot{R} = CA - r\dot{F},$$

$$q = a\left(y_d, i - \frac{\tilde{p}}{p}, \frac{W}{p}\right) + x(\pi, a) + G_R,$$
$$0 < a_y < 1, \quad a_i < 0, \quad a_w > 0,$$
$$y_d = \frac{p_h}{p} q + \frac{iN}{p} + \frac{ri_f F}{p} - T,$$
$$\frac{M}{p} = L\left(i, q, \frac{W}{p}\right),$$
$$L_i < 0, \quad L_q > 0, \quad 0 < L_w < 1,$$
$$W = M + N + rF,$$
$$g = 0,$$
$$\dot{N} = 0, \quad N > 0,$$
$$\dot{R} = 0, \quad R = 0,$$
$$\dot{M} = 0. \tag{A.16.59}$$

---

[35] Actually for $u \to +\infty$ we fall back in the case of instantaneous adjustment in private expenditure, where the crucial stability condition is $\eta > 0$, as we have shown above.

Before going on to its analysis a few observations are in order. We first note that the fifth equation is valid as a first approximation. The precise relation is obtained by comparing the alternative consisting of holding an amount of funds z in domestic currency (obtaining $z(1+i)$ at the end of the period considered) with the alternative consisting of transforming those funds into an amount z/r of foreign currency, obtaining, at the end of the same period, $(z/r)(1+i_f)$ of foreign currency which, transformed into domestic currency at the expected exchange rate $(r+\tilde{r})$ gives — in the asset holder's expectations — an amount $(r+\tilde{r})(z/r)(1+i_f)$ of domestic currency[36]. By equating the two operations and rearranging terms we get

$$i = i_f + \tilde{r}/r + (\tilde{r}/r)i_f.$$

The term $(\tilde{r}/r)i_f$ is usually ignored as being of the second order of magnitude, and we shall conform to this simplification. The approximation remains even when — as is more correct in continuous time — we use continuous compounding: in this case, in fact, the alternatives to be equated are ze^i and $(z/r)e^{i_f}(r+\tilde{r})$, whence

$$e^i = (1+\tilde{r}/r)e^{i_f},$$

whence, if we take the natural logarithms and use the approximation $\ln(1+\tilde{r}/r) = \tilde{r}/r +$ higher order terms, we get

$$i = i_f + \tilde{r}/r + \text{ higher order terms}.$$

Apart from these technical matters, it should be noted that the same relation being examined is obtained by considering a risk-neutral speculator who, anticipating an exchange-rate variation $\tilde{r}$, shifts funds (out of or into the country under consideration according as $\tilde{r} \gtrless 0$ respectively) so as to earn the difference between the current exchange rate and that which will hold in the future according to his expectations. In doing this, however, the speculator must take into account the interest rate which he loses in the country from which funds are shifted and the interest rate which he earns in the country into which funds are shifted, as we showed in Chap. 10, especially Eq. (10.21). From this equation, by ignoring the term δ_t and observing that $\tilde{r} - r \equiv \tilde{r}$, we get the relation (in the symbology used here) $\tilde{r}/r = i - i_f$.

A second observation concerns the equations that come last but two and last but one: the constancy of N goes together with a preexisting amount of national bonds ($N > 0$), whilst the perfect exchange-rate flexibility (and so the instantaneous equilibrium in the balance of payments) makes the existence of a stock of international reserves unnecessary, so that this is assumed to be zero.

Finally, we show, in relation to net exports x, that $x_\pi > 0$ means that the critical elasticities condition occurs. If we denote exports in physical terms by $ex(\pi)$ and

---

[36] It should also be noted that, with rational expectations and efficient foreign exchange markets, the expected spot rate coincides with the current forward exchange rate, so that this reasoning holds for covered interest arbitrage as well.

physical imports by $m(\pi,a)$, in monetary terms (in domestic currency) we get

$$p_h ex(\pi) - rm(\pi,a), \quad ex_\pi < 0, \; m_\pi > 0, \; 0 < m_a < 1,$$

and so, in real terms (that is, in terms of domestic output)

$$x(\pi,a) = ex(\pi) - \frac{rm(\pi,a)}{p_h} = ex(\pi) - \frac{1}{\pi} m(\pi,a).$$

Therefore

$$x_\pi = ex_\pi + \frac{1}{\pi^2} m - \frac{1}{\pi} m_\pi = \frac{m}{\pi^2} \left(\frac{ex}{\frac{1}{\pi} - m} \cdot \frac{\pi}{ex} ex_\pi + 1 - \frac{\pi}{m} m_\pi \right)$$

$$= \frac{m}{\pi^2} \left(-\frac{ex}{\frac{1}{\pi} - m} \eta_{ex} + 1 - \eta_m \right),$$

where $\eta_{ex} \equiv -(\pi/ex) ex_\pi, \eta_m \equiv (\pi/m) m_\pi$. If the critical elasticities condition holds, that is if

$$\frac{ex}{\frac{1}{\pi} - m} \eta_{ex} + \eta_m > 1,$$

then $x_\pi < 0$, and vice versa.

By way of suitable substitutions, model (A.16.59) can be boiled down to the three equations of monetary, real, and balance-of-payments equilibrium:

$$\frac{M}{p_h^\alpha r^{1-\alpha}} - L\left(i_f + \frac{\tilde{r}}{r}, q, \frac{M+N+rF}{p_h^\alpha r^{1-\alpha}}\right) = 0, \tag{A.16.59.1}$$

$$a\left[\left(\frac{p_h}{r}\right)^{1-\alpha}(q - G_R) + \frac{ri_f F}{p_h^\alpha r^{1-\alpha}}, i_f + \alpha\left(\frac{\tilde{r}}{r} - \frac{\tilde{p}_h}{p_h}\right), \frac{M+N+rF}{p_h^\alpha r^{1-\alpha}}\right]$$

$$+ x\left(\frac{p_h}{r}, a[\ldots]\right) + G_R - q = 0, \tag{A.16.59.2}$$

$$r\dot{F} = p_h x\left(\frac{p_h}{r}, a[\ldots]\right) + r i_f F. \tag{A.16.59.3}$$

Almost all substitutions are self-evident; thus we only make the following observations. Given the assumptions $g=0$ and $R=0$, the expression $(iN/p) - T$ which appears in the definition of y_d can be written, by using the definition of g and the assumptions, as $-(p_h/p) G_R$. If we then consider the definition of p, we have $(p_h/p) = (p_h/r)^{1-\alpha}$; from all this the expression which replaces y_d in a follows. As regards the real interest rate, we observe that

$$\frac{\dot{p}}{p} = \alpha \frac{\dot{p}_h}{p_h} + (1-\alpha)\frac{\dot{r}}{r},$$

and so

$$\frac{\tilde{p}}{p} = \alpha \frac{\tilde{p}_h}{p_h} + (1-\alpha)\frac{\tilde{r}}{r},$$

whence, as $i = i_f + \tilde{r}/r$, we have

$$i - \frac{\tilde{p}}{p} = i_f + \alpha \left(\frac{\tilde{r}}{r} - \frac{\tilde{p}_h}{p_h} \right),$$

where the term $\tilde{p}_h/p_h$ will ultimately disappear owing to the assumption of a constant p_h (if, on the contrary, one wishes to extend the model to the consideration of a variable p_h, this term must be kept. For the case of p_h variable, not considered here, see Branson and Buiter, 1983, Sect. 9.5).

We now analyze the two cases of static and rational expectations.

A.16.5.2 Static Expectations

A.16.5.2.1 Short-Run Equilibrium

In the case of static expectations, $\tilde{r} = 0$. Let us begin by examining short-run equilibrium, in which all the stocks are considered exogenously given. This amounts to considering the subset consisting in Eqs. (A.16.59.1) and (A.16.59.2), which form a system of two equations in the two unknowns r and q. According to the implicit-function theorem we can express r and q as differentiable functions of M, N, F, G_R, and so perform exercises in comparative statics, provided that the Jacobian of those two equations with respect to r and q is different from zero. We have

$$J = \begin{vmatrix} -(1-\alpha)\frac{M}{pr} + L_w \frac{M+N-\alpha W}{pr} & -L_q \\ -(1+x_a)\left\{ a_y \left[(q-G_R)(1-\alpha)\frac{\pi^{1-\alpha}}{r} - \frac{\alpha i_f F}{p} \right] + \frac{a_w}{pr}(M+N-\alpha W) \right\} - \frac{\pi}{r}x_\pi & (1+x_a)a_y\pi^{1-\alpha} - 1 \end{vmatrix} \quad (A.16.60)$$

For future reference we define the following expressions

$$\begin{aligned}
\Omega_1 &\equiv (1-\alpha)\frac{M}{pr} - L_w \frac{M+N-\alpha W}{pr} > 0, \\
\Omega_2 &\equiv (1+x_a)\left\{ a_y \left[(q-G_R)(1-\alpha)\frac{\pi^{1-\alpha}}{r} - \frac{\alpha i_f F}{p} \right] \right. \\
&\quad \left. + \frac{a_w}{pr}(M+N-\alpha W) \right\} + \frac{\pi}{r}x_\pi < 0, \\
\Omega_3 &\equiv 1 - (1+x_a)a_y\pi^{1-\alpha} > 0,
\end{aligned} \quad (A.16.61)$$

where the assumptions made on the signs reflect the following hypotheses.

The positivity of Ω_1 reflects the hypothesis that an exchange-rate depreciation, by raising the general price level, causes a decrease in the real money stock greater in absolute value than the possible decrease in the demand for money in real terms. We have said "possible" because this latter decrease only occurs when the stock of real wealth W/p decreases, which in turn only comes about when the country is a net debtor to the rest of the world, i.e. when the stock of private net foreign assets is negative ($F<0$). In this case the exchange-rate depreciation, by raising the domestic-currency value of this debt, causes a decrease in nominal wealth W, which, together with the increase in the price level, definitely brings about a decrease in real wealth W/p. If, on the contrary, the country is a net creditor ($F>0$), the exchange-rate depreciation causes an increase in nominal wealth, which in principle might more than offset the increase in the price level, thus causing real wealth to increase. In this second case real money demand increases, and Ω_1 is certainly positive. But it may be positive also in the previous case if L_w is fairly small, that is, if money is "dominated" by other financial assets in the wealth holders' portfolio equilibrium (many writers believe that because of this dominance, L_w is practically nil).

The negativity of Ω_2 reflects the hypothesis that an exchange-rate depreciation increases the total (domestic plus foreign) demand for domestic output. An exchange-rate depreciation, on the one hand, has a favourable effect on net exports x and hence on total demand if, as was assumed above — see Sect. A.16.5.1 — the critical elasticities condition holds; this effect is captured by the term $(\pi/r)x_\pi$. On the other hand, the depreciation has depressive effects on absorption. The first of these occurs when the depreciation decreases real wealth (the conditions for this decrease have been discussed above): this effect is captured by the term $(a_w/rp)(M+N-\alpha W)$. The second depressive effect is due to the fact that the worsening in the terms of trade (because of the depreciation) reduces the real income corresponding to any given level of domestic production: this is captured by the term $a_y(q-G_R)(1-\alpha)(\pi^{1-\alpha}/r)$. This effect is however contrasted by the increase in income due to the increased domestic-currency value of interest income on the stock of net foreign assets (if this stock is positive; in the contrary case the increase in interest payments will enhance the depressive effect); this is captured by the term $-a_y(\alpha i_f F/p)$. In conclusion, $\Omega_2<0$ if we assume that the expansionary effects via elasticities prevail over the depressive effects.

Finally, Ω_3 is positive owing to the assumption that an increase in domestic output causes an increase in the total demand for it by less than the increase in output. This has already been discussed in the text, note 24.

This said, we can write the Jacobian (A.16.60) as

$$J=\Omega_1\Omega_3-L_q\Omega_2>0, \tag{A.16.60.1}$$

where the positivity is ensured by the assumptions made above on the various Ω's. Thus in a neighbourhood of the equilibrium point there exist the differentiable functions

$$r=r(M,N,F,G_R), \quad q=q(M,N,F,G_R). \tag{A.16.62}$$

The effects on equilibrium of changes in the exogenous variables can be ascertained by way of the suitable partial derivatives, which can be calculated by differentiating Eqs. (A.16.59.1) – (A.16.59.2), account being taken of (A.16.62). If we consider, for example, a change in government expenditure, we get

$$-\Omega_1 \frac{\partial r}{\partial G_R} - L_q \frac{\partial q}{\partial G_R} = 0,$$

$$-\Omega_2 \frac{\partial r}{\partial G_R} - \Omega_3 \frac{\partial q}{\partial G_R} + \Omega_3 = 0,$$

(A.16.63)

whence

$$\frac{\partial r}{\partial G_R} = -\Omega_3 L_q / J < 0,$$

$$\frac{\partial q}{\partial G_R} = \Omega_1 \Omega_3 / J > 0.$$

(A.16.63.1)

The signs – which derive from the assumptions made above – lend support to the statement made in Sect. 16.6.3, as regards the effectiveness of fiscal policy.

In a similar way we obtain the effects of a change in the stock of money by way of an open market operation:

$$\frac{\partial r}{\partial M} - \frac{\partial r}{\partial N} = \frac{1}{p} \Omega_3 / J > 0,$$

$$\frac{\partial q}{\partial M} - \frac{\partial q}{\partial N} = \frac{1}{p} \Omega_2 / J > 0,$$

(A.16.64)

which confirm the statements in the text.

The same procedure will give the effects of a change in the stock of net foreign assets:

$$\frac{\partial r}{\partial F} = -\left[L_w \frac{r}{p} \Omega_3 + (1+x_a) \frac{r}{p} (a_w + a_y i_f) L_q \right] / J < 0,$$

$$\frac{\partial q}{\partial F} = \left[\Omega_1 (1+x_a) \frac{r}{p} (a_w + a_y i_f) + L_w \frac{r}{p} \Omega_2 \right] / J > 0,$$

(A.16.65)

where the sign of $\partial q/\partial F$ is based on the additional hypothesis that L_w is sufficiently small. An increase in F shifts the RR schedule to the right (see Fig. 16.7) through the wealth effect on absorption: domestic production increases and the exchange rate appreciates.

A.16.5.2.2 Long-Run Equilibrium

As we said in Sect. 16.6.3, in the long-run equilibrium, F is constant: this amounts to setting $\dot{F}=0$ in (A.16.59.3) and considering F as an endogenous variable. The system to be examined is now made up of the three equations (A.16.59.1), (A.16.59.2), (A.16.59.3) – where $\tilde{r}=0$ and $\dot{F}=0$ – whose Jacobian with respect to the three variables r,q,F turns out to be

$$J_1 = \begin{vmatrix} -\Omega_1 & -L_q & -L_w\dfrac{r}{p} \\ -\Omega_2 & -\Omega_3 & (1+x_a)\dfrac{r}{p}(a_y i_f + a_w) \\ -\Omega_4 & -p_h x_a a_y \pi^{1-\alpha} & -\Omega_5 \end{vmatrix}, \qquad (A.16.66)$$

where $\Omega_1, \Omega_2, \Omega_3$ are as defined above in (A.16.61), and

$$\Omega_4 \equiv x_\pi \pi^2 - i_f F + p_h x_a \left\{ a_y \left[(q - G_R)(1-\alpha)\dfrac{\pi^{1-\alpha}}{r} - \dfrac{\alpha i_f F}{p} \right] \right.$$

$$\left. + \dfrac{a_w}{rp}(M + N - \alpha W) \right\} < 0, \qquad (A.16.67)$$

$$\Omega_5 \equiv r\left(p_h x_a \dfrac{a_y i_f + a_w}{p} + i_f \right) < 0.$$

The negativity of Ω_4 is ensured when a depreciation improves the balance of payments. The elasticity effect (which goes in the right direction because we have assumed that the critical elasticities condition occurs) is strengthened (if we assume $F > 0$) by the increased domestic-currency value of interest receipts from abroad and by the decrease in absorption due to the terms-of-trade effect and the wealth effect.

The negativity of Ω_5 reflects the assumption that the improvement in the interest-income account due to the increase in F is more than offset by the deterioration in the net exports account due to the higher absorption determined by the wealth effect.

If we expand the determinant (A.16.66), we get

$$J_1 = -\Omega_1 \left[\Omega_3 \Omega_5 + p_h x_a a_y \pi^{1-\alpha}(1+x_a)\dfrac{r}{p}(a_y i_f + a_w) \right]$$

$$+ L_q \left[\Omega_2 \Omega_5 - \Omega_4 (1+x_a)\dfrac{r}{p}(a_y i_f + a_w) \right]$$

$$- L_w \dfrac{r}{p} [\Omega_3 p_h x_a a_y \pi^{1-\alpha} + \Omega_3 \Omega_4] > 0, \qquad (A.16.66.1)$$

where the positivity of J_1 depends on the assumptions made on the various Ω's.

Thus in a neighbourhood of the equilibrium point there exist the following differentiable functions

$$r = r(M, N, G_R), \quad q = q(M, N, G_R), \quad F = F(M, N, G_R), \qquad (A.16.68)$$

which allow us to determine the effects of monetary and fiscal policy on the long-run equilibrium values. To simplify this determination, we shall assume, following Branson and Buiter (1983, p. 267) that the wealth effect in the demand for money (which has already been discussed above) is negligible, so that $L_w = 0$.

To begin with, we consider a change in government expenditure and get

$$-\Omega_1 \frac{\partial r}{\partial G_R} - L_q \frac{\partial q}{\partial G_R} = 0,$$

$$-\Omega_2 \frac{\partial r}{\partial G_R} - \Omega_3 \frac{\partial q}{\partial G_R} + (1+x_a)\frac{r}{p}(a_y i_f + a_w)\frac{\partial F}{\partial G_R} + \Omega_3 = 0, \quad (\text{A}.16.69)$$

$$-\Omega_4 \frac{\partial r}{\partial G_R} - p_h x_a a_y \pi^{1-\alpha} \frac{\partial q}{\partial G_R} - \Omega_5 \frac{\partial F}{\partial G_R} + p_h x_a a_y \pi^{1-\alpha} = 0,$$

whence, by solving and indicating for brevity only the signs of the elements of the various determinants (when this indication is sufficient to determine the sign of the determinant), we obtain

$$\frac{\partial r}{\partial G_R} = \frac{\begin{vmatrix} 0 & - & 0 \\ - & - & + \\ + & + & + \end{vmatrix}}{J_1} = \frac{-}{+} < 0, \quad \frac{\partial q}{\partial G_R} = \frac{\begin{vmatrix} - & 0 & 0 \\ + & - & + \\ - & + & + \end{vmatrix}}{J_1} = \frac{+}{+} > 0,$$

$$\frac{\partial F}{\partial G_R} = \frac{\begin{vmatrix} -\Omega_1 & -L_q & 0 \\ -\Omega_2 & -\Omega_3 & -\Omega_3 \\ \Omega_4 & -p_h x_a a_y \pi^{1-\alpha} & -p_h x_a a_y \pi^{1-\alpha} \end{vmatrix}}{J_1} \quad (\text{A}.16.70)$$

$$= \frac{L_q[\Omega_2 p_h x_a a_y \pi^{1-\alpha} + \Omega_3 \Omega_4]}{J_1}$$

$$= \frac{L_q[\pi^2 x_\pi (1 - a_y \pi^{1-\alpha}) - i_f F \Omega_3 + p_h x_a \Omega_6]}{J_1} = \frac{-}{+} < 0,$$

where

$$\Omega_6 \equiv a_y\left[(q - G_R)(1-\alpha)\frac{\pi^{1-\alpha}}{r} - \frac{\alpha i_f F}{p}\right] + \frac{a_w}{rp}(M + B - \alpha W) > 0. \quad (\text{A}.16.71)$$

In a similar way we calculate

$$\frac{\partial r}{\partial M} - \frac{\partial r}{\partial N} = \frac{\begin{vmatrix} - & - & 0 \\ 0 & - & + \\ 0 & + & + \end{vmatrix}}{J_1} = \frac{+}{+} > 0,$$

$$\frac{\partial q}{\partial M} - \frac{\partial q}{\partial N} = \frac{\begin{vmatrix} - & - & 0 \\ + & 0 & + \\ - & 0 & + \end{vmatrix}}{J_1} = \frac{+}{+} > 0 \quad (\text{A}.16.72)$$

$$\frac{\partial F}{\partial M} - \frac{\partial F}{\partial N} = -\frac{1}{p}\frac{[\pi^2 x_\pi(1 - a_y\pi^{1-\alpha}) - i_f F\Omega_3 + p_h x_a \Omega_6]}{J_1} = \frac{+}{+} > 0.$$

Let us now briefly comment on the results. An expansionary fiscal policy causes an increase in domestic production and an appreciation in the exchange rate (which in the short run, on the contrary, depreciated); the stock of net foreign assets decreases. The lower F causes the RR schedule to shift to the left relative to the new short-run equilibrium, in relation to which the exchange rate depreciates and output decreases: with respect to the initial equilibrium, however, the exchange rate appreciates and output increases. Thus the long-run equilibrium will be placed at an intermediate point between the initial equilibrium and the short-run equilibrium determined by the impact effect of the increase in G_R.

An expansionary monetary policy, on the contrary, raises output above its new short-run equilibrium level, and causes the exchange rate to appreciate with respect to its new short-run equilibrium value. This appreciation, however, is not so great as to bring it back to its initial value, with respect to which it shows a depreciation. The stock of net foreign assets increases.

After examining the comparative statics, let us examine the stability of the long-run equilibrium, by way of the dynamic equation (A.16.59.3). The idea is that the system *moves in time through a succession of short-run equilibria*, and we must ascertain whether this succession converges towards the long-run equilibrium point. It would be theoretically possible also to examine the *disequilibrium dynamics* of the system, that is, allowing for the possibility that r and q are *outside* of their short-run equilibrium, but this would greatly complicate the analysis.

To study the *equilibrium dynamics* of the system, we substitute the short-run equilibrium values of r and q — given by the solution of Eqs. (A.16.59.1) and (A.16.59.2), i.e. the functions (A.16.62) — in Eq. (A.16.59.3) and we obtain a first-order differential equation in F, given the exogenous variables. This equation is

$$\dot{F} = \frac{p_h}{r} x\left(\frac{p_h}{r}, a[\ldots]\right) + i_f F, \qquad (A.16.73)$$

where r and q are functions of F by way of (A.16.62). If we linearize Eq. (A.16.73) at the equilibrium point, we get

$$\dot{\bar{F}} = [\pi x_a a_y \pi^{1-\alpha} \frac{\partial q}{\partial F} - \pi x_a a_y (q - G_R)(1-\alpha) \frac{\pi^{1-\alpha}}{r} \frac{\partial r}{\partial F}$$

$$+ \pi x_a a_y \frac{\alpha i_f F \pi^{-\alpha}}{r} \frac{\partial r}{\partial F} + \pi x_a a_y i_f \pi^{-\alpha} + \pi x_a a_w \frac{r}{p}$$

$$- \pi x_a a_w \frac{M+F-\alpha W}{pr} \frac{\partial r}{\partial F} - \frac{\pi}{r}(x + \pi x_\pi) \frac{\partial r}{\partial F} + i_f] \bar{F}, \qquad (A.16.73.1)$$

where, as usual, a bar over the variable denotes the deviations from equilibrium.

The necessary and sufficient stability condition is that the expression in square brackets which multiplies $\bar{F}$ is negative. This condition is what Branson and Buiter (1983, p. 269) call the "*super Marshall-Lerner condition*", a simpler version of which was given in Branson (1977).

The stability condition implies that if, for example, F is higher than its long-run equilibrium value, the current account must show a deficit, whence a capital inflow to equilibrate the overall balance and so a decrease in F (a capital inflow means a decrease in foreign assets or an increase in foreign liabilities: in both cases the stock of net foreign assets decreases).

The critical elasticities condition does, of course, operate in the right direction, because a greater value of F causes, in the short-run, the exchange rate to appreciate [$\partial r/\partial F < 0$ from Eqs. (A.16.65)] and this brings about a deterioration in the trade balance[37], if the critical elasticities condition holds. This effect is captured by the term[38]

$$-\frac{\pi}{r}(x+\pi x_\pi)\frac{\partial r}{\partial F}<0.$$

On the other hand a greater value of F implies, *ceteris paribus*, an improvement in the investment income account (term i_f), which tends to offset the previous effect. This improvement does, however, raise disposable income and so absorption, which makes the trade balance deteriorate; this effect is captured by the term

$$\pi x_a a_y i_f \pi^{-\alpha}<0.$$

In the short-run equilibrium, a greater F brings about a higher output [$\partial q/\partial F>0$: see Eqs. (A.16.65)], which increases absorption and thus causes the trade balance to deteriorate, as is shown by the term

$$\pi x_a a_y \pi^{1-\alpha}\frac{\partial q}{\partial F}<0.$$

The exchange-rate appreciation due to the higher F ($\partial r/\partial F<0$, as said above) has two other effects on income. Firstly, it improves the terms of trade, thus raising real income and hence absorption, with a consequent deterioration in the trade balance, as shown by the term

$$-\pi x_a a_y (q-G_R)(1-\alpha)\frac{\pi^{1-\alpha}}{r}\frac{\partial r}{\partial F}<0;$$

secondly, it reduces the domestic-currency value of interest payments from abroad (we are assuming $F>0$), which works in the opposite direction, as shown by the term

$$\pi x_a a_y \frac{i_f F \alpha \pi^{-\alpha}}{r}\frac{\partial r}{\partial F}>0.$$

A greater F also means — *ceteris paribus* — greater wealth and hence a greater absorption, which causes the trade balance to deteriorate; this effect is captured

---

[37] In what follows "trade balance" is used in the sense of "net exports" as defined in Sect. A.16.5.1.
[38] Since we are using foreign-currency-denominated magnitudes (F), we must consider net exports in terms of foreign currency, which — according to the definition explained in Sect. A.16.51 — are x. Thus, $\partial(\pi x)/\partial r = (x+\pi x_\pi)\frac{d\pi}{dr} = -\frac{\pi}{r}(x+\pi x_\pi)$.

by the term

$$\pi x_a a_w \frac{r}{p} < 0.$$

Finally, the exchange-rate appreciation caused by higher F reduces the price level and so raises real wealth[39], which, via an increase in absorption, causes the balance of trade to deteriorate, as shown by the term

$$-\pi x_a a_w \frac{M+N-\alpha W}{rp} \frac{\partial r}{\partial F} < 0.$$

As we see, almost all the additional effects (additional with respect to the effect due to the elasticities) on the balance of trade work in the right direction, so that this balance is likely to deteriorate as a consequence of the greater F. In opposition to this, there is the improvement in the investment income account (term i_f already commented on), so that it is not possible to establish on *a priori* grounds whether the current account deteriorates (in which case the stability condition is fulfilled) or improves.

A.16.5.3 Rational Expectations

In the case of rational expectations, $\tilde{r} = \dot{r}$ and so system (A.16.59.1) – (A.16.59.3) must be examined from the dynamic point of view also in the short run. It should be emphasized that the long-run equilibrium is the same as in the case of static expectations, since even with rational expectations, long-run equilibrium implies $\dot{r} = 0$, $\dot{F} = 0$. From this a very important result follows, namely that the comparative-static analysis carried out on the long-run equilibrium in the static expectations case — see Eqs. (A.16.66) through (A.16.72) — holds without modifications in the rational expectations case as well.

On the contrary, the analysis of the dynamics is different, due to the presence of the term $\dot{r}/r$ in the various equations. If we consider system (A.16.59.1) – (A.16.59.3), where $\tilde{r} = \dot{r}$, and perform a linear approximation at the long-run equilibrium point, we get

$$\dot{\bar{r}} = H_{11}\bar{r} + H_{12}\bar{F},$$
$$\dot{\bar{F}} = H_{21}\bar{r} + H_{22}\bar{F}, \qquad (A.16.74)$$

where (all the following expressions are, of course, evaluated at the equilibrium point)

---

[39] This is under the assumption that the capital loss (which comes about when $F > 0$, whose domestic-currency value decreases as a consequence of the exchange-rate appreciation) does not offset the decrease in the price level completely. If $F < 0$ the problem does not arise, as there will also be a capital gain.

$$H_{11} \equiv (-\Omega_3 \Omega_1 + L_q \Omega_2) \Omega_7 > 0,$$

$$H_{12} \equiv -\left[\Omega_3 L_w \frac{r}{p} + L_q(1+x_a)(a_w + a_y i_f)\frac{r}{p})\right]\Omega_7 > 0,$$

$$H_{21} \equiv -\frac{\pi x_a a_i \alpha}{r}\Omega_1 \Omega_7$$

$$+ \left(-\frac{L_i}{r} x_a a_y \pi^{2-\alpha} + \frac{\pi x_a a_i \alpha}{r} L_q\right)\Omega_2 \Omega_7 - \frac{1}{r}\Omega_4 \gtreqless 0, \quad (A.16.75)$$

$$H_{22} \equiv -\frac{\pi x_a a_i \alpha}{r}\frac{L_w r}{p}\Omega_7$$

$$- \left(-\frac{L_i}{r} x_a a_y \pi^{2-\alpha} + \frac{\pi x_a a_i \alpha}{r} L_q\right)(1+x_a)(a_w + a_y i_f)\frac{r}{p}\Omega_7 + \frac{1}{r}\Omega_5 \gtreqless 0.$$

The Ω's subscripted from 1 through 6 are as previously defined, whilst Ω_7 is defined as

$$\Omega_7 \equiv \left[\Omega_3 \frac{L_i}{r} + \frac{(1+x_a)a_i}{r}\alpha L_q\right]^{-1} < 0. \quad (A.16.75.1)$$

The signs of the H's derive from the assumptions on the signs of the Ω's and the various partial derivatives.

The differential equation system (A.16.74) determines the time path of the exchange rate and of the stock of net foreign assets; the time path of domestic output is determined by the equation, always derived from the linearization of system (A.16.59.1)–(A.16.59.3),

$$\bar{q} = \left[-\frac{(1+x_a)a_i \alpha}{r}\Omega_1 - \frac{L_i}{r}\Omega_2\right]\Omega_7 \bar{r}$$

$$+ \left[-\frac{(1+x_a)a_i}{r}\alpha L_w \frac{r}{p}\right.$$

$$+ \frac{L_i}{r}(1+x_a)(a_w + a_y i_f)\frac{r}{p}\right]\Omega_7 \bar{F}. \quad (A.16.76)$$

If we assume that an increase in F causes the trade balance to deteriorate by more than it improves the investment income account, the sign of H_{22} will be positive[40]. Thus the pattern of signs in the coefficient matrix of system (A.16.74) is

$$\begin{bmatrix} + & + \\ ? & - \end{bmatrix}.$$

This means that, in the phase plane (r, F), the $\dot{r} = 0$ schedule slopes negatively whilst the $\dot{F} = 0$ schedule can be either positively (if $H_{21} < 0$) or negatively (if

---

[40] The coefficient H_{22} can, in fact, be interpreted in a similar way — *mutatis mutandis* — as the multiplicative coefficient of $\bar{F}$ in Eq. (A.16.73.1).

$H_{21}>0$) sloping. We have, in fact

$$\left(\frac{dr}{dF}\right)_{\dot{r}=0} = -\frac{H_{12}}{H_{11}} < 0, \quad \left(\frac{dr}{dF}\right)_{\dot{F}=0} = -\frac{H_{22}}{H_{21}} \gtreqless 0. \qquad (A.16.77)$$

In the former case (positive slope of $\dot{F}=0$) the determinant of the matrix is certainly negative and the equilibrium point is certainly a *saddle point* (see Gandolfo, 1980, pp. 435–42), so that a unique convergent trajectory (coinciding with one of the two asymptotes of the saddle point) will exist, as described by SS in Fig. 16.9; any point outside SS will move away from equilibrium.

In the latter case (negative slope of $\dot{F}=0$), for the determinant of the matrix to be negative the $\dot{F}=0$ schedule must be steeper than the $\dot{r}=0$ one, namely $(H_{22}/H_{21}) > (H_{12}/H_{11})$, whence $H_{11}H_{22}-H_{21}H_{12}<0$ and the equilibrium point will again be a saddle point. When this condition does not occur, the long-run equilibrium point will be singular point of a different nature (a *node* or a *focus*), and the results of the analysis will change.

We conclude by noting that in the case of static expectations the system by definition always moves along the $\dot{r}=0$ schedule, and — if the system is stable — will reach the same long-run equilibrium which, as we have already noted, is identical with both types of expectations.

A.16.6 Forward Market Intervention

The monetary authorities' intervention in the forward market has already been mentioned in Sect. 12.4.3. Here we wish briefly to comment on the thesis (see, for example, Sohmen, 1966, 1969) according to which, by stabilizing the forward exchange rate (by way of intervention in the relative market) and letting the spot exchange rate fluctuate freely, the monetary authorities would on the one hand avoid hindrance to traders who cover on the forward market (as these would find a fairly stable forward exchange rate), and on the other achieve balance-of-payments equilibrium, provided of course that the suitable conditions on the elasticities hold.

This thesis, if valid in a partial equilibrium framework (in which, that is, only the exchange markets, and the effects on these of exchange-rate variations, are considered), is no longer generally valid in a more general framework (such as that examined in the present chapter), in which macroeconomic equilibrium etc., is considered besides foreign-exchange market equilibrium. In this framework, in fact, variations in the spot exchange rate influence the rest of the economy which in turn feeds back on foreign exchange markets (both spot and forward). To avoid further burdening of an already overcrowded chapter we refer the reader to Casprini (1976); on the interactions between macroeconomic equilibrium and forward exchange market, see also Levin (1970), Argy and Porter (1972), Eaton and Turnovsky (1984).

References

Allen, P.R. and P.B. Kenen, 1980
Argy, V. and M.G. Porter, 1972
Behnke, E.-A., 1980
Branson, W.H., 1977
Branson, W.H., 1979
Branson, W.H. and W.H. Buiter, 1983
Branson, W.H. and D.W. Henderson, 1985
Casprini, F., 1973
Casprini, F., 1976
Chacholiades, M., 1978, Chaps. 17 and 18
Cuthbertson, K., 1979, Chap. 3
Deardoff, A.V. and R.M. Stern, 1978a
Deardoff, A.V. and R.M. Stern, 1978b
De Grauwe, P., 1983
Dixon, R., 1983
Dornbusch, R., 1980, Chaps. 11, 12, 13
Dornbusch, R. and S. Fischer, 1980
Eaton, J. and S.J. Turnovsky, 1984
Fleming, J.M., 1962
Floyd, J.E., 1985, Chaps. 8, 9
Frenkel, J.A and A. Razin, 1987
Gandolfo, G., 1975
Gandolfo, G., 1980, Part II, Chap. 9, Sect. 6
Gandolfo, G., 1981, Sect. 1.2
Godley, W. and F. Cripps, 1983
Goldstein, M., 1980
Gylfason, T. and J.F. Helliwell, 1983
Harberger, A.C., 1950
Herin, J.A. Lindbeck and J. Myhrman (eds), 1977
Himarios, D., 1987
Kawai, M., 1985
Keynes, J.M., 1936, Chap. 22; Chap. 24, Sect. IV
Lai, C.-C. and C.C. Chen, 1984
Laursen, S. and L.A. Metzler, 1950
Lawrence, C., 1984
Levin, J.H., 1970
Levin, J.H., 1980
Levin, J.H., 1986
Marston, R.C., 1985
Martinengo, G., 1978
McCallum, J. and D. Vines, 1981
Modigliani, F. and H. Askari, 1973
Mundell, R.A., 1963
Mudell, R.A., 1968, Chaps. 17 and 18
Mussa, M., 1979
Niehans, J., 1984, Chaps. 7, 10–13, 15
Obstfeld, M., 1982
Persson, T. and L.E.O. Svensson, 1985
Pitchford, J.D., 1985
Shinkai, Y., 1975
Sinn, H.W., 1983
Sohmen, E., 1966
Sohmen, E., 1969, Chaps. IV and V
Stern, R.M., 1973, Chap. 10
Svensson, L.E.O. and A. Razin, 1983
Tobin, J. and J.E. DeMacedo, 1980
Tower, E., 1980
Turnovsky, S.J. 1983
Vines, D., 1976
von Neuman Whitman, M., 1970
Witte, W.E., 1983
Yeager, L.B., 1976, Chap. 9

17 International Capital Movements and Other Problems

17.1 Introduction

International capital movements have been mentioned several times in previous chapters (see, for example, Sects. 7.7, 10.2 – 10.4, 11.1, 12.4, 15.4 – 15.6; Chap. 16, passim). The purpose of the next sections is to bring these together in a unified picture, and to examine the causes and effects of the main types of capital movements in detail; for convenience the traditional distinction between short-term and long-term movements will be maintained. It should be stressed that for obvious reasons our examination will be made from the point of view of international monetary economics, so that we shall ignore − except for a very brief mention − the important problem of the behaviour of multinational corporations in carrying out direct investment, a problem which more properly belongs to the theory of the firm, as we shall see in Sect. 17.3.

The transfer problem is treated here (whereas it is often treated in conjunction with the foreign multiplier) because, although it has a broader significance, it helps to throw light on the effects on the balance of payments of certain types of capital movements.

The last section examines the relations between balance of payments and growth; as both the Keynesian and the monetarist view of the balance of payments examined in the two previous chapters bear upon this topic, we have treated it here in a unified manner instead of in those chapters separately.

17.2 Short-Term Capital Movements and Foreign-Exchange Speculation

17.2.1 The Main Types of Short-Term Capital Movements

The main short-term capital movements are those due to *foreign-exchange arbitrage, covered interest arbitrage, commercial hedging,* and *foreign-exchange speculation*[1]. These have already been described in Sects. 10.2 – 10.4 and 12.4, where we also examined their nature and functions. Here we wish to consider a

---

[1] Other types of short-term capital movements are commercial credits (those which have a maturity of less than one year). These, being related to international trade in commodities, can give rise − insofar as the agent concerned wishes to cover against exchange risks − to the hedging operations described in Sect. 10.3.

17.2 Short-Term Capital Movements and Foreign-Exchange Speculation 339

problem that we have not treated previously, namely the economic role of speculation, a hotly debated topic of great importance also outside international economics. On the one hand, in fact, it is claimed that speculators, by buying when the price is low and reselling when the price is high, help to smooth out and dampen down the fluctuations of the price around its normal value, so that their operations are beneficial (*stabilizing speculation*). On the other, the possibility is stressed that speculators buy precisely when the price is rising in order to force a further rise and then profit from the difference (bullish speculation: the case of bearish speculation is perfectly symmetrical), so that their operations *destabilize* the market. It does not therefore seem possible to reach an unambiguous theoretical conclusion, as we shall see below.

This said in general, let us pass to the examination of foreign-exchange speculation, in particular of speculation on the *spot* market. The asset concerned is foreign exchange, whose price in terms of domestic currency is the (spot) exchange rate. Therefore, if speculators anticipate a depreciation (i.e. if the expected exchange rate is higher than the current one), they will demand foreign exchange (simultaneously supplying domestic currency) in the expectation of reselling it at a higher price and so earning the difference[2]. Conversely they will supply foreign exchange (simultaneously demanding domestic currency) if the expected exchange rate is lower than the current one.

In order better to examine the effects of speculation, we must distinguish a fixed exchange-rate regime of the adjustable peg type (see Sect. 10.5) and a freely flexible exchange-rate regime.

Under an adjustable peg regime (such as the Bretton Woods system), speculation is normally destabilizing, for a very simple reason. Since the regime allows once-and-for-all parity changes in the case of fundamental disequilibrium, in a situation of a persistent and serious balance-of-payments disequilibrium it will be apparent to all in which direction the parity change — if any — will take place, so that speculation is practically risk-free (the so-called *one-way option*). The worst that can happen to speculators, in fact, is that the parity is not changed, in which case they will only lose the cost of transferring funds, the possible interest differential against them for a limited period of time, and the possible difference between the buying and selling prices (which is very small, given the restricted margins of oscillation around parity). It goes without saying, that these speculative transfers of funds make the disequilibrium worse and thus make the parity change more and more necessary: they are *intrinsically destabilizing*. Among the most sensational cases of this type of speculation, those that occurred on the occasion of the parity changes of the pound sterling (devaluation of November, 1967), of the French franc (devaluation of August, 1969), and of the Deutschmark (revaluation of October, 1969) are usually pointed out. In fact, in the case of a fundamental disequilibrium of the deficit type, the pressure on the exchange rate is in the sense of a devaluation, and the authorities are compelled, as we know, to sell foreign exchange to defend the given parity. Now speculators

---

[2] It goes without saying that the expected difference will have to be greater than the net costs of the speculative operation, as explained in Sect. 10.4.1. A similar observation holds in the case of an expected appreciation.

demand foreign exchange[3]: this demand has to be added to the demand deriving from the fundamental deficit and, by increasing the pressure on the exchange rate, may cause the monetary authorities' defence to collapse[4] (this defence might otherwise have been successful in the absence of speculation). A similar reasoning holds, *mutatis mutandis*, in the case of a fundamental disequilibrium in the surplus direction.

Under a freely flexible exchange-rate system, the situation is different. First of all, the uncertainty about the future path of the exchange rate increases the risk and so tends to put a brake on speculative activity. But the fundamental issue consists in examining the destabilizing or stabilizing[5] nature of speculation, to which we now turn.

17.2.2 Flexible Exchange Rates and Speculation

According to one school of thought, speculation under flexible exchange rates is necessarily stabilizing. The basic argument of those supporting this claim is that speculation is profitable insofar as it is stabilizing: consequently, destabilizing speculators lose money and must leave the market, where only stabilizing speculators, who make profits, remain. Here is a well-known quotation on the matter from Friedman (1953, p. 175): "People who argue that speculation is generally destabilizing seldom realize that this is largely equivalent to saying that speculators lose money, since speculation can be destabilizing in general only if speculators sell when the currency is low in price and buy it when it is high".

But the equation destabilization = losses (and so stabilization = profits) does not seem generally valid, as can be easily argued. Assume, for example, that the non-speculative exchange-rate (i.e. the one occurring in the absence of speculation) follows a cyclically oscillating path around a constant average value. If speculators concentrate their sales of foreign currency immediately after the upper turning point (point A in Fig. 17.1) and their purchases immediately after the lower turning point (point B), an acceleration of both the downwards and the upwards movement (as shown by the broken lines) follows, with an increase in the amplitude and/or frequency of the oscillations. The effect is destabilizing, and it is self-evident that speculators, by selling the foreign currency at a higher price than that at which they purchase it, make profits.

One can also point out the case, already mentioned above, of bullish or bearish speculation (much like that which takes place in the Stock Exchange). This leaves out of consideration any normal or "average" reference value such as that drawn in Fig. 17.1. Bullish speculators, well aware of the effects that their action will have

---

[3] In the case of a parity change, this change is usually fairly large, since the monetary authorities wish to get enough room so as not to fall once more into the same situation of deficit shortly after. Therefore the change expected by speculators is certainly greater than the cost (if any) of the operation.

[4] For an interesting theoretical study on the collapse time of a regime of fixed exchange rates under speculative attack, see Flood and Garber (1984).

[5] Although the notions of "stabilizing" and "destabilizing" may, at first sight, look intuitive, it is by no means easy to find a rigorous measure. See Gandolfo (1971), Kohlhagen (1979), Orosel (1984).

17.2 Short-Term Capital Movements and Foreign-Exchange Speculation

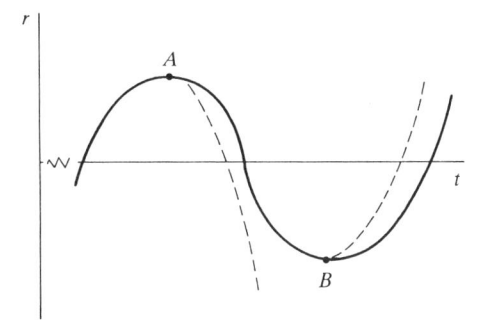

Fig. 17.1. An example of destabilizing speculation

on the price[6] (in this case the exchange rate), buy foreign exchange with the aim of forcing an increase in its price; their intervention will be followed by other, less sagacious, operators hoping to make a killing by purchasing an asset (in this case, the foreign exchange) which is appreciating. When the exchange rate has depreciated sufficiently, the initial speculators sell the foreign exchange they bought in the first place (which may well give rise to a wave of sales and an abrupt fall in the price): they have certainly made profits and just as certainly destabilized the market. Naturally in this example someone has to bear the losses and will leave the market, but will be replaced by someone else who wishes to have a go. The idea that professional speculators might on the average make profits while a changing body of "amateurs" regularly loses large sums was already considered by Friedman (1953, p. 175), but he dismissed it as unlikely. On the contrary, other writers (see, for example, Glahe, 1966) believe that the existence of professional and non-professional speculators is the norm (into the latter category fall those traders who occasionally speculate by exploiting the leads and lags of trade) and show that if one group has positive profits and the other negative profits, the net effect may in general be either stabilizing or destabilizing.

Another interesting example of profitable and destabilizing speculation was given by Kemp (1963). Let us assume that non-speculators' excess demand for foreign exchange is the $E_n(r)$ curve drawn in Fig. 17.2. This curve gives rise to three equilibrium points: r_1, r_2, r_3, of which the first and third are stable and the second unstable, as can readily be verified by reasoning in the way shown in Sect. 12.3 (see Fig. 12.1). We also assume that initially the exchange rate is at r_1, where in the absence of speculation it would remain.

Now speculation comes in with an excess demand for foreign exchange equal to E_s, which joins E_n and so causes the overall excess demand curve to shift to the right, to the position $E_n + E_s$; a new *single* equilibrium point, r_4, corresponds to this new curve. Since r_4 is a stable equilibrium point, the exchange rate will start depreciating and moving towards r_4 from r_1; if the flow of speculative demand E_s

---

[6] This implies that the market is not perfectly competitive (by definition, under perfect competition each of a great numer of agents considers the market price as a datum which he cannot modify). Actually the foreign-exchange speculative market is essentially oligopolistic, since the possibility — in normal times — of existing and operating profitably depends essentially on the information possessed by the speculator, which in turn implies an organization and a cost beyond the reach of most people, as only certain operators (banks, multinational corporations, etc.) can afford them.

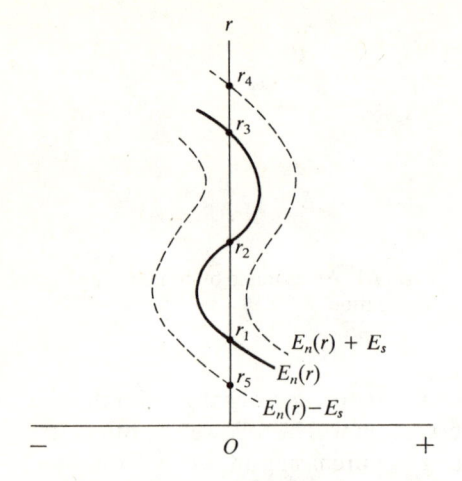

Fig. 17.2. An example of profitable and destabilizing speculation

continued long enough, the exchange rate would tend to reach r_4. However, we assume that immediately after r has reached r_2 speculators stop buying and withdraw from the market. The market's excess demand curve goes back to its initial position E_n, but since r_2 is an unstable point, the exchange rate will go on depreciating, moving towards the stable point r_3. When the exchange rate has arrived in proximity to r_3, the speculators — who are holding speculative stocks of foreign exchange purchased at rates of exchange ranging between r_1 and r_2 — put the whole operation into reverse. They enter the market as sellers, so that the aggregate excess demand curve shifts to the left, to the position $E_n - E_s$. A new single equilibrium point, r_5, corresponds to this new curve, and since it is a stable point, the exchange rate will start appreciating towards it. However, we assume that speculators, after having liquidated their position, withdraw from the market when the exchange rate reaches r_2. The aggregate excess demand curve goes back to the original position E_n, and the exchange rate converges to the stable equilibrium point r_1, thus completing its cycle.

Speculators, then, have purchased foreign exchange at prices included between r_1 and r_2 and have sold it at higher prices, ranging between r_3 and r_2. The profitability of their operations is undoubted, as is the fact that they have destabilized the market by causing a fluctuation $r_1 - r_3 - r_1$ in the exchange rate, which in their absence would have remained at r_1.

For further considerations and a survey of earlier debates (between Telser, Baumol and others), we refer the reader to Gandolfo (1971); other examples of profitable and destabilizing speculation are given by Williamson (1973b), Hart (1977), Witte (1978), Orosel (1984), Ljungqvist (1992).

It should be stressed that it would *not* be correct to argue, from what we have said, that under flexible exchange rates speculation is *always* destabilizing. It is, in fact, quite possible for speculators to behave as described by Friedman, in which case their stabilizing effect is self-evident. It has even been shown that there are cases in which speculation stabilizes an otherwise unstable flexible-exchange-rate regime (i.e., one which would have been unstable in the absence of speculation): see, for example, Britton (1970); Driskill and McCafferty (1980); McKinnon (1983); Levin (1983a).

Thus we have seen that, whilst under an adjustable peg regime[7] speculation is generally destabilizing[8], under flexible exchange rates it may have either effect, so that the question we started from has no unambiguous answer. Even this apparently inconclusive answer is of importance, as it denies general validity to both the statements, that speculation is generally stabilizing and that it is generally destabilizing.

Neither does the question seem solvable on the basis of the empirical evidence[9], which has given contradictory results. This is not surprising, if one bears in mind that the nature of speculation is, more than other economic phenomena, strictly related to political, historical and institutional circumstances, so that it becomes difficult if not impossible to obtain general answers, but it is necessary to consider each case separately.

As regards *forward speculation*, we refer the reader to what we said in Sects. 10.4 and 12.4. We simply remind the reader here that forward speculation by itself does *not* give rise, at the moment in which it is undertaken, to any transfer of funds: only when the contract matures will there be a (positive or negative) excess demand for (spot) foreign exchange, deriving from the liquidation of the contract.

We conclude with the observation that the volatility of short-term speculative capital flows is one of the major problems of the international monetary system. This topic will be taken up again in Chap. 20, Sect. 20.6.

17.3 Long-Term Capital Movements

The main types of private long-term capital movements are *portfolio investment* and *direct investment*[10]. The difference between the two is that the direct investor seeks to have, on a lasting basis, an effective voice in the management of a nonresident enterprise, whilst portfolio investment is of a purely financial nature.

In general, the typical direct investment is in ordinary shares (equities) and the operator is usually a multinational corporation. Portfolio investment covers government bonds, private bonds, bonds issued by international organizations, preference shares, equities (but not so as to gain control over the corporation), various kinds of other securities (certificates of deposit, marketable promissory

---

[7] For an examination of the effects of speculation under a crawling peg regime see, for example, Levin (1977) and Bhandari (1984).

[8] It should be noted that in what we have said so far, there is an implicit judgement that destabilizing speculation is harmful. This judgement is generally shared, whether implicitly or explicitly. Friedman (1960) has tried to oppose it, by arguing, for example, that "destabilizing" speculation (in an adjustable peg regime) compels the monetary authorities to make the parity adjustment, thus accelerating the attainment of the new equilibrium.

[9] It should be stressed that, as the theory refers to freely flexible exchange rates, the empirical evidence derived from the managed float that has prevailed since 1973 is not relevant (we shall come back to the problem of speculation in the managed float in Sects. 18.3 and 18.4). For the previous historical periods, see the studies cited by Sohmen (1969, Chap. III) and by Stern (1973, pp. 95–107).

[10] Other types of long-term capital movements are international loans and commercial credits, naturally with a maturity of more than one year.

notes, etc.). At this point the problem arises of determining the percentage of ownership of an enterprise above which one can talk of control.

It is true, of course, that full legal control is achieved by owning just over 50% of the equities (or other form of ownership of the enterprise), but in the case of big corporations with a widely distributed ownership among numerous small shareholders a much lower percentage is often sufficient to achieve the actual control of the corporation. Thus a conventional accounting solution is inevitable.

Most countries, therefore, rely on the percentage of ownership of the voting stock in an enterprise. Some countries use more than one percentage (for example according to whether investment is in foreign enterprises by residents or in domestic enterprises by nonresidents, or depending on the degree of dispersion of foreign ownership among foreign investors, etc.). In general the percentage chosen as providing evidence of direct investment is low, usually ranging from 25% down to 10%, with a tendency towards the lower end of the range. As regards the United States, the item *direct investment abroad* covers capital transactions between foreign enterprises and US residents who hold at least a 10% ownership interest in the foreign enterprises. The item *direct investment in the United States* covers capital transactions between US enterprises and non-US residents who have at least a 10% ownership interest in the US enterprises (through 1973, foreign direct investment in the US was based on a criterion of 25% ownership).

Let us now come to a brief consideration of theoretical problems.

Portfolio investment, once assumed to be a function of differential yields and of risk diversification, but without a precise framework to fit in, has received an adequate theoretical placing within the general *theory of portfolio selection*. This theory — which has already been treated in Sects. A.10.3.2 and 15.6.2 — states that given a certain amount of funds (wealth) to be placed in a certain set of admissible[11] domestic and foreign assets, and given the rates of return and the direct and cross risk coefficients of the various assets, first the set of *efficient*[12] portfolios is determined, then the *optimum* portfolio in this set is determined by using the investor's utility function. To put it another way, given the stock of wealth, the *optimum stock* of each of the various assets included in the portfolio is a function of the rates of return and risk coefficients of all assets as well as of the "tastes" of the wealth holder (at the same rates of return and risk coefficients, the portfolio of a risk-averse investor will be different from that of a risk lover).

Now, since portfolio investment is an aggregate of *flows*, it is self-evident that these arise if, and only if, the currently owned *stocks* of the various assets relevant to the balance of payments (that is, of foreign financial assets owned by residents, and of domestic financial assets owned by nonresidents) are *different* from the respective optimum stocks. As soon as these are reached by way of the adjustment flows, the flows themselves cease.

Therefore, according to this theory, the existence of continuous flows of portfolio investment derives *both* from the fact that the elements (yields, risk,

---

[11] That is, we exclude illegal financial assets, such as, for example, clandestine capital movements etc., which are mentioned in Sect. A.11.2.

[12] A portfolio, that is a given allocation of funds among the various assets, is efficient if a greater return can be achieved only by accepting a greater risk (or a lower risk can be obtained only by accepting a lower return). See Sect. A.10.3.2.

tastes) underlying the optimum *composition*[13] are not constant but change through time (since the optimum composition changes as they change, continuous adjustment flows will be required) *and* from the fact that the stock of wealth is not itself a constant but changes through time, so that even if the composition were constant, the desired stocks of the various relevant assets change just the same and so adjustment flows take place.

This is a very plausible picture, as even a casual look at world financial markets will confirm that yields and risks are in a state of continual change in all directions (we neglect tastes, not because they are not important, but because they are not directly observable); the stock of financial wealth is also a magnitude in continual evolution.

Thus the theory of portfolio selection is capable of giving a consistent and satisfactory explanation of portfolio investment.

The problem of *direct investment* is much more complicated and does not seem susceptible to a single simple explanation. First of all, it is necessary to dissipate a possible misunderstanding due to the confusion between the *real* and the *financial* aspects of direct investment. Many analyses, in fact, consider direct investment in the context of the theory of international factor mobility treated by the pure theory of international trade (see Sect. 7.7): according to this view, direct investment is nothing more nor less than the movement of the productive factor "(real) capital" between countries. If one accepted this point of view, the causes and effects of direct investment would be those already analyzed by the pure theory of international trade. As regards the *causes*, these should be seen essentially in the existence of different rewards to capital in different countries (this implies that the factor price equalization theorem — see Sect. 4.3 — does not hold), due both to the presence of tariffs (we remember that by the Stolper-Samuelson theorem — see Sect. 5.4.1 — there is a precise relationship between tariffs and factor rewards) and to other elements (such as complete specialization, factor-intensity reversals, etc.). As regards the *effects* on the host country, these could be analyzed by using first of all the Rybczynski theorem (see Sect. 6.4), because the view under consideration implies that direct investment brings about an increase in the capital stock of the country which receives it, and Rybczynski's theorem is the appropriate tool for analyzing the effects of an increase in factor endowments. The problem of the possible repatriation of profits should then be dealt with (if this repatriation were complete, the case might occur in which it entirely absorbs the increase in national income due to the increase in output made possible by the increase in the stock of capital).

All these problems have been fully dealt with in Sects. 7.7 and A.7.6, to which the reader is referred. What we wish to stress is that this formulation, if perfectly valid in the context of the pure theory of international trade, is no longer valid with certainty in the context of international monetary economics. A direct investment does *not* necessarily mean an increase in the physical capital stock of the host

---

[13] It should be remembered that according to the theory of portfolio selection, the composition of both efficient and optimum portfolios is independent of the stock of wealth, which has the role of a scale variable. In other words, one first determines the composition (i.e., the fractions of total wealth allocated to the various assets) and then the stocks of the various assets themselves, by applying these fractions to the stock of wealth.

country. If, for example, the multinational corporation x of country 1 buys the majority of the equities of corporation y in country 2 (previously owned by country 2's residents) the only thing that has happened is an inflow of financial capital (the payment for the equities) into country 2, whose stock of physical capital is *exactly the same* as before[14]. It goes without saying that insofar as the multinational x subsequently transfers entrepreneurship, known-how, etc, to y, there will be "real" effects on country 2, but this is a different story. It has indeed been observed that direct investment is strongly industry-specific: in other words, it is not so much a flow of capital from country 1 to country 2 but rather a flow of capital from industry α of country 1 to industry α of country 2. The typical enterprise which makes direct investment is usually a big corporation which operates in a market with a high product differentiation, and, for this corporation, direct investment is often an alternative to exporting its products, as the ownership of plant in foreign countries facilitates the penetration of foreign markets (see Sect. 8.5).

From this point of view it is clear that the theory of direct investment belongs to the theory of the firm and, to be precise, to the theory of multinational firms (which has had an enormous development in recent times), rather than to general international economics. Therefore we refer the reader to the relevant literature, amongst which Caves (1982) and Buckley and Casson (1985). Reference is made to that literature also for the study of the effects of direct investment on the host country, which are the subject of heated debate. We merely mention the fact that among the pros, the transfer of entrepreneurship and new technology to the host country is pointed out, whilst among the cons the critics point out the exploitation of the host economy (for example when the outflow of repatriated profits becomes higher than the inflow of direct investment), the possible diminution in its sovereignty (the subsidiary responds to the instructions of the parent company rather than to those of the local authorities), the possible checkmating of its economic policies (for example a restrictive monetary policy can be nullified by the subsidiary which has recourse to the financial market of the country of residence of the parent company). An objective balance between the pros and cons is probably impossible, partly because of the political questions that come into play.

17.4 The Transfer Problem

17.4.1 Introductory Remarks

Let us consider a two-country (country 1 and country 2) world, and suppose that country 1 makes a transfer of funds to country 2. The transfers traditionally considered are war reparations[15], donations and the transfers of funds related to

---

[14] This reasoning can of course be applied by analogy to all kinds of financial capital movements (including the clandestine flows treated in Sect. A.11.2).

[15] Indeed, although the transfer problem had already been studied in remote times, the culmination of the debate was in relation to the war reparations that Germany had to pay after the first World War; especially noteworthy is the debate between Keynes (1929) and Ohlin (1929).

long-term capital movements (direct investment, portfolio investment, international loans, etc.).

Although donations and war reparations are unilateral transfers whilst capital movements are bilateral ones[16] (see Sect. 11.1), in the *current period* both types of transactions give rise to the transfer of purchasing power from one country to another. It has therefore been correctly noted that an abrupt increase (by a cartel of producers) in the price of an input not substitutable in the short term (and so having a rigid short-term demand), such as for example oil, also gives rise to a transfer, from the importing to the producing countries.

Thus, in general, a transfer takes place whenever there is an international movement of funds temporarily (for example, the case of a loan, which will subsequently be repaid) or definitively (for example, the case of war reparations) without any *quid pro quo*[17].

Besides the *financial* aspect of the transfer, we must also consider its *real* effects, that is the movement of goods between country 1 and 2 induced by the movement of funds. The *transfer problem* consists in ascertaining whether, account being taken of all the secondary effects induced by the transfer, the balance of payments of the transferor (say, country 1) improves by a sufficient amount to "effect" the transfer. To be precise, in theory, three cases are possible:

(a) Country 1's balance of trade improves by less than (the absolute amount of) the transfer. In this case the transfer is said to be *undereffected*, and country 1's current account balance worsens.
(b) Country 1's trade balance improves by an amount exactly equal to the transfer. In this case the transfer is said to be *effected*, and country 1's current account does not change.
(c) Country 1's trade balance improves by more than the transfer, which is then said to be *overeffected*; country 1's current account improves.

The problem, is, then, to find the conditions under which each of the three possible cases occurs. In the context of the traditional theory one can distinguish the *classical* and the *Keynesian* transfer theory. We shall deal with both, and then examine the problem from a more recent point of view (Sect. 17.4.3).

17.4.2 The Traditional Setting

The basic proposition of the *classical* theory is that the transfer will be undereffected, effected, overeffected, according as the sum of those proportions of the expenditure changes in the two countries which fall on imports (in our simple model they can be identified with the marginal propensities to spend on imports) is less than, equal to, or greater than unity.

---

[16] It goes without saying that, when a loan is granted, there is a transfer of funds in one direction, whilst, when the loan is repaid, a transfer in the opposite direction will take place; in the case of a gradual repayment there will be a series of transfers. One can use a similar argument in the case of the subsquent disinvestment of funds transferred for direct or portfolio investment purposes.

[17] In the case of a loan, of course, the *quid pro quo* exists in the form of an increase in the stock of indebtedness etc., written in the books, but we are looking at the *actual* flow of purchasing power.

The underlying assumptions are that the two countries are in continuous full employment and were in external equilibrium before the transfer; in both, the entire income is spent in the purchase of goods[18]; prices and exchange rate are constant. It is also assumed that the transfer is financed and disposed of in such a way as to reduce the aggregate expenditure of the transferor (country 1) and increase the aggregate expenditure of the transferee (country 2), by the amount of the transfer; this rules out any multiplier effects.

It follows that country 1's imports will decrease by an amount equal to its marginal propensity to spend on imports (μ_1) applied to the expenditure reduction, i.e. to the value of the transfer, and country 2's imports (which are country 1's exports) will increase by an amount equal to its marginal propensity to spend on imports (μ_2) applied to the expenditure increase, i.e. to the value of the transfer. Thus we shall have three effects on country 1's balance of payments:

(i) initial deterioration by an amount equal to the transfer, T;
(ii) improvement due to lower imports, by an amount $\mu_1 T$;
(iii) improvement due to higher exports, by an amount $\mu_2 T$.

The sum of these gives the overall change in the balance of payments:

$$\Delta B_1 = -T + \mu_1 T + \mu_2 T = (\mu_1 + \mu_2 - 1) T. \tag{17.1}$$

It is then clear that the balance of payments will improve ($\Delta B_1 > 0$: overeffected transfer), remain unchanged (effected transfer), deteriorate (undereffected transfer) according as the sum $\mu_1 + \mu_2$ is greater than, equal to, less than unity.

In the case of an overeffected or undereffected transfer, the balance of payments which was initially in equilibrium shows a surplus or deficit respectively, and — since in the classical theory no multiplier effects can take place — the only way to restore external equilibrium is by a *modification in the terms of trade* (which can come about either through a change in the absolute price levels under a gold standard regime, or through an exchange-rate variation: see Sects. 15.2 and 12.1), which will bring about adjustment provided that the suitable elasticity conditions are fulfilled. The traditional opinion was that the sum of the marginal propensities to spend on imports was likely to be smaller than one, so that the transfer would be undereffected and the terms of trade would have to move *against* country 1, to allow the further adjustment via relative prices to take place.

The *Keynesian* theory[19] differs from the classical theory in two respects. Firstly, it drops the assumption that the transferor's aggregate expenditure increases, and the transferee's decreases, by the amount of the transfer. It is, in fact, quite possible that the transfer is financed in such a way that aggregate expenditure in country 1 decreases by less, the difference coming out of saving, and that it is disposed of in such a way that aggregate expenditure in country 2

---

[18] These assumptions were already met with in the pure theory of international trade: see Chap. 3, especially Sects. 3.1 – 3.3.

[19] To avoid misunderstandings it is as well to inform the reader that Keynes, in the debate with Ohlin already cited, was reasoning on the basis of the classical theory. The Keynesian theory is not due to Keynes, but to subsequent authors, notably Metzler (1942b), Machlup (1943, Chap. IX), and Johnson (1956a), to the last of whom our treatment owes much.

increases by less, the difference going to the increase of saving. Secondly, any change in aggregate expenditure due to the transfer is to be taken as an *exogenous* change which gives rise to multiplicative effects on income in both countries (assumed to be underemployed) which have to be accounted for in calculating the induced changes in imports.

The chain of effects is thus much more complicated than that present in the classical theory, and can be summed up as follows:

(1) initial deterioration in country 1's balance of payments by an amount equal to the transfer, T;
(2) changes, concomitant to the transfer, in the autonomous components of expenditure in both countries (including the autonomous components of imports, $\Delta m_{01}, \Delta m_{02}$);
(3) multiplier effects of these changes on both countries' income (via multiplier with foreign repercussions);
(4) induced changes in imports, $\mu_1 \Delta y_1$ and $\mu_2 \Delta y_2$.

The net result of all these effects can be determined only through a formal analysis, based on the multiplier with foreign repercussions treated in Sect. 13.3. For this purpose we introduce the following relations

$$\Delta C_{01} = -b'_1 T, \qquad \Delta C_{02} = b'_2 T,$$
$$\Delta I_{01} = -h'_1 T, \qquad \Delta I_{01} = h'_2 T, \qquad (17.2)$$
$$\Delta m_{01} = -\mu'_1 T, \qquad \Delta m_{02} = \mu'_2 T,$$

where $\Delta C_{01}, \Delta I_{01}, \Delta m_{01}$ denote, as usual, the changes (concomitant to the transfer) in the exogenous components of country 1's expenditure functions, and b'_1, h'_1, μ'_1 are coefficients which relate these exogenous changes to the transfer (the minus sign indicates that these changes are negative, as country 1 is the transferor); the primes are used to distinguish them from the marginal propensities, which refer to the induced changes depending on income. Similar considerations hold for country 2, the transferee.

If we examine country 1's balance of payments, we see that

$$\Delta B_1 = -T + (\Delta m_{02} - \Delta m_{01}) + (\mu_2 \Delta y_2 - \mu_1 \Delta y_1), \qquad (17.3)$$

which are the effects mentioned in points (1),(3),(4) above, in that order. If we substitute Δm_{02} and Δm_{01} from (17.2) into (17.3) and also substitute the expressions for Δy_1 and Δy_2 coming from the foreign multiplier (the effects mentioned in point (2) above) we get, after some manipulations (see Sect. A.17.2), the result that the transfer will be overeffected, effected, undereffected ($\Delta B_1 \gtreqless 0$), according as

$$\mu'_1 + \mu'_2 \gtreqless 1 + \frac{\mu_1}{1 - b_1 - h_1}(1 - b'_1 - h'_1)$$
$$+ \frac{\mu_2}{1 - b_2 - h_2}(1 - b'_2 - h'_2), \qquad (17.4)$$

that is, according as the sum of the proportions of the transfer by which the *exogenous* expenditure on imports is altered by the financing (μ'_1) and disposal

(μ'_2) of the transfer is greater than, equal to, less than the critical value expressed by the right-hand side of Eq. (17.4).

This result, due to Johnson (1956a), is contrary to results previously found by other writers, such as Machlup (1943) and Metzler (1942b). These writers — in the context of the Keynesian theory and under the assumption that the sum of the marginal propensity to consume and the marginal propensity to invest is lower than one in both countries — had found that the transfer is necessarily undereffected and had contrasted this result of the Keynesian transfer theory with that of the classical one, according to which, as we have seen above, the transfer can in principle also be effected or overeffected. However, the result of Machlup and Metzler was due to particular additional assumptions, namely

(a) the transfer does not directly affect the demand for imports (μ'_1 and μ'_2 are zero) and changes the demand for domestic goods either by the amount of the transfer (the magnitudes ($b'_1+h'_1$) and ($b'_2+h'_2$) are equal to one) or not at all (these magnitudes are zero);

or

(b) the transfer affects the various demands exactly as any income change (in each country the primed parameters are equal to the corresponding unprimed ones: $b'=b$, etc.).

It is then easy to verify, by simple substitutions, that in both cases (a) and (b), inequality (17.4) is fulfilled with the sign $<$, so that $\Delta B_1 < 0$. It is thus possible to state that (17.4) is the general case[20], which includes the others as particular cases.

In the case of a not effected transfer, the balance of payments, which was assumed to be in equilibrium prior to the transfer, will show an imbalance. It is then usual to state that, at this point, the various adjustment mechanisms (examined in the previous chapters) come into play, and will restore external equilibrium provided that the relevant stability conditions are satisfied.

If, for example, one is considering the current account balance, then an exchange-rate variation has to be brought into the picture, and the equilibrating effects of this variation will depend on whether the condition examined in Sect. 14.3 is fulfilled; the fact that this condition has to be used instead of those examined in Sect. 12.2, depends on the circumstance that one must account for the further income changes caused by the exchange-rate variation. Thus, for example, in the case of an undereffected transfer, an exchange-rate depreciation will come about (and thus a deterioration in the terms of trade), which will restore external equilibrium, if condition (14.12) occurs [or, in the case of a two-country model, condition (A.14.26)].

If, instead, the overall balance of payments is considered, one can use one of the models of macroeconomic equilibrium in an open economy, under either fixed (Sects. 15.4 ff.) or flexible (Sects. 16.2. ff.) exchange rates.

This, as we said, is the standard opinion which, however, needs to be commented on at some length to arrive at an alternative point of view.

---

[20] According to Metzler (1973a), the price of this generality is the ambiguity in the results, as nothing can be inferred about ΔB_1 unless something is known about the relative values of the primed and unprimed propensities (p. 89).

17.4.3 Observations and Qualifications

The traditional opinion represents a simplification because it amounts to saying that the effectuation of the transfer can be separated into two phases. The first consists of ascertaining whether the transfer is effected, by applying the chosen model (either the classical or the Keynesian). If it is not, there will remain a balance-of-payments disequilibrium, which must be corrected by some adjustment process (second phase). This process is a change in the terms of trade (according to the classical theory), or some other adjustment process (excluding, of course, the multiplier mechanism which has already worked itself out in the first phase of the Keynesian approach).

But, more rigorously, the transfer problem ought to be tackled *from the very beginning* in the context of the adjustment process chosen for the second phase in the two-stage traditional approach (note that this phase is not only possible but very likely, since the conditions for the transfer to be effected are unlikely to occur).

This approach does not present any special difficulty, because *the transfer problem can be examined as any comparative static problem* in the context of the model chosen; it excludes, however, the possibility of enunciating a *general theory* of the transfer, as the traditional approach (whether classical or Keynesian) proposed to do. In fact, different comparative-static results and so different conditions for the transfer to be effected will prevail according as one or the other model is used. From this point of view condition (17.4), once believed to be "*the*" general condition, is nothing more than the condition deriving from the application of the multiplier model with repercussions (described in Sect. 13.3) to the transfer problem.

Simply in order to illustrate how the alternative approach can be used, we now show the way the transfer problem can be examined in the context of the model of macroeconomic equilibrium in a standard Keynesian-type open model under fixed exchange rates, as described in Sect. 15.4.

It goes without saying that, as this is a flow model, the implicit assumption is that the transfer is itself a flow; besides, we are in the context of a small country model.

The point of departure consists in finding out the *initial* impact of the transfer on the balance of payments and income of the transferor, so as to determine the shifts in the various schedules and the new equilibrium point. For this purpose we can accept what was said in relation to the Keynesian transfer theory at points (1) and (2) in Sect. 17.4.2: indeed, the idea that the transfer is associated with changes in the autonomous components of the expenditure functions of the two countries has a general validity which goes beyond the Keynesian transfer theory.

The initial impact of the transfer on the balance of payments will then be given by the expression

$$-T + (\Delta m_{02} - \Delta m_{01}) = (\mu'_1 + \mu'_2 - 1) T, \qquad (17.5)$$

where we have used Eqs. (17.2). This expression can be either positive or negative: in the former case the *BB* schedule will shift to the right, in the latter to the left (see Fig. 17.3).

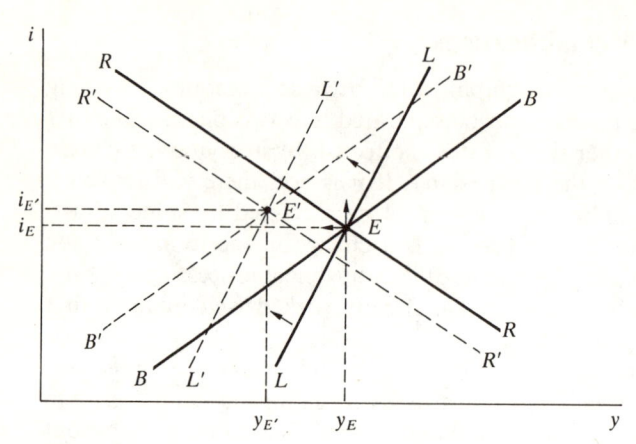

Fig. 17.3. The transfer problem in the context of the standard macroeconomic model under fixed exchange rates

As regards the impact effect of the transfer on income, this will be

$$\Delta C_{01} + \Delta I_{01} + \Delta m_{02} - \Delta m_{01} = (\mu'_1 + \mu'_2 - b'_1 - h'_1)T, \quad (17.6)$$

which can be either positive or negative: in the former case the RR schedule will shift to the right, in the latter to the left. Note that, if one assumes[21] that $b'_1 + h'_1 < 1$, then (17.6) is positive when (17.5) is positive. The converse is not true, however, so that we can eliminate only one of the four theoretically possible combinations and we are left with three to be examined. We shall limit ourselves to an examination of only one, for example that in which both (17.5) and (17.6) are negative. The situation can be analyzed graphically by way of the method explained in Sect. 15.4.4. Consider Fig. 17.3, where E is the initial equilibrium point. In the case before us, both BB and RR will shift to the left, for example to $B'B'$ and $R'R'$. At E we have a balance-of-payments deficit and so a decrease in the supply of money (the LL schedule shifts to the left), so that the resulting excess demand for money causes the interest rate to increase (arrow pointing upwards from E). At E there is also an excess supply of goods and so income tends to decrease (arrow pointing leftwards from E).

The reader will have recognized the dynamic adjustment process described in Sect. 15.4.3. We assume that the stability conditions mentioned there occur, so that the system will converge to its new equilibrium point E': as we said at the end of Sect. 15.4.4, the process of transition from the old to the new equilibrium is ensured by the stability conditions.

At the new equilibrium point E', income will be lower, the interest rate higher and the money supply lower[22] than at the initial equilibrium point E. But we are

---

[21] This seems a plausible assumption, as it amounts to assuming that the process of financing the transfer leads to an exogenous change in the transferor's aggregate expenditure by an amount smaller than the transfer, the difference coming out of dissaving.

[22] Whilst income is necessarily lower, the interest rate is not necessarily higher, as the reader can verify graphically (this is related to the magnitude of the marginal propensity to aggregate spending). Consequently the money supply is not necessarily lower (this is related to the slope of the LL schedule relative to that of the BB schedule). See Sect. A.17.2.

not so much interested in this as in the fact that at E' *balance-of-payments equilibrium* prevails: the transfer is *effected*. This is worthy of note because this is a case in which the transfer would be undereffected according to the Keynesian transfer theory. In fact, as we have assumed that (17.5) is negative, we have $\mu'_1 + \mu'_2 < 1$ and so inequality (17.4) — under the assumptions that the sum of the marginal propensity to consume and the marginal propensity to invest is less than one in both countries and also that $b'_i + h'_i < 1$ — is necessarily fulfilled with the $<$ sign.

Thus we find the confirmation of the statement made above, that it is not possible to enunciate general rules or formulae as regards the effectuation of the transfer, since the result — for the same initial situation — will depend on the type of model being utilized to analyze the transfer problem.

We conclude this section with some observations aimed at avoiding confusion.

We said at the beginning (Sect. 17.4.1) that the transfer problem consists in determining whether the transferor (country 1) will achieve the trade surplus necessary to effect the transfer. This is equivalent to saying that after the financial transfer, country 1 "transfers" goods to country 2 (a real transfer) through the trade surplus (which means that country 1 has released to country 2 goods having a value greater than that of the goods acquired) so as to obtain the funds required to effect the initial financial transfer. From this point of view it has often been stated that *the transfer problem can be considered as the "inversion" of the balance-of-payments problem*, since any actual balance-of-payments disequilibrium involves a real transfer from the surplus to the deficit country. Therefore, the problem of rectifying balance-of-payments disequilibria can be framed as the problem of creating either a real transfer of equal amount in the opposite direction (i.e. from the deficit to the surplus country) or a financial transfer from the surplus to the deficit country.

All this is undoubtedly true in the traditional context, in which the focus of the analysis is the current account. In this context the only way of effecting the initial transfer of funds is to achieve a trade surplus (i.e. to make a real transfer) and, inversely, a deficit country, by receiving (in value) more goods than it releases, receives a real transfer. But as soon as one considers the *overall* balance of payments which includes capital movements, none of the above statements is necessarily true any longer. The initial transfer of funds can also be effected by way of a capital flow determined by an increase in the interest rate (actually this is what happens in the model underlying Fig. 17.3) and, inversely, a deficit country can be in deficit because, though it enjoys a trade surplus (so that it makes, instead of receiving, a real transfer), it suffers from a higher deficit in the capital account. It is therefore advisable, when one reads the literature on the transfer problem, to pay a great deal of attention to the context in which the writer develops the argument.

17.5 Exports, Growth, and the Balance of Payments

The relations between growth and international economics can be examined both in the context of the pure theory of international trade (for which see Chap. 6) and in the context of open-economy macroeconomics, as we shall do in this section.

The macroeconomic theory of growth, after the pioneering contributions of Harrod (1948), Solow (1956) and Swan (1956), and Kaldor (1957), gave rise in the late fifties and in the sixties to an immense literature, which we cannot even mention here (the reader is referred, for example, to the textbooks by Burmeister and Dobell, 1970, and Wan, 1971). Nor is it possible to give an adequate treatment of all those models attempting an extension to an open economy of the various growth models, originally conceived for a closed economy. We shall therefore only treat — and at that very briefly — two questions which in our opinion deserve a closer examination:

(a) whether it is possible to talk of a mechanism of *export-led* growth;
(b) whether, given an economic system which is growing for internal causes, this growth has favourable or unfavourable effects on the system's balance of payments.

17.5.1 Export-led Growth

The basic idea is that the increase in exports exerts a favourable effect on investment and productivity, so that a country with rapidly expanding exports will see its growth enhanced; an underemployment situation is, of course, assumed. The two best-known and pioneering models in this vein are the Lamfalussy (1963) and the Beckerman (1962) models, which can be considered as complementary.

The *Lamfalussy model* (which we propose to treat following the revisions of Caves (1970) and of Stern (1973)), starts from the assumption that the investment ratio (to income) depends also on the ratio of exports to income, i.e.

$$\frac{I}{y} = h'\frac{x}{y} + h, \tag{17.7}$$

where the symbols have the usual meanings and the variables are expressed in real terms, in a context of rigid prices and exchange rates. The parameter h can be interpreted as the usual marginal propensity to invest: in fact, if we multiply through by y, we get

$$I = h'x + hy. \tag{17.7.1}$$

The parameter h' reflects the assumption that a rate of expansion of exports higher than that of the other components of national income causes an increase in the desired investment rate, for example because the sectors producing exportables are the most innovating sectors as they are exposed to international competition.

Saving is a function not only of income (as in the traditional Keynesian model) but also of the change in income, to account for the fact that growth may have a positive influence on the average propensity to save (for example because the distribution of income will change in favour of categories with a higher propensity to save). Thus the proportional saving function is

$$\frac{S}{y} = s'\frac{\Delta y}{y} + s, \qquad (17.8)$$

where s is the marginal propensity to save (as can be verified by multiplying through by y) and s' represents the effect of growth. The import equation also embodies a marginal effect (μ') for growth in income:

$$\frac{m}{y} = \mu'\frac{\Delta y}{y} + \mu, \qquad (17.9)$$

where μ is the marginal propensity to import.

The equation for the determination of income in an open economy

$$S + m = I + x, \qquad (17.10)$$

closes the model. If we divide both sides of Eq. (17.10) by y, we get

$$\frac{S}{y} + \frac{m}{y} = \frac{I}{y} + \frac{x}{y}, \qquad (17.11)$$

whence, by substituting the previous equations into it and solving for the rate of growth of income, we get

$$\frac{\Delta y}{y} = \frac{1+h'}{s'+\mu'}\frac{x}{y} + \frac{h-\mu-s}{s'+\mu'}. \qquad (17.12)$$

From this equation we immediately see that an increase in x/y has a favourable influence on the rate of growth of income.

The *Beckerman model* differs from the Lamfalussy model because it more directly focusses on productivity, prices, and wages. The basic equations of the model are

$$\frac{\Delta x}{x} = \alpha + \beta\left(1 - \frac{p}{p_f}\right), \quad \alpha > 0, \, \beta > 0, \qquad (17.13)$$

$$\frac{\Delta Q}{Q} = \gamma + \delta\frac{\Delta x}{x}, \quad \gamma > 0, \, \delta > 0, \qquad (17.14)$$

$$\frac{\Delta w}{w} = \theta + \lambda\frac{\Delta Q}{Q}, \quad \theta > 0, \, 0 < \lambda < 1, \qquad (17.15)$$

$$\frac{\Delta p}{p} = \frac{\Delta w}{w} - \frac{\Delta Q}{Q}. \qquad (17.16)$$

The export equation relates the rate of growth of exports to the terms of trade, that is, as the exchange rate is rigid by assumption, to the ratio of domestic (p) to foreign (p_f) prices: if this ratio is less than one this means that domestic prices are lower than foreign prices and so exports are enhanced, with a favourable effect on the rate of growth of exports themselves; conversely in the opposite case. The parameter α represents the average rate of growth of world trade (exports), so that Eq. (17.13) states that when domestic goods compete favourably with foreign goods ($p<p_f$), the country's exports will grow at a higher proportional rate than the world average, and conversely in the opposite case.

The second equation considers productivity (Q) and directly relates its rate of growth to the rate of growth of exports. The reason behind this link is similar to that already commented on in Lamfalussy's model: since the sectors which are producing exportables are generally the most innovative and those in which the productivity increases are the largest, a more rapid growth in these sectors has beneficial effects on the productivity of the whole economic system, which are added to the rate of increase of productivity (γ) due to other factors (technical progress etc.).

The third equation incorporates a precise assumption on the rate of growth of the money wage rate, which states that it grows both for exogenous factors (wage negotiations, etc.), represented by the rate θ, and for the increase in productivity, but in such a way that any increase in the rate of growth of productivity raises the rate of growth of the wage rate by a *smaller* amount, as reflected in the assumption that the coefficient λ is strictly included between zero and one.

The fourth equation expresses the rate of growth of prices as the difference between the rate of growth of the wage rate and the rate of growth of productivity. This can be interpreted either along neoclassical lines or by assuming a price-formation equation based on a markup on unit labour costs. In the former case, the condition of equality between the value of the (marginal) productivity of a factor and its reward, when applied to labour, gives $pQ=w$, whence by simple manipulations[23] Eq. (17.16) is obtained. In the latter case the markup equation is $p=g(w/Q)$, where $g>1$ is the markup coefficient and Q is interpreted as the average productivity: simple manipulations[24] will again yield Eq. (17.16).

If we substitute the third equation into the fourth we get

$$\frac{\Delta p}{p} = \theta + (\lambda-1)\frac{\Delta Q}{Q}, \tag{17.16.1}$$

from which we see that, thanks to the assumption $0<\lambda<1$, an increase in productivity has a favourable effect on prices, as it tends to curb their rate of increase.

Let us now assume that at a certain moment the country has a competitive advantage in trade, that is, $p<p_f$. From Eqs. (17.13) and (17.14), we see that the rate of growth of productivity is enhanced; consequently — Eq. (17.16.1) — the rate of increase in prices is depressed. It follows that, as the rate of increase of foreign prices is exogenously given, the initial price disparity is accentuated, hence the rate of growth of productivity is enhanced, and so on and so forth. Thus a kind of "virtuous circle" exports-productivity (and hence growth in income) starts off.

---

[23] If one considers the changes and neglects the second order of smalls, one gets $Q\Delta p + p\Delta Q = \Delta w$; by dividing through by $pQ=w$ and rearranging terms one obtains Eq. (17.16).

[24] From the formal point of view the equation can be written as $pQ=gw$. Since g is a constant, the equation for the changes is $Q\Delta p + p\Delta Q$; by dividing through by $pQ=gw$ and rearranging terms Eq. (17.16) is immediately obtained.

It goes without saying that this circle may also be vicious: if the country has a competitive disadvantage ($p > p_f$), the rate of growth of exports (and hence of productivity) is depressed; this raises the rate of growth of prices and so further increases the disadvantage, etc.

Both the Beckerman and the Lamfalussy models have been criticized especially as regards the basic assumptions, which have been regarded as unwarranted or oversimplified (for example, the inflationary mechanism is more complicated than that embodied in Eq. (17.16), etc.). This criticism is sensible, but it must not lead us to reject the idea than an export-led growth mechanism exists. This idea, however, can receive adequate treatment only in much more complicated models, which we cannot deal with here (for an example, see Gandolfo and Padoan, 1990). For a revival of the theory of export-led growth, see Thirlwall (1980), McCombie (1985), McGregor and Swales (1985).

17.5.2 Growth and the Balance of Payments

Let us now consider the second problem. In the context of a simple Keynesian model with rigid prices and exchange rates, and given *exogenously* the time path of exports, the obvious conclusion is that growth for internal causes has an unfavourable effect on the balance of payments. In fact, the more income grows, the more imports grow, so that, given the path of exports, the balance of payments (in the sense of balance on goods and services) is affected unfavourably. It follows that growth finds a limitation in the balance-of-payments restraint or, more precisely, in the international reserves restraint (which enable the country to finance its balance-of-payments deficits, but only up to the point below which reserves cannot be allowed to fall).

But some writers (see, for example, Mundell, 1968) point to the experience of countries that have grown rapidly in the post-World War II period (Germany, France, Italy, etc.) and enjoyed a surplus, as evidence to the contrary. This would however be easy to rebut by showing that this experience is not in itself sufficient evidence, as these countries might well have enjoyed export-led growth, in which case it is not surprising that growth *and* balance-of-payments surplus have gone hand in hand. In fact if we again take up, for example, the Lamfalussy model explained in Sect. 17.5.1, and express the balance of payments as a function of the rate of growth of income, we get

$$\frac{x-m}{y} = \frac{s' - h'\mu'}{1+h'} \frac{\Delta y}{y} + \frac{s - h - h'\mu}{1+h'}, \qquad (17.17)$$

from which we see that when income growth is led by exports, the balance of payments will be favourably or unfavourably affected according as

$$s' - h'\mu' \gtreqless 0. \qquad (17.17.1)$$

This inequality can in principle occur with any sign, and so, if it occurs with the $>$ sign, income growth will favourably affect the balance of payments.

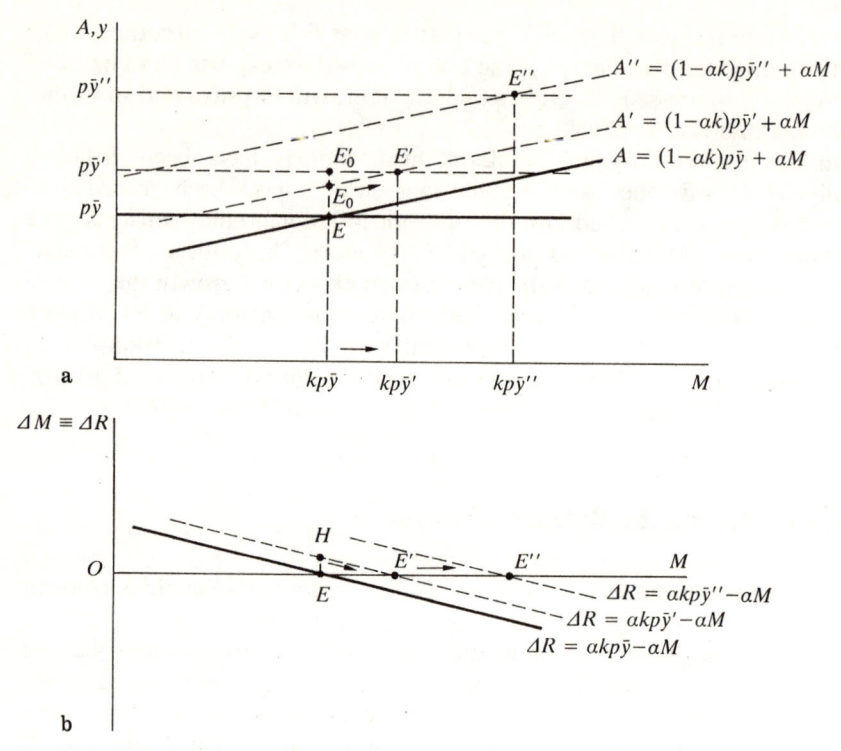

Fig. 17.4. Growth and the balance of payments according to the MABP

To avoid confusion, it is therefore necessary to use models in which the rate of growth of income is *not* causally related to exports through an export-led mechanism: only in this way, in fact, the question under consideration can be answered unambiguously. We shall therefore assume that income growth is due to internal factors and is not of the export-led type.

In this framework the answer will depend on the type of model that we use. From the point of view of the traditional Keynesian model the answer given at the beginning of this section remains valid. On the contrary, the answer is exactly the opposite if one uses the monetary approach to the balance of payments (MABP) explained in Sect. 15.3.

In fact, if one assumes that income is growing (always remaining at the full employment level) and that prices and the exchange rate are rigid, it follows from the MABP that the balance of payments will improve. This is so because an increase in income raises the demand for money and so, at unchanged stock of money, an excess demand for money will come about which will generate a balance-of-payments surplus through the mechanism described in Sect. 15.3. It is true that, by increasing the stock of money, this surplus will reduce the excess demand for money and so will tend to eliminate itself automatically; but the continuing income growth will again give rise to an excess demand for money and so the balance-of-payments surplus will be recreated by a continual knock-on effect.

This phenomenon can be easily described graphically by taking up Fig. 15.2 again. In Fig. 17.4 the initial equilibrium point is E. Income grows, for example to $\bar{y}'$, so that the various schedules shift to the positions indicated by the broken lines. We immediately see from panel (b) of the figure that now a *surplus* of HE (equal to $E'_0 E_0$ in panel (a) of the figure) corresponds to the initial point E (which is no longer an equilibrium point: the new equilibrium point is E'). The increase in the stock of money generated by the surplus makes the economic system move towards E', as can be seen from panel (a) of the figure. In the course of this movement the surplus tends to disappear, but in the meantime income continues to grow, and goes from $\bar{y}'$ to, say, $\bar{y}''$: the schedules shift to the second position indicated by the broken lines with a double prime, and so on and so forth.

It goes without saying that this phenomenon is valid insofar as the basic model is valid, so that those who do not accept the MABP (see the criticism at the end of Sect. 15.3.3) will not accept the thesis that growth favourably affects the balance of payments. Leaving aside this debate, it is necessary to point out a somewhat paradoxical consequence of the thesis in question, which arises as soon as we abandon the small country framework. In fact, if we look at the problem from a world point of view and bear in mind that it is not possible for all countries to have a balance-of-payments surplus at one and the same time, it follows that countries with positive income growth and balance-of-payments surpluses will have to be matched by countries with negative income growth and balance-of-payments deficits. There would then seem to be a kind of exploitation of the latter group by the former, a situation which cannot be maintained in the long run, unless places are swapped every now and then.

For further considerations on the relations between growth and the balance of payments see Sect. A.17.3.

Appendix

A.17.1 Speculation

The debate on speculation under flexible exchange rates treated in Sect. 17.2.2 can be condensed into two questions:

(a) whether profitable speculation is necessarily stabilizing, or, on the contrary, whether profitable *and* destabilizing speculation can exist;
(b) whether speculation can stabilize an otherwise unstable market (that is, one without the presence of speculation). Note that here "stabilizing" has a stronger meaning than usual: the problem is not, in fact, to make an already stable market more stable (stabilizing speculation in a weak sense), but to make a market stable which is in itself unstable, where unstable means a time path of the exchange rate which diverges — monotonically or with explosive oscillations — from its equilibrium or reference value (stabilizing speculation in a strong sense).

Question (a) has already been answered in the text: the counterexample by Kemp does, in fact, satisfactorily show the possibility of profitable and destabilizing speculation (for a general treatment see Orosel, 1984), nor could it be rebutted by observing that it requires the presence of multiple equilibria: we know, in fact (see Sect. 12.3), that multiple equilibria are not an extraordinary event.

As regards question (b), let us consider a very simple example, that is, a foreign-exchange market where initially only commercial operators are present and such that the condition of critical elasticities is *not* fulfilled. In this case, as we know from the analysis carried out in Chap. 12 (see especially Sect. A.12.2), the foreign-exchange market is unstable. We now introduce speculators and assume that they behave *à la Friedman* (1953), that is, they purchase foreign exchange when its price is low (i.e. when the exchange rate is below its normal value) and sell it when its price is high (i.e. when the exchange rate is above its normal value).

If by "normal" value we mean the equilibrium exchange rate[25], we can write the speculators' excess demand for foreign exchange as

$$E_s(r) = a(r_e - r), \quad (A.17.1)$$

where the linear form has been used for simplicity's sake and $a > 0$ is a parameter which reflects the intensity of intervention of speculators. Note that Eq. (A.17.1) is of the same type as Eq. (A.12.35) discussed in Sect. A.12.3: the assumption that we have introduced is, in fact, equivalent to assuming that speculators anticipate a return of the exchange rate to its equilibrium value.

The total excess demand for foreign exchange is now

$$E(r) = -B'(r) + E_s(r), \quad (A.17.2)$$

where

$$B'(r) = \frac{1}{r} p_x x(r) - p_m m(r) \quad (A.17.2.1)$$

represents the excess demand coming from traders. The usual dynamic behaviour assumption of the exchange rate varying in relation to excess demand for foreign exchange gives the equation

$$\frac{dr}{dt} = kE(r), \quad k > 0, \quad (A.17.2.2)$$

whence, by linearizing at the equilibrium point,

$$\frac{d\bar{r}}{dt} = -k\left(\frac{dB'}{dr} + a\right)\bar{r}. \quad (A.17.3)$$

The stability condition is

$$\frac{dB'}{dr} + a > 0. \quad (A.17.4)$$

---

[25] It is a common opinion of many writers on this topic that speculators are better informed than the other agents and so are able to evaluate the equilibrium exchange rate with a fair degree of accuracy (in the case of rational expectations, they know it precisely). This opinion could be discussed, but the discussion is not of interest to us here.

We know from the analysis in Chap. 12 — see (A.12.5) — that dB'/dr depends on the elasticities; as we have assumed that the critical condition does *not* occur, dB'/dr will be negative and so — as stated above — in the absence of speculation ($a=0$) the equilibrium is unstable. The presence of speculation has a stabilizing effect in a strong sense: in fact, for a sufficiently great (i.e. for a sufficiently intense intervention of speculators), condition (A.17.4) will be fulfilled notwithstanding the negativity of dB'/dr.

The very simple model presented here can be rendered more complex by introducing adjustment lags (like those underlying the J-curve, discussed in Sect. A.14.3), rational expectations, etc.: see, for example, Britton (1970), Levin (1983a), and the references quoted by the latter. The basic idea does however remain the same, that is, that a foreign-exchange market, which is unstable in the absence of speculation, can be rendered stable by the introduction of speculative activity, *provided that the intervention of speculators is sufficiently intense*.

We conclude by observing that all the analyses so far mentioned consider only the foreign-exchange market and, as regards exports and imports, consider only their dependence on the exchange rate via elasticities (which, to be correct, must be taken as partial elasticities: see Sect. 12.2.3); all the other variables are, therefore, explicitly or implicitly considered as exogenous. For an interesting attempt at examining speculation in the context of a macroeconomic model of an economy see Casprini (1974); see also Minford (1978) and Eaton and Turnovsky (1984).

A.17.2 The Transfer Problem

The Keynesian transfer problem can be readily analyzed by way of the foreign-multiplier formulae derived in Chap. 13, especially in Eqs. (A.13.20). If we adopt the same symbols as there, we have

$$dB_1 = -T + d\alpha_{2m} - d\alpha_{1m} + \mu_2 dy_2 - \mu_1 dy_1, \qquad (A.17.5)$$

whence, if we let

$$d\alpha_{1C} = -b'_1 T, \; d\alpha_{1I} = -h'_1 T, \; d\alpha_{1m} = -\mu'_1 T,$$
$$d\alpha_{2C} = b'_2 T, \; d\alpha_{2I} = h'_2 T, \; d\alpha_{2m} = \mu'_2 T, \qquad (A.17.6)$$

and substitute these expressions in (A.13.20), we get

$$dy_1 = \frac{(1-b_2-h_2)(-b'_1-h'_1+\mu'_2+\mu'_1) + \mu_2(-b'_1-h'_1+b'_2+h'_2)}{|J|} T, \qquad (A.17.7)$$

$$dy_2 = \frac{(1-b_1-h_1)(b'_2+h'_2-\mu'_1-\mu'_2) + \mu_1(-b'_1-h'_1+b'_2+h'_2)}{|J|} T,$$

where

$$|J| = (1-b_1-h_1+\mu_1)(1-b_2-h_2+\mu_2) - \mu_1\mu_2 \qquad (A.17.8)$$

is positive owing to the stability conditions (A.13.24).

If we now substitute (A.17.7) into (A.17.5) where we also substitute $d\alpha_{2m}$ and $d\alpha_{1m}$, as defined in (A.17.6), after simplifications we get

$$dB_1 = [\mu'_1 + \mu'_2 - \frac{\mu_1}{1-b_1-h_1}(1-b'_1-h'_1)$$

$$- \frac{\mu_2}{1-b_2-h_2}(1-b'_2-h'_2)$$

$$-1]\frac{(1-b_1-h_1)(1-b_2-h_2)}{|J|}T. \qquad (A.17.9)$$

Therefore, if we adopt the assumption — usually made in transfer theory — that $(1-b_1-h_1)$ and $(1-b_2-h_2)$ are both positive[26], dB_1 will be positive, zero, or negative according as the expression in square brackets in (A.17.9) is positive, zero, or negative, whence (17.4) in the text.

It is just as easy to analyze the transfer problem in the context of the standard macroeconomic model of an open economy: all what is required, in fact, is an exercise in comparative statics on the model treated in Chap. 15, especially section A.15.3. If we introduce the transfer T as a parameter and assume that it alters the exogenous components of expenditure as shown in (A.17.5), we get[27]

$$y = d(y,i) + x_0 + (-b'_1 - h'_1 + \mu'_1 + \mu'_2)T,$$

$$x_0 - m(y,i) + K(i) + (\mu'_1 + \mu'_2 - 1)T = 0, \qquad (A.17.10)$$

$$L(y,i) - M = 0,$$

where $T=0$ initially. If we differentiate the system with respect to T (we already know from the analysis of Sect. A.15.3.3, that the relevant Jacobian is different from zero) we get

$$(1-d_y)\frac{\partial y}{\partial T} - d_i\frac{\partial i}{\partial T} = -b'_1 - h'_1 + \mu'_1 + \mu'_2,$$

$$m_y\frac{\partial y}{\partial T} + (m_i - K_i)\frac{\partial i}{\partial T} = \mu'_1 + \mu'_2 - 1, \qquad (A.17.11)$$

$$L_y\frac{\partial y}{\partial T} + L_i\frac{\partial i}{\partial T} - \frac{\partial M}{\partial T} = 0,$$

---

[26] It should be remembered from the stability analysis carried out in Sect. A.13.2, that of these expressions one may also be positive and the other negative, so that the positivity of both is an *additional* assumption.

[27] It should be observed that, in the text, we have considered the transfer as influencing the *variations* in the exogenous components, whilst in (A.17.10) it apparently influences the levels. If, however, we remember that $T=0$ *initially*, so that in the *new* situation $dT=T$, then the difference disappears.

from which

$$\frac{\partial y}{\partial T} = \frac{(\mu'_1+\mu'_2-b'_1-h'_1)(K_i-m_i) - (\mu'_1+\mu'_2-1)d_i}{D},$$

$$\frac{\partial i}{\partial T} = \frac{-(1-d_y)(\mu'_1+\mu'_2-1) + m_y(\mu'_1+\mu'_2-b'_1-h'_1)}{D}, \quad (A.17.12)$$

$$\frac{\partial M}{\partial T} = \frac{(\mu'_1+\mu'_2-b'_1-h'_1)[L_im_y+L_y(K_i-m_i)] - (\mu'_1+\mu'_2-1)[L_i(1-d_y)+L_yd_i]}{D},$$

where

$$D \equiv (1-d_y)(K_i-m_i) - m_yd_i. \quad (A.17.12.1)$$

If (as assumed in Sect. 17.4.2), $\mu'_1+\mu'_2-b'_1-h'_1<0$, and $\mu'_1+\mu'_2-1<0$, then — account being taken of the signs of the various partial derivatives and since $D>0$ by the stability conditions — we find

$$\frac{\partial y}{\partial T} < 0, \quad \frac{\partial i}{\partial T} \gtrless 0, \quad \frac{\partial M}{\partial T} \gtrless 0. \quad (A.17.13)$$

As regards the interest rate, we observe that, since $\mu'_1+\mu'_2-1<\mu'_1+\mu'_2-b'_1-h'_1<0$, the derivative $\partial i/\partial T$ will certainly be positive if $-(1-d_y) < -m_y$. In other words, the interest rate will increase if

$$d_y + m_y < 1, \quad (A.17.13.1)$$

i.e. if the marginal propensity to aggregate spending (which, given the definition of d_y, equals $b+h$) is less than one.

As regards the stock of money, it will decrease ($\partial M/\partial T<0$) if $L_im_y+L_y(K_i-m_i)>0$, i.e. if

$$\frac{m_y}{K_i-m_i} < -\frac{L_y}{L_i}, \quad (A.17.13.2)$$

that is — if we remember Eqs. (A.15.31) — if the slope of BB is smaller than that of LL.

This analysis, it should be remembered, is valid in the context of a small country model; a more general analysis could be carried out in the context of a two-country model, for example, by using the model which was used for other purposes in Sect. A.16.3.2.

A.17.3 Exports, Growth, and the Balance of Payments

Besides the Lamfalussy and Beckerman models, various other models of export-led growth have been produced (see, for example, Thirlwall, 1980; McGregor and Swales, 1985; McCombie, 1985). These models are, however, too simple to be capable of embodying all the complicated interrelations between the numerous real and financial variables involved in the phenomenon of export-led growth. An attempt in the direction of a more complete model has been carried out by

Gandolfo and Padoan (1990), but this is too cumbersome a model to examine here.

As regards the thesis that growth can have favourable effects on the balance of payments in the context of the MABP, the original enunciation by Mundell (1968) is based on a model containing errors, as shown by Reid (1973) and Wein (1974). It is however possible to show the validity of the thesis under consideration, by correctly formalizing it.

For this purpose we shall again take up the model explained in Sect. A.15.2 and consider the system of differential equations

$$\frac{dM}{dt} = \alpha(kpy - M),$$
$$\frac{dy}{dt} = \lambda y, \qquad (A.17.14)$$

where, for simplicity of notation, we have omitted the bar over the symbol y (which, it will be remembered, denotes full employment income).

The first equation is already known, the second expresses the hypothesis that full employment income grows in time at the rate λ. This system can be solved explicitly (see, for example, Gandolfo, 1980, Part II, Chap. 8); the solution is

$$y(t) = y_0 e^{\lambda t},$$
$$M(t) = \left(M_0 - \frac{\alpha k p y_0}{\alpha + \lambda}\right) e^{-\alpha t} + \frac{\alpha k p y_0}{\alpha + \lambda} e^{\lambda t}, \qquad (A.17.15)$$

where M_0 and y_0 are the initial values of y and M. Since we have, as we know

$$B(t) = dR/dt = dM/dt, \qquad (A.17.16)$$

by differentiating the second equation in (A.17.15) with respect to time, we obtain

$$B(t) = -\alpha\left(M_0 - \frac{\alpha k p y_0}{\alpha + \lambda}\right) e^{-\alpha t} + \frac{\alpha \lambda k p y_0}{\alpha + \lambda} e^{\lambda t}. \qquad (A.17.17)$$

From this equation we see that, since the first term tends to zero asymptotically whilst the second is positive and increasing, in the long run the balance of payments will definitely show an increasing surplus. To ascertain what happens in the short-run, we must know the initial situation in the balance of payments. If, as assumed in the text, the system is initially in equilibrium (that is, the stock of money is equal to the demand for money, hence absorption equals income and the balance of payments is in equilibrium), then

$$M_0 = kpy_0, \qquad (A.17.18)$$

so that Eq. (A.17.17) becomes

$$B(t) = \frac{-\alpha \lambda k p y_0}{\alpha + \lambda} e^{-\alpha t} + \frac{\alpha \lambda k p y_0}{\alpha + \lambda} e^{\lambda t}$$
$$= \frac{\alpha \lambda k p y_0}{\alpha + \lambda} e^{\lambda t} (1 - e^{-(\alpha + \lambda)t}). \qquad (A.17.17.1)$$

Since the term $e^{-(\alpha+\lambda)t}$ is smaller than one for all $t>0$ and decreases as time goes on, the balance of payments will show a surplus from the instant that immediately follows time zero.

But it is also possible that the system is *not* initially in equilibrium, for example because there is an excessive money stock (in which case the balance of payments will start from an initial deficit) or insufficient (in which case the balance of payments will start from an initial surplus). To examine these cases formally let us introduce a constant a which measures the excess ($a>0$) or deficiency ($a<0$) of money supply at the initial time, that is

$$M_0 = kpy_0 + a. \tag{A.17.18.1}$$

Equation (A.17.17) now becomes

$$B(t) = \left(-\alpha a - \frac{\alpha\lambda kpy_0}{\alpha+\lambda}\right)e^{-\alpha t} + \frac{\alpha\lambda kpy_0}{\alpha+\lambda}e^{\lambda t}$$

$$= \frac{\alpha\lambda kpy_0}{\alpha+\lambda}e^{\lambda t}(1-e^{-(\alpha+\lambda)t}) - \alpha a e^{-\alpha t}. \tag{A.17.17.2}$$

From this last equation we see that, when $a<0$ (initial balance-of-payments surplus), $B(t)$ will be *a fortiori* positive for all $t>0$. If, on the contrary, $a>0$ (initial deficit), then the balance of payments will remain in deficit in the short-run; this deficit, however, will gradually disappear and become an ever-increasing surplus. The critical value t^* of t — that is, the point in time at which the balance of payments from a situation of deficit becomes zero (equilibrium) to show a surplus immediately after — can be easily calculated from (A.17.17.2) by setting $B(t)=0$ there. Simple passages yield the exponential equation

$$e^{(\alpha+\lambda)t} = \frac{(\alpha+\lambda)a + \lambda kpy_0}{\lambda kpy_0}, \tag{A.17.19}$$

which, as the right-hand side is positive, admits of a unique real and positive solution, given by

$$t^* = \frac{1}{\alpha+\lambda}\ln\frac{(\alpha+\lambda)a + \lambda kpy_0}{\lambda kpy_0}, \tag{A.17.20}$$

from which we see that the greater is a, i.e. the greater the initial deficit, the greater will be t^*. This is intuitive, since the greater is the initial deficit, the more time will be needed — *ceteris paribus* — to eliminate it.

For further considerations on the relations between growth and the balance of payments see, for example, Komiya (1969), Johnson (1972), Purvis (1972), Chen (1975), McGregor and Swales (1985), Padoan (1993). On the problem of the "stages" of the balance of payments in relation to growth see, for example, Fischer and Frenkel (1974) and Katz (1982).

References

Beckerman, W.H., 1962
Bhandari, J.S., 1984
Britton, A.J.C., 1970
Buckley, P.J. and M. Casson, 1985
Burmeister, E. and A.R. Dobell, 1970
Casprini, F., 1974
Caves, R., 1970
Caves, R.E., 1982
Chacholiades, M., 1978, Chap. 12
Chen, C.-N., 1975
Chipman, J.S., 1974
Driskill, R. and S. McCafferty, 1980
Eaton, J. and S.J. Turnovsky, 1984
Fischer, S. and J.A. Frenkel, 1974
Flood, R.P. and P.M. Garber, 1984
Friedman, M., 1953
Friedman, M., 1960
Gandolfo, G., 1971
Gandolfo, G., 1980, 236–242
Gandolfo, G. and P.C. Padoan, 1990
Glahe, F.R., 1966
Harrod, R.F., 1939
Hart, O.D., 1977
Johnson, H.G., 1956a
Johnson, H.G., 1972
Kaldor, N., 1957
Katz, L., 1982
Kemp, M.C., 1963
Kemp, M.C., 1964, Chap. 18
Keynes, J.M., 1929
Kohlhagen, S.W., 1979
Komiya, R., 1969
Lamfalussy, A., 1963
Levin, J.H., 1977
Levin, J.H., 1983a
Ljungqvist, L., 1992
Machlup, F., 1943, Chap. IX
Machlup, F., 1964a, Part Five
McCombie, J.S.L., 1985
McGregor, P.G. and J.K. Swales, 1985
McKinnon, R.I., 1983
Metzler, L.A., 1942b
Metzler, L.A., 1973a
Metzler, L.A., 1973b
Minford, P., 1978
Mundell, R.A., 1968, Chap. 9
Niehans, J., 1984, Part II
Ohlin, B., 1929
Orosel, G., 1984
Padoan, P.C., 1993
Price, L.D.D. and G.E. Wood, 1974
Purvis, D.D., 1972
Reid, F.J., 1973
Sohmen, E., 1969, Chap. III
Solow, R.M., 1956
Stern, R.M., 1973, Chaps. 3, 8, 11
Swan, T., 1956
Sweeney, R.J., 1985
Taylor, D., 1982
Thirlwall, A.P., 1980, Chaps. 10 and 11
Wan, H.Y., Jr., 1971
Wein, J., 1974
Williamson, J., 1973b
Witte, W., 1978
Yeager, L.B., 1976, Chap. 12

18 The Exchange Rate

18.1 Introduction

The problem of the best exchange-rate regime (fixed or flexible exchange rates) was the subject of a heated debate in the fifties and sixties, which — among other things — also produced a series of proposals for intermediate or limited-flexibility regimes. It was a debate based mainly on theoretical arguments, because — as the prevailing regime at that time was the Bretton Woods adjustable peg (see Sect. 10.5) — the effects of a generalized system of flexible exchange rates could not be observed. Nor was the empirical evidence drawn from other historical periods of much help, given the profound economic changes occurring in those years.

This debate is examined in Sect. 18.2, whilst Sect. 18.3 examines the renewal of the debate in the light of the experience of the managed float, which is still under way. The specific problem of the "vicious" circle is examined in a section on its own (18.4).

Finally, the problem of the determination of the exchange rate and, in particular, of the equilibrium exchange rate, already touched upon in previous chapters (see, for example, Sects. 12.3, 14.3, 16.6) finds its natural place in this chapter (Sects. 18.5 and 18.6).

18.2 The Traditional Arguments

It may seem that the old debate on fixed and flexible exchange rates has been made obsolete by international monetary events, as the international monetary system abandoned the Bretton Woods fixed exchange rate regime (of the adjustable peg type) in the early seventies, and is now operating under a managed float regime mixed with others (see Sect. 10.5.4); nor does it seem likely that freely flexible exchange rates will be adopted or fixed ones will return. However, a general outline of the traditional arguments is not without its uses, because many of these crop up again now and then. The reference to aspects already treated in previous chapters will allow us to streamline the exposition; for a more detailed survey of the old debate the reader can consult, for example, Clement, Pfister, and Rothwell (1967, Chap. 6) and the references therein. In examining the main pros and cons of the two systems it should be borne in mind that the arguments for one system often consist of arguments against the other.

The birth of a Keynesian economic policy about 1950 explains one of the main criticisms then directed at the existing system of fixed parities. This system, it was argued, in many instances created dilemma cases between external and internal equilibrium (see Sect. 15.5.1). Only after the diffusion of external convertibility and interest-sensitive capital flows did the theoretical possibility of solving the dilemma cases (by way of an appropriate mix of fiscal and monetary policy) arise, as shown in Sect. 15.5.2. However, the numerous criticisms levelled at the policy mix solution (see Sect. 15.5.2.1) gave good reason to the advocates of flexibility to point out the importance of exchange-rate flexibility for the achievement of external equilibrium, so as to be able to use fiscal and monetary policy to solve internal problems without burdening these tools with external problems.

The critics of flexibility pointed out the serious consequences for international trade and investment that would derive from a situation of uncertainty on the foreign exchange markets (whence higher risks). But the advocates replied that foreign exchange risks can be hedged by way of the forward market (see Sect. 10.3), and pointed out that habitual use of this market would stimulate its development and efficiency, so that forward cover could be obtained at moderate cost. On the contrary, the lack of development of an efficient and "thick" forward market under the adjustable peg regime[1], meant that, when parity changes were expected, forward cover could be obtained only at a prohibitive cost. Furthermore, the possibility — which actually became a reality on several occasions — of parity changes, did *not* generate that certainty which the advocates of the adjustable peg claimed against the uncertainty of flexible exchange rates.

Among the further criticisms against fixed exchange rates two more points are worthy of note. One is the observation that this regime has a distortionary effect on markets when the relative competitiveness of two countries varies. If the exchange rate does not reflect this variation because it is fixed, it then means that an additional advantage is created for the country with the lower rate of inflation against the country with the higher one. The former, in fact, sells its commodities to the latter at increasing prices (under the assumption that the exporting country adjusts the price of its exports towards the price of similar goods in the importing country) while maintaining the same rate of conversion, notwithstanding the fact that the latter's currency has been losing purchasing power. It should be added that the country with the lower rate of inflation will probably see a decrease in its exports of capital (capital outflows) and an increase in its imports of capital (capital inflows), which may give rise to a disparity in the growth of the two countries.

The second point is that the maintenance of fixed parities ultimately amounts to subsidizing firms engaged in international trade, as it implies the use of public

---

[1] Under normal conditions, all agents expect parities to remain fixed, so that there is no incentive for them to have recourse to the forward market. It is only in the case of fundamental disequilibrium that agents begin to fear parity changes. But, by the very nature of the adjustable peg, their expectations will be unidirectional, so that there will either be only a demand for forward exchange (if a devaluation is expected) by importers and other agents who have to make future payments abroad, or else only a supply of forward exchange (if a revaluation is expected) by exporters and other agents who are due to receive future payments from abroad. Thus in both cases the other side of the market will be absent, i.e. there will be no supply (if a devaluation is expected) or no demand (if a revaluation is expected) to match the demand and supply respectively. This means that banking intermediaries will procure the forward cover at costs practically corresponding to the expected devaluation or revaluation.

18.2 The Traditional Arguments

funds to absorb part of the risks inherent in private international transactions, and so involves a possible misallocation of resources (unless there is a diversion of social costs and benefits from private ones, which, however, has to be demonstrated). As Lanyi (1969, p. 7) aptly put it, "if one should ask an economist whether it is *necessarily* (italics added) desirable to subsidize industry X while not subsidizing industry Y, he would immediately reply in the negative". Therefore the answer to the question "are we *necessarily* (italics added) better off because international commerce is subsidized through the government's bearing the exchange risk, while most types of domestic commerce receive no government assistance in risk-bearing?" must also be in the negative.

Among the advantages of flexible exchange rates the advocates included, in addition to the greater freedom of economic policy to achieve internal equilibrium, already mentioned above, the following:

(a) the possibility of protecting domestic price stability by an appreciating exchange rate with respect to countries with a higher inflation rate. The existence was also claimed of an insulating power against disturbances of a real nature (see, however, Sect. 16.4);

(b) the greater effectiveness of monetary policy: a restrictive monetary policy, for example, by causing a capital inflow, brings about an appreciation in the exchange rate, with depressive effects on aggregate demand which reinforce those already due to the increase in the interest rate; the opposite is true in the case of an expansionary monetary policy (see, however, Sect. 16.3);

(c) the lower need for international reserves, as the elimination of possible deficits is ensured by the exchange-rate flexibility.

Among the disadvantages of flexible exchange rates, in addition to the increased risk in international transactions, already mentioned above, the critics included the following:

(1) the possible non-verification of the critical elasticities condition (see Sects. 12.2, 12.3, 14.3) would make the system unstable (see, however, Sect. 12.3.2);

(2) the possible presence of destabilizing speculation; the advocates of flexible exchange rates, however, pointed out the undoubtedly destabilizing nature of speculation under the adjustable peg and argued for its stabilizing nature under flexible exchange rates (this debate has been treated in Sect. 17.2);

(3) the resource reallocation costs of flexible rates, which induce resource movements into and out of export and import-competing domestic industries (see, however, Thursby, 1981);

(4) the loss of monetary discipline, as the need for restrictive monetary policies in the presence of inflation is reduced if there is no external constraint; the advocates of flexible rates, however, pointed out that an excessive exchange-rate depreciation is as good as an excessive reserve loss as an indicator of the need for monetary restriction;

(5) last but not least, what has become one of the main arguments against flexible exchange rates, i.e. their alleged inflationary bias due to a ratchet effect of exchange-rate movements on prices: a depreciation, by raising the domestic prices of imported final goods and of imported intermediate goods, raises the domestic general price level, whilst an appreciation does not bring it down at

all or not as much. Hence the possibility of a "vicious circle" of depreciation-inflation. This topic will be dealt with at some length in Sect. 18.4.

It seems difficult, if not impossible, to strike a balance between all the arguments for and against the two regimes. The reason for the impossibility of declaring one regime definitely superior from the theoretical point of view lies, in our opinion, in the fact that neither one has inferior costs and superior benefits on all counts, so that costs and benefits will have to be weighted according to a social preference function, which may vary from country to country (and from period to period in the same country).

18.3 The Experience of the Managed Float

18.3.1 Introduction

On August 15, 1971, the United States of America announced to the world a series of measures amongst which the imposition of a 10% additional tax on imports and the *"de jure" inconvertibility of the US dollar into gold*. Although, as mentioned in Sect. 10.5.3, the dollar had long been inconvertible *de facto*[2], the official declaration of its *de jure* inconvertibility was the beginning of the end of the Bretton Woods era. Subsequent consultations with other countries led to the Smithsonian Agreement in December, 1971, in which new par values or central rates of the main currencies with respect to the dollar were established, and the margins of fluctuation were widened to $\pm 2.25\%$ of these rates. For their part, the USA eliminated the additional tariff and devalued the dollar with respect to gold from $ 35 to $ 38 per ounce (in February, 1973, this price was further increased to $ 42.22, and in 1976 it was abolished: see Sect. 19.1).

The realignment of the various currencies brought into being at the Smithsonian Conference with the aim of giving a certain stability to exchange rates was short-lived. In fact, severe balance-of-payments difficulties soon compelled various countries to abandon the fixed exchange rate (adjustable peg) regime for a (managed) float: the first to float was the pound sterling (June, 1972), then the Italian lira (January-February 1973)[3]. In March, 1973, the EEC (European Economic Community) countries agreed to let their currencies float

---

[2] It should be noticed that the official convertibility of the US dollar into gold put, at least in theory, restraints on the conduct of the US monetary policy (and, more generally, on US economic policy). See, for example, Argy (1981), Chaps. 3 and 6.

[3] Some countries, amongst them Italy, adopted a *two-tier* (or *dual*) exchange rate, that is a regime where there are two distinct markets for foreign exchange: one for commercial (or, more generally, current account) transactions, where a "commercial" exchange rate (usually fixed) exists, and the other for the residual transactions, where a "financial" exchange rate (usually floating, more or less cleanly) is determined. The two markets must of course be completely separated, otherwise no spread could exist between the commercial and the financial exchange rate; the administrative measures required to bring about this segregation need not concern us here. The idea behind a two-tier market is to isolate the current account from disturbances deriving from possible destabilizing capital flows. This implies that the financial exchange rate is left completely free so as to equilibrate the capital account, whilst the commercial exchange rate is fixed or under a heavily managed float. The relative pros and cons of a *perfect* two-tier market are

vis-à-vis the dollar whilst maintaining fixed parities (with predetermined margins) among themselves; this was called a *joint float*. The same countries had previously (in March-April, 1972) agreed to create the *"snake"* in the *"tunnel"*, i.e. to restrict the margins of fluctuation around their partner-country parities to $\pm 1.125\%$ (snake) whilst maintaining the Smithsonian margins of $\pm 2.25\%$ (the tunnel) around the parities vis-à-vis non-partner countries. This was clearly an attempt at moving towards a *currency area*, but — as mentioned above — balance-of-payments difficulties led Italy and then France to abandon the snake and let their currencies float (England had been floating since June 1972). This attempt was taken up again more formally in 1979 with the creation of the EMS (European Monetary System), which will be dealt with at some length in Sect. 18.7.

Italy and England were exempted from the March 1973 agreement (together with Ireland, which pegged its currency to the pound sterling); these countries maintained the float vis-à-vis all currencies. In January, 1974, the French franc was compelled to abandon that agreement and float; after returning in July, 1975, France had to abandon it again in March, 1976. In 1973 other countries as well (amongst them Japan and Switzerland) had decided to let their currencies float; Canada had been under a managed float since 1970. With the Kingston (Jamaica) Agreement in January, 1976, the floating exchange-rate regime has been legalized within the IMF[4].

In March 1979, as mentioned above, the EEC countries constituted the EMS, which involves an adjustable peg regime (with relatively wide margins) among the partner countries and a float vis-à-vis non-partner countries (see Sect. 19.5).

18.3.2 New Light on an Old Debate?

The very brief description given in the previous section (further details on the international monetary system will be given in Sect. 19.1) was meant to provide the reader with the minimum of historical perspective better to appreciate the renewal of the debate on fixed versus flexible exchange rates. Many, in fact, wonder why the empirical evidence accumulated since 1972–3 on floating

---

a matter of debate (for a theoretical analysis of dual exchange markets see, for example, Flood, 1978; Adams and Greenwood, 1985, and references therein); all agree, however, that for an actual two-tier market to approach the ideal theoretical form, the two markets must be effectively segregated. Otherwise, in fact, on the one hand the financial market comes to lose any practical importance and, on the other, clandestine capital movements (which, as we know, take place through current account transactions: see Sect. A.11.2) are stimulated and a "parallel" market develops. This is what actually happened, for example, in Italy, so that in March, 1974, the dual market — which had lost any practical importance — was abolished. For a detailed description of actual two-tier markets see International Monetary Fund, *Annual Report on Exchange Restrictions* (years 1971 through 1974, and the current year for indication of those countries still maintaining dual exchange markets).

[4] This agreement does contemplate the possibility of returning to a system of "stable but adjustable" parities should the Fund ascertain that the presuppositions exist and with a majority of 85%. In the meantime each country is free to adopt the exchange-rate regime it wishes although it must notify its decision to the IMF and accept the surveillance of the Fund, which requires that certain very general obligations be respected.

exchange rates is not used to throw new (and possibly conclusive) light on the various arguments examined in Sect. 18.2. But the evaluation of this evidence requires an important warning: the theoretical regime of flexible exchange rates contemplates *free* flexibility, that is, with no control nor interference on the part of the monetary authorities. This is definitely *not* the case of the managed float, which is what we have been observing. Therefore, it would be wrong simply to extend the results of the managed float experience to flexible exchange rates proper.

This said, the impression that one gets from the observation of twenty-five years of managed floats is that the claims of the advocates of the two extreme regimes in favour of the supported regime and against the other were rather exaggerated. To put it differently, the fluctuation has proved to be neither the panacea that advocates of flexible rates (opponents of fixed rates) claimed, nor the disaster that opponents of flexible rates (advocates of fixed rates) predicted.

An in-depth examination of the empirical evidence would be outside the scope of the present book, so that we shall only give a brief outline (with the exception of the vicious circle problem, on which see Sect. 18.4), referring the reader to the relevant literature, e.g. Federal Reserve Bank of Boston (1978), Artus and Young (1979), Goldstein (1980), Corden (1983), Dunn (1983), Farrell et al. (1983), Shafer and Loopesko (1983), International Monetary Fund (1984), Arndt et al. eds. (1985), Vlaene and de Vries (1992).

As regards the problem of *external adjustment*, it does not seem that a substantial equilibrium in the various countries' balances of payments (either on current account or overall) has come about; concomitantly, large stocks of *international reserves* have had to be kept on hand by the various countries. But one should bear in mind that in the seventies various oil crises (of which the first, at the end of 1973, was particularly serious: see Sect. 19.1) came about. Against these, flexible exchange rates are impotent, because of the short-run price rigidity of the demand for oil and the low short-run price elasticity of imports of oil-exporting countries. One must therfore wonder what would have happened under fixed exchange rates, namely whether the balance-of-payments disequilibria would have been greater than those actually observed.

The hoped-for (greater) *autonomy of monetary policy* has not come about. This is not surprising, if one thinks that monetary independence can be achieved only if exchange-rate flexibility is such as to maintain the balance of payments always in equilibrium, so that there are no effects on the domestic money stock; but this might require exchange-rate variations so ample and frequent as to be undesirable because of their side effects[5]. As a matter of fact in the early eighties the European countries have often asked the USA to ease its monetary policy so that they could ease theirs and avoid making undesired monetary restrictions at home. It has been rightly pointed out that, whilst in the Bretton Woods era the European countries had to follow US monetary policy to prevent excessive

---

[5] Leaving aside the problem of inflation which will be dealt with subsequently, the exchange-rate variations influence the current account insofar as resources move into and out of export and import-competing domestic industries, hence causing possible resource reallocation costs (already mentioned under point (3) of the criticism against flexible rates, at the end of Sect. 18.2).

oscillations in their balances of payments, in the floating exchanges era the same countries have again had to follow US monetary policy to prevent excessive oscillations in their exchange rates vis-à-vis the dollar. The reasons are different, but a constraint on monetary policy exists in both regimes.

International trade does not seem to have been negatively influenced by exchange-rate variability, and has continued growing at sustained rates, but of course it is not easy to ascertain whether it would have grown more (or less) if exchange rates had been fixed.

The exchange-rate variability has been high, but no evidence seems to exist for destabilizing *speculation* of the explosive type described in Sect. 17.2. Speculative episodes have undoubtedly taken place, which — since the regime was a managed float with a more or less heavy intervention of the monetary authorities, sometimes to support a certain (not officially declared) level of the exchange rate — have been more similar to those which occurred under the adjustable peg than to those feared by the opponents of flexible exchange rates. One of the main contributions to the volatility of exchange rates seems to have been given by the huge capital movements induced by interest arbitrage (of course, insofar as these movements were not covered, they also contained a speculative element).

One of the main problems which the individual countries and the international monetary system have had to face since the beginning of the managed float era is *inflation* (still an acute problem for several countries). It is fair to point out that the inflation concomitant to floating exchange rates had its roots in the previous fixed-exchanges era, but many wonder whether the float, though not the cause of inflation, has not been an amplifying agent. This will be dealt with in the next section, but we wish to conclude the present treatment with a very simple observation. The experience of the European Monetary System (which will be dealt with in Sect. 19.5) shows that, from its inception to the present, many parity realignments have taken place among the partner countries. Now, if this has been necessary within a currency area formed by countries already linked by economic integration agreements (the EEC), it would have been *a fortiori* necessary for other less integrated countries if all the world had been under an adjustable peg in the same period. In other words, it is presumable that a system of fixed exchange rates at world level could not have held out. A return to an international monetary system based on fixed exchange rates does not seem likely in the foreseeable future.

Let us conclude by mentioning a problem related to the managed float, i.e. the criteria for the *authorities' intervention* in the foreign exchange market (see also Sect. 10.5). Various criteria are in principle possible: one consists in contrasting excessive movements (if any) of the exchange rate in either direction (*leaning against the wind*), another in managing the exchange rate towards a desired value or zone (*target approach*). The latter can in turn take various forms, according to whether the authorities wish to use the exchange rate (insofar as they can) as a *tool* to achieve certain targets (this would be, for example, the case of the new Cambridge school treated in Sect. 16.5) or wish to guide it towards its *equilibrium* value (on the equilibrium exchange rate see Sect. 18.5). In any case the member countries of the IMF have agreed (Second Amendment to the Articles of Agreement of the Fund, which came into force in March, 1978) to adhere to certain general principles in their interventions in the exchange markets, amongst which that of not manipulating exchange rates in order to prevent effective balance of payments adjustment or in order to gain an unfair competitive advantage over other members. The Fund, according to this Amendment, shall exercise firm surveillance over the exchange rate policies of members, which must consult with the Fund in establishing these policies.

For a treatment of these problems both from a theoretical point of view and from the point of view of actual practice, see, for example, Argy (1982), Branson (1984), Shelburn (1984), Bhandari ed. (1985), Williamson (1985).

18.4 The Vicious Circle of Depreciation-Inflation

18.4.1 Introductory Remarks

The "depreciation-inflation vicious circle" is a situation in which an exchange-rate depreciation causes a domestic price increase such as to prevent the hoped-for benefits of the depreciation (gain of competitiveness and restoration of balance-of-payments equilibrium) from coming about, thus calling for a new depreciation, and so on and so forth. The opposite "virtuous circle" between exchange-rate appreciation and price stability or deflation also exists, to which one can apply a reasoning symmetrical to that carried out below in relation to the vicious circle (the symmetry is not perfect, however, given the downward rigidity of prices).

The danger of the vicious circle, should the existence of this circle be proved, is self-evident. It, in fact, would preclude the use of exchange-rate depreciation as a means to restore equilibrium in the current account balance and, if the depreciation were imposed by capital account disequilibria (remember that the depreciationary pressures on the exchange rate come from the overall payment imbalance), it would give rise to domestic inflationary effects etc., such as to undermine the economic stability of the country affected by it.

The problems arising in the study of the vicious circle are many, but, at the cost of drastic simplification for didactic purposes, they can be condensed into two questions:

(1) does a depreciation-inflation circle exist?
(2) if so, is this circle *really* vicious?

In the first question we have purposely omitted the adjective vicious; i.e. we are only asking whether *causality links* exist between depreciation and inflation which go from depreciation to inflation *and* from inflation to depreciation. The presence of these links is, in fact, a necessary, but not sufficient, condition for the phenomenon under examination to occur.

For the circle to be really vicious, the inflation induced by the depreciation must be such as to *prevent* the hoped-for benefits of the depreciation from coming about, as we said at the beginning.

The next two sections will be dedicated to a brief examination of the two above questions: for complete surveys and references we refer the reader to Mastropasqua (1984) and Spaventa (1983). It is as well to point out that the vicious circle problem is only one aspect of the phenomenon of inflation in open economies, whose complete treatment is outside the scope of the present textbook; we refer the reader, for example, to Krause and Salant (1977), Lindbeck ed. (1979), Ahmad (1984).

18.4.2 The Depreciation-Inflation Circle

The problem of a depreciation-inflation circle, as has been shown by De Cecco (1983), was already present in 17th century writers, and was hotly debated in the 1920s. We shall, for brevity, refer only to the contemporary debate. The literature on the circle has followed two different approaches: that of the so-called *causality tests*, and that of *structural macroeconomic models.*

Causality tests are statistical tests aimed at finding the existence, if any, of a "causality" between two variables (in the case under consideration these are the exchange rate and the price level). It should be noted that the "causality" referred to is to be understood in a statistical sense (to be clarified presently) which does not necessarily coincide with the concept in use in the hard sciences (physics, chemistry, etc.) and in economic theory, but we leave this problem to philosophers of science. Loosely speaking, a variable x is said to "cause" another variable y if, by using the current and past values of x in addition to the past values of y, it is possible to obtain a statistically better prediction of the current value of y than by using the past values of y only. If, besides the fact that x causes y, it is also true that y causes x (in the definition, simply interchange x and y), then two-way or bidirectional causality (also called feedback) is said to exist between x and y.

This brief technical premise (for a detailed treatment of causality and of the relative tests the reader is referred to Geweke, 1984) is necessary to understand that the existence of a depreciation-inflation (or exchange rate-price level) circle is proved, according to this approach, by the existence of causality between the exchange rate and the general price level. It goes without saying that causality must be *bidirectional*, as the presence of mere *unidirectional* causality (from the exchange rate to prices *or* vice versa) is not enough to prove the existence of the circle.

The studies which have followed this approach have not given unequivocal results. A study by Falchi and Michelangeli (1977) finds the circle only as regards Italy, whilst in the UK causality is undirectional (from prices to the exchange rate, but not vice versa); in the other two countries considered (France and Germany) the result of the test is negative, as it reveals no causality in either direction.

A subsequent study by Kawai (1980) examines ten industrialized countries and finds the presence of the circle not only in Italy, but also in Belgium, the Netherlands, Switzerland and Japan (in the last two the circle would be of the virtuous type). Contrary to Falchi and Michelangeli's results, Kawai does not find any causality in the UK.

The methodological validity of causality testing has given rise to a heated debate and many writers believe it to be an unsuitable tool to prove causality in the sense used in economic theory (for a survey and references see Conway et al, 1983). We do not wish to examine this controversy here, but even allowing the validity of these tests, there are two important *economic* problems they leave unsolved which are particularly serious in the case at hand. Firstly, they do not tell us anything about the transmission mechanism through which the bidirectional causality exchange rates-prices comes about, and so do not give us any suggestion as to possible policy interventions. Secondly, they do not answer the second question made at the beginning, i.e. whether the circle, if it exists, is really vicious. The answer to this question can, in fact, only be given through dynamic structural models, as we shall see in Sect. 18.4.3.

The *second approach* consists, as we said, in building structural macroeconomic models, where the relations between the main macroeconomic variables are adequately modelled, so as to explain the circle, find its ultimate economic cause(s) and hence derive policy suggestions to influence it. This is certainly an approach that is more consistent with the way of thinking of an economist, but a problem immediately arises. As we know and have seen in the previous chapters, there are many schools of thought in (open economy) macroeconomics. The vision of the functioning of the economy and so of the transmission mechanisms is different, often drastically different, from one school to the other; different will then be the explanation of the circle and the policy suggestions.

Some writers (for example Bilson, 1979a, Bond, 1980) see a wrong monetary policy as the primary cause of the circle. An excessive increase in the money supply influences the exchange rate immediately (causing it to depreciate) and the real sector only afterwards (because of the much higher adjustment speeds of financial with respect to real markets: this point will be considered in Sect. 18.5.3). The exchange-rate depreciation causes an increase both in aggregate demand and in imported inflation. Inflation is also fed by the excess demand and by expectations of further price increases, and ultimately causes a deterioration in the balance of payments; hence the need for further depreciation, etc.. The appropriate therapy is monetary discipline.

Other writers (for example Basevi and De Grauwe, 1977) believe that downward price rigidity is the explanation for the circle. As a consequence of an initial expansionary monetary shock, the exchange rate depreciates (the idea is always that of a higher adjustment speed of financial markets with respect to real ones) but by an excessive amount with respect to its long-run equilibrium value (the overshooting phenomenon). A price increase then inevitably follows, and the downward price rigidity frustrates any subsequent monetary restriction. This policy, in fact, brings about an exchange rate appreciation which, however, is *not* followed by a price decrease. As prices remain high, balance-of-payments deficits will reappear, the exchange-rate will depreciate again, inflation will be boosted, etc.. In this situation the appropriate therapy is intervention in the foreign exchange market to prevent the exchange rate from deviating from its long-run equilibrium value.

A model which is based on a completely different view is that by Modigliani and Padoa-Schioppa (1978). It includes a price-formation mechanism by way of a markup on production costs and a wage-indexation mechanism (by which wages are linked to prices). In this context, any exchange-rate depreciation causes an increase in production costs (because imported intermediate inputs cost more in domestic currency) and so in prices; hence an increase in wages and, as these are a component of production costs, a new price increase etc. The loss in competitiveness caused by the price increases gives rise to a balance-of-payments deficit due to the deterioration in the current account, hence a new exchange-rate depreciation, and so on and so forth. The therapy, in this case, consists in breaking the circle by acting on unit labour costs.

It would be possible to continue with other models (for exhaustive surveys see Mastropasqua, 1984, and Spaventa, 1983), but the sample shown is sufficient to prove our assertion, that the explanations of the circle and the therapies suggested are widely different according to the view of the various authors, as is often the case in economic theory.

It is however possible, in our opinion, to move towards an *eclectic* model, which does not embrace any one of the competing theories but takes the best from each at the theoretical level, then uses appropriate econometric tools to determine the empirical validity of the theoretical hypothesis (it is, for example, possible to *ascertain* whether financial markets adjust more rapidly than real markets instead of merely assuming this to be true). Such a model must obviously be dynamic and multi-equational, as it is necessary to consider the interrelations between real and financial variables, stocks and flows, etc., in a dynamic context. For a step in this direction see, for example, Gandolfo and Padoan (1990).

We observe, in conclusion, that according to the second approach the existence of the circle is in any case proven.

18.4.3 Is the Circle Really Vicious?

To further clarify what we said in Sect. 18.4.1, we point out that the depreciation-inflation circle can either die away spontaneously or perpetuate itself and (even) become explosive: only in the latter case is it correct, in our opinion, to talk of a really vicious circle.

By a circle which dies away spontaneously we mean a situation of the following type: given a $d\%$ exchange-rate depreciation, prices increase *less* than proportionally, say by $p\%$ (where $p<d$); this increase is followed by a new depreciation which is, however, smaller than the previous one (say $d'\%$, where $d'<d$), hence a new price increase but by a smaller percentage than before, say by $p'\%$, where $p'<p$, and so on and so forth. As can be seen, depreciation and inflation converge to zero, *ceteris paribus,* so that the circle works itself out spontaneously and cannot be said to be vicious. Completely different is the case in which the above percentages are non-decreasing or increasing ($p \geq d, d' \geq d, p' \geq p$, etc.): the circle is really vicious!

In order to be able to answer the question asked in the title of this section a structural *dynamic* model is necessary, which must also be estimated econometrically. Time does in fact play an essential role, for example to determine the *adjustment lags*. These are extremely important, as it is self-evident that the situation is completely different when the $p\%$ inflation determined by a $d\%$ depreciation comes about in one month or in six months or after several years; the same applies to the inflation-to-depreciation causation. The longer the adjustment lags are, the less worrying is the circle. It is also self-evident that the importance of the parameters (amongst which the relative adjustment speeds of the various markets) which determine the dynamic convergence or divergence of the circle and the length of the adjustment lags is so crucial that their values *cannot* be assumed on *a priori* grounds but must be estimated econometrically with the utmost care. Further elaboration on this point would take us beyond the scope of a textbook; we simply point out that a step in this direction has been taken by the Gandolfo and Padoan (1990) model, and that the econometric estimates for Italy seem to indicate that the circle is slowly converging on its own, with relatively long mean time-lags. This implies that, as regards Italy, the managed flexibility of the exchange rate is, insofar as it can be implemented, a useful tool of economic policy. Results for other countries might, of course, be totally different.

18.5 Exchange-Rate Determination: Theory

The problem of the forces that determine the exchange rate and, in particular, its equilibrium value, is self-evident under flexible exchange rates but is also important under limited flexibility and even under fixed exchange rates (if the fixed rate is not an equilibrium one, the market will put continuing pressure on it and compel the monetary authorities to intervene on the exchange market, etc.). This problem has already been mentioned in several places (see, e.g., Sects. 12.3, 14.3, 16.2, 16.6); in this section we gather up the threads and try to give a general treatment. This is not easy, since various competing theories exist, of which we shall try to give a balanced view; for general surveys of the problems treated in this section see, for example, Dornbusch (1983), Isard (1978), Krueger (1983), Mussa (1984), MacDonald (1988), Baillie and McMahon (1989), de Jong (1991), MacDonald and Taylor (1992).

18.5.1 The Purchasing-Power-Parity Theory

The oldest theory of exchange-rate determination is probably the purchasing power-parity (henceforth PPP) theory, commonly attributed to Cassel (1918) even though – as usual – precursors in earlier times are not lacking (on this point see Officer, 1982). Two versions of the PPP are distinguished, the *absolute* and the *relative* one. According to the *absolute* version, the exchange rate between two currencies equals the ratio between the values, expressed in the two currencies considered, of the same typical basket containing the same amounts of the same commodities. If, for example, such a basket is worth US$ 12,000 in the United States and DM 20,000 in Germany, the $/DM exchange rate will be 0,60 (60 cents per DM). According to the relative version, the percentage *variations* in the exchange rate equal the percentage variations in the ratio of the price levels of the two countries (the percentage variations in this ratio are approximately equal to the difference between the percentage variations in the two price levels, or *inflation differential*).

In both versions the PPP theory is put forward as a *long-run* theory of the equilibrium exchange rate, in the sense that in the short-run there may be marked deviations from PPP which, however, set into motion forces capable of bringing the exchange rate back to its PPP value in the long term. The problems arise when one wants better to specify this theory, which implies both a precise singling out of the price indexes to be used and the determination of the forces acting to restore the PPP: the two questions are, in fact, strictly related.

Those who suggest using a price-index based on internationally traded commodities only, believe that PPP is restored by international commodity arbitrage which arises as soon as the internal price of a traded good deviates from that prevailing on international markets, when both prices are expressed in a common unit (the *law of one price*).

On the contrary, those who maintain that a general price-index should be used, think that people appraise the various currencies essentially for what these can buy, so that — in free markets — people exchange them in proportion to the respective purchasing power.

Others suggest using cost-of-production indexes, in the belief that international competition and the degree of internationalization of industries are the main forces which produce PPP.

A fourth proposal suggests the use of the domestic inflation rates starting from various assumptions:

(a) the real interest rates are equalized among countries;
(b) in any country the nominal interest rate equals the sum of the real interest rate and the rate of inflation (the Fisher equation);
(c) the differential between the nominal interest rates of any two countries is equal (if one assumes risk-neutral agents) to the expected percentage variation in the exchange rate (for this relation, see Sects. 10.7.2 and 10.7.4).

From these assumptions it follows that there is equality between the expected percentage variations (which, with the further assumption of perfect foresight, will coincide with the actual ones) in the exchange rate and the inflation differential.

None of these proposals is without its drawbacks and each has been subjected to serious criticism which we cannot go into here, so that we shall only mention a few points. For example, the commodity-arbitrage idea was criticized on the grounds that it presupposes free mobility of goods (absence of tariffs and other restrictions to trade) and a constant ratio, within each country, between the prices of traded and non-traded goods: the inexistence, even in the long run, of these conditions, is a well-known fact. Besides, the law of one price presupposes that traded goods are highly homogeneous, another assumption often contradicted by fact and by the "new" theories of international trade (see Chap. 8), which stress the role of product differentiation.

The same idea of free markets, of both goods and capital, lies at the basis of the other proposals, which run into trouble because this freedom does not actually exist. Cassel himself, it should be noted, had already singled out these problems and stated that they were responsible for the deviations of the exchange-rate from the PPP.

These deviations, which make the PPP theory useless to explain the behaviour of exchange rates in the short-run, were one of the reasons which induced most economists to abandon it in favour of the exchange-market approach. It should however be pointed out that the PPP theory has been taken up again by the monetary approach (which will be dealt with in Sect. 18.5.3), and used as an indicator of the long-run trend in the exchange rate.. For empirical studies on the PPP theory see Frenkel (1981), Hakkio (1984), Rush and Husted (1985).

18.5.2 The Traditional Flow Approach

This approach, also called the balance-of-payments view or the exchange-market approach, starts from the observation that the exchange rate[6] is actually determined in the foreign exchange market by the demand for and supply of foreign exchange, and that it moves (if free to do so) to bring these demands and supplies into equality and hence (if no intervention is assumed) to restore equilibrium in the balance of payments. In fact, according to Nurkse's definition (1945), the equilibrium exchange rate is "... that rate which, over a certain period of time, keeps the balance of payments in equilibrium" (p. 5 of the reprint).

That the exchange rate is determined in the foreign exchange market by the demand for and supply of foreign exchange is an irrefutable fact (we do, of course, exclude centrally planned economies, etc.), but it is precisely in determining these demands and supplies that most problems arise.

The traditional flow approach sees these as pure flows, deriving — in the older version — from imports and exports of goods, which in turn depend on the exchange rate and — after the Keynesian-type models — also on national income. This approach has been widely described before, in particular in Sects. 12.3, 12.4, A.12.2, A.12.3 and in Sects. 14.3, A.14.2 – A.14.4, to which we refer the reader; we only remember that it gives rise to the critical elasticity-sum conditions in various versions (including the one deriving from the synthesis with the absorption approach). For further details on this approach see, for example, Gandolfo (1979).

The introduction of capital movements as a further component of the demand for and supply of foreign exchange does not alter this view insofar as these movements are also seen as pure flows: this is, for example, the case of the model described in Sect. 16.2.

This approach can be criticized for several shortcomings, amongst which the fact that it neglects stock adjustments, a point that we have already treated extensively (see, for example, Sects. 15.4.3.1, 15.6.3, 16.6.1). It should however be stressed that, if on the one hand the criticism must induce us to consider the traditional approach inadequate in its specification of the determinants of the demands for and supplies of foreign exchange, on the other, it does not affect the fact that it is the interaction between these demands and supplies which actually determines the exchange rate.

---

[6] For brevity, we shall talk of "exchange rate" in the sense of the set of exchange rates between the various currencies. A similar observation holds for the foreign exchange market.

18.5.3 The Modern Approach: Money and Assets in the Determination of the Exchange Rate

18.5.3.1 Introductory Remarks

As Dornbusch (1983) notes, the modern approach (also called the *asset-market approach*) takes the exchange rate as the relative price of monies (the monetary approach) or as the relative price of bonds (the portfolio approach). The two views differ as regards the assumptions made on the substitutability between domestic and foreign bonds, given however the common hypothesis of perfect capital mobility (Murphy and Van Duyne, 1980; Frankel, 1983). The monetary approach assumes perfect substitutability between domestic and foreign bonds, so that asset holders are indifferent as to which they hold, and bond supplies become irrelevant. Conversely, in the portfolio approach domestic and foreign bonds are imperfect substitutes, and their supplies become relevant.

To avoid confusion it is as well to recall the distinction between (perfect) capital mobility and (perfect) substitutability (see Sect. 10.7.6)[7]. Perfect capital mobility means that the actual portfolio composition adjusts instantaneously to the desired one. This, in turn, implies that – if we assume no risk of default or future capital controls, etc. – *covered interest parity* must hold (see Sect. 10.7.1). Perfect substitutability is a stronger assumption, as it means that asset holders are indifferent as to the composition of their bond portfolios (provided of course that both domestic and foreign bonds have the same expected rate of return expressed in in a common numéraire). This, in turn, implies that *uncovered interest parity* must hold (see Sect. 10.7.2).

It is important to note that according to some writers (see, for example, Helliwell and Boothe, 1983), the condition of covered interest parity itself becomes a theory of exchange-rate determination (the *interest parity model,* where interest parity may be expressed either in nominal or real terms), if one assumes that the forward exchange rate is an accurate and unbiased predictor of the future spot rate (see Sect. 10.7.5): it would in fact suffice, in this case, to find the determinants of the expected future spot exchange rate to be able to determine, given the interest rates, the current spot rate.

Since classifications are largely a matter of convenience (and perhaps of personal taste) we have chosen to follow the dichotomy based on the perfect or imperfect substitutability between domestic and foreign bonds within the common assumption of perfect capital mobility.

18.5.3.2 The Monetary Approach

The monetary approach to the balance of payments has been treated in Sects. 15.3 and A.15.2; we only recall that it assumes the validity of PPP as a long-run theory. Now, if one assumes fixed exchange rates, as in Chap. 15, then the monetary approach determines the effects of (changes in) the stock of money (which is an

---

[7] As Frankel (1983) notes, earlier analyses (see, for example, Mundell 1963) implicitly took perfect capital mobility to require perfect asset substitutability, but the distinction between these is useful; Dornbusch and Krugman (1976) were among the first to introduce this distinction.

endogenous variable) on the balance of payments and vice versa; if one assumes flexible exchange rates the same approach (with the money stock exogenous) becomes a theory of exchange-rate determination, as can easily be shown (Bilson, 1978). If we again take up the model explained in Sect. 15.3 and for brevity consider only the equilibrium relations (i.e., we neglect the adjustment process set into motion by discrepancies between money demand and supply) we get

$$\begin{aligned} M &= kpy, \\ M_f &= k_f p_f y_f, \\ p &= rp_f. \end{aligned} \quad (18.1)$$

The first two equations express monetary equilibrium in the two countries[8], whilst the third is the PPP equation. For simplicity's sake, we assume the rest-of-the-world variables as exogenously given. Then, under fixed exchange rates, the third equation determines the domestic price-level p, whilst the first determines the equilibrium domestic money-stock M[9]. In the case of flexible exchange rates, the domestic stock of money becomes exogenous, so that the first equation determines p and the third determines the exchange rate. After simple manipulations we get

$$r = \frac{M}{M_f} \cdot \frac{k_f y_f}{ky}, \quad (18.2)$$

from which we see that, as stated in Sect. 18.5.3.1, the exchange rate is the relative price of two monies, i.e. of the two money-stocks M and M_f (the other variables are given exogenously).

In this model the interest rate is not explicitly present, but it can be introduced by assuming that the demand for money in real terms is also a function of i, that is

$$\begin{aligned} M &= pL(y,i), \\ M_f &= p_f L_f(y_f,i_f), \\ p &= rp_f, \end{aligned} \quad (18.3)$$

whence

$$r = \frac{M}{M_f} \cdot \frac{L_f(y_f,i_f)}{L(y,i)}. \quad (18.4)$$

From this equation it can clearly be seen that — *ceteris paribus* — an increase in the domestic money-stock brings about a depreciation in the exchange rate, whilst an increase in national income causes an appreciation, and an increase in the domestic interest rate causes a depreciation. These conclusions, especially the last two, are in sharp contrast with the traditional approach, where an increase in income, by raising imports, tends to make the exchange rate depreciate, whilst an increase in the interest rate, by raising capital inflows (or reducing capital outflows), brings about an appreciation in the exchange rate.

---

[8] For notational simplicity we have eliminated the bar over y and y_f, it being understood that these are exogenously given.

[9] In the case of a divergence of the current from the equilibrium value, the adjustment described in Sect. 15.3 will set into motion and automatically restore equilibrium.

These (surprisingly) different conclusions are however perfectly consistent with the vision of the MABP, described in Sect. 15.3. For example an increase in income raises the demand for money; given the money stock and the price level, the public will try to get the desired additional liquidity by reducing absorption, which causes a balance-of-payments surplus, hence the appreciation. This appreciation, by simultaneously reducing the domestic price level p (given that PPP holds), raises the value of the real money-stock (M/p increases), and so restores monetary equilibrium. Similar reasoning explains the depreciation in the case of an increase in i (the demand for money falls, etc.).

The monetary approach to the exchange rate can be made more sophisticated by introducing additional elements (arbitrage relations between i and i_f, sticky prices which do not immediately reflect PPP, the possibility that domestic agents hold foreign money, etc.: see Sect. A.18.2.4), but its basic message remains that which we have described, and so it will be accepted from the theoretical point of view (apart from problems of empirical evidence, which will be treated below, Sect. 18.6) insofar as one thinks that the criticisms mentioned in Sect. 15.3 can be overcome: further critical remarks are contained in Rabin and Yeager (1982) and in Sect. 18.5.4 below.

18.5.3.3 The Portfolio Approach

This approach, in its simplest version, is based on a model of portfolio choice between domestic and foreign assets. As we know from the theory of portfolio selection examined more than once in this volume (see Sect. 15.6.2, 16.6.1, 17.3), asset holders will determine the composition of their bond portfolios[10], i.e. the shares of domestic and foreign bonds on the basis of considerations of (expected) return and risk. If perfect substitutability between domestic and foreign assets existed, then uncovered interest parity should hold, that is

$$i = i_f + \tilde{r}/r \tag{18.5}$$

where $\tilde{r}$ denotes the expected change in the exchange rate over a given time interval; i and i_f are to be taken as referring to the same interval. In the case of imperfect substitutability this relation becomes

$$i = i_f + \tilde{r}/r + \delta. \tag{18.5.1}$$

Hence, with imperfect substitutability a divergence may exist between i and $(i_f + \tilde{r}/r)$; the extent of this divergence will - *ceteris paribus* - determine the allocation of wealth (W) between national (N) and foreign (F) bonds. If, for simplicity's sake, we make the small-country assumption, i.e. we assume that domestic bonds are held solely by residents[11], because the country is too small for its assets to be of interest to foreign investors, we can write

---

[10] To simplify to the utmost, we follow Frankel (1983) in considering solely bonds; the introduction of money would not alter the substance of the results (see, for example, Krueger, 1983, Sect. 4.3.2). Alternatively, one could assume that asset holders make a two-stage decision, by first establishing the allocation of their wealth between money and bonds, and then allocating this second part between domestic and foreign bonds.

[11] The model can be extended to consider the general case without substantially altering the results, provided that residents of any country wish to hold a greater proportion of their wealth as domestic bonds (the so-called *preferred local habitat* hypothesis): see Frankel (1983).

$$W = N^d + rF^d, \tag{18.6}$$

where the demands are expressed, in accordance with portfolio selection theory, as

$$\begin{aligned} N^d &= g(i - i_f - \tilde{r}/r)\,W, \\ rF^d &= h(i - i_f - \tilde{r}/r)\,W, \end{aligned} \tag{18.7}$$

wehre $g(\ldots) + h(\ldots) = 1$ because of (18.6). If we impose the equilibrium condition that the amounts demanded should be equal to the given quantities existing (supplied), we get

$$N^d = N^s, \quad F^d = F^s, \tag{18.8}$$

and so, by substituting into (18.7) and dividing the second by the first equation there, we obtain

$$\frac{rF^s}{N^s} = \psi(i - i_f - \tilde{r}/r), \tag{18.9}$$

where $\psi(\ldots)$ denotes the ratio between the $h(\ldots)$ and $g(\ldots)$ functions. From Eq. (18.9) we can express the exchange rate as a function of the other variables

$$r = \frac{N^s}{F^s}\psi(i - i_f - \tilde{r}/r). \tag{18.10}$$

Equation (18.10) shows that the exchange rate can be considered as the relative price of two stocks of assets, since it is determined — given the interest differential corrected for the expectations of exchange-rate variations — by the relative quantities of N^s and F^s.

The basic idea behind all this is that the exchange rate is the variable which adjusts instantaneously so as to keep the (international) asset markets in equilibrium. Let us assume, for example, that an increase occurs in the supply of foreign bonds from abroad to domestic residents (in exchange for domestic currency) and that (to simplify to the utmost) expectations are static ($\tilde{r} = 0$). This increase, *ceteris paribus*, causes an instantaneous appreciation in the exchange rate. To understand this apparently counter-intuitive result, let us begin with the observation that, given the foreign-currency price of foreign bonds, their domestic-currency price will be determined by the exchange rate. Now, residents will be willing to hold (demand) a higher amount of foreign bonds, *ceteris paribus*, only if the domestic price that they have to pay for these bonds (i.e., the exchange rate) is lower. In this way the value of $rF^d = rF^s$ remains unchanged, as it should remain, since all the magnitudes present on the right-hand side of Eqs. (18.7) are unchanged, and the market for foreign assets remains in equilibrium ($F^d = F^s$) at a higher level of F and a lower level of r.

18.5.3.4 Interaction Between Current and Capital Accounts

The simplified model that we have described is a partial equilibrium model, as it does not consider the determinants of the interest rate(s) and the possible

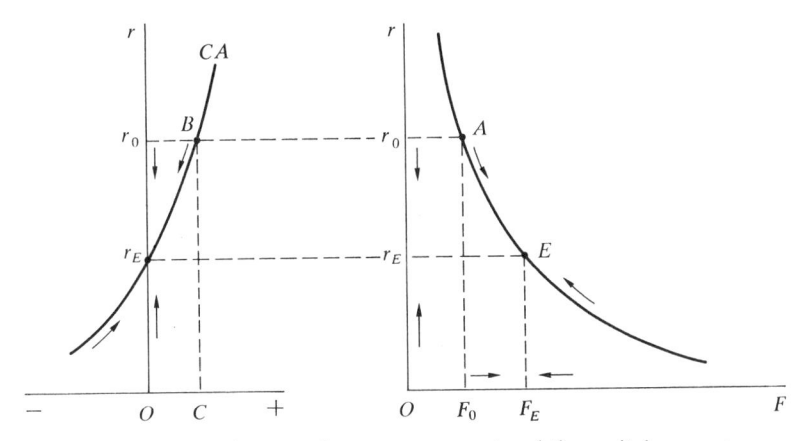

Fig. 18.1. Interaction between the current account and the capital account

interaction between the current account and the capital account in the determination of the exchange rate. As regards this interaction, we consider a model suggested by Kouri (1983a, but the idea was set forth by this author long before that date). As usual we simplify to the utmost by assuming static expectations, absence of domestic bonds in foreign investors' portfolio, an exogenously given interest differential. Thanks to these assumptions, the stock of foreign bonds held in domestic investors' portfolios becomes an inverse function of the exchange rate. In fact, from the portfolio equilibrium described in Sect. 18.5.3.3, we have (in what follows we use F to denote the equilibrium stock of foreign bonds held by residents, $F = F^d = FR^s$)

$$rF = h(i - i_f - \tilde{r}/r)\, W, \tag{18.11}$$

so that, given i, i_f, W, and letting $\tilde{r} = 0$ (static expectations), the right-hand side of Eq. (18.11) becomes a constant, hence the relation of inverse proportionality between r and F.

As regards the current account, Kouri assumes that its balance is an increasing function of the exchange rate (i.e. the critical elasticities condition occurs). The long-run equilibrium can prevail only when both the current account and the capital account are in equilibrium. In the opposite case, in fact, since any current-account disequilibrium is matched by a capital-account disequilibrium in the opposite sense[12], the latter will cause a variation in the stock of foreign assets held by residents and so a variation in the exchange rate, which will feed back on the current account until this is brought back to equilibrium.

To illustrate this mechanism we can use Fig. 18.1, where the left-hand panel shows the current account (CA) as a function of the exchange rate (the positive slope means, as we have said, that the critical elasticities condition occurs); the

---

[12] As we know from balance-of-payments accounting, the algebraic sum of the current account and the capital account is necessarily zero (see Sect. 11.1). Here the implicit assumption is that there are no compensatory (see Sect. 11.2) capital movements, i.e. that there is no official intervention (the exchange rate is perfectly and freely flexible). Under this assumption all capital movements are autonomous and originate from private agents.

right-hand panel shows the relation between r and F, which is a rectangular hyperbola as its equation is (18.11).

The long-run equilibrium corresponds to the exchange-rate r_E, where the current account (and so the capital account) is in equilibrium. Let us assume, for example, that the exchange rate happens to be r_0, hence a current account surplus OC; the initial stock of foreign assets (which corresponds to r_0) is F_0. The current-account surplus is matched by a capital outflow, i.e. by an increase in foreign assets; thus the residents' stock of foreign bonds increases (from F_0 towards F_E, which is the equilibrium stock) and so the exchange rate appreciates (point A moves towards point E). This appreciation reduces the current-account surplus; the process goes on until equilibrium is reached.

The case of an initial exchange rate lower than r_E is perfectly symmetrical (current-account deficit, decrease in the stock of domestically held foreign assets, exchange rate depreciation, etc.). This — Kouri concludes — explains why the exchange rate of a country with a current account surplus (deficit) tends to appreciate (depreciate); he labels this phenomenon the *acceleration hypothesis*.

Although this is a highly simplified model, it serves well to highlight the features of the interaction between the current account and the capital account. This interaction, it should be emphasized, does not alter the fact that in the short-run the exchange rate is always determined in the asset market(s), even if it tends towards a long-run value (r_E) which corresponds to current-account equilibrium. All the above reasoning, in fact, is based on the assumption that Eq. (18.11) holds instantaneously as an equilibrium relation, so that any change in F *immediately* gives rise to a change in r, which feeds back on the current account, which "follows" the exchange-rate behaviour. The assumption of instantaneous equilibrium in asset markets, or (at any rate) of *a much higher adjustment speed of asset markets compared to that of goods markets*, is thus essential to the approach under consideration. Thanks to this assumption, in fact, the introduction of goods markets and so of the current account does not alter the nature of the relative price of two assets attributed to the exchange rate in the short run.

More sophisticated models, in which the simplifying assumptions adopted here are dropped (see, for example, Kouri, 1983a), do not alter the fundamental conclusion stated above.

18.5.4 The Exchange Rate in Macroeconometric Models

Let us begin with some remarks on the modern approach. As Kouri (1983a, 1983b) – an author who is certainly not against the modern approach – aptly put it, if it is true by definition that the exchange rate is the relative price of two monies, it is vacuous to state that it is determined by the relative supplies of (and demands for) the two monies. To borrow a comparison of his (1983b, p. 36), it is also true that the (money) price of steel is a relative price between steel and money, but nobody would analyze the determination of the price of steel in terms of supply of and demand for money: what one should do is to understand the determinants of the supply of and demand for steel and the mechanism which brings these into equilibrium in the steel market, and so determines the price of steel as well as the quantity exchanged. Exactly the same considerations apply, according to Kouri, to the exchange rate, which is a price actually determined in the foreign exchange market through the demand for and supply of foreign exchange. This lack of, or insufficient, consideration of the foreign exchange market is, in Kouri's opinion, the main shortcoming of the modern theory. In fact, no theory of exchange-rate determination can be deemed satisfactory if it does not explain how the variables that it considers crucial (whether they are the stocks of money or the stocks of assets or expectations or whatever) actually translate into supply and demand in the foreign exchange market which, together with supplies and demand coming from other sources, determine the exchange rate. For further considerations on the modern theory see Tobin (1982) and Rabin and Yeager (1982).

We fully agree with these considerations of Kouri's which, of course, are not to be taken to mean that the modern approach is useless. Indeed, we believe that neither the traditional nor the modern theory is by itself a satisfactory explanation: is this we share Dornbusch's opinion who, after listing the basic views on exchange-rate determination stated "I regard any one of these views as a partial picture of exchange rate determination, although each may be especially important in explaining a particular historical episode" (Dornbusch, 1983, p. 45). In fact, as we have already observed, the determinants that we are looking for are both real and financial, derive from both pure flows and stock adjustments, with a network of reciprocal interrelationships in a disequilibrium setting. It follows that only an eclectic approach is capable of tackling the problem satisfactorily, and from this point of view we believe that models like that of Branson and Buiter (1983) explained in Sect. 16.6, or of Ahtiala (1984) and of Gylfason and Helliwell (1983) – who independently share the same point of view – are a step forward in the right direction (it should be remembered that the Branson and Buiter model also determines the exchange rate among the other endogenous variables, and the same is true for the Ahtiala and the Gylfason-Helliwell models). More complex models seem however called for, because – as soon as one considers the exchange rate as one among the various endogenous variables which are present in the model of an economic system – simple models[13] like those which have been described in this book are no longer sufficient. One should move toward economy – wide macroeconom(etr)ic models. When doing this, however, one should pay much attention to the way in which exchange-rate determination is dealt with.

In order to put this important topic into proper perspective, we first introduce the distinction between models where there is a specific equation for the exchange rate and models where the exchange rate is implicitly determined by the balance-of-payments equation (thus the exchange rate is obtained by solving out this equation). From the mathematical point of view the two approaches are equivalent, as can be seen from the following considerations.

---

[13] In the sense that, notwithstanding the formal difficulty of many of these, they can account for only a very limited number of variables and aspects of the real world, and must ignore others which may have an essential importance (as, for example, the distinction between consumption and investment, which are usually lumped together in an aggregate expenditure function).

Let us consider the typical aggregate foreign sector of any economy-wide macroeconomic model, and let CA denote the current account, NFA the stock of net foreign assets of the private sector, R the stock of international reserves. Then the balance-of-payments equation simply states that

$$CA + \Delta NFA + \Delta R = 0. \tag{18.12}$$

Introduce now the following functional relations:

$$CA = f(E, \ldots), \tag{18.13}$$

$$\Delta NFA = g(E, \ldots), \tag{18.14}$$

$$\Delta R = h(E, \ldots), \tag{18.15}$$

$$E = \varphi(\ldots), \tag{18.16}$$

where E is the exchange rate and the dots indicate all the other explanatory variables, that for the present purposes can be considered as exogenous. These relations do not require particular explanation. We only observe that the reserve-variation equation, Eq. (18.15), represents the (possible) monetary authorities' intervention in the foreign exchange market, also called the monetary authorities' *reaction function*.

Since system (18.12)–(18.16) contains five independent equations in four unknowns, it is over-determined, and so we can drop one equation. Which equation we drop is irrelevant from the mathematical point of view but not from the point of view of economic theory. From the economic point of view there are three possibilities:

a) we drop the capital-movement equation (18.14) and use the balance-of-payments equation (18.12) to determine capital movements *residually* (i.e., once the rest of the model has determined the exchange rate, the reserve variation, and the current account).

b) we drop the reserve-variation equation (18.15) and use the balance-of-payments equation to residually determine the change in international reserves.

c) we drop the exchange-rate equation (18.16) and use the balance-of-payments equation as an implicit equation that determines the exchange rate. The exchange-rate, in other words, is determined by solving it out of the implicit equation (18.12). More precisely, if we substitute from Eqs. (18.13)–(18.15) into Eq. (18.12), we get

$$f(E, \ldots) + g(E, \ldots) + h(E, \ldots) = 0, \tag{18.17}$$

which can be considered as an implicit equation in E. This can be in principle solved to determine E, which will of course be a function of all the other variables represented by the dots.

Since the functions f, g and h represent the excess demands for foreign exchange coming from commercial operators (the current account), financial private operators (private capital flows), and monetary authorities (the change in international reserves), what we are doing under approach (c) *is simply to determine the exchange rate through the equilibrium condition in the foreign exchange market (the equality between demand and supply of foreign exchange).*

It should be stressed that if one uses the balance-of-payments definition to determine the exchange rate one is not necessarily adhering to the traditional or "flow" approach to the exchange rate, as was once incorrectly believed. A few words are in order to clarify this point. Under approach (c) one is simply using the fact that the exchange rate is determined in the foreign exchange market, which is reflected in the balance-of-payments equation, under the assumption that this market clears instantaneously. This assumption is actually true, if we include the (possible) monetary authorities' demand or supply of foreign exchange as an item in this market; this item is given by eq. (18.15), which defines the monetary authorities' reaction function. As we have already observed above, in fact, no theory of exchange-rate determination can be deemed satisfactory if it does not explain how the variables that it considers crucial (whether they are the stocks of assets or the flows of goods or expectations or whatever) actually translate into supply and demand in the foreign exchange market which, together with supplies and demands coming from other sources, determine the exchange rate. When all these sources – including the monetary authorities through their reaction function in the foreign exchange market, eq. (18.15) – are present in the balance-of-payments equation, this equation is no longer an identity (like Eq. (11.11) in Chap. 11), but becomes a market-clearing condition. Thus it is perfectly legitimate (and consistent with any theory of exchange-rate determination) to use the balance-of-payments equation to calculate the exchange rate once one has specified behavioral equations for *all* the items included in the balance of payments.

For future reference we call models of type A the models based on approaches (a) and (b), in which the exchange-rate equation (18.16) is kept, and models of type B those based on approach (c).

As we have said above, the various cases are equivalent mathematically but not from the economic point of view. In models of type A, in fact, it is in any case necessary to specify an equation for exchange-rate determination, and hence adhere to one or the other theory explained in the previous sections. Besides, these models leave the foreign exchange market (of which the balance-of-payments equation is the mirror) out of the picture. On the contrary, the foreign exchange market is put at the centre of the stage in models of type B. Hence, these models are not sensitive to possible theoretical errors made in the specification of the exchange-rate equation (18.17)

For a survey of exchange-rate determination in actual economy-wide macroeconometric models see Gandolfo, Padoan and Paladino (1990b).

18.6 Exchange-Rate Determination: Empirical Studies

18.6.1 Introduction

Everybody knows that "explanation" and "prediction" are not necessarily related. Geologists, for example, have very good explanations for earthquakes, but are as yet unable to predict them with any useful degree of accuracy. The effects of putting certain substances together in certain proportions were accurately predicted by alchemists long before the birth of chemistry (prediction without explanation). However, as Mark Blaug (1980, p. 9) notes, "...when offered an explanation that does not yield a prediction, is it because we cannot secure all the relevant information about the initial conditions, or is it because (...) we are being handed chaff for wheat?".

Exchange rate determination offers a good example of this dilemma. Surprisingly enough, no rigorous test of the true predictive accuracy of the structural models of exchange rate determination which constitute the modern theory explained in Sect. 18.5.3 was carried out before the studies of Meese and Rogoff (1983a, 1983b; see also 1988). The in-sample predictive accuracy, in fact, is not a good test, for it simply tells us that the model fits the data reasonably well. What Meese and Rogoff did was to examine the *out-of-sample* predictive performance of these models. As a benchmark they took the simple random-walk model, according to which the forecast, at time t, of the value of a variable in period $t+1$, is the current (at time t) value of the variable. To avoid possible confusion, it is as well to stress that to compare the forecasts of a model with those of the random walk does *not* mean that one is assuming that the exchange rate does indeed follow a random walk process (it might or might not, which is irrelevant for our present purposes). It simply means taking as benchmark the simplest type of forecast, which is that of the random walk. This benchmark amounts to assuming a *naïf* agent who has no idea of how the exchange rate will evolve, and feels that increases or decreases are equally likely.

It should not be difficult to perform better than this *naïf* scheme. Instead, what Meese and Rogoff found was that the structural models failed to outperform the random-walk model even when the actual realized values of the explanatory variables were used (*ex post* forecasts[14]). The choice of *ex post* forecasts was made by Meese and Rogoff to prevent a possible defence of the structural models, namely that they do not perform well only because of the forecast errors of the exogenous variables that one has to use to forecast the exchange rate as endogenous variable (Meese and Rogoff, 1983a, p. 10).

We feel that, if one aims at testing the theoretical validity of a model, one should put the model in the most favourable situation for giving predictions, and that these should be true predictions (namely out of sample). If, this notwithstanding, the model fails, then there is certainly something wrong in the model, and "we are being handed chaff for wheat". This methodological vision amounts to following the Meese and Rogoff procedure, by now standard in all empirical studies of the exchange rate.

---

[14] For the student who has no econometric background we recall that by *ex post* forecasts we mean the following procedure. Given a data sample, say from 1970 to 1990, one uses a subsample, say from 1970 to 1985, to estimate the equation(s) of the model. The estimated equations are then used to generate true out-of-sample forecasts over the period left out of the estimation procedure (1986–1990), using however the *actual values of the exogenous variables observed in that period*. In other words, it is as if a hypothetical forecaster acting in 1985 possessed perfect foresight as regards the exogenous variables, having only to forecast the endogenous variable (in our case, the exchange rate), naturally using the equations estimated with the data up to 1985.

18.6.2 The Reactions to Meese and Rogoff, and the Way Out

The result of Meese and Rogoff haven been updated and confirmed in several later studies, for example Alexander and Thomas (1987), Gandolfo, Padoan and De Arcangelis (1993), and have led to two opposite categories of reactions. On the one hand, there are those who try to improve the performance of the structural models by all means (for example by using more sophisticated techniques, such as error-correction models, time-varying coefficients, etc.), but without appreciable improvement except in sporadic cases (for suveys of this approach see Gandolfo, Padoan, Paladino, 1990b, and Gandolfo, Padoan, De Arcangelis, 1993). On the other hand, there are those who take the failure of the structural models as a failure of economic theory and as showing the necessity of moving towards pure time-series techniques ("prediction without explanation").

We do not agree with either view. In our opinion, the basic fact is that the traditional structural models of exchange-rate determination are of the single-equation, semi-reduced form type, which is inadequate to capture all the complex phenomena underlying the determination of the exchange rate, as we have already observed in Sect. 18.5.4. To adapt a similitude coined by Edgeworth for other purposes (see Vol. I of the present textbook, p. 47), there is more than meets the eye in the movement of the exchange rate: this movement, in fact, should be considered as attended with rearrangement of all the main economic variables, just "as the movement of the hand of a clock corresponds to considerable unseen movements of the machinery" (1905, p. 70). In order to explain the movement of the hands of a clock one must have a model of the underlying machinery, and to explain the movement of the exchange rate one must have an economy-wide macroeconometric model. Thus, in front of the failure of the standard structural models, the proper course of action is neither to try to improve their performance by all means nor to abandon the structural models approach. Instead, the proper course of action is to move away from the single-equation, semi-reduced form models, toward suitable economy-wide macroeconometric models capable of capturing all the complex associations between the exchange rate and the other variables (both real and financial, both stocks and flows) of a modern economy.

We have been advocating this systemic approach for many years, starting from non-suspect years, that is when the models now rejected by the data were on the crest of a wave (see, for example, Gandolfo, 1976, p. 6; 1979, p. 102; 1981, p. 171; 1986, pp. II.402–403), and we are happy to see that this idea is gaining ground. As Isard writes in his survey (1987, p. 15; see also 1988), the hope is that "models that simultaneously take account of a complete system of macroeconomic relationships will be able to improve on the single-equation, semi-reduced form models in capturing all the associations between exchange rates, interest rate differentials, and other variables". We wish to add that not every macroeconometric model is inherently suitable for this purpose. In fact, since the exchange rate is just one of the endogenous variables of an economy-wide model, its determination occurs in conjunction with the determination of the other endogenous variables, in a general (dis)equilibrium setting where stocks and flows, real and financial variables, etc., all interact. Thus, economy-wide macroeconometric models that embody a partial view of exchange-rate determination (in the sense that they, like the single-equation models, take account only of some factors), are not suitable to fulfill our hopes.

In the next section we briefly summarize the results that we have obtained from our macroeconometric model of the Italian economy.

18.6.3 An Economy-Wide Model Beats the Random Walk

The economy-wide macroeconometric model that we have used is the MARK V version of the Italian continuous time model, for whose details we refer the reader to Gandolfo and Padoan (1990). Just a few words are in order on the fact that the model is not only specified but also estimated in *continuous time* (instead of assuming and using discrete time-intervals as in conventional econometrics). It has been demonstrated (see, for example, Gandolfo, 1981) that one can actually estimate the parameters of a continuous-time model on the basis of the discrete-time observations available. One practical advantage of the continuous-time approach is that one can produce forecasts for any time interval and not only for the time unit inherent in the data. This is particularly important in our case. In fact, we had to use quarterly data in estimation (as this is an economy-wide model, most series – in particular national accounting data – were on a quarterly basis). However, we wanted to produce out-of-sample forecasts of the exchange rate not only for quarterly intervals but also for other intervals, such as one month ahead, one of the intervals considered by Meese and Rogoff. Another important advantage of the continuous time approach that is relevant in the present context is the estimation of adjustment speeds.

In fact, a basic problem in the theoretical debate on exchange-rate determination is the question of the adjustment speeds in the various markets. If one believes that asset markets adjust instantaneously or at least have adjustment speeds which are very high and in any case much higher than those of goods markets, then it follows that it is the flows related to asset markets which have immediate effects on the exchange rate (see above, Sect. 18.5.3.3). But if this is not true, then the other markets also are relevant for determining the exchange rate, and the asset market approach is not a correct way of describing the process of exchange rate determination. Now, the continuous time approach enables us to determine the adjustment speeds rigorously (whichever the length of the observation interval); therefore, by using the balance-of-payments equation in which all the relevant variables are present and *come from adjustment equations with their specific estimated adjustment speeds,* we do not impose any arbitrary constraint on the data but let them speak for themselves.

Let us now come to the *exchange rate* (as representative exchange rate we have taken the Lira/US$ rate), which is determined through the balance-of-payments equation. Thus the model follows approach *B* according to our classification. The choice has been made on the grounds that the specification of an exchange-rate determination equation would have induced us to accept one or the other theory, whereas the balance-of-payments equation is more "neutral" once it is properly treated as explained in Sect. 18.5.4. This of course shifts the problem onto the specification of capital movements and of official intervention.

Capital movements are modelled according to the portfolio approach with non-instantaneous adjustment: the current stock of net foreign assets (as determined by portfolio theory) moves toward the desired stock with an adjustment speed which is estimated. As regards the monetary authorities' intervention, it is modelled as a reaction function, which is rather complicated. It contains, in fact, elements specific to the exchange-rate regime (fixed or floating) as well as elements of permanent nature, such as the leaning-against-the-wind policy and the desired reserves/imports ratio.

This said, let us come to the out-of-sample forecasts of the exchange rate. Our models has consistently outperformed the random walk (which in turn outperformed the traditional structural models). The results are shown in detail in Gandolfo, Padoan, Paladino (1990a, b) and in Gandolfo, Padoan, De Arcangelis (1993). Here we limit ourselves to give the order of the RMSE (root mean square error) of dynamic forecasts, which has been around 2.5%, as compared with 7–8% of the random walk and much higher values as regards the traditional models.

These results confirm the opinion that to outperform the random walk it is necessary to move away from the conventional single-equation, semi-reduced form structural models, toward suitable economy-wide macroeconometric models. Our Italian continuous time model is an eclectic model in which all the relevant interactions between real and financial variables, and stocks and flows, are present in a dynamic setting where the usual simplifying assumptions (PPP, UIP, etc.) are not used. It is comforting for economic theory to know that our model has been able to outperform the random walk.

Appendix

A.18.1 A Disequilibrium Model of Real and Financial Accumulation in an Open Economy

In the text – in order to validate statements on the convergence of the vicious circle (Sect. 18.4.3) and on exchange-rate forecasting (Sect. 18.6.3) – we have referred to a model by Gandolfo and Padoan. This is an eclectic model, in the sense that both real and financial variables, both stocks and flows, etc., are present, with no *a priori* prevalence given to any one. Each variable adjusts with an adjustment speed to be determined empirically (not by *a priori* assumptions) to its partial equilibrium or desired value: this is a setting of disequilibrium dynamics, though the model possesses a steady-state growth path (with damped oscillations around it) which is structurally stable.

From the formal point of view the model is specified in continuous time, as a system of non-linear stochastic differential equations, and is econometrically estimated in continuous time in accordance with suitable methods (see, for example, Gandolfo, 1981). These, amongst other advantages, allow us to obtain rigorous estimates of the adjustment speeds whichever the period of time inherent in the data, and so the values of these adjustment speeds can be obtained even if the adjustment speed of a variable is such as to bring the variable itself to equilibrium within the observation interval.

Since the model consists of a set of twenty-four non-linear stochastic differential equations, even a cursory examination of its theoretical and formal features, and of its empirical results, would require too much space, so that we refer the reader to the source (Gandolfo and Padoan, 1990).

A.18.2 The Modern Approach to Exchange-Rate Determination

A.18.2.1 The Monetary Approach

Let us take up Eq. (18.12), which expresses the simplest form of the monetary approach to the exchange rate, and assume that the money-demand function has the form

$$\frac{L}{p} = L_0 e^{-\varepsilon i} y^\eta, \qquad (A.18.1)$$

where ε is the semi-elasticity of money demand with respect to the interest rate and η the real-income elasticity of the same demand. Let us also assume that these functions are internationally identical in our two-country world, so that the parameters $L_{0f}, \varepsilon_f, \eta_f$ are equal to the corresponding parameters L_0, ε, η. Then, if we substitute (A.18.1) into (18.4) and take the natural logarithms, we get

$$\ln r = (\ln M - \ln M_f) + \varepsilon(i - i_f) - \eta(\ln y - \ln y_f). \qquad (A.18.2)$$

Besides, since, with perfect substitutability between domestic and foreign assets, relation (18.5) must hold, we have

$$i = i_f = \tilde{r}/r, \qquad (A.18.3)$$

which can be substituted into (A.18.2). In its turn the expected rate of variation in the exchange rate, as PPP is assumed to hold also in expectations, equals the difference between the expected rates of inflation

$$\tilde{r}/r = \tilde{p}/p - \tilde{p}_f/p_f, \qquad (A.18.4)$$

so that

$$i - i_f = \tilde{p}/p - \tilde{p}_f/p_f, \qquad (A.18.5)$$

and so, by substitution into (A.18.2), we get

$$\ln r = (\ln M - \ln M_f) - \eta(\ln y - \ln y_f) + \varepsilon(\tilde{p}/p - \tilde{p}_f/p_f). \qquad (A.18.2.1)$$

If we further assume that the time-path of income is exogenously given and that expectations are rational, the expected inflation rate coincides with the proportional rate of change in the money supply, so that

$$\ln r = (\ln M - \ln M_f) - \eta(\ln y - \ln y_f) + \varepsilon(\dot{M}/M - \dot{M}_f/M_f). \qquad (A.18.2.2)$$

Equations (A.18.2), (A.18.2.1) and (A.18.2.2) are alternative formulations of the simple version of the monetary approach. However, there is also a more sophisticated version which, though accepting the validity of PPP in the long run, acknowledges that in the short-run the exchange rate may deviate from PPP because of price stickiness. According to this version, what happens in the short run is that, for example, an increase in the money stock does not cause an immediate increase in prices owing to their stickiness, but has the effects described in the Mundellian model (see Sect. 16.3.1): the interest rate tends to decrease, and the incipient capital outflow causes the exchange rate to depreciate. This depreciation, however, is greater than that required by long-run PPP (the overshooting phenomenon, already treated in Sect. 16.6.4). To be precise, the amount by which the depreciation is greater than required is exactly such that the expected future appreciation (agents with rational expectations do in fact know that in the long run the exchange rate will have to conform to PPP) precisely offsets the interest differential that has come about.

It follows from the above reasoning that Eq. (A.18.2) and its alternative formulations hold as long-run relations, which we can express by replacing $\ln r$ with $\ln \hat{r}$ into them, where $\ln \hat{r}$ denotes the long-run equilibrium value of the exchange rate satisfying PPP. We must now determine exchange-rate expectations: in these, both a short-run and a long-run component are present. In the short-run, agents believe that the exchange rate will tend towards its PPP value with a certain speed of adjustment α; and they expect that, when it has reached this value, it will move in accordance with the inflation differential as expressed in (A.18.4) (which, in this version of the model, is also a long-run relationship). Thus we have.

$$\tilde{r}/r = -\alpha(\ln r - \ln \hat{r}) + (\tilde{p}/p - \tilde{p}_f/p_f). \quad (A.18.6)$$

With integrated financial markets and perfect asset substitutability Eq. (A.18.3) continues to hold, so that, by substituting in Eq. (A.18.6) and by solving for $(\ln r - \ln \hat{r})$, we have

$$\ln r - \ln \hat{r} = -(1/\alpha)[(i - \tilde{p}/p) - (i_f - \tilde{p}_f/p_f)]. \quad (A.18.7)$$

The expression in square brackets on the right-hand side is the differential between the *real* interest rates. If we now replace $\ln \hat{r}$ with its PPP value given by (A.18.2.1), we finally obtain

$$\ln r = (\ln M - \ln M_f) - \eta(\ln y - \ln y_f)$$
$$-\frac{1}{\alpha}(i - i_f) + \left(\frac{1}{\alpha} + \varepsilon\right)(\tilde{p}/p - \tilde{p}_f/p_f), \quad (A.18.8)$$

which is the *sticky-price version* (sometimes called the *overshooting version*) of the monetarist model. It can be readily seen that the simple version (A.18.2) is a particular case of (A.18.8), which comes about when the adjustment speed α tends to infinity and Eq. (A.18.5) holds instantaneously.

A.18.2.2 The Portfolio Approach

The essential feature of the portfolio approach is imperfect substitutability between domestic and foreign assets, so that Eq. (A.18.3) is no longer valid and must be replaced with

$$\tilde{r}/r = i - i_f - \delta, \tag{A.18.3.1}$$

where δ, which denotes the divergence between the interest differential and the expected proportional variation in the exchange rate, is a *risk coefficient* or *risk premium* that asset holders demand on domestic-currency assets relative to foreign currency assets, given the existing stocks of wealth, of assets, and given the expected relative rates of return on the various assets. In other words, δ is the exchange risk premium that must be expected, over and above the interest differential, for asset holders to be indifferent at the margin between uncovered holdings of domestic bonds and foreign bonds.

Instead of pursuing the way outlined in the text, which leads one to introduce the stocks of the various assets, which cannot be easily observed, it is expedient to follow an alternative route, which leads one to express the risk premium in terms of easily observable variables, and then to introduce the result in the equation of the monetary approach. As has been shown by various writers — for example Dooley and Isard (1983) and Hooper and Morton (1982), to whom we refer the reader — the risk premium can be expressed in terms of various factors, amongst which mainly the cumulative imbalances in the current account[15] (or more restrictively, in the trade account) of the two countries[16], that is

$$\delta = \beta_0 + \beta_1 \sum_{j=0}^{t} x_j + \beta_2 \sum_{j=0}^{t} x_{fj}, \tag{A.18.3.2}$$

where x_j is the current account balance of the home country in period j, x_{fj} the current account balance of the rest of the world, and $\beta_0, \beta_1, \beta_2$ are coefficients. It should be noted that the cumulative current accounts could also be taken to represent empirically the role of "news" in exchange-rate determination (the role of news is examined in Sect. 16.6.4, from the theoretical point of view).

If we use Eq. (A.18.3.1) instead of Eq. (A.18.3), in the place of Eq. (A.18.8) we obtain the equation

$$\ln r = (\ln M - \ln M_f) - \eta(\ln y - \ln y_f)$$
$$- \frac{1}{\alpha}(i - i_f) + \left(\frac{1}{\alpha} + \varepsilon\right)(\tilde{p}/p - \tilde{p}_f/p_f) + \frac{1}{\alpha}\delta, \tag{A.18.8.1}$$

and so, by substituting (A.18.3.2) into (A.18.8.1), we get

---

[15] An elementary explanation (Shafer and Loopesko, 1983, p. 30) is the following. As time passes, financial wealth is transferred from the deficit to the surplus countries. If we assume that residents of any country, *ceteris paribus*, have a preference for assets denominated in their own currency (the preferred local habitat assumption, already mentioned in note 11) this redistribution of wealth alters the relative demands for assets. The currency of a deficit country depreciate to a point from which agents expect it to subsequently appreciate, thus establishing a risk premium.

[16] In a two-country world the two countries' current accounts are mirror-images of each other. In practice one refers to two countries out of n, so that their current accounts are no longer necessarily symmetric.

$$\ln r = \frac{\beta_0}{\alpha} + (\ln M - \ln M_f) - \eta(\ln y - \ln y_f)$$
$$- \frac{1}{\alpha}(i - i_f) + \left(\frac{1}{\alpha} + \varepsilon\right)(\tilde{p}/p - \tilde{p}_f/p_f) \qquad \text{(A.18.9)}$$
$$+ \frac{\beta_1}{\alpha} \sum_j x_j + \frac{\beta_2}{\alpha} \sum_j x_{fj},$$

where all the variables are to be taken at time t.

Equation (A.18.9) is the general form of the asset-market approach which includes, as particular cases, both Eq. (A.18.2) and Eq. (A.18.8).

A.18.2.3 Empirical studies

The models considered by Meese and Rogoff were the flexible-price (Frenkel-Bilson) monetary model, the sticky-price (Dornbusch-Frankel) monetary model, and the sticky-price (Hooper-Morton) asset model. They did not consider the Hooper-Morton model with risk because it had been rejected by Hooper-Morton themselves since the coefficient of the term representing risk has the wrong sign, but we shall include this version for completeness of exposition.

The quasi-reduced forms of the four models can be subsumed under the following general specification:

$$e_t = a_0 + a_1(m - m_f)_t + a_2(y - y_f)_t + a_3(i_s - i_{sf})_t + a_4(i_L - i_{Lf})_t$$
$$+ a_5(\overline{CA} - \overline{CA}_f)_t + a_6\bar{K}_t + u_t, \qquad \text{(A.18.10)}$$

where the subscript f denotes the foreign country, t is time, and

e = logarithm of the spot exchange rate (price of foreign currency)
m = logarithm of the money supply
y = logarithm of real income
i_s = short-term interest rate
i_L = long-term interest rate
$\overline{CA}$ = cumulated trade balance
$\bar{K}$ = cumulated capital movements balance
u = disturbance term.

The four models are derived as follows:

(FB) Frenkel-Bilson: $a_1 > 0, a_2 < 0, a_3 > 0, a_4 = a_5 = a_6 = 0$;
(DF) Dornbusch-Frankel: $a_1 > 0, a_2 < 0, a_3 < 0, a_4 > 0, a_5 = a_6 = 0$;
(HM) Hooper and Morton: $a_1 > 0, a_2 < 0, a_3 < 0, a_4 > 0, a_5 < 0, a_6 = 0$;
(HMR) Hooper and Morton with risk: $a_1 > 0, a_2 < 0, a_3 < 0, a_4 > 0, a_5 < 0, a_6 > 0$.

The FB and DF models are monetary models, the difference being that the FB model assumes PPP in both the short and the long run, while the DF model assumes PPP only in the long run and allows for sticky prices in the short run. The Hooper-Morton model is a model which draws from both the monetary and the portfolio approach to exchange-rate determination. In the HM formulation it follows the *DF* model but introduces the effects of trade-balance surpluses: a persistent domestic (foreign) trade-balance surplus (deficit) indicates an appreciation of the long-run exchange rate. It should be noted that *HM* allowed for different coefficients on the domestic and foreign cumulated trade balances, but it is usual to follow Meese and Rogoff (1983b) in assuming that domestic and foreign trade balance surpluses have an effect on the exchange rate of equal magnitude but opposite sign. Finally, the *HMR* model introduces imperfect asset substitutability hence a risk premium, that we approximate by $\bar{K}$ following Dooley and Isard (1983).

Subsequent studies by Somanath (1986) suggested that, contrary to the findings of Meese and Rogoff, the introduction of the lagged dependent variable among the explanatory variables improved the forecasting ability of the model, indicating a non-instantaneous adjustment of the actual exchange rate to its equilibrium value as given by the right-hand-side of eq. (A.18.10). Thus one should also test the lagged version of the four above models, that is

$$e_t = a_0 + a_1(m - m_f)_t + a_2(y - y_f)_t + a_3(i_s - i_{sf})_t + a_4(i_L - i_{Lf})_t$$
$$+ a_5(\overline{CA} - \overline{CA_f})_t + a_6\bar{K}_t + a_7 e_{t-1} + u_t. \qquad (A.18.11)$$

It has also been suggested that error correction models (*ECM*) may be better suited for theories that postulate long-run relationships such as, for example, the long-run proportionality between the exchange rate and relative money stocks in the monetary models. In fact, Sheen (1989) found that a modified monetary model (in which *PPP* was dropped and certain restrictive assumptions were made about the generation of the expected future values of the predetermined variables) with an *EC* term outperformed the *RW* in out-of-sample forecasts of the Australian $/US$ exchange rate.

The basic idea of the *ECM* formulation is simply that a certain fraction of the disequilibrium is corrected in the following period. The *ECM* specification of the four models under consideration is

$$\Delta e_t = a_0 + a_1(\Delta m - \Delta m_f)_t + a_2(\Delta y - \Delta y_f)_t + a_3(\Delta i_s - \Delta i_{sf})_t$$
$$+ a_4(\Delta i_L - \Delta i_{Lf})_t + a_5(\Delta \overline{CA} - \Delta \overline{CA_f})_t + a_6\Delta\bar{K}_t + a_7(e - m + m_f)_{t-1}$$
$$+ a_8 e_{t-1} + u_t. \qquad (A.18.12)$$

The *ECM* specification is equivalent to the cointegration between the relevant variables (Engle and Granger, 1987), in our case between the exchange rate and the relative money stocks. A test of $a_7 = 0$ is a test of both the *ECM* specification and the long-run proportionality; the cointegration between the exchange rate and the relative money supplies can be further tested by running the cointegrating regression of Engle and Granger and applying various unit root tests (e.g. Fuller, 1976; Dickey and Fuller, 1981).

As stated in the text, the application of these models (including the *ECM* version) to the Lira/US$ exchange rate has been a dismal failure: see Gandolfo, Padoan, Paladino (1990a, b) and Gandolfo, Padoan, De Arcangelis (1993).

Among the various reasons that Meese and Rogoff adduced for the poor performance of the structural exchange rate models, "parameter instability" (Meese and Rogoff, 1983a, p. 18) is briefly cited and justified by possible structural breaks due to specific episodes that occured in the Seventies. Apart from the peculiarity of the sample, a more theoretical justification for parameter instability can be found in the presence of changes of regime, or also as an extension of Lucas' critique. Parameter instability can be dealt with using the time-varying-coefficients (*TVC*) methodology. It should however be noted that the problem in applying *TVC* models is to find a meaningful economic explanation for how the structural coefficients should vary, i.e., why they follow a supposed stochastic process (see Schinasi and Swamy, 1987).

In addition, it should be noticed that the use of the rolling regression technique to obtain forecasts (as was done by Meese and Rogoff, 1983a) is stochastically equivalent to the use of a *TVC* model where a particular random process – i.e., the multivariate *RW* – is imposed to the coefficients (see Alexander and Thomas, 1987):

$$e_t = x_t \beta_t + u_t,$$

$$\beta_t = \beta_{t-1} + \varepsilon_t,$$

where $\varepsilon_t = NIID(0; \Sigma)$ and $E[u_t | x_t] = 0$.

Gandolfo, Padoan and De Arcangelis (1993) have used a *TVC* model of the so-called "return-to-normality" type: the coefficients are assumed to follow a generic *ARMA* stationary process around a constant term and are not restricted to the multivariate *RW* process, as in the above model. In other words, this model is equivalent to a restricted Kalman filter where the state variables are deviations from a mean value and follow a stationary process, i.e., the eigenvalues of the transformation matrix, H, are all less than one in absolute value:

$$e_t = x_t \beta_t + u_t,$$

$$(\beta_t - \bar{\beta}) = H(\beta_{t-1} - \bar{\beta}) + \varepsilon_t.$$

Despite the more general framework, the main drawback of this approach still remains: as Schinasi and Swamy (1987) observe in their conclusions, this drawback is the lack of "sound and rigorous economic principles" (p. 28) to explain the evolution process of the *TVC*'s. See also Schinasi and Swami, 1989.

The results of this *TVC* model have however remained poor, and have not outperformed the random walk (Gandolfo, Padoan, De Arcangelis, 1993). Similarly poor results have been obtained by De Arcangelis (1992) with another type of *TVC* model, based on a Bayesian approach. Thus it does not seem that parameter instability is responsible for the poor performance of the standard structural models of exchange-rate determination.

Let us come finally to the results of our continuous-time macroeconometric model of the Italian economy. We first clarify a technical point. In discrete-time models it is usual to make the distinction between (a) single-period (or "static") forecasts and (b) multi-period (or "dynamic") forecasts. The former are those obtained by letting the lagged endogenous variables take on their actual observed values; the latter are those obtained by letting the lagged endogenous variables take on the values forecast by the model for the previous period(s). The equivalent distinction in continuous time models is made according to whether the solution of the differential equation system is (a) recomputed each period, or

(b) computed once and for all. In case (a) the differential equation system is re-initialized and solved n times (if one wants forecasts for n periods), each time using the observed values of the endogenous variables in period t as initial values in the solution, which is then employed to obtain forecasts for period $t+1$. This is equivalent to the single period forecasts in discrete models. In case (b) the observed values of the endogenous variables for a given starting period are used as initial values in the solution of the differential equation system, which is then employed for the whole forecast period. This is equivalent to the dynamic forecasts in discrete models. Although it is a well known fact that dynamic forecasts are generally less good than static ones because the errors cumulate, we decided to use dynamic forecasts to test the predictive performance of our model, because these are the only ones which can be employed to produce forecasts for a time interval different from that inherent in the data.

The basic random-walk model was used as the benchmark, although some authors suggest that comparing multi-step-ahead predictions of structural models with one-step-ahead predictions of the random-walk model gives the random-walk model an unfair advantage over structural models which do not include a lagged dependent variable; in this case a multi-step-ahead (with or without drift) prediction of the random walk is on a more equal footing with the structural model's predictions (Schinasi and Swamy, 1987). The reason for our choice is that a continuous time model specified as a differential equation system embodies all the relevant dynamics, including the one that discrete-time models try to capture by introducing lagged dependent variables as explanatory variables.

Our results are consistently better than the random walk, as stated in the text. The thesis that a suitable economy-wide model would outperform the random walk has been lent further support by Howrey (1994), who – building on work of Gandolfo, Padoan, Paladino (1990b) – shows that exchange-rate forecasts obtained by the Michigan quarterly econometric model of the U.S. perform better than the random walk.

A.18.2.4 Currency Substitution

An interesting theoretical development of the monetary approach to the exchange rate is to be seen in currency-substitution models. In all the models analyzed here a common assumption is that residents can hold domestic money but cannot hold foreign currency (they can, of course, hold foreign securities). Currency-substitution models abandon this assumption, so that residents can hold both domestic and foreign currency. Since, by definition, money is the riskless asset and can be assumed to be non-interest bearing[17], the problem arises of determining how residents will allocate their (real) wealth between domestic and foreign currency. The general criterion is always that of relative expected returns expressed in a common standard, for example domestic currency. The expected real return on domestic is the opposite of the expected rate of domestic

---

[17] The fact that in some countries checking accounts, which are to be considered money for all purposes, bear interest, is an institutional problem that we shall ignore.

inflation, $-\tilde{p}/p$. The expected real return of foreign money equals the difference between the expected proportional rate of change of the exchange rate (the price of foreign currency in terms of domestic currency) minus the expected rate of domestic inflation. The expected differential in returns is thus $\tilde{r}/r$ which, in the case of rational expectations (perfect foresight) equals $\dot{r}/r$. To avoid burdening an already overcrowded chapter we refer the reader to the relevant literature (see, for example, Calvo and Rodriguez, 1977; Ortiz and Solis, 1982; Canto and Miles, 1983; Salin ed., 1984; Daniel, 1985; Koustas and Ng, 1992; Canzoneri and Diba, 1993). We make only two observations. The first is that these models are limited in that the menu offered usually contains only two assets (domestic and foreign money); for a more general approach in which domestic and foreign securities are also considered in a general portfolio balance model, see Cuddington (1983) and Branson and Henderson (1985). The second concerns one of the interesting implications of currency substitution models, which is that a high degree of currency substitution may put pressure on the countries, whose currencies are concerned, to move towards a monetary union. According to some writers (see, for instance, Melvin, 1985), this may have been a more important reason for the move towards the EMS than any of the reasons examined in the traditional optimum currency area framework.

References

Adams, C. and J. Greenwood, 1985
Ahmad, J., 1984
Ahtiala, P., 1984
Aizenmann, J., 1984
Alexander, D. and L.R. Thomas, 1987
Allen, P.R. and P.B. Kenen, 1980, Part V
Argy, V., 1981
Argy, V., 1982
Arndt, S.W., R.J. Sweeney and T.D. Willet (eds.), 1985
Artus, J.R. and J.H. Young, 1979
Asheim, G.B., 1984
Backus, D., 1984
Baillie, R.T. and P.T. McMahon, 1989
Basevi, G. and P. De Grauwe, 1977
Basevi, G. and P. De Grauwe, 1978
Batchelor, R.A. and G.E. Wood (eds.), 1982
Bergsten, C.F. et al. (eds.), 1970
Bernholz, P., M. Gäartner and E.W. Heri, 1985
Bhandari, J.S., 1982
Bhandari, J.S., 1984
Bhandari, J.S. (ed.), 1985
Bhandari, J.S. and B.H. Putnam (eds.), 1983
Bigman, D., 1983
Bigman, D. and T. Taya (eds.), 1980
Bigman, D. and T. Taya (eds.), 1983
Bilson, J.F.O., 1978
Bilson, J.F.O., 1979a
Bilson, J.F.O., 1979b
Bilson, J.F.O. and R.C. Marston (eds.), 1984
Blaug, M., 1980
Blundell-Wignall, A., 1984
Bond, M.E., 1980
Branson, W.H., 1984
Branson, W.H. and W.H. Buiter, 1983
Branson, W.H. and D.W. Henderson, 1985
Calvo, G.A. and C.A. Rodriguez, 1977
Canto, V.A. and M.A. Miles, 1983
Canzoneri, M.B. and B.T. Diba, 1993
Cassel, G., 1918
Claassen E. and P. Salin (eds.), 1983
Clement, M.O., R.L. Pfister and K.J. Rothwell, 1967, Chap. 6
Cohen, B.J., 1981
Conway, R.K., P.A.V.B. Swamy and J.F. Yanagida, 1983
Cooper, R.N. et al. (eds.), 1982
Corden, W.M., 1983
Cuddington, J.T., 1983
Daniel, B.C., 1985
De Arcangelis, G., 1992
De Cecco, M., 1983
De Grauwe, P., 1983, Chaps. 12 and 16
De Grauwe, P., M. Fratianni and M.K. Nabli, 1985

De Grauwe, P., M. Janssens and H. Leliaert, 1985
De Grauwe, P. and T. Peeters (eds.), 1983
De Jong, E., 1991
Dickey, D.A. and W.A. Fuller, 1981
Dooley, M. and P. Isard, 1983
Dornbusch, R., 1983
Dornbusch, R. and P. Krugman, 1976
Dunn, R.M., 1983
Edgeworth, F.Y., 1905
Engle, R.P. and C.W.J. Granger, 1987
Falchi, G. and M. Michelangeli, 1977
Fama, E.F., 1984
Farrell, V.S., D.A. DeRosa and T.A. McCown, 1983
Federal Reserve Bank of Boston, 1978
Flood, R.P., 1978
Fratianni, M. and T. Peeters (eds.), 1978
Frankel, J.A., 1983
Frankel, J.A., 1984
Frenkel, J.A., 1981
Frenkel, J.A. and M.L. Mussa, 1985, Sect. 4
Frenkel, J.A. (ed.), 1983
Frenkel, J.A. and H.G. Johnson (eds.), 1978
Fuller, W.A., 1976
Gandolfo, G., 1976
Gandolfo, G., 1979
Gandolfo, G., 1981
Gandolfo, G., 1986
Gandolfo, G. and P.C. Padoan, 1990
Gandolfo, G., P.C. Padoan and G. Paladino, 1990a
Gandolfo, G., P.C. Padoan and G. Paladino, 1990b
Gandolfo, G., P.C. Padoan and G. De Arcangelis, 1993
Geweke, J., 1984
Goldstein, M., 1980
Gylfason, T. and J.F. Helliwell, 1983
Hakkio, C.S., 1984
Helliwell, J.F., 1979
Helliwell, J.F. and P.M. Boothe, 1983
Hoffman, D.L. and D.E. Schlagenhauf, 1985
Hooper, P. and J. Morton, 1982
Horne, J., 1983
Howrey, P., 1994
Ingram, J.C., 1973
International Monetary Fund, 1984
Isard, P., 1978
Isard, P., 1987
Isard, P., 1988
Johnson, H.G. and A.K. Swoboda (eds.), 1973
Kawai, M., 1980
Klein, L.R. and W.E. Krelle (eds.), 1983
Kouri, P.J.K., 1983a
Kouri, P.J.K., 1983b
Koustas, Z. and K.S. Ng, 1992
Krause, L.B. and W.S. Salant (eds.), 1977
Krueger, A.O., 1983
Lanyi, A., 1969
Levich, R.M., 1985
Levin, J.H., 1977
Levin, J.H., 1983b
Lindbeck, A. (ed.), 1979
MacDonald, R., 1988
MacDonald, R. and M.P. Taylor, 1992a, b
Martin, J.P. and A. Smith (eds.), 1979
Masera, R.S. and R. Triffin (eds.), 1984
Mastropasqua, C., 1984
Meese, R.A., 1984
Meese, R.A. and K. Rogoff, 1981
Meese, R.A. and K. Rogoff, 1983a
Meese, R.A. and K. Rogoff, 1983b
Meese, R.A. and K. Rogoff, 1985
Meese, R.A. and K. Rogoff, 1988
Melvin, M., 1985
Modigliani, F. and T. Padoa-Schioppa, 1978
Mundell, R.A., 1961
Mundell, R.A., 1963
Murphy, R.G. and C. Van Duyne, 1980
Mussa, M., 1976
Mussa, M., 1984
Niehans, J., 1984, Chap. 18
Nurkse, R., 1945
Obstfeld, M. and A.C. Stockman, 1985
Officer, L.H., 1982
Ortiz, G. and L.F. Solis, 1982
Persson, T., 1984
Rabin, A.A. and L.B. Yeager, 1982
Rush, M. and S. Husted, 1985
Salin, P. (ed.), 1984
Sassanpour, C. and J. Sheen, 1984
Schinasi, G.J. and P.A.V.B. Swami, 1987
Schinasi, G.J. and P.A.V.B. Swami, 1989
Shafer, J.R. and B.E. Loopesko, 1983
Sheen, J., 1989
Shelburn, M.R., 1984
Somanath, V.S., 1986
Spaventa, L., 1983
Thursby, M.C., 1981
Tobin, J., 1982
Triffin, R., 1982
Vlaene, J.H. and C.G. De Vries, 1992
Various Authors, 1978
Wallich, H. and J.A. Gray, 1980
Williams, H.R., 1973
Williamson, J., 1985
Williamson, J. (ed.), 1981
Woo, W.T., 1985

19 The Theory of Monetary Integration and the European Monetary System

19.1 Introduction

As in the case of commercial integration (see Vol. I, Sect. 5.8), also in the case of monetary integration there are various degrees on integration, from the simple currency area to the full monetary union (with a single currency). However, while in the case of commercial integration the various degrees of integration can be classified precisely, the same is not true in the case of monetary integration, where a certain amount of terminological confusion exists. Thus a preliminary conceptual and terminological clarification is called for. A good starting point is the definition given in a report to the EEC Council and Commission, commonly known as the Werner Report (1970). It identifies a first set of conditions (called "necessary conditions" by the subsequent Delors Report, 1989) to define a monetary union:

1) within the area of a monetary union, currencies must be fully and irreversibly convertible into one another;
2) par values must be irrevocably fixed;
3) fluctuation margins around these parities must be eliminated;
4) capital movements must be completely free.

The second set of conditions identified in the Werner Report concerns the *centralization of monetary policy*. In particular, this centralization should involve all decisions concerning liquidity, interest rates, intervention on the exchange markets, management of reserves, and the fixing of currency parities vis-à-vis the rest of the world.

Finally, in the Werner Report the adoption of a single currency, though not indispensable for the creation of a monetary union, is considered preferable to maintaining the various national currencies. This is so for psychological and political factors, as the adoption of a single currency would demonstrate the irreversible nature of the undertaking.

Some authors (for example Ingram, 1973) take the first set of elements listed in the Werner Report and call it *monetary integration*. In practical usage this latter definition is then simplified to fixed exchange rates and freedom of capital movements. Other authors, on the contrary, take the view that monetary integration must imply something more. For example, Corden (1972) states that monetary integration consists of two elements:

1) "complete exchange-rate union," *i.e.* irrevocably fixed exchange rates and centralization of exchange-rate policy towards the rest of the world and of part of monetary policy, by a supranational body;
2) "convertibility," namely complete elimination of any control on international (within the area) transactions on both current and capital accounts.

Other authors, however, use "monetary integration" as the analogous, in international monetary theory, of the term "commercial integration" used as a generic term in trade theory. Monetary integration, in other words, is taken as the generic term that contains various categories (including the process of transition from a simple currency union to a full monetary union).

Be it as it may, from the point of view of economic theory the starting point of any analysis of monetary integration (we shall take this term in the generic meaning) is the theory of optimum currency areas. These will be examine in the next section. We shall next analyse the common monetary policy prerequisite (Sect. 3) and the problem of the single currency (Sect. 19.4). A section on the European Monetary System (EMS) will follow (Sect. 19.5), and the final section 19.6 will examine the prospective European monetary union.

19.2 The Theory of Optimum Currency Areas

The notion of *optimum currency area* (introduced by Mundell, 1961) is an evolution of the concept of currency area.

A currency area is a group of countries which have a common currency (in which case full monetary integration prevails) or which, though maintaining different national currencies, have permanently and rigidly fixed exchange rates among themselves and full convertibility of the respective currencies into one another; instead, the exchange rates vis-à-vis non-partner countries are flexible. The problem consists in determining the appropriate domain of a currency area[1] (hence the adjective *optimum*) and, specifically, whether the adhesion of a country to a currency area (to be set up or already existing) or its remaining in one is beneficial. Optimality can be judged in various manners, for example on the basis of the capability of maintaining external equilibrium without unemployment at home and with price stability.

As various authors point out, two approaches can be distinguished in the theory of optimum currency areas. The first is the traditional approach, which tries to single out a crucial criterion to delimit the appropriate domain. The second is the cost-benefit approach, which believes that the participation in a currency area has both benefits and costs, so that optimality has to be evaluated by a cost-benefit analysis. Both approaches will be dealt with in the following sections.

---

[1] Theoretically defined, optimum currency areas do not necessarily correspond to national frontiers, as they might include part of a nation only. But as it would not be viable, we shall not consider this case.

19.2.1 The Traditional Approach

Several single criteria to delimit the domain of an optimum currency area can be found in the literature, since different authors have singled out different criteria as crucial. The reader wishing to trace the origins of the different criteria that we are to examine can consult Ishiyama (1975), Tower and Willet (1976), Allen and Kenen (1980, Chap. 14).

(a) One criterion is that of *international factor mobility*: countries between which this mobility is high can profitably participate in a currency area, whilst exchange rates should be flexible between countries with a low factor mobility between them. With a high factor mobility, in fact, international adjustment would resemble the adjustment between different regions of the same country (interregional adjustment), between which, obviously, no balance-of-payments problem exists. Let us assume, for example, that there is a decline in the exports of a region to the rest of the country because of a fall in the demand by the rest of the country for the output of an industry located in that region. The region's income and consumption decrease and, to ease the transition to a situation of lower real income, it is necessary for the region to get outside financing to be able to consume more than the value of output (high mobility of capital, possibly stimulated by policy interventions). Furthermore, the unemployed workers can move to other regions and find a job there (high mobility of labour). A similar process would take place at the international level. It is also clear that, in the absence of the postulated factor mobility, the elimination of the imbalances described above would require exchange-rate variations.

(b) A second criterion is that of the *degree of openness* of the economy, as measured by the relative importance of the sectors producing internationally traded goods or tradeables (both exportables and importables) and the sectors producing non-traded goods. A country where traded goods are a high proportion of total domestic output can profitably participate in a currency area, whilst it had better adopt flexible exchange rates in the opposite case. Let us assume that a highly open economy incurs a balance-of-payments deficit: if this is cured by an exchange-rate depreciation, the change in relative prices will cause resources to move from the non-traded goods sector to the traded goods one, so as to meet the increased (foreign) demand for exports and the higher (domestic) demand for import subsitutes. This implies huge disturbances (amongst which possible inflationary effects) in the non-traded goods sector because of its relative smallness[2]. In this situation it would be more effective to adopt fixed exchange rates and expenditure-reducing policies which reduce imports and free for exportation a sufficient amount of exportables previously consumed domestically.

(c) A third criterion is that of *product diversification*. A country with a high productive diversification will also export a wide range of different products (see, for example, Sects. 8.3 ff.). Now, if we exclude macroeconomic events which influence the whole range of exports (for example a generalized

---

[2] This is, in another form, the resource-reallocation-cost argument against flexible exchange rates already mentioned in Sect. 18.2.

inflation which causes the prices of all domestically produced goods to increase), in the normal course of events commodities with a fine or brilliant export performance will exist beside commodities with a poor export performance. It is self-evident that these offsetting effects will be very feeble or will not occur at all when exports are concentrated in a very limited number of commodities. On the average, therefore, the total exports of a country with a high product diversification will be more stable than those of a country with a low one. Since the variations in exports influence the balance of payments and so — *ceteris paribus* — give rise to pressures on the exchange rate, it follows that a country with high product diversification will have less need for exchange-rate changes and so can tolerate fixed exchange rates, whilst the contrary holds for a country having low product diversification.

(d) A fourth criterion is that of the degree of *financial integration*. It partially overlaps with criterion (a), but it is especially concerned with capital flows as an equilibrating element of payments imbalances. If there is a high degree of international financial integration, no need will exist for exchange-rate changes in order to restore external equilibrium, because slight changes (in the appropriate direction) in interest rates will give rise to sufficient equilibrating capital flows; in this situation it is possible to maintain fixed exchange rates within the area where financial integration exists. It goes without saying that a condition for financial integration is the elimination of all kinds of restrictions on international capital movements.

(e) A fifth criterion is that of the *similarity in rates of inflation*. Very different inflation rates do, in fact, cause appreciable variations in the terms of trade and so, insofar as these influence the flows of goods, give rise to current-account disequilibria, which may require offsetting exchange-rate variations. When, on the contrary, the rates of inflation are identical or very similar, there will be no effect on the terms of trade and so — *ceteris paribus* — an equilibrated flow of current-account transactions will take place (with fixed exchange rates) within the currency area.

(f) A sixth criterion is that of the *degree of policy integration*. Policy integration can go from the simple coordination of economic policies among the various partner countries to a situation in which these surrender their monetary and fiscal sovereignty to a single supranational monetary authority (necessary for consistently managing the international reserves of the area and the exchange-rates of the partner countries vis-à-vis the rest of the world, for achieving an appropriate distribution of the money supply within the area, etc.) and a single supranational fiscal authority (necessary to coordinate taxation, transfer payments and other measures — for example in favour of those workers who remain unemployed notwithstanding full labour mobility, etc.). It is clear that this ideal situation presupposes complete economic integration (on which see Sect. 5.8) which, in turn, cannot be achieved without some form of political integration.

All the above-listed criteria — with the exception of the last one, which is almost a truism, as it amounts to saying that when there is full economic and political integration there also is monetary integration — have been criticized as incomplete and partial. As a matter of fact, the reader who has followed us through the previous chapters will readily see that all these criteria stress only one or the other element present in the adjustment processes of the balance of payments under the various exchange-rate regimes, and that these elements can be subjected to the same criticism examined in the previous chapters. Just as an example, the criterion of financial integration and so of the equilibrating influence of capital flows is susceptible to the same criticisms examined in Sect. 15.4.3.1 (burden of interest payments, stocks and flows, etc.).

19.2.2 The Cost-Benefit Approach

Participation in a currency area involves benefits but also costs, so that to take the best course of action a careful determination of both is necessary by weighing these costs and benefits through some kind of social preference function. It is self-evident that the final decision will depend on the set of weights chosen; as these may vary from country to country (and from period to period in the same country), no general rule can be given. What we shall do is to describe the benefits and costs, following the already cited works (Ishiyama, 1975; Tower and Willet, 1976; Allen and Kenen, 1980, Chap. 14; see also Denton ed., 1974, and Robson, 1987) with some additional considerations.

The main benefits include the following:

(1) A permanently fixed exchange rate eliminates speculative capital flows between the partner countries. This, of course, depends on the confidence in the fixity of the exchange rates within the area, as in the opposite case, destabilizing speculation (of the type which affected the adjustable peg system: see Sect. 17.2) would inevitably come about.
(2) The saving on exchange reserves. The members no longer need international reserves for transactions within the area, exactly as in the case of regions within a country. This, of course, will occur when the credibility of the fixed exchange rates is complete, whilst in the initial stages it may be necessary to hold the same amount of pre-union reserves to ensure the agreed exchange-rate rigidity, i.e. to enforce the fixed parities established within the area.
(3) Monetary integration can stimulate the integration of economic policies and even economic integration. The idea is that participation in a currency area, and so the obligation to maintain fixed exchange rates vis-à-vis the other members, compels all members to make their economic policies uniform (in particular anti-inflationary policies) with those of the most "virtuous" member, at the same time making more credible domestically the statements of a firm intention to pursue a strong policy against inflation. This is essentially the same argument of monetary discipline already set forth in general in the debate on fixed versus flexible rates (see Sect. 18.2), strengthened by the fact that the commitment to maintain fixed exchange rates within the area would be felt more strongly than the commitment to defend a certain parity vis-à-vis the rest of the world as under the Bretton Woods regime. Another argument, however, suggests that monetary

agreements might give rise to more inflation. This might happen (Rogoff, 1985) when the national policy authority is involved in a policy game with other institutional agents (trade unions, etc.).

The argument of the uniformization of inflation rates has been the subject of much debate. Firstly, it has been noted that it curiously turns the position of the traditional approach upside down: we have in fact seen in Sect. 19.2.1, criterion (e), that according to the traditional approach the similarity in the rates of inflation is a *precondition* for taking part in an (optimal) currency area, whilst it now becomes a (beneficial) *effect* of taking part. Secondly, many nonmonetarist writers deny that the achievement of a common rate of inflation is ontologically a benefit, and observe that different countries may have different propensities to inflate: some are more or less inflation-shy, others more or less inflation-prone, and this reflects a different structure of their national preference function.

In effect, some confusion seems to exist in relation to this argument. Benefits (1) and (2) are fairly objective ones, in the sense that they do not presuppose the adhesion to a particular school of thought or to a particular preference function (practically everybody agrees that allocative efficiency, elimination of destabilizing speculation, saving on international reserves, are benefits). On the contrary, the equalization of the inflation rates is not considered universally desirable. From this point of view the traditional approach seems more neutral, because it only states that *if* there is similarity in inflation rates, *then* ground exist for participating in a currency area.

Behind the idea that monetary integration is conducive to economic integration there is, if one looks carefully, a psychological expedient of the following type. Assuming that a certain number of countries wish to effect an *economic union* (in the sense explained in Sect. 5.8), and assuming also that some of these are not able to implement domestically and as an expression of their autonomy the policies which bring about the characteristics necessary to an economic union (one of these characteristics is the uniformity in inflation rates), then *monetary integration* may well be a useful *instrument* to enable them to implement those policies. This reasoning is based on the belief (or hope) that society is affected by a kind of "economic policy illusion", in the sense that it is not willing to accept certain economic policies as an expression of its own autonomy, but it is willing to accept them if these are presented as deriving from external conditioning, i.e. required by the participation in a currency area. How justified is this belief, is an empirical matter; in general one can only observe that a common currency can certainly be brought into being and manifest all its advantages when it is established as the final step of a process of economic integration, whilst one can doubt its effectiveness as a tool to compel the refractory countries to realize the conditions necessary for economic integration.

(4) Besides the advantages listed above there may also be advantages of a political type, in the sense that a currency area (and, more generally, an economic union: see Sect. 5.8.2) carries more weight than the single countries in negotiating as a whole with outside parties. This of course requires that, although the exchange rates vis-à-vis non members are flexible, the currency area adopts a common exchange policy towards outside currencies. This is in

the nature of things when the area adopts a common currency in the strict sense, whilst it not so easily and automatically realizable when the individual members maintain their respective national currencies. In fact, the currency of any member may turn out to be stronger or weaker than those of other members with respect to outside currencies which are key currencies in international transactions (as for example the US dollar). This may give rise to tensions within the currencies of the area (remember what was said in Sect. 10.2, about cross rates), unless there is a coordination of the interventions on the foreign exchange rates; as an extreme case one can envisage a pool of all the international reserves of the partner countries with respect to outside countries and a unified management of this pool.

Let us now come to the *costs*, amongst which we list the following:

(1) loss of autonomy in monetary and exchange policy of the individual members. The financial integration and the related perfect capital mobility makes monetary policy impotent (see Sect. 16.3.1); in the case of full integration the central banks of the members will merge into one supranational central bank. The disappearance of a possible policy tool such as the managed variations in the exchange rate may give rise to serious problems if wage rates, productivity, and prices, have different trends in different member countries. These problems may become particularly severe in the case of shocks coming from outside the area.

(2) Constraints on national fiscal policy. It is true that fiscal policy — for the same reasons for which monetary policy is ineffective — is fully effective under fixed exchange rates (see Sect. 16.3.1), but this is true for an isolated country. In the case of a country belonging to a currency area, its fiscal policy may be constrained by the targets of the area as a whole (for example to maintain a certain equilibrium in the area's balance of payment vis-à-vis the rest of the world). And since the joint management of the single members' fiscal policies is carried out in the interest of the majority, it may happen that some member is harmed (unless a vetoing power is given to each member, in which case, however, there is the risk of a complete paralysis).

(3) Possible increase in unemployment. Assuming that the area includes a country with low inflation and an external surplus, this country will probably become dominant and compel the other members (with greater inflation and an external deficit) to adjust, because — as there are no means to compel the former country to inflate — the deficit countries will have to take restrictive measures which will lead to a decrease in employment. The writers of the monetarist school claim that in the long-run every country will be better off thanks to the lower rate of inflation, but, even allowing this to be true, the problem remains of determining how long is the long-run, as it is clear that in the short-run there are costs to be borne.

(4) Possible deterioration of previous regional disequilibria. "Regional" is here used in the strict sense, i.e. referring to single regions within a member country. Since the international mobility of capital (in the absence of controls) is higher than the international mobility of labour, the greater possibilities of finding better-rewarded uses of capital in other countries of the area, together with the relatively low international labour mobility, may

aggravate the development problems of the underdeveloped regions of a country. It should be noted that this negative effect occurs insofar as what was listed as the first criterion in the traditional approach (the high international mobility of *all* factors) does not occur, but it seems in any case likely that international labour mobility is lower than that of capital.

Having thus listed the benefits and costs, we conclude by pointing out that the already mentioned problem of weighing them is quite similar to that of weighing the benefits and costs of an economic union (see Sect. 5.8). The problem will be again touched upon in Sect. 19.7, in relation to the examination of the EMS (European Monetary System).

19.2.3 The Common Monetary Unit and the Basket-Currency

The problem of the common monetary unit, of course, necessarily arises only in what one could define as the *maximal* form of currency area (i.e. a full monetary integration), because in the *minimal* form (i.e. that which only establishes fixed exchange rates between the members) all that is needed is the declaration of the bilateral parities between the currencies of the members, namely the so-called *parity grid*. Given n members the parity grid will contain $n(n-1)$ bilateral exchange rates, since each currency has $(n-1)$ bilateral exchange rates with all the others; it should however be remembered from Sect. 10.2, that it is sufficient to know $(n-1)$ bilateral exchange rates to determine all. However, also in the minimal form it is possible to define a currency unit of the area which performs certain functions (see below, Sect. 19.5.2) although the members retain their own currencies.

From the theoretical point of view there are two possible ways to define the common currency unit. The first is to use a unit external to the area, namely not coinciding with any one of the members' currencies or combination of these, for example gold. The second consists in defining a unit internal to the area, which may be either the currency of a member or a combination of their currencies to be duly defined. The first way is not considered advisable by many writers because it does not permit a suitable regulation of international liquidity (see Sect. 20.1: actually, gold — once the basis of the international monetary system — has been demonetized, as we shall see in that section). The second way, as we have said, presents two options: the internationalization of the currency of a member or the definition of a *composite unit*, consisting in a bundle or combination of the various currencies belonging to the area. The former option implies that one of the members of the area is the dominant country, with all the inherent problems, as was the case of the Bretton Woods system (see Sect. 10.5.2 and 20.1), which might be considered as a currency area at the world level with the US dollar as the dominant currency. The latter option implies the definition of a "basket" of currencies (hence the name of *currency basket* or *basket-currency*), which contains predetermined and fixed amounts of the single currencies belonging to the area. These amounts are established by a common agreement in accordance with some criterion which usually refers to the relative economic importance of the various members[3].

In formal terms, if $q_1, q_2, \ldots, q_n$ are the amounts of the various currencies which make up the basket-currency, this (denoted by N) is defined by the set of numbers

$$\{q_1, q_2, \ldots, q_n\} = 1N. \tag{19.1}$$

An alternative way of expressing the same notion is

q_1 units of currency $1 + q_2$ units of currency $2 + \ldots + q_n$ units of currency $n \rightarrow 1N$, \hfill (19.2)

where the arrow instead of the $=$ sign indicates that the left-hand side is not really an arithmetic sum (it is not, in fact, possible to add heterogeneous magnitudes) but an operation which defines the contents of N. Naturally, given the bilateral (fixed) exchange rates r_{ks} (see Sect. 10.2), it is possible to define the *value* of N in terms of any one of the component currencies, that is the *exchange rate* of the jth currency with respect to N, as

$$R_j = \sum_{k=1}^{n} q_k r_{kj}, \quad j = 1, 2, \ldots, n, \tag{19.3}$$

where $r_{jj} = 1$. It is also possible to define a *weight* (b_j) of each currency in the basket, given by the ratio between the amount of the currency in the basket and the value of the basket in terms of the same currency, that is[4]

$$b_j = \frac{q_j}{\sum_{k=1}^{n} q_k r_{kj}}, \quad j = 1, 2, \ldots, n \tag{19.4}$$

where it must, of course, be

$$\sum_{j=1}^{n} b_j = 1, \tag{19.5}$$

i.e., the sum of the weights equals unity.

The option of the basket-currency also has its drawbacks, as we shall see later in relation to the EMS.

Therefore none of the solutions examined seems optimal, as all are a compromise between various and often opposite requirements. Many writers believe that the optimal solution would be for the area to create a *new* currency which should be entirely fiduciary (with no relation either with elements external to the system or with the members' currencies, issued and regulated by a supranational Central Bank) and would circulate throughout the area, exactly as

---

[3] It should be noted that, in general, a basket-currency is not necessarily linked to a currency area, as it can also be defined and used independently of the existence of a currency area. This is the case, for example, of the International Monetary Fund's *Special Drawing Right*, on which see Sect. 20.1.4.

[4] As can be seen from (19.4), the weights – given the quantities q_j – change as the r_{kj} change. Thus the definition of a currency basket in terms of (fixed) weights is equivalent to that in terms of fixed quantities only if the bilateral exchange rates are irrevocably fixed.

the US dollar is the currency circulating in all the States of the USA. But it is clear that this solution could be envisaged only *after* full economic and political integration had come about.

19.3 The Common Monetary Policy Prerequisite

We examine whether a common monetary policy is only desirable or also necessary for monetary integration to be viable. To analyse this question let us begin by recalling a few well-known interest-rate-parity conditions (see Sect. 10.7). Given perfect capital mobility, we must distinguish the cases of perfect and imperfect asset substitutability (see Sect. 10.7.6). With perfect asset substitutability, uncovered interest parity must hold, i.e.

$$i_h = i_f + \frac{\tilde{r}-r}{r}. \tag{19.6}$$

With imperfect asset substitutability, condition (19.6) has to be modified by the introduction of a risk premium δ, namely

$$i_h = i_f + \frac{\tilde{r}-r}{r} + \delta. \tag{19.7}$$

Let us begin by considering Eq. (19.6). In a currency area (and in higher degrees of monetary integration), exchange rates are irrevocably fixed, hence $(\tilde{r}-r)/r = 0$ and, consequently,

$$i_h = i_f. \tag{19.8}$$

With perfect asset substitutability only the money stock matters (see Sect. 18.5.3.1), so that we can consider only money-market equilibrium (demand for money = supply of money) at home and abroad. Thus we have

$$P_h L_h(Y_h, i_h) = M_h, \tag{19.9}$$

$$P_f L_f(Y_f, i_f) = M_f. \tag{19.10}$$

Even if we take the price levels and the outputs as given, the three equations (19.8)–(19.10) form an undetermined system, which is unable to determine the four unknowns (the two money supplies and the two interest rates). Thus, there is a fundamental indeterminacy of the money supply and the interest rate in this two-country system. It follows that the two countries will have to agree (implicitly or explicitly) on the conduct of monetary policy. We must stress that the apparent absence of agreement can simply be due to the presence of an implicit agreement. The typical implicit agreement is asymmetric, in the sense that it is based on the dominannt role of one country. This means that one country sets its money supply according to its own criteria and the other country adapts its money stock.

Suppose, for example, that the foreign country is the "dominant" country and fixes M_f. Then Eq. (19.10) determines i_f, which sets i_h by Eq. (19.8). Finally, Eq. (19.9) determines M_h. Thus country 1 must set its money supply at this level.

If it does otherwise, the currency area will break down. In fact, suppose for example that the home country tries to fix a higher money supply. This will depress i_h below i_f. As a consequence, immediate and disrupting capital flows from home to abroad will take place, unless controls on capital flows are introduced (but such controls are hardly compatible with monetary integration). These flows will lead to expectations of a future exchange rate adjustment and to the breakdown of the exchange rate commitment.

Explicit agreements on the conduct of the overall monetary policy are, on the contrary, of the cooperative type. This requires that countries agree to cooperate in setting their money stocks (or interest rates). This presents the well known free-riding problem (Hamada, 1985), the same kind of problem that has been treated at length in the theory of international price cartels (see Vol. I, § 5.5.3). In general, this means that once a cooperative agreement has been reached, there are usually incentives for one partner to do something else than was agreed upon. This follows from the fact that, by so doing, the partner will be better off, if the other partners do not retaliate (for example by reneging on the agreement). Thus some institutional mechanism has to be devised to avoid the free-riding problem.

These considerations confirm the essential importance of viable agreements on the conduct of monetary policy within the currency area. We have illustrated this proposition by the simplest model possible, but the results do not change substantially with more complicated models, such as those based on Eq. (19.7) instead of Eq. (19.8). This would require the introduction of the stocks of assets (money and other financial assets) and the determination of the portfolio-balance equilibrium.

19.4 The Single-Currency Problem

This problem is best examined in the context of cost-benefit analysis. In fact, the demonstration that the adoption of a single currency is required for the elimination of the inefficiencies linked to the coexistence of national currencies, is not a proof of the necessity of a single currency. What it shows is that a single currency is somehow better than the fixity of exchange rates, not that it is essential for a monetary union. Thus the proper framework is that of cost-benefit analysis.

In general, the full advantages of a monetary union can be obtained only through the perfect substitutability of all the union members' currencies in the three basic functions of money: unit of account, means of payment, and store of value. Once the credibility of the irrevocable fixity of exchange rates is firmly established, perfect substitutability in the unit-of-account and store-of-value functions does not present particular problems. Problems are present, on the contrary, in the means-of-payment function. Transaction costs create a wedge between buying and selling rates, since foreign exchange operators charge a cost for their service. These costs could be eliminated for private agents if the authorities subsidize the conversion between the various national currencies. This, however, would simply shift the costs onto the union's budget. In practice bid-ask spreads are such that, by simply converting one currency into another, one after each other, and finally reverting to the initial currency in, say, a fifteen-member union (such as the future European Monetary Union), without actually *spending* a penny one might well end up with less than 40% of the initial amount! In addition, these spreads are likely to vary from contry to country in the union, thus altering the degree of substitutability among currencies.

Let us now come to the examination of the main benefits and costs of a single currency (for a complete treatment see Emerson et al., 1992; De Grauwe, 1992, Part I). The benefits are due to the fact that a single currency *by definition* eliminates a number of problems and shortcomings inherent in the use of several national currencies. These are:

(1) The elimination of imperfections in the substitutability of currencies, as detailed above.
(2) The elimination of any possibility, even if remote, of changes in par values. The expression "irrevocably fixed exchange rate" has no practical significance. Although the international community tries to observe the rule *"pacta sunt servanda,"* history is full of examples of "irrevocable commitments" to fixed exchange rates that have broken down. The reason is simple: assuming that national governments behave rationally, they will evaluate the costs and benefits of the fixed exchange rate union, as shown in Sect. 19.2.2. If the costs become overwhelming with respect to the benefits, the government concerned may be tempted to change the parity, even if this means breaking an international agreement. This is by no means an impossible occurrence. The evaluation of the costs and benefits, in fact, may vary over time, for example in relation to economic conditions *and/or* to preference functions of different governments. Thus a fixed exchange rate system does not eliminate the risk that a temporary change in this evaluation might lead a member country to alter the parity. Rational economic agents know this, hence the possibility of speculative capital flows and of an uncertain climate for businesses.
(3) The elimination of destabilizing speculative capital flows within the union, due to expectations of parity changes as detailed under (2).
(4) The elimination of the need for intra-union international reserves, required to make the commitment credible and to offset possible speculative capital flows.
(5) We have shown in Sect. 19.3 that a common monetary policy is necessary for a monetary union. A single currency would greatly facilitate the conduct of this overall monetary policy, and would eliminate free-riding problems.
(6) A single currency would carry more international weight and enable the union to reap the benefits of seignorage. In addition, the interventions in the foreign exchange market vis-à-vis other currencies would be greatly facilitated and would require a smaller amount of international reserves vis-à-vis the rest of the world.

The main costs that have been stressed are the following:

(1) Costs for the transformation of the system of payments. These include the costs of changing existing monetary values into the new currency, the costs of changing coin machines, etc.

(2) The psychological cost to the public of introducing the new currency and their getting used to it. It is not sufficient to declare a currency legal tender for this to be used willingly in a country in the place of the existing national currency. A new currency cannot be merely imposed by legislative act, but must gain social consensus and be accepted by the market. Thus the authorities will have to ensure that the new currency performs the functions of money at least as efficiently as the existing national currencies. This process of convincing the public is not without costs.

(3) This point is usually presented as an advantage of the fixed exchange rate system, rather than as a cost of the single-currency system. It is called the "currency competition" argument. Several currencies in competition, so the argument goes, stimulate each national monetary authority in the group to pursue a lower rate of inflation and, more generally, a stable value of its respective currency. This does not seem a theoretically well-founded argument. A system based on competition between monetary policies will result either in the breakdown of the fixed exchange rate commitment or in the dominance of one currency, as shown in Sect. 19.3

To conclude, we observe that the benefits of a single currency seem much greater than the costs. From this, of course, it does not follow that a single currency is necessary for a monetary union. It is preferable, but not indispensable. There is, however, a further consideration that points to the necessity of a single currency. We have already mentioned above, under entry (2) of the list of benefits, the problems related to maintaining fixed parities. In the absence of capital controls (whose elimination necessarily accompanies the formation of a monetary union), 'permanently fixed exchange rate' is an oxymoron, as Portes (1993, p. 2) aptly puts it. No matter what governments say, speculators know that exchange rates between distinct national currencies exist only to be changed. And – confronted with one-way bets thanks to fixed exchange rates, and having practically unlimited resources thanks to free capital mobility – they can indeed compel the authorities to change the parities, as the crises of the EMS (see Sect. 19.5.5) have shown. Hence there is a strong suspect that a monetary union maintaining distinct national currencies with "permanently fixed exchange rates" would not be viable.

The same considerations can throw light on the issue of the process of transition to a monetary union with a single currency. Two approaches are possible: the gradual approach and the "shock therapy", the latter meaning the sudden introduction of the single currency. With the gradual approach there is the cost-of-credibility question. A major problem in the road to a monetary union is to convince the private sector that the commitment of the national authorities to monetary union is credible. An obvious way of achieving credibility would be to introduce a common currency immediately. A gradual approach (such as that adopted by the Maastricht Treaty, on which see below, Sect. 19.6) may not convince the private sector, because the commitment to a fixed exchange rate is not sufficiently credible. This may make it very costly the attempt to maintain a fixed exchange rate. The costs are the loss of competitiveness if fixed exchange rates generate overvaluation in an inflation-prone economy and (as happened in the September-October 1992 EMS crisis, on which see below, Sect. 19.5.5) the loss of international reserves to defend the parity against speculative attacks. If the defence is successful, we have a gain in credibility to be counted on the side of benefits. But if the defence is unsuccessful, we only have the cost, which can be measured precisely as an opportunity cost.

The single currency issue is not disjunct from the central bank issue. Once a single currency has been decided upon, the necessity arises of the centralization of monetary policy in a single supranational body. This is the union's central bank, which could be of the federal type to take advantage of the long experience that national central banks have built up over the years. We shall briefly take it up again in Sect. 19.6.

19.5 The European Monetary System

19.5.1 Introduction

On 13th March 1979 the EEC countries (with the exception of Britain), in application of the Bremen Agreement of 7th July 1978, gave birth to a currency area called the European Monetary System (henceforth EMS) and based on a unit of account called the European Currency Unit (ECU; it should be noted that this acronym considered as a word, is in French the name of an ancient French coin).

In Sects. 19.5.1–19.5.5 and A.19.1 we shall give a fairly detailed treatment of the EMS. Not only European students but also students in non-European countries might wish to have a textbook source to satisfy their curiosity or to examine wheter currency areas are appropriate for other parts of the world. In any case, a segmentation of this section has been made so that those only wishing to get a general idea can read Sect. 19.5.1 (and perhaps also Sect. 19.5.5) and skip the rest.

The EMS is based on three elements: the exchange rate mechanism (ERM), the European Currency Unit (ECU), the credit mechanisms. As regards the ERM, the member countries declare their bilateral parities (giving rise to a so called 'parity grid'), around which the actual exchange rates can oscillate within predefined margins. These margins were originally $\pm 2.25\%$ ($\pm 6\%$ in exceptional cases), and have been widened to $\pm 15\%$ from 2 August 1993 (see below, Sect. 19.5.5)[5]. The first committment of the ERM is that the participating countries are obliged to intervene in the foreign exchange market when the market exchange rate hit one of the fluctuation margins (using if necessary the Very Short Term Financing Facility, on which see below). The second committment of the ERM requires central rates to be modified only by collective agreement, with no unilateral action on the part of any partner.

---

[5] Actually the margins are asymmetric, namely $+2.275\%$ and -2.225% in the case of the band having total width 4.5%; $+6.18\%$ and -5.82% in the case of the 12% band; $+16.11\%$ and -13.881% in the case of the 30% band. The technical reasons for this asymmetry are explained in Sect. A.19.2.3.

As far as the ERM is concerned, the EMS – with reference to the classification in Sect. 10.5.3 – belongs to the category of limited-flexibility exchange systems, and is a combination of the adjustable peg and the wider band, i.e. an adjustable band system.

The EMS is therefore a currency area *sui generis,* as it officially contemplates the possibility of parity changes. What does then differentiate the EMS from the old snake mentioned in Sect. 18.3.1? One of the distinguishing features, in the original intentions, was the ECU and its role in the EMS. In fact, as we have seen in Sect. 19.2.3, it is when a currency area intends to move towards monetary union that the need for the definition of a common currency unit arises.

The introduction of the ECU was in fact a manifestation of "political will". Indeed, in the negotiations which gave rise to the EMS, the greatest controversies took place in relation to the definition of the operational rules which were to guide the central banks' interventions to maintain their currencies at the given parities with one another. One of the mechanisms considered was simply that of defining a parity grid (see Sect. 19.2.3) with an obligation on the part of each country to intervene on the foreign exchange market when its currency had reached one of the margins of fluctuation with respect to any other currency; in practice, nothing more nor less than the old snake. Another mechanism considered was that of defining a basket-currency, to wit the ECU, in terms of which to determine the central rates (parities) of the individual currencies and the respective margins of fluctuation, and so also the obligation to take corrective action in case of divergence.

This was by no means a useless debate, as the mechanisms imply quite different obligations to corrective action. If a single currency, for example the Deutschmark, should begin to deviate too much from its central rate, the second mechanism would require corrective action solely by the Bundesbank (Germany's Central Bank), whilst the first mechanism would require correcting action by *all* central banks. In other words, the ECU mechanism allows to single out the currency which, by diverging too much from the weighted average of the ECU basket, can be considered responsible for the disequilibrium and so has to take corrective action alone; on the contrary, the parity grid mechanism puts the burden of intervention on all currencies, including those not responsible for the disequilibrium. It is, in fact, a simple mathematical property of bilateral exchange rates (see Sect. 10.2) that $r_{ks}r_{sk}=1$, so that if a currency approaches a margin with respect to all the others, all the others will approach the opposite margin.

It was not necessary to be prophets to understand that anticipations of a strong Deutschmark suggested the ECU mechanism to the countries with weaker currencies (amongst them Italy), whilst Germany preferred the parity-grid mechanism. The compromise that was reached was to maintain the parity-grid mechanism as the basis for the *obligation* to take corrective action, and to use the ECU (a) as the unit of reference to define the central rates (parities) of the grid, and (b) as the basis for defining an "indicator of divergence", i.e. an indicator of a currency's divergence from its central ECU price, with the proviso that when this indicator exceeds a certain threshold (the "threshold of divergence"), this results in a *presumption* that the authorities concerned will correct the situation by adequate measures (in the form of exchange market interventions or of internal policy measures). To put it another way, the crossing of the ECU-defined threshold of divergence was intended as a kind of alarm-bell to warn that a currency was deviating too much (though not having yet reached the maximum bilateral margin against any other currency), and so it was presumed that *this* currency would take corrective action (but it was not obliged to: the obligation came into force only when a bilateral margin was reached).

The third element of the EMS is a set of measures of monetary cooperation and of monetary help to currencies under pressure, which will be dealt with in Sect. 19.5.4, after having examined the ECU and the indicator of divergence.

19.5.2 The ECU

As any basket-currency, the ECU is made of given quantities of the various currencies. Its composition, from the beginning to 16th September 1984, has been the following:

$$\begin{aligned}
&\text{Italian Lire } 109 \\
&+ \text{German D-Marks } 0.828 \\
&+ \text{Belgian Francs } 3.80 \\
&+ \text{French Francs } 1.15 \\
&+ \text{Dutch Guilders } 0.286 \\
&+ (\text{UK Pounds Sterling } 0.0885) \\
&+ \text{Irish Punts } 0.00759 \\
&+ \text{Danish Krones } 0.217
\end{aligned} \quad \rightarrow \text{one ECU}, \qquad (19.11)$$

while on 17th September 1984 its composition was changed in

$$\begin{aligned}
&\text{Italian Lire } 140 \\
&+ \text{German D-Marks } 0.719 \\
&+ \text{Belgian Francs } 3.85 \\
&+ \text{French Francs } 1.31 \\
&+ \text{Dutch Guilders } 0.256 \\
&+ (\text{UK Pounds Sterling } 0.0878) \\
&+ \text{Irish Punts } 0.00871 \\
&+ \text{Danish Krones } 0.219 \\
&+ (\text{Greek Drachmas } 1.15)
\end{aligned} \quad \rightarrow \text{one ECU}. \qquad (19.12)$$

It should be noted that the pound, and, since 17th September 1984, the newcomer, the drachma, although not participating in the exchange rate agreement and hence under no obligation to maintain given bilateral parities against any other currency of the area etc., were included in the basket. Another observation is that the quantity of Belgian francs also accounts for Luxembourg (which forms a monetary union with Belgium).

Finally, on 21st September 1989 the composition of the ECU was modified into

Italian lire 151.8
+ German D-Marks 0.6242
+ Belgian Francs 3.431
+ French Francs 1.332
+ Dutch Guilders 0.2198
+ (UK Pounds Sterling 0.08784) → one ECU (19.13)
+ Irish Punts 0.008552
+ Danish Krones 0.1976
+ (Greek Drachmas 1.44)
+ Spanish Pesetas 6.885
+ (Portuguese Escudos 1.393)

We observe that, of the two newcomers, one currency (the peseta) also accepted the exchange rate agreement, while the other (the escudo) initially did not, but took part in this agreement later, in 1992. In 1991 the UK pound entered the exchange rate agreement, but left it in September 1992, as did the lira (see Sect. 19.5.5).

The initial composition of the ECU was identical with that of the pre-existing European Unit of Account (EUA), established in 1974 for purely accounting purposes. In the EUA the quantities of the various currencies had been determined so as to yield weights which reflected the respective countries' relative importance (measured by various indicators, such as national income, foreign trade, population) in the EEC. We must dwell on this point to get it right.

If we consider the set (19.4), we see that it relates three groups of elements: the weights (b), the quantities (q) and the bilateral exchange rates (r). Given any two of these, set (19.4) enables one to determine the third: given the weights and the bilateral exchange rates it is possible to determine the quantities, etc.. Now, when the EUA was established, the weights were given as shown above and, given the bilateral exchange rates then existing, the quantities were determined by using set (19.4)[6]. These are the quantities which made up the EUA and which, as stated above, also made up the initial ECU – see (19.11) – and remained unchanged except for the two modifications, in 1984 and 1989, for the reasons that we shall explain presently.

Thus the quantities, after having been determined as unknowns through set (19.4) as shown above, became a datum in the ECU; it follows that, given the bilateral rates, the unknowns are the weights. To put it differently, set (19.4) now determines the weights given the quantities and the bilateral rates. At this point it is important to distinguish between the weights corresponding to the bilateral central rates (parities), i.e. the *central weights*, and the weights corresponding to the current bilateral exchange rates (which, as we know, may deviate from the parities within the prescribed margins), i.e. the *current weights*. In the parity grid, the bilateral central rates are fixed and hence the central weights are fixed: they change only if and when a change in the bilateral central rates (a so-called *realignment*) is agreed upon by the member countries, as provided for in the EMS agreement. The current weights, on the contrary, change through time as the actual market bilateral exchange rates change.

---

[6] From the mathematical point of view they are determined up to a scalar multiple. See Sect. A.19.2.1.

From (19.4) it can be readily seen that the weight of a currency varies inversely with that currency's bilateral market (or central, as the case may be) exchange rates: if, for example, currency j depreciates with respect to currency k (i.e., r_{kj} increases), the weight h_j decreases and, conversely, the weight h_k of currency k increases.

In Table 19.1, besides the predetermined weights of the various currencies in the EUA, we have given their quantities determined as explained above, their weights at the outset of the EMS [obtained through (19.4) by applying the bilateral parities in force on the eve of the EMS to the said quantities], their central rates with respect to the ECU at the same time [obtained by inserting the same data in (19.3)]; their central weights and rates determined by the last realignment before the modification of the composition of the basket (for brevity we have not given all the previous realignments, of which there were seven); the new quantities of the various currencies with the relative central weights and rates resulting from the new basket which came into force on 17th September 1984 after the five-year revision of the weights provided for by the EMS Agreement (on that occasion, the currency of the new EEC member, Greece, was also included in the basket); the realignment of January 1987; the new basket which came into force on 21st September 1989 (which also reflects the entry of the peseta and the escudo); the situation in force from August 1993. We shall ignore, for the moment, the threshold of divergence, on which see Sect. 19.5.3.

It is important to stress that any new composition of the ECU not only reflects the entrance of new countries into the EEC, but also, and especially, the necessity that the weights be brought again into line with the relative economic importance of the members (this was the main reason for the inclusion in the Articles of Agreement of the EMS of the proviso of a five-year revision of the weights, mentioned a moment ago). For example, as a consequence of the several realignments of the bilateral parities, the central weights (which, as we know, change when the bilateral parities change) had become more and more distorted, in the sense that they no longer reflected the relative economic importance of the members. And since these realignments had always been in the direction of a revaluation of the D-Mark, the distortion was in favour of this currency (and of the Dutch guilder, traditionally a follower of the D-Mark) and against the others: the D-Mark had increased its weight from the initial 33% to 37% and the Dutch guilder from 9% to 11.3%, the Italian lira had decreased its own from 9.5% to 7.8%, the French franc from 19.8% to 16.7%, etc. (see Table 19.1). Therefore, the new quantities have been determined such that the weights again reflect the relative economic importance of the members, through a calculation like that described at the beginning (given the weights and the bilateral parities, set (19.4) can be used to determine the quantities) *and* with the constraint (provided for in the Articles of Agreement of the EMS) that the central ECU-rates remained the same, namely that those holding after the change in the quantities were the same as those holding immediately before the change. It goes without saying that this proviso is applicable only to those currencies that were already present in the basket; for the new-comers (such as the drachma)[7] there is a degree of freedom settled by negotiation.

---

[7] In order to leave the bilateral central rates and the central ECU-rates unchanged after the entry of the drachma, while at the same time giving this currency a central ECU-rate not too different from its market exchange rate, a further "fictitious" realignment of the "notional" parities of the pound was made when the composition of the ECU was changed. This had no practical consequence as the pound is not party to the exchange rate agreement.

19.5 The European Monetary System   421

Table 19.1. Composition of the ECU, central weights and rates[a], threshold of divergence

Currency	Weights in the EUA (March 1975)	Quantities	ECU on 13th March 1979			ECU on 18th May 1983		
			Central weights %	Central rates (units of national currency)	Threshold of divergence ±%	Central weights %	Central rates (units of national currency)	Threshold of divergence ±%
Italian Lira	14.0	109	9.49	1148.15	4.07	7.77	1403.49	4.15
German D-Mark	27.3	0.828	32.98	2.51064	1.13	36.93	2.24184	1.06
Belgian/Lux. Franc	8.2	3.80	9.64	39.4582	1.53	8.46	44.9008	1.54
French Franc	19.5	1.15	19.83	5.79831	1.35	16.73	6.87456	1.41
Dutch Guilder	9.0	0.286	10.51	2.72077	1.51	11.32	2.52595	1.50
(UK Pound Sterling)[b]	17.5	0.0885	13.34	0.663247	1.46	15.07	0.587087	1.43
Irish Punt	1.5	0.00759	1.15	0.662638	1.67	1.05	0.725690	1.67
Danish Krone	3.0	0.217	3.06	7.08592	1.64	2.67	8.14104	1.64
(Greek Drachma)[b]	–	–	–	–	–	–	–	–

Currency	ECU on 17th September 1984 (new composition)				ECU on 17th January 1987		
	Quantities	Central weights %	Central rates (units of national currency)	Threshold of divergence ±%	Central weights %	Central rates (units of national currency)	Threshold of divergence ±%
Italian Lira	140	9.98	1403.49	4.05	9.44	1483.58	4.08
German D-Mark	0.719	32.08	2.24184	1.15	34,93	2.05853	1.10
Belgian/Lux. Franc	3.85	8.57	44.9008	1.54	9.07	42.4582	1.53
French Franc	1.31	19.06	6.87456	1.37	18.97	6.90403	1.37
Dutch Guilder	0.256	10.13	2.52595	1.52	11.04	2.31943	1.50
(UK Pound Sterling)[b]	0.0878	14.98	0.587087	1.43	11.87	0.739615	–
Irish Punt	0.00871	1.20	0.725690	1.67	1.14	0.768411	1.67
Danish Krone	0.219	2.69	8.14104	1.64	2.79	7.85212	1.64
(Greek Drachma)[b]	1.15	1.31	87.4813	1.67	0.76	150.792	–

Currency	ECU on 21th September 1989 (new composition)				ECU on 2nd August 1993		
	Quantities	Central weights %	Central rates (units of national currency)	Threshold of divergence ±%	Central weights %	Central rates (units of national currency)	Threshold of divergence ±%
Italian Lira[c]	151.8	10.24	1483.58	4.040	8.47	1793.19	–
German D-Mark	0.6242	30.33	2.05853	1.176	32.02	1.94964	7.65
Belgian/Lux. Franc	3.431	8.09	42.4584	1.556	8.53	40.2123	10.29
French Franc	1.332	19.30	6.90403	1.362	20.37	6.53883	8.96
Dutch Guilder	0.2198	9.49	2.31943	1.528	10.01	2.19672	10.12
(UK Pound Sterling)[b,d]	0.08784	11.89	0.739615	–	11.16	0.786749	–
Irish Punt	0.008552	1.12	0.768411	1.669	1.06	0.808628	11.13
Danish Krone	0.1976	2.53	7.85212	1.645	2.66	7.43679	10.95
(Greek Drachma)[b]	1.44	0.96	150.792	–	0.54	264.513	–
Spanish Peseta	6.885	5.16	133.804	4.268	4.46	154.250	10.75
(Portuguese Escudo)[b,e]	1.393	0.89	157.26	–	0.72	192.854	11.17

[a] The central weights are consistent with the central rates.
[b] Country that did not participate in the ERM at the date shown in the various tables.
[c] The lira left the ERM on 17th September 1992.
[d] The UK pound, that had joined the ERM in 1991, left it on 17th September 1992.
[e] The escudo joined the ERM in 1992.

Table 19.2. Grid of bilateral parities in the EMS and compulsory intervention points[a] (as of 2nd August 1993)

	100 BLF	100 DKR	100 FF	100 DM	100 IRL	100 HFL	100 ESC	100 PST	ECU
Belgian/Lux. Franc (BLF)		627.880 540.723 465.665	714.030 614.977 529.660	2,395.20 2,062.55 1,776.20	57.7445 49.7289 42.8260	2,125.60 1,830.54 1,576.45	24.2120 20.8512 17.9570	30.2715 26.0696 22.4510	— 40.2123 —
Danish Krones (DKR)	21.4747 18.4938 15.9266		132.0660 113.7320 97.9430	442.968 381.443 328.461	10.6792 9.19676 7.92014	393.105 338.537 291.544	4.47770 3.8568 3.3209	5.5985 4.8213 4.1529	— 7.4368 —
French Francs (FF)	18.800 16.2608 14.0050	102.1000 87.9257 75.7200		389.480 335.386 288.810	9.38950 8.08631 6.96400	345.650 297.661 256.350	3.93700 3.39056 2.91990	4.92250 4.23911 3.65050	— 6.5388 —
D-Marks (DM)	5.63000 4.84837 4.17500	30.4450 26.2162 22.5750	34.6250 29.8164 25.6750		2.80000 2.41105 2.07600	90.7700 88.7526 86.7800	1.17400 1.01094 0.87100	1.46800 1.26395 1.08800	— 1.9496 —
Irish Punt (IRL)	2.33503 2.01090 1.73176	12.6261 10.8734 9.36403	14.3599 12.3666 10.6500	48.1696 41.4757 35.7143		42.7439 36.8105 31.7007	0.486881 0.419295 0.361092	0.608731 0.524232 0.451462	— 0.8086 —
Dutch Guilders (HFL)	6.34340 5.46286 4.70454	34.3002 29.5389 25.4385	39.0091 33.5953 28.9381	115.2350 112.6730 110.1675	3.15450 2.71662 2.33952		1.32266 1.13906 0.98094	1.65368 1.42413 1.22644	— 2.1967 —
Portuguese Escudes (ESC)	556.890 479.590 413.020	3,011.20 2,593.24 2,233.30	3,424.80 2,949.37 2,540.00	11,481.10 9,891.77 8,517.90	276.938 238.495 205.389	10,194.30 8,779.18 7,560.50		145.180 125.027 107.670	— 192.854 —
Spanish Pesetas (PST)	445.418 383.589 330.342	2,408.50 2,074.15 1,786.20	2,739.30 2,358.98 2,031.50	9,191.20 7,911.72 6,812.80	221.503 190.755 164.276	8,153.70 7,021.83 6,047.10	92.8760 79.9828 68.8800		— 154.250 —

[a] Germany and the Netherlands have bilaterally decided to keep the previous 4.50% band vis-à-vis each other rather than using the new 30% band.

In Table 19.2 we have given the parity grid as of August 1993 and the compulsory intervention points. The parity grid is in principle derived from the central ECU-rates, since the statutes of the EMS dictate that "each currency will have an ECU-related central rate and the central rates will be used to establish a grid of bilateral parities". Formally, given the quantities (q_k) and the ECU central rates (R_j), set (19.3) can be solved for the r_{kj}'s [account being taken of Eqs.(10.1) and following equations]. This proviso is intended to stress the role of the ECU as the denominator (numéraire) of the exchange rate mechanism.

No data are present in Table 19.2 for the pound sterling, the lira, and the drachma since, as we said, these currencies, though present in the ECU basket, do not take part in the exchange rate agreement. Naturally, by the same procedure described a moment ago, it is possible to compute "notional" bilateral parities also for these currencies.

19.5.3 The Indicator of Divergence

In Table 19.1, the "threshold of divergence" column(s) are related to the socalled *indicator of divergence* (ID). This indicator, fruit of the compromise between those who wanted a new system based entirely on the ECU and those who wanted something just like the old snake (see Sect. 19.5.1), has the task of signalling the direction and extent of a currency's deviation from the "barycentre" of the system as characterized by the currency's central rate in terms of the ECU.

In fact, the deviation from the bilateral central rate between any two currencies does not in itself show which country is responsible for the strains in the system. If, for example, the bilateral exchange rate between currency *x* and currency *y* shows that more units of *x* are needed to buy one unit of *y* and, conversely, that less units of *y* are needed to buy one unit of *x*, this may be due either to depreciating phenomena on the part of currency *x* or to appreciating phenomena on the part of currency *y*. Therefore, the change in the current bilateral exchange rate is not in itself able to discriminate between the two cases. In order to single out the deviating currency — onto which the responsibility for taking corrective action would be shifted — it is necessary to be able to attribute the variations in its exchange rate exclusively to its movements: we face the problem of expressing in absolute terms the value, and the changes in that value, of assets (currencies) which change in value with respect to one another. Hence the solution of giving the ECU the function of numéraire of the system and of deriving from it an appropriate index of the divergence of a currency.

This index, that is, the *indicator of divergence*, is defined as the ratio between the actual divergence spread (i.e., the percentage deviation of the ECU-rate of a currency from its central ECU-rate) and the maximum divergence spread, that is, for any currency *j*,

$$\text{ID}_{jt} = \frac{s_{jt}}{\max s_j} \times 100, \qquad (19.14)$$

where s_{jt} is the actual divergence spread of currency *j* at time *t* and max s_j the maximum divergence spread. The multiplication by 100 serves to express the indicator as a figure ranging in absolute value between zero and one hundred in order to facilitate comparisons.

As regards the maximum divergence spread, it is the maximum percentage by which the market rate of the ECU in terms of a specific currency can appreciate or depreciate against the ECU central rate of that currency. This maximum spread must not be confused with the maximum margin of fluctuation around the bilateral parities: in fact, as it is referred to the ECU, it will depend on this margin *and* on the central weight of currency j, that is (for the details see Sect. A.19.1.2)

$$\max s_j = m_j(1 - b_j), \tag{19.15}$$

where m_j is the maximum percentage margin around the bilateral parities, that is, once 2.25 or 6, now 15.

As we said above, the indicator of divergence will be a number included between zero (when $s_{jt}=0$, i.e. no divergence) and 100 (when $s_{jt}=\max s_{jt}$, i.e. maximum divergence); by convention, the ID will be given a positive (negative) sign when the divergence is due to an appreciation (depreciation) of the currency in terms of the ECU.

The alarm bell rings when the indicator of divergence reaches 75 in absolute value, i.e. 75% of the maximum divergence spread. Thus a *threshold of divergence* is defined for each currency j as that value of the actual divergence spread s_{jt} which gives rise to a value of 75 of the indicator of divergence. From Eqs. (19.14) and (19.15) it is easy to see that the threshold of divergence (s_{djt}) for currency j is numerically equal to

$$s_{djt} = 0.75 \, m_j(1 - b_j). \tag{19.16}$$

When a currency reaches its divergence threshold, the *presumption* to act mentioned in Sect. 19.5.1 is triggered. The threshold of divergence are given in the relevant columns of Table 19.1.

It can easily be seen from Eq. (19.16) that the smaller is the (central) weight of a currency in the ECU, the smaller will be the threshold of divergence of this currency (at the same m_j), and vice versa. The reason for defining the divergence indicator (and hence the divergence threshold) with this property is that the weight of a currency influences its deviation from the average by making this deviation look lower; an offset to this phenomenon is obtained by defining the threshold divergence at levels which are the lower, the higher is the weight of the currency.

To put the same thing another way, since the ECU is a basket-currency, the ECU-rate of a currency will change every time changes occur in the market bilateral exchange rates of that currency, but by less than these changes: if, for example, currency j depreciates or appreciates by a certain amount, say $x\%$, against all other EMS currencies, its ECU-rate will tend to reflect this movement only in part. In fact, since in that rate the part accounted for by currency j is unchanged (as it is equal to the number of units of currency j in the ECU), the variation of the ECU-price of this currency will be less than $x\%$: only slightly less if currency j's weight is low, but much less if this weight is high. Thus the larger the weight of a currency in the ECU, the less the ECU-rate of that currency will be influenced by variations in its bilateral exchange rates.

The inverse relationship between the threshold of divergence and the weight tries to obviate this phenomenon, but is not always successful. It is in fact possible that the effect described above is such that the alarm bell does not ring (i.e., the divergence threshold is not crossed) even if a currency is deviating too much, and it is also possible that the alarm bell may ring for an "innocent" currency whilst quite a different currency is responsible for the deviation. We refer the reader to Sect. A.19.2.2 for the general proof. Actually, in the crisis of the lira vis-à-vis the DM (August–September 1992), the divergence threshold was crossed by neither the DM nor the lira, though both currencies crossed the bilateral margins several times.

In conclusion, if the aim behind the divergence indicator was to define an indicator able to single out the deviating currencies objectively and so to avoid both the asymmetries in the burden of intervention and adjustment (which under fixed exchange rates falls prevalently on the shoulders of the weaker currencies) and the subjective discussions as to which currency must adjust (or undergo a realignment, in the case in which the situation requires changes in the central rates), then it seems that this aim has not been achieved. In practice, the divergence indicator soon fell into desuetude.

19.5.4 Monetary Cooperation within the EMS

When the presumption of intervention is put into practice or when a compulsory intervention limit is reached, the corrective actions taken will be those usually undertaken in a fixed exchange rate regime: first of all, intervention in the foreign exchange market by the central bank(s) concerned which sell or buy foreign exchange, then monetary and other domestic policy measures; if all these actions are unsuccessful or cannot be pursued beyond certain limits, changes in central rates will be negotiated (a realignment). To facilitate these corrective actions the articles of agreement of the EMS also provided for monetary cooperation based on the European Monetary Cooperation Fund (EMCF) existing since 1973 (in January 1994 the EMCF has been replaced by the EMI: see Sect. 19.6.1). This cooperation consists of three credit mechanisms to partner countries: *very short-term financing, short-term monetary support,* and *medium-term financial assistance.*

Under article 17 of the Articles of Agreements of the EMS, each participating central bank has "contributed" to the EMCF 20% of its gold holdings and 20% of its gross dollar reserves and has been credited by the EMCF with an amount of ECUs corresponding to these contributions. We have put "contributed" in inverted commas because the ownership of the reserves cannot be juridically transferred to the EMCF (for this to be possible, formal legislative bills would have be approved by the national Parliaments). Thus these contributions take the form of three-month revolving swaps against ECUs between each central bank and the EMCF. Actually, the monetary cooperation passes through the EMCF only in accounting terms, since in practice it takes the form of credit granted by one partner country to another, as we shall see.

The *very short-term financing* is a credit facility, unlimited in amount, which the participating central banks grant to each other through the EMCF in order to permit interventions in Community currencies. These operations are denominated in ECUs and have a duration of 75 days; the interest rate, formerly equal to a weighted average of the official discount rates of all EEC central banks, is now calculated as a weighted average of the money market interest rates of the member countries (the weights are the same as the respective currencies' weights in the ECU). When a financing operation falls due, the debtor can settle it either in the creditor's currency or by transferring ECUs (this transfer takes the form of credit and debit entries in the relevant accounts with the EMCF), with the proviso that the creditor central bank shall not be obliged to accept settlement by means of ECUs of an amount ("payment ratio") of more than 50% of its claim. The balance, if any, shall be settled by transferring other reserve components (convertible currencies and SDRs; gold is excluded except for specific agreements between the central banks involved) in accordance with the composition of the debtor central bank's reserves. The 50% limit was later relaxed: if a central bank is a net debtor in ECUs to the system (i.e. if its assets in ECUs are smaller than its forward sales of ECUs to the EMCF), it is obliged to accept full settlement in ECUs up to the point where its ECU position balances, after which it can again invoke, if it is the case, the 50% payment ratio.

The *short-term monetary support* is intended to help meet financing needs arising from temporary balance-of-payments deficits and is based on credits which the participating central banks grant directly to each other for a duration of three months, renewable at most twice for an identical period at the request of the beneficiary central bank. Unlike the very short-term financing, the short-term monetary support is limited in amount, because it is based on a system of debtor and creditor quotas. This system establishes, for each central bank, both its borrowing entitlement — i.e., the maximum amount of credit that it may receive globally from all the other central banks (the debtor quota, which may be increased in exceptional cases by a "rallonge" mechanism) — and its financing obligations, i.e., the maximum amount of credit that it may be called on to grant globally (the creditor quota).

The *medium-term financial assistance* provides for the granting of credits to member countries experiencing difficulties, or seriously threatened with difficulties, as regards their balance of payments in the medium term; the duration is between two and five years. This assistance is granted by the EEC Council and is conditional, since the borrower country has to agree to certain economic and monetary measures (aimed at restoring equilibrium) established by the Council, which also establishes the interest rate, the duration, the repayment terms, etc. As with short-term monetary support, each member country is required to grant credit only up to a specific commitment ceiling, whilst no official ceiling is put on the loans that a country may receive (but, as rule, no country will be granted loans amounting to more than 50% of the total amount of the commitment ceilings).

In the Basle accord of 10th June 1985, the Committee of the Governors of the central banks participating in the EMS approved a series of proposals for strengthening the EMS in general and the ECU in particular, amongst which:

(a) the abolition, in the circumstances explained above, of the rule (concerning the repayment of loans granted under the very short-term financing) that no

central bank shall be obliged to accept settlement by means of ECUs of an amount more than 50% of its claim which is being settled;
(b) the creation of a new "mobilisation mechanism" of ECUs (besides the very short-term financing facility) in the provision of foreign exchange by the member central banks for their interventions on foreign exchange markets;
(c) the market-oriented remuneration of ECUs already mentioned above, i.e. the calculation of the interest rate on ECU balances by a weighted average of the money market interest rates of the member countries (instead of the official discount rates);
(d) the possibility for non-EMS central banks and international monetary institutions to hold ECUs when accorded the status of "Other Holder".

Further strengthening measures for the EMS were introduced in the 1987 Basle-Nyborg accord, amongst which:

a) the possibility of using the very short term financing facility also in the case of intra-marginal intervention, namely intervention in the foreign exchange market before the bilateral exchange rate reaches the margins;
b) the possibility of reacting to pressures on exchange rates also through coordinated changes in the interest rates of the countries concerned.

It should also be noted that, besides official initiatives to spread the use of the ECU among private agents (for example, the issuing of government bonds denominated in ECUs and with an ECU-related coupon), this use has been spontaneously growing (for example, the issuing of private bonds denominated in ECUs, short- and medium-term banking operations in ECUs, etc.; for a survey see the Istituto Bancario San Paolo's *ECU Newsletter*).

19.5.5 The EMS and the Theory of Optimum Currency Areas

By and large, the functioning of the EMS can be divided into three periods: the first goes from its inception to January 1987; the second from January 1987 to middle 1992; the third from middle 1992 to the time of writing (February 1994).

The first period is characterized by frequent realignments, that enabled the system to work like an improved Bretton Woods system at the EEC level. In the second period there was a substantial exchange rate stability: the last true realignment took place in January 1987 (the realignment on the occasion of the definition of the new ECU basket in September 1989, and the realignment on the occasion of the entry of the lira in the narrow band in 1991 has a purely technical nature). In this period the EMS became a fairly stable currency area. In 1991 the Italian lira, that from the inception of the EMS had opted for the wider ($\pm 6\%$) margins, decided to enter the narrow ($\pm 2.25\%$) band. The British pound, that had remained out of the exchange-rate agreement from the beginning of the EMS, decided to enter it.

Several reasons are set forth to explain this stability. The most often quoted are the monetary discipline effect and the wish to pave the way for the European monetary union. The monetary discipline argument has already been treated in Sect. 19.2.2, point 3. As regards the second motive, it is clear that the movement towards a monetary union (see below, Sect. 19.6.1) requires that exchange rates be maintained fixed.

In the third period the system fell into a deep crisis. In September 1992 the lira first depreciated by 7% and then had to abandon the exchange rate agreement to float. Also the pound left the exchange rate agreement to float. The contingent motives that are invoked to explain this crisis are various, and start from the negative result of the Danish referendum to ratify the Maastricht Treaty (on which see below, Sect. 19.6) and from the consequent confusion on the juridical effects that this refusal would have had on the process of European monetary unification (a new referendum in 1993 approved the Treaty). The uncertainty was increased by the announcement that also in France the Treaty would have been subjected to a referendum in September 1992, whose results were dubious (in fact, the result of this referendum gave only slightly more that 51% in favour of the Maastricht Treaty). Another element that is often indicated is the refusal (due to internal motives of fight against inflation) of the German central bank to lower interest rates so as to discourage the speculative inflow of capital into Germany. In these conditions, international speculators attacked the structurally weaker currencies of the EMS, namely the lira and the pound.

The same motive (i.e., the refusal of the Bundesbank to lower interest rates) is set forth, together with the breakdown of the so called "Franco-German axis", to explain the still more serious crisis of 31st July–1st August 1993, when – after massive speculative attacks against the French franc and other currencies, it was decided to increase the margins of oscillation around bilateral parities from $\pm 2.25\%$ to $\pm 15\%$ (except for the Dutch Guilder-German DM rate; these two currencies maintain the old margin between themselves). It is clear that the notion itself of fixed exchange rates is devoid of meaning when applied to rates that can move within a 30% band, so that it would be more correct to speak of a target zone (on which see Sect. 20.8.3).

Be it as it may, the above-mentioned motives are contingent motives, that only serve to cause the underlying disequilibria to explode. The crises of September 1992 and July 1993 clearly show the impossibility of maintaining fixed exchange rates among countries with divergent economic fundamentals, divergent monetary policies, and perfect capital mobility. An impossibility which is well known since the Bretton Woods era. From the more theoretical point of view, we refer the reader to what we have said in general in Sects. 16.3.1 (on perfect capital mobility under fixed exchange rates), 17.2.1 (on speculation under fixed exchange rates), 19.3 (on the common monetary policy prerequisite), and to what we shall explain in Sect. 20.6 (on perfect capital mobility and foreign exchange crises).

The crisis in the EMS brings us to the next question, namely whether the EMS is an optimum currency area.

If one adopts the traditional approach (see Sect. 19.2.1), then one can say that not all of the criteria for considering the EMS an optimum currency area are fulfilled: factor mobility is, at least in principle, present (it is provided for in the EEC statutes), and the criteria of openness and of product diversification are also satisfied. Financial integration is also present, thanks to the full liberalization of capital movements. Similarity in inflation rates has been and still seems to be a chimera, and equally chimerical appears the integration of economic policies both within the area and with respect to the rest of the world: within the area there is the problem of the *hierarchic* relations between strong and weak currencies; with respect to the rest of the world there is the problem of the lack of a common policy vis-à-vis outside currencies, especially the US dollar (for an indepth examination of these problems see, for example, Martinengo and Padoan, 1983). Those who believe that the last criteria are the most important, hold the opinion that the EMS cannot be considered an optimum currency area, as shown by the crises mentioned above (for a contrary view see Bini Smaghi and Vori, 1993).

The situation is more complicated if one adopts the cost-benefit approach. The costs listed in Sect. 19.2.2 have more or less occured in most member countries. The benefits have been much less observed, partly because a true fixity of exchange rates has not been realised (see what we said on the ECU in the previous sections), so that advantages (1) and (2) of the list in Sect. 19.2.2 do not seem to have come about. In point of fact the only true advantage, which has been and is greatly emphasized by the supporters of the EMS, is number (3) of that list, and, to a lesser extent, number (4). At the moment, however, it does not seem that the EMS has greatly contributed to the process of economic integration within the EEC countries, though not all hope is dead.

To evaluate the EMS in accordance with this approach it is necessary, as we have said in general, to give weights to the various costs and benefits (even the hope of an advantage can be given a weight, though in the probabilistic sense). The obvious consideration, from a European point of view, is an elementary one: nowadays (and still more in the future) no European country belonging to the EEC is able to compete *single-handed* with the outside economic and political giants (USA, Japan, in the future possibly China and other countries or groups of countries). Only by merging into a single politico-economic entity may these European countries hope to deal on an equal footing with these giants and avoid becoming provinces of the empire(s). If this argument has a paramount weight in the policy maker's (or the reader's) preference functions, then even a very small probability will make advantage (4) preponderant with respect to the costs, which are by no means negligible.

19.6 Towards the European Monetary Union?

19.6.1 The Maastricht Treaty and the Gradual Approach to Monetary Union

The European Council (composed of the Heads of State or Government of the countries forming the European Community), held in the Dutch town of Maastricht on 9–10 December 1991, approved a Treaty containing important modifications to the 1958 Treaty of Rome (which gave rise to the EEC). The final version of the Maastricht Treaty was signed on 7th February 1992 in Maastricht. We have already touched upon the Danish and French referendum for the approval of this Treaty (Sect. 19.5.5). Here we shall deal with the main innovations introduced by the Treaty as regards the European Union (for a general evaluation see Eichengreen, 1993). This Union is also called EMU, an acronym that stands for Economic and Monetary Union as well as for European Monetary Union (note, however, that the official denomination is simply European Union). The Treaty, adopting the strategy suggested by a report of the Committee for the Study of Economic and Monetary Union (commonly known as the Delors Report, 1989), envisages the movement to EMU in three stages the first of which, already begun in 1990, is further strengthened in the Treaty, that then goes on to lay out the second and third stages in detail.

I) The *first stage* (1990–1993) consists of the following main measures:

(I.1) abolition of any restriction to capital movements, both within the EC and with respect to third countries. The latter movements may be subjected to restrictions but only if they threaten the functioning of the Union, and in any case cannot be imposed for more than a six-month period.

(I.2) prohibition of financing the public deficit through the central bank.

(I.3) adoption of programmes of long-run convergence, in particular as regards price stability and public finance issues.

(I.4) adoption of the narrow band by all countries; avoidance of frequent realignments; prohibition of any modification of the composition of the ECU basket until its transformation in the single European currency.

II) The *second stage* (1994–6/8) is aimed at securing the convergence of the economies of the EEC countries and to pave the way for the third stage. It contemplates the following main measures:

(II.1) control of the public deficit and debt, with the aim of reducing the former to 3% of GDP and the latter to 60% of GDP.

(II.2) constitution of the European Monetary Instute (EMI), with the task – amongst others – to coordinate the monetary policies and to pave the way for the European System of Central Banks that will come into being the stage III; the EMI absorbs the tasks of the EMCF (see Sect. 19.5.4) and will dissolve on the starting day of stage three.

(II.3) obligation on the part of the member countries to conform domestic legislative provisions concerning their central banks to the principles of the Union.

(II.4) elimination of any automatic solidarity commitment to aid member countries faced with problems.

The *third stage* will begin on 1st January 1997 or 1st January 1999 at the latest. More precisely, at the end of 1996 the European Council will meet and decide whether the majority of member countries satisfies certain *convergence criteria:* in the affirmative case, the third stage will begin on 1st January 1997. In the negative case, the third stage will be postponed but not later than 1st January 1999, when it will in any case begin with the participation of those countries that meet the convergence criteria. The other countries will obtain a temporary derogation and enter when they have satisfied the criteria. Let us now examine the convergence criteria, which are the following:

(a) an inflation rate (as measured by the rate of increase of the consumer price index) that does not exceed by more than 1.5 percentage points the rate of inflation of the three best performing countries (i.e., those having the three lowest inflation rates);
(b) a long-term nominal interest rate (measured on the basis of long-term government bonds) that does not exceed by more than 2 percentage points the average of those same three countries;
(c) an exchange rate that has respected the normal fluctuation margins in the last two years;
(d) a public deficit and debt that satisfies the criteria detailed under II.1 above.
The measures contemplated in the third stage, that gives rise to the European Union proper, are the following:

(III.1) creation of the European System of Central Banks (ESCB), which consists of the national central banks plus the European Central Bank (ECB), to be founded. The ESCB has the task of taking all decisions concerning monetary policy, including the control of the money supply, with the *primary* objective of maintaining price stability and the *subordinate* (i.e., without prejudice to the objective of price stability) objective of supporting the general economic policies in the Community.
(III.2) the bilateral exchange rates will be irrevocably fixed, as well as those vis-à-vis the ECU, that will become a currency by full right.
(III.3) the ECU will replace the single national currencies at the earliest possible date.
(III.4) the Community will be entitled to apply appropriate sanctions against the countries which infringe the EC financial regulations after joining stage three.
(III.5) the position of those countries that were granted a derogation (and were therefore temporarily left out of the Union: see above) will be reconsidered every two years.

After this description of the various stages, we shall consider in more detail two important points: the establishment of the ESCB (see the next section) and the nature of the convergence criteria (see Sect. 19.6.3).

19.6.2 The Institutional Aspects

The ESCB consists of the ECB, to be established, and the existing central banks of the member countries. The ECB will be managed by an Executive Committee consisting of the Chairman, the Vice-chairman, and four more members, and by a Governing Council consisting of the governors of the national central banks plus the six components of the Executive Committee. The components of the Executive Committee are appointed by common accord of the Heads of state or government for a period of eight years and cannot be reappointed. This relatively long term in office and the non-renewability of the appointment are directed at insulating monetary policy makers from political pressure. In fact, the principle of independence of the central bank has been fully accepted: the ESCB will decide in autonomy, namely without either seeking or taking instructions from national governments or supranational EC authorities. The Community authorities and the national governments agree to respect this principle and not to seek to influence the members of the decision making bodies of the ESCB.

As we said, the ESCB is responsible for all monetary policy decisions, with the primary objective of price stability and the subordinate objective of giving support to the economic policy of the Union. It will also have the task of carrying out intervention in foreign exchange markets, holding and managing the official international reserves of the member countries, promoting the orderly functioning of the payment system. Besides, the ESCB shall contribute to the smooth conduct of the prudential supervision activity of the single national authorities over credit institutions.

Can we say that – once adopted the ECU as the single European currency – the ESCB will function like a true central bank of the Union? The answer to this question requires examination of the functions of a central bank. If one believes that, in addition to conducting monetary policy, a central bank should also act as "lender of last resort" and have the power of surveillance over the banking system, then the answer is clearly in the negative. The closest that one finds in the Treaty is article 105(5): "The ESCB shall contribute to the smooth conduct of policies pursued by the competent authorities relating to the prudential supervision of credit institutions and the stability of the financial system". But of course to "contribute" means that the supervisory power remains with the single national authorities. Actually, under article 105(6) it is possible to confer upon the ECB specific tasks concerning the prudential supervision, but only through an unanimous deliberation of the European Council acting "on a proposal from the Commission and after consulting the ECB and after receiving the assent of the European Parliament".

It is in principle possible to separate monetary policy from prudential supervision, as has been done in various European countries (Germany for example) by conferring the responsibility for prudential supervision upon a national agency separate from the central bank. One reason for doing so is that price stability might conflict with prudential supervision. Price stability, in fact, might require high interest rates, which might conflict with the wish of keeping interest rates low so as to help banks' debtors in avoiding default (which could weaken the balance sheets of banks). If this is the idea, then the solution would have been to create an EC agency endowed with the prudential supervision power. But this has not been contemplated in the Treaty, with the result that the Union shall have a single currency and a centralized monetary policy, but no centralized prudential supervison. Financial integration is already so advanced, and will be so complete in stage three, that it will be impossible to contain banking and financial crises within national boundaries. The lack of a centralized lender of last resort possessing powers of surveillance and regulation will certainly be a problem.

Table 19.3. Convergence Indicators, 1991–94[1]

Country	Inflation (%)				Long term interest rate (%)				Public deficit (% of GDP)				Public debt (% of GDP)				Exchange rate band criterion			
	1991	1992	1993	1994	1991	1992	1993	1994	1991	1992	1993	1994	1991	1992	1993	1994	1991	1992	1993	1994[2]
Belgium	3.2	2.4	2.7	2.5	9.3	8.6	7.2	7.5	6.8	7.1	7.0	5.4	133.6	135.1	142.2	142.6	yes	yes	no	no
Denmark	2.4	2.1	1.2	1.9	9.3	9.0	7.3	7.5	3.2	2.6	4.6	4.6	64.6	68.8	80.4	82.2	yes	yes	no	no
France	3.2	2.4	2.1	1.7	9.0	8.6	6.7	6.9	2.1	3.9	5.7	5.6	35.5	39.4	43.9	48.1	yes	yes	no	no
Germany	3.5	4.0	4.1	3.1	8.5	7.9	6.4	6.8	3.2	2.6	3.3	3.1	42.1	44.8	48.9	53.6	yes	yes	no	no
Greece	19.5	15.9	14.4	11.1	:	:	:	:	14.4	14.3	16.3	17.9	103.9	110.2	145.2	154.0	no	no	no	no
Ireland	3.2	2.9	1.4	2.1	9.2	9.1	7.7	7.9	2.0	2.3	2.3	2.5	97.0	94.5	99.0	93.1	yes	yes	no	no
Italy	6.4	5.3	4.5	4.0	13.2	13.3	11.3	10.5	10.2	9.5	9.5	9.5	101.2	108.2	118.3	123.3	no	no	no	no
Luxembourg	3.1	3.1	3.6	2.2	8.2	7.9	7.2	7.4	−2.3	0.3	−1.4	0.4	4.9	5.8	6.8	7.9	yes	yes	no	no
Netherlands	3.9	3.7	2.6	2.9	8.7	8.1	6.7	7.1	2.5	3.5	2.9	3.6	79.0	79.7	81.2	82.2	yes	yes	no	no
Portugal	11.4	8.9	6.5	5.9	18.3	15.4	12.5	10.5	6.6	3.3	7.1	6.2	69.4	61.7	66.6	70.2	no	no	no	no
Spain	5.9	5.9	4.6	4.9	12.4	12.2	10.2	9.4	4.9	4.5	7.3	7.2	45.2	48.2	55.9	61.4	no	no	no	no
UK	5.8	3.7	1.6	2.4	10.1	7.5	7.9	8.1	2.8	6.4	7.7	6.0	35.8	41.7	48.2	50.5	no	no	no	no
EMU	4.4	3.7	2.9	3.4	11.1	11.1	9.6	9.4	3	3	3	3	60	60	60	60	yes	yes	yes	yes

[1] *Source:* our elaboration on data from *European Economy* (European Commission), *International Financial Statistics* (IMF), and *Main Economic Indicators* (OECD), various issues. The data for 1994 are forecasts.
The data on public debt refer to total general government consolidated gross debt (*including* the debt outstanding from the financing of public enterprises), in conformity with the definition of the European Commission.
The symbol : means not available. In the Public deficit data, a minus (−) means a surplus.
[2] If the 15% band that was adopted after the crisis of 1993 (see Sect. 19.5.4) is interpreted (as some suggest) as the "normal fluctuation margins", then all countries adhering to the exchange rate mechanism would satisfy this criterion.

19.6.3 Conclusion

The title of section 19.6 contains a question mark. It is now time to explain why.

We have seen that the satisfaction of the convergence criteria is the precondition for stage three, namely for the realization of the Union proper. The aim of these criteria is clearly to prevent the destabilization of the Union by the premature admission of countries whose economic fundamentals are not compatible with a permanently fixed exchange rate. Each of these criteria can be, and has been criticized on economic grounds: see, for example, Begg et al. 1991; Eichengreen, 1992. There is particularly severe criticism on the the criteria concerning public deficit and debt; see, for example, Bean, 1992; Buiter et al., 1993. But in our opinion there something more fundamentally wrong, that cannot be eliminated by changing one or the other criterion. To show this let us look at Table 19.3, where we have collected the data for the years 1991–94. The last row, titled EMU, contains the values of the convergence indicators calculated as explained above. The only additional point to explain is that the inflation rate of the three most virtuous countries has been calculated as an *average* of the three lowest-inflation countries (on this point, article 109j(1) of the Treaty and the relative Protocol give no indication).

The Maastricht Treaty has been signed in February 1992. Now, in 1991 only two countries (France and Luxembourg) satisfied all criteria: even Germany would have been left out! In 1992, 1993 and 1994 (data for 1994 are preliminary forecasts at the time of writing) no country satisfied all criteria, with a clear deterioration of the indices.

When *no* country can satisfy the criteria there must be something more fundamentally wrong than one or the other criterion.

It is evident that the Maastricht Treaty has adopted the gradualist approach to monetary union, as opposed to the called "shock therapy" approach, which consists of the sudden (or at least very quick) introduction of a *complete* monetary union, i.e., with a common currency. One of the main reasons for the shock therapy is that, as we have already pointed out several times (see, for example, Sect. 19.4), in the absence of capital controls (whose elimination necessarily accompanies the single market), 'permanently fixed' exchange rates are a chimera. Hence it is the extended transitional period contemplated by the Maastricht Treaty that may contain in itself the germs of the procrastination of the Union well beyond 1st January 1999.

Appendix

A.19.1 Fiscal Policy in a Monetary Union

We have seen in the text (Sect. 19.3) that a common monetary policy is a prerequisite for a viable monetary union. But what about fiscal policy? Levin (1983b) found a beggar-my-neighbour effect of fiscal policy in a three-country model of the IS-LM type (a two-country currency area with a floating exchange rate vis-à-vis the rest of the world considered as country 3). Namely, a fiscal expansion in one country of the area causes a contraction in the other country's national income. If this were generally true the necessity of a common fiscal policy would be obvious – no country in a union would be willing to accept such contractionary effects. It was however shown by Sauernheimer (1984), with a model that is a generalization of Levin's, that Levin's finding depends on the assumption of price rigidity. If this assumption is relaxed, the outcome becomes indeterminate, but a taxonomy can be made. The same results were later rediscovered by Moutos and Scarth (1988), with the same kind of model as Sauernheimer's. Here we shall follow Sauernheimer's treatment, with slight changes in notation to conform with ours.

The area consists of two countries with a permanently fixed exchange rate normalised at unity (hence we could as well apply the model to a monetary union with a single currency), with a floating exchange rate vis-à-vis the rest of the world. The rest of the world (ROW) is considered exogenous. The basic equations of the model are

$$S_1(y_1) = I_1(i_1) + \bar{G}_1 + B_{12}(y_1, y_2, p_2/p_1) + B_{13}(y_1, y_3, r\bar{p}_3/p_1), \quad (A.19.1)$$
$$\underset{-}{} \qquad \underset{- \ + \ +}{\phantom{B_{12}(y_1, y_2, p_2/p_1)}} \underset{- \ + \ +}{\phantom{B_{13}(y_1, y_3, r\bar{p}_3/p_1)}}$$

$$S_2(y_2) = I_2(i_2) + \bar{G}_2 + B_{21}(y_1, y_2, p_2/p_1) + B_{23}(y_2, y_3, r\bar{p}_3/p_2), \quad (A.19.2)$$
$$\underset{-}{} \qquad \underset{+ \ - \ -}{\phantom{B_{21}}} \underset{- \ + \ +}{\phantom{B_{23}}}$$

$$\overline{M_1 + M_2} = p_1 L_1(y_1, i_1) + p_2 L_2(y_2, i_2), \quad (A.19.3)$$
$$\underset{+ \ -}{} \underset{+ \ -}{}$$

$$i_1 = i_2 = \bar{i}_3, \quad (A.19.4)$$

where the subscripts 1,2 refer to the countries forming the currency area while the subscript 3 refers to ROW. A bar over a variable denotes that the variable is exogenous. The signs below the arguments in the functions represent the signs of the partial derivatives. The symbols have the usual meaning: S = private saving, y = national income (output), I = private investment, i = nominal interest rate, B_{ij} = trade balance or net exports of country i with respect to country j, p_i = price of country i's domestically produced goods, r = exchange rate of the area vis-à-vis the rest of the world, M_i = country i's money supply. All expenditure variables are measured in real terms, namely in units of the country's goods. Note that to assume the partial derivative of each member country's trade balance (vis-à-vis the ROW) with respect to terms of trade to be positive, implies the assumption that the critical elasticities condition is satisfied (the proof is exactly like that given in Sect. A.16.1).

The first and second equation define the aggregate demand sector of the model (instead of $S(y) = I(i) + \ldots$ one could also write $y = C(y) + I(i) + \ldots$). The third equation is the sum of the two countries' monetary equilibrium conditions, $M_i = p_i L_i(y_i, i_i)$, and reflects the assumption that the *total* money supply of the union is exogenous while that in the single member countries is endogenous. The fourth equation expresses perfect capital mobility *à la Mundell* (on this point see Sects. 10.7.6 and 16.3.1) not only within the currency area but also between the area and the ROW. Hence the area's interest rate is exogenously given by the ROW's interest rate.

In Levin's model, "the domestic price of each country's domestically produced good is taken to be constant and normalized at unity on the assumptions of fixed money wages and constant returns in production" (Levin, 1983b, pp. 330–331). Hence equations (A.19.1)–(A.19.3) – if we replace both i_1 and i_2 with $\bar{i}_3$ – form a system in the three endogenous variables y_1, y_2, r, from which we can obtain Levin's result by standard comparative statics methods. The economic rationale of this result is easy to see, if we consider for a moment the union as a whole vis-à-vis the rest of the world. We know from Mundell's analysis (see Chap. 16, Sect. 16.3.1) that fiscal policy under perfect capital mobility, flexible exchange rates and price rigidity is completely ineffective. Thus the union's overall income will not change as a consequence of a fiscal expansion. Hence, if now look at the two regions (countries) in the union, it follows that an expansion in one country must cause a depression in the other, since the total is unchanged.

The Sauernheimer model modifies Levin's model by introducing variable prices according to mark-up pricing over a money wage rate that varies through indexation effects. Thus we have

$$p_i = (1 + g_i)(L/y)_i w_i, \tag{A.19.5}$$

where g_i is the fixed mark-up coefficient, $(L/y)_i$ is the (fixed) labour-input coefficient and w_i is the money wage rate in country $i = 1, 2$. The money wage rate, in turn, depends on the general (consumer) price index in the country (for example through an indexation mechanism)

$$w_i = \omega_i(I_i), \quad 0 \leq \mathrm{d}w_i/\mathrm{d}I_i \leq 1, \tag{A.19.6}$$

where

$$I_i = \alpha_{i1}p_1 + \alpha_{i2}p_2 + \alpha_{i3}r\bar{p}_3, \quad \alpha_{i1} + \alpha_{i2} + \alpha_{i3} = 1, \tag{A.19.7}$$

is a weighted average of the prices of the three goods available to consumers. Note that the case $\omega_{i,I} \equiv \mathrm{d}w_i/\mathrm{d}I_i = 0$ means a rigid wage rate, $\omega_{i,I} = 1$ means complete indexation.

Equations (A.19.5)–(A.19.7) form a subset that allows us to express p_1, p_2 in terms of the exchange rate r and the data ($\bar{p}_3$, etc.). Thus we have

$$p_i = \varphi_i(r, \ldots), \quad i = 1, 2. \tag{A.19.8}$$

For future reference let us compute the derivatives of the functions φ_i with respect to r. If we substitute I_i from Eq. (A.19.7) into (A.19.6) and then the result into Eq. (A.19.5), we get

$$p_i - (1 + g_i)(L/y)_i \omega_i(\alpha_{i1}p_1 + \alpha_{i2}p_2 + \alpha_{i3}r\bar{p}_3) = 0, \tag{A.19.9}$$

whose solution gives the functions φ_i. To compute the derivatives $p_{i,r} \equiv \partial p_i / \partial r$, we apply the implicit function theorem. With no loss of generality we can normalize $\bar{p}_3$ at one and choose units such that $p_i = w_i = r$ in the initial situation (this implies choosing output units such that $(1 + g_i)(L/y)_i = 1$). Thus we have

$$(1 - \omega_{1,I}\alpha_{11})p_{1,r} - \omega_{1,I}\alpha_{12}p_{2,r} = \omega_{1,I}\alpha_{13}$$
$$-\omega_{2,I}\alpha_{21}p_{1,r} + (1 - \omega_{2,I}\alpha_{22})p_{2,r} = \omega_{2,I}\alpha_{23}. \tag{A.19.10}$$

Solving this system we get

$$p_{1,r} = \frac{\omega_{1,I}[\alpha_{13}(1-\omega_{2,I}\alpha_{22}) + \omega_{2,I}\alpha_{12}\alpha_{23}]}{(1-\omega_{1,I}\alpha_{11})(1-\omega_{2,I}\alpha_{22}) - \omega_{1,I}\omega_{2,I}\alpha_{12}\alpha_{21}},$$

$$p_{2,r} = \frac{\omega_{2,I}[\alpha_{23}(1-\omega_{1,I}\alpha_{11}) + \omega_{1,I}\alpha_{21}\alpha_{13}]}{(1-\omega_{1,I}\alpha_{11})(1-\omega_{2,I}\alpha_{22}) - \omega_{1,I}\omega_{2,I}\alpha_{12}\alpha_{21}},$$

(A.19.11)

where both the numerator and the denominator are positive given the definitions of the α's and ω's, except when $\omega_{i,I}$ is zero, in which case $p_{i,r}$ is zero. Also note that $p_{i,r} = 1$ when $\omega_{i,I} = 1$. In general, the weights α and the functions ω will be different in the two countries of the currency area, hence $p_{1,r} \neq p_{2,r}$ (except in the two extreme cases).

If we now substitute Eqs.(A.19.8) into Eqs. (A.19.1)–(A.19.3), where we have also replaced both i_1 and i_2 with $\bar{i}_3$, we can determine y_1, y_2, r in the variable-price case under consideration and perform our comparative statics exercises. In fact, provided that the Jacobian of this system with respect to the endogenous variables y_1, y_2, r is different from zero at the equilibrium point, we can express these variables as differentiable functions of the exogenous variables and compute the relevant partial derivatives by the implicit function theorem. We are interested in $\partial y_i/\partial G_j$, so as to ascertain whether and under which conditions the beggar-my-neighbour effect can materialize.

We compute $\partial y_i/\partial G_1$ (the case $\partial y_i/\partial G_2$ is symmetric) by differentiating system (A.19.1)–(A.19.3) with respect to G_1. For simplicity of notation we define $\mu_{ij} = -\partial B_{ij}/\partial y_i$ ($i = 1, 2; j = 1, 2, 3; i \neq j$), i.e. country i's partial marginal propensity to import from country j; $\mu_i = \Sigma_{j \neq i} \mu_{ij}$, i.e. country i's overall marginal propensity to import. We also define $p = p_2/p_1$, the area's internal relative price. Note that, by definition, in the initial situation we have $B_{12} + B_{21} \equiv 0$, from which $\partial B_{12}/\partial y_1 + \partial B_{21}/\partial y_1 = 0$, $\partial B_{12}/\partial y_2 + \partial B_{21}/\partial y_2 = 0$, $\partial B_{12}/\partial p + \partial B_{21}/\partial p = 0$. Finally, we define $S_{iy} = \partial S_i/\partial y_i$, $y_{iG_1} = \partial y_i/\partial G_1$, $B_{ij,p} = \partial B_{ij}/\partial p$, $B_{i3,r} = \partial B_{i3}/\partial r$, $r_{G_1} = \partial r/\partial G_1$, $L_{iy} = \partial L_i/\partial y_i$.

The differentiation of system (A.19.1)–(A.19.3) with respect to G_1 yields

$$(S_{1y} + \mu_1)y_{1G_1} - \mu_{21}y_{2G_1} \quad -[B_{12,p}(p_{2,r} - p_{1,r}) + B_{13,r}(1 - p_{1,r})]r_{G_1} = 1,$$
$$-\mu_{12}y_{1G_1} + (S_{2y} + \mu_2)y_{2G_1} + [B_{12,p}(p_{2,r} - p_{1,r}) - B_{23,r}(1 - p_{2,r})]r_{G_1} = 0,$$
$$L_{1y}y_{1G_1} + L_{2y}y_{2G_1} + [L_1 p_{1,r} + L_2 p_{2,r}]r_{G_1} = 0.$$

(A.19.12)

Solving this linear system we obtain

$$y_{1G_1} = \frac{(S_{2y} + \mu_2)[L_1 p_{1,r} + L_2 p_{2,r}] - L_{2y}[B_{12,p}(p_{2,r} - p_{1,r}) - B_{23,r}(1 - p_{2,r})]}{\Delta},$$

$$y_{2G_1} = \frac{\mu_{12}[L_1 p_{1,r} + L_2 p_{2,r}] + L_{1y}[B_{12,p}(p_{2,r} - p_{1,r}) - B_{23,r}(1 - p_{2,r})]}{\Delta},$$

$$r_{G_1} = \frac{-\mu_{12}L_{2y} - L_{1y}(S_{2y} + \mu_2)}{\Delta},$$

where Δ, the determinant of system (A.19.12), is positive when $p_{1,r}=p_{2,r}$; when $p_{1,r} \neq p_{2,r}$ this determinant will be positive if $B_{12,p}$ is not too large. At any rate, Δ is assumed to be positive (Sauernheimer, 1984).

From inspection of Eqs. (A.19.13) it can be seen that r_{G_1} is negative, while the signs of y_{1G_1}, y_{2G_1} are indeterminate. The appreciation in the union's exchange rate is not a surprise – it is a standard effect of fiscal policy under perfect capital mobility and flexible exchange rates. When the union is considered as a whole we can, in fact, apply the well-known Mundell results (see Chap. 16, Sect. 16.3.1). The indeterminacy of the signs of y_{1G_1}, y_{2G_1} shows that the beggar-my-neigbour effect is just a possibility, whose materialization depends on the presence of price rigidity (Levin's assumption). In fact, the indeterminacy of the signs of the numerators of the fractions giving y_{1G_1}, y_{2G_1} depends on the presence of the terms $p_{i,r}$. Following Sauernheimer, we examine four main cases.

1) $p_{1,r}=p_{2,r}=0$.

This is the fix-price case. The numerator of y_{1G_1} becomes $L_{2y}B_{23,r}>0$, while that of y_{2G_1} is $-L_{1y}B_{23,r}<0$. Thus the beggar-my-neighbour effect is present, unless $B_{23,r}=0$, namely when there is no relative price effect on country 2's net exports to the rest of the world, a case that we can rule out. Also note that the overall income of the union increases, remains constant or decreases according as $L_{2y} \gtreqless L_{1y}$. When $L_{2y}=L_{1y}$, the two countries of the union are so similar that they can be considered as a single country, and we are back in the traditional Mundell setting (see Chap. 16, Sect. 16.3.1). Fiscal policy under perfect capital mobility and rigid prices is ineffective; the result of an exchange rate appreciation is also standard. Now, if the union's total income is unchanged, then it is obvious that an expansion in one member country causes a depression in the other, as we have already noted above.

2) $p_{1,r}=p_{2,r}=1$.

This is the case of complete wage indexation. Levin's result is no longer true. In fact, not only the numerator of y_{1G_1} but also the numerator of y_{2G_1} is positive (if we exclude the abnormal case $\mu_{12}=0$, which means that country 1 does not import anything from country 2). Hence both countries' income increases, and, of course, the union's income increases. Again, if we consider the union as a whole, we know that the effectiveness of fiscal policy under perfect capital mobility and flexible exchange rates is restored owing to the effects on the real money supply of the price changes induced by the exchange-rate variations (see Chap. 16, Sect. 16.6.3). Note however that, when indexation is not complete, i.e. $0 < p_{1,r}=p_{1,r}<1$, prices fall less than proportionally to the exchange rate appreciation, and the effect on country 2's income is again indeterminate, while y_{1G_1} is certainly positive. As regards the union as a whole, if $L_{1y} \simeq L_{2y}$ the union's income increases.

3) $1=p_{1,r}>p_{2,r}=0$.

In this case the union's internal relative price (p_2/p_1) changes. We now have $y_{1G_1}>0$, but the sign of y_{2G_1} is indeterminate. This indeterminacy is due to relative price effects in the union, that were not present in the previous cases. Actually, there is an expansionary effect on the aggregate demand for country 2's output due to the tendency of this country's exports to country 1 to increase (term μ_{12} in the numerator of y_{2G_1}). But this effect is counteracted by the diversion of country 2's aggregate demand toward goods produced in countries 1 and 3, due to relative price effects. First, the exchange-rate appreciation diverts demand toward country 3's goods. Second, this appreciation works on the union's internal prices asymmetrically (due to a lack of harmonisation in wage policies), because it causes a decrease in country 1's prices but has no effect on country 2's prices. From this it follows a diversion of country 2's aggregate demand toward country 1's goods induced by the change in the intra-union relative price. Thus the lack of harmonisation of wage policies aggravates country 2's employment problems deriving from the lack of coordination of aggregate demand policies. It should however be noted, as Sauernheimer points out, that changes in relative prices cannot be avoided even with fully coordinated policies when the countries in the union have very different requirements of imported inputs, so that different price-effects of exchange-rate changes cannot be avoided.

4) $1 \geq p_{2,r} > p_{1,r} = 0$.

This is particularly interesting case, because country 1 – notwithstanding the fiscal expansion and the increase in the union's real quantity of money (due to the price decline induced by the appreciation in the exchange rate) – may suffer an income contraction ($y_{1G_1} < 0$). This, again, is due to a relative price effect: while country 1's prices are rigid, country 2's prices are flexible and decline due to the exchange-rate appreciation. The ensuing relative price effect diverts country 1's aggregate demand toward country 2' goods. Besides, there is the diversion of country 1's demand towards country 3's goods due to the exchange rate appreciation. If the sum of these effects is sufficiently strong, country 1 will suffer a depression.

We observe, in conclusion, that within-currency-area beggar-my-neighbour effects are a serious possibility, though not a certainty as in Levin's model. Hence the coordination of fiscal and wage policies should be taken into consideration in addition to the (necessary) common monetary policy.

A.19.2 Some Properties of Basket-Currencies in General and of the Indicator of Divergence in Particular

A.19.2.1 The Basket-Currency

A.19.2.1.1 The Sum of the Weights

The first point to show is that, given a basket-currency, the sum of the weights as defined in the text, Eq. (19.4), must equal one. This may seem self-evident, but to show it rigorously a few manipulations are required. To begin with, we note that the price of the unitary basket (the basket-currency) in terms of currency i equals the price of the basket-currency in terms of currency j multiplied by the bilateral exchange rate r_{ji}, i.e.

$$r_{ji} R_j = R_i, \text{ for all } i, j. \tag{A.19.14}$$

In fact, if we use the definition of R_j given in Eq. (19.3), we have

$$r_{ji}R_j = r_{ji}\sum_{k=1}^{n} q_k r_{kj} = \sum_{k=1}^{n} q_k r_{kj} r_{ji}, \qquad (A.19.15)$$

where r_{ji} has been brought under the summation sign since it is a constant. Now, given the triangular arbitrage relations explained in Eq. (10.3), we have $r_{kj}r_{ji} = r_{ki}$, and so by substituting this in Eq. (A.19.15) we get

$$r_{ji}R_j = \sum_{k=1}^{n} q_k r_{ki}. \qquad (A.19.16)$$

The summation on the right-hand side of (A.19.16) is exactly the definition of R_i, hence (A.19.14).

Let us now consider the sum of the weights

$$\sum_{j=1}^{n} b_j = \frac{q_1}{R_1} + \frac{q_2}{R_2} + \ldots + \frac{q_n}{R_n}. \qquad (A.19.20)$$

If we multiply both numerator and denominator of the first fraction on the r.h.s. by r_{1i}, both numerator and denominator of the second fraction by r_{2i}, etc., we obtain

$$\sum_{j=1}^{n} b_j = \frac{q_1 r_{1i}}{r_{1i}R_1} + \frac{q_2 r_{2i}}{r_{2i}R_2} + \ldots + \frac{q_n r_{ni}}{r_{ni}R_n}. \qquad (A.19.21)$$

Given Eq. (A.19.14), the denominators $r_{ji}R_j$ are all equal to R_i, thus we can rewrite (A.19.21) as

$$\sum_{j=1}^{n} b_j = \frac{\sum_{k=1}^{n} q_k r_{ki}}{R_i}, \qquad (A.19.22)$$

which equals one because the numerator of the fraction on the r.h.s. is nothing more nor less than R_i.

A.19.2.1.2 Solution for the Quantities

The fact that the weights add up to one is crucial to ensure the possibility of uniquely solving set (19.4) for the quantities; this solution is required when one wishes to determine the quantities given the weights and the bilateral parities (see Sect. 19.5.2). A general proof is the following. System (19.4) can be written as

$$\begin{aligned} b_1 q_1 + b_1 r_{21} q_2 + \ldots + b_1 r_{n1} q_n &= q_1, \\ b_2 r_{12} q_1 + b_2 q_2 \phantom{{}+b_2 r_{22} q_2} + \ldots + b_2 r_{n2} q_n &= q_2, \\ b_n r_{1n} q_1 + b_n r_{2n} q_2 + \ldots + \phantom{b_n r_{nn} q_n +{}} b_n q_n &= q_n, \end{aligned} \qquad (A.19.23)$$

which is a homogeneous system. To study its solution we perform a few simple manipulations to put it in an alternative form which will enable us to use powerful theorems concerning positive matrices.

If we multiply through the first equation by r_{12}, the third by r_{32},..., the ith by r_{i2},..., the nth by r_{n2}, and use the relations (10.1) and (10.3), we get the equivalent system

$$b_1 r_{12} q_1 + b_1 q_2 + ... + b_1 r_{n2} q_n = r_{12} q_1,$$
$$b_2 r_{12} q_1 + b_2 q_2 + ... + b_2 r_{n2} q_n = q_2, \quad \text{(A.19.24)}$$
$$\cdots\cdots\cdots\cdots\cdots\cdots\cdots\cdots\cdots\cdots\cdots\cdots$$
$$b_n r_{12} q_1 + b_n q_2 + ... + b_n r_{n2} q_n = r_{n2} q_n.$$

We now define new variables $Q_i = r_{i2} q_i$, $i = 1, 2, ..., n$, ($r_{22} = 1$), and write the system in matrix form

$$\mathbf{BQ} = \mathbf{Q}, \quad (\mathbf{B} - \mathbf{I})\mathbf{Q} = \mathbf{0}, \quad \text{(A.19.25)}$$

where

$$\mathbf{B} \equiv \begin{bmatrix} b_1 & b_1 & \cdots & b_1 \\ b_2 & b_2 & \cdots & b_2 \\ \cdot & \cdot & & \cdot \\ b_n & b_n & \cdots & b_n \end{bmatrix} \quad \text{(A.19.26)}$$

is the matrix of the weights, $\mathbf{Q}$ the column vector of the Q_i, $\mathbf{I}$ the identity matrix. Since $\mathbf{B}$ is a positive matrix, we can apply the Perron theorem (see, for example, Gantmacher, 1959, pp. 64 ff.) according to which the characteristic vector associated with the dominant characteristic root (which is simple, real and positive) of $\mathbf{B}$ is positive and unique up to a scalar multiple. Since all the column sums of $\mathbf{B}$ are unity (the sum of the weights is one), the dominant characteristic root of $\mathbf{B}$ is unity as well (Gantmacher, 1959, p. 76). It follows that, in (A.19.25), $\mathbf{Q}$ is the characteristic vector associated with the dominant root and so is positive and unique up to a scalar multiple. Having thus determined the Q_i and as the r_{i2} are known by assumption, the q_i are immediately determined up to a scalar multiple. The fixation of this arbitrary scale factor, and hence the determination of the actual quantities, is a matter of convenience or of consistency (if, for example, the central ECU-rates are to remain the same after an exogenous change in the weights, this will provide the necessary constraints).

A.19.2.1.3 Other Properties

Let us now consider other properties of basket-currencies. The change in the price of the basket in terms of any one member currency (i.e., the change in any R) is a weighted average of the changes in the bilateral exchange rates of that currency. If we define

$$a_{ij,t} = \frac{r_{ij,t} - r_{ij,t-1}}{r_{ij,t-1}}, \quad \text{(A.19.27)}$$

where $a_{ij,t}$ is the proportional change in the bilateral rate (note that $a_{ij,t} = 0$ for $i = j$), we have

$$r_{ij,t} = (1 + a_{ij,t}) r_{ij,t-1}. \quad \text{(A.19.28)}$$

The proportional change in R_i, which we denote by $s_{i,t}$, is given by (henceforth Σ_k is taken to mean $\sum_{k=1}^{n}$)

$$s_{i,t} = \frac{R_{i,t} - R_{i,t-1}}{R_{i,t-1}} = \frac{\Sigma_k r_{ki,t} q_k - \Sigma_k r_{ki,t-1} q_k}{\Sigma_k r_{ki,t-1} q_k}$$

$$= \frac{\Sigma_k r_{ki,t-1}(1+a_{ki,t}) q_k - \Sigma_k r_{ki,t-1} q_k}{\Sigma_k r_{ki,t-1} q_k} = \frac{\Sigma_k r_{ki,t-1} q_k a_{ki,t}}{\Sigma_k r_{ki,t-1} q_k}$$

$$= \Sigma_k a_{ki,t} \frac{r_{ki,t-1} q_k}{\Sigma_k r_{ki,t-1} q_k}, \quad (A.19.29)$$

and so, if we define

$$b_{ki,t-1} \equiv r_{ki,t-1} q_k / \Sigma_k r_{ki,t-1} q_k \equiv r_{ki,t-1} q_k / R_{i,t-1}, \quad (A.19.30)$$

we get

$$s_{i,t} = \Sigma_k a_{ki,t} b_{ki,t-1}, \quad (A.19.31)$$

that is, the proportional change in R_i is a weighted average of the proportional changes in the bilateral exchange rates; the weights are $b_{ki,t-1}$, each of which indicates the weight, in the value of the basket in terms of currency i, of currency k (also expressed in terms of currency i). Since $R_i = r_{ki} R_k$ by Eq. (A.19.14), this weight is exactly that (at time $t-1$) of currency k in the basket-currency as defined in Eq. (19.4), so that

$$s_{i,t} = \Sigma_k a_{ki,t} b_{k,t-1}. \quad (A.19.32)$$

In a regime in which market rates can float, though within predetermined margins, the weight that a currency has at any moment may vary through time. If we denote by $\Delta b_{i,t}$ the proportional change, we have

$$\Delta b_{i,t} = \frac{b_{i,t} - b_{i,t-1}}{b_{i,t-1}} = \frac{q_i/R_{i,t} - q_i/R_{i,t-1}}{q_i/R_{i,t-1}} = \frac{R_{i,t-1} - R_{i,t}}{R_{i,t}}$$

$$= \frac{R_{i,t-1} - R_{i,t-1}(1+s_{i,t})}{R_{i,t-1}(1+s_{i,t})} = -\frac{s_{i,t}}{1+s_{i,t}}. \quad (A.19.33)$$

By using (A.19.32), we have

$$\Delta b_{i,t} = -\frac{\Sigma_k a_{ki,t} b_{k,t-1}}{1 + \Sigma_k a_{ki,t} b_{k,t-1}}. \quad (A.19.34)$$

Therefore, when the bilateral exchange rates change, a change occurs both in the weights and in the exchange rates with respect to the basket-currency. If, for example, currency i appreciates with respect to all the others ($a_{ki,t} < 0$), it also appreciates with respect to the basket currency ($s_{i,t} < 0$), and, besides, its weight increases ($\Delta b_{i,t} > 0$). The opposite is true in the case of a generalized depreciation of a currency.

It follows that strong currencies, i.e. those with a tendency to appreciate, will see an increase in their importance in the basket-currency to the detriment of weak currencies. This can be most clearly seen in the case of a uniform proportional change in the bilateral exchange rates of a currency, i.e. $a_{ki,t} = a_{i,t}$. If we consider Eq. (A.19.32) and remember that $a_{ii,t} = 0$ by definition, we get

$$s_{i,t} = a_{i,t} \sum_{k \neq i} b_{k,t-1}, \qquad (A.19.35)$$

whence – since $\sum_{k \neq i} b_{k,t-1} = 1 - b_{i,t-1}$, because the sum of the weights is one – we have

$$s_{i,t} = a_{i,t}(1 - b_{i,t-1}). \qquad (A.19.36)$$

If we consider any other currency j (which by assumption varies only with respect to currency i) – by using Eq. (A.19.32) and taking account of the fact that $a_{kj,t} = 0$ except for $k = i$ – we have that

$$s_{j,t} = \sum_k a_{kj,t} b_{k,t-1} = a_{ij,t} b_{i,t-1}, \qquad (A.19.37)$$

where

$$a_{ij,t} = -\frac{a_{ji,t}}{1 + a_{ji,t}} = -\frac{a_{i,t}}{1 + a_{i,t}}; \qquad (A.19.38)$$

the last passage is due to the fact that $a_{ji,t} = a_{i,t}$ by assumption. To understand (A.19.38) it is sufficient to use the triangular arbitrage relations (10.3). Since $r_{ij} r_{ji} = 1$ for any t, it is also true that $r_{ij,t}(1 + a_{ij,t})r_{ji,t-1}(1 + a_{ji,t}) = 1$, whence $(1 + a_{ij,t})(1 + a_{ij,t}) = 1$. By solving for $a_{ij,t}$ we get (A.19.38).

We can easily see from Eq. (A.19.36) that the change in the price of the basket-currency in terms of the currency which varies uniformly with respect to all the others will be smaller, the greater is the weight of this currency, whilst the opposite will happen, given Eq. (A.19.37), to the other currencies. To put it another way, the basket-currency will follow the highest-weight currency, which will maintain a fairly stable value (exchange rate) in terms of the numéraire (the basket-currency), whilst the exchange rates of the other currencies with respect to the numéraire will change by a (proportional) amount close to the proportional change in their respective bilateral exchange rates with respect to the "heavy" currency.

Since this mechanism operates in the same way when, given a parity grid, the bilateral central rates are occasionally realigned, the result is that the strong currencies will tend to take on an overwhelming weight in the basket currency. To offset this bias it is then necessary to change the composition of the basket-currency, as was done when defining the new ECU in 1984 and 1989 [see Eq. (19.31)].

Further considerations on the properties of basket-currencies with specific reference to the ECU are contained in Masera (1987, Appendix II); for the properties of a generalized system of basket-currencies see Asheim (1984).

A.19.2.2 The Indicator of Divergence

We must first point out that the formula actually used in the calculations is slightly more complicated than that given in the text – see Eqs. (19.6) and (19.7) – because it is necessary to account for the fact that some currencies, though contained in the ECU, do not take part in the exchange agreement, so that their market bilateral rates may exceed the maximum margins permitted to the other currencies. To obviate these problems the formula used for the participating countries in the case in which one or more of the non participating currencies diverge from the other currencies by more than the maximum margins is

$$ID_{jt} = \frac{s_{jt} - \Sigma_i(a_{ij,t} - m_j)b_i}{m_j(1-b_j)} \times 100, \quad \begin{array}{l} j \neq i \\ i = \text{non participating country.} \end{array} \qquad (A.19.39)$$

Let us now examine the problems related to the indicator of divergence. Spaventa (1982) has demonstrated several properties (or, as he calls them, "algebraic properties but economic improprieties") of the divergence indicator. One of these is that, although the bilateral exchange rate between two currencies is at the maximum margin, their indicator may not reach the respective divergence threshold (property E in Spaventa's list).

To show this, let us assume that $a_{ij} = \pm m$, where i, j are the two currencies considered and the bilateral margin m has been assumed identical (we thus ignore the complications introduced because of the non-participating currencies as shown above); we must check whether the conditions

$$-s_{di} < s_i < s_{di}, \quad -s_{dj} < s_j < s_{dj}, \qquad (A.19.40)$$

are verified, i.e. the ECU-rates of both currencies do *not* reach the threshold. Since, owing to (A.19.14), the proportional rates of change of r_{ji}, R_j, and R_i are related by the relation[8]

$$a_{ji} + s_j = s_j, \qquad (A.19.41)$$

we can, by using (A.19.41), rewrite (A.19.40) in the form

$$-s_{di} < s_i < s_{dj} + a_{ji}, \quad -s_{dj} + a_{ji} < s_i < s_{di}. \qquad (A.19.42)$$

These conditions can be verified, for $|a_{ji}| = m$, provided that the weighted rate of change of the other currencies with respect to the currencies considered falls within a certain range. Firstly consider Eq. (A.19.32) and rewrite it as

$$s_i = a_{ji}b_j + \sum_{k \neq i,j} a_{ki}b_k. \qquad (A.19.43)$$

---

[8] For simplicity, following Spaventa, we use the rates of change in continuous time rather than in discrete time as before [note that Eqs. (A.19.41) hold for any value of s and so also for s_d]. The passage to discrete time does not alter the results. Also note that for notational brevity we omit the time subscripts.

By using (A.19.43) we can then rewrite (A.19.42) in the form

$$-s_{di} < a_{ji}b_j + \sum_{k \neq i,j} a_{ki}b_k < s_{dj} + a_{ji},$$

$$-s_{dj} + a_{ji} < a_{ji}b_j + \sum_{k \neq i,j} a_{ki}b_k < s_{di}, \qquad (A.19.44)$$

whence

$$-s_{di} - a_{ji}b_j < \sum_{k \neq i,j} a_{ki}b_k < s_{dj} + a_{ji}(1-b_j),$$

$$-s_{dj} + a_{ji}(1-b_j) < \sum_{k \neq i,j} a_{ki}b_k < s_{di} - a_{ji}b_j, \qquad (A.19.45)$$

and so, for $a_{ji} = -m$ we have, from the first equation in (A.19.45),

$$-s_{di} + mb_j < \sum_{k \neq i,j} a_{ki}b_k < s_{dj} - m(1-b_j), \qquad (A.19.46)$$

whilst for $a_{ji} = m$ we have, from the second,

$$-s_{dj} + m(1-b_j) < \sum_{k \neq i,j} a_{ki}b_k < s_{di} - mb_j. \qquad (A.19.47)$$

Inequalities (A.19.46) and (A.19.47) give the intervals of $\sum_{k \neq i,j} a_{ki}b_k$ which verify the proposition in question; these intervals – which can be determined numerically – are altogether plausible (see Spaventa, 1982).

A second property is that, when the previous case occurs, it may happen that a third currency, which does not reach its bilateral margin with respect to any other currency, does nevertheless reach the threshold. In referring the reader to Spaventa (1982) for the proof, and for the examination of numerous other properties, we fully agree with his observation that a system of margins around ECU-rates and a system of margins around bilateral parities, apart from their relative merits and demerits, both have an internal consistency, and that the divergence indicator attempts to capture some features of both systems, but the resulting hybrid loses the internal consistency of each.

A.19.2.3 The Asymmetry in the Bilateral Margins

We conclude our treatment by examining the technical reasons behind the asymmetry in the bilateral margins actually used to determine the obligatory intervention points in the EMS, given a band of a predetermined total width.

This asymmetry is required to achieve the symmetry in the attainment of the obligatory intervention points by the currency which is appreciating and the currency which is depreciating. When currency i is appreciating with respect to currency j, currency j is simultaneously depreciating with respect to currency i, and logic requires that, when currency i reaches its (lower) margin vis-à-vis currency j, currency j simultaneously reaches its (upper) margin vis-à-vis currency i. Now, with infinitesimal changes, the appreciation of i and the depreciation of j are perfectly symmetrical[9]; but with discrete changes they are not, because if currency i appreciates by $x\%$ with respect to currency j, currency j depreciates by a different amount than $x\%$ (in absolute value) with respect to currency i. In fact, as we have already shown above in relation to Eq. (A.19.38), we have the following relations (for brevity we omit the time subscript)

$$a_{ij} = -\frac{a_{ji}}{1+a_{ji}}, \quad a_{ji} = -\frac{a_{ij}}{1+a_{ij}}, \qquad (A.19.48)$$

where a_{ij} denotes the propertional rate of change of r_{ij} – see Eq. (A.19.27) – and a_{ji} that of r_{ji}; generally speaking, $a_{ij} \neq -a_{ji}$.

To calculate the margins which make the attainment of the respective obligatory intervention points symmetrical for the appreciating and depreciating currency given a band of total width b, let us assume that currency i is appreciating with respect to currency j (as is self-evident, the latter is depreciating with respect to the former). Thus r_{ji} is decreasing ($a_{ji} < 0$) and r_{ij} is increasing ($a_{ij} > 0$), where of course conditions (A.19.48) must be satisfied. The obligation to intervene is triggered when the sum of the deviations equals the width of the band (b), that is, account being taken of the assumed signs, when

$$a_{ij} - a_{ji} = b, \text{ where } a_{ji} = -a_{ij}/(1+a_{ij}). \qquad (A.19.49)$$

This is a system of two equations in two unknowns; by simple manipulations we get

$$a_{ij}^2 + (2-b)a_{ij} - b = 0, \qquad (A.19.50)$$

which, as $b > 0$, always has two real roots, one positive and the other negative (the latter must be ignored given the assumption that $a_{ij} > 0$). Having thus obtained the solution for a_{ij}, one immediately obtains $a_{ji} = a_{ij} - b$.

With $b = 0.045$ (a band of 4.5%) we get $a_{ij} = 0.02275$ (upper intervention limit for currency j), hence $a_{ji} = -0.02225$ (lower intervention limit for currency i). Since the indexes i and j can be interchanged, it follows that for all currencies with a 4.5% band the upper margin (the maximum depreciation permitted) is 2.275% above the bilateral parities, and the lower margin (the maximum appreciation permitted) is 2.225% below the bilateral parities. In the case of $b = 0.12$ we get $+6.18\%$ and -5.82% respectively, and for $b = 0.30$ we have $+16.119\%$ and -13.881%.

---

[9] In fact, by differentiating with respect to time the familiar relation $r_{ij}r_{ji} = 1$ and denoting by a dot the time derivative, we have $\dot{r}_{ij}r_{ji} + r_{ij}\dot{r}_{ji} = 0$, whence — if we divide through by $r_{ij}r_{ji}$ — we get $\dot{r}_{ij}/r_{ij} + \dot{r}_{ji}/r_{ji} = 0$, namely $\dot{r}_{ij}/r_{ij} = -\dot{r}_{ji}/r_{ji}$. This means that the proportional rate of change in the exchange rate of currency j with respect to currency i and that in the exchange rate of currency i with respect to currency j are equal in absolute value and with opposite sign.

References

Allen, P.R. and P.B. Kenen, 1980, Part V
Artus, P. and C. Dupuy, 1992
Asheim, G.B., 1984
Bean, C.R., 1992
Begg, D. et al., 1991
Bini Smaghi, L., 1990
Bini Smaghi, L. and S. Vori, 1993
Bordo, M.D. and B. Eichengreen (eds.), 1993
Buiter, W. et al., 1993
Canzoneri, M.B., V. Grilli and P.R. Masson, 1992
Casella, A., 1992
Cooper, R.N. et al. (eds.), 1982
Corden, W.M., 1972, 1983
De Grauwe, P., 1992
Delors Report, 1989
Denton, G. (ed.), 1974
De Vries, T., 1980
Dowd, K., 1989
EC Commission, 1990
Eichengreen, B., 1992, 1993
Emerson, M. et al., 1992
Fratianni, M., J. von Hagen and C. Waller, 1992
Gantmacher, F.R., 1959, Chap. III, Sect. 2
Giavazzi, F., S. Micossi and M. Miller (eds.), 1988
Gros, D. and N. Thygesen, 1992
Hamada, K., 1985
HMT (Her Majesty Treasury), 1989
Ingram, J.C., 1973
Ishiyama, Y., 1975
Istituto Bancario San Paolo, *ECU Newsletter*
Johnson, H.G. and A.K. Swoboda (eds.), 1973
Levin, J.H., 1983b
Martinengo, G. and P.C. Padoan, 1983
Masera, R.S., 1987
Masson, P.R. and M.P. Taylor, 1992
Masson, P.R. and M.P. Taylor (eds.), 1993
McKinnon, R.I., 1963
Moutos, T. and W. Scarth, 1988
Mundell, R.A., 1961
Padoan, P.C., 1988
Portes, R., 1993
Robson, P., 1987, Chap. 6
Rogoff, K., 1985
Salin, P. (ed.), 1984
Sauernheimer, K., 1984
Spaventa, L., 1982
Spaventa, L., 1983
Tower, E. and T.D. Willet, 1976
Triffin, R., 1982
Various Authors, 1982
Werner Report, 1970

20 Problems of the International Monetary System

20.1 Key Events in the Postwar International Monetary System

20.1.1 Introductory Remarks

Although a detailed description of the international monetary system in the period after the Second World War is outside the scope of the present work, a very brief treatment of the key events is necessary to provide the minimum amount of information necessary to set the theoretical problems against their institutional and historical background (for detailed treatment we refer the reader, e.g., to Triffin, 1968; Meier, 1982; Solomon, 1982; Scammell, 1987; Tew, 1988; Grubel, 1984; Federal Reserve Bank of Boston, 1984; De Grauwe, 1989; Kenen et al., 1994).

As we have already mentioned in Sect. 10.5, the postwar international monetary system was reconstructed on the basis of the Bretton Woods agreements (1944), which gave birth to the IMF (International Monetary Fund) and to the IBRD (International Bank for Reconstruction and Development, also called World Bank) and laid the foundations for international monetary cooperation. The Fund was set up to deal with monetary matters; the World Bank (as its full name says) to promote a flow of long-term loans for purposes of reconstruction and development. The Fund was of course seen as centre of the international monetary system, and it is unfortunately impossible to examine even cursorily the debate between the plans of White and Keynes, who had completely different ideas as to the role of the future Fund.

The member countries agreed to tie their currencies to gold (or to the US dollar, which was the same thing, as the dollar was then officially convertible into gold at the official price of $ 35 per ounce) by declaring a par value or parity, with the obligation of keeping the actual exchange rate within narrow margins ($\pm 1\%$) of this parity. The features of the system qualified it as a gold exchange standard, though a "limping" one (see Sect. 10.5) and mitigated by the possibility of altering the parity, as we shall see presently. However, for various reasons most countries used the facility for converting their dollar reserves into gold very moderately or not at all, so that the system became a *de facto* dollar standard. The *de facto* inconvertibility of the US dollar became a *de jure* one in 1971, as we have mentioned in Sect. 18.3.1.

20.1 Key Events in the Postwar International Monetary System

The countries participating in the IMF also agreed to change their currencies' parity solely in the case of fundamental disequilibrium, and even then with certain limitations: changes up to 10% were discretional, whilst for greater changes the country had first to obtain the Fund's assent. For its part the IMF also had a support role for currencies in difficulty, by using its general resources to extend financial assistance.

Another element in the agreement was the undertaking made by each member to eliminate foreign exchange restrictions and restore the convertibility of its currency, after the necessary transitional period (generalized convertibility was restored at the end of the fifties), so as to contribute to the establishment of a multilateral system of payments.

The obligation to maintain the par value (typical of fixed exchange rates), coupled with the possibility of changing it as described above, caused this regime to be dubbed an adjustable peg system. Obviously it was a compromise between (irrevocably) fixed exchange rates and flexible rates, and it is clear that the degree of closeness to one or the other end depended essentially on the interpretation given to the concept of "fundamental disequilibrium" (not defined in the Articles of Agreement of the Fund) and to the frequency of the possible parity changes. The interpretation implicitly adopted in practice was usually restrictive, in the sense that the par value had to be defended at all costs, and changed only when further defence was impossible. This, amongst other consequences, gave rise to the continuing application of restrictive domestic measures in the case of balance-of-payments difficulties and to destabilizing speculative capital flows (see Sect. 17.2). It should also be noted that, whilst in the intention of the Bretton Woods agreements the burden of adjusting balance-of-payments disequilibria was to be equally shared by both deficit and surplus countries, in practice this burden fell mostly on the shoulders of deficit countries only. As a matter of fact, the so-called *scarce currency clause* — which gave the Fund the power formally to declare a member's currency scarce, with several consequences, amongst which the automatic authorisation for any other member to impose limitations on the freedom of exchange operations in the scarce currency — was practically never applied. Thus the principle of joint responsibility of surplus and deficit countries for disequilibrium became a dead letter.

Among the main events in the working of the postwar international monetary system are the following (in chronological order):

(a) the restoration of the convertibility of the currencies of the major industrialized countries;
(b) the formation of the Euro-dollar market;
(c) the creation of the Special Drawing Rights (SDR) within the Fund;
(d) the *de jure* inconvertibility into gold of the US dollar in 1971 and the subsequent abandonment of the par value by all major currencies, which adopted a managed float system (the collapse of the Bretton Woods system);
(e) the acquisition of enormous dollar surpluses by the oil exporting countries and the consequent "recycling" problem;
(f) the demonetization of gold and the legalization of the float;
(g) the creation of the European Monetary System;
(h) the international debt crisis.

Any choice of a limited number of events is inevitably arbitrary and reflects the idiosyncrasies of the writer. While pleading guilty, we believe that most events listed above would be considered by most writers as key events in the international monetary system. A very brief treatment of each of these (or reference to other parts of the book, in which an event has already been treated previously) will now be given.

20.1.2 Convertibility

The restoration of the convertibility of currencies, which is indispensable for a multilateral system of payments and trade, was one of the purposes of the IMF. "Convertibility" of a currency is not to be taken here as under the gold standard (convertibility into gold) nor as unlimited convertibility (which means that anybody — resident or nonresident — can freely convert domestic currency into foreign exchange) but as *nonresident convertibility* or convertibility of foreign-held balances of domestic currency. This means that a nonresident (as defined in Sect. 11.1), for example a foreign exporter, who has acquired a domestic currency balance, is entitled to freely obtain the conversion of this into foreign exchange, which may be his own currency or any other currency participating in the convertibility agreement. It is self-evident that, in the absence of convertibility, the nonresident is obliged to spend the domestic currency in the purchase of domestic goods, services, etc., or to transfer it to someone else (for example, an importer in his own country) who has to pay for the purchase of domestic goods, etc. This means a *bilateral* settlement of international exchanges which hampers trade; the fostering of world trade requires a *multilateral* system of payments which, in turn, requires nonresident convertibility.

It is important to point out that in the Articles of Agreement of the IMF, convertibility of the currencies into one another was provided for as regards current transactions, whilst controls over capital movements were not prohibited. The articles — in consideration of the abnormal conditions expected to prevail in the postwar period — also provided for the exemption from convertibility when the domestic situation of a country would have made convertibility impossible. As a matter of fact, the necessities of postwar reconstruction induced all countries (except the USA) to avail themselves of this proviso. It was not until December 1958 that the pound sterling and twelve other European currencies shed restrictions, which had the effect of securing convertibility, which was full for the pound and the D-mark, whilst the other currencies maintained a very limited part of the previous bilateral payment agreements. This move was soon followed by many other currencies, so that by 1961 generalized convertibility prevailed. This passage to convertibility and hence to a (limping) gold exchange standard (as we have said the US dollar was convertible into gold for central banks) rendered more evident the problem of international liquidity (see below, Sect. 20.1.4).

20.1.3 Euro-dollars

The Euro-dollar market was born in the fifties, when deposits denominated in US dollars were placed with European banks (in the sense of banks resident in

Table 20.1. Estimated Xenocurrency market size (at end of period, billions of dollars) and growth rates

Year	Gross market size	Net market size	Growth rates, %	
			in gross size	in net size
1964	19	14	–	–
1965	20	17	5.3	21.4
1966	25	21	25.0	23.5
1967	32	25	28.0	19.0
1968	46	34	43.8	36.0
1969	65	50	41.3	47.1
1970	86	65	32.3	30.0
1971	150	85	74.7	30.8
1972	210	110	40.0	29.4
1973	315	160	50.0	45.5
1974	395	220	25.4	37.5
1975	485	255	22.8	15.9
1976	595	314	22.7	23.1
1977	740	379	24.4	20.7
1978	949	478	28.2	26.1
1979	1245	584	31.2	22.2
1980	1574	797	26.4	36.5
1981	1950	1034	23.9	29.7
1982	2164	1191	11.0	15.2
1983	2280	1248	5.4	4.8
1984	2614	1274	14.6	2.1
1985	3137	1485	20.0	16.6
1986	3973	1770	26.6	19.2
1987	4959	2220	24.8	25.4
1988	5505	2390	11.0	7.7
1989	6164	2640	12.0	10.5
1990	7217	3350	17.1	28.8
1991	7443	3615	3.1	7.9
1992	7352	3660	–0.1	1.2
Average yearly compound rate, 1964–92			23.7	22.0

Source: our elaboration on data published in *World Financial Markets* (various issues) by Morgan Guaranty Trust Co. of New York, and in the *Annual Report* by Bank for International Settlements (various issues).

Europe according to the residency criteria illustrated in Sect. 11.1), which used them to extend dollar loans. As explained in Sect. 10.6, a European bank can also hold deposits and extend loans in currencies other than the dollar (and, of course, other than the currency of the country where the bank is resident), in which case we talk of *Euro-currencies*. Still more generally, the term *Xeno-currency* (and *Xeno-market*) has been suggested by Machlup (1972, p. 120) to include deposits and loans denominated in currencies other than that of the country where the bank – whether European or non-European – is resident.

The "mystery story" of the origins of the Euro-dollar market was briefly mentioned in Sect. 10.6; for further historical details see, for example, Johnston (1983). Here we give some data on the size of the Euro-currency market.

Estimates[1] of the size of the Euro-market are published by various sources; the best known are those of the Bank for International Settlements (BIS) of Basle, and (in the past) those of the Morgan Guaranty Trust Company of New York. It is as well to warn the reader that the estimates are often revised: it is therefore advisable to keep in mind that the data in Table 20.1 are subject to revision.

The estimates are based on data provided by banks located in major European countries, in Canada, Japan, the U.S. (international banking facilities only), and in the various "offshore" centres (the Bahamas, Bahrain, Cayman Islands, Hong Kong, Netherlands Antilles, Panama, Singapore, etc.). The greatest part of Xeno-currencies consists of US dollars: around 80% of the total up to the 1980s; subsequently this percentage has been decreasing in favour of other currencies, mainly D-marks and yens.

Thus "Euro-currency market" is to be understood in the broad sense, i.e. in the sense of "Xeno-currency market" in Machlup's terminology. Indeed, although European banks still account for the greatest part of the total, the presence and growing importance of the other international banking centres listed above, and the fact that not only dollars and European currencies, but also other currencies (for example yen) are involved, makes the terms Euro-market and Euro-currency somewhat misleading. In fact, one now also hears the terms "Asia-currency" and "Asia-currency market". Therefore the terms Xeno-currency and Xeno-currency market to indicate the whole market seem more to the point. However, it is still common practice to use "Euro-currency" and "Euro-currency market" in the broad sense; in any case, no danger of confusion exists as long as one clearly defines what one means. Finally, the difference between the gross and net size is that the latter excludes interbank liabilities within the market area.

For a theoretical treatment of the Euro-currency market see below, Sects. 20.3 and 20.4.

20.1.4 Special Drawing Rights

The creation of SDRs (*Special Drawing Rights*), which was decided — after many years of discussion and formulation of plans — at the 1967 Rio de Janeiro Annual Meeting of the IMF, is best seen in conjunction with the problem of international liquidity. "International liquidity" is usually taken to cover those financial assets available for use by a country's monetary authorities in meeting balance-of-payments needs and in intervening on the foreign exchange market. This concept leaves undefined the range of actual assets to be considered as international liquidity, which thus may be wider or narrower. Some writers suggest the inclusion in international liquidity not only of the reserve of international means of payment but also the borrowing capacity of individual central banks, so that international liquidity would be taken to mean the capacity of any central bank to meet its foreign obligations, and would thus become a still vaguer concept (Machlup, 1964b).

---

[1] The procedure for calculating these estimates is described, for example, in Johnston (1983, Chap. 3).

Although it must be recognized that from the theoretical point of view there may be a difference between "international reserves" and "international liquidity", to avoid confusion we take these as synonymous: in fact, the definition of international liquidity that we have given above coincides with the concept of international reserves.

As regards the range of assets which are taken to be international reserves, the convention usually adopted is to limit this range to the following assets: reserves of gold and foreign exchange, reserve position in the IMF[2], and — after 1970, the year in which the agreement of 1967 was put into practice — the SDRs; for the countries belonging to the EMS there also are ECUs, within the limits clarified in Sect. 19.5.

Now, if we ignore the reserve position in the Fund (which is a small part of the total: see Table 20.2 below), and consider gold and foreign exchange, it must be observed that the determination of their amount depends on elements which are in fact arbitrary and unrelated to the needs of the international monetary system. The increase in the stock of gold depends on this metal being produced by only a few countries, and this production cannot easily be made to increase or decrease in accordance with these needs. As regards foreign exchange, most of it (see Table 20.2) consists of US dollars, whose accumulation by every country (other than the USA) is obviously related to a deficit in the US balance of payments. But a situation of continuing deficits in the US balance of payments weakens the dollar. Hence the *Triffin dilemma* (so named because the first to clearly state it was R.

---

[2] The reserve position in the Fund is given by what was once called the "gold tranche position", plus the country's lending to the Fund, if any. The gold tranche position, after the demonetization of gold (see Sect. 20.1.7), is now called the reserve tranche position (henceforth r.t.p.). To understand what the r.t.p. is, it should be remembered that any member country has to pay out a quota to the Fund; this payment is usually made partly in the member's currency (75% of the quota) and partly in SDRs (once in gold, hence the earlier denomination). The amount of the member's currency owned by the Fund increases when the country buys another currency from the Fund in exchange for its own and, vice versa, decreases when another member buys from the Fund the currency of the country under consideration. Now, the r.t.p. of a country equals the total of the country's quota minus the Fund's holdings of this country's currency; thus it will be equal to, smaller or greater than, the SDR percentage of the quota, according as the Fund's holdings of the country's currency are equal to, greater or smaller than, the amount initially paid out by the country to the Fund. In the latter case (i.e. when the amount of a country's currency owned by the Fund is smaller than 75% of the country's quota because other countries have purchased this currency from the Fund) it was customary to talk of "super gold (now reserve) tranche position". The drawing (i.e. the purchase of foreign currency from the Fund in exchange for domestic currency) is automatic — namely no assent on the part of the Fund is required — within the limits of the r.t.p., which gives it a status identical with that of foreign exchange reserves. When the r.t.p. falls to zero the automaticity disappears, and further drawings are conditional, i.e. require the Fund's assent.

A numerical example may help to clarify the notion of r.t.p.. Let us assume that, in the initial situation, the Fund owns 75 units of currency x and that country's x quota is 100 (measured in the currency of country x). The r.t.p. is $100-75=25$, i.e. the SDR part of the quota. If another country borrows 35 of x from the Fund, the Fund's holdings of x drop to 40, and country's x r.t.p. is now $100-40=60$. Conversely, if — starting from the same initial situation — country x sells 15 units of its currency to the Fund to purchase other currencies, the Fund's holdings of x rise to 90 and the r.t.p. of this country is $100-90=10$. It is thus clear that the r.t.p. of a country can vary between zero and 100% of its quota (when the Fund's holdings of that country's currency have fallen to zero because other countries have bought it from the Fund).

Table 20.2. World international reserves and their composition (millions of US dollars at end of period)

Years	Gold "Official" valuation[a]	Gold "Market" valuation[b]	SDR	Reserve position in the Fund	Foreign exchange	Composition of foreign exchange reserves, %[c]								Total reserves	
						$	Pound Sterling	French Franc	Swiss Franc	Netherlands Guilder	Deutsche Mark	Jap. Yen	Unspecified curr.	Total	Total[d]	Total[e]
1950	33,320	—	—	1,672	13,333	—	—	—	—	—	—	—	—	—	48,325	
1951	33,582	—	—	1,713	13,469	—	—	—	—	—	—	—	—	—	48,764	
1952	33,619	—	—	1,777	13,991	—	—	—	—	—	—	—	—	—	49,387	
1953	34,085	—	—	1,891	15,350	—	—	—	—	—	—	—	—	—	51,326	
1954	34,723	—	—	1,845	16,452	—	—	—	—	—	—	—	—	—	53,020	
1955	35,156	—	—	1,880	16,731	—	—	—	—	—	—	—	—	—	53,767	
1956	35,855	—	—	2,278	17,770	—	—	—	—	—	—	—	—	—	55,903	
1957	37,079	—	—	2,313	17,050	—	—	—	—	—	—	—	—	—	56,442	
1958	37,819	—	—	2,557	17,077	—	—	—	—	—	—	—	—	—	57,453	
1959	37,764	—	—	3,250	16,111	—	—	—	—	—	—	—	—	—	57,125	
1960	37,918	—	—	3,570	18,494	—	—	—	—	—	—	—	—	—	59,982	
1961	38,753	—	—	4,159	19,134	—	—	—	—	—	—	—	—	—	62,046	
1962	39,159	—	—	3,795	19,698	—	—	—	—	—	—	—	—	—	62,852	
1963	40,217	—	—	3,940	22,690	—	—	—	—	—	—	—	—	—	66,847	
1964	40,717	—	—	4,155	24,218	67.6	21.5	1.5	0.2	0.0	0.1	0.0	9.1	100.0	69,090	
1965	41,776	—	—	5,377	24,018	66.4	22.3	1.5	0.1	0.0	0.2	0.0	9.4	100.0	71,171	
1966	40,801	—	—	6,331	25,898	67.8	21.8	1.7	0.2	0.0	0.2	0.0	8.3	100.0	72,830	
1967	39,424	—	—	5,748	29,409	68.0	19.4	1.7	0.2	0.0	0.4	0.0	10.3	100.0	74,581	
1968	38,758	—	—	6,488	32,585	60.9	21.3	1.3	0.3	0.0	0.5	0.0	15.8	100.0	77,831	
1969	38,952	—	—	6,726	33,068	59.1	20.1	1.1	0.6	0.0	0.7	0.0	18.5	100.0	78,746	
1970	37,026	—	3,124	7,697	45,465	77.2	10.4	1.1	0.7	0.1	1.9	0.0	8.7	100.0	93,312	
1971	39,080	48,693	6,377	6,895	82,020	77.4	8.7	1.1	1.1	0.1	3.3	0.0	8.3	100.0	134,372	143,155
1972	38,748	71,656	9,430	6,867	105,040	78.6	7.1	1.0	1.0	0.3	4.6	0.0	7.5	100.0	160,085	192,064
1973	43,159	137,771	10,624	7,441	124,155	76.1	5.6	0.9	1.4	0.5	7.1	0.1	8.1	100.0	185,379	278,722
1974	43,720	232,024	10,845	10,828	156,417	77.8	6.5	1.1	1.5	0.4	6.1	0.1	6.9	100.0	221,810	408,339
1975	41,740	166,708	10,260	14,778	162,577	79.5	3.9	0.7	1.6	0.6	6.3	0.5	6.5	100.0	229,355	352,451
1976	41,243	158,121	10,056	20,606	187,946	76.5	1.8	1.2	2.3	0.9	9.0	2.0	5.9	100.0	259,851	374,905
1977	43,756	202,733	9,879	21,973	247,518	77.9	1.7	1.6	2.4	0.9	9.2	2.3	4.3	100.0	323,126	553,121
1978	47,277	234,374	10,566	19,332	292,049	75.6	1.7	1.3	2.3	0.9	11.0	3.2	4.2	100.0	369,224	554,181
1979	43,545	483,581	16,439	15,492	329,141	72.8	2.0	1.4	2.7	1.1	12.6	3.5	4.0	100.0	404,617	843,027

20.1 Key Events in the Postwar International Monetary System

Year														
1980	42,515	561,431	15,060	21,473	373,582	66.7	3.0	1.7	3.2	1.3	15.1	4.2	4.8	100.0	452,900	971,147
1981	38,764	378,3	19,102	24,819	348,039	69.4	2.2	1.4	2.8	1.2	13.2	4.1	5.7	100.0	430,724	761,996
1982	36,567	432,746	19,575	28,080	317,499	68.5	2.5	1.4	2.7	1.0	12.5	4.2	7.2	100.0	401,721	794,458
1983	34,653	360,796	15,095	40,949	324,070	69.1	2.6	1.2	2.4	0.8	11.9	4.2	7.8	100.0	414,767	740,138
1984	32,458	291,904	16,144	40,747	339,987	70.0	2.9	0.8	2.0	0.7	12.6	5.8	5.2	100.0	429,336	691,319
1985	36,645	310,408	20,005	42,543	382,404	65.0	3.0	0.9	2.3	1.0	15.2	8.0	4.6	100.0	481,742	755,497
1986	40,806	370,997	23,845	43,226	445,338	67.1	2.5	0.8	2.0	1.1	14.6	7.9	4.0	100.0	553,284	883,48
1987	47,045	458,665	28,675	44,641	647,249	67.8	2.4	0.8	2.0	1.2	14.4	7.5	3.8	100.0	767,444	1179,08
1988	44,653	388,907	27,147	38,047	665,594	64.6	2.7	1.0	2.0	1.1	15.6	7.7	5.3	100.0	775,293	1119,55
1989	43,365	378,095	26,920	33,473	716,357	60.2	2.7	1.4	1.5	1.1	19.0	7.7	6.3	100.0	820,200	1154,95
1990	46,839	362,219	28,957	33,787	844,929	57.5	3.4	2.3	1.4	1.1	18.6	8.8	6.8	100.0	954,309	1269,72
1991	47,040	332,281	29,397	37,031	894,688	58.5	3.6	2.8	1.4	1.1	16.5	9.4	6.8	100.0	1008,15	1293,37
1992	44,770	310,021	17,692	46,615	915,664	62.9	3.7	2.4	1.3	0.8	13.1	8.5	7.3	100.0	1024,70	1289,95

Source: our elaboration on data from IMF (Annual Report; International Financial Statistics, Supplement on international reserves). The IMF gives the data in SDRs; we have converte them in US dollars by using the end-of-period $/SDR exchange rate.

a "Official" valuation: 1950–1971 (Dec. 18), $35/oz; 1971 (Dec. 19)–1973 (Feb. 11), $38/oz; 1973 (Feb. 12)–1974 (June 30), $42.22/oz; since July 1994, SDR 35/oz.

b The valuation at market prices uses the London market price at the end of the last working day of the year considered.

c Since 1979, the dollar value of ECUs issued in exchange for part of the dollar reserves of the central banks of EMS countries (see Sect. 19.5.3) is included in the $ component; the SDR value of ECUs issued in exchange for part of the gold reserves is not included in the total shown in the table. The percentages may not add up to 100 because of rounding.

d With gold at the official valuation

e With gold at the market valuation

Triffin, 1960): to avoid a shortage in international liquidity, the United States would have to run balance-of-payments deficits, and this would undermine confidence in the dollar; on the other hand, the cessation of the US deficits to strengthen the dollar would create a liquidity shortage. The agreement to introduce SDRs reflects, amongst other things, an attempt at creating a new form of international reserve asset unrelated to any particular currency and intended to become a true *fiat money* issued by the IMF.

The value of the SDR was initially fixed in terms of gold (with the same content as the 1970 US dollar); in July 1974 it was transformed into a basket-currency (see Sect. 18.6.3). The currencies composing the basket were initially 16, then reduced to 5 in 1981 (in parentheses we give the amounts of each currency in one SDR): US dollar (0.54), D-mark (0.46), yen (34), pound sterling (0.071), French franc (0.74). It is important to note that the newly created SDRs are allocated by the IMF to member countries in proportion to their quotas and that they are indeed fiat money, though their use is subject to certain limitations[3].

In order to make the SDR competitive with reserve currencies, it was decided to attribute an interest on holdings of it, depending on the short-term interest rates of the countries whose currencies compose the basket. Besides, the SDR has been given the role of numéraire of the international monetary system, in the sense that any declaration of a par value by a country to the Fund is to be made with reference to the SDR and not to gold or dollars. Finally, after the demonetization of gold (see below, Sect. 20.1.7) the 25% of all quota increases (and of quota subscriptions by new members) once to be paid in gold, is paid in SDRs (or in the currencies of other countries specified by the Fund, with the concurrence of the issuers, or in any combination of SDRs and these currencies).

The role of SDRs in international liquidity is however quantitatively irrelevant, as can be seen from Table 20.2.

On the problem of international liquidity and in particular of the demand for international reserves, see below, Sect. 20.2. Here we only mention the plan for the creation of a *substitution account within the IMF*. This plan aimed at strengthening the role of the SDR and, at the same time, at solving the problem of not weakening the dollar should some countries wish to change the composition of their international reserves by selling dollars in exchange for other reserve currencies. The idea was that official holders of dollars could deposit them with the IMF in exchange for claims denominated in SDRs. But the plan was dropped both because of disagreement on how that should be done and because the dollar was getting stronger: the official holders wanted to keep their dollars, not turn them in for SDRs.

Another proposal is to issue SDRs in favour of countries that have been recently joining the international monetary system while owning negligible amounts of international reserves. For the most part these are Eastern-European countries belonging to the former communist bloc. The group of the most

---

[3] Initially the use of SDRs to settle payment imbalances between member countries was subjected to a partial "reconstitution requirement", whereby members were obliged to maintain, over time, a minimum average level of SDRs holdings as a percentage of their net cumulative allocation. This was eliminated in April 1981; other limitations, however, still persist, for example as regards the maximum total amount of SDRs that a country is obliged to accept.

industrialised countries (G-7 or G-10) has acknowledged that these countries' lack of reserves is a problem that might jeopardize the stability of the international monetary system. According to some authors (for example Polak, 1994, Sect. 3) a SDR allocation mechanism is much more suitable than other mechanisms.

20.1.5 Collapse of Bretton Woods

The events that are identified with the collapse of the Bretton Woods system have already been described in Sect. 18.3, to which we refer the reader. We only add that where the Jamaica Agreement of January 1976 contemplated the possibility of returning to a generalized regime of "stable but adjustable" par values, the reference was not to an adjustable peg of the Bretton Woods type, which has proved to be no longer viable, but to a regime which should ensure a better flexibility than the adjustable peg. Thus the problem of the choice of the appropriate exchange-rate regime is far from obsolete, and we refer the reader to Sects. 18.2–18.3 for a discussion of the various possible alternatives.

It is now as well to examine the causes of the collapse of the Bretton Woods regime. We first briefly recall the features of this system (see Sect. 10.5).

In the Bretton Woods system the country at the centre of the system, or dominant country (the United States) guaranteed the convertibility of its currency into gold at a fixed price. The other participating countries, in turn, guaranteed the convertibility of their currencies into dollars at a fixed exchange rate. Hence the system was, in fact, a gold exchange standard of the limping type (since the convertibility of dollars into gold was limited to central banks). It should be noted that generalised convertibility was fully actuated only in 1959, so that the life span of the regime was a dozen years. There is no doubt that the Bretton Woods regime of convertibility and fixed exchange rates was very near to a regime with a single world currency. And, in fact, it brought about great benefits, amongst which the impetus to the growth of international trade. We must then ask ourselves why it didn't last longer.

The answer to this question is generally based on the "Triffin dilemma" (that we have mentioned in Sect. 20.1.4), from the name of the economist who formulated it in 1960. In a growing world with growing trade, there is a growing world demand for money for transaction purposes. In the system under consideration, this amounts to a growing demand for dollars. This does not seem to be a problem, because the United States can supply all the required dollars simply by incurring balance-of-payments deficits. But this process poses the problem of the convertibility of dollars into gold. Since the gold stock owned by the US cannot grow at the same rate as the growth of dollars held by the rest-of-the-world central banks, there is a loss of confidence in the ability of the US to guarantee convertibility. If, on the other hand, the United States brought their balance of payments into equilibrium, the international monetary system would suffer from a liquidity shortage, with the possible collapse of international trade. Hence the dilemma: if the US allow the increase in international liquidity through deficits in their balance of payments, the international monetary system is bound to collapse for a confidence crisis; if, on the other hand, they do not allow such an increase, the world is condemned to deflation.

In addition to the Triffin dilemma, two other concurring causes are brought into play: the rigidity of the system and the "seignorage" problem. The rigidity of the system was due to the fact that the idea of "fixed but adjustable" exchange rates *(adjustable peg)* was interpreted, as observed in Sect. 10.5, in the restrictive sense. That is to say, the parity was to be defended by all means, and was to be changed only when any further defence turned out to be impossible. Hence the external adjustment could not come about through reasonably frequent exchange-rate variations, but through deflationary policies.

The seignorage problem was related to the reserve-currency role of the dollar. This enabled the US to acquire long-term assets to carry out direct investment abroad in exchange for short-term assets (the dollars). These dollars were usually invested by the rest-of-the-world central banks in short-term US Treasury bills, that carried a relatively low interest and whose purchasing power was slowly but steadily eroded by US inflation. This problem was much felt by several countries (especially by France under De Gaulle) and, though not being an essential cause, certainly weakened the will to save the system when it came under pressure.

The Triffin dilemma is the commonly accepted explanation of the collapse of the Bretton Woods system. But there is an alternative explanation, put forth by Paul De Grauwe (1989, Ch. 4). This explanation (hints of which can be found in Niehans, 1978) is based on Gresham's law ("bad money drives out good money"). This law, originally stated for a bimetallic standard (gold-silver, etc.), can be applied to any monetary system based on the use of two moneys whose relative price (or conversion rate) is officially fixed by the authorities, who commit themselves to buying and selling the moneys at the official price. If one of the two currencies becomes relatively abundant, its price in the private market will tend to decrease: economic agents will then buy it there and sell it to the authorities at the official price, which is higher. In the same way they obtain the scarce currency from the authorities at a cheaper price than in the private market. This means that the scarce currency will go out of the monetary circuit to be used for non-monetary purposes (hoarding etc.). Only the abundant currency will remain in use in the monetary circuit.

Now, if we apply this law to the gold-dollar system, it can be seen that the increase in dollars was not matched by an increase in the gold stock, and that the official price was losing credibility. In fact, while the purchasing power of dollars (in terms of goods and services) was decreasing because of inflation, it remained fixed in terms of gold. Thus the so-called "gold pool", made up of the central banks of the most industrialised countries (see Sect. 20.1.7), that acted buying and selling gold in the private market with the aim of stabilizing its price at the official level, was faced with increasing gold demand from the private sector at the given official price ($ 35/oz). The ensuing gold loss compelled the gold pool to discontinue any intervention and leave the private price free, maintaining the official price for transactions between central banks only. The August 1971 official declaration of inconvertibility of the dollar (see Sect. 18.3) was just the *de jure* acknowledgment of a *de facto* situation, namely the functioning of the system as a *dollar standard*.

If one accepts this analysis of De Grauwe's, the corollary follows that, even if the Triffin dilemma were hypothetically solved, the working of Gresham's law would not make it advisable a "return to gold" (as some still advocate).

Whichever explanation is accepted for the collapse of Bretton Woods, the following fundamental point should be stressed: to base the international monetary system on fixed exchange rates is tantamount to assuming that the world as whole is an optimum currency area. If this assumption is not true (and it does not seem that the Bretton Woods system was an optimum currency area for all participants), then the system is bound to collapse.

20.1.6 Petrodollars

The repeated increases in oil prices[4] charged since October 1973 by the oil producing and exporting countries united in the OPEC cartel (Organization of Petroleum Exporting Countries), gave rise to serious balance-of-payments problems in the importing countries and to the accumulation of huge dollar balances (also called petrodollars) by these countries, as oil was paid in dollars. In 1974 the (flow) financial surplus of the OPEC countries was about $ 56 billion, which mirrored an equal overall deficit of the oil importing countries vis-à-vis OPEC countries. About two-thirds of this deficit concerned industrial countries, the remaining third the non-oil-producing developing countries (also called the "Fourth World"). The problem of financing the oil deficits was particularly acute given the suddenness and the amount of the price increases, and was solved by means of the so-called *recycling* process, through which the oil surpluses of the OPEC countries were lent back (indirectly) to the deficit countries. The recycling process operated mostly through market mechanisms, both international (the Euro-dollar market) and national (the US and UK financial markets), and for the rest through *ad hoc* mechanisms. Since the OPEC countries invested their petrodollar surpluses in the Euro-dollar market and in the US and UK financial markets, the deficit countries could borrow the dollars that they needed by applying to the Euro-dollar market and to the US and UK financial markets. The *ad hoc* mechanisms concerned both bilateral agreements between an oil importing and an oil exporting country, and agreements brought into being by international organizations. The latter included the IMF's "oil facility" brought into being in 1974 (and discontinued in 1976) and financed by borrowing agreements between the IMF and other countries (mostly oil producing countries) with the aim of granting loans, with certain conditions, to countries facing balance-of-payments disequilibria due to oil deficits. The agreements also included borrowing facilities created within the EEC and OECD organisations.

The recycling process was of course a short-run solution as it did not solve the problem of the elimination of the oil surpluses and deficits. This can be examined

---

[4] To set the problem into proper perspective it should be pointed out that these increases occurred after a long period of low oil prices, which, though stable in nominal terms, had actually been decreasing in real terms. Many people wonder therefore whether a more far sighted policy (on the part of all those concerned), of gradual price increases in the period before 1973, might not have avoided the problems created by the huge and sudden 1973 price increase.

in the context of the transfer problem (see Sect. 17.4), and in the context of the theory of cartels (see Sect. 5.5.3). The long-run predictions[5] of this theory seem to have come true, since in the last few years the OPEC countries have been experiencing balance-of-payments difficulties.

20.1.7 Demonetization of Gold

The problem of the function of gold in the international monetary system and of its price has been solved by the Jamaica Agreement of 1976 (referred to above), which ruled the *demonetization* of gold, thus removing the privileged status that gold had previously enjoyed, with the ultimate aim of making it like any other commodity.

The Bretton Woods Agreement gave gold a central place in the international monetary system, as was clear from the obligation on the part of members to pay out twenty-five per cent of their IMF quota in gold and to declare the par value of their currencies in terms of gold or, alternatively, in terms of the US dollar (which was the same thing, since the dollar was convertible into gold at the irrevocably fixed price of $ 35 per ounce). The maintenance of this official price of gold was an easy matter until the end of the fifties. But in 1960 problems began to arise because of the fact that the free market price of gold, quoted in some financial centres (mainly London), began to diverge from the official price, mostly because of speculative hoarding. To counter this, the central banks of eight countries, by the Basle Agreements of 1961 and 1962, constituted the so-called *Gold Pool*, which — by using the gold provided by the central banks themselves — had the task of intervening on the free market to stabilize the gold price, by buying (selling) gold when its price fell (rose) beyond certain limits with respect to the official price. In this way a single price of gold prevailed. But in 1968 the Gold Pool was discontinued, because of huge losses of gold due to increasing speculative pressures on the market, and the two-tier market for gold was established: the official market for the transactions between central banks, at the agreed price of $ 35 per ounce, and the free market, where the price was formed by the free interplay of supply and demand; the central banks agreed not to intervene on the free market.

The increase in the official price of gold to $ 38 and then to $ 42.44 (see Sect. 18.3.1) did not solve the problem of the gold-reserve freeze, due to the fact that no central bank was willing to meet its international payments by releasing gold at the official price when the market price was much higher. Partial solutions were found within the EEC (1974), with the settlement in gold of payment imbalances at an official gold price related to the market price. However, the general problem of the function of gold remained, and there were two main schools of thought.

The first aimed at maintaining the monetary function of gold as the paramount international means of payment and suggested the revaluation of its official price to bring it close to the market price. The second aimed (a) at eliminating this function and (b) at replacing gold with an international fiduciary

---

[5] We recall from Sect. 5.5.3, that according to this theory there exist long-run forces which lead to the progressive erosion of the cartel's power.

means of payments, as had happened in the individual national economic systems (where the link with gold had long been eliminated and replaced by fiduciary money). The second school prevailed within the IMF, and this is reflected in the Kingston (Jamaica) Agreement of January 1976 [in which, only point (a) is fully accepted]. As regards gold, the main provisos of this Agreement are the following:

(1) The elimination of the function of gold as numéraire of the system, i.e. as common denominator of par values of currencies and as the unit of value of the SDR.
(2) The abolition of the official price of gold.
(3) The abolition of any obligation on the part of member countries to make payments to the Fund in gold, in particular as regards quota increases and interest payments.
(4) The authorization for the Fund to return one sixth of its gold (25 million ounces), at the official price of grams 0.888671 per SDR, to the countries which were members as of 31st August 1975, in proportion to their quotas at the same date and in accordance with certain procedures. This return has been carried out.
(5) The authorization for the Fund to sell another sixth of its gold for the benefit of developing countries which were members as of 31st August 1975. A part of the profit (excess of the selling price over the old book value), proportional to these countries' quotas, was to be transferred directly to them, whilst the remaining part was to be used for subsidized loans through a newly created Trust Fund. These gold sales were to be carried out by the IMF, acting as agent of the Trust Fund, through auctions over a period of four years, as has in fact been done.
(6) The possibility for the Fund (the IMF) to release its residual stock of gold (but only after a decision taken each time by a majority of 85%) through further returns or sales. In the latter case the profits are to be disposed of in prescribed ways.
(7) The obligation for the Fund to avoid stabilizing the gold price (or otherwise regulating the gold market) as a consequence of its sales of gold.
(8) The member countries pledged themselves to cooperate with the Fund and with one another in the management of reserve assets, with the aim of enhancing te role of the SDR as the principal reserve asset (this was the only concession made to point (b) above).

As a consequence of this Agreement, the countries of the Group of Ten stipulated an arrangement (to which other countries adhered) under which they may sell and buy gold at market-related prices, provided this does not involve pegging the price of gold or increasing the total stock of gold then held by the Fund and the Group of Ten.

In parallel to the demonetization[6] of gold the role of the SDR was strengthened (see above, Sect. 20.1.4).

---

[6] It should be noted that here "demonetization" — in the sense of the elimination of the function of gold as common denominator of par values, etc., as described above — has a different meaning from the one it has in balance-of-payments accounting (see Sect. 11.1.3.II).

Although gold has been demonetized, it is still owned by central banks, and included in their international reserves. However, the central banks intervene in the foreign exchange market and meet their country's international payment obligations by using foreign exchange and possibly other reserve assets (SDRs, ECUs), but not gold as such, which — after the demonetization — has to be "mobilized" before it can be used. The problem then arises of the value that has to be given to gold holdings by central banks. The "official" price of 35 SDRs per ounce (see Table 20.2) is merely conventional, and in practice each country adopts its own criteria, which in general relate the valuation in some way to the market price. In Table 20.2 we have also given the market-price valuation.

What is clear is that if several countries simultaneously were to realize their gold by selling it on the free market, the price would crash. This is so because the gold market — on which the price is formed in accordance with the law of supply and demand — could not stand the impact of huge gold sales; therefore, the mobilizability of gold reserves is by no means an easy matter. One possibility would be to use gold as collateral to obtain loans, i.e. to pledge it as security for repayment of the loan, but, given the wide swings in its price, it would not be easy to fix a price. Another possibility is that put into being in the EMS, where ECUs are created against the contribution of reserves (gold amongst them) to the EMCF and can be mobilized according to certain rules (see Sect. 18.7.4).

It must be acknowledged that the problem is not easy to solve and that further studies are required (see, for example, Falchi and Masera, 1982, and Quadrio Curzio ed., 1982, especially Part III).

20.1.8 The EMS

The European Monetary System has been treated in detail in Sect. 19.5, to which we refer the reader.

20.1.9 The International Debt Crisis

This term refers to the incapability of the governments of some developing countries (mainly in Latin America) to service their foreign debt, namely to pay the interest and/or repay the principal as scheduled. The beginning of this crisis is usually placed in August 1982, when the Mexican government informed the US Treasury, the IMF, and the creditor foreign banks that it could no longer service its foreign debt. Similar cases had already occured previously, but the fact that the country concerned was Mexico, an oil producing country and with a debt of more than US $ 80 billion of the time, shook the international financial markets. The example of Mexico was soon followed by several other Latin-American countries.

The reasons why these countries had indebted themselves are clear (mainly the financing of ambitious development programs). The reasons for their difficulties are also clear: the hoped-for huge export increases with which to get the foreign exchange to service the debt did not materialize, partly because of the unfavourable international economic situation. But to create a debt situation there must be two parties, the debtor and the lender who supplies the funds. Hence we must examine the reasons why the main international banks had so easily granted huge amounts of credit to the countries under consideration. A widely shared thesis starts from the oil shocks (see above, Sect. 20.1.6). These had generated huge financial surpluses in the OPEC countries, that had deposited them with the main international banks in London and in the United States. The enormous funds received by these banks raised the issue of how they could profitably utilise the money. A good outlet was found to be the lending to less developed countries in the course of industrializing their economies (the Newly Industrializing Countries or NICs). The fact that the debt was incurred by governments or guaranteed by governments made the risk of default look fairly low. Paradoxically, it were the increasing prices of the export goods of the countries (hence increasing proceeds in foreign currency) rather than the industrialization to give confidence to the lending banks, so much so that about one half of the stock of debt outstanding in 1992 had been contracted in the last two years.

Be it as it may, the international debt crisis has given rise to serious problems, not only for the creditor banks but also for the governments of the countries to which these banks belong, and for the international monetary system. The possible bankruptcy of these banks, in fact, would create serious dangers for both the national monetary system and the international monetary system. Although several general proposals and plans have been put forward (the Baker plan, the Brady plan, and so on: see Pilbeam, 1992, Ch. 15), in practice the international debt problem has been tackled on a case by case approach, through a combination of measures that can be summarized into three categories:

(a) modifications in the structure and nature of the debt, for example by *rescheduling,* i.e. lengthening the time horizon of the debt (so that the repayment installments become smaller) or postponing the payment of interest and/or principal to some date in the future. Another measure in this category consists of *debt-equity swaps,* namely part of the debt is exchanged, through third parties, for equities of corporate firms of debtor countries.
(b) economic reforms in debtor countries, which are usually summed up in the d-triad: devaluation, deflation, deregulation. These are the macroeconomic measures usually suggested by the IMF to debtor countries. Their aim is to improve the economic situation of debtor countries and hence these countries' capability of servicing the debt. In the short run these measures may however have strong negative effects on employment and so turn out to be politically destabilizing for debtor countries.
(c) debt forgiveness. This can take place in various ways (in addition to simply writing off part of the debt): for example, by allowing the debtor to buy back its debt at a huge discount, or by drastically reducing the interest rate.

Given the very different nature of the situation and prospects of debtor countries, it is difficult if not impossible to make generalizations. Hence the case-by-case approach seems indeed the most suitable.

20.2 International Liquidity and the Demand for International Reserves

20.2.1 Introductory Remarks

The problem of the "adequacy" of international liquidity and the related problem of the demand for international reserves are moot questions, far from being solved, notwithstanding innumerable studies; for surveys of the earlier literature we refer the reader to Flanders (1971), Grubel (1971), Williamson (1973), Cohen (1975), Claassen (1976).

As we have already seen above (Sect. 20.1.4), international liquidity and international reserves are often used as synonyms, although they are not. International reserves are financial assets representing liquid international purchasing power in the the hands of the monetary authorities. International liquidity, as we have already said, is a broader concept and also includes access to loans as well as the monetary authorities' ability to convert illiquid assets into liquid purchasing power through international asset markets. A further distinction is made between "owned" and "borrowed" reserves. The former, unlike the latter, have no offsetting foreign liability of the monetary authorities. There is a last distinction to be recalled: that between official and private international liquidity. The former only includes liquid international assets held by the monetary authorities, while the latter includes all the foreign liquid assets held by residents of the country.

Some maintain that, given the huge increase in international asset markets, the problem of international liquidity, once prominent, is now less important if not irrelevant. With free international asset markets, a creditworthy country (just like a creditworthy firm) can borrow all the liquidity it needs. This opinion cannot be shared, as not all countries in need of international liquidity are equally creditworthy (think of the East-European countries). In any case, the problem remains of what determines the need for, or the adequacy of, international liquidity. To this problem we now turn.

According to an old definition, international liquidity can be considered "adequate" when it allows the countries suffering from balance-of-payments deficits to finance these without having to undertake adjustment policies which are undesirable for the growth of their economies and international trade. This definition was rightly criticized because it inevitably leads one to say that international liquidity is always inadequate, as no reasonable amount of it will be sufficient to allow financing without adjusting balance-of-payments deficits (by way of more or less undesirable policies).

If we consider official international reserves, since the holders and users are the central banks of the various countries, the problem can be seen from the point of view of the central banks' demand for international reserves: international liquidity should then be considered adequate when its actual amount equals the amount which is *desired* in accordance with this demand function.This, as Machlup (1966) points out, is quite different from determining the *need* for international reserves on the basis of allegedly *objective* parameters (such as, for example, a particular ratio of reserves to imports, etc.) as was once customary, because a demand also implies subjective elements and may not be entirely justifiable on the basis of objective ones. In this respect the often cited "Mrs. Machlup's wardrobe rule" is an amusing analogy. After having set forth an analogy between the number of dresses that Mrs. Machlup wants and the amount of reserves that central bankers want, Machlup amends it in the sense of stressing the annual *addition* to Mrs. Machlup's wardrobe: "She does not really care so much whether she has 25 or 52 dresses, if only she gets a few new dresses each year. This ambition is the correct analogue of the central banker's ambition. He is not so much concerned whether his reserve ratio (to his liabilities or to the total money supply) is 47 or 74 per cent, if only his reserves increase, however modestly, and do not decrease" (Machlup, 1966, p. 201). Machlup's thesis is that it cannot be reasonably said of any particular amount of reserves that it is adequate, and that any country will take adjusting measures, if it sees that its stock of reserves, whatever their amount, is on the decrease. It follows that the only way to avoid undesirable measure is to cause the stock of reserves to *increase*.

Machlup's thesis, however, has not been generally accepted, and many writers have continued to explore the possibility of finding the determinants of the demand for international reserves by central banks. From this point of view it is possible to single out two main approaches to the problem, the *interpretative* or *descriptive approach* and the *optimizing* one[7]. The former aims at finding, by way of theoretical and empirical studies, the determinants which explain the demand for international reserves which actually emanates from central banks. The latter approach aims at determining the optimum level of international reserves (in accordance with one or other criterion of optimality), irrespective of whether this optimum level is what is actually demanded. If we make a distinction widely used in general economics, we may say that the descriptive approach belongs to *positive* economics, the optimizing approach to *normative* economics[8], since an obvious suggestion deriving from the optimizing approach is that the actual level of international reserves should be brought to the optimum level when the two are different.

20.2.2 The Descriptive Approach

The basic idea underlying this approach is that central banks demand international reserves for motives analogous to those for which people demand money in accordance with traditional demand-for-money theory.

There is, firstly, the transactions motive: the lack of synchronization between international payments and receipts requires the availability of a stock of means of

---

[7] A different distinction has been suggested by Hipple (1974), between the *transactions approach* and the *disturbances approach*. This classification only partially coincides with the classification that we have adopted in the text, as the entire optimizing approach and part of the studies classified in the descriptive approach may be included in the disturbances approach.

[8] Other writers, however, do not identify the positive theory with the descriptive approach and the normative theory with the optimizing approach: see Williamson (1973a), who includes both approaches in the positive theory, as — in his opinion — normative questions are those concerned with the management of the system.

payment. It should be noted that the international payments imbalances in question are the regular and recurring (hence anticipated) ones such as those due to seasonal factors; some writers also include possible random fluctuations.

There is, secondly, the precautionary motive, according to which countries usually wish to hold balances to meet sudden and unexpected events which may cause a decline in receipts or an increase in payments (crop failures, abnormal changes in capital movements, exceptional drops in foreign demand or increases in foreign prices, political unrest, etc.).

The speculative motive is more difficult to make concrete; it is usually related to the fact that reserve assets — insofar as they give a yield — are an alternative use of national resources.

Once the motives have been determined, the problem arises of singling out the factors to include as independent variables in the demand-for-reserves function. Traditionally the main variable considered was the *period of financial covering of imports*, that is, how long the current flow of imports can be maintained if the existing stock of reserves are used for this purpose. This period can be calculated simply by taking the reserve/imports ratio; thus the demand for reserves is an increasing function of imports. It was however noted that the desired period, and so the desired reserve/imports ratio (hereafter called the reserve ratio), cannot be considered constant, but depends in its turn on a number of variables, amongst which (the list is taken from Flanders, 1971, p. 24):

(1) The instability of exports: the higher this instability, the higher the reserve ratio.
(2) The efficiency of the private market in foreign exchange and foreign credit: the more efficient this market, the lower the reserve ratio.
(3) The opportunity cost of holding reserves (measured, for example, by the yield of productive investment forgone): the higher this cost, the lower the reserve ratio.
(4) The rate of return on reserves: the higher this return, the higher the reserve ratio.
(5) The variability of reserves (due to the variability in payment imbalances): the higher this variability, the higher the risk of remaining without reserves and the higher the reserve ratio.
(6) The willingness to change the exchange rate instead of financing payment deficits: insofar as these changes are effective in restoring external equilibrium, a greater willingness to use them implies a lower reserve ratio.
(7) The willingness to accept the cost of adjustment (by tools other than exchange-rate changes, for example restrictive domestic policies) of balance-of-payments deficits: the higher this willingness, the lower the need to finance disequilibria and the lower the reserve ratio.
(8) The existence of inventories of traded goods: if a country has sizeable inventories of traded goods (both exports and imports) the reserve ratio will be lower, as the country can use these goods as substitutes for reserves.
(9) The cost of international borrowing. An alternative to holding reserves is to borrow abroad when the need arises. The higher this cost (where cost is measured not only by interest rate, but also by terms of repayment, ease of obtaining the credit, etc.), the higher the reserve ratio.

(10) Income, which in monetary theory is often considered to be a determinant of the demand for money over and above the effect of the volume of transactions.

The problem of discriminating among these explanatory variables (to which others could be added) is by no means easy, despite the help given by econometric studies. The main difficulty of these studies is, in fact, the data problem. The demand for reserves is a desired or *ex ante* concept, which may not coincide with the observed *ex post* value. To assume that the demand for reserves is always equal to the observed stock of reserves, is tantamount to assuming that the central banks are capable of maintaining the actual stock of reserves instantaneously equal to its desired value. This is unrealistic and is, in any case, contradicted by what central banks themselves say. A possible solution to this problem could be to hypothesize a partial adjustment equation of the type

$$\Delta R = \alpha (\hat{R} - R), \quad 0 < \alpha < 1, \tag{20.1}$$

where $\hat{R}$ denotes the desired level[9] of reserves – which is a function of the various explanatory variables considered – and R the *observed* stock of reserves. Equation (20.1) states that the adjustment of the actual to the desired stock of reserves is not instantaneous, but takes place gradually through time in accordance with the adjustment coefficient α.

Even this formulation is not, however, fully satisfactory, because – especially during periods of turbulence on foreign exchange markets – if the central banks have to intervene in these markets and so use their reserve holdings, these may well move in an opposite direction to the desired one (which is that specified in Eq. (20.1) above). This might suggest the inclusion of further variables in Eq. (20.1) to represent the above interventions (see, for example, Giustiniani, 1985).

A second difficulty derives from the fact that reserve changes feed back on the other macroeconomic variables (for example on the money supply) and so on some of the explanatory variables in the demand-for-reserves function. This is the simultaneity problem, very well known in econometrics, which leads one to believe that the estimates of an isolated equation for the demand for reserves, outside the context of an economy-wide simultaneous model, will necessarily give seriously biased estimates.

All the above considerations may serve to explain why the attempts at estimating single equations for the demand for reserves along the lines explained above have generally given poor results: these range from the "dismal failure" of Flanders (1971, p. 43), to the more satisfactory findings of Frenkel (1983: see, however, Purvis 1983, for a criticism). An element that seems in any case to be empirically relevant is the opportunity cost (see point 3 above). It turns to be a significant determinant of the demand for international reserves. This result holds both when the cost is measured as the difference between the yield on reserves and the marginal productivity of an alternative investment in fixed

---

[9] In the case in which the dependent variable is the reserve ratio, the equation will be written in terms of $\hat{R}/IMP$ and R/IMP; alternatively, but not equivalently, one could include IMP among the explanatory variables and use Eq. (20.1).

capital (Ben-Bassat and Gottlieb, 1992a) and when it is measured as the interest rate at which the monetary authorities can borrow in international financial markets (Landell-Mills, 1989).

In any case – and this is an interesting result that we have already mentioned in Sect. 18.3.2 – it does not seem that the passage from fixed to floating exchange rates has significantly reduced the demand for reserves (see, for example, Heller and Khan, 1978; Holden and Holden, 1979; Batten, 1982; Frenkel, 1983). This result, which some writers have considered as surprising, is — in our opinion — to be considered totally plausible, if only one remembers that the existing regime of floating exchange rates is actually a managed float, where central banks intervene in the foreign exchange markets. In fact, as it seems that the criteria adopted to manage the float (see Sect. 18.3.2) have required continuing, heavy interventions, it is by no means surprising that the reserve needs have remained high.

20.2.3 The Optimizing Approach

This approach aims at determining the optimum level of international reserves by way of a maximizing procedure, and has been developed along two main lines.

The first is that of *cost-benefit-analysis*, which entails beginning by singling out the costs and benefits of holding reserves; the optimum level of these will then be determined by maximizing the difference between benefits and costs.

The second line begins by finding a *social welfare function* (or an objective function of the policy maker), which has the reserve level among its arguments; this function is then maximized subject to all the constraints of the problem.

It is possible to make a further distinction based on the static or dynamic nature of the optimizing process; this distinction can be applied to both lines previously distinguished.

It should be noted that the descriptive approach must not be seen as totally distinct from the optimizing approach. As a matter of fact many explanatory variables considered by the former are again found in the latter, as for example when one singles out costs and benefits.

Let us now begin by briefly examining the cost-benefit line; in general, the optimum will be found by equating marginal costs and benefits. The first example of this kind of analysis applied to reserve holding is Heller's (1966) which, thanks to its simplicity, allows a clear illustration of the procedure.

The cost of holding reserves is an opportunity cost, given by the difference between the yield that the resources held in the form of reserves would have if employed productively at home (this yield is identified with the social yield on capital) and the yield on reserve assets[10]. The latter is assumed to be lower that the former, so that the opportunity cost is positive. It is also assumed that the above yields are constant, so that the net marginal opportunity cost of reserves, denoted by i, is constant.

The benefits consist in the fact that the use of reserves enables the country to finance a possible balance-of-payments deficit instead of having to adjust. In the

---
[10] Or, more exactly, on that part of reserves that can be invested so as to obtain a yield whilst remaining liquid. This excludes gold, unless one considers possible increases or decreases in gold prices as a positive or negative yield.

simple model used by Heller (fixed exchange rates, no capital movements, etc.) the only way of adjusting to an external deficit is to reduce national income to the point where the consequent reduction in imports eliminates the deficit. If we consider a deficit of D, an equal reduction in imports (Δm) will be required to eliminate it, and since $\Delta m = \mu \Delta y$, income will have to decrease by D/μ. Therefore, if we assume that the marginal propensity to import is constant, the marginal benefit will be $1/\mu$. This benefit, however, is not certain, as it will occur only in the case where a cumulative balance-of-payments deficit of a certain magnitude actually occurs. Thus we must multiply the marginal benefit by prob(R_j), the probability of the occurence of j consecutive deficits of a size necessitating the use of the jth reserve unit. Thus the optimum condition turns out to be

$$\text{prob}(R_j) \frac{1}{\mu} = i, \tag{20.2}$$

whose solution (see Sect. A.20.1) yields the optimum reserve level.

It is self-evident that this is a very much simplified model, which is rendered more complex if one introduces the possibility of adjusting to external deficits not only by income decreases but also by exchange-rate variations (Kreinin and Heller, 1973), by interest-rate changes (W. Sellekaerts and B. Sellekaerts, 1973), and so on; in addition, the monetary authorities can borrow abroad (Alessandrini, 1975). Other refinements can be introduced by extending the time horizon into the future and going more deeply into the probabilistic aspect (Hamada and Ueda, 1977; Frenkel and Jovanovic, 1981). However, the basic idea remains the same as that set forth by Heller; what changes is the determination of costs and benefits.

As regards the *maximization of the policy maker's utility* (or of the social welfare) *function*, the initial step is to single out the arguments of this function. The first studies (Clark, 1970; Kelly, 1970) assume that this objective function depends positively on the level and negatively on the variability of income. As regards the constraint, one must take into consideration the fact that random disturbances to the balance of payments can be offset either by financing, i.e. using reserves, or by adjusting, i.e. causing income variations (the reasoning is exactly like that made in the cost-benefit analysis above). In the former case there will be a lower income level due to the income sacrificed in holding reserves (i.e., the alternative return which these assets could yield), whilst in the second case there will be a higher income variability[11]. It is thus possible to construct a trade-off between the level of income and its variability. By maximizing the objective function subject to this constraint one obtains the optimum point from which one can derive the optimum level of reserves.

These models also are very simplified: as regards the structure of the economy, the determination of the arguments of the objective function, the implicit assumption of the symmetry of the adjustment policies (on the contrary – as Claassen, 1976, notes – the pressure on the monetary authorities is quite different

---

[11] The question is complicated by the fact that the context is stochastic and that the policy maker must also take into account the probability of running out of reserves (or, more realistically, of their falling below a minimum acceptable level), but the basic idea is that set forth in the text.

according to whether they face a deficit or a surplus, and it also is quite different according as they are indebted to abroad, as noted by Ben Bassat and Gottlieb, 1992b). They have, however, the merit of showing the complementarity between reserve policy and the other policy instruments in achieving external and internal equilibrium. This aspect is even more evident in the studies which refine the analysis by improving on the simplifications mentioned above (for these studies we refer the reader to Hipple, 1974; Claassen, 1976; Ben Bassat and Gottlieb, 1992b) and by considering the problem in an intertemporal maximization framework (see, for example, Nyberg and Viotti, 1976).

It should be noted, as a conclusion to this overview of the optimizing approach, that once one has determined the optimum reserve stock by way of one of the procedures described above, it is possible to quantify it numerically, either by giving *a priori* values to the relevant parameters or by estimating them by econometric methods. Then the optimum stock can be compared with the actual reserve level so as to draw concrete indications (for example, that actual reserves are insufficient, or excessive, or ill distributed among countries), as has been done by many of the authors cited. However, the oversimplification inherent in all the models examined (even in those formally more complex), which consider only a small part of reality, suggests that one should take these indications with a great caution.

20.2.4 The Problem of the Composition of International Reserves

In the previous sections we have talked of international reserves as if these were a single entity. Actually, as we know – see Sect. 20.1.4 – international reserves are made up of various assets, and we must now study their composition (this is given in detail in Table 20.2).

The problem of the composition of international reserves was mainly studied, until the end of the sixties, by examining the choice between gold and US dollars (see, for example, Kenen, 1963; Hageman, 1969). This focus was justified by the fact that these were the preponderant components.

After the crisis of the dollar standard which took place in 1971 and the subsequent collapse of the Bretton Woods system and the demonetization of gold (see Sect. 20.1.7), attention shifted onto the process of diversification within the stock of foreign exchange held by central banks, due to the emergence of new currencies which play the role of *vehicle currencies*, i.e. of international means of payment. The most promising line of research in this direction seems to be that which applies to this problem the theory of portfolio selection, duly enlarged by other considerations (Chrystal, 1977; Heller and Knight, 1978; Ben-Bassat, 1980, 1984; Roger, 1993).

Before briefly examining these studies, it is however necessary to ask why particular currencies become an international means of payment. This depends in part on historical accident but also – as Swoboda (1968, p. 10) observes – on economic factors which it is possible to single out.

Firstly, there are the *costs of converting* foreign exchange assets into domestic currency. For instance, traders will prefer to conduct transactions in US dollars rather than in Italian lire if the exchange costs from dollars to domestic currency are lower than those from lire to domestic currency. Asset-exchange costs depend inversely on the size of the market for a particular currency, owing to the presence of economies of scale in financial intermediation. This size partly depends, in turn, on the size of the foreign transactions (volume of foreign trade and balance-of-payments structure) of the country which issues the currency.

Secondly, since asset holders are in general risk-averse, the financial market of a vehicle currency must show *"depth, breadth, and resiliency"*, so that the risk of capital loss (if investors want to sell an asset denominated in that currency) is low.

Thirdly, the *expected behaviour of the currency's exchange rate* plays a role, since, if the currency is expected to fluctuate wildly, it is unlikely to be a good candidate for use as a vehicle currency.

According to Swoboda, it is also interesting to note the self-reinforcing tendency towards the use of a particular currency as vehicle currency. In fact, the more a currency is used as an international means of payments, the lower the asset exchange costs become and the more its use in international payments will expand.

On the other hand, a vehicle currency may cease to be such, if the necessary conditions cease (this was, for example, the case of the pound sterling, replaced by the US dollar), although this loss of status does not usually take place abruptly, but gradually. But the self-reinforcing mechanism noted above may be so strong that a currency may keep its status as vehicle even if one of the basic conditions fails, as is the case of the US dollar, which remains the main vehicle currency (see below) notwithstanding its wide swings on exchange markets.

On the basis of the data given in Table 20.2, it turns out that the main vehicle currency is always the US dollar, and that the importance of the German mark and the Japanese yen has been on the increase, notwithstanding the reluctance of the respective countries to permit this to come about. In fact, on the one hand, the use of a currency as a vehicle can give the issuing country certain advantages, such as, for example, the so-called *seignorage*[12], consisting in the fact that the country can use its own currency to settle balance-of-payments deficits, etc. On the other, it can give the country certain disadvantages, such as constraints — dictated by the need to stabilize the exchange rate — on its domestic economic policy, the possible upsetting of its domestic financial markets due to the investment or disinvestment of reserves by foreign central banks, etc. These disadvantages are, of course, inversely proportional to the economic, financial, etc. strength of the issuing country, and this partly explains the *"benign neglect"*[13] of the US monetary authorities as to the behaviour of the US dollar on foreign exchange markets (this situation, however, has been changing in recent times).

Let us now go back to the study of the problem of the composition of international reserves. The application of the theory of portfolio selection (whose general principles we have often mentioned: see, e.g., Sects. 15.6.2, 16.6.1, 17.3) to this problem starts from the idea that a central bank allocates its wealth — made

---

[12] For an analysis of this problem see, for example, Grubel (1969), Wijkman (1981).

[13] This expression was coined during the dollar standard period of the sixties, to denote that the USA did not take any policy actions to alleviate its balance-of-payments problems (nor should it have done, according to one school of thought: see McKinnon, 1979, p. 256).

up of its international reserves[14] — among the various vehicle currencies so as to achieve an efficient portfolio (minimum risk for a given yield or maximum yield for a given risk), much as a private asset-holder allocates his wealth. However, as Heller and Knight (1978) observe, this straightforward extension of the private asset-holder's behaviour to a central bank's behaviour is not correct for a number of reasons, the main one being that a central bank has much wider tasks and objectives than the mere optimization of its portfolio. Therefore, besides the principles underlying the choice of an efficient portfolio, a central bank will also take into account the prevailing exchange-rate arrangements, the structure of international trade and payments of the country, etc, in determining to what extent its foreign exchange portfolio should be concentrated or diversified.

If, for example, country x pegs its exchange rate to currency y [15], it is presumable that country x's central bank will allocate a relatively greater proportion of its reserves to holdings of currency y (with respect to the average of the other countries). It is also presumable that the quantity of a particular vehicle currency held by a country will be an increasing function of the amount of trade (and, more generally, of international transactions) of that country with the country which issues the vehicle currency.

The studies, already cited, of Chrystal (1977), Heller and Knight (1978), Ben-Bassat (1980, 1984), Dooley et al. (1989), all take this point of view, though with different emphasis, and obtain interesting empirical results (se also Sect. A.20.2).

20.3 The Traditional Analysis of Euro-Markets

20.3.1 General Remarks and the Simple Multipliers

The analytical explanation of the enormous development of Euro-dollar deposits, and more generally of the Euro-currency market, whose size has been illustrated in Table 20.1, gave rise to a heated theoretical debate. Whilst referring the reader to the texts of Bell (1973), Dufey and Giddy (1979), Johnston (1983), Gibson (1989) for exhaustive surveys of the literature, we begin our necessarily brief treatment by observing that the theories of the expansion of Euro-deposits are generally classified into two broad categories.

The first is the *traditional school* or *(fixed) multiplier approach*, which explains Euro-deposits by a multiplier mechanism analogous to that used in traditional monetary theory to explain deposit creation within a single country. The second rejects the fixed multiplier approach of the traditional school and takes the *portfolio approach*, analogous to that which is used in the modern theory of the domestic money supply or "new view" of money.

---

[14] For the reason that we have often mentioned (the demonetization of gold: see Sect. 20.1.7), in recent studies the gold component of reserves is excluded and the analysis focusses on the composition of the item "foreign exchange assets" (also called "convertible currencies"). It should also be noted that, for some currencies, it is possible to place them in alternative financial centres: for example, US dollars can be either placed in the US domestic financial market or in the Euro-dollar market. This is true for all Xeno-currencies. For simplicity's sake we ignore these additional complications (on which see, for example, Heller and Knight, 1978).

[15] As we have already mentioned in Sect. 10.5.4, after the collapse of the Bretton Woods regime, any country may choose any exchange-rate regime, though it must first notify its decision to the IMF and observe certain general principles. Many countries adopt a regime in which they peg their currency to a given foreign currency (usually the US dollar, but also the French franc and other currencies: see Table 10.1).

20.3 The Traditional Analysis of Euro-Markets

In this section we deal with the traditional approach, whilst the modern one will be taken up in the Sect. 20.4. In Sect. 20.5, we shall examine the (positive and negative) effects of Euro-markets (in the broad sense of Xeno-markets) with particular regard to their implications for national monetary policies and to the problem of their control.

Let us assume, in accordance with the traditional approach, that there is an initial (non-bank) deposit of H dollars with a Euro-bank[16]; we take dollars as the example, but the reasoning can be applied to any Xeno-currency, although with the appropriate modifications.

The Euro-bank will hold[17] a fraction c of this deposit by way of reserve (it should be noted that, as no legal requirements on the reserve ratio exist as regards Euro-deposits, the reserve ratio c will be purely voluntary, dictated by experience, convention, etc.) and will lend the rest. We must now distinguish various possibilities as to the end of the $(1-c)H$ dollars loaned by the bank:

(a) they can end up outside the Euro-banking system, i.e. they remain in the hands of the public (which can either keep them or deposit them in a US bank);

(b) they can be converted into another currency, in which case they will end up in the hands of a central bank[18] (other than the US Federal Reserve System), thus augmenting its international reserves;

(c) they can be redeposited with the Euro-banking system.

In case (a) that is the end of the process. In case (b) we must examine the behaviour of the central bank: it might, in fact, in its turn deposit part of the reserve increase with the Euro-banking system. For the moment we ignore this possibility (which will be examined later on), so that the process comes to an end also in case (b).

On the contrary, in case (c) the process goes on, and we must distinguish two sub-cases: that in which the entire loan is redeposited with the Euro-bank and that in which — given a leakage coefficient g — only a part $(1-g)$ of the loan is redeposited with the Euro-bank. The leakage coefficient may be due either to the fact that the public keeps part of the loan in its hands in cash or redeposits it outside the Euro-banking system.

In the first sub-case the Euro-bank receives an additional amount of deposits equal to $(1-c)H$. Since an amount $c(1-c)H$ will be held as reserve, the Euro-bank will lend the difference $(1-c)H-c(1-c)H=(1-c)^2H$, and so on. The redepositing chain from the initial deposit is then

$$H+(1-c)H+(1-c)^2H+\ldots+(1-c)^nH+\ldots \qquad (20.3)$$

---

[16] Analogously to the traditional analysis of the domestic deposit multiplier (with which the reader is assumed to be familiar), we consider the banking system as a whole, so that "Euro-bank" is taken to mean the "Euro-currency banking system" even if not specified.

[17] As a matter of fact the dollars will not be physically with the Euro-bank, as this will usually keep them in sight deposits with the US banking system. This is, however, irrelevant for our purposes.

[18] To be precise, this is true only if the currency is not another Euro-currency. But if it is, we are in case (c).

i.e. an infinite geometric series with first term H and common ratio $(1-c)$, whose sum is

$$\Delta D = \frac{1}{1-(1-c)} H = \frac{1}{c} H, \tag{20.4}$$

which is the final increase in deposits (ΔD) corresponding to an initial deposit of H dollars with the Euro-bank. It can be easily checked that when the increase in deposits reaches the value given by Eq. (20.4) the process comes to an end because the Euro-bank will hold all the H dollars by way of reserve; we have, in fact,

$$c\Delta D = c\frac{1}{c}H = H. \tag{20.5}$$

In the second sub-case the Euro-bank receives an additional amount of deposits equal to $(1-g)(1-c)H$. Since an amount $c(1-g)(1-c)H$ will be held as reserve, the Euro-bank will lend the difference $(1-g)(1-c)H - c(1-g)(1-c)H = (1-g)(1-c)^2 H$, of which a fraction $(1-g)$, i.e. an amount $(1-g)^2(1-c)^2 H$ will be redeposited, and so on. The redepositing chain is now

$$H + (1-g)(1-c)H + (1-g)^2(1-c)^2 H + \ldots + (1-g)^n(1-c)^n H + \ldots \tag{20.6}$$

whence the familiar multiplier formula

$$\Delta D = \frac{1}{1-(1-c)(1-g)} H, \tag{20.7}$$

which is the final increase in deposits corresponding to an initial deposit H when there is a leakage.

20.3.2 More Sophisticated Multipliers

Up to now there is nothing new with respect to the conventional deposit multiplier in a closed monetary economy. A new case may take place in case (b) or, more precisely, in a combination of case (b) with case (c). Not only private agents, but also central banks carry out transactions in the Euro-dollar market, both by depositing part of their international reserves there and by borrowing from it when the need arises. This may occur for various reasons, both economic (for example a higher yield) and noneconomic (for example political: see Sect. 10.6). Be it as it may, we assume that all central banks (other than the US Federal Reserve System) deposit an identical fraction v of their reserve increases with the Euro-banking system. We also make the additional simplifying assumption that the leakage examined in case (c) is entirely converted by the public into other currencies, so that the amount $g(1-c)H$ goes to increase the central banks' reserves, which then deposit a fraction v of it, i.e. an amount $vg(1-c)H$ with the Euro-market.

20.3 The Traditional Analysis of Euro-Markets

Thus, when the Euro-bank makes a loan of $(1-c)H$, it will get back an amount $(1-g)(1-c)H$ from the public and an amount $vg(1-c)H$ from central banks. Thus the additional amount of deposits received is

$$(1-g)(1-c)H + vg(1-c)H = (1-c)(1-g+vg)H, \tag{20.8}$$

of which a fraction c, i.e. an amount $c(1-c)(1-g+vg)H$, will be held by the Euro-bank by way of reserve, and the difference $[(1-c)(1-g+vg)H] - [c(1-c)(1-g+vg)H] = (1-c)^2(1-g+vg)H$ will be lent. Of this loan the public will keep a fraction g and convert it into other currencies (the central banks involved will then also deposit a fraction v of the new reserve increase with the Euro-bank), and will redeposit the fraction $(1-g)$ with the Euro-bank. Thus the new round gives a further deposit increase of

$$(1-g)(1-c)^2(1-g+vg)H + vg(1-c)^2(1-g+vg)H$$
$$= (1-c)^2(1-g+vg)^2 H. \tag{20.9}$$

The redepositing chain is now

$$H + (1-c)(1-g+vg)H + (1-c)^2(1-g+vg)^2 H + \ldots \tag{20.10}$$

whence we get the final increase in Euro-deposits

$$\Delta D = \frac{1}{1-(1-c)(1-g+vg)} H. \tag{20.11}$$

Thus the presence of a depositing activity of central banks with the Eurodollar market *increases* the value of the multiplier, as can be seen from the fact that the fraction on the right-hand side of Eq. (20.11) is greater than the fraction on the right-hand side of Eq. (20.7).

No particular difficulties exist in dropping the simplifying assumption that the leakage is entirely converted by the public into other currencies. More realistically, we may assume that a fraction g_1 of the loan received by the public leaks out of the Euro-currency system, and a fraction g_2 is converted into other currencies. In this case the public which has received a loan of $(1-c)H$ Euro-dollars, leaks an amount $g_1(1-c)H$ out of the Euro-currency system, converts an amount $g_2(1-c)H$ into other currencies, and redeposits the remaining part, i.e. $(1-g_1-g_2)(1-c)H$, with the Euro-bank. If we assume, as above, that central banks deposit a fraction v of the reserve increase with the Euro-banking system, the second round will give an increase in Euro-deposits equal to

$$(1-g_1-g_2)(1-c)H + vg_2(1-c)H = (1-c)[1-g_1-g_2(1-v)]H. \tag{20.12}$$

By applying the usual procedure we get the geometric series

$$H + (1-c)[1-g_1-g_2(1-v)]H + (1-c)^2[1-g_1-g_2(1-v)]^2 H + \ldots \tag{20.13}$$

whence we obtain the final increase in Euro-deposits

$$\Delta D = \frac{1}{1-(1-c)[1-g_1-g_2(1-v)]} H. \tag{20.14}$$

It is important to note that in the case in question, i.e. when the public converts part of the Euro-dollar loans into other currencies and the central banks involved deposit part of their reserve increase with the Euro-dollar banking system, there is a sort of creation of dollar reserves, since, when the process is over, the central banks will end up with an amount of dollars (in the form of Euro-dollar deposits) greater than that which they would have had if they had not deposited part of the inflow of dollars with the Euro-banking system. In fact, either by the usual geometric series method[19] or by simply observing that, under the assumptions made, a fraction $g_2(1-c)\Delta D$ of the total increase in Euro-deposits is converted into other currencies, we get the final increase in the central banks' dollar reserves – account being taken of Eq. (20.14) –

$$\Delta R = \frac{g_2(1-c)}{1-(1-c)[1-g_1-g_2(1-v)]} H. \qquad (20.15)$$

It can easily be seen that $\Delta R = 0$ if $g_2 = 0$, i.e. if the public converts no part of the Euro-dollar loan into other currencies. Also, the greater is v (the fraction of the increment in reserves that central banks deposit with the Euro-banking system), the greater will be ΔR.

The traditional analysis can be extended ad lib so as to derive more and more complicated multipliers (see, for example, Swoboda, 1978; Johnston, 1981), but the basic idea remains the same. Essentially, it is based on two presuppositions: that the various parameters which appear in the formulae are given and constant (or at least fairly stable), and that the demand for Euro-dollar loans accomodates any increase in lending (irrespective of the conditions) that the Euro-banks wish to undertake, so that the technical limits to the expansion of deposits represented by the various multipliers are always reached.

20.4 The Portfolio Approach to Euro-Markets

The presuppositions of the traditional theory are rejected by the portfolio approach. This approach, as we have said, consists in the application to the Euro-market of the "new view" of money and banking theory in a closed economic system; the new view — with which we must assume the reader to be familiar — is credited mainly to Tobin (1963) and is also called the Yale approach. We only note that the modern approach — as well as the traditional one — presupposes

---

[19] The initial increment in the central banks' reserves, as we have seen, $g_2(1-c)H$. The second round of deposits – see Eq. (20.12) – gives rise to loans by an amount of $(1-c)^2[1-g_1-g_2(1-v)]H$, of which the fraction g_2 accrues to central banks, and so on. Thus we get the geometric series

$$g_2(1-c)H + g_2(1-c)^2[1-g_1-g_2(1-v)]H + \ldots$$
$$= g_2(1-c)\{H+(1-c)[1-g_1-g_2(1-v)]H+\ldots\},$$

which equals (20.13) multiplied by $g_2(1-c)$.

20.4 The Portfolio Approach to Euro-Markets

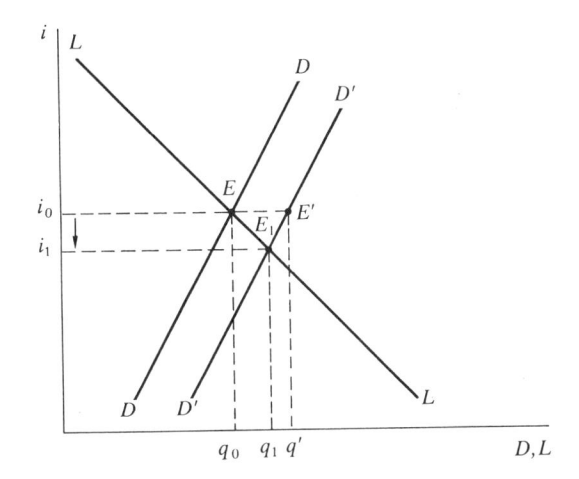

Fig. 20.1. The portfolio approach to the Euro-market

that the maturity structures of both assets and liabilities match perfectly (on this problem see, for example, Niehans and Hewson, 1976).

According to the new view, there is no substantial distinction between money and other assets and between banks and other non-bank financial intermediaries, which all operate in a market environment where there are demands for and supplies of financial assets depending on yields and risks. These considerations are the more relevant for the Euro-market insofar as it is subjected to no legal minimum reserve ratio[20]. Thus, to take an example, the Euro-bank will be willing to reduce the coefficient c if — *ceteris paribus* — the interest rate that it can earn on loans increases sufficiently, and vice versa. Similar considerations can be made as regards the other coefficients which are present in the various multipliers examined in the previous section. It follows that the first presupposition of the traditional theory — the constancy of the said coefficients — is invalid. The multipliers are not fixed but change as circumstances change (and, in fact, the modern approach is sometimes called the *flexible multiplier* approach), so that any analysis of the Euro-market based on the calculation of multipliers is not very helpful, as is also shown by the disparate estimates that have been obtained (Crockett, 1976, footnote 9 to p. 382, reports that the values of the multipliers resulting from the various estimates range from 0.5 to 100!).

The second presupposition of the traditional theory is also invalid, because the demand for loans in the Euro-market will be a decreasing function — *ceteris paribus* — of the interest rate.

This said, it is possible to give an idea — in a partial equilibrium context — of how the portfolio approach determines the size of the Euro-market by way of a simple diagram. In Fig. 20.1 we have drawn the demand (LL) for loans and the

---

[20] It should be noted that this absence enhances the conclusions of the new view, but is not essential. This approach, in fact, could be applied even if — as is the case for domestic money — there were a legal minimum reserve ratio: it will then be the free reserve ratio that will be sensitive to the interest rate.

supply (DD) of loan funds (deposits)[21] as functions of the interest rate with the usual normal slopes. Following Hewson and Sakakibara (1974), we make the simplifying assumptions that Euro-banks hold zero reserves and that the margin between the deposit and loan rates is zero[22]. Under these conditions the equilibrium interest rate (i_0) is determined where the supply of loan funds to banks (deposits) equals the demand for funds from banks (loans); concomitantly, the size of the market (q_0) is determined.

Let us now assume that, at the given initial equilibrium interest rate (i_0) there is an exogenous inflow of new deposit funds to the Euro-banking system (the H of the traditional analysis), so that the schedule of the supply of loan funds from the Euro-banks shifts to the right to $D'D'$. This — at an unchanged position of the demand-for-loans schedule and at the given initial interest rate i_0 — causes an excess supply of loan funds and hence a decrease in the interest rate. This decrease will, on the one hand, stimulate the demand for loan funds, and on the other depress the supply of these, so that the new equilibrium will not be situated at E' but at E_1. Hence — owing to the decrease in the interest rate from i_0 to i_1 — the (final) increase in Euro-deposits will be q_0q_1 (whilst the initial increase is q_0q'). What has happened is that some marginal holders of Euro-currency deposits have shifted their funds out of the Euro-market (because of the decrease in the Euro-interest rate), thus partly offsetting the initial inflow.

If we so wish we can calculate an "implicit" or "ex post" multiplier, defined as q_0q_1/q_0q', i.e. as the ratio of the final to the initial increase in deposits: from the diagram it is clear that this multiplier is smaller than one. But it is self-evident that only by knowing the form and the position of the demand and supply schedules (which depend on i and on all the other variables that we have assumed constant under the *ceteris paribus* clause) can we perform that calculation: we are faced with a flexible multiplier.

The above analysis can be formally developed in a general equilibrium context, thus obtaining formulae which express the flexible multiplier as a function of the interest rate and of all the other relevant variables (see Sect. A.20.3).

20.5 An Evaluation of the Costs and Benefits of Xeno-Markets

One of the topics in international monetary economics where widely divergent opinions exist is that of the effects of the Euro-market (in the broad sense of Xeno-market). What we shall do is to try to list the main advantages and disadvantages that have been advanced in the literature (for details the reader is referred to Argy, 1981; Johnston, 1983; Mayer, 1985), so as to give the basic elements for a kind of cost-benefit analysis. In neither list are items arranged in increasing or decreasing order of importance.

---

[21] Since the Euro-banks are assumed to operate so as to equate the volume of loans and deposits, it is possible to identify the supply of loan funds with the demand for deposits.

[22] The removal of these simplifying assumptions would not change the substance of the analysis: see Johnston, 1981.

20.5 An Evaluation of the Costs and Benefits of Xeno-Markets

To begin with, we list the disadvantages.

(C1) The market in question is a source which helps to feed speculative capital movements; given its size (see Table 19.1) it follows that if these movements were of the destabilizing type (see Sect. 17.2), no central bank (nor even any pool of central banks) would be able to oppose them. Thus this market allows speculation to gain an overwhelming victory over the central banks.

(C2) The market increases international capital mobility, and so contributes to the loss of effectiveness of national monetary policies under fixed exchange rates (as we know, given perfect capital mobility, a country's monetary policy becomes ineffective under fixed exchange rates: see Sect. 16.3.1). The market sets limits to national economic policies also under the managed float. For example, a restrictive monetary policy can be thwarted by the fact that national economic agents borrow funds on the Xeno-market. Besides, the capital inflow related to this borrowing tends to cause the exchange rate to appreciate and, if the monetary authorities do not wish this to occur (for example to avoid a loss of competitiveness of national exporters), they must intervene and buy foreign exchange, which entails an increase in the domestic money supply and hence sterilization problems.

(C3) The growth in the market and so in world liquidity is considered to be one of the causes of the acceleration in world inflation in the early seventies.

(C4) The market is based on a "paper pyramid", which may collapse at any moment (especially if the Xeno-banks grant medium-term or even long-term loans whilst having mostly short-term liabilities), with catastrophic consequences, partly because the Xeno-banking system has no equivalent of the national banking system's lender of last resort[23].

(C5) The market's capability for creating international reserves is not only a threat to international liquidity, as already listed under (C3), but also implies that international monetary authorities lose control over the growth of world reserves.

(C6) The possibility of borrowing on the Xeno-market enables the central banks to finance balance-of-payments deficits beyond what is opportune and so to avoid making the necessary adjustments.

Economists worried with these negative aspects believe that it is necessary to move towards a strict control of Xeno-markets by way of international agreements, and some even believe that their "immediate death should be engineered with a maximum of speed and a minimum of fuss" (Hogan and Pearce, 1982, pp. 127–8).

---

[23] In a national banking system, a bank with liquidity troubles because the maturities of assets do not match those of liabilities, can apply to the central bank which, if it so wishes, can grant unlimited credit and so avoid the bank's collapse. A Euro-bank which, say, deals in Euro-dollars and has liquidity problems, can obtain help from its central bank within the (theoretical) limits of the international reserves of the latter, so that — unless the Federal Reserve System comes into play — a collapse of the Euro-banking system is quite possible. On the problems of the lender of last resort in an international context see, for example, Guttentag and Herring (1983).

Let us now list the advantages.

(B1) The market acts as an intermediary between agents wishing to lend and agents wishing to borrow, who belong to different countries. In this manner the situation of imperfect competition prevailing in national credit markets is reduced, and the efficiency of the capital market increased. The contribution to capital mobility is not so great as to give rise to the disadvantages listed under (C2).

(B2) The intermediation function of the market is beneficial not only to private agents but also to central banks, which have an additional source from which they can borrow to finance balance-of-payments deficits.

(B3) The contribution of the market to the recycling of petrodollars has proved invaluable: suffice it to recall that in 1974, the most dramatic year following the first oil price increase, no less than 40% [24] of the financial surplus of OPEC countries was deposited by these countries with the Euro-market and from here recycled to the countries suffering from oil deficits. Should there arise crises in the future (concerning oil or other things) the market will be able to fulfil an analogous task, thus preventing a collapse of the international monetary system.

Those economists who are more sensitive to these positive aspects are against any form of control of a market whose growth, after all, is beneficial.

As in any case of cost-benefit analysis, to strike a balance it is necessary to give a weight to each cost and benefit, a task in which subjective elements are necessarily introduced. Thus we shall only offer a few general considerations which may help the reader in forming a personal opinion:

(a) some controversial points are (implicitly or explicitly) due to different conceptions of the functioning of Xeno-markets. Only if one accepts the traditional theory (Sect. 20.3) of the creation of Euro-currencies can one unhesitatingly subscribe to point (C3) – which entails in addition the adhesion to a monetarist view of inflation, not shared by all – and to points (C4), (C5). If, on the contrary, one accepts the new view (Sect. 20.4), one must acknowledge that the capacity of the Euro-market for creating liquidity is limited, so that the causes of the increase in international liquidity etc., must be looked for elsewhere. Another example of difference in point of view is that of the relations between the Euro-market and capital mobility: some consider higher capital mobility (due to the relaxation of the restrictions on capital movements and to the expansion of multi-national corporations) to have caused the Euro-market to grow, and not vice versa. Even if one does not accept this view (opposite to that underlying point (C2) above), one must acknowledge that, at least, there is a bidirectional relationship.

(b) The effects which are considered to be positive by some, are considered to be negative by others, and this also reflects different theoretical points of view.

---

[24] In absolute terms the amount was about $ 22.5 bn out of a total of about $ 56 bn.

The "adjustment or financing" dilemma is reflected in the conflict between (C6) and (B2). It is clear that the supporters of some automatic mechanism which restores equilibrium in international trade and payments (like, for instance, the gold standard or the MABP: see Sects. 15.2 and 15.3) will stress (C6), whilst the advocates of discretionary interventions will emphasize (B2) as this enables the authorities, if not to eliminate, at least to dilute the painfulness of the adjustment over time[25].

(c) If we exclude the two extreme positions (rigid control or even suppression of Xeno-markets on the one hand; full freedom on the other) there is the intermediate position – which, mediating between the two extremes, shows a belief in the usefulness of Xeno-markets but also in the usefulness of some kind of control to avoid possible abuses and dangers (Masera, 1981; Johnston, 1983, Chaps. 10 and 11). This position, however, meets with practical difficulties due to the fact that the controls – whatever their nature (for technical details we refer the reader to the works of Masera and Johnston cited) – would have to be *universal,* otherwise the only result would be that Xeno-deposits would simply shift from the centres subjected to controls to the centres without controls. But this universality seems hard to achieve, because the countries which are Xeno-banking centres (and which belong to various continents in the world), "reap significant benefits (in the from of foreign exchange earning, tax revenues and some employment) from these activities" (Argy, 1981, p. 86). Thus the question is still open.

20.6 International Capital Flows and Foreign Exchange Crises

20.6.1 Introduction

Complete liberalization of capital movements undoubtedly makes speculation easier. Speculation can easily cause foreign exchange crises. The typical Bretton-Woods-era phenomenon (a currency under speculative attack that is compelled to devalue after having run out of international reserves in the vain defence of the parity) is now much easier for two reasons: the absence of capital controls (under Bretton Woods system capital controls were allowed, even considered normal) and the greater relative stock of privately owned international financial assets. This stock is vastly superior to the stock of international reserves owned by any country or group of countries. The events in the European Monetary System in September 1992 and July 1993 (see Sect. 19.5.5) are a clear example. Exchange rate expectations play of course a prominent role in determining the outcome of the tug-of-war between speculators and central banks. Speculative capital flows can of course destabilize a floating exchange rate as well, causing undesirable excessive volatility.

---

[25] It is as well to bear in mind that theoretical conceptions are not always consistent when the Euro-market is concerned: for example, many inveterate advocates of economic liberalism (who invoke automatic mechanisms of adjustment of the balance-of-payments, no intervention of the monetary authorities, and, in general, laissez-faire), are the same ones who strongly invoke a rigid control and even the suppression of a free market such as the Euro-market substantially is.

It should also be pointed out that these phenomena give rise to problems which go beyond the foreign exchange market and the capital market, but concern the whole economic system. Hence an adequate study of them should be carried out in the context of an economy-wide dynamic macro model. This is the subject of the present section, where we shall also examine the role of exchange-rate expectations and a potential remedy, suggested by Tobin (1978), to the possible negative consequences of capital liberalization.

20.6.2 The Basic Case

We know from Sects. 16.3 and 19.3 that with perfect capital mobility and fixed exchange rates monetary policy is ineffective. But there is more to it than that: the same type of model also shows that any attempt to pursue a monetary policy incompatible with international equilibrium will give rise to so huge capital flows that a foreign exchange crisis is inevitable. This is exactly what happens in the context of our continuos time macrodynamic model, already mentioned in Sect. 18.6.3. We recall that capital flows are modelled according to a disequilibrium portfolio approach, where the adjustment speed of the actual to the desired (or partial equilibrium) stock of net foreign assets plays an essential role. With imperfect capital mobility (due to capital controls) this speed is low, while it is very high (to denote an almost instantaneous adjustment) when there is perfect capital mobility.

The model indicated that, passing from a situation of low to one of very high values of the adjustment speed under consideration, after a period (lasting about three years) of apparent exchange rate stability a foreign exchange crisis would occur, and the whole system would become unstable, with negative consequences on all the variables (including the rate of growth of real income). This was of course a *ceteris paribus* result, namely the only change was the adjustment speed of capital flows. In Italy, complete capital liberalization took place in 1990, no other policy change was taken (the *ceteris paribus* clause was indeed satisfied), the exchange rate remained apparently stable for about two years and a half, then the foreign exchange crisis of September 1992 hit the lira. This is exactly exactly in line with the predictions of the model (which are not of the *ex post* type, but were made in 1989–90).

The next step is to examine the role of exchange-rate expectations.

20.6.3 Exchange Rate Expectations and the Credibility Problem

For the reasons that will be made clear below, we considered only two types of expectations (and combinations thereof): extrapolative and regressive (or 'normal') expectations.

The former simply mean that, if a change has taken place, a further change in the same directions is expected. It is a rather coarse type of expectations, which is however suitable for describing phenomena of loss of confidence in a currency. Regressive or normal expectations, on the contrary, imply that economic agents have an idea of a normal, long-run value of the variable under consideration so that, whenever the current value is different from the normal one, they expect the current value sooner or later to move toward (or "regress" to) the normal one. It seems plausible to assume the PPP value as the long-run normal exchange rate, also because the model possesses a steady-state path on which the exchange rate is at its PPP value (see Gandolfo and Padoan, 1990). Hence rational agents, who know the model (and the fact that its steady state is stable) have this normal value in mind.

It is fairly obvious that extrapolative expectations are bound to have a destabilizing effect whereas normal expectations will have a stabilizing effect. The reason for considering these two types of expectations is related to the argument put forth by Frankel (1988a). From surveys of the forecasts of the agents operating in the foreign exchange market, Frankel concludes that those who forecast at shorter horizons display destabilizing expectations because they tend to extrapolate recent trends, while those who operate with relatively longer horizons tend to have regressive, or stabilizing expectations. The reasons for this different behaviour are to be seen, according to Frankel, in the fact that short-term traders in the foreign exchange market have to show to their superiors (typically, bank executives) that they are able to make profits over a much shorter time period than that over which the performance of longer-term traders is evaluated. Independently of the reason, we believe that Frankel's distinction is correct, since it corresponds to the distinction between "occasional" and "permanent" speculators introduced long ago by Cutilli and Gandolfo (1963, 1972, 1973).

In the light of this distinction, one should not only consider the two extreme cases (all agents are of the same type, *i.e.* with either extrapolative or normal expectations), but also the intermediate ones. These are the cases where there are agents of the two types operating simultaneously in the market. The outcome will obviously depend on the relative intensity of action of the two categories (Cutilli and Gandolfo, op. cit.), that can vary in the course of time. This relative intensity is in turn dependent on, amongst other elements, the *credibility* of the monetary authorities. In fact, if the market believes that the monetary authorities' commitment to a fixed parity is credible, then normal expectations will prevail. It is thus possible to examine the credibility problem in the context of our model.

The agents holding extrapolative expectations have, as is obvious, a strong destabilizing effect, but this effect is neutralized by the introduction of agents holding regressive expectations. This introduction has been performed gradually increasing the relative weight of the latter agents. To understand the economic meaning of this experiment it is necessary to point out that in the model one of the variables that determines the monetary authorities's behaviour in exchange rate intervention is international competitiveness. This amounts to assuming that the authorities intervene so as to maintain the exchange rate not too far from its long run PPP value. Hence an increasing weight of normal expectations in determining market behaviour may reflect the fact that the market considers such a policy commitment as increasingly credible. In other words a variable weight of normal expectations reflects a change in the policy regime (as far as exchange rate intervention is concerned) which is credible. The results of our simulations show that by increasing the weight of regressive expectations the model does in fact follow a stable behaviour.

20.6.4 The Tobin Tax

Tobin (1978, 1994) suggested a tax (with a modest rate) on all foreign-exchange transactions as a means of "throwing sand in the wheels" of international speculation, namely of contrasting speculative capital flows without disturbing medium-long term 'normal' flows. Such a tax should be applied on all foreign-exchange transactions (both inflows and outflows) independently of the nature of the transaction. This is necessary to avoid the practically insurmountable enforcement problem of distinguishing between foreign exchange transactions for "speculative" purposes and for other purposes. Such a tax, in fact, given its modest rate would not be much of a deterrent to anyone contemplating the purchase of a foreign security for longer-term investing, but it might discourage the spot trader who is now accustomed to buying foreign exchange with the intention of selling it a few hours later, and who would have to pay the tax every time it buys or sells foreign exchange.

The Tobin tax on capital flows is a tax on the relevant foreign exchange transactions, but it can be translated into an equivalent tax on interest income. It is, in fact, equivalent either to a tax on foreign interest income at a rate which is an increasing function of the Tobin tax rate θ, or to a negative tax (*i.e.*, a positive subsidy) on domestic interest income at a rate which is an increasing function of θ (for the proof see Gandolfo and Padoan, 1992).

It is then easy to examine the introduction of a Tobin tax by suitably modifying the interest-rate differential on which capital flows depend. In such a way the effects of this introduction on the macroeconomic system can be examined taking account of all the dynamic interrelations between the relevant variables. The results of our simulations show that the introduction of a Tobin tax provides a crucial contribution to the stabilization of the system with full capital liberalization. However there is more to it than that. A Tobin tax allows the system to operate with a lower level of the domestic interest rate as it makes the constraint represented by the foreign interest rate less stringent. This obviously gives more room for domestic financial policy (in terms of e.g. the financing of the domestic public debt).

The argument against such a tax is well known: if not all countries adopt it, then the business would simply go to the financial centres where the tax is not present. Hence a cooperation at the world level (or at least at the level of areas such as the European Community) is necessary.

20.7 International Policy Coordination

20.7.1 Policy Optimization, Game Theory, and International Coordination

The international policy coordination problem was already mentioned in Sect. 15.5.3 in the context of the traditional fixed exchange rate model. Here we give a general treatment starting from the observation that – as a consequence of the ever increasing economic interdependence of the various countries – the

Table 20.3. Payoff matrix of the International policy game

Europe	United States	
	Contraction	Expansion
Contraction	Recession in both countries; $B=0$	No employment change; B favourable to Europe
Expansion	No employment change; B favourable to U.S.	Boom in both countries; $B=0$

economic policies of a country influence (and are influenced by) the economic situation and the economic policy stance in other countries.

From the terminological point of view, 'coordination' and 'cooperation' are usually considered as synonyms. Some authors, however, take 'coordination' as implying a significant modification of domestic policies in recognition of international interdependence, namely as something more than cooperation (which in turn is something more than simple 'consultation'). We shall use 'cooperation' and 'coordination' interchangeably.

As any case of strategic interdependence, international cooperation can be interpreted in terms of game theory. The players are the governments of the various countries, that adopt various 'strategies' (the policy actions) to pursue their objectives (employment, balance of payments, etc.). Each combination of strategies will give rise to a precise result in terms of each country's objectives. Table 20.3 illustrates the simple case of two countries (USA and Europe), two targets (employment and current account balance) and two strategies (expansionary and restrictive economic policy) under fixed exchange rates.

If both countries expand, both will be better off in terms of employment and there will also be current account balance. If both adopt a contractionary policy, both will suffer a recession though reaching current account balance. If one expands and the other contracts, there will be no employment change in either country, but the expanding country will suffer a deterioration in the current account (the current account of the contracting country will of course improve). In terms of game theory we are in the so-called 'prisoner's dilemma' situation. If one country expands and the other does not, the latter will gain (in terms of current account balance) at the expense of the former. Without coordination, it is impossible to reach the optimal situation in which both countries expand.

In reality no economic policy consists of two alternatives only (expansion/contraction in our example), but can vary in more or less continuous manner from restriction to expansion. Furthermore, even a partial fulfilment of a target (maybe at the expense of another target) has a value. This means that the government of a country does not carry out its economic policy in a fixed-target context (in our example this would be a given level of employment and equilibrium in the current account balance), but in a flexible-target context. The flexible-target approach means that there is a trade-off among the various

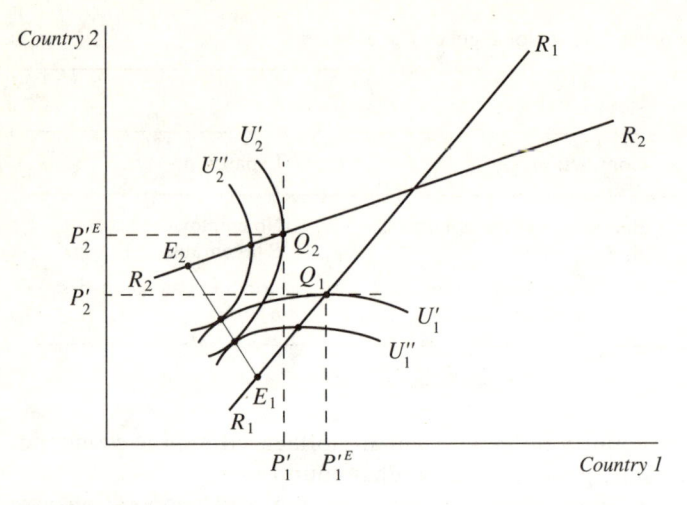

Fig. 20.2. The Hamada diagram

targets, in the sense that a higher fulfilment of a target can compensate for a lower fulfilment of another, given a social welfare function. The policy maker aims at maximizing the social welfare function, which depends on the degree of fulfilment of the objectives, given the constraints (represented by the economic system and the other countries' actions). This more general framework can be represented by a diagram due to Hamada (1974, 1985).

If we assume that the policy configuration of each country can be represented by a synthetic and continuous variable, we can show the policy configurations of the two countries on the axes of a diagram like Fig. 20.2. The policy configuration of country 1 is shown on the horizontal axis, while the policy configuration of country 2 is shown on the vertical axis. A point in the diagram thus represents a combination of the two countries' policy configurations, which will give rise to a well-defined result in terms of the two countries' targets. This result will of course depend on the underlying model representing international interdependence, on which more below (Sect. 20.7.2). The welfare level corresponding to the result will depend on each country's social welfare function. Such a function has a maximum corresponding to the best possible result for the country concerned (the bliss point). Let us assume that E_1, E_2, are the points which give rise to the maximum welfare for country 1 and country 2 respectively. We can then draw around these points the welfare indifference curves of the two countries. A welfare indifference curve of a country is the locus of all points (combinations of the two countries' policy configurations) that give rise to results (in terms of the country's targets) which are considered equivalent by the country under consideration. Let us consider country 1: since we have assumed that the bliss point corresponds to E_1, any other point in the diagram represents a lower welfare. The closer the indifference curve is to point E_1, the better off country 1 is: any policy combination that puts it on indifference curve U_1'' is preferred to any policy combination that puts it on U_1'. The welfare indifference curves are closed curves around the bliss point, but for graphical simplicity we have drawn them only partly. In a similar way we can draw country 2's welfare indifference curves around point E_2. Let us note in passing that in the special case of no interdependence (total independence) the indifference curves of country 1 would be vertical straight lines and those of country 2 horizontal straight lines. In this case each country could achieve its optimal welfare independently of the policy pursued by the other country. Hence the case for coordination is based on the presence of international interdependence (see Martinez, 1991, for the proof that interdependence is necessary, though not sufficient, for coordination to be welfare improving).

In the case of interdependence, the first step of the constrained-optimum problem that each country has to solve is to determine its welfare-maximizing policy configuration for any given policy configuration of the other country. Let us consider, for example, country 1, and let us assume that country 2 adopts the policy configuration represented by point P_2'. If we draw from this point a straight line parallel to country 1's axis, we see that the highest indifference curve that country 1 can reach is U_1', tangent to the aforesaid straight line. U_1', in fact, is the indifference curve nearest to E_1 compatibly with the given policy choice of country 2 (the constraint). Hence, given P_2', the optimal choice for country 1 is policy $P_1'^E$. Going on in like manner, we obtain a set of points that give rise to the R_1R_1 curve, called the *policy reaction function* of country 1 (for graphical simplicity we have drawn it linear).

In a similar way we obtain country 2's policy reaction curve. Given for example country 1's policy configuration P_1', the indifference curve of country 2 which is nearest to the bliss point E_2 is the curve tangent to the straight line originating from P_1' and parallel to country 2's axis.

In the diagram we also have drawn a segment joining the two ideal points $E_1., E_2$, which is the locus of all points where the two countries' indifference curves are tangential to one another. This locus is a Pareto-optimal or contract curve, since in each of these points the property holds that it is not possible to increase the welfare of one country without decreasing the other country's welfare.

We can now use the Hamada diagram to illustrate what happens without coordination, and the advantages of coordination. In Fig. 20.3 we have drawn the two policy reaction curves obtained as explained above, and we now want to know what will be the behaviour of the two countries.

Let us begin by considering a non-cooperative behaviour, that can take on various forms. The most commonly used are the Cournot-Nash and Stackelberg scenarios.

In the former, each country maximizes its welfare by choosing its own optimal policy taking as given the policy configuration of the other country, on the assumption that this configuration is beyond its influence. Given for example country 1's policy P_1^0, country 2 will choose P_2^0 on its own reaction function. In its turn country 1, taking as given country 2's P_2^0, will change its policy to P_1' on its own reaction curve; country 2 will then react to P_1' by changing its policy to P_2' and so forth, until point N is reached. This is the Cournot-Nash equilibrium, where the welfare achieved is U_1^N for country 1 and U_2^N for country 2.

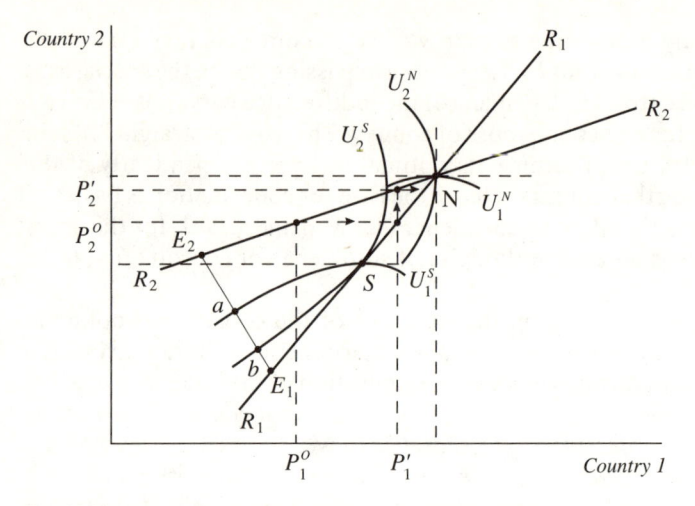

Fig. 20.3. Game theory and the gains from coordination

The Stackelberg or leader-follower solution is obtained when one country (for example, country 2) is dominant (the *leader*) and takes account of the fact that its actions influence the other country's decisions, while the *follower* country behaves like in the previous case. The leader knows the reaction curve of the follower and hence country 2 knows that country 1 will react to the leader's policy choices by choosing a policy along the R_1R_1 curve. Thus country 2 maximizes its welfare function taking account of this curve as a constraint. This means that country 2 will choose the highest indifference curve compatible with the constraint. This curve is U_2^S, which is tangential to R_1R_1 at point S. In fact, U_2^S is country 2's indifference curve that is nearest to E_2 compatibly with R_1R_1.

It can be seen that in the Stackelberg equilibrium point S, country 2 (the leader) obtains a welfare level clearly higher than in the Cournot-Nash equilibrium, while the follower may or may not be better off. Both equilibria are however inefficient, since they do not lie on the contract curve E_1E_2. Both countries could be better off if they agreed to cooperate: if they coordinate their policies they can reach a point on the segment ab of the contract curve. Any such point is clearly superior to both the Cournot-Nash and the Stackelberg equilibrium. The precise point where the two countries will end up will of course depend on the relative bargaining power.

20.7.2 The Problem of the Reference Model and the Obstacles to Coordination

If coordination is favourable to all, why is it not universally adopted, and why many talk of obstacles to coordination? Let us first note that forms of 'weak' international cooperation (or 'consultation', according to the terminology introduced in Sect. 20.7.1) are very frequent. All countries hold routine consultations in the context of various international economic organizations such as the IMF. The industrialised countries routinely consult with one another in the context of the OECD; the seven and the five most industrialised countries hold the G7 and G5 summits respectively, and there are several other subsets of countries holding routine consultations. But here we are dealing with policy coordination proper, and we focus on economic rather than political obstacles.

The first and foremost impediment can be illustrated by an illuminating analogy due to Cooper (1989). It took over seventy years (from 1834 to 1907) – he observes – for the various countries to reach an agreement on the best way to prevent the spread of virulent diseases such as cholera. The reason is that in the 19th century there were two completely different theories or models on the transmission of such diseases: the 'miasmatic' and the 'contagionist'. Miasmatists held that infectious diseases were not transmitted by diseased persons but originated in environmental 'miasms'. Contagionists supported the view that such diseases were transmitted by contact with diseased persons. Now, "epidemiology in the nineteenth century was much like economics in the twentieth century: a subject of intense public interest and concern, in which theories abounded but where the scope for controlled experiment was limited" (Cooper). Hence both views had the support of the scientific community. It is clear that the age-old technique of quarantining ships infected (or suspected of being infected) was a decisive measure according to the contagionist theory, but a pointless measure for the miasmatists. Quarantine represented a severe burden on trade and shipping, the cost of which would have been unequally shared, as the greater part of merchandise and passenger trade was carried out by Britain (a country that, not surprisingly, vigorously supported the miasmatist theory). Hence an agreement on the means to prevent the spread of virulent diseases could not be reached until the validity of the contagionist model was demonstrated. Thus, as Cooper observes, the world was in a situation in which all agreed on the objectives (the prevention of the spread of virulent diseases), but sharp disagreement existed on the instruments and on the related cost sharing, because of the conflicting views on the theory that could explain the facts.

In economics all agree on the objectives: high employment, and growth without inflation are universally considered as desirable. The attached weights may be different in different countries, but this is normal given the different welfare functions of the various countries, and does not cause particular problems. It is the lack of agreement on the model that explains the transmission of the effects of economic policies (both domestically and from one country to another) that determines the impossibility of international policy coordination to fight unemployment, low (or negative) growth, inflation as the case may be. In Fig. 20.2 we have taken for granted the existence of a model – no matter which – accepted by all countries. In the contrary case there is no ground at all for carrying out the analysis.

A further problem is model uncertainty. Assuming that all countries agree on a model, it might happen that this model turns out to be wrong. Cooperation based on an incorrect model might be negative rather than positive.

These problems have given rise to an ample literature (see, e.g., Buiter and Marston eds., 1985; Feldstein ed., 1988; Branson, Frenkel and Goldstein eds., 1990; Blommestein ed. 1991; Carraro et al. eds., 1991), that has amongst others tackled the question of the consequences of uncertainty on the 'true' model. The conclusion has been that the case of internationally coordinated policies based on an invalid model can give rise to a lower welfare than the case of no coordination. Ghosh and Masson (1991), have introduced the assumption that policy makers have a learning ability, namely the ability of adjusting the model towards the true model by modifying it through the observation of the policy results. In this case international policy coordination is better than no coordination. The theoretical debate is still open.

In addition to these theoretical problems, there are practical problems, the most important of which are the free rider problem and the third-country problem.

The free rider problem is a typical problem of all cooperative equilibria (including all kinds of agreements) in games of the prisoner's dilemma type. Even if the various countries happen to be in a situation in which cooperation is beneficial to all, the problem remains of how to ensure that all countries participating in the cooperative equilibrium respect the agreement. In terms of Table 20.3, each country – taking the other country's expansionary policy for granted – has the incentive not to respect the agreement and take a restrictive policy, leaving the burden of expansion on the other country. Each country tries to move from the last cell in the payoff matrix to a cell outside the main diagonal. Such a behaviour causes retaliation from the other country, and we are back in the non-cooperative inferior situation. Hence institutional mechanisms have to be devised and introduced to enforce the cooperative agreement.

The third-country problem is related to the fact that the agreement to coordinate usually includes only a subset of the countries of the world. It may then happen that the coordinated policies undertaken by the participating countries have a negative effect on non-participating countries. These third countries could react by carrying out policies that negatively affect the cooperating countries, which might then ultimately be worse off. For example, suppose that country 1 and 2 cooperate and decide to deflate their economies. The adverse effects on country 3's exports may lead this country to deflate as well. This aggravates the recession in country 1 and 2 above what they had anticipated in deciding their coordinated policy, making them worse off than if they had not jointly deflated.

20.8 Proposals for the International Management of Exchange Rates

20.8.1 Introduction

We have already mentioned the current international monetary 'non system' (see Sect. 10.5.4). It is a generally held opinion of both policy makers and researchers that it would be desirable to prevent excessive (and often disrupting) oscillations of the exchange rates of the major currencies. There is however no agreement on the best way to reach this goal. Among the various proposals the best known are the Tobin tax, McKinnon's global monetary objective, and John Williamson's target zones. The Tobin tax has already been treated in Sect. 20.6.4; here we shall deal with the two other proposals.

20.8.2 McKinnon's Global Monetary Objective

This proposal was set forth in the 1970s by Ronald McKinnon, who has later perfectioned it (see McKinnon, 1988). It is based on fixed exchange rates (that he considers superior to flexible rates) integrated by a precise intervention rule to be followed by the monetary authorities.

According to McKinnon, the main cause for exchange-rate volatility is currency substitution. In a world practically free from controls on international capital flows, private international economic agents (multinational enterprises, portfolio investors, etc.) wish to hold a basket of various national currencies. McKinnon holds that the overall demand for this currency basket is, like the traditional domestic demand for domestic money, a stable function (the Friedman thesis extended to international economics), but that the desired *composition* of the global basket may be very volatile. This implies that the control of the single national domestic supplies is unsuitable, and that Friedman's monetary rule (according to which the money supply must grow at a constant predefined rate) should be shifted from the national to the international level.

In practice this means that, once the nominal exchange rates (McKinnon suggests a PPP rule) and the rate of growth of the world money supply have been fixed, the national monetary authorities' interventions in the foreign exchange markets to maintain the fixed parities should consists of *non sterilized* purchases and sales of foreign currencies. Such interventions cause changes (an increase in the case of a purchase of foreign exchange, a decrease in the case of a sale) in the national money supplies. Thus the currency substitution desires of the international agents, which are the cause of the excess demands and supplies of the various currencies, give rise to changes in the national money supplies while leaving the world money supply unchanged and the exchange rates fixed. Hence currency substitution will have no effect on the national economies.

This proposal has been criticized for various reasons. The first and foremost concerns the foundation itself of the proposal: currency substitution seems to be neither the main cause of exchange-rate volatility nor the main determinant of exchanges rates. Rather, it is *asset* substitution concerning assets denominated in the various currencies that appears to have a much greater role. Besides – the critics continue – by fixing nominal exchange rates no room is left for real exchange-rate adjustments. These adjustments might be required not so much because of differences in inflation rates (these could not occur according to the proposal), but to offset different productivity changes in the various countries. For a clear exposition of the various criticisms see Dornbusch (1988).

20.8.3 John Williamson's Target Zones

The idea of trying to combine the advantages of both fixed and flexible exchange rates while eliminating the disadvantages of both is at the basis of this proposal (antecedents of which can be found in the gliding wider band and in the oscillating exchange rates proposals – see Sect. 10.5.3). John Williamson (1985) and his coworkers (see, for example, Edison, Miller and Williamson, 1987) have elaborated this idea in much detail, giving rise to the target zone proposal, which is based on two main elements.

The first is the calculation of a fundamental equilibrium exchange rate (FEER), defined as that exchange rate 'which is expected to generate a current account surplus or deficit equal to the underlying capital flow over the cycle, given that the country is pursuing internal balance as best it can and not restricting trade for balance of payments reasons' (Williamson, 1985, p. 14). Such a rate should be periodically recalculated to take account of the change in its fundamental determinants (for example the relative inflation rates); thus it must not be confused with a fixed central parity.

The second element is the possibility for the current exchange rate to float within wide margins around the FEER (at least $\pm 10\%$). These margins should be 'soft' margins, namely there would be no obligation for the monetary authorities to intervene when the current exchange rate hits a margin; this is aimed at preventing destabilizing speculation of the kind that was present in the Bretton Woods system.

The target zone proposal has been criticized for various reasons (see Frenkel and Goldstein, 1986). We shall just point out two of them. The first is the difficulty of calculating the FEER. Even by using the most sophisticated econometric techniques and models, there remains a rather wide error margin. The second concens the 'credibility' of the target zone. A target zone is viable only if economic agents find it credible. The experience of the European Monetary System (see Sect. 19.5.4), which before August 1993 could be considered as a target zone with narrower margins, shows that the monetary authorities, even when there are monetary cooperation agreements like in the ERM, are helpless when credibility lacks.

The credibility problem has been theoretically studied in several models that can be divided into first-generation and second-generation models. First-generation models are based on simplified assumptions: economic agents are convinced that the exchange rate will not go beyond the margins and that the central parity will not be changed. Second-generation models are based on more general assumptions: economic agents assign non-zero probabilities to both events (the exchange rate going beyond the margins and the central parity being changed). For a survey of these models see Svensson (1992) and De Arcangelis (1994).

Appendix

A.20.1 The Optimum Level of International Reserves and the Theory of Economic Policy

A.20.1.1 The Cost-Benefit Approach

As an example of this approach we take Heller's model (1966) which – as explained in Sect. 20.2.3, Eq. (20.2) – gives rise to the optimum condition

$$\text{Prob}(R_j)\frac{1}{\mu}=i,\ i\mu=\text{Prob}(R_j), \qquad (A.20.1)$$

where $\text{Prob}(R_j)$ denotes the probability of having to use adjustment as a means of achieving external equilibrium. This probability is given by the probability of the occurrence of a number of consecutive deficits whose total size is such that the stock of reserves R_j is used up. To determine this probability, the author introduces two simplifying assumptions:

(a) the stochastic process underlying the behaviour of international reserves held by a country is a random walk[26] of the symmetric type, so that the probabilities of an increase and a decrease (of the same absolute value) are equal to each other and so both are equal to 1/2. To put it differently, the probability of the occurrence of a balance-of-payments surplus of a certain size h is equal to the probability of the occurrence of a deficit of the same size h.

(b) all changes in international reserves expected in the future are equal in absolute value; this common value, denoted by h, is the "typical amount of imbalance given by the average absolute change in international reserves which the country in question experienced during the recent past" (Heller, 1966, p. 302).

Thanks to these assumptions, it is easy to determine the probability that we are seeking. In fact, the probability of the occurrence of j consecutive deficits of (absolute) size h such that

$$jh=R_j, \qquad (A.20.2)$$

i.e. such that the amount of reserves R_j held by the country is used up, is given by the multiplication theorem for probabilities; that is

$$\text{Prob}(R_j)=(0.5)^j. \qquad (A.20.3)$$

If we substitute (A.20.3) into (A.20.1) we get

$$(0.5)^j=i\mu, \qquad (A.20.1.1)$$

---

[26] For the elementary notions on stochastic processes that we use in this appendix, see any textbook, for example Cox and Miller (1980).

whence, by solving for j,

$$j = \frac{\log(i\mu)}{\log(0.5)}. \tag{A.20.4}$$

By substituting (A.20.4) into (A.20.2) we obtain the reserve level that we are seeking,

$$\hat{R} = h\frac{\log(i\mu)}{\log(0.5)}, \tag{A.20.5}$$

which is the optimum stock of reserves on the basis of the cost-benefit analysis.

Heller's model can be, and was, criticized from various points of view; the possible extensions have already been mentioned in Sect. 20.2.3, so that we now pass on to the other approach: that based on the maximization of a welfare function.

A.20.1.2 The Maximization of a Welfare Function

As an example of this second approach to the determination of the optimum reserve level, we shall first consider Kelly's model (1970). The utility function expressing the country's preferences depends on the level and variability of income. The reduction in income caused by tying up resources in reserves is

$$y' - y = Ri, \tag{A.20.6}$$

where y' is the level of income which could be attained if no reserves were held and y is the level which is obtained when an amount of reserves R is held, at their (net) opportunity cost i. Since we are working within a probabilistic framework, we must consider the expected values (denoted by the symbol E applied to the relevant variable), so that the argument $E(y') - E(y)$ will enter with a negative marginal utility in the utility function. Also negative will be the marginal utility of income variability as measured by the variance (V) around its expected level when no reserves are held. Kelly considers the quadratic (dis)utility function

$$U = -a[E(y') - E(y)]^2 - b[y - E(y)]^2, \quad a > 0, \, b > 0, \tag{A.20.7}$$

and then by substituting from (A.20.6) and taking expected values he gets expected utility as

$$E(U) = -ai^2 E(R)^2 - bV(y). \tag{A.20.7.1}$$

Let us now determine the constraint. If we start from an initial equilibrium situation and consider only current transactions, the change in reserves in any period t will be given by the change in exports (considered exogenous) minus the change in imports (considered endogenous) i.e

$$\Delta R_t = \Delta x_t - \Delta m_t. \tag{A.20.8}$$

To determine the endogenous change in imports Kelly introduces an import response coefficient f which links Δm to Δx and depends on the willingness of the authorities to allow income to change as exports change, due to external disturbances. This coefficient can be considered as the product of the effect of a change in exports on income (denoted by $g=\Delta y/\Delta x$)[27] and the marginal propensity to import μ, so that $f=\mu g$.

Thus by letting $\Delta m = f\Delta x$, we have

$$\Delta R = \Delta x(1-f). \tag{A.20.9}$$

We now compute the variances of reserves and income, $V(R)$ and $V(y)$, which turn out to be

$$V(R) = E(\Delta R^2), \quad V(y) = E(\Delta y^2). \tag{A.20.10}$$

If we substitute (A.19.9) and the definition of g in (A.19.10), we get

$$V(R) = E[\Delta x^2(1-f)^2] = V(x)(1-f)^2, \tag{A.20.11}$$

$$V(y) = E(g^2 \Delta x^2) = g^2 V(x). \tag{A.20.12}$$

Let us assume now that there is some minimum reserve level, R', below which the authorities do not wish the actual reserve level to fall (R' may also be zero, which amounts to saying that the authorities are willing to accept the eventuality of running out of reserves). Since we are in a stochastic context, the authorities will establish an (arbitrarily) small probability level e such that

$$P[R < R'/E(R), V(R)] = e. \tag{A.20.13}$$

Equation (A.20.13) tells us that the probability that reserves fall below R', given the average level (expected value) and the variance of reserves, equals e. This equation is the constraint in the problem. To be able to solve the problem it is necessary to take an explicit probability density function, which Kelly assumes to be

$$e = cV(R)/E(R)^2, \tag{A.20.14}$$

which has the property that, given e, $dE(R)/dV(R) > 0$; this is a property typical of any regularly behaved probability density function.

If we combine (A.20.14) and (A.20.11) we get

$$E(R) = \sqrt{c/e}\, S(R) = \sqrt{c/e}\, S(x)(1-f), \tag{A.20.15}$$

where $S(\ldots) \equiv \sqrt{V(\ldots)}$ is the standard deviation. From (A.20.12) we obtain $g = S(y)/S(x)$ and, letting $f=\mu g$ and substituting into Eq. (A.20.15), we obtain the final form of the constraint

$$E(R) = \sqrt{c/e}\,[S(x) - \mu S(y)]. \tag{A.20.16}$$

We must now minimize[28] the function (A.20.7.1) with respect to $E(R)$ and $S(y)$ with the constraint (A.20.16). For this purpose we form the Langrangian

$$L = -ai^2 E(R)^2 - bV(y) + \lambda\{E(R) - \sqrt{c/e}\,[S(x) - \mu S(y)]\}, \tag{A.20.17}$$

---

[27] As a matter of fact g will be a multiplier (see Chap. 13), corrected for possible policy interventions.

[28] Since U is defined as a *dis*-utility, it is self-evident that it should be minimized and not maximized.

where λ is a Lagrange multiplier. The first order conditions[29] for an extremum are

$$\frac{\partial L}{\partial E(R)} = -2ai^2 E(R) + \lambda = 0,$$

$$\frac{\partial L}{\partial S(y)} = -2bS(y) + \lambda \sqrt{c/e}\, \mu = 0, \quad\quad\quad\quad (A.20.18)$$

$$\frac{\partial L}{\partial \lambda} = E(R) - \sqrt{c/e}\,[S(x) - \mu S(y)] = 0.$$

By simple manipulations[30] we get the optimum average level of reserves $\widehat{E(R)}$, which turns out to be

$$\widehat{E(R)} = \frac{S(x)}{\sqrt{e/c} + \sqrt{c/e}\, \mu^2 i^2 (a/b)}. \quad\quad\quad\quad (A.20.19)$$

Thus — given the standard deviation of exogenous shocks, $S(x)$, and the various structural parameters — it is possible to determine the optimum level of reserves. This is an increasing function of $S(x)$ and of b (the marginal disutility of income variability) and a decreasing function of a (the marginal disutility of income variations), of i (the opportunity cost of reserves), and of μ (the marginal propensity to import). Finally, optimum reserves will vary inversely with e (the probability of reserves falling below the minimum specified level) except in particular cases[31].

A.20.1.3 Intertemporal Maximization and the Normative Theory of Economic Policy

As we have said in Sect. 20.2.3, the approach to the optimum reserve level based on the maximization of a welfare function can be extended in various directions. We examine here the model by Nyberg and Viotti (1976), who consider the problem in an intertemporal maximization framework and in the presence of capital movements. This model will also give us the cue for some considerations on the theory of economic policy in general.

The basic model is the standard Keynesian-type model under fixed exchange rates (see Sects. 15.4 and 15.5), that we rewrite here (with a slightly different symbology)

$$y = A(y,i) + x - m(y) + G,$$

$$L(y,i) = M, \quad\quad\quad\quad (A.20.20)$$

$$\dot{R} = x - m(y) + K(y,i).$$

---

[29] Following Kelly, we shall consider solely the first-order conditions.
[30] Solve the first equation for λ and substitute the result in the second, which is then used to express $S(y)$ in terms of $E(R)$. Then substitute the result in the third equation and obtain the result given in Eq. (A.20.19).
[31] Whilst the previous results are immediately evident by simply inspecting Eq. (A.20.19), this last result requires the computation of the partial derivative $\partial \widehat{E(R)}/\partial e$, which turns out to be negative unless a is much greater than b.

The third equation defines the changes in reserves, which is equal to the surplus or deficit in the balance of payments (a dot over the variable denotes the time derivative). The policy instruments are government expenditure (G) and the money supply (M). In the traditional analysis (see Sect. 15.5) the basic assumption is that the policy maker manages the instruments so as to achieve the prescribed targets: full employment and external equilibrium (note that the latter amounts to saying that the policy maker wishes to maintain a constant level of international reserves).

Nyberg and Viotti take a different approach, one already suggested by Williamson (1971)[32], which consists in the intertemporal maximization of a welfare function subject to the constraints imposed by the positive economy as represented by model (A.20.20). They assume that the policy maker's utility (or objective function) U depends positively on income and the stock of reserves, and negatively on the rate of interest[33], i.e.

$$U = U(y, i, R). \tag{A.20.21}$$

It should be pointed out that U denotes the *instantaneous* utility; if one were in the context of a static model one would then — as in Kelly's model treated in Sect. A.20.1.2 – maximize U subject to the constraint of model (A.20.20). In a dynamic context the policy maker acts to maximize utility over time, i.e. the objective is to maximize

$$\Omega = \int_0^\infty e^{-rt} U(y, i, R) \, dt, \tag{A.20.22}$$

which represents the present value of total utility over the entire period of time (which goes from zero — the current moment — to the farthest future — infinity —, but it would also be possible to consider a finite time period). The constant r is the social rate of discount or rate of social time preference, which represents the way the policy maker weighs the future with respect to the present (the idea is that the more distant the utility enjoyed, the less weight it should be given).

Thus the optimization problem can be expressed as

$$max \ \Omega = \int_0^\infty e^{-rt} U(y, i, R) \, dt$$

subject to (A.20.23)

$$\dot{R} = x - m(y) + K(y, i),$$

where y and i are functions of the two instruments G and M through the first two equations in set (A.20.20); it follows that the only "state variable" is R. Problem (A.20.23) is a typical *dynamic optimization problem,* which can be solved by

---

[32] The idea of intertemporal maximization is of course much older and underlies all the optimal economic growth literature, which dates back at least to the work of Ramsey in 1928: see, for example, Intriligator (1971, Chap. 16) for a treatment of optimal economic growth and references to the literature.

[33] "Having the rate of interest as a target variable may seem a bit unusual, but is very realistic in many countries (such as Sweden) where high priority is given to keeping down housing costs" (Nyberg and Viotti, 1976, p. 127).

applying Pontryagin's *maximum principle* (see, for example, Intriligator, 1971, Chap. 14). For this purpose we form the *Hamiltonian*

$$H = e^{-rt} \{U(y,i,R) + \lambda[x - m(y) + K(y,i)]\}, \qquad (A.20.24)$$

and set to zero its partial derivatives[34] with respect to the instruments after elimination of the term e^{-rt}; thus we obtain

$$\frac{\partial H}{\partial G} = [U_y - \lambda(m_y - K_y)]y_G + (U_i + \lambda K_i)i_G = 0,$$

$$\frac{\partial H}{\partial M} = [U_y - \lambda(m_y - K_y)]y_M + (U_i + \lambda K_i)i_M = 0. \qquad (A.20.25)$$

If we now add the canonical equations (with the opportune boundary conditions at terminal time and at initial time)

$$\frac{d}{dt}(e^{-rt}\lambda) = -\frac{\partial H}{\partial R}, \quad \lim_{t \to \infty} e^{-rt}\lambda = 0,$$

$$\dot{R} = \frac{\partial H}{\partial \lambda}, \quad R(0) = R_0, \qquad (A.20.26)$$

and consider Eqs. (A.20.25) and (A.20.26) together, we shall obtain the solution to the problem. We refer the reader to Nyberg and Viotti (1976) for a complete examination of the solution and only consider the optimal path of reserves, which is obtained through the differential equation system (A.20.26). If we perform the partial differentiation operations on H indicated in that system we get

$$\dot{\lambda} = r\lambda - U_R,$$

$$\dot{R} = x - m(y) + K(y,i). \qquad (A.20.26.1)$$

By letting $\dot{R} = 0$, $\dot{\lambda} = 0$, we find the stationary equilibrium point (singular point) of the system, (R^*, λ^*). In the phase plane we get the phase diagram illustrated in Fig. A.20.1. The curve $\dot{\lambda} = 0$ is decreasing because of the assumption of decreasing marginal utility of reserves ($U_{RR} < 0$). In fact, from $r\lambda - U_R = 0$ we get

$$\left(\frac{d\lambda}{dR}\right)_{\dot{\lambda}=0} = \frac{U_{RR}}{r} < 0. \qquad (A.20.27)$$

The condition $\dot{R} = 0$ instead gives rise to a straight line parallel to the R axis: in fact, since R does not appear in the equation $x - m(y) - K(y,i) = 0$, we have

$$\left(\frac{d\lambda}{dR}\right)_{\dot{R}=0} = 0. \qquad (A.20.28)$$

---

[34] For brevity we use subscripts to denote partial derivatives: $U_y \equiv \partial U/\partial y$, etc. We also note that the derivatives y_G etc. are obtained after expressing y and i as functions of G and M by way of the first two equations in set (A.20.20); the relevant Jacobian is assumed to be different from zero: see below, in the text.

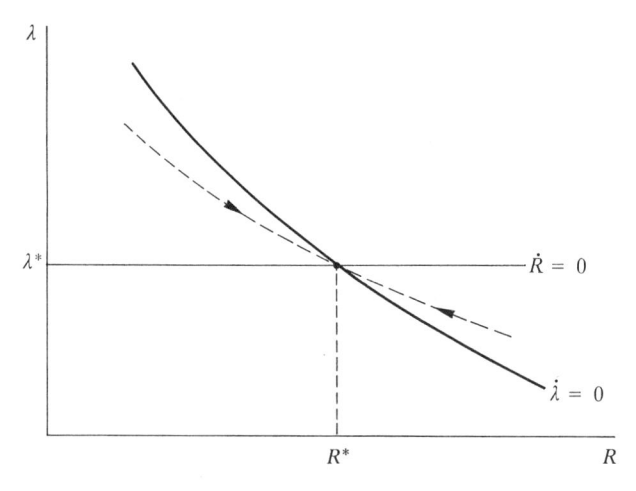

Fig. A.20.1. The dynamics of the optimum reserve level

We could now analyze the stability of the equilibrium point by way of an arrow diagram, but it is more rigorous to determine the nature of the singular point by way of mathematical analysis. For this purpose we perform a linear approximation of system (A.20.26.1) at the singular point. Since y and i are functions of G and M, which in turn depend on λ through the optimum conditions (A.20.25), we obtain

$$\dot{\bar{\lambda}} = r\bar{\lambda} - U_{RR}\bar{R}, \quad \dot{\bar{R}} = Q\bar{\lambda}, \quad (A.20.29)$$

where (the derivatives are, as usual, taken at the equilibrium point)

$$Q \equiv -(m_y - K_y)y_\lambda + K_i i_\lambda, \quad y_\lambda = y_M M_\lambda + y_G G_\lambda, \quad i_\lambda = i_M M_\lambda + i_G G_\lambda, \quad (A.20.29.1)$$

and the bars over the symbols denote deviations from equilibrium. The sign of Q is essential to determine the nature of the singular point, so that we must carefully examine the expressions which appear in (A.20.29.1). From the first two equations in set (A.20.20) we can, as stated more than once, express y and i as functions of G and M provided that the Jacobian

$$|J_1| = \begin{vmatrix} 1 - A_y + m_y & -A_i \\ L_y & L_i \end{vmatrix} = L_i(1 - A_y + m_y) + A_i L_y \quad (A.20.30)$$

is different from zero. The usual assumptions on the signs of the partial derivatives ($0 < A_y < 1 + m_y$, $0 < m_y < 1$, etc.) allow us to ascertain that $|J_1| > 0$. We can thus calculate the derivatives we are interested in and obtain

$$y_G = L_i/|J_1| > 0, \quad i_G = -L_y/|J_1| > 0, \quad (A.20.31)$$
$$y_M = A_i/|J_1| > 0, \quad i_M = (1 - A_y + m_y)/|J_1| < 0.$$

In order to calculate the derivatives M_λ and G_λ we consider the optimum conditions (A.20.25). Account being taken of (A.20.31), Eqs. (A.20.25) can be satisfied if, and only if,

$$U_y - \lambda(m_y - K_y) = 0, \quad (A.20.25.1)$$
$$U_i + \lambda K_i = 0.$$

Since y and i are functions of M and G as shown above, we could use set (A.20.25.1) to express M and G as functions of λ and then calculate the partial derivatives M_λ and G_λ to be substituted in Eqs. (A.20.29.1). Alternatively, and more simply, we can use Eqs. (A.20.25.1) to express y and i directly as functions of λ and then compute the dirivatives y_λ and i_λ that we are interested in. This is possible provided that the Jacobian of Eqs. (A.20.25.1) with respect to y, i is different from zero. This Jacobian is

$$|J_2| = \begin{vmatrix} U_{yy} - \lambda(m_{yy} - K_{yy}) & U_{yi} - \lambda(m_{yi} - K_{yi}) \\ U_{iy} + \lambda K_{iy} & U_{ii} + \lambda K_{ii} \end{vmatrix} \quad \text{(A.20.32)}$$

If we assume, as Nyberg and Viotti do, that the utility function is separable ($U_{yi} = U_{iy} = 0$) and that the balance-of-payments equation is linear (all second-order derivatives of m and K are zero), our Jacobian reduces to

$$|J_2| = U_{yy} U_{ii} > 0, \quad \text{(A.20.32.1)}$$

where the positivity derives from the assumption of decreasing marginal utilities. Thus we have

$$y_\lambda = (m_y - K_y)/U_{yy} < 0, \quad i_\lambda = -K_i/U_{ii} > 0, \quad \text{(A.20.33)}$$

where, following Nyberg and Viotti, we have introduced the further assumption that $m_y - K_y > 0$, namely that the Johnson effect (see Sect. 15.5.2.1, point 4), measured by K_y, is smaller than the marginal propensity to import. Given these results and assumptions, it turns out that Q is positive.

The characteristic equation of system (A.20.29) is

$$\begin{vmatrix} r - \mu & -U_{RR} \\ Q & -\mu \end{vmatrix} = \mu^2 - r\mu + QU_{RR} = 0, \quad \text{(A.20.29.1)}$$

so that, since the succession of the signs of the coefficients is $+ - -$, the roots are real, one positive and one negative; hence the singular point is a *saddle point* (Gandolfo, 1980, Part III, Chap. 3, §5.2). This means that there will be one and only one optimal trajectory converging towards the stationary equilibrium (which is that drawn with a broken curve in fig. A.19.1) which will determine the time path of the optimal reserve level. Still using the linear approximation (A.20.29) this path turns out to be

$$R(t) = R^* + (R_0 - R^*) e^{\mu t}, \quad \text{(A.20.34)}$$

where μ is the negative root of the characteristic equation (A.20.29.1). As regards the problem we are interested in, we could stop here, but it is important briefly to mention some general considerations on the *normative theory of economic policy* or *optimizing approach to economic policy*.

The traditional theory of the Meade-Tinbergen type, which is still widely used, is based, as we have seen in Sect. 15.5, on the instrument-target approach. The optimizing approach — instead of starting from prescribed values of the targets — defines an objective function (which can be a social welfare function, a preference function of the policy maker, a loss function, etc.) which is maximized (subject to the constraint consisting of the model which represents the positive economy) in a static or dynamic context. From this optimization process, amongst other results, one obtains the optimum values (or the optimal time paths, if we are in a dynamic context) of the instruments.

For example, in the Nyberg and Viotti model, once the optimal path of R has been obtained as shown above, it is possible to obtain the time paths of λ, of the instruments M and G, and, of course, of the other target variables y and i; all these paths are optimal because they are derived by way of the described optimization procedure. See Nyberg and Viotti (1976) for details.

This approach is undoubtedly interesting and its diffusion is on the increase, but its practical application meets with several difficulties (for example, the determination of the objective function or, more simply, of the weights to be given to the various objectives). Research on this approach is going on, but, as it pertains to the general theory of quantitative economic policy, which lies outside the limits of the present book, we refer the reader to the relevant literature (see, for example, Hughes Hallet and Rees, 1983, and references therein).

A.20.2 The Composition of International Reserves

The studies of Ben-Bassat (1980, 1984) examine the problem within the framework of the theory of portfolio selection and taking into account the basket of currencies used to pay for imports, since reserves are held, amongst other reasons, to meet import payment needs. As is known, the portfolio selection approach requires one first to determine the set of efficient portfolios (minimum risk for any given return, or, equivalently, maximum return for any given risk).

If we assume that risk can be represented by the variance, the standard mean-variance problem can be formulated as

$$min \; \sigma^2 = \sum_{i=1}^{n} a_i^2 \sigma_i^2 + 2 \sum_{i=1}^{n} \sum_{j=1, j>i}^{n} a_i a_j R_{ij} \sigma_i \sigma_j$$

subject to (A.20.35)

$$\varrho = \sum_{i=1}^{n} a_i \varrho_i, \quad \sum_i a_i = 1, \; a_i \geq 0,$$

where a_i is the optimum share (to be found) of currency i in the portfolio, σ_i^2 is the variance of the returns on currency i, R_{ij} is the correlation coefficient between the returns on currencies i and j, and ϱ_i is the return on currency i. Problem (A.20.35) requires one to minimize the overall variance of the portfolio (σ^2) taken as a measure of risk, for any given overall return ϱ.

It is in the definition of the return on currency i (and so of its variance) that the notion of the basket of import currencies (which enter into the basket with weights derived from their actual utilization in import payments) comes into play. The return on currency i is, in fact, defined in terms of the interest rate on funds placed in currency i (denoted by r_i), account being taken of the variation in the exchange rate of currency i with respect to the basket of import currencies (this variation is denoted by E_i). Thus we get

$$1 + \varrho_i = \frac{1 + r_i}{1 + E_i}, \quad \varrho_i = \frac{1 + r_i}{1 + E_i} - 1, \quad \text{(A.20.35.1)}$$

from which we see that $\varrho_i = r_i$ if currency i does not change of value with respect to the basket, whilst $\varrho_i \lessgtr r_i$ according to whether currency i depreciates ($E_i > 0$) or appreciates ($E_i < 0$) with respect to the basket. This is an ingenious expedient, as it uses the concept of basket-currency (see Sect. 19.2.3), defined concretely in terms of the import currencies, to correct the interest rate on each currency.

It is self-evident that, as the import currency basket is different from country to country, the return on the same currency i will be different in different countries, so that the set of efficient portfolios will have to be computed separately for each country.

Once the efficient set has been determined, the optimum portfolio will be determined by maximizing the utility function of the agent (in this case the central bank of the country considered) under the constraint of the efficient set. This utility function is assumed to be increasing with respect to return and decreasing with respect to risk.

In the (ϱ, σ^2) plane the problem is then to find the highest-indexed indifference curve compatible with the efficient set. Since the utility function (and hence the indifference map) is not given, Ben-Bassat solves the problem by using Sharpe and Lintner's market price theory (CAPM), according to which the optimum portfolio of risky assets is determined at the point of tangency between the efficiency curve and the straight line which rises from the riskless asset return. It is usual to take the rate of interest on Treasury bills as the riskless asset rate; in the case in question, since the objective function is a currency basket, Ben-Bassat uses the average of the interest rates on Treasury bills in these currencies, expressed in terms of the import basket.

By this procedure the author calculates the optimum reserve composition for 69 countries, then aggregates the results[35] into two groups of countries (the semi-industrialized and developing countries, and the industrialized countries; the latter are further divided into snake countries and floaters) and compares them with the actual reserve composition. The results are given in the following table (adapted from Ben-Bassat, 1980, p. 294, and 1984, pp. 12–13).

As the author points out, the correspondence between the actual and optimum reserve composition is much closer for the semi-industrialized and developing countries than for the industrialized countries. In the latter group the correspondence is so poor that one is led to believe that in these countries the profit-risk factor is of secondary importance. This, we might add, lends support to the argument of those who believe that the optimizing approach, relevant from the point of view of normative economics, is hardly (if at all) useful in explaining the *actual* behaviour of central banks.

For another interesting study of optimal portfolio diversification across currencies see de Macedo (1982) who, however, refers to private international investors rather than to central banks. See also Dooley et al. (1989).

---

[35] This requires that each country's portfolio be given a weight; the weights used by Ben-Bassat are the reserves of the countries.

Table A.20.1. Optimal and actual currency composition of foreign exchange reserves, 1976 and 1980 (per cent)

Currency	Semi-industrialized and developing countries				Industrialized countries								
					Snake countries				Floaters			
	1976		1980		1976		1980		1976		1980	
	Optimal	Actual	Optimal	Actual	Optimal	Actual	Optimal	Actual	Optimal	Actual	Optimal	Actual
Dollar	58	72	55	64	48	98	47	86	70	74	62	79
Pound sterling	2	3	11	5	0.1	0.02	15	1	2	3	10	1
D-mark	13	10	9	19	8	1	11	7	11	8	9	11
Others	27	15	25	12	44	1	27	6	7	15	19	9
Total	100	100	100	100	100	100	100	100	100	100	100	100
Mean return	9.5	8.7	9.3	8.9	9.6	7.1	9.4	8.0	8.7	8.4	9.1	8.5
Standard deviation	7.8	6.7	5.4	5.0	7.9	16.0	5.1	10.8	5.0	4.2	5.6	4.5

A.20.3 A Portfolio Model of the Euro-Market

In this section we explain the model of Niehans and Hewson (1976; see also Niehans, 1984), which, though adopting some simplifying assumptions, lends itself well to the illustration of the portfolio or new approach to the Euro-dollar market. For other models in the same line see, e.g., Hewson and Sakakibara (1974, 1976), Freedman (1977), Knight (1977), Herring and Marston (1977), Johnston (1981, 1983).

The model starts from some known definitional and accounting relations and then introduces the appropriate behavioural functions into them. Only liquid assets (denominated in dollars)[36] held by the (nonbank) public are considered (M^*), and it is assumed that they consist of currency (C) and sight deposits, which can be held both with US banks (D) and with Euro-banks (e), so that we have

$$M^* = C + D + e. \qquad (A.20.36)$$

Given a certain amount of monetary base ($\bar{B}$), exogenously determined by the USA, this will be held partly by the public (C) and partly by US banks as bank reserves (R), so that

$$C + R = \bar{B}. \qquad (A.20.37)$$

The balance-sheet identity of US banks is

$$L + R = D + r, \qquad (A.20.38)$$

where the assets are the loans (L) and the reserves (R), whilst the liabilities are the deposits, made up of the public's deposits (D) and the Euro-banks' deposits (r): the latter, in fact, are assumed to hold all their dollar reserves (related to their Euro-dollar operations) with US banks. The balance-sheet identity of Euro-banks is

$$l + r = e, \qquad (A.20.39)$$

where the assets are loans (l) and reserves (r), whilst the liabilities are the Euro-dollar deposits (e).

Having thus completed the definitional and accounting framework, we now pass to the behavioural relationship. We first have the US banks' demand for reserves as a function of the volume of total deposits

$$R = R(D+r), \quad 0 < R_D < 1. \qquad (A.20.40)$$

More generally, one could consider R as also depending on interest rates, but for simplicity the influence of interest rates is disregarded. Another simplification is that the Euro-banks' reserves are assumed to be independent of Euro-deposits

---

[36] Thus we ignore portfolio choices among other assets (bonds etc.), possibly denominated in different currencies. For more complex models which take this wider spectrum of assets into account see, for example, Hewson and Sakakibara (1976) and Freedman (1977). We also inform the reader that, in order to facilitate comparison with the original source, we shall use the same symbology as Niehans and Hewson.

and of any other variables in the model, so that they can be taken as exogenous. As the authors point out, this simplification does not seem excessively unrealistic, and, if anything, it would tend to bias the result in favour of a higher value of the multiplier which will be derived below.

If we denote by I and i, respectively, the US and the Euro-market interest rates and disregard — in each market — the spread between the borrowing and lending rates, we can write the supply of deposits by the public (which depends on the two interest rates and on total liquid assets) as the following functions

$$\begin{aligned} D &= D(I,i,M^*), & D_I &> 0, & D_i &< 0, & 0 &< D_M < 1, \\ e &= e(I,i,M^*), & e_I &< 0, & e_i &> 0, & 0 &< e_M < 1, \\ L &= L(I,i), & L_I &< 0, & L_i &> 0, \\ l &= l(I,i), & l_I &> 0, & l_i &< 0, \end{aligned} \quad \text{(A.20.41)}$$

where the signs of the partial derivatives are self-evident.

The equilibrium interest rates are determined by equating the supply of deposits (after due allowance for reserves) and the demand for loans in each market. Thus, if we substitute the various functions (A.20.41) in the previous equations, and if we also substitute C from (A.20.37) into (A.20.36), we get the system

$$\begin{aligned} M^* &= \bar{B} - R(D+r) + D(I,i,M^*) + e(I,i,M^*), \\ L(I,i) + R(D+r) &= D(I,i,M^*) + r, \\ l(I,i) + r &= e(I,i,M^*). \end{aligned} \quad \text{(A.20.42)}$$

This system determines the three unknowns I, i, M^*, whence we can determine the size of the Euro-market, e. To ascertain the effects on e of an exogenous shift of the public's deposits from US banks to Euro-banks, we introduce a shift parameters α to be deducted from D and added to e. Thus we get the following system in implicit form (note that the parameter α cancels out in the first equation)

$$\begin{aligned} M^* - \bar{B} + R(D+r) - D(I,i,M^*) - e(I,i,M^*) &= 0, \\ L(I,i) + R(D+r) - D(I,i,M^*) + \alpha - r &= 0, \\ l(I,i) + r - e(I,i,M^*) - \alpha &= 0. \end{aligned} \quad \text{(A.20.42.1)}$$

By using the implicit function theorem, we can express I, i and M^* as differentiable functions of α if the Jacobian of Eqs. (A.20.42.1) with respect to these three variables is different from zero, i.e.

$$J = \begin{vmatrix} 1 - (1-R_D)D_M - e_M & -(1-R_D)D_I - e_I & -(1-R_D)D_i - e_i \\ -(1-R_D)D_M & -(1-R_D)D_I + L_I & -(1-R_D)D_i + L_i \\ -e_M & l_I - e_I & l_i - e_i \end{vmatrix} \neq 0.$$

(A.20.43)

If this condition occurs, we can use the method of comparative statics to determine the final effect of α on e, which is

$$de = \left(e_I \frac{dI}{d\alpha} d\alpha + e_i \frac{di}{d\alpha} d\alpha + e_M \frac{dM^*}{d\alpha} d\alpha \right) + d\alpha, \quad (A.20.44)$$

where $d\alpha$ is the initial effect (the initial shift of deposits) whilst the expression in parentheses is the sum of the induced effects, which come from the effects that the initial shift causes on the endogenous variables I, i, M^*. Equations (A.20.44) can also be written as

$$\frac{de}{d\alpha} = 1 + \left(e_I \frac{dI}{d\alpha} + e_i \frac{di}{d\alpha} + e_M \frac{dM^*}{d\alpha} \right), \quad (A.20.44.1)$$

which represents the *flexible* Euro-dollar multiplier. Whether this multiplier is greater or smaller than one thus depends on the induced effects, i.e. on the expression in parentheses; to determine it, it is necessary to calculate $dI/d\alpha$, $di/d\alpha$, $dM^*/d\alpha$. For this purpose we must check whether J is indeed different from zero and, if possible, determine its sign. The correspondence principle of Samuelson (see, for example, Gandolfo, 1980) can be applied here: it can in fact be shown that $J > 0$ if the equilibrium is stable.

The dynamic system that we are going to set up for the examination of stability is based on standard assumptions, namely that in each market the interest rate varies in relation to the excess demand for loans; we also add the (inessential) assumption that there is an adjustment lag in the equation of the public's total liquid assets, which — dynamically speaking — takes the form of a partial adjustment equation. We thus obtain the following differential equation system

$$\frac{dM^*}{dt} = k_1\{[B - R(D+r) + D(I,i,M^*) + e(I,i,M^*)] - M^*\}, \quad k_1 > 0,$$

$$\frac{dI}{dt} = k_2\{[L(I,i) + R(D+r)] - [D(I,i,M^*) + r]\}, \quad k_2 > 0, \quad (A.20.45)$$

$$\frac{di}{dt} = k_3\{[l(I,i) + r] - e(I,i,M^*)\}, \quad k_3 > 0,$$

where the k's represent adjustment speeds. If we linearize system (A.20.45) at the equilibrium point and consider the deviations from equilibrium, we get

$$\frac{d\mathbf{x}}{dt} = \mathbf{KHx}, \quad (A.20.46)$$

where $\mathbf{x} = \{\bar{M^*}, \bar{I}, \bar{i}\}$ is the vector of the deviations from equilibrium (these are denoted by a bar over the variable), $\mathbf{K}$ is the diagonal matrix of the adjustment speeds and $\mathbf{H}$ is the coefficient matrix defined as

$$\mathbf{H} \equiv \begin{bmatrix} e_M + (1-R_D)D_M - 1 & (1-R_D)D_I + e_I & (1-R_D)D_i + e_i \\ -(1-R_D)D_M & -(1-R_D)D_I + L_I & -(1-R_D)D_i + L_i \\ -e_M & l_I - e_I & l_i - e_i \end{bmatrix}.$$

$$(A.20.47)$$

The characteristic equation of system (A.20.46) is

$$-\lambda^3 + c_1\lambda^2 - c_2\lambda + k_1 k_2 k_3 |\mathbf{H}| = 0, \tag{A.20.48}$$

where $|\mathbf{H}|$ denotes the determinant of the matrix $\mathbf{H}$. Among the necessary stability conditions (Gandolfo, 1980) there is the condition

$$k_1 k_2 k_3 |\mathbf{H}| < 0, \text{ i.e. } |\mathbf{H}| < 0. \tag{A.20.49}$$

It can easily be checked that $|\mathbf{H}|$ coincides with J (with the sign of the elements of the first row changed), so that, by the rules on determinants,

$$-|\mathbf{H}| = J > 0. \tag{A.20.50}$$

Thus the correspondence principle enables us to ascertain that J is positive. It is then possible to differentiate Eqs. (A.20.42.1) with respect to α, account being taken of the fact that M^*, I, i are functions of α. We thus get the system

$$[1 - (1-R_D)D_M - e_M]\frac{dM^*}{d\alpha} - [(1-R_D)D_I + e_I]\frac{dI}{d\alpha}$$
$$- [(1-R_D)D_i + e_i]\frac{di}{d\alpha} = 0,$$

$$-(1-R_D)D_M \frac{dM^*}{d\alpha} + [-(1-R_D)D_I + L_I]\frac{dI}{d\alpha} \tag{A.20.51}$$
$$+ [-(1-R_D)D_i + L_i]\frac{di}{d\alpha} = -1,$$

$$-e_M \frac{dM^*}{d\alpha} + (l_I - e_I)\frac{dI}{d\alpha} + (l_i - e_i)\frac{di}{d\alpha} = 1.$$

If we solve this system for $dM^*/d\alpha$, $dI/d\alpha$, $di/d\alpha$, and insert the resulting expressions into Eq. (A.20.44.1), after some simplifications and rearrangement of terms, we get the equation

$$\frac{de}{d\alpha} = 1 + \frac{N}{J}, \tag{A.20.52}$$

where

$$N = (1-R_D)\{[e_I D_i - e_i D_I] + (1-D_M)[e_i(L_I + l_I) - e_I(L_i + l_i)]$$
$$+ e_M[D_i(L_I + l_I) - D_I(L_i + l_i)]\}$$
$$+ R_D[e_i(L_I + l_I) - e_I(L_i + l_i)]. \tag{A.20.53}$$

In order to evaluate expression (A.20.53) and so establish whether the flexible multiplier (A.20.52) is higher or lower than one, we must introduce a further plausible assumption, namely that each rate of interest has a greater influence on its own market than on the other market. To put the same thing another way, the US interest rate (I) has an influence on L and D which is greater in absolute value than its influence on l and e, whilst the Euro-dollar interest rate (i) has a stronger effect on l and e than on L and D. This gives rise to the inequalities

$$|L_I| > |l_I|, \quad |l_i| > |L_i|, \quad |D_I| > |e_I|, \quad |e_i| > |D_i|. \tag{A.20.54}$$

Thanks to (A.20.54) it is possible to establish that, of the four expressions in square brackets on the r.h.s. of (A.20.53), the first, second and fourth are negative, whilst the third is positive. The negative expressions tend to make N smaller and so to push the multiplier below unity, whilst the positive one has the opposite effect. This means that a high marginal propensity to hold Euro-dollars (represented by high values of e_M) tends to raise the multiplier. It is however likely, though not certain, that the multiplier will be below one, as it is presumable that the negative expressions in N prevail over the positive one, so that N is likely to be negative; hence $de/d\alpha < 1$. It should be noted that — whilst in the simplified analysis presented in the text (Fig. 20.1 in Sect. 20.4), in which the cross effects of the various interest rates on the various markets have not been considered, the multiplier was sure to be below one — now this result is only likely. In any case, we are not facing a simple fixed-coefficient multiplier as in the traditional analysis, but a *flexible* multiplier in the sense already explained.

A.20.4 Capital Liberalization and Foreign Exchange Crises

A.20.4.1 Introduction

According to the portfolio view, capital movements are not pure flows but represent the adjustment of the desired to the actual stock of net foreign assets. Now, the parameter representing the adjustment speed depends not only on the behaviour of economic agents but also on the presence of capital controls hence on an institutional arrangement – in the sense that a low adjustment speed is due to the fact that agents are not free immediately to adjust the actual to the desired stock of net foreign assets. To put the same concept in other words, the desired stock of *NFA* (net foreign assets) depends on fundamentals, the adjustment speed reflects institutional features such as capital controls.

More precisely, the dynamic version of the portfolio approach to capital movements starts from an equation of the following type:

$$DNFA = \alpha(\widehat{NFA} - NFA), \tag{A.20.55}$$

where D denotes the differential operator d/dt, $\alpha > 0$ the adjustment speed, and NFA the stock of net foreign assets. $\widehat{NFA} = \varphi(...)$ is the *desired* stock, which depends on fundamentals (the arguments of the function φ, such as the interest rate differential, etc. These will be specified later on). In equation (A.20.55), a low value of α reflects capital controls. In the presence of capital controls, in fact, economic agents are not free immediately to adjust the actual to the desired stock of net foreign assets. While the desired stock of net foreign assets depends on fundamentals, the adjustment speed reflects institutional features such as capital controls.

In this context, the transition to a regime with higher capital mobility is equivalent to an increase in α or, which is the same thing, a decrease in the mean time lag of adjustment. In continuous time, the mean time lag is given by the reciprocal of α, and measures the time required for about 63% of the discrepancy between desired and actual values to be eliminated by the adjustment process.

A.20.4.2 The Actual Specification

Let us take a closer look at the capital movement equation, which is specified as follows:

$$D \log NFA = \alpha_{24} \log (\widehat{NFA}/NFA) + \alpha_{25} \log \left(\frac{PMGS_f \cdot E \cdot MGS}{PXGS \cdot XGS} \right), \alpha_{25} > 0, \tag{A.20.56}$$

where:

$$\widehat{NFA} = \gamma_{11} e^{\beta_{19}[i_f + \log(FR/E) - i_{TIT}]} (PY)^{\beta_{20}} (PF_f \cdot E \cdot YF)^{-\beta_{21}}. \tag{A.20.57}$$

This equation has a twofold nature. First of all, the stock of net foreign assets (NFA) adjusts to its desired value $\widehat{NFA}$. The latter reflects the portfolio view, in which the scale variables are proxied by the domestic (PY) and foreign ($PF_f \cdot E \cdot YF$) money incomes. Given the scale variables the level of $\widehat{NFA}$ is determined by the interest differential term corrected for exchange rate expectations; these are proxied by the ratio of the forward to the spot exchange rate (FR/E).

The second element in the equation refers to capital movements which are not strictly related to portfolio considerations, but rather to trade flows. The ratio of the value of imports to the value of exports is meant to capture the effect of commercial credits on the capital account. A trade deficit – i.e. ($PMGS_f \cdot E \cdot MGS/PXGS \cdot XGS) > 1$; hence $\log(\ldots) > 0$ – is partly financed through commercial credits from abroad, hence an increase in foreign liabilities ($D \log NFA < 0$).

The interest differential term is also included in the interest rate equation. This is consistent with the idea that the domestic interest rate moves to close the discrepancy between its current value and the covered interest parity value. In fact, under perfect mobility and infinite elasticity of arbitrage funds the relation

$$i_{TIT} = i_f + (FR - E)/E \tag{A.20.58}$$

should hold. Considerations of imperfect capital mobility can however explain the presence of a gap between the two members. This, in turn, gives rise to a (policy managed) movement of i_{TIT} aimed at the reduction of the gap.

Given the relevance of the topic some further considerations on the modelling of exchange rate expectations seem appropriate. Let us recall from Chap. 10 (Sect. 10.7) two interest-rate parity conditions. In an open economy with perfect capital mobility, perfect asset substitutability, and risk neutral agents, *uncovered interest parity* holds, *i.e.*

$$i_{TIT} = i_f + D\tilde{E}/E, \tag{A.20.59}$$

where $D\tilde{E} = \tilde{E} - E$ is the expected variation in the exchange rate. If we assume –

according to the portfolio approach – imperfect substitutability between domestic and foreign assets, the interest-parity relation becomes

$$i_{TIT} = i_f + D\tilde{E}/E + \delta, \qquad (A.20.60)$$

where δ is a risk premium.

However, if we take account of imperfect capital mobility, neither relation (A.20.59) nor relation (A.20.60) will hold. A discrepancy between i_{TIT} and the right-hand-side of either Eq. (A.20.59) or Eq. (A.20.60) will not, in fact, cause an instantaneous and huge amount of capital flow. What will take place is a limited amount of capital flow, as described by the first term on the r.h.s. of Eq. (A.20.56). This flow will also cause a tendency of i_{TIT} to move to close the discrepancy; the speed of this adjustment depends, inter alia, on the degree of the authorities' control on capital movements. Precisely, we have not included it explicitly. The observed discrepancy between i_{TIT} and $(i_f + D\tilde{E}/E)$, therefore, reflects both imperfect capital mobility and imperfect asset substitutability. This enables us tu keep this discrepancy even under perfect capital mobility.

The problem of exchange rate expectations – as we have mentioned – has been solved by using the forward exchange rate. From the formal point of view, $\log(FR/E) \simeq (FR-E)/E$ if we expand in Taylor's series and neglect all higher order terms. From the substantial point of view, in an efficient foreign exchange market with rational expectations, the forward exchange rate is an unbiased predictor of the future spot exchange rate (see Sect. A.10.4.1). Hence the expected spot rate can be represented by the forward rate. But what if the foreign exchange market is not efficient and expectations are not rational, as empirical evidence seems to suggest? (see, for example, Ito, 1990, and Takagi, 1991). Let us introduce the concept of "plausible" expectations, *i.e.* expectations which use easy and plausible information in a simple way, as opposed to rational expectations which use all the existing information efficiently. Now, in the context of plausible expectations a reasonable candidate for representing the expected spot exchange rate remains the forward exchange rate, irrespective of the efficiency of the market. First of all, we observe that in some cases the forward exchange rate ouperforms all other forecasts based on econometric analyses (random walk, ARIMA, PPP, uncovered interest parity, various versions of the monetary model: see Hogan, 1986). Secondly, even admitting that the forward exchange rate is generally not the best unbiased predictor of future spot rates, the problem remains of how agents involved in international transactions form their expectations. The proliferation of exchange-rate forecasting services may suggest that agents rely on these forecasts, but are these better than the forward exchange rate? The findings of Goodman (1979), Levich (1980), Blake, Beenstock, and Brasse (1986), indicate that the forward exchange rate is a predictor of future spot rates which is not worse (and sometimes better) than the predictions of the exchange-rate forecasting services. In addition, the forward exchange rate has no cost. Thus it seems reasonable to assume that a rational agent (not necessarily in the sense of an agent holding rational expectations, but in the general sense of *homo economicus*) uses the forward rate. It should also be noted that the forward exchange rate, which is considered an exogenous variable for estimation purposes, becomes an endogenous variable in the long run (see Gandolfo and Padoan, 1990).

This as regards the estimated version of the model. When one passes from a situation of capital controls to perfect capital mobility, it is plausible to think that exchange rate expectations undergo a modification as well. Hence the necessity arises of considering different hypotheses about the formation of these expectations, as detailed in the text.

A.20.4.3 The Method of Analysis

The first cue to a possible destabilising effect of capital liberalisation was given by sensitivity analysis. By *sensitivity analysis* we here mean the analysis of the effects of changes in the parameters on the characteristic roots of the model (for a general treatment see Gandolfo, 1992). This can be performed in a general way by computing the partial derivatives of these roots with respect to the parameters. If we call **A** the matrix of the linear approximation of the original non-linear system, we can compute $\partial \mu_i / \partial \mathbf{A}$, where μ_i denotes the $i-th$ characteristic root of **A**. Now, the partial derivative of one real root with respect to α_{24} is positive and very large in relative terms, which implies that the model becomes unstable for sufficiently high capital mobility. This is a worrying result, but sensitivity analysis indicates some possible stabilizing effects. Both an increase in the adjustment speed of imports and an increase in the adjustment speed of exports have a stabilizing effect on the same root. The implication seems to be that the destabilizing impact of an increase in capital mobility can be counteracted by an increase in goods mobility: when one frees capital movements one must also have free trade in goods and services.

Further indications on the effects of higher capital mobility may be obtained through simulation analysis. The results of the simulations are described in the text; for a full account see Gandolfo and Padoan (1992) and Gandolfo et al. (1994).

A.20.5 The Policy Coordination Problem

We consider a very simple two-country model (Frankel, 1988b), in which each country has three targets (real output, current account balance, inflation rate) and two policy instruments (fiscal and monetary policy). As is usual in this type of problem, the policy maker's welfare function is expressed as a loss function, namely as a function of the deviations of the actual values of the targets from an assumed ideal value or optimum. Furthermore, this loss function is assumed to be quadratic for mathematical convenience. The optimal policy problem consists in minimising the loss function. For simplicity's sake we remain in the static context rather than considering a dynamic optimization framework.

Let us denote by y, x, π the deviations of real output, current account, inflation rate from the respective optimum values in the home country; an asterisk will denote the rest-of-the world variables. Hence we have the two welfare (loss) functions

$$W = \frac{1}{2}y^2 + \frac{1}{2}w_x x^2 + \frac{1}{2}w_\pi \pi^2,$$
$$W^* = \frac{1}{2}y^{*2} + \frac{1}{2}w_x^* x^{*2} + \frac{1}{2}w_\pi^* \pi^{*2},$$
(A.20.61)

where the w's represent the weights placed on the current account and on the inflation rate relative to the weight placed on output. By g (government expenditure) and m (money supply) we denote the two instruments.

For our purposes it is irrelevant the kind of model(s) used to represent our two-country world system. It is enough to observe that, whichever the model(s) used, the interdependence of the two economies will give rise to the functions

$$\begin{aligned} y &= y(m, g, m^*, g^*), \\ x &= x(m, g, m^*, g^*), \\ \pi &= \pi(m, g, m^*, g^*), \\ y^* &= y^*(m, g, m^*, g^*), \\ x^* &= x^*(m, g, m^*, g^*), \\ \pi^* &= \pi^*(m, g, m^*, g^*), \end{aligned} \tag{A.20.62}$$

where the nature of the functions and the various partial derivatives with respect to the policy variables (these derivatives are also called *policy multipliers*) depend on the underlying structural model(s). Hence the welfare functions can ultimately be written in terms of the policy instruments, namely

$$\begin{aligned} W &= \omega(m, g, m^*, g^*), \\ W^* &= \omega^*(m, g, m^*, g^*). \end{aligned} \tag{A.20.63}$$

When there is only one policy instrument per country (or each country's policy instruments can be bundled into one), we have the diagrams described in the text (Figs. 20.2 and 20.3). Note, however, that in these diagrams the welfare is taken in the conventional way rather than as a loss function.

The marginal welfare effects of changes in the instruments are given by

$$\begin{aligned} \frac{\partial W}{\partial m} &= y \frac{\partial y}{\partial m} + x w_x \frac{\partial x}{\partial m} + \pi w_\pi \frac{\partial \pi}{\partial m}, \\ \frac{\partial W}{\partial g} &= y \frac{\partial y}{\partial g} + x w_x \frac{\partial x}{\partial g} + \pi w_\pi \frac{\partial \pi}{\partial g}, \\ \frac{\partial W}{\partial m^*} &= y \frac{\partial y}{\partial m^*} + x w_x \frac{\partial x}{\partial m^*} + \pi w_\pi \frac{\partial \pi}{\partial m^*}, \\ \frac{\partial W}{\partial g^*} &= y \frac{\partial y}{\partial g^*} + x w_x \frac{\partial x}{\partial g^*} + \pi w_\pi \frac{\partial \pi}{\partial g^*}, \\ \frac{\partial W^*}{\partial m} &= y^* \frac{\partial y^*}{\partial m} + x^* w_x^* \frac{\partial x^*}{\partial m} + \pi^* w_\pi^* \frac{\partial \pi^*}{\partial m}, \\ \frac{\partial W^*}{\partial g} &= y^* \frac{\partial y^*}{\partial g} + x^* w_x^* \frac{\partial x^*}{\partial g} + \pi^* w_\pi^* \frac{\partial \pi^*}{\partial g}, \\ \frac{\partial W^*}{\partial m^*} &= y^* \frac{\partial y^*}{\partial m^*} + x^* w_x^* \frac{\partial x^*}{\partial m^*} + \pi^* w_\pi^* \frac{\partial \pi^*}{\partial m^*}, \\ \frac{\partial W^*}{\partial g^*} &= y^* \frac{\partial y^*}{\partial g^*} + x^* w_x^* \frac{\partial x^*}{\partial g^*} + \pi^* w_\pi^* \frac{\partial \pi^*}{\partial g^*}. \end{aligned} \tag{A.20.64}$$

The first-order conditions for an overall optimum require all these derivatives to equal zero ($\partial W/\partial m = 0$, and so on). In the case in which each country ignores the effects of its policy actions on the other country (a Nash noncooperative equilibrium), we need only the two first ($\partial W/\partial m = \partial W/\partial g = 0$) and the two last ($\partial W^*/\partial m^* = \partial W^*/\partial g^* = 0$) equations for the solution. But this solution is clearly suboptimal. With the values of m, g, m^*, g^* thus obtained, in fact, there is no reason why the other optimum conditions ($\partial W/\partial m^* = 0$, etc.) should be satisfied. This shows that the cooperative solution is superior.

The set of optimum conditions also clearly illustrates the obstacles to coordination. As Frankel observes, the actual process of policy coordination can be ideally divided into three stages. At the first stage, each country has to decide what policy changes by the other countries would best suit its interests, and – on the other hand – what changes in its policy it would be willing to concede in the other countries' interest. At the second stage, the countries must negotiate the distribution of the gains from coordination. At the third stage, rules must be set to enforce the agreement and avoid the free rider problem (see Sect. 20.7.2).

It is already at the first stage that three kinds of uncertainty might hamper the very beginning of the coordination process. These are (Frankel, 1988):

(a) uncertainty about the initial position of the economy with respect to the ideal values (we all know that macroeconomic data are often revised by substantial amounts). In terms of our optimum equations, the initial values y, x, π are not known with certainty (the same holds, of course, for the rest of the world): the policy maker does not know where it stands exactly.
(b) uncertainty about the correct weights to be put on the various possible target variables. Different values of the w's might give rise to different results.
(c) uncertainty about the effects of a policy change (domestic or foreign) on the relevant variables (both domestic and foreign). This is the most serious kind of uncertainty, because it means that policy makers do not know the policy multipliers. Hence what should they ask the other countries for, and what should they give up in turn?

Disagreement over the "true" model is clearly one of the main reasons for type (c) uncertainty (see Sect. 20.7.2).

These three types of uncertainty are also present in domestic policy-making, but at the international level they are more severe, due to the international spillover effects ($\partial y/\partial m^*$, $\partial y^*/\partial m$, etc.). These are essential for the determination of the cooperative optimum, and are much more difficult to determine than the domestic effects of domestic policies. This difficulty is further aggravated by disagreement over the "true" model, especially when models embodying different visions of the functioning of an economy yield different results already at the qualitative level (i.e. at the level of the signs of the policy multipliers).

A.20.6 Target Zones

The target zone proposal has given rise to a burgeoning theoretical literature, aimed at evaluating the credibility of a target zone. This literature – for an exhaustive survey see De Arcangelis (1994) – is very interesting but does not give any practical indication on how the central rate or FEER should be calculated – which, after all, is what the target zone proposal is all about. Such calculations (Williamson and Miller, 1987; Williamson, 1993) can be performed using macroeconometric models, in which targets and instruments are clearly specified. Suppose, for example, that the targets are the level of output (y) and the balance of payments (B), and that the policy instruments are fiscal (G) and monetary (M) policy. The model endogenously determines y, B, as well as the exchange rate, r (on exchange-rate determination in macroeconometric models see Sect. 18.5.4). The reduced form of the model allows to express the endogenous variables in terms of the policy instruments, namely

$$y = f(G, M, \mathbf{Z}_1),$$
$$B = h(G, M, \mathbf{Z}_2), \qquad (A.20.65)$$
$$r = g(G, M, \mathbf{Z}_3),$$

where $\mathbf{Z}_i$, $i = 1, 2, 3$ are vectors (not necessarily distinct) of other exogenous variables. From the first and second equation, given the targets y^*, B^*, and assuming that the conditions on the Jacobian are satisfied, we can express G and M in terms of the targets, namely

$$G^* = G(y^*, B^*, \mathbf{Z}_1, \mathbf{Z}_2),$$
$$M^* = M(y^*, B^*, \mathbf{Z}_1, \mathbf{Z}_2). \qquad (A.20.66)$$

If we now substitute these values in the third equation, we get

$$r^* = g(G^*, M^*, \mathbf{Z}_3) = g(y^*, B^*, \mathbf{Z}_1, \mathbf{Z}_2, \mathbf{Z}_3) \qquad (A.20.67)$$

which is the expression of the FEER in terms of the targets and the set of exogenous variables of the model. This approach, which is based on the traditional Meade-Tinbergen target-instrument approach, can give rise to problems when the number of targets and (independent) instruments are unequal. Hence an optimal control approach is preferable.

In general, given a loss function of the policy maker (it is usually expressed in terms of the deviations of the actual paths of the variables from some desired path), the optimal control problem can be formulated as

$$\min_{\{\mathbf{u}(t)\}} J = -\int_{t_0}^{t_1} I(\mathbf{x}, \mathbf{u}, t) dt$$
$$\text{sub } \dot{\mathbf{x}} = \mathbf{f}(\mathbf{x}, \mathbf{u}, t),$$
$$\mathbf{x}(t_0) = \mathbf{x}_0, \qquad (A.20.68)$$
$$\mathbf{x}(t_1) = \mathbf{x}_1,$$

where I is the loss function, $\mathbf{x}$ the vector of endogenous variables, $\mathbf{u} \in U$ the vector of control variables belonging to a set U, t time (including other exogenous variables), and $\dot{\mathbf{x}} = \mathbf{f}(\mathbf{x}, \mathbf{u}, t)$ is the dynamic econometric model of the economy, whose initial and terminal states are $\mathbf{x}_0$ and $\mathbf{x}_1$. The specification of the econometric model as a set of differential equations is not just for mathematical convenience, since continuous time econometric models can actually be estimated (see Sect. 18.6.3 and A.20.4). Note that, if the model is not already a first-order system in normal form (because in the specification there are higher-order time derivatives and in some equations the time derivatives also appear on the right hand side), it will have to be reduced to this form. This can be done by well-known mathematical methods (see, for example, Gandolfo, 1980, pp. 402–403).

The solution to this standard optimal control problem can be obtained through Pontryagin's maximum principle, which implies defining the Hamiltonian

$$H(\lambda, \mathbf{x}, \mathbf{u}, t) = I(\mathbf{x}, \mathbf{u}, t) + \lambda \mathbf{f}(\mathbf{x}, \mathbf{u}, t), \qquad (A.20.69)$$

where λ is a vector of costate variables. One then applies the following conditions

$$\begin{aligned} &\max_{\{\mathbf{u} \in U\}} H \quad t_0 \le t \le t_1, \\ &\dot{\mathbf{x}} = \partial H / \partial \lambda, \quad \mathbf{x}(t_0) = \mathbf{x}_0, \\ &\dot{\lambda} = -\partial H / \partial \mathbf{x}, \quad \lambda(t_1) = \mathbf{0}. \end{aligned} \qquad (A.20.70)$$

Note that the equations of motion for the state variables are the model, since $\partial H / \partial \lambda = \mathbf{f}(\mathbf{x}, \mathbf{u}, t)$.

For our purposes, let us suppose that the exchange rate is a control variable. This of course is not true, but what we are doing is to carry out an exercise to determine the optimal path of the exchange rate. This exercise is relevant for two reasons.

First, it can serve as a rational starting point for the determination of the central rate of the target zone. Instead of using the fixed target approach implicit in the Meade-Tinbergen method, the optimizing method allows for flexibility in the targets, which appear in the loss function with their appropriate weight reflecting the policy maker's preferences. Hence the optimal path of the exchange rate contains all the relevant information to constitute a guideline for the monetary authorities in their management of the actual exchange rate.

Second, if all countries participating in the target zone agreement perform the excercise (each using its preferred econometric model and its own welfare function – no need to impose a common model and a common welfare function!), it will be easy to determine the consistency of the cross rates emerging from the exercise. Consequently, it will be easy to determine the necessary adjustments so as to establish a mutually consistent set of 'optimal' exchange rates as the basis for the target zone. The use by each national authority of its preferred econometric model and its own welfare function avoids all the problems – already mentioned in Sect. 20.7.2 – due to the lack of agreement on the reference model. Hence the use of multicountry models – unless accepted by all countries – is not advisable in this context.

References

Alessandrini, S., 1975
Argy, V., 1981
Batten, S.D., 1982
Bell, G., 1973
Ben-Bassat, A., 1980
Ben-Bassat, A., 1984
Ben-Bassat, A. and Gottlieb D., 1992a, 1992b
Blake, D., M. Beenstock and V. Brasse, 1986
Blommestein, H.J. (ed.), 1991
Branson, W.H., Frenkel, J.A. and M. Goldstein (eds.), 1990
Buiter, W.H. and R.C. Marston, 1985
Carraro, C., Laussel, D., Salmon, M. and A. Sonbeyran (eds.), 1991
Chrystal, K.A., 1977
Claassen, E.M., 1976
Clark, P.B., 1970
Cohen, B.J., 1975
Cooper, R.N., 1989
Cox, D.R. and H.D. Miller, 1980
Crockett, A.D., 1976
Cutilli, B. and G. Gandolfo, 1963, 1972, 1973
De Arcangelis, G., 1994
De Grauwe, P., 1989
de Macedo, J.B., 1982
Dooley, M.P., J.S. Lizondo and D.J. Mathieson, 1989
Dornbusch, R., 1988
Dufey, G. and I.H. Giddy, 1978
Edison, H.J., Miller, M.H. and J. Williamson, 1987
Falchi, G. and R.S. Masera, 1982
Federal Reserve Bank of Boston, 1984
Feldstein, M. (ed.), 1988
Flanders, M.J., 1971
Frankel, J.A., 1988a, b
Frankel, J.A. and M. Goldstein, 1986
Freedman, C., 1977
Frenkel, J.A., 1983
Frenkel, J.A. and B. Jovanovic, 1981
Gandolfo, G., 1980, Part III, Chap. 1, Sect. 2
Gandolfo, G. and P.C. Padoan, 1988, 1990, 1992
Ghosh, A.R. and P.R. Masson, 1991
Gibson, H.D., 1989
Giustiniani, A., 1985
Goodman, S.H., 1979
Grubel, H.G., 1969
Grubel, H.G., 1971
Grubel, H.G., 1984
Guttentag, J. and R. Herring, 1983
Hageman, H.A., 1969
Hamada, K., 1974, 1985
Hamada, K. and K. Ueda, 1977
Heller, H.R., 1966
Heller, H.R. and M.S. Khan, 1978
Heller, H.R. and M. Knight, 1978
Henderson, D.W. and D.G. Waldo, 1983
Herring, R.J. and R.C. Marston, 1977
Hewson, J. and E. Sakakibara, 1974
Hewson, J. and E. Sakakibara, 1976
Hipple, F.S., 1974
Hogan, W.P., 1986
Hogan, W.P. and I.F. Pearce, 1982
Holden, P. and M. Holden, 1979
Hughes Hallet, A. and H. Rees, 1983
Intriligator, M.D., 1971, Chaps. 11 and 14
Ito, T., 1990
Johnston, R.B., 1981
Johnston, R.B., 1983
Kelly, M.G., 1970
Kenen, P., 1963
Kenen, P., F. Papadia and F. Saccomanni (eds.), 1994
Klopstock, F.H., 1968
Knight, M.D., 1977
Kreinin, M.E. and H.R. Heller, 1973
Krugman, P., 1984
Krugman, P., 1993
Landell-Mills, J.M., 1989
Lee, B., 1973
Levich, R.M., 1980
Machlup, F., 1964b
Machlup, F., 1966
Machlup, F., 1970a
Machlup, F., 1972
Marston, R.C., 1985
Martinez Oliva, J.C., 1991
Masera, R., 1981
Mayer, H., 1979
Mayer, H., 1985
McKinnon, R.I., 1977
McKinnon, R.I., 1979
McKinnon, R.I., 1988
Meier, G.M., 1982
Niehans, J., 1978
Niehans, J., 1984, Chap. 9
Niehans, J. and J. Hewson, 1976
Nyberg, L. and S. Viotti, 1976
Pilbeam, K., 1992
Polak, J.J., 1994
Purvis, D.D., 1983
Quadrio Curzio, A. (ed.), 1982
Roger, S., 1993
Scammell, W.M., 1987
Sellekaerts, W. and B. Sellekaerts, 1973
Solomon, R., 1982
Svensson, L.E.O., 1992
Swoboda, A.K., 1968
Swoboda, A.K., 1978
Swoboda, A.K., 1980
Takagi, S., 1991
Tew, B., 1988
Tobin, J., 1963
Tobin, J., 1978, 1994
Triffin, R., 1960
Triffin, R., 1968
Various Authors, 1973
von Furstenberg, G.M., 1982
Wijkman, P.M., 1981
Williamson, J.H., 1971
Williamson, J., 1973a
Williamson, J., 1985, 1993

21 The Problem of Integration Between the Pure Theory of International Trade and International Monetary Economics

21.1 Introduction

In international economics it is customary to distinguish between the *pure theory of international trade* and *international monetary theory* (see Sects. 1.1 and 10.1). The former (which has an essentially microeconomic nature) deals with international trade on the assumption that trade takes place in the form of barter, whilst the latter (which is essentially of a macroeconomic nature) deals with the problems deriving from balance-of-payments disequilibria in a monetary economy, etc., (for details see Sects. 1.1 and 11.4). It is also customary to treat these two branches of international economics separately, and we have not departed from standard practice. But one may wonder whether a more general theory exists, which integrates pure and monetary theory. On the problem of this integration it is possible to advance two preliminary considerations:

(a) the integration must be attempted by taking into account the theoretical framework into which one places the problem;

(b) the integration can be understood, and attempted, at two levels of increasing generality. At the first level money is considered solely as a medium of exchange. To put it differently, money is only a veil having no influence on the underlying real variables but serving only as a reference unit. At the second level, money (possibly together with other financial assets) has an influence of its own on the real part of the system, so that, for the determination of the (equilibrium) values of the real variables, it is no longer irrelevant whether money is present or the economy operates under barter: the model does not dichotomize.

The significance of the problem is so great that it goes beyond the realm of international economics and concerns the whole of economic theory, so that an adequate treatment would require a book of its own. Thus we shall only make some brief general considerations and refer the reader to the relevant literature.

In the frame of reference of the classical theory of international trade the integration should be understood at the first level. As a matter of fact, it is commonly agreed that, for the classical writers, money was indeed a veil, whose presence did not alter the results obtained in the barter theory of international trade. For this purpose it is sufficient to recall what David Ricardo (the founder of the classical theory of comparative costs) and John Stuart Mill (who introduced the concept of international supply and demand or reciprocal demand) had to say on this subject.

Ricardo (1817; p. 137 of the 1951 reprint) writes: "Gold and silver having been chosen for the general medium of circulation, they are, by the competition of commerce, distributed in such proportions amongst the different countries of the world, as to accomodate themselves to the natural traffic which would take place if no such metals existed, and the trade between countries were purely a trade of barter".

Similarly, J. S. Mill holds that the introduction of money does not alter the results found under the assumption of barter trade, and concludes: "The result of the preceding discussion cannot be better summed up than in the words of Ricardo [Ricardo's passage given above is then quoted]" (Mill, 1848; p. 625 of the 1961 reprint).

It would be possible to show formally how the integration (at the first level, as we have said) can be carried out provided that certain simplifying assumptions are adopted so that an unequivocal monetary "dress" can be given to the pure-theory "body". The latter is that described in Chap. 2; the monetary aspect (i.e. the balance-of-payments adjustment mechanism) is basically the Humean price-specie-flow mechanism (accepted by Ricardo and, in general, by most classical writers) described in Sect. 15.2. The reader who so wishes can consult, for example, Gandolfo (1966).

In the framework of the neoclassical model of international trade (to which the Heckscher-Ohlin theory also belongs), the integration becomes much more complex; for details of the various attempts so far (implicitly or explicitly) suggested we refer the reader to the literature (see, e.g., Kemp, 1964, Chaps. 16 and 19; Cutilli, 1967, essay I; Vicarelli, 1972; Takayama, 1972, Chap. 9; Negishi, 1972, Part 6; Prachowny, 1975; Allen and Kenen, 1980; Gale, 1983, Chap. 6). We simply point out here that, among other things, these attempts use the wealth effect already adopted in the attempts at integrating real and monetary phenomena in a closed economy (see, for example, Patinkin, 1965).

The debate on whether these attempts are to be considered adequate is by no means over, nor is the debate on the role of money in general equilibrium models of both the microeconomic and the macroeconomic type, and on the relationship between these. At this point the problem involves still more general and deeper questions, which we can only mention in passing.

21.2 An Epistemological Problem

The problem from which we started in fact goes right to the very roots of macroeconomics — whether referring to a closed economy or an open economy — that is, the debate on the *microeconomic foundations of macroeconomics* (see, e.g., Weintraub, 1977, 1979; Harcourt, 1977; Sinclair, 1983; Fitoussi, 1983; Perry, 1984; Janssen, 1991; Mayer, 1993).

Does a macroeconomic theory exist as an autonomous discipline, or — in order to give rigour and significance to the study of macroeconomic variables — is it necessary to start from the study of the single underlying microeconomic units, and then derive the behaviour of the macro variables by aggregation? It is self-evident that, if the latter thesis is accepted, macroeconomics (in the broad sense, i.e. including also monetary economics, both internal and international), as is usually practised, has no rigour, for it is based on somewhat vague, doubtful, and questionable extensions to the macroeconomic variables of "behaviours" peculiar to microeconomic agents. In support of the former thesis it has been observed that the whole is more than the sum of its parts and that, in any case, the macroeconomic variables can have a "behaviour" peculiar to themselves, not necessarily derivable from the study of the behaviour of the individual underlying units.

This is a problem which in its turn goes far beyond the realm of economics to enter into that of epistemology in general. The problem of the description of collective behaviour independently of, and with entirely new concepts compared to, the microscopic description of the single particles (atoms, electrons, protons, and so on towards more and more elementary particles) is, in fact, on the agenda of the so-called "hard" sciences (physics, chemistry, etc.). The study of those collective phenomena of *self-organization* — i.e., of those phenomena in which the macroscopic variable behaves as if the single microscopic units acted together by some kind of tacit mutual understanding — is the subject, amongst others, of *synergetics* (Haken, 1978, 1983). This approach, though discussed mainly in physics, chemistry, and biology, seems to offer fruitful insights also for economists (see, for example, the remarks in Gandolfo and Padoan, 1984). But here we must call a halt, so as not to stray too far from the subject of this book, and refer the reader to the relevant literature.

References

Allen, P.R. and P.B. Kenen, 1980, Parts I and II
Cutilli, B., 1967, Saggio I
Fitoussi, J.P., 1983
Gale, D., 1983
Gandolfo, G., 1966
Gandolfo, G. and P.C. Padoan, 1984
Haken, H., 1978
Haken, H., 1983
Harcourt, G.C. (ed.), 1977
Janssen, M.C.W., 1991
Kemp, M.C., 1964, Chaps. 16 and 19

Mayer, T., 1993
Mill, J.S., 1848
Negishi, T., 1972, Part 6
Patinkin, D., 1965
Perry, G.L., 1984
Prachowny, M.F.J., 1975, Chaps. 1−3
Ricardo, D., 1817
Sinclair, P.J.N., 1983
Takayama, A., 1972, Chap. 9
Vicarelli, F., 1972
Weintraub, E.R., 1977
Weintraub, E.R., 1979

Bibliography

Adams, C. and J. Greenwood, 1985, Dual Exchange Rate Systems and Capital Controls: An Investigation, Journal of International Economics **18**, 43–64

Advisory Committee on the Presentation of Balance of Payments Statistics, 1976, Report, Survey of Current Business **56**, June, 18–27

Ahmad, J., 1984, Floating Exchange Rates and World Inflation, London, Macmillan

Ahtiala, P., 1984, A Synthesis of the Macroeconomic Approaches to Exchange Rate Determination, European Economic Review **24**, 117–136

Aizenmann, J., 1984, Modelling Deviation from Purchasing Power Parity (PPP), International Economic Review **25**, 175–191

Alessandrini, S., 1975, Financing Policies and the Demand for International Reserves, Ricerche Economiche, No. 3–4, 370–395

Alexander, S.S., 1952, Effects of a Devaluation on a Trade Balance, International Monetary Fund Staff Papers **2**, 263–278; reprinted in: R.E. Caves and H.G. Johnson (eds.), 1968, 359–373

Alexander, S.S., 1959, Effects of a Devaluation: A Simplified Synthesis of Elasticities and Absorption Approaches, American Economic Review **49**, 22–42

Alexander, D. and L.R. Thomas, 1987, Monetary/Asset Models of Exchange Rate Determination: How Well Have they Performed in the 1980s? International Journal of Forecasting **3**, 53-64

Aliber, R.Z. (ed.), 1969, The International Market for Foreign Exchange, New York, Praeger.

Allen, P.R. and P.B. Kenen, 1980, Asset Markets, Exchange Rates, and Economic Integration: A Synthesis, Cambridge University Press

Angell, J.W., 1926, The Theory of International Prices, Harvard University Press

Aoki, M., 1981, Dynamic Analysis of Open Economies, New York, Academic Press

Argy, V., 1981, The Postwar International Money Crisis: An Analysis, London, Allen & Unwin

Argy, V., 1982, Exchange-Rate Management in Theory and Practice, Princeton Studies in International Finance No. 50, International Finance Section, Princeton University

Argy, V. and K.W. Clements, 1982, The Forward Rate as a Predictor of the Spot Rate: An Analysis of Four Major Currencies, Economies et Sociétés **16**, 569–596

Argy, V. and M.G. Porter, 1972, The Forward Exchange Market and Effects of Domestic and External Disturbances under Alternative Exchange Rate Systems, IMF Staff Papers **19**, 503–532

Arndt, S.W., R.J. Sweeney and T.D. Willet (eds.), 1985, Exchange Rates, Trade & the U.S. Economy, Cambridge (Mass.), Ballinger

Artus, J.R. and J.H. Young, 1979, Fixed and Flexible Exchange Rates: A Renewal of the Debate, IMF Staff Papers **26**, 654-698

Artus, P. and C. Dupuy, 1992, Can There Be a "New EMS"?, Journal of International and Comparative Economics **1**, 199-229

Asheim, G.B., 1984, Properties of a System of Currency Baskets, Journal of International Economics **16**, 311–318

Backus, D., 1984, Empirical Models of the Exchange Rate: Separating the Wheat from the Chaff, Canadian Journal of Economics **17**, 824–846

Bailey, R.W., R.T. Baillie and P.C. McMahon, 1984, Interpreting Econometric Evidence of Efficiency in the Foreign Exchange Market, Oxford Economic Papers **36**, 67–85

Baillie, R.T. and P.T. McMahon, 1989, The Foreign Exchange Market: Theory and Econometric Evidence, Cambridge (UK), Cambridge University Press

Bain, A.D., 1973, Surveys in Applied Economics: Flow of Funds Analysis, Economic Journal **83**, 1055–1094

Balogh, T. and P.P. Streeten, 1951, The Inappropriateness of Simple Elasticity Concepts in the Analysis of International Trade, Bulletin of the Oxford Institute of Statistics **12**, 65–77

Basevi, G. and P. De Grauwe, 1977, Vicious and Virtuous Circles: A Theoretical Analysis and a Policy Proposal for Managing Exchange Rates, European Economic Review **10**, 277–301

Basevi, G. and P. De Grauwe, 1978, Vicious and Virtuous Circles and the Optica Proposal: A Two-Country Analysis, in: M. Fratianni and T. Peeters (eds.), 144–157

Batchelor, R.A. and G.E. Wood (eds.), 1982, Exchange Rate Policy, London, Macmillan

Batten, S.D., 1982, Central Banks Demand for Foreign Reserves under Fixed and Floating Exchange Rates, Federal Reserve Bank of St. Louis Review **64**, 20–30

Bean, C., 1992, Economic and Monetary Union in Europe, Journal of Economic Perspectives **6**, 31-52

Beckerman, W.H., 1962, Projecting Europe's Growth, Economic Journal **72**, 912-925

Begg, D. et al., 1991, European Monetary Union – The Macro Issues, London, CEPR

Behnke, E.-A., 1980, International Transmission of Business Cycles – The Sohmen-Laursen-Metzler Effect, in: J.S. Chipman and C.P. Kindleberger (eds.), 257–267

Bell, G., 1973, The Euro-Dollar Market and the International Financial System, London, Macmillan

Ben-Bassat, A., 1980, The Optimal Composition of Foreign Exchange Reserves, Journal of International Economics **10**, 285–295

Ben-Bassat, A., 1984, Reserve-Currency Diversification and the Substitution Account, Princeton Studies in International Finance No. 53, International Finance Section, Princeton University

Ben-Bassat, A. and D. Gottlieb, 1992a, On the Effects of Opportunity Cost on International Reserve Holdings, Review of Economics and Statistics **74**, 329-332

Ben-Bassat, A. and D. Gottlieb, 1992b, Optimal International Reserves and Sovereign Risk, Journal of International Economics **33**, 345-362

Bergsten, C.F. et al. (eds.), 1970, Approaches to Greater Flexibility of Exchange Rates: The Bürgenstock Papers, Princeton University Press

Bernholz, P., M. Gäartner and E.W. Heri, 1985, Historical Experiences with Flexible Exchange Rates: A Simulation of Common Qualitative Characteristics, Journal of International Economics **19**, 21–45

Bernstein Report, see Review Committee etc.

Bhagwati, J.N. and H.G. Johnson, 1960, Notes on Some Controversies in the Theory of International Trade, Economic Journal **70**, 74–93; reprinted in: J. Bhagwati, 1983, International Factor Mobility – Essays in International Economic Theory, Vol. 2 (R.C. Feenstra ed.), Cambridge (Mass.), MIT Press, 433–452

Bhagwati, J.N. and H.G. Johnson, 1961, Notes on Some Controversies in the Theory of International Trade: Rejoinder, Economic Journal **71**, 427–430

Bhandari, J.S., 1982, Exchange Rate Determination and Adjustment, New York, Praeger

Bhandari, J.S., 1984, Speculation and the Crawling Peg: Some Further Issues, Zeitschrift für die gesamte Staatswissenschaft **140**, 528–536

Bhandari, J.S. (ed.), 1985, Exchange Rate Management under Uncertainty, Cambridge (Mass.), MIT Press

Bhandari, J.S. and B.H. Putnam (eds.), 1983, Economic Interdependence and Flexible Exchange Rates, Cambridge (Mass.), MIT Press

Bickerdicke, C.F., 1920, The Instability of Foreign Exchange, Economic Journal **30**, 118–122

Bigman, D., 1983, Exchange Rate Determination: Some Old Myths and New Paradigms, in: D. Bigman and T. Taya (eds.), 1983, 73–102

Bigman, D. and T. Taya (eds.), 1980, The Functioning of Floating Exchange Rates: Theory, Evidence, and Policy Implications, Cambridge (Mass.), Ballinger

Bigman, D. and T. Taya (eds.), 1983, Exchange Rate and Trade Instability: Causes, Consequences, and Remedies, Cambridge (Mass.), Ballinger

Bilson, J.F.O., 1978, The Current Experience with Floating Exchange Rates: An Appraisal of the Monetary Approach, American Economic Review **68**, Papers and Proceedings, 392-397

Bilson, J.F.O., 1979a, The Vicious Circle Hypothesis, IMF Staff Papers **26**, 1-37

Bilson, J.F.O., 1979b, Recent Developments in Monetary Models of Exchange Rate Determination, IMF Staff Papers **26**, 201–223

Bilson, J.F.O. and R.C. Marston (eds.), 1984, Exchange Rate Theory and Practice, University of Chicago Press

Bini Smaghi, L., 1990, Progressing towards European Monetary Unification: Selected Issues and Proposals, Roma, Banca d'Italia, Temi di Discussione del Servizio Studi No. 133

Bini Smaghi, L. and S. Vori, 1993, Rating the EC as an Optimal Currency Area, Roma, Banca d'Italia, Temi di Discussione del Servizio Studi No. 187

Black, J., 1957, A Geometrical Analysis of Foreign Trade Multiplier, Economic Journal **67**, 240–243

Black, S.W., 1973, International Money Markets and Flexible Rates, Studies in International Finance No. 32, International Finance Section, Princeton University

Blake, D., M. Beenstock and V. Brasse, The Performance of UK Exchange Rate Forecasters, Economic Journal **96**, 986–999

Blaug, M., 1980, The Methodology of Economics, Cambridge (UK), Cambridge University Press

Blommestein, H.J. (ed.), 1991, The Reality of International Economic Policy Coordination, Amsterdam, North-Holland

Blundell-Wignall, A., 1984, Exchange Rate Modelling and the Role of Asset Supplies: The Case of the Deutschemark Effective Rate 1973 to 1981, Manchester School **52**, 14–27

Bond, M.E., 1980, Exchange Rates, Inflation, and Vicious Circles, IMF Staff Papers **37**, 679–711

Bordo, M.D. and B. Eichengreen (eds.), 1993, A Retrospective on the Bretton Woods System, Chicago, Chigaco University Press

Branson, W.H., 1974, Stocks and Flows in International Monetary Analysis, in: A. Ando, R. Herring and R. Marston (eds.), International Aspects of Stabilization Policies, Federal Reserve Bank of Boston, Conference Series No. 12, 27–50

Branson, W.H., 1976, Portfolio Equilibrium and Monetary Policy with Foreign and Non-Traded Assets, in: E. Claassen and P. Salin (eds.), 240–249

Branson, W.H., 1977, Asset Markets and Relative Prices in Exchange Rate Determination, Sozialwissenschaftliche Annalen des Instituts für höhere Studien **1**, 69–89; reprinted as Reprint in International Finance No. 20, International Finance Section, Princeton University

Branson, W.H., 1979, Exchange Rate Dynamics and Monetary Policy, in: A Lindbeck (ed.), 189–224

Branson, W.H., 1984, Exchange Rate Policy after a Decade of "Floating", in: J.F.O. Bilson and R.C. Marston (eds.), 79–117

Branson, W.H. and W.H. Buiter, 1983, Monetary and Fiscal Policy and Flexible Exchange Rates, in: J.S. Bhandari and B.H. Putnam (eds.), Chap. 9

Branson, W.H. and D.W. Henderson, 1985, The Specification and Influence of Asset Markets, in: R.W. Jones and P.B. Kenen (eds.), Chap. 15

Branson, W.H., J.A. Frenkel and M. Goldstein (eds.), 1990, International Policy Coordination and Exchange Rate Fluctuations, Chicago, University of Chicago Press

Britton, A.J.C., 1970, The Dynamic Stability of the Foreign-Exchange Market, Economic Journal **80**, 91–96

Brown, B., 1983, The Forward Market in Foreign Exchange, London, Croom Helm

Bruce, N. and D. Purvis, 1985, The Specification of Goods and Factor Markets in Open Economy Macroeconomic Models, in: R.W. Jones and P.B. Kenen (eds.), Chap. 16

Brunner, K. and A.H. Meltzer, 1976, Monetary and Fiscal Policy in Open, Interdependent Economies with Fixed Exchange Rates, in: E. Claassen and P. Salin (eds.), 327–359

Buckley, P.J. and M. Casson, 1985, The Economic Theory of the Multinational Enterprise, London, Macmillan

Buiter, W.H. and R.C. Marston (eds.), 1985, International Economic Policy Coordination, Cambridge University Press

Buiter, W., G. Corsetti and N. Roubini, 1993, Excessive Deficits: Sense and Nonsense in the Treaty of Maastricht, Economic Policy **16**, 57–100

Burmeister, E. and A.R. Dobell, 1970, Mathematical Theories of Economic Growth, New York, Macmillan

Calvo, G.A. and C.A. Rodriguez, 1977, A Model of Exchange Rate Determination under Currency Substitution and Rational Expectations, Journal of Political Economy **85**, 617–625

Canto, V.A. and M.A. Miles, 1983, Exchange Rates in a Global Monetary Model with Currency Substitution and Rational Expectations, in: J.S. Bhandari and B.H. Putnam (eds.), 158–175

Canzoneri, M.B., V. Grilli and P.R. Masson, 1992, Establishing a Central Bank: Issues in Europe and Lessons from the US, Cambridge (UK), Cambridge University Press

Carraro, C., D. Laussel, M. Salmon and A. Soubeyran (eds.), 1991, International Policy Coordination, Oxford, Blackwell

Casella, A., 1992, Participation in a Currency Union, American Economic Review **82**, 847–863

Casprini, F., 1973, Politica fiscale e monetaria in un'economia aperta, Note Economiche **6**, 96–124

Casprini, F., 1974, Cambi flessibili, speculazione e politiche di stabilizzazione: un modello integrato, Note Economiche **7**, No.5

Casprini, F., 1976, Interventi sul mercato a termine e tassi di cambio flessibili, Rivista di Politica Economica **56**, 602–616

Casprini, F., 1977, Sugli effetti perversi della svalutazione: una analisi di disequilibrio, Giornale degli Economisti e Annali di Economia **36**, 169–185

Casprini, F., 1984, L'efficienza del mercato dei cambi. Analisi teorica e verifica empirica, Siena, Facolta' di Scienze Economiche e Bancarie, Quaderni dell'Istituto di Economia, n. 22

Cassel, G., 1918, Abnormal Deviations in International Exchanges, Economic Journal **28**, 413–415

Caves, R., 1970, Export-Led Growth: The Post-War Industrial Setting, in: W.A. Eltis, M.FG. Scott and J.N. Wolfe (eds.), Induction, Growth and Trade: Essays in Honour of Sir Roy Harrod, Oxford University Press, 234–255

Caves, R.E., 1982, Multinational Enterprise and Economic Analysis, Cambridge University Press

Caves, R.E. and H.G. Johnson (eds.), 1968, Readings in International Economics, London, Allen & Unwin

Chacholiades, M., 1971, The Sufficiency of Three-Point Arbitrage to Insure Consistent Cross Rates of Exchange, Southern Economic Journal **38**, 86–88

Chacholiades, M., 1978, International Monetary Theory and Policy, New York, McGraw-Hill

Chen, C.-N., 1975, Economic Growth, Portfolio Balance, and the Balance of Payments, Canadian Journal of Economics **8**, 24–33

Chipman, J.S., 1974, The Transfer Problem Once Again, in: G. Horwich and P.A. Samuelson (eds.), 19–78

Chipman, J.S., 1978, A Reconsideration of the "Elasticity Approach" to Balance-of-Payments Adjustment Problems, in: J.S. Dreyer (ed.), Breadth and Depth in Economics: Fritz Machlup – The Man and His Ideas, Lexington (Mass.), D.C. Heath, 49–85

Chipman, J.S. and C.P. Kindleberger (eds.), 1980, Flexible Exchange Rates and The Balance of Payments – Essays in Memory of Egon Sohmen, Amsterdam, North-Holland

Christ, C.F., 1979, On Fiscal and Monetary Policies and the Government Budget Restraint, American Economic Review **69**, 526–538

Chrystal, K.A., 1977, Demand for International Media of Exchange, American Economic Review **67**, 840–850

Claassen, E.M., 1976, The Optimizing Approach to the Demand for International Reserves: A Survey, in: E. Claassen and P. Salin (eds.), 1976, 73–115

Claassen, E. and P. Salin (eds.), 1976, Recent Issues in International Monetary Economics, Amsterdam, North-Holland

Claassen, E. and P. Salin (eds.), 1983, Recent Issues in the Theory of Flexible Exchange Rates, Amsterdam, North-Holland

Clark, P.B., 1970, Optimum International Reserves and the Speed of Adjustment, Journal of Political Economy **78**, 356–376

Clement, M.O., R.L. Pfister and K.J. Rothwell, 1967, Theoretical Issues in International Economics, Boston, Houghton Mifflin

Clower, R.W. and D.W. Bushaw, 1954, Price Determination in a Stock-Flow Economy, Econometrica **22**, 328–343

Cohen, B., 1969, Balance-of-Payments Policy, Harmondsworth, Penguin

Cohen, B.J., 1975, International Reserves and Liquidity, in: P.B. Kenen (ed.), International Trade and Finance, Cambridge University Press, 411–451

Cohen, B.J., 1981, The European Monetary System: An Outsider's View, Essays in International Finance No. 142, International Finance Section, Princeton University

Commission of the European Communities, 1990, Economic and Monetary Union, Brussels, 21 August 1990
Conway, R.K., P.A.V.B. Swamy and J.F. Yanagida, 1983, The Impossibility of Causality Testing, Special Studies Paper No. 178, Division of Research and Statistics, Federal Reserve Board, Washington (D.C.)
Cooper, R.N., 1969, Macroeconomic Policy Adjustment in Interdependent Economies, Quarterly Journal of Economics **83**, 1 – 24
Cooper, R.N., 1985, Economic Interdependence and Coordination of Economic Policies, in: R.W. Jones and P.B. Kenen (eds.), Chap. 23
Cooper, R.N. (ed.), 1969, International Finance – Selected Readings, Harmondsworth, Penguin
Cooper, R.N. et al. (eds.), 1982, The International Monetary System under Flexible Exchange Rates: Global, Regional, and National – Essays in Honor of Robert Triffin, Cambridge (Mass.), Ballinger
Cooper, R.N., 1989, International Cooperation in Public Health as a Prologue to Macroeconomic Cooperation, in: R.N. Cooper et al. (eds.), Can Nations Agree? Issues in International Economic Cooperation, Washington (DC), Brookings Institution, Studies in International Economics Series, 178-254
Corden, W.M., 1972, Monetary Integration, Essays in International Finance No. 93, Princeton University, International Finance Section
Corden, W.M., 1983, The Logic of the International Monetary Non-System, in: F. Machlup, G. Fels and H. Müller-Groeling (eds.), Reflections on a Troubled World Economy, London, Macmillan, 59 – 74
Courant, R., 1962, Differential and Integral Calculus, Glasgow, Blackie & Sons, Vol. II
Cox, D.R. and H.D. Miller, 1980, The Theory of Stochastic Processes, London, Chapman and Hall
Crockett, A.D., 1976, The Euro-Currency Market: An Attempt to Clarify Some Basic Issues, IMF Staff Papers **23**, 375 – 386
Cuddington, J.T., 1983, Currency Substitution, Capital Mobility, and Money Demand, Journal of Money and Finance **2**, 111-133
Cuthbertson, K., 1979, Macroeconomic Policy, London, Macmillan
Cutilli, B., 1967, Saggi critici di economia inernazionale, Milano, Giuffré
Cutilli, B. and G. Gandolfo, 1963, The Role of Commercial Banks in Foreign Exchange Speculation, Banca Nazionale del Lavoro Quarterly Review, No. 65, 216 – 231
Cutilli, B. and G. Gandolfo, 1972, Wider Band and "Oscillating Exchange Rates", Economic Notes **1**, 111 – 124
Cutilli, B. and G. Gandolfo, 1973, Un contributo alla teoria della speculazione in regime di cambi oscillanti, Roma, Ente per gli studi monetari bancari e finanziari Luigi Einaudi, Quaderno di ricerche n. 10
Daniel, B.C., 1985, Monetary Autonomy and Exchange Rate Dynamics under Currency Substitution, Journal of International Economics **19**, 119 – 139
Deardoff, A.V. and R.M. Stern, 1978a, The Terms-of-Trade Effect on Expenditure: Some Evidence from Econometric Models, Journal of International Economics **8**, 409 – 414
Deardoff, A.V. and R.M. Stern, 1978b, Modelling the Effects of Foreign Prices on Domestic Price Determination: Some Econometric Evidence and Implications for Theoretical Analysis, Banca Nazionale del Lavoro Quarterly Review **31**, 333 – 353
Deardoff, A.V. and R.M. Stern, 1979, What Have we Learned from Linked Econometric Models? A Comparison of Fiscal-Policy Simulations, Banca Nazionale del Lavoro Quarterly Review **32**, 415 – 432
De Arcangelis, G., 1992, Time-Varying Parameters and Exchange Rate Forecasting, University of Rome "La Sapienza", CIDEI Working Paper No. 14
De Arcangelis, G., 1994, Exchange Rate Target Zone Modeling: Recent Theoretical and Empirical Contributions, Economic Notes **23**, 74-115
De Cecco, M., 1983, The Vicious/Virtuous Circle Debate in the Twenties and in the Seventies, Banca Nazionale del Lavoro Quarterly Review, No. 146, 285-303
De Cecco, M. (ed), 1983, International Economic Adjustment: Small Countries and the European Monetary System, Oxford, Blackwell

De Grauwe, P., 1983, Macroeconomic Theory for the Open Economy, Hampshire, Gower Publishing Co
De Grauwe, P., M. Fratianni and M.K. Nabli, 1985, Exchange Rates, Money and Output — The European Experience, London, Macmillan
De Grauwe, P., M. Janssens and H. Leliaert, 1985, Real-Exchange-Rate Variability from 1920 to 1926 and 1973 to 1982, Princeton Studies in International Finance No. 56, International Finance Section, Princeton University
De Grauwe, P. and T. Peeters (eds.), 1983, Exchange Rates in Multicountry Econometric Models, London, Macmillan
De Grauwe, P., 1989, International Money: Post-War Trends and Theories, Oxford, Clarendon Press
De Grauwe, P., 1992, The Economics of Monetary Integration, Oxford, Oxford University Press
De Grauwe, P. and L. Papademos (eds.), 1990, The European Monetary System in the 1990's, London, Longman
De Jong, E., 1991, Exchange Rate Determination and Optimal Economic Policy under Various Exchange Rate Regimes, Berlin Heidelberg, Springer-Verlag
Delors Report, 1989, Report on Economic and Monetary Union in the European Community, Brussels, 12 April 1989
De Macedo, J.B., 1982, Portfolio Diversification across Currencies, in: R.N. Cooper et al. (eds.), 69–100
Denton, G. (ed.), 1974, Economic and Monetary Union in Europe, London, Croom Helm
De Vries, T., 1980, On the Meaning and Future of the European Monetary System, Essays in International Finance No. 138, International Finance Section, Princeton University
Dickey, D.A. and W.A. Fuller, 1981, Likelihood Ratio Statistics for Autoregressive Time Series with a Unit Root, Econometrica **49**, 1057–1072
Dixon, R., 1983, On the New Cambridge School, Journal of Post Keynesian Economics **5**, 289–294
Dooley, M. and P. Isard, 1983, The Portfolio Model of Exchange Rates and Some Structural Estimates of the Risk Premium, IMF Staff Papers **30**, 683–702
Dooley, M.P. and J.R. Shafer, 1983, Analysis of Short-Run Exchange Rate Behaviour: March 1973 to November 1981, in: D. Bigman and T. Taya (eds.), 1983, 43–69
Dooley, M.P., J.S. Lizondo and D.J. Mathieson, 1989, The Currency Composition of Foreign Exchange Reserves, IMF Staff Papers **36**, 385–434
Dornbusch, R., 1975, Exchange Rates and Fiscal Policy in a Popular Model of International Trade, American Economic Review **65**, 859–871
Dornbusch, R., 1980, Open Economy Macroeconomics, New York, Basic Books Inc.
Dornbusch, R., 1983, Exchange Rate Economics: Where Do We Stand?, in: J.S. Bhandari and B.H. Putnam (eds.), 45–83
Dornbusch, R., 1988, Doubts About the McKinnon Standard, Journal of Economic Perspectives **2**, 105–112
Dornbusch, R. and P. Krugman, 1976, Flexible Exchange Rates in the Short Run, Brookings Papers on Economic Activity, No. 3, 537–575
Dornbusch, R. and S. Fischer, 1980, Exchange Rates and the Current Account, American Economic Review **70**, 960–976
Dornbusch, R. and J.A. Frenkel, 1984, The Gold Standard Crisis of 1847, Journal of International Economics **16**, 1–27
Dowd, K., 1989, The Case Against a European Central Bank, World Economy **12**, 361–372
Driskill, R. and S. McCafferty, 1980, Speculation, Rational Expectations, and Stability of the Foreign Exchange Market, Journal of International Economics **10**, 91–102
Dufey, G. and I.H. Giddy, 1978, The International Money Market, Englewood Cliffs (N.J.), Prentice-Hall
Dunn, R.M., 1983, The Many Disappointments of Flexible Exchange Rates, Essays in International Finance No. 154, International Finance Section, Priceton University
Eaton, J. and S.J. Turnovsky, 1984, The Forward Exchange Market, Speculation, and Exchange Market Intervention, Quarterly Journal of Economics **99**, 45–69
Edgeworth, F.Y., 1905, Review of H. Cunynghame's Book A Geometrical Political Economy, Economic Journal **15**, 62–71

Edison, H.J., M.H. Miller and J. Williamson, 1987, On Evaluating and Extending the Target Zone Proposal, Journal of Policy Modeling **9**, 199–227

Eichengreen, B., 1993, European Monetary Unification, Journal of Economic Literature **31**, 1321–1357

Einzig, P., 1961, The Dynamic Theory of Forward Exchange, London, Macmillan

Einzig, P., 1966, A Textbook on Foreign Exchange, 2nd ed., London, Macmillan

Ellis, H.S. and L.A. Metzler (eds.), 1949, Readings in the Theory of International Trade, Philadelphia, Blakiston

Emerson, M., D. Gros, A. Italianer, J. Pisani-Ferry, H. Reichenbach, 1992, One Market, One Money, Oxford, Oxford University Press

Engle, R.P. and C.W.P. Granger, 1987, Co-integration and Error Correction: Representation, Estimation and Testing, Econometrica **55**, 251–276

Falchi, G. and R.S. Masera, 1982, The Role of Gold in Central Banks' Reserve Composition, in: A. Quadrio Curzio (ed.), 245–262

Falchi, G. and M. Michelangeli, 1977, Interazione fra tasso di cambio e inflazione: una verifica empirica della tesi del circolo vizioso, in: Contributi alla ricerca economica, No. 7, Roma, Banca d'Italia, 51–74

Fama, E.F., 1970, Efficient Capital Markets: A Review of Theory and Empirical Work, Journal of Finance **22**, 383–417

Fama, E., 1976, Foundations of Finance, New York, Basic Books

Fama, E.F., 1984, Forward and Spot Exchange Rates, Journal of Monetary Economics **14**, 319–338

Farrell, V.S., D.A. DeRosa and T.A. McCown, 1983, Effects of Exchange Rate Variability on International Trade and Other Economic Variables: A Survey of the Literature, Board of Governors of the Federal Reserve System, Staff Studies No. 130, Washington (D.C.)

Federal Reserve Bank of Boston, 1978, Managed Exchange-Rate Flexibility: The Recent Experience, Conference Series No. 20, Boston

Federal Reserve Bank of Boston, 1984, The International Monetary System: Forty Years after Bretton Woods (Proceedings of a Conference Held at Bretton Woods, New Hampshire, May 1984), Conference Series No. 28, Boston

Feldstein, M.S., 1968, Uncertainty and Forward Exchange Speculation, Review of Economics and Statistics **50**, 182–192

Feldstein, M. (ed.), 1988, International Economic Cooperation, Chicago, University of Chicago Press

Fellner, W. et al., 1966, Maintaining and Restoring Balance in International Payments, Princeton University Press

Ferrara, L., 1984, Il moltiplicatore in mercato aperto nelle analisi dell'interdipendenza internazionale: teoria e evidenza empirica, unpublished "tesi di laurea", Facoltà di Economia e Commercio, Università di Roma

Fischer, S. and J.A. Frenkel, 1974, Economic Growth and Stages of the Balance of Payments: A Theoretical Model, in: G. Horwich and P.A. Samuelson (eds.), 503–521

Fitoussi, J.P., 1983, Modern Macroeconomic Theory: An Overview, in: J.P. Fitoussi (ed.), Modern Macroeconomic Theory, Oxford, Blackwell

Flanders, M.J., 1971, The Demand for International Reserves, Studies in International Finance No. 27, International Finance Section, Princeton University

Fleming, J.M., 1962, Domestic Financial Policy under Fixed and under Floating Exchange Rates, IMF Staff Papers **9**, 369–379. Reprinted in: R.N. Cooper (ed.), 1969, 291–303, and in: J.M. Fleming, 1971, 237–248

Fleming, J.M., 1971, Essays in International Economics, London, Allen & Unwin

Fleming, J.M. and R.A. Mundell, 1964, Official Intervention on the Forward Exchange Rate: A Simplified Analysis, IMF Staff Papers **11**, 1–17; reprinted in: J.M. Fleming, 1971, 249–267

Flood, R.P., 1978, Exchange Rate Expectations in Dual Exchange Markets, Journal of International Economics **8**, 65–77

Flood, R.P. and P.M. Garber, 1984, Collapsing Exchange-Rate Regimes: Some Linear Examples, Journal of International Economics **17**, 1–13

Floyd, J.E., 1985, World Monetary Equilibrium, Oxford, Philip Allan

Frankel, J.A., 1983, Monetary and Portfolio Models of Exchange Rate Determination, in: J.S. Bhandari and B.H. Putnam (eds.), 84–115

Frankel, J.A., 1984, Tests of Monetary and Portfolio Balance Models of Exchange Rate Determination, in: J.F.O. Bilson and R.C. Marston (eds.), 239–260

Frankel, J.A., 1988a, International Capital Mobility and Exchange Rate Volatility, in: N.S. Fieleke (ed.), International Payments Imbalances in the 1980, Boston, Federal Reserve Bank of Boston Conference Series No. 32, 162–188

Frankel, J.A., 1988b, Obstacles to International Macroeconomic Policy Coordination, Princeton Studies in International Finance No. 64, Princeton, Princeton University, International Finance Section

Fratianni, M. and T. Peeters (eds.), 1978, One Money for Europe, London, Macmillan

Fratianni, M., J. von Hagen and C. Waller, 1992, The Maastrich Way to EMU, Essays in International Finance No. 187, Princeton University, International Finance Section

Freedman, C., 1977, A Model of the Euro-Dollar Market, Journal of Monetary Economics **8**, 139–161

Frenkel, J.A., 1981, The Collapse of Purchasing Power Parities During the 1970's, European Economic Review **16**, 145–165

Frenkel, J.A., 1983, International Liquidity and Monetary Control, in: G.M. von Furstenberg (ed.), 65–109

Frenkel, J.A., T. Gylfason and J.F. Helliwell, 1980, A Synthesis of Monetary and Keynesian Approaches to Short-Run Balance-of-Payments Theory, Economic Journal **90**, 582–592

Frenkel, J.A. and B. Jovanovic, 1981, Optimal International Reserves: A Stochastic Framework, Economic Journal **91**, 507–514

Frenkel, J.A. and M.L. Mussa, 1980, The Efficiency of Foreign Exchange Markets and Measures of Turbulence, American Economic Review **70**, Papers and Proceedings, 374–381

Frenkel, J.A. and M.L. Mussa, 1985, Assets Markets, Exchange Rates, and the Balance of Payments, in: R.W. Jones and P.B. Kenen (eds.), Chap. 14

Frenkel, J.A. (ed.), 1983, Exchange Rates and International Macroeconomics, University of Chicago Press

Frenkel, J.A. and H.G. Johnson (eds.), 1976, The Monetary Approach to the Balance of Payments, London, Allen & Unwin

Frenkel, J.A. and H.G. Johnson (eds.), 1978, The Economics of Exchange Rates: Selected Studies, London, Addison-Wesley

Frenkel, J.A. and M. Goldstein, 1986, A Guide to Target Zones, IMF Staff Papers **33**, 633–673

Frenkel, J.A. and A. Razin, 1987, The Mundell-Fleming Model a Quarter Century Later, IMF Staff Papers **34**, 567–620

Frevert, P., 1967, A Theoretical Model of the Forward Exchange Rate: Part 1, International Economic Review **8**, 153–167, and Part 2, idem, 307–325

Friedman, M., 1953, The Case for Flexible Exchange Rates, in: M. Friedman, Essays in Positive Economics, University of Chicago Press, 157–203

Friedman, M., 1960, In Defence of Destabilizing Speculation, in: R.W.P. Pfouts (ed.), Essays in Economics and Econometrics, University of North Carolina Press, 133–141

Frydman, R. and M.D. Goldberg, 1993, Is There a Connection Between Exchange Rate Dynamics and Macroeconomic Fundamentals?, in: H. Frisch and A. Wörgötter (eds.), Open-Economy Macroeconomics, London, Macmillan

Fuller, W.A., 1976, Introduction to Statistical Time Series, New York, Wiley

Gale, D., 1983, Money: In Disequilibrium, Cambridge University Press

Gandolfo, G., 1966, La teoria classica del meccanismo di aggiustamento della bilancia dei pagamenti, Economia Internazionale **19**, 397–432

Gandolfo, G., 1970, Aggiustamento della bilancia dei pagamenti ed equilibrio macroeconomico, Milano, Franco Angeli

Gandolfo, G., 1971, Tentativi di analisi teorica in tema di cambi flessibili e speculazione, L'Industria, No. 1, 40–60

Gandolfo, G., 1974, Politica monetaria e fiscale in regime di cambi fissi: il "problema del coordinamento", Rassegna Economica **38**, 613–634

Gandolfo, G., 1975, Sulla trasmissione internazionale delle perturbazioni in vari regimi di cambi, Quaderni dell'Economia Sarda **5**, 103–110

Gandolfo, G., 1976, Il tasso di cambio di equilibrio: teoria ed evidenza empirica, Milano, ISEDI

Gandolfo, G., 1979, The Equilibrium Exchange Rate: Theory and Empirical Evidence, in: M. Sarnat and G.P. Szegö (eds.), International Finance and Trade, Cambridge (Mass.), Ballinger, Vol. I, 99–130

Gandolfo, G., 1980, Economic Dynamics: Methods and Models, Amsterdam, North-Holland

Gandolfo, G., 1981, Qualitative Analysis and Econometric Estimation of Continuous Time Dynamic Models, Amsterdam, North-Holland

Gandolfo, G. and P.C. Padoan, 1984, A Disequilibrium Model of Real and Financial Accumulation in an Open Economy: Theory, Evidence and Policy Simulations, Berlin Heidelberg New York Tokyo, Springer-Verlag

Gandolfo, G. and P.C. Padoan, 1988, Conseguenze della liberalizzazione dei movimenti di capitale: un'analisi sistemica, Note Economiche, No. 2, 5–27

Gandolfo, G. and P.C. Padoan, 1990, The Italian Continuous Time Model: Theory and Empirical Results, Economic Modelling **7**, 91–132

Gandolfo, G., P.C. Padoan and G. Paladino, 1990a, Structural Models vs Random Walk: The Case of the Lira/$ Exchange Rate, Eastern Economic Journal **16**, 101–113

Gandolfo, G., P.C. Padoan and G. Paladino, 1990b, Exchange Rate Determination: Single Equation or Structural Models? Journal of Banking and Finance **14**, 965–992

Gandolfo, G. and P.C. Padoan, 1992, Perfect Capital Mobility and the Italian Economy, in E. Baltensperger and H.-W. Sinn (eds.), Exchange Rate Regimes and Currency Unions, London, Macmillan, 26–61

Gandolfo, G., G. De Arcangelis and P.C. Padoan, 1993, The Theory of Exchange Rate Determination, and Exchange Rate Forecasting, in H. Frisch and A. Wörgötter (eds.), Open-Economy Macroeconomics, London, Macmillan, 332–352

Gantmacher, F.R., 1959, Applications of the Theory of Matrices, New York, Interscience (also as Vol. Two of F.R. Gantmacher, 1959, The Theory of Matrices, New York, Chelsea). Pages refer to the Interscience edition

Geweke, J., 1984, Inference and Causality in Economic Time Series Models, in: Z. Griliches and M.D. Intriligator (eds.), Handbook of Econometrics, Amsterdam, North-Holland, Vol. 2, 1101–1144

Giavazzi, F., S. Micossi and M. Miller (eds.), 1988, The European Monetary System, Cambridge, Cambridge University Press

Gibson, H.D., 1989, The Eurocurrency Market, Domestic Financial Policy and International Instability, London, Macmillan

Giustiniani, A., 1985, Domanda di riserve internazionali ed interventi sul mercato dei cambi: alcune considerazioni, Quaderni Sardi di Economia **15**, 3–22

Glahe, F.R., 1966, Professional and Non-Professional Speculation, Profitability and Stability, Southern Economic Journal **23**, 43–48

Godley, W. and F. Cripps, 1983, Macroeconomics, Oxford University Press

Goldstein, M., 1980, Have Flexible Exchange Rates Handicapped Macroeconomic Policy?, Special Papers in International Economics No. 14, International Finance Section, Princeton University

Goodman, S.H., 1979, Foreign Exchange Forecasting Techniques: Implications for Business and Policy, Journal of Finance **3**, 415–427

Goodwin, R.M., 1980, World Trade Multipliers, Journal of Post Keynesian Economics **2**, 319–344; reprinted in: R.M. Goodwin, 1983, Essays in Linear Economic Structure, London, Macmillan, 30–56

Gros, D. and N. Thygesen, 1992, European Monetary Integration: From the European Monetary System to European Monetary Union, London, Longman

Grubel, H.G., 1966, Forward Exchange, Speculation, and the International Flow of Capital, Stanford University Press

Grubel, H.G., 1968, International Diversified Portfolios: Welfare Gains and Capital Flows, American Economic Review **58**, 1299–1314

Grubel, H.G., 1969, The Distribution of Seignorage from International Liquidity Creation, in: R.A. Mundell and A.K. Swoboda (eds.), Monetary Problems of the International Economy, Chicago University Press, 269–282

Grubel, H.G., 1971, The Demand for International Reserves: A Critical Review of the Literature, Journal of Economic Literature **9**, 1148–1166

Grubel, H.G., 1977, International Economics, Homewood (Ill.), Irwin

Grubel, H.G., 1984, The International Monetary System, 4th ed., Harmondsworth, Penguin

Guttentag, J. and R. Herring, 1983, The Lender-of-Last Resort Function in an International Context, Essays in International Finance No. 151, International Finance Section, Princeton University

Gylfason, T. and J.F. Helliwell, 1983, A Synthesis of Keynesian, Monetary, and Portfolio Approaches to Flexible Exchange Rates, Economic Journal **93**, 820–831

Haberler, G., 1949, The Market for Foreign Exchange and the Stability of Balance of Payments: A Theoretical Analysis, Kyklos 3, 193–218; reprinted in: R.N. Cooper (ed.), 1969, 107–134

Hageman, H.A., 1969, Reserve Policies of Central Banks and Their Implications for U.S. Balance of Payments Policy, American Economic Review **59**, 62–77

Hahn, F.H., 1977, The Monetary Approach to the Balance of Payments, Journal of International Economics **7**, 231–249; reprinted in: F. Hahn, 1984, Equilibrium and Macroeconomics, Oxford, Basil Blackwell, 237–258

Haken, H., 1978, Synergetics – An Introduction, Berlin Heidelberg New York Tokyo, Springer-Verlag (3rd ed., 1983)

Haken, H., 1983, Advanced Synergetics, Berlin Heidelberg New York Tokyo, Springer-Verlag

Hakkio, C.S., 1984, A Re-Examination of Purchasing Power Parity: A Multi-Country and Multi-Period Study, Journal of International Economics **17**, 265–277

Halm, G.N., 1965, The "Band" Proposal: The Limits of Permissible Exchange Rate Variations, Special Papers in International Economics No. 6, International Finance Section, Princeton University

Hamada, K., 1974, Alternative Exchange Rate System and the Interdependence of Monetary Policies, in: R.Z. Aliber (ed.), National Monetary Policies and the International Financial System, Chicago, University of Chicago Press

Hamada, K., 1985, The Political Economy of International Monetary Interdependence, Cambridge (Mass.), MIT Press

Hamada, K. and K. Ueda, 1977, Random Walks and the Theory of Optimal International Reserves, Economic Journal **87**, 722–742

Harberger, A.C., 1950, Currency Depreciation, Income and the Balance of Trade, Journal of Political Economy **58**, 47–60; reprinted in: R.E. Caves and H.G. Johnson (eds.), 1968, 341–358

Harcourt, G.C. (ed.), 1977, Microeconomic Foundations of Macroeconomics, London, Macmillan

Harrod, R.F., 1933, International Economics, Cambridge University Press

Harrod, R.F., 1939, An Essay in Dynamic Theory, Economic Journal **49**, 14–33. Reprinted in: A.H. Hansen and R.V. Clemence (eds.), 1953, Readings in Business Cycles and National Income, New York, Norton, 200–219; J.E. Stiglitz and H. Uzawa (eds.), 1969, Readings in the Modern Theory of Economic Growth, Cambridge (Mass.), MIT Press, 14–31; A. Sen (ed.), 1970, Growth Economics: Selected Readings, Harmondsworth, Penguin, 43–64

Hart, O.D., 1977, On the Profitability of Speculation, Quarterly Journal of Economics **91**, 579–597

Hawkins, D. and H.A. Simon, 1949, Note: Some Conditions of Macroeconomic Stability, Econometrica **17**, 245–248

Heller, H.R., 1966, Optimal International Reserves, Economic Journal **76**, 296–311

Heller, H.R. and M.S. Kahn, 1978, The Demand for International Reserves under Fixed and Floating Exchange Rates, IMF Staff Papers **26**, 699–724

Heller, H.R. and M. Knight, 1978, Reserve-Currency Preferences of Central Banks, Essays in International Finance No. 131, International Finance Section, Princeton University

Helliwell, J.F., 1979, Policy Modelling of Foreign Exchange Rates, Journal of Policy Modelling **1**, 425–444

Helliwell, J.F. and P.M. Boothe, 1983, Macroeconomic Implications of Alternative Exchange Rate Models, in: P. De Grauwe and T. Peeters (eds.), 21–53

Helliwell, J.F. and T. Padmore, 1985, Empirical Studies of Macroeconomic Interdependence, in: R.W. Jones and P.B. Kenen (eds.), Chap. 21

Henderson, D.W. and D.G. Waldo, 1983, Reserve Requirements on Eurocurrency Deposits: Implications for the Stabilization of Real Output, in: J.S. Bhandari and B.H. Putman (eds.), 350–383

Herin, J., A. Lindbeck and J. Myhrman (eds.), 1977, Flexible Exchange Rates and Stabilization Policy, London, Macmillan

Herring, R.J. and R.C. Marston, 1977, National Monetary Policies and International Financial Markets, Amsterdam, North-Holland

Hewson, J. and E. Sakakibara, 1974, The Euro-Dollar Deposit Multiplier: A Portfolio Approach, IMF Staff Papers **21**, 307–328

Hewson, J. and E. Sakakibara, 1976, A General Equilibrium Approach to the Eurodollar Market, Journal of Money, Credit and Banking **8**, 297–323

Hicks, J.R., 1937, Mr. Keynes and the 'Classics', Econometrica **5**, 147–159; reprinted in: J.R. Hicks, 1967a, Chap. 7

Hicks, J.R., 1967a, Critical Essays in Monetary Theory, Oxford University Press

Hicks, J.R., 1967b, The Pure Theory of Portfolio Selection, in: J.R. Hicks, 1967a, Chap. 6

Hicks, J.R., 1967c, The 'Classics' Again, in: J.R. Hicks, 1967a, Chap. 8

Hicks, J.R., 1981, IS-LM: An Explanation, Journal of Post Keynesian Economics **3**, 139–154

Himarios, D., 1987, Devaluation, Devaluation Expectations and Price Dynamics, Economica **54**, 299–313

Himarios, D., 1989, Do Devaluations Improve the Balance of Payments? The Evidence Revisited, Economic Inquiry **27**, 143–168

Hipple, F.S., 1974, The Disturbances Approach in the Literature of the Demand for International Reserves, Studies in International Finance No. 35, International Finance Section, Princeton University

Hirschman, A.O., 1949, Devaluation and the Trade Balance: A Note, Review of Economics and Statistics **31**, 50–53

HMT, 1989, An Evolutionary Approach to the European Monetary Union, London, UK Treasury

Hoffman, D.L. and D.E. Schlagenhauf, 1985, The Impact of News and Alternative Theories of Exchange Rate Determination, Journal of Money, Credit and Banking **17**, 328–346

Hogan, L.I., 1986, A Comparison of Alternative Exchange Rate Forecasting Models, Economic Record **62**, 215–223

Hogan, W.P. and I.F. Pearce, 1982, The Incredible Eurodollar, London, Allen & Unwin

Holden, P. and M. Holden, 1979, Exchange Rate Policy and the Demand for International Reserves, Rivista Internazionale di Scienze Economiche e Commerciali **26**, 232–246

Holzman, F.D. and A. Zellner, 1958, The Foreign-Trade and Balanced Budget Multipliers, American Economic Review **48**, 73–91

Hooper, P. and J. Morton, 1982, Fluctuations in the Dollar: A Model of Nominal and Real Exchange Rate Determination, Journal of International Money and Finance **1**, 39–56

Horne, J., 1983, The Asset Market Model of Balance and Finance **2**, 89–109

Horwich, G. and P.A. Samuelson (eds.), 1974, Trade, Stability, and Macroeconomics: Essays in Honor of L.A. Metzler, New York, Academic Press

Howrey, E.P., 1994, Exchange Rate Forecasts with the Michigan Quarterly Econometric Model of the U.S. Economy, Journal of Banking and Finance **18**, 27–41

Hsieh, D.A., 1984, Tests of Rational Expectations and No Risk Premium in Forward Exchange Markets, Journal of International Economics **17**, 173–184

Hughes Hallet, A. and H. Rees, 1983, Quantitative Economic Policies and Interactive Planning, Cambridge University Press

Hume, D., 1752, Of the Balance of Trade, in: D. Hume, Political Discourses, Edinburgh. Reprinted in: D. Hume, 1955, Writings on Economics (E. Rotwein ed.), London, Nelson, 60 ff., and (partially) in: R.N. Cooper (ed.), 1969, 25–37

IMF (International Monetary Fund), Annual Report on Exchange Rates and Exchange Restrictions, Washington (D.C.)

IMF, Balance of Payments Statistics Yearbook; International Financial Statistics (monthly), Washington (D.C.)

IMF, 1948, Balance of Payments Manual, 1st ed., Washington (D.C.); 2nd ed., 1950; 3rd ed., 1961; 4th ed., 1977; 5th ed., 1993

IMF, 1949, Balance of Payments Yearbook 1938, 1946, 1947, Washington (D.C.)

IMF, 1984, Exchange Rate Volatility and World Trade, Occasional Paper No. 28, Washington (D.C.)
Ingram, J.C., 1973, The Case for European Monetary Union, Princeton Essays in International Finance No. 98, Princeton University, International Finance Section
Intriligator, M.D., 1971, Mathematical Optimization and Economic Theory, Englewood Cliffs (N.J.), Prentice-Hall
Isard, P., 1978, Exchange-Rate Determination: A Survey of Popular Views and Recent Models, Princeton Studies in International Finance No. 42, International Finance Section, Princeton University
Isard, P., 1987, Lessons from Empirical Models of Exchange Rates, IMF Staff Papers **34**, 1–28
Isard, P., 1988, Exchange-rate Modeling: An Assessment of Alternative Approaches, in: R.C. Bryant et al. (eds.), Empirical Macroeconomics for Interdependent Economies, Washington (D.C.), Brookings Institution, 183–201
Ishiyama, Y., 1975, The Theory of Optimum Currency Areas: A Survey, IMF Staff Papers **22**, 344–383
Istituto Bancario San Paolo, ECU Newsletter (Quarterly Journal), Torino
Ito, T., 1990, Foreign Exchange Rate Expectations: Micro Survey Data, American Economic Review **80**, 434–449
Janssen, M.C.W., 1991, What Is This Thing Called Microfoundations?, History of Political Economy **23**, 687–712
Johnson, H.G., 1956a, The Transfer problem and Exchange Stability, Journal of Political Economy **44**, 212–225; reprinted (with additions) in: H.G. Johnson, 1958b, 168–195; in: R.E. Caves and H.G. Johnson (eds.), 1968, 148–171; and in: R.N. Cooper (ed.), 1969, 62–86
Johnson, H.G., 1956b, A Simplification of Multi-Country Multiplier Theory, Canadian Journal of Economics and Political Science **22**, 244–246; reprinted in: H.G. Johnson, 1958b, 196–199
Johnson, H.G., 1958a, Towards a General Theory of the Balance of Payments, in H.G. Johnson, 1958b, Chap. VI. Reprinted in: R.E. Caves and H.G. Johnson (eds.), 1968, 374–388, and in: R.N. Cooper (ed.), 1969, 237–255
Johnson, H.G., 1958b, International Trade and Economic Growth, London, Allen & Unwin
Johnson, H.G., 1965, Some Aspects of the Theory of Economic Policy in a World of Capital Mobility, Rivista Internazionale di Scienze Economiche e Commerciali **12**, 545–559. Reprinted in: Various Authors, 1966, Essays in Honour of Marco Fanno, Padova, Cedam, 345–359, and in: H.G. Johnson, 1972, Further Essays in Monetary Economics, London, Allen & Unwin, 151–166
Johnson, H.G., 1972, The Monetary Approach to Balance-of-Payments Theory, in: H.G. Johnson, Further Essays in Monetary Economics, London, Allen & Unwin, 229–249, and in: M.B. Connolly and A.K. Swoboda (eds.), 1973, International Trade and Money, London, Allen & Unwin, 206–224
Johnson, H.G., 1977a, The Monetary Approach to the Balance of Payments: A Nontechnical Guide, Journal of International Economics **7**, 251–268
Johnson, H.G., 1977b, The Monetary Approach to Balance of Payments Theory and Policy: Explanation and Policy Implications, Economica **44**, 217–229
Johnson, H.G. and A.K. Swoboda (eds.), 1973, The Economics of Common Currencies, London, Allen & Unwin
Johnston, R.B., 1981, Theories of the Growth of the Euro-Currency Market: A Review of the Euro-Currency Deposit Multiplier, BIS Economic Papers, No. 4, Bank for International Settlements, Basle
Johnston, R.B., 1983, The Economics of the Euro-Market: History, Theory and Policy, London, Macmillan
Jones, R.W. and P.B. Kenen (eds.), 1985, Handbook of International Economics, Vol. II, Amsterdam, North-Holland
Jonson, P.D. and H.I. Kierzkowski, 1975, The Balance of Payments: An Analytic Exercise, Manchester School of Economics and Social Studies **43**, 105–133
Kaldor, N., 1939, Speculation and Economic Stability, Review of Economic Studies **7**, 1–27; reprinted, with revisions, in: N. Kaldor, 1960, Essays on Economic Stability and Growth, London, G. Duckworth, 17–58
Kaldor, N., 1957, A Model of Economic Growth, Economic Journal **67**, 591–624; reprinted in: N. Kaldor, 1960, Essays in Economic Stability and Growth, London, G. Duckworth, 259–300
Katz, L., 1982, The Cost of Borrowing, the Terms of Trade and the Determination of External Debt, Oxford Economic Papers **34**, 332–345

Kawai, M., 1980, Exchange Rate-Price Causality in the Recent Floating Period, in: D. Bigman and T. Taya (eds.), 1980, 197–219

Kawai, M., 1985, Exchange Rates, the Current Account and Monetary-Fiscal Policies in the Short Run and in the Long Run, Oxford Economic Papers **37**, 391–425

Kelly, M.G., 1970, The Demand for International Reserves. American Economic Review **60**, 655–667

Kemp, M.C., 1963, Profitability and Price Stability, The Review of Economics and Statistics **45**, 185–189

Kemp, M.C., 1964, The Pure Theory of International Trade, Englewood Cliffs (N.J.), Prentice Hall

Kenen, P., 1963, Reserve Asset Preferences of Central Banks and Stability of the Gold Exchange Standard, Studies in International Finance No. 10, International Finance Section, Princeton University

Kenen, P.B., 1965, Trade, Speculation, and the Forward Exchange Market, in: R.E. Caves et al. (eds.), Trade, Growth and the Balance of Payments − Essays in Honor of G. Haberler, Chicago, Rand McNally, 134–169

Kenen, P.B., 1985, Macroeconomic Theory and Policy: How the Closed Economy Was Opened, in: R.W. Jones and P.B. Kenen (eds.), Chap. 13

Kenen, P., F. Papadia and F. Saccomanni (eds.), 1994, The International Monetary System, Cambridge (UK), Cambridge University Press

Kennedy, C. and A.P. Thirlwall, 1979, The Input-Output Formulation of the Foreign Trade Multiplier, Australian Economic Papers **18**, 173–180

Kennedy, C. and A.P. Thirlwall, 1980, The Foreign Trade Multiplier Revisited, in: D.A. Currie and W. Peters (eds.), Contemporary Economic Analysis, Vol. 2, London, Croom Helm, 79–100

Keynes, J.M., 1923, A Tract on Monetary Reform, London, Macmillan; reprinted as Vol. IV of The Collected Writings of J.M. Keynes, London, Macmillan for the Royal Economic Society, 1971

Keynes, J.M., 1929, The German Transfer Problem, Economic Journal **39**, 1–7. Reprinted in: H.S. Ellis and L.A. Metzler (eds.), 1949, 161–169, and in: The Collected Writings of J.M. Keynes, Vol. XI, 451–459, London, Macmillan for the Royal Economic Society, 1983

Keynes, J.M., 1936, The General Theory of Employment, Interest and Money, London, Macmillan; reprinted as Vol. VII of The Collected Writings of J.M. Keynes, London, Macmillan for the Royal Economic Society, 1973

Kindleberger, C.P., 1969, Measuring Equilibrium in the Balance of Payments, Journal of Political Economy **77**, 873–891

Kindleberger, C.P., 1973, International Economics, 5th ed., Homewood (Ill.), Irwin

Kindleberger, C.P., 1980, Myths and Realities of the Forward-Exchange Market, in: J.S. Chipman and C.P. Kindleberger (eds.) 27–38

Kindleberger, C.P. and P.H. Lindert, 1978, International Economics, 6th ed., Homewood (Ill.), Irwin

Klein, L.R. and W.E. Krelle (eds.), 1983, Capital Flows and Exchange Rate Determination, Supplementum 3 to Zeitschrift für Nationalökonomie

Klopstock, F.H., 1968, The Euro-Dollar Market: Some Unresolved Issues, Essays in International Finance No. 65, International Finance Section, Princeton University

Knight, M.D., 1977, Euro-Dollars, Capital Mobility and the Forward Exchange Market, Economica **44**, 1–21

Kohlhagen, S.W., 1979, The Identification of Destabilizing Foreign Exchange Speculation, Journal of International Economics **9**, 321–340

Komiya, R., 1969, Economic Growth and the Balance of Payments: A Monetary Approach, Journal of Political Economy **77**, 35–48

Kouri, P.J.K., 1983a, Balance of Payments and the Foreign Exchange Market: A Dynamic Partial Equilibrium Model, in: J.S. Bhandari and B.H. Putnam (eds.), 116–156

Kouri, P.J.K., 1983b, Intertemporal Balance of Payments Equilibrium and Exchange Rate Determination, Discussion Papers on International Economics and Finance No. 5, Roma, Banca d'Italia

Koustas, Z. and K.-S. Ng, 1991, Currency Substitution and Exchange Rate Dynamics: A Note, Atlantic Economic Journal **19**, 47–50

Krause, L.B. and W.S. Salant (eds.), 1977, Worldwide Inflation: Theory and Recent Experience, Washington (D.C.), Brookings Institution

Kreinin, M. E. and H.R. Heller, 1973, Adjustment Costs, Optimal Currency Areas and International Reserves, in: W. Sellekaerts (ed.), International Trade and Finance: Essays in Honour of Jan Tinbergen, London, Macmillan, 127–140

Kreinin, M. and L. Officer, 1978, The Monetary Approach to the Balance of Payments: A Survey, Princeton Studies in International Finance No. 43, International Finance Section, Princeton University

Krueger, A.O., 1983, Exchange-Rate Determination, Cambridge University Press

Krugman, P., 1984, The International Role of the Dollar, Theory and Prospect, in: J.F.O. Bilson and R.C. Marston (eds.), 261–278

Krugman, P., 1993, What Do We Need to Know About the International Monetary System?, Essays in International Finance No. 190, Princeton University, International Finance Section

Laffer, A.B. and M.A. Miles, 1982, International Economics in an Integrated World, Glenview (Ill.), Scott Foresman & Co

Lai, C.-C. and C.-C. Chen, 1984, Flexible Exchange Rates, Tight Money Effects, and Macroeconomic Policy, Journal of Post Keynesian Economics **7**, 129–133

Lamfalussy, A., 1963, Contribution à une théorie de la croissance en économie ouverte, Recherches Economiques de Louvain **29**, 715–734

Landefeld, J.S., O.G. Whichard and J.H. Lowe, 1993, Alternative Frameworks for U.S. International Transactions, Survey of Current Business **73**, 50–61

Landell-Mills, J.M., 1989, The Demand for International Reserves and Their Opportunity Cost, IMF Staff Papers **36**, 708–732

Lanyi, A., 1969, The Case for Floating Exchange Rates Reconsidered, Essays in International Finance No. 72, International Finance Section, Princeton University

Laursen, S. and L.A. Metzler, 1959, Flexible Exchange Rates and the Theory of Employment, Review of Economics and Statistics **32**, 281–299; reprinted in: L.A. Metzler, 1973c, 275–307

Lawrence, C., 1984, The Role of Information in the International Business Cycle, Journal of International Economics **17**, 101–120

Lederer, W., 1963, The Balance of Foreign Transactions: Problems of Definition and Measurement, Special Papers in International Economics No. 5, International Finance Section, Princeton University

Lee, B., 1973, The Euro-Dollar Multiplier, Journal of Finance **28**, 867–874

Lerner, A.P., 1944, The Economics of Control, New York, Macmillan

Levich, R.M., 1978, Further Results on the Efficiency of Markets for Foreign Exchange, in Federal Reserve Bank of Boston, 1978, 58–80

Levich, R.M., 1980, Analysing the Accuracy of Foreign Exchange Advisory Services: Theory and Evidence, in: R.M. Levich and C. Whilborg (eds.), Exchange Rate Exposure, D.C. Heath, Lexington

Levich, R.M., 1985, Empirical Studies of Exchange Rates: Price Behavior, Rate Determination and Market Efficiency, in: R.W. Jones and P.B. Kenen (eds.), Chap. 19

Levin, J.H., 1970, Forward Exchange and Internal-External Equilibrium, University of Michigan, Michigan International Business Studies No. 12

Levin, J.H., 1977, Speculation and the Crawling Peg, Economica **44**, 57–62

Levin, J.H., 1980, The Dynamics of Stabilization Policy under Flexible Exchange Rates: A Synthesis of the Asset and Neo-Keynesian Approaches, Oxford Economic Papers **32**, 411–426

Levin, J.H., 1983a, The J-Curve, Rational Expectations, and the Stability of the Flexible Exchange Rate System, Journal of International Economics **15**, 239–251

Levin, J.H., 1983b, A Model of Stabilization Policy in a Jointly Floating Currency Area, in: J.S. Bhandari and B.H. Putnam (eds.), 329–349

Levin, J.H., 1986, Monetary-Fiscal Policy Assignment under Flexible Exchange Rates: A Synthesis of the Asset and Neo-Keynesian Approaches, De Economist **134**, 467–478

Levy, H. and M. Sarnat, 1972, Investment and Portfolio Analysis, New York, Wiley

Lewis, K.K., 1992, Peso Problem, in: P. Newman, M. Milgate, J. Eatwell (eds.), The New Palgrave Dictionary of Money and Finance, Vol. 3, London, Macmillan

Lindbeck, A. (ed.), 1979, Inflation and Employment in Open Economies, Amsterdam, North-Holland

Lizondo, J.S., 1983, Foreign Exchange Futures Prices under Fixed Exchange Rates, Journal of International Economics **14**, 69–84

Ljungqvist, L., 1992, Destabilizing Exchange Rate Speculation: A Counterexample to Milton Friedman, Seminar Paper 125, Institute for International Economic Studies, Stockholm

MacDonald, R., 1988, Floating Exchange Rates: Theories and Evidence, London, Unwin Hyman

MacDonald, R. and M.P. Taylor, 1989, Interest Rate Parity: Some New Evidence, Bulletin of Economic Research **41**, 255–274

MacDonald, R. and M.P. Taylor, 1990, International Parity Conditions, in: Courakis, A.S. and M.P. Taylor (eds.), Private Behaviour and Government Policy in Interdependent Economies, Oxford, Clarendon Press, 19–52

MacDonald, R. and M.P. Taylor, 1992, Exchange Rate Economics: A Survey, IMF Staff Papers **39**, 1–57

MacDonald, R. and M.P. Taylor (eds.), 1992, Exchange Rate Economics, Aldershot, Elgar

Machlup, F., 1939, The Theory of Foreign Exchanges, Economica (New Series) **6**, 375–397; reprinted in: H.S. Ellis and L.A. Metzler (eds.), 1949, 104–158, and, with revisions, in: F. Machlup, 1943, Chap. I

Machlup, F., 1943, International Trade and the National Income Multiplier, Philadelphia, Blakiston; reprinted 1965 by Kelley, New York

Machlup, F., 1950, Three Concepts of the Balance of Payments and the So-Called Dollar-Shortage, Economic Journal **60**, 46–68: reprinted in: F. Machlup, 1964a, 69–92

Machlup, F., 1955, Relative Prices and Aggregate Spending in the Analysis of Devaluation, American Economic Review **45**, 255–278; reprinted in: F. Machlup, 1964a, 171–194

Machlup, F., 1956, The Terms of Trade Effects of Devaluation upon Real Income and the Balance of Trade, Kyklos **9**, 417–452; reprinted in: F. Machlup, 1964a, 195–222

Machlup, F., 1958, Equilibrium and Disequilibrium: Misplaced Concreteness and Disguised Politics, Economic Journal **68**, 1–24; reprinted in: F. Machlup, 1964a, 110–135

Machlup, F., 1964a, International Payments, Debts, and Gold, New York, Scribner's Sons

Machlup, F., 1964b, The Fuzzy Concepts of Liquidity, International and Domestic, in: F. Machlup, 1964a, 245–259

Machlup, F., 1966, The Need for Monetary Reserves, Banca Nazionale del Lavoro Quarterly Review **19**, 175–222

Machlup, F., 1970a, Euro-Dollar Creation: A Mystery Story, Banca Nazionale del Lavoro Quarterly Review **23**, 119–137

Machlup, F., 1970b, The Forward Exchange Market: Misunderstandings Between Practitioners and Economists, in: C.F. Bergsten et al. (eds.), 297–306

Machlup, F., 1972, Euro-Dollars, Once Again, Banca Nazionale del Lavoro Quarterly Review **25**, 119–137

Magee, S.P., 1973, Currency Contracts, Pass-Through, and Devaluation, Brookings Papers on Economic Activity, No. 1, 303–323

Markowitz, H., 1952, Portfolio Selection, Journal of Finance **7**, 77–91

Markowitz, H., 1959, Portfolio Selection, New York, Wiley

Marston, R.C., 1985, Stabilization Policies in Open Economies, in: R.W. Jones and P.B. Kenen (eds.), Chap. 17

Martin, J.P. and A. Smith (eds.), 1979, Trade and Payments Adjustment under Flexible Exchange Rates, London, Macmillan

Martinengo, G., 1978, Cambi flessibili e collaborazione tra paesi deficitari ed eccedentari nell'aggiustamento degli squilibri, Quaderni Sardi di Economia **8**, 127–135

Martinengo, G., 1981, The Equilibrium Exchange Rate: A Critical Survey, in: G. Gandolfo, 1981, 129–169

Martinengo, G. and P.C. Padoan, 1983, Lo SME e il dollaro: interdipendenza e gerarchia nei rapporti tra aree valutarie, Napoli, ESI

Martinez Oliva, J.C., 1991, One Remark on Spillover Effects and the Gains from Coordination, Oxford Economic Papers **43**, 172–176

Masera, R.S., 1974, The J-Curve: UK Experience after the 1967 Devaluation, Metroeconomica **26**, 40–62

Masera, R., 1981, The Euro-Currency Markets: Their Development, the Problem of Their Control and Their Role in the International Monetary System, in: Various Authors, Mercati monetari internationali e inflazione (atti della tavola rotonda su "Inflazione e sistema monetario internazionale", Rome, 20–21 October 1980), Università degli Studi di Roma, Facoltà di Scienze Politiche

Masera, R.S., 1987, L'unificazione monetaria e lo SME, Bologna, Il Mulino

Masera, R.S. and R. Triffin (eds.), 1984, Europe's Money: Problems of European Monetary Coordination and Integration, Oxford University Press

Masson, P.R. and M.P. Taylor, 1992, Common Currency Areas and Currency Unions: An Analysis of the Issues, Part I and Part II, Journal of International and Comparative Economics **1**, 231–250 and 265–294

Masson, P.R. and M.P. Taylor (eds.), 1993, Policy Issues in the Operation of Currency Unions, Cambridge (UK), Cambridge University Press

Mastropasqua, C., 1984, Il circolo vizioso svalutazione-inflazione: teoria ed evidenza empirica, Quaderni Sardi di Economia **14**, 3–37

Mayer, H., 1979, Credit and Liquidity Creation in the International Banking Sector, BIS Economic Papers, No. 1, Bank for International Settlements, Basle

Mayer, H., 1985, Interaction between the Euro-Currency Markets and the Exchange Markets, BIS Economic Papers, No. 15, Bank for International Settlements, Basle

Mayer, T., 1993, How Much Do Microfoundations Matter?, University of Munich, CES Working Paper 32

McCallum, J. and D. Vines, 1981, Cambridge and Chicago on the Balance of Payments, Economic Journal **91**, 439–453

McCombie, J.S.L., 1985, Economic Growth, the Harrod Foreign Trade Multiplier and the Hicks Super-Multiplier, Applied Economies **17**, 55–72

McCormick, F., 1977, A Multiperiod Theory of Forward Exchange, Journal of International Economics **7**, 269–282

McCulloch, J.H., 1975, Operational Aspects of the Siegel Paradox, Quarterly Journal of Economics **89**, 170–172

McGregor, P.G. and J.K. Swales, 1985, Professor Thirwall and Balance of Payments Constrained Growth, Applied Economics **17**, 17–32

McKinnon, R.I., 1963, Optimum Currency Areas, American Economic Review **52**, 717–724

McKinnon, R.I., 1969, Portfolio Balance and International Payments Adjustment, in: R.A. Mundell and A.K. Swoboda (eds.), Monetary Problems of the International Economy, University of Chicago Press, 199–234

McKinnon, R.I., 1977, The Euro-Currency Market, Essays in International Finance No. 125, International Finance Section, Princeton University

McKinnon, R.I., 1979, Money in International Exchange, Oxford University Press

McKinnon, R.I., 1983, The J-Curve, Stabilizing Speculation, and Capital Constraints on Foreign Exchange Dealers, in: D. Bigman and T. Taya (eds.), 103–127

McKinnon, R., 1988, Monetary and Exchange Rate Policies for International Financial Stability: A Proposal, Journal of Economic Perspectives **2**, 83–103

McKinnon, R.I. and W. Oates, 1966, The Implications of International Economic Integration for Monetary, Fiscal and Exchange Rate Policy, Princeton Studies in International Finance No. 16, International Finance Section, Princeton University

Meade, J.E., 1948, National Income, National Expenditure and the Balance of Payments. Part I, Economic Journal **58**, 483–505 (continued in 1949, EJ **59**, 17–39)

Meade, J.E., 1951, The Theory of International Economic Policy, Vol. I: The Balance of Payments, Oxford University Press

Meade, J.E., 1964, The International Monetary Mechanism, Three Banks Review, September, 3–25

Meese, R.A., 1984, Is the Sticky Price Assumption Reasonable for Exchange Rate Models?, Journal of International Money and Finance **3**, 131–139

Meese, R.A. and K. Rogoff, 1981, Empirical Exchange Rate Models of the Seventies: Are Any Fit to Survive? International Finance Discussion Paper No. 184, Federal Reserve Board, Washington, D.C.

Meese, R.A. and K. Rogoff, 1983a, Empirical Exchange Rate Models of the Seventies: Do They Fit Out of Sample?, Journal of International Economics **14**, 3–24

Meese, R.A. and K. Rogoff, 1983b, The Out-of-Sample Failure of Empirical Exchange Rate Models: Sampling Error or Misspecification?, in: J.A. Frenkel (ed.), 67–105

Meese, R.A. and K. Rogoff, 1985, Was it Real? The Exchange Rate-Interest Differential Relationship, 1973–1984, paper presented at the Conference of the Society for Economic

Dynamics and Control, London, 26—28 June, 1985, also circulated as International Finance Discussion Paper No. 228, Federal Reserve Board, Washington, D.C.
Meese, R.A. and K. Rogoff, 1988, Was It Real? The Exchange Rate – Interest Differential Relation over the Modern Floating-Rate Period, Journal of Finance **43**, 933–948
Meier, G.M., 1982, Problems of a World Monetary Order, Oxford University Press
Melvin, M., 1985, Currency Substitution and Western European Monetary Unification, Economica **52**, 79—91
Metzler, L.A., 1942a, Underemployment Equilibrium in International Trade, Econometrica **10**, 97–112; reprinted in: L.A. Metzler, 1973c, 258–274
Metzler, L.A., 1942b, The Transfer Problem Reconsidered, Journal of Political Economy **50**, 397–414; reprinted in: H.S. Ellis and L.A. Metzler (eds.), 1949, 179–187, and in: L.A. Metzler, 1973c, 50–69
Metzler, L.A., 1949, The Theory of International Trade, in: H.S. Ellis (ed.), A Survey of Contemporary Economics, Philadelphia, Blakiston, Chap. 6, Sect. III; reprinted in: L.A. Metzler, 1973c, 1–50
Metzler, L.A., 1950, A Multiple Region Theory of Income and Trade, Econometrica **18**, 329–354; reprinted in: L.A. Metzler, 1973c, 516–544
Metzler, L.A., 1973a, Imported Raw Materials, the Transfer Problem and the Concepts of Income, in: L.A. Metzler, 1973c, 70–94
Metzler, L.A., 1973b, Flexible Exchange Rates, the Transfer Problem, and the Balanced Budget Theorem, in: L.A. Metzler, 1973c, 95–111
Metzler, L.A., 1973c, Collected Papers, Harvard University Press
Milana, C., 1984, Le importazioni di beni intermedi nel moltiplicatore del reddito di un'economia aperta, ISPE Working Papers, Roma, Istituto di Studi per la Programmazione Economica
Mill, J.S., 1848, Principles of Political Economy, London, Parker, 1st ed.; 9th ed., London, Longmans, Green & Co., 1885; new edition (ed. by M.J. Ashley), London, Longmans, Green & Co., 1909, reprinted 1961 by A.M. Kelley, New York
Miller, N.C., 1978, Monetary vs. Traditional Approaches to Balance-of-Payments Analysis, American Economic Review **68**, Papers and Proceedings, 405—411
Minford, P., 1978, Substitution Effects, Speculation and Exchange Rate Stability, Amsterdam, North-Holland
Miyazawa, K., 1960, Foreign Trade Multiplier, Input-Output Analysis and the Consumption Function, Quarterly Journal of Economics **74**, 53—64; reprinted in: K. Miyazawa, 1976, Input-Output Analysis and the Structure of Income Distribution, Berlin Heidelberg, Springer-Verlag, 43—58
Modigliani, F. and H. Askari, 1973, The International Transfer of Capital and the Propagation of Domestic Disturbances under Alternative Payment Systems, Banca Nazionale del Lavoro Quarterly Review **26**, 295—310; reprinted in: F. Modigliani, 1980, Collected Papers (ed. by A. Abel), Cambridge (Mass.), MIT Press, Vol. 3, 321—337
Modigliani, F. and T. Padoa-Schioppa, 1978, The Management of an Open Economy with "100% plus" Wage Indexation, Essays in International Finance no. 130, International Finance Section, Princeton University; reprinted in: F. Modigliani, 1980, Collected Papers (ed. by A. Abel), Cambridge (Mass.), MIT Press, Vol. 3, 220—259
Mood, A.M., F.A. Graybill and D.C. Bos, 1974, Introduction to the Theory of Statistics, 3rd edition, New York, McGraw-Hill
Morishima, M., 1984, The Economics of Industrial Society, Cambridge University Press
Moutos, T. and W. Scarth, 1988, Stabilization Policy within a Currency Area, Scottish Journal of Political Economy **35**, 387–397
Mundell, R.A., 1961, A Theory of Optimum Currency Areas, American Economic Review **51**, 509–517; reprinted in: R.A. Mundell, 1968, Chap. 12
Mundell, R.A., 1962, The Appropriate Use of Monetary and Fiscal Policy under Fixed Exchange Rates, IMF Staff Papers **9**, 70—79; reprinted in: R.A. Mundell, 1968, Chap. 16
Mundell, R.A., 1963, Capital Mobility and Stabilization Policy under Fixed and Flexible Exchange Rates, Canadian Journal of Economics and Political Science **29**, 475—485. Reprinted in: R.E. Caves and H.G. Johnson (eds.), 1968, 487—499, and in: R.A. Mundell, 1968, Chap. 18

Mundell, R.A., 1965, The Homogeneity Postulate and the Laws of Comparative Statics, Econometrica **33**, 349–356; reprinted in: R.A. Mundell, 1968, Chap. 7

Mundell, R.A., 1968, International Economics, New York, Macmillan

Mundell, R.A., 1971, Monetary Theory: Inflation, Interest and Growth in the World Economy, Pacific Palisades (California), Goodyear

Murphy, R.G. and C. Van Duyne, 1980, Asset Market Approaches to Exchange Rate Determination: A Comparative Analysis, Weltwirtschaftliches Archiv **116**, 627–655

Mussa, M., 1976, The Exchange Rate, the Balance of Payments and Monetary and Fiscal Policy under a Regime of Controlled Floating, Scandinavian Journal of Economics **78**, 229–248; reprinted in: J.A. Frenkel and H.G. Johnson (eds.), 1978, 47–65

Mussa, M., 1979, Macroeconomic Interdependence and the Exchange Rate Regime, in: R. Dornbusch and J. Frenkel (eds.), International Economic Policy, Baltimore, Johns Hopkins University Press, 160–204

Mussa, M., 1984, The Theory of Exchange Rate Determination, in: J.F.O. Bilson and R.C. Marston (eds.), 13–78

Muth, J.F., 1960, Optimal Properties of Exponentially Weighted Forecasts, Journal of the American Statistical Association **55**, 299–306

Muth, J.F., 1961, Rational Expectations and the Theory of Price Movements, Econometrica **29**, 315–335

Myhrman, J., 1976, Balance-of-Payments Adjustment and Portfolio Theory: A Survey, in: E. Claassen and P. Salin (eds.), 1976, 203–237

Negishi, T., 1972, General Equilibrium Theory and International Trade, Amsterdam, North-Holland

Niehans, J., 1984, International Monetary Economics, Oxford, Philip Allan

Niehans, J. and J. Hewson, 1976, The Euro-Dollar Market and Monetary Theory, Journal of Money, Credit and Banking **8**, 1–27

N.I.E.S.R., 1968, The Economic Situation. The Home Economy, National Institute Economic Review, No. 44, 4–17

Nurkse, R., 1945, Conditions of International Monetary Equilibrium, Essays in International Princeton University; reprinted in: H.S. Ellis and L.A. Metzler (eds.), 1949, 3–34

Nyberg, L. and S. Viotti, 1976, Optimal Reserves and Adjustment Policies, in: E.M. Claassen and P. Salin (eds.), 1976, 124–145

Nyberg, L. and S. Viotti, 1979, Limited Instrument Flexibility and the Assignment Principle, Oxford Economic Papers **31**, 177–186

Obstfeld, M., 1982, Aggregate Spending and the Terms of Trade: Is There a Laursen and Metzler Effect?, Quarterly Journal of Economics **97**, 251–270

Obstfeld, M. and A.C. Stockman, 1985, Exchange Rate Dynamics, in: R.W. Jones and P.B. Kenen (eds.), Chap. 18

O'Connell, J., 1984, Stock Adjustment and the Balance of Payments, Economic Notes, No. 1, 136–144

Officer, L.H., 1982, Purchasing Power Parity and Exchange Rates: Theory, Evidence and Relevance, Greenwich (CT.), JAI Press

Ohlin, B., 1929, The Reparation Problem: A Discussion. I. Transfer Difficulties, Real and Imagined. Economic Journal **39**, 172–178; reprinted in: H.S. Ellis and L.A. Metzler (eds.), 1949, 170–178

Orosel, G., 1984, Profitable Speculation and Price Stability, Jahrbücher für Nationalökonomie und Statistik **199**, 485–501

Ortiz, G. and L.F. Solís, 1982, Currency Substitution and Monetary Independence: The Case of Mexico, in: R.N. Cooper et al. (eds.), 217–233

Oudiz, G. and J. Sachs, 1984, Macroeconomic Policy Coordination among the Industrial Economies, Brookings Papers on Economic Activity, No. 1, 1–64

Padoan, P.C., 1988, The Political Economy of Currency Agreements, Rivista di Diritto Valutario e di Economia Internazionale **37**, 907–936

Padoan, P.C., 1993, Competitività, crescita e bilancia dei pagamenti, in: C.A. Bollino and P.C. Padoan (eds.), Il circolo virtuoso: Commercio e flussi finanziari in un'Europa allargata, Bologna, il Mulino, 167–185

Patinkin, D., 1965, Money, Interest, and Prices, New York, Harper & Row, 2nd ed.
Pentecost, E.J., 1991, Econometric Approaches to Empirical Models of Exchange Rate Determination, Journal of Economic Surveys **5**, 71–96
Perry, G.L., 1984, Real Transfers in Fixed Exchange Rate Systems and the International Adjustment Mechanism, Journal of Monetary Economics **13**, 349–369
Persson, T. and L.E.O. Svensson, 1985, Current Account Dynamics and the Terms of Trade: Harberger-Laursen-Metzler Two Generations Later, Journal of Political Economy **93**, 43–65
Petit, M.L., 1985, Path Controllability of Dynamic Economic Systems, Economic Notes, No. 1, 26–42
Pilbeam, K., 1992, International Finance, London, Macmillan
Pitchford, J.D., 1985, The Insulation Capacity of a Flexible Exchange Rate System in the Context of External Inflation, Scandinavian Journal of Economics **87**, 44–65
Polak, J.J., 1947, The Foreign Trade Multiplier, American Economic Review **37**, 889–897
Polak, J.J., 1957, Monetary Analysis of Income Formation and Payments Problems, IMF Staff Papers **6**, 1–50; reprinted in: Various Authors, 1977, 15–64
Polak, J.J., 1994, The International Monetary Issues of the Bretton Woods Era: Are They Still Relevant?, in: P. Kenen, F. Papadia and F. Saccomanni (eds.)
Portes, R., 1993, EMS and EMU after the Fall, World Economy **16**, 1–15
Prachowny, M.F.J., 1975, Small Open Economies, Lexington (Mass.), D.C. Heath
Prais, S.J., 1961, Some Mathematical Notes on the Quantity Theory of Money in an Open Economy, IMF Staff Papers **8**, 212–226; reprinted in: Various Authors, 1977, 147–161
Price, L.D.D. and G.E. Wood, 1974, Another Case of Profitable Destabilizing Speculation: A Note, Journal of International Economics **4**, 217–220
Purvis, D.D., 1972, More on Growth and the Balance of Payments: The Adjustment Process, Canadian Journal of Economics **5**, 531–540
Purvis, D.D., 1983, Comment (on Frenkel, 1983), in: G.M. von Furstenberg (ed.), 115–116
Putnam, B.H. and D.S. Wilford (eds.), 1978, The Monetary Approach to International Adjustment, New York, Praeger
Quadrio Curzio, A. (ed.), 1982, The Gold Problem: Economic Perspectives (Proceedings of the World Conference on Gold held in Rome, 1982), Oxford University Press for the Banca Nazionale del Lavoro and Nomisma
Rabin, A.A. and L.B. Yeager, 1982, Monetary Approaches to the Balance of Payments and Exchange Rates, Essays in International Finance No. 148, International Finance Section, Princeton University
Reid, F.J., 1973, Mundell on Growth and the Balance of Payments: A Note, Canadian Journal of Economics **6**, 592–595
Review Committee for Balance of Payments Statistics, 1965, The Balance of Payments Statistics of the United States: A Review and Appraisal, Washington (D.C.), US Government Printing Office
Ricardo, D., 1817, On the Principles of Political Economy and Taxation, London, J. Murray. Reprinted as Vol. I of The Works and Correspondence of David Ricardo (ed. by P. Sraffa), Cambridge University Press for the Royal Economic Society, 1951
Riehl, H. and R.M. Rodriguez, 1977, Foreign Exchange Markets, New York, McGraw-Hill
Robinson, J., 1937, The Foreign Exchanges, in: J. Robinson, Essays in the Theory of Employment, Oxford, Blackwell; reprinted in: H.S. Ellis and L.A. Metzler (eds.), 1949, 83–103
Robinson, R., 1952, A Graphical Analysis of the Foreign Trade Multiplier, Economic Journal **62**, 546–564
Robson, P., 1984, The Economics of International Integration, 2nd ed., London, Allen & Unwin
Roger, S., 1993, The Management of Foreign Exchange Reserves, BIS Economic Papers No. 38
Rogoff, K., 1985, Can International Monetary Policy Cooperation Be Counterproductive?, Journal of International Economics **18**, 199–217
Rose, A.K. and Y.L. Yellen, 1989, Is There a J-Curve?, Journal of Monetary Economics **24**, 53–68
Rotondi, Z., 1989, La trasmissione internazionale delle perturbazioni in cambi fissi e flessibili, unpublished thesis, University of Rome La Sapienza, Faculty of Economics and Commerce
Rush, M. and S. Husted, 1985, Purchasing Power Parity in the Long-Run, Canadian Journal of Economics **18**, 137–145

Salin, P. (ed.), 1984, Currency Competition and Monetary Union, The Hague, M. Nijhoff
Samuelson, P.A., 1980, A Corrected Version of Hume's Equilibrating Mechanisms for International Trade, in: J.S. Chipman and C.P. Kindleberger (eds.), 141–158
Sassanpour, C. and J. Sheen, 1984, An Empirical Analysis of the Effects of Monetary Disequilibria in Open Economies, Journal of Monetary Economics **13**, 127–163
Sauernheimer, K., 1984, 'Fiscal Policy' in einer Wechselkursunion, Finanzarchiv **42**, 143–157
Scammell, W.M., 1987, The Stability of the International Monetary System, Totowa (NJ), Littlefield
Schinasi, G.J. and P.A.V.B. Swamy, 1987, The Out-of-Sample Forecasting Performance of Exchange Rate Models When Coefficients are Allowed to Change, Special Studies Paper 212, Division of Research and Statistics, Federal Reserve Board, Washington (DC). Revised version published in 1989 with the same title in: Journal of International Money and Finance **8**, 375–390
Schumpeter, J.A., 1954, History of Economic Analysis, Oxford University Press
Scitovsky, T., 1969, Money and the Balance of Payments, London, Allen & Unwin
Sellekaerts, W. and B. Sellekaerts, 1973, Balance of Payments Deficits, the Adjustment Cost and the Optimum Level of International Reserves, Weltwirtschaftliches Archiv **109**, 1–18
Shafer, J.R. and B.E. Loopesko, 1983, Floating Exchange Rates after Ten Years, Brookings Papers on Economic Activity, No. 1, 1–70
Sheen, J., 1989, Modelling the Floating Australian Dollar: Can the Random Walk be Encompassed by a Model Using a Permanent Decomposition of Money and Output?, Journal of International Money and Finance **8**, 253–276
Shelburn, M.R., 1984, Rules for Regulating Intervention under a Managed Float, Princeton Studies in International Finance No. 55, International Finance Section, Princeton University
Shinkai, Y., 1975, Stabilization Policies in an Open Economy: A Taxonomic Discussion, International Economic Review **16**, 662–681
Shone, R., 1980, The Monetary Approach to the Balance of Payments: Stock-Flow Disequilibria, Oxford Economic Papers **32**, 200–209
Siegel, J.J., 1972, Risk, Interest, and Forward Exchange, Quarterly Journal of Economics **86**, 303–309
Sinclair, P.J.N., 1983, The Foundations of Macroeconomics and Monetary Theory, Oxford University Press
Sinn, H.W., 1983, International Capital Movements, Flexible Exchange Rates, and the IS-LM Model: A Comparison between the Portfolio-Balance and the Flow Hypothesis, Weltwirtschaftliches Archiv **119**, 36–63
Sinn, H.-W., 1989, Expected Utility and the Siegel Paradox, Zeitschrift für Nationalökonomie **50**, 257–268
Sohmen, E., 1961, Notes on Some Controversies in the Theory of International Trade: A Comment, Economic Journal **71**, 423–426
Sohmen, E., 1966, The Theory of Forward Exchange, Princeton Studies in International Finance No. 17, International Finance Section, Princeton University
Sohmen, E., 1969, Flexible Exchange Rates, 2nd ed., University of Chicago Press
Solomon, R., 1982, The International Monetary System, 1945–1981, New York, Harper & Row
Solow, R.M., 1956, A Contribution to the Theory of Economic Growth, Quarterly Journal of Economics **70**, 65–94. Reprinted in: P.K. Newman (ed.), 1968, Readings in Mathematical Economics, Baltimore, Johns Hopkins, Vol. II, 142–171; J.E. Stigliz and H. Uzawa (ed.), 1969, Readings in the Modern Theory of Economic Growth, Cambridge (Mass.), MIT Press, 58–87; A Sen (ed.), 1979, Growth Economics: Selected Readings, Harmondsworth, Penguin, 161–192
Somanath, V.S., 1986, Efficient Exchange Rate Forecasts: Lagged Models Better than the Random Walk, Journal of International Money and Finance **5**, 195–220
Spaventa, L., 1982, Algebraic Properties and Economic Improprieties of the "Indicator of Divergence" in the European Monetary System, in: Various Authors, 1982, 1−34, and in: R.N. Cooper et al. (eds.), 259−277
Spaventa, L., 1983, Feedbacks between Exchange Rate Movements and Domestic Inflation: Vicious and Not so Virtuous Circles, Old and New, International Social Science Journal **97**, 517−534

Spraos, J., 1953, The Theory of Forward Exchange and Recent Practice, Manchester School of Economics and Social Studies **21**, 87–117

Spraos, J., 1959, Speculation, Arbitrage and Sterling, Economic Journal **59**, 1–21

Stein, J.L., M. Rzepczynski and R. Selvaggio, 1983, A Theoretical Explanation of the Empirical Studies of Future Markets in Foreign Exchange and Financial Instruments, Financial Review **18**, 1–32

Stern, R.M., 1973, The Balance of Payments: Theory and Economic Policy, Chicago, Aldine

Stern, R.M. et al., 1977, The Presentation of the Balance of Payments: A Symposium, Essays in International Finance No. 123, International Finance Section, Princeton University

Stern, R.M., J. Francis and B. Schumacher, 1976, Price Elasticities in International Trade: An Annotated Bibliography, London, Macmillan

Stolper, W.F., 1950, The Multiplier, Flexible Exchanges and International Equilibrium, Quarterly Journal of Economics **64**, 559–582

Stuvel, G., 1951, The Exchange Stability Problem, Oxford, Blackwell

Svensson, L.E.O., 1992, An Interpretation of Recent Research on Exchange Rate Target Zones, Journal of Economic Perspectives **6**, 119-144

Svensson, L.E.O. and A. Razin, 1983, The Terms of Trade and the Current Account: The Harberger-Laursen-Metzler Effect, Journal of Political Economy **91**, 97–125

Swan, T., 1955, Longer Run Problems of the Balance of Payments, paper presented at the Congress of the ANZAAS, Melbourne. Published in: H.W. Arndt and M.W. Corden (eds.), 1963, The Australian Economy: A Volume of Readings, Melbourne, Cheshire Press, 384–395; reprinted in: R.E. Caves and H.G. Johnson (eds.), 1968, 455–464

Swan, T., 1956, Economic Growth and Capital Accumulation, Economic Record **32**, 334–361. Reprinted in: P.K. Newman (ed.), 1968, Readings in Mathematical Economics, Baltimore, Johns Hopkins, Vol. II, 172–199; J.E. Stigliz and H. Uzawa (eds.), 1969, Readings in the Modern Theory of Economic Growth, Cambridge (Mass.), MIT Press, 88–115

Sweeney, R.J., 1985, Stabilizing or Destabilizing Speculation? Evidence From the Foreign Exchange Markets, in: S.W. Arndt, R.J. Sweeney and T.D. Willet (eds.), 107–123

Swoboda, A.K., 1968, The Euro-Dollar Market: An Interpretation, Essay in International Finance No. 64, International Finance Section, Princeton University

Swoboda, A.K., 1976, Monetary Approaches to Balance of Payments Theory, in: E. Claassen and P. Salin (eds.), 1976, 3–23

Swoboda, A.K., 1978, Gold, Dollars, Euro-Dollars, and the World Money Stock under Fixed Exchange Rates, American Economic Review **68**, 625–642

Swoboda, A.K., 1980, Credit Creation in the Euro-Market: Alternative Theories and the Implications for Control, Occasional Paper No. 2, Group of Thirty, New York

Takagi, S., 1991, Exchange Rate Expectations: A Survey of Survey Studies, IMF Staff Papers **38**, 156-183

Takayama, A., 1972, International Trade: An Approach to the Theory, New York, Holt Rinehart and Winston

Takayama, A., 1978, The Wealth Effect, the Capital Account, and Alternative Policies under Fixed Exchange Rates, Quarterly Journal of Economics **92**, 117–147

Taylor, D., 1982, Official Intervention in the Foreign Exchange Market, or, Bet against the Central Bank, Journal of Political Economy **90**, 356–368

Tew, B., 1988, The Evolution of the International Monetary System 1945-88, London, Hutchinson

Thirlwall, A.P., 1979, The Interaction between Income and Expenditure in the Absorption Approach to the Balance of Payments, Journal of Macroeconomics **1**, 237–240

Thirlwall, A.P., 1980, Balance-of-Payments Theory and the United Kingdom Experience, London, Macmillan

Thursby, M.C., 1981, The Resource Reallocation Costs of Fixed and Flexible Exchange Rates: A Multi-Country Extension, Journal of International Economics **11**, 487–493

Tobin, J., 1958, Liquidity Preference as Behavior towards Risk, Review of Economic Studies **25**, 65–86; reprinted in: J. Tobin, 1971, Essays in Economics – Vol. 1: Macroeconomics, Amsterdam, North-Holland, Chap. 15

Tobin, J., 1963, Commercial Banks as Creators of "Money", in: D. Carson (ed.), Banking and Monetary Studies, Homewood (Ill.), Irwin, 408–419. Reprinted in: J. Tobin and D. Hester (eds.), 1967, Financial Markets and Economic Activity, Cowles Fundation Monograph No.

21, New York, Wiley, Chap. 1, and in: J. Tobin, 1971, Essays in Economics, Vol. 1: Macroeconomics, Amsterdam, North-Holland, Chap. 16

Tobin, J., 1969, A General Equilibrium Approach to Monetary Theory, Journal of Money, Credit, and Banking **1**, 15-29; reprinted in: J. Tobin, 1971, Essays in Economics, Vol. 1: Macroeconomics, Amsterdam, North-Holland, 322-338

Tobin, J., 1978, A Proposal for International Monetary Reform, Eastern Economic Journal **4**, 153-159

Tobin, J., 1980, Asset Accumulation and Economic Activity, Oxford, Blackwell

Tobin, J., 1982, The State of Exchange Rate Theory: Some Sceptical Observations, in: R.N. Cooper et al. (eds.), 115-128

Tobin, J., 1994, A Currency Transaction Tax, Why and How, paper presented at the CIDEI Conference on Globalization of Markets, University of Rome "La Sapienza", 27-28 October 1994. Forthcoming as CIDEI Working Paper, and to be published in JOICE

Tobin, J. and J.B. De Macedo, 1980, The Short-Run Macroeconomics of Floating Exchange Rates: An Exposition, in: J.S. Chipman and C.P. Kindleberger (eds.), 5–28

Tower, E., 1980, Effective Market Classification, the New Cambridge School of Economic Policy and the Choice between Fixed and Floating Exchange Rates, in: J.S. Chipman and C.P. Kindleberger (eds.), 231–255

Tower, E. and T.D. Willet, 1976, The Theory of Optimum Currency Areas and Exchange Rate Flexibility, Special Papers in International Economics No. 11, International Finance Section, Princeton University

Triffin, R., 1960, Gold and the Dollar Crisis, Yale University Press

Triffin, R., 1968, Our International Monetary System: Yesterday, Today and Tomorrow, New York, Random House

Triffin, R., 1982, The European Monetary System and the Dollar in the Framework of the World Monetary System, Banca Nazionale del Lavoro Quarterly Review, No. 142, 245-267

Tseng, K.K., 1993, Forward Intervention, Risk Premium and the Fluctuations of International Financial Market, Economia Internazionale **46**, 276-287

Tsiang, S.C., 1958, A Theory of Foreign Exchange Speculation under a Floating Exchange System, Journal of Political Economy **66**, 399-418

Tsiang, S.C., 1959, The Theory of Forward Exchange and Effects of Government Intervention on the Forward Exchange Market, IMF Staff Papers **7**, 75–106

Tsiang, S.C., 1961, The Role of Money in Trade-Balance Stability: Synthesis of the Elasticity and Absorption Approaches, American Economic Review **51**, 912–936. Reprinted in: R.E. Caves and H.G. Johnson (eds.), 1968, 389–412, and in: R.N. Cooper (ed.), 1969, 135–164

Tsiang, S.C., 1975, The Dynamics of International Capital Flows and Internal and External Balance, Quarterly Journal of Economics **89**, 195–214

Turnovsky, S.J., 1983, Exchange Market Intervention Policies in a Small Open Economy, in: J.S. Bhandari and B.H. Putman (eds.), 286–311

United States Department of Commerce-Bureau of Economic Analysis, Survey of Current Business (monthly), Washington (D.C.), US Government Printing Office

Various Authors, 1973, A Debate on the Eurodollar Market, Quaderni di Ricerche n. 11, Ente per gli studi monetari, bancari e finanziari Luigi Einaudi, Roma

Various Authors, 1977, The Monetary Approach to the Balance of Payments, Washington (D.C.), IMF

Various Authors, 1978, Purchasing Power Parity: A Symposium, Journal of International Economics **8**, May

Various Authors, 1982, Seminar on the Indicator of Divergence in the European Monetary System, Discussion Papers on International Economics and Finance No. 1, Roma, Banca d'Italia

Vicarelli, F., 1972, Verso un'integrazione fra teoria pura e teoria monetaria del commercio internazionale, Economia Internazionale **25**, febbraio e novembre

Viner, J., 1937, Studies in the Theory of International Trade, London, Allen & Unwin

Vines, D., 1976, Economic Policy for an Open Economy: Resolution of the New School's Elegant Paradoxes, Australian Economic Papers **15**, 207-229

Vlaene, J.-M. and C.G. De Vries, 1992, International Trade and Exchange Rate Volatility, European Economic Review **36**, 1311-1322 von Furstenberg, G.M., 1982, New Estimates of the Demand for Non-Gold Reserves under Floating Exchange Rates, Journal of International Money and Finance **1**, 81–95

von Furstenberg, G.M. (ed.), 1983, International Money and Credit: The Policy Roles, Washington, International Monetary Fund

von Neumann Whitman, M., 1970, Policies for Internal and External Balance, Special Papers in International Economics No. 9, International Finance Section, Princeton University

von Neumann Whitman, M., 1975, Global Monetarism and the Monetary Approach to the Balance of Payments, Brookings Papers on Economic Activity, No. 3, 539–583

Wallich, H. and J.A. Gray, 1980, Stabilization Policy and Vicious and Virtuous Circles, in: J.S. Chipman and C.P. Kindleberger (eds.), 49–65

Wan, H.Y., Jr., 1971, Economic Growth, New York, Harcourt Brace Jovanovich Inc.

Wein, J., 1974, Growth and the Balance of Payments: A Comment on Mundell, Economic Journal **84**, 621–623

Weintraub, E.R., 1977, The Microfoundations of Macroeconomics: A Critical Survey, Journal of Economic Literature **15**, 1–23

Weintraub, E.R., 1979, Microfoundations: The Compatibility of Microeconomics and Macroeconomics, Cambridge University Press

Wijkman, P.M., 1981, Seignorage, Financial Intermediation, and the International Role of the Dollar, 1960–1971, Seminar Paper No. 173, Institute for International Economic Studies, University of Stockholm

Willet, T.D. and F. Forte, 1969, Interest Rate Policy and External Balance, Quarterly Journal of Economics **83**, 242–262

Williams, H.R., 1973, Exchange Rate Systems, the Marginal Efficiency of Investment, and Foreign Direct Capital Movements, Kyklos **26**, 58–73

Williamson, J.H., 1965, The Crawling Peg, Essays in International Finance No. 90, International Finance Section, Princeton University

Williamson, J.H., 1971, On the Normative Theory of Balance-of-Payments Adjustment, in: G. Clayton, J.C. Gilbert, R. Sedgwick (eds.), Monetary Theory and Monetary Policy in the 1970s, Oxford University Press, 235–256

Williamson, J., 1973a, Surveys in Applied Economics: International Liquidity, Economic Journal **83**, 685–746

Williamson, J., 1973b, Another Case of Profitable Destabilizing Speculation, Journal of International Economics **1**, 77–83

Williamson, J., 1976, The Benefits and Costs of an International Monetary Nonsystem, in: E.M. Bernstein et al., Reflections on Jamaica, Essays in International Finance No. 115, International Finance Section, Princeton University

Williamson, J., 1985, The Exchange Rate System, rev. ed., Washington (D.C.), Institute for International Economics

Williamson, J. (ed.), 1981, Exchange Rate Rules: The Theory, Performance and Prospects of the Crawling Peg, London, Macmillan

Williamson, J., 1993, Equilibrium Exchange Rates: An Update, Washington, Institute for International Economics

Witte, W., 1978, Another Case of Profitable Destabilizing Speculation: A Comment, Journal of International Economics **8**, 135-138

Witte, W.E., 1983, Policy Interdependence under Flexible Exchange Rates: A Dynamic Analysis of Price Interactions, in: J.S. Bhandari and B.H. Putnam (eds.), 312-328

Woo, W.T., 1985, The Monetary Approach to Exchange Rate Determination under Rational Expectations: The Dollar-Deutschmark Rate, Journal of International Economics **18**, 1–16

Wood, G., 1991, Valuation Effects, Currency Contract Impacts and the J-Curve: Empirical Estimates, Australian Economic Papers **30**, 148–163

Yeager, L.B., 1976, International Monetary Relations: Theory, History and Policy, 2nd ed., New York, Harper & Row

Name Index

(Numbers followed by n refer to footnotes, and those followed by r to the References at the end of each chapter)

Adams, C. 371n, 401r
Advisory Committee on the Presentation of Balance of Payments Statistics 82, 86r
Ahmad, J. 375, 401r
Ahtiala, P. 387, 401r
Aizemann, J. 401r
Alessandrini, S. 469, 516r
Alexander, S. S. 159, 160, 162, 173, 174, 186r
Alexander, D. 391, 399, 401r
Aliber, P. R. 49r
Allen, P. R. 272r, 337r, 401r, 405, 407, 447r, 518, 519r
Angell, J. W. 272r
Aoki, M. 272r
Argy, V. 49r, 122r, 272r, 336, 337r, 370n, 374, 401r, 478, 481, 516r
Arndt, S. W. 372, 401r
Artus, J. R. 372, 401r, 447r
Asheim, G. B. 401r, 444, 447r
Askari, H. 286, 337r

Backus, D. 401r
Bailey, R. W. 121n, 122r
Baillie, R. T. 122r, 378, 401r
Bain, A. D. 86r
Balogh, T. 122r
Bank for International Settlements 452
Basevi, G. 376, 401r
Batchelor, R. A., 401r
Batten, S. D. 468, 516r
Baumol, W. J. 342
Bean, C. R. 434, 447r
Beckerman, W. H. 354, 355, 357, 363, 366r
Beenstock, M. 510, 516r
Begg, D. 434, 447r
Behnke, E. A. 337r
Bell, G. 49r, 516r
Ben-Bassat, A. 468, 470, 472, 501, 502, 516r
Bergsten, C. F. 401r
Bernholz, P. 401r
Bernstein, E. M. 82, 83, 86r
Bhagwati, J. 103, 122r

Bhandari, J. S. 343n, 366r, 374, 401r
Bickerdicke, C. F. 96, 122r
Bigman, D. 401r
Bilson, J. F. O. 376, 382, 397, 401r
Bini Smaghi, L. 429, 447r
Black, J. 121, 122r, 158r
Blake, D. 510, 516r
Blaug, M. 390, 401r
Blommestein, H. J. 489, 516r
Blundell-Wignall, A. 401r
Bond, M. E. 376, 401r
Boothe, P. M. 381, 402r
Bordo, M. D. 447r
Branson, W. H. 230, 272r, 295n, 297, 299, 327, 330, 332, 337r, 374, 387, 401, 401r, 489, 516r
Brasse, V. 510
Britton, A. J. C. 342, 361, 366r
Brown, B. 49r
Bruce, N. 272r
Brunner, K. 272r
Buckley, P. J. 346, 366r
Buiter, W. H. 272r, 297, 299, 327, 330, 332, 337r, 387, 401r, 434, 447r, 489, 516r
Burmeister, E. 354, 366r
Bushaw, D. W. 204, 272r

Calvo, G. A. 401, 401r
Canto, V. A. 401, 401r
Canzoneri, M. B. 401, 401r, 447r
Carraro, C. 489, 516r
Casella, A. 447r
Casprini, F. 110, 121n, 122r, 179, 186r, 227, 272r, 279, 336, 337r, 361, 366r
Cassel, G. 378, 379, 401r
Casson, M. C. 346, 366r
Caves, R. E. 346, 354, 366r
Chacholiades, M. 37, 49r, 122r, 158r, 272r, 311, 337r, 366r
Chen, C. C. 295n, 337r, 365, 366r
Chipman, J. S. 88n, 122r, 366r
Christ, C. F. 236n, 272r
Chrystal, K. A. 470, 472, 516r
Claassen, E. M. 401r, 464, 469, 470, 516r

Name Index

Clark, P. B.   469, 516r
Clement, M. O.   122r, 367, 401r
Clower, R. W.   204, 272r
Cohen, B. J.   49r, 86r, 401r, 464, 516r
Conway, R. K.   375, 401r
Cooper, R. N.   228, 272r, 401r, 447r, 489, 516r
Corden, W. M.   372, 401r, 403, 447r
Courant, R.   251, 272r
Cox, D. R.   493n, 516r
Cripps, F.   290
Crockett, D.   477, 516r
Cuddington, J. T.   401, 401r
Cuthberston, K.   337r
Cutilli B.   25, 49r, 120, 121, 122r, 483, 516r, 518, 519r

Daniel, B. C.   401, 401r
De Arcangelis, G.   391, 393, 398, 399, 401r, 402r, 492, 514, 516r
De Cecco, M.   375, 401r
De Grauwe, P.   231n, 232, 234n, 272r, 337r, 376, 401r, 402r, 414, 447r, 448, 458, 459, 516r
De Jong, E.   378, 401r
De Macedo, J. B.   337r, 502, 516r
De Vries, T.   447r
De Vries, C. G.   372
Deardoff, A. V.   157, 158r, 182n, 186r, 285n, 295, 337r
Delors (Report), 403, 430, 447r
Denton, G.   407, 447r
DeRosa, D. A.   402r
Diba, B. T.   401, 401r
Dickey, D. A.   398, 402r
Dixon, R. I.   337r
Dobell, A. R.   354, 366r
Dooley, M. P.   121, 122r, 396, 398, 402r, 472, 502, 516r
Dornbusch, R.   36, 49r, 122r,158r, 186r, 190, 248, 272r, 337r, 378, 381, 381n, 387, 397, 402r, 491, 516r
Dowd, K.   447r
Driskill, R.   342, 366r
Dufey, G.   472, 516r
Dunn, R. N.   372, 402r
Dupuy, C.   447r

Eaton, J.   109, 122r, 336, 337r, 361, 366r
EC Commission   447r
Edgeworth, F. Y.   391, 402r
Edison, H. J.   492, 516r
Eichengreen, B.   430, 434, 447r
Eizing, P.   9n, 21n, 49r, 122r
Emerson, M.   414, 447r
Engle, R. P.   398, 402r

Falchi, G.   375, 402r, 462, 516r
Fama, E. F.   49r, 121n, 122r, 402r
Farrell, V. S.   372, 402r
Federal Reserve Bank of Boston   372, 402r, 448, 516r
Feldstein, M. S.   107n, 122r, 489, 516r
Fellner, W.   63n, 86r
Ferrara, L.   157, 158r
Fischer, S.   337r, 365, 366r
Fitoussi, J. P.   518, 519r
Flanders, M. J.   464, 466, 467, 516r
Fleming, J. M.   110, 122r, 205, 272r, 337r
Flood, R. P.   340n, 366r, 371n, 402r
Floyd, J. E.   272r, 337r
Forte, F.   272r
Frankel, J. A.   36, 49r, 381, 381n, 383n, 397, 402r, 483, 511, 513, 516r
Fratianni, M.   401r, 402r, 447r
Freedman, C.   504, 504n, 516r
Frenkel, J. A.   121n, 122r, 190, 196, 196n, 205, 272r, 337r, 365, 366r, 380, 397, 402r, 467, 468, 469, 489, 492, 516r
Frevert, P.   107, 122r
Friedman, M.   340, 341, 343n, 360, 366r
Froot, K. A.   35, 49r
Fuller, W. A.   398, 402r

Gaartner, M.   401r
Gale, D.   518, 519r
Gandolfo, G.   25, 49r, 113, 120, 122r, 123, 146, 147, 150, 151, 154, 157, 158r, 179, 181, 186r, 190, 196n, 227, 238n, 243, 250, 257, 260n, 263n, 265n, 268, 272r, 286, 306, 311, 317, 322, 323, 336, 337r, 340n, 342, 357, 364, 366r, 377, 378, 380, 389, 391, 392, 393, 394, 398, 399, 400, 402r, 483, 484, 500, 506, 507, 511, 515, 516r, 518, 519, 519r
Gantmacher, F. R.   155, 158r, 441, 447r
Garber, P. M.   340n, 366r
Geweke, J.   375, 402r
Ghosh, A. R.   490, 516r
Giavazzi, F.   447r
Gibson, H. D.   472, 516r
Giddy, I. H.   472, 516r
Giustiniani, A.   467, 516r
Glahe, F. R.   341, 366r
Godley, W.   290, 337r
Goldstein, M.   289, 337r, 372, 402r, 489, 492, 516r
Goodman, S. H.   510, 516r
Goodwin, R. M.   158r
Gottlieb, D.   468, 470
Granger, C. W. J.   398, 402r
Greenwood, J.   371n, 401r
Grilli, V.   447r

Gros, D. 447r
Grubel, H. G. 105, 106, 110, 272r, 448, 464, 516r
Guttentag, J. 479n, 516r
Gylfason, T. 272r, 337r, 387, 402r

Hageman, H. A. 470, 516r
Hahn, F. H. 204, 272r
Haken, H. 519, 519r
Hakkio, C. S. 49r, 380, 402r
Halm, G. N. 24, 49r
Hamada, K. 413, 447r, 469, 486, 516r
Harberger, A. C. 164n, 182n, 186r, 285n, 337r
Harcourt, G. C. 518, 519r
Harrod, R. F. 24n, 123n, 158r, 354, 366r
Hart, O. D. 342, 366r
Hawkins, D. 158r
Heller, H. R. 468, 469, 470, 471, 472, 493, 494, 516r
Helliwell, J. F. 157, 158r, 272r, 337r, 381, 387, 402r
Henderson, D. W. 295n, 337r, 401, 401r, 516r
Heri, E. W. 401r
Herin, J. 337r
Herring, R. J. 109, 122r, 479n, 504, 516r
Hewson, J. 477, 478, 504, 504n, 516r
Hicks, J. R. 43, 44, 45, 49r, 205n, 272r
Himarios, D. 95, 122r, 337r
Hipple, F. S. 465n, 470, 516r
Hirschman, A. O. 122r
HMT (Her Majesty Treasury) 447r
Hoffman, D. L. 402r
Hogan, W. P. 479, 510, 516r
Holden, M. 468, 516r
Holden, P. 468, 516r
Holzman, F. D. 145, 158r
Hooper, P. 396, 397, 402r
Horne, J. 402r
Howrey, P. 400, 402r
Hsieh, D. A. 121n, 122r
Hughes Hallet, A. 501, 516r
Hume, D. 73, 187, 188, 196n, 272r
Husted, S. 380, 402r

I. M. F. (International Monetary Fund) 23, 28, 29, 49r, 50, 52, 64, 64n, 86r, 371n, 372, 402r, 448, 449, 452, 453, 456, 459, 461, 462, 472n
Ingram, J. C. 402r, 403, 447r
Intriligator, M. D. 497n, 498, 516r
Isard, P. 378, 392, 396, 398, 402r
Ishiyama, Y. 405, 407, 447r
Istituto Bancario San Paolo, 427, 447r
Ito, J. 510, 516r

Janssens, M. 402r, 518, 519r
Johnson, H. G. 86r, 88, 103, 122r, 157, 158r, 164, 186r, 196, 196n, 214n, 226, 272r, 348n, 350, 365, 366r, 402r, 447r, 451
Johnston, R. B. 452n, 472, 476, 478, 478n, 481, 504, 516r
Jonson, P. D. 272r
Jovanovic, B. 469, 516r

Kahn, R. 290
Kaldor, N. 16, 17, 17n, 44, 49r, 354, 366r
Katz, L. 365, 366r
Kawai, M. 305, 337r, 375, 402r
Kelly, M. G. 469, 494, 495, 496n, 497, 516r
Kemp, M. C. 341, 366r, 518, 519r
Kenen, P. B. 74, 86r, 105, 107n, 122r, 272r, 337r, 401r, 405, 407, 447r, 448, 470, 516r, 518, 519r
Kennedy, C. 141, 141n, 144, 158r
Keynes, J. M. 13, 16, 16n, 49r, 105, 105n, 122r, 158r, 293, 337r, 346n, 366r
Khan, M. S. 468, 516r
Kierzkowski, H. 272r
Kindleberger, C. P. 49r, 86r, 121n, 122r, 158r
Klein, L. R. 402r
Klopstock, F. H. 516r
Knight, M. D. 470, 471, 472, 504, 516r
Kohlhagen, S. W. 340n, 366r
Komiya, R. 365, 366r
Kouri, P. J. K. 385, 386, 402r
Koustas, Z. 401, 402r
Krause, L. B. 375, 402r
Kreinin, M. E. 272r, 469, 516r
Krelle, W. E. 402r
Krueger, A. O. 378, 383n, 402r
Krugman, P. R. 36, 49r, 381n, 402r, 516r

Laffer, A. B. 272r
Lai, C. C. 295n, 337r
Lamfalussy, A. 354, 355, 356, 357, 363, 366r
Landefeld, J. S. 83, 86r
Landell-Mills, J. M. 468, 516r
Lanyi, A. 369, 402r
Laursen, S. 164, 164n, 182, 186r, 284, 285, 337r
Laussel, D. 516r
Lawrence, C. 289, 337r
Lederer, W. 76, 83, 86r
Lee, B. 516r
Leliaert, H. 402r
Lerner, A. P. 95, 96, 122r
Levich, R. M. 122r, 402r, 510, 516r
Levin, J. H. 110, 122r, 336, 337r, 342, 343n, 361, 366r, 402r, 434, 435, 436, 447r
Levy, H. 44, 49r

Lewis, K.K. 48, 49r
Lindbeck, A. 375, 402r
Lindert, P. 49r
Lizondo, J.S. 48, 49r, 516r
Ljungqvist, L. 342, 366
Loopesko, B.E. 372, 396n, 402r

MacDonald, R. 35, 36, 47, 48, 49r, 378, 402r
Machlup (Mrs) 465
Machlup, F. 29, 49r, 63, 64n, 86r, 122r, 158r, 160, 161, 186, 348n, 350, 366r, 451, 452, 464, 465, 516r
Magee, S.P. 172, 173, 186
Markowitz, H. 43, 49r, 230n, 272r
Marshall, A. 96
Marston, R.C. 109, 122r, 272r, 289, 337r, 401r, 489, 504, 516r
Martin, J.P. 402r
Martinengo, G. 288n, 337r, 447r
Martinez–Oliva, J.C. 516r
Masera, R.S. 186r, 402r, 444, 447r, 462, 481, 516r
Masson, P.R. 447r, 490, 516r
Mastropasqua, C. 374, 377, 402r
Mathieson, D.J. 516r
Mayer, H. 478, 516r
Mayer, T. 518, 519r
McCafferty, S. 342, 366r
McCallum, J. 290, 291, 291n, 337r
McCombie, J.L.S. 157, 158r, 357, 363, 366r
McCormick, F. 110, 121, 122r
McCown, T.A. 402r
McCulloch, J.H. 49, 49r
McGregor, P.G. 357, 363, 365, 366r
McKinnon, R.I. 49r, 122r, 230, 272r, 342, 366r, 447, 471, 490, 491, 516r
McMahon, P.C. 122r, 378, 401r
Meade, J.E. 24, 49r, 86r, 138n, 144, 158r, 500, 514, 515
Meese, R.A. 390, 391, 392, 397, 398, 399, 402r
Meier, G.M. 448, 516r
Melvin, M. 401, 402r
Meltzer, A.H. 122r, 150, 186, 272r
Metzler, L.A. 138n, 154, 157, 158r, 164, 164n, 182, 284, 285, 337r, 348n, 350, 350n, 366r
Michelangeli, M. 375, 402r
Micossi, S. 447r
Milana, C. 141, 142n, 158r
Miles, M.A. 272r, 401, 401r
Mill, J.S. 517, 518, 519r
Miller, H.D. 204, 493n, 516r
Miller, N.C. 272r
Miller, M. 447r, 492, 514, 516r

Minford, P. 361, 366r
Miyazawa, K. 138, 138n, 141n, 144, 158r
Modigliani, F. 286, 337, 376, 402r
Mood, A.M. 48, 49r
Morgan Guaranty Trust Co. 29, 452
Morishima, M. 49r, 122r
Morton, J. 396, 397, 402r
Moutos, T. 435, 447r
Mundell, R.A. 36, 49r, 75, 86r, 110, 122r, 157, 158r, 196, 205, 224, 224n, 235n, 272r, 279, 280, 337r, 357, 364, 366r, 381n, 402r, 404, 447r
Murphy, R.G. 381, 402r
Mussa, M.L. 121n, 272r, 289, 337r, 378, 402r
Muth, J.F. 46, 49r
Myhrman, J. 272r

N.I.E.S.R. 172, 186r
Nabli, M.K. 401r
Negishi, T. 518, 519r
Neild, R. 290
Ng, K.S. 401, 402r
Niehans, J. 49r, 122r, 186r, 190, 196n, 202, 248, 272r, 337r, 366r, 402r, 458, 477, 504, 504n, 516r
Nurske, R. 380, 402r
Nyberg, L. 272r, 470, 496, 497, 497n, 498, 500, 501, 516r

O'Connell, J. 236, 272r
Oates, W.R. 230, 272r
Obstfeld, M. 182n, 186r, 285n, 337r, 402r
Officer, L.H. 272r, 378, 402r
Ohlin, B. 346n, 366r
Orosel, G. 340n, 342, 360, 366r
Ortiz, G. 401, 402r
Oswald, J. 196n
Oudiz, G. 272r

Padmore, T. 157, 158r
Padoa Schioppa, T. 376
Padoan, P.C. 357, 364, 365, 366r, 377, 378, 389, 391, 392, 393, 394, 398, 399, 400, 402r, 447r, 483, 484, 511, 516r, 519, 519r
Paladino, G. 389, 391, 393, 398, 400, 402r
Papadia, F. 516r
Patinkin, D. 518, 519r
Pcarcc, I.F. 479
Peeters, T. 402r
Perry, G.L. 518, 519r
Persson, T. 182n, 186r, 285n, 337r, 402r
Petit, M.L. 272r
Pfister, R.L. 367, 401r
Pichford, G.D. 289, 337r
Pilbeam, K. 463, 516r
Polak, J.J. 123, 158r, 272r, 457, 516r

Porter, M. G.   336, 337r
Portes, R.   415, 447r
Posner, M. V.   290
Prachowny, M. F. J.   518, 519r
Prais, S. J.   272r
Price, L. D. D.   366r
Purvis, D. D.   272r, 366r, 467, 516r
Putman, B. H.   272r, 365, 401r

Ouadrio Curzio, A.,   462, 516r

Rabin, A. A.   204, 272r, 383, 387, 402r
Razin, A.   182n, 205, 272r, 285n, 337r
Rees, H.   501, 516r
Reid, F. J.   364, 366
Review Committee for Balance of Payments Statistics   86r
Ricardo, D.   517, 518, 519r
Riehl, H.   49r
Robinson, J.   96, 122r
Robinson, R.   132, 158r
Robson, P.   407, 447r
Rodriguez, C. A.   401, 401r
Rodriguez, R. M.   49r
Roger, S.   470, 516r
Rogoff, K.   272r, 390, 391, 392, 397, 398, 399, 402r, 408, 447r
Rose, A. K.   173, 186r
Rothwell, K. J.   368, 401r
Rotondi Z.   157, 158r
Rush, M.   380, 402r
Rybczynski, T. M.   345
Rzepczynski, T.   122r

Saccomanni, F.   516r
Sachs, J.   272r
Sakakibara, E.   478, 504, 504n, 516r
Salant, W. S.   375, 402r
Salin, P.   44, 401, 401r, 402r, 447
Salmon, M.   516r
Samuelson, P. A.   196n, 243, 272r
Sarnat, M.   49r
Sassanpour, C.   402r
Sauernheimer, K.   435, 438, 499, 447
Scammell, W. M.   448, 516r
Scarth, W.   435, 447r
Schinasi , G. J.   399, 402r
Schlagenhauf, D. E.   402r
Schumpeter, J. A.   189, 272r
Schwartz, C. F.   83
Scitovsky, T.   186
Sellekaerts, B.   469, 516r
Sellekaerts, H.   469, 516r
Selvaggio, R.   122r
Shafer, J. R.   121n, 122r, 372, 396n, 402r
Sheen, J.   398, 402r
Shelburn, M. R.   374, 402r

Shinkai, Y.   279, 337r
Shone, R.   272r
Siegel, J. J.   48, 49r
Sinclair, P. J. N.   518, 519r
Sinn, H.-W.   49, 49r, 337r
Smith, M. Alasdair M.   402r
Sohmen, E.   49r, 95, 103, 122r, 336, 337r, 343n, 366r
Solis, L. F.   401, 402r
Solomon, R.   448, 516r
Solow, R. M.   354, 366
Somanath, V. S.   398, 402r
Sonbeyran, A.   516r
Spaventa, L.   375, 377, 402r, 444, 445, 447r
Spraos, J.   19, 49r, 105, 122r
Stein, J. L.   121, 122r
Stern, R. M.   49r, 83, 86, 95, 105n, 122r, 157, 158r, 182n, 186r, 272r, 285n, 295, 337r, 343n, 354, 366r
Stockman, A. C.   402r
Stolper, W. F.   164n, 186r
Stuvel, G.   122r
Svensson, L. E. O.   182n, 186r, 285n, 337r, 492, 516r
Swales, J. K.   357, 363, 365
Swamy, P. A. V. B.   399, 401r, 402r
Swan, T.   186, 354, 366r
Sweeney, R. J.   366r, 401r
Swoboda, A. K.   272r, 402r, 447r, 470, 476, 516r

Takagi , S.   510, 516r
Takayama, A.   272r, 518, 519r
Taya, T.   401r
Taylor, D.   366r
Taylor, M. P.   35, 47, 48, 49r, 378, 402r, 447r
Telser, L. G.   342
Tew, B.   448, 516r
Thaler, R. H.   35, 49r
Thirlwall, A. P.   141, 141n, 142n, 144, 186r, 204, 272r, 357, 363, 366r
Thomas, L. R.   391, 399, 401r
Thursby, M. C.   369, 402r
Thygesen, N.   447r
Tinbergen, J.   220, 221n, 500, 514, 515
Tobin, J.   43, 49r, 230n, 237n, 272r, 337r, 387, 402r, 476, 482, 484, 490, 491, 516r
Torrens, R.   24
Tower, E.   337r, 405, 407, 447r
Triffin, R.   83, 402r, 447r, 448, 453, 456, 457, 459, 516r
Tseng, K. K.   110, 122r
Tsiang, S. C.   16, 17, 18, 19, 44, 49r, 105, 122r, 163, 164, 164n, 186r, 227, 272r
Turnovsky, S. J.   109, 122r, 336, 337r, 361, 366r

Ueda, K.   469, 516r
United Nations   52, 71
United States Department of Commerce, Bureau of Economic Analysis   76, 86r

Van Duyne, C.   381
Various Authors   272r, 402r, 447r, 516r
Vicarelli, F.   518, 519r
Viner, J.   196n, 272r
Vines, D.   290, 291, 291n, 337r
Viotti, S.   272r, 470, 496, 497, 497n, 498, 500, 501, 516r
Vlaene, J. M.   372, 402r
Von Furstenberg, G. M.   516r
Von Hagen, J.   447r
Von Neumann Whitman, M.   227, 272r, 279, 337r
Vori, S.   429, 447r

Waldo, D. G.   516r
Waller, C.   447r
Wallich, H.   402r

Wan, H. Y. Jr.   354, 366r
Wein, J.   364, 366r
Weintraub, E. R.   518, 519r
Werner (Report)   403, 447r
Wijkman, P. M.   471, 516r
Wilford, D. S.   272r
Willet, T. D.   272r, 401r, 405, 407, 447
Williams, H. R.   402r
Williamson, J. H.   24, 24n, 25, 49r, 342, 366r, 374, 402r, 464, 465n, 490, 491, 492, 497, 514, 516r
Witte, W. E.   289, 337r, 342, 366r
Woo, W. T.   402r
Wood, G.   173, 186, 366r, 401r
World Bank   52, 448

Yanagida, J. F.   401r
Yeager, L. B.   49r, 86, 110, 122r, 204, 272r, 337r, 366r, 383, 387, 402r
Yellen, J. L.   173, 186
Young, J. H.   372

Zellner, A.   145

Subject Index

(Numbers followed by n refer to footnotes)

Absorption approach 72n, 159–161, 198
– and elasticity approach 161–164
– – controversy between 161–162
– – synthesis between 162–164, 173–174
Acceleration hypothesis 386
Accounting principles in the balance of payments 52ff
Adjustable peg 23, 372, 449
Adjustment lag 173, 178ff, 264, 322, 378, 506
Adjustment or financing dilemma 199–200, 464, 466, 469–470, 481, 493ff
Adjustment speeds 179, 386, 392, 393–394, 395, 510
Advance deposit requirements 20
Appreciation 90
Arbitrage
– on foreign exchange 6–8, 15, 36–37, 338
– – n-point 36–37
– – three-point or triangular 7–8, 440, 443
– – two-point 6–7
– on goods 199, 379
– on interest 5, 13–14, 30ff, 104–106, 109, 120, 206, 338, 381
(see also Covered interest arbitrage; Forward arbitrage; Interest-rate-parity conditions)
Arbitrage incentive 105n
Asset market approach 381ff, 386, 394–399
Asset substitutability
– and capital mobility 35–36, 381
– imperfect 35, 381
– perfect 35, 381
Assets 16ff, 68, 73, 226, 230ff, 263–265, 476
– and balance-of-payments adjustment 73
– – under fixed exchange rates 187ff, 234ff, 265ff
– – under flexible exchange rates 273ff, 289ff, 295, 297ff, 324ff
– and exchange rate determination 381ff, 394–399
Assignment of instruments to targets (see Assignment problem)

Assignment problem 223–225, 256–257, 289–290, 292–295, 307ff, 318ff (see also Effective market classification)

Backwardation 11n
Balance of indebtedness 62
Balance of payments 4, 50, 52
– accounting 52ff
– adjustment processes (see Balance-of-payments adjustment processes)
– and national accounts 67ff
– definition of 50–51
– equilibrium and disequilibrium 63ff
– overall 65
– stages of 365
Balance-of-payments adjustment processes 73ff
– absorption (see Absorption approach)
– and internal and external balance
– – under fixed exchange rates 220ff, 254ff
– – under flexible exchange rates 279ff, 307ff
– and foreign multiplier (see Foreign multiplier)
– and portfolio approach
– – under fixed exchange rates 230ff
– – under flexible exchange rates 295ff
– and standard macroeconomic equilibrium
– – under fixed exchange rates 205ff
– – under flexible exchange rates 273ff
– classical price-specie-flow mechanism 187ff, 241–243
– exchange-rate based (partial equilibrium) 87ff
– monetary approach 196ff
– money and other assets in
– – under fixed exchange rates 187ff
– – under flexible exchange rates 273ff
– under fixed exchange rates 123ff, 187ff
– under flexible exchange rates 87ff, 159ff, 273ff
Balance of trade 65
Balance on goods and services 65

Subject Index

Bank for International Settlements 451, 452
Banknotes 5
Basic balance 65
Basket currency 28, 28n, 410–411, 418ff, 439ff, 501–502 (see also ECU; SDR)
BB schedule 167–168, 169–172, 175, 207–209, 210, 213, 215–219, 222n, 248, 250, 251, 274–276, 280–283, 287, 301, 313, 352
Bear 18
Beggar-my-neighbour 293
Benign neglect 471, 471n
Bid-offer spread 5
Bretton Woods
– agreement 22ff, 460
– system 22ff, 370, 411, 448–450, 457–459
Budget constraint 68-69, 70–72
Budget deficit 69, 70, 72, 234, 236–241 passim, 291, 292, 297, 299, 318, 430, 433
– financing of 71–72, 236–241 passim, 318, 430
Bull 18
Burden of interest payments 215–216, 226, 250–251, 279

Capital account 52–57 passim, 60–62
Capital and financial account 52
Capital mobility 222, 405, 412, 480
– and effectiveness of economic policy 222, 222n, 279–284, 301
– and asset substitutability 35–36
– and foreign exchange crises 481ff
– and transmission of disturbances 285–289, 312ff
Capital movement liberalization 481
– and foreign exchange crises 482, 508ff
Capital movements
– accounting rules for 52ff
– and balance-of-payments adjustment
– – under fixed exchange rates 206–207, 208–209, 210ff, 214n, 217, 222, 226, 234, 236
– – under flexible exchange rates 278–279, 279ff, 298, 305ff
– and foreign exchange crises 481ff
– and Tobin tax 484, 491
– and transfer theory 347, 351, 353, 362–363
– and transmission of disturbances 285–289, 312ff
– arbitrage induced 13–14
– autonomous and accomodating 64
– clandestine 84–85
– payment of interest on 215–216, 226, 250–251
– pure flows and stock adjustment 216, 298, 333, 344, 508, 509
– speculative (see Speculation)

– various classifications of 60-62 (see also Arbitrage; International investment; Speculation)
Capital transfers 60, 346 (see also Capital movements)
Cartels 347, 459, 460n
C. i. f. and F. o. b. 57–58, 85
Coins 5
Commercial balance 65
Commercial credits (loans) 8ff, 106, 338n, 343n, 509
Compensatory
– capital movements 64
– official financing 64–65
Composition
– of international reserves 454–455, 470–472, 501–503
– of portfolio 43–44, 230ff, 295ff, 344, 344n
Condition of neutrality in covered interest arbitrage 14, 38, 105, 121
Contango 11n
Convertibility 21–22, 403, 404, 449, 450
– of the US dollar, suspension of 23, 370, 457
Cooperation (see International policy coordination)
Coordination of economic policies (see International policy coordination)
Covered interest arbitrage 13–14, 104–106, 109, 120, 206, 338
Covered interest parity 31
Covering alternatives 10ff
Crawling peg 24
Credibility 36, 413, 482–483
Currency areas 373, 404ff
– common currency 410–412
– optimum 404ff
– – and EMS 427–429
– – and monetary integration 404, 406, 407–408
– – cost-benefit approach 407–410
– – traditional approach 405–407
Currency basket 28, 28n, 410–411, 418ff, 439ff, 501–502
– definition of the weights 411
Currency competition 415
Currency-contract period 172
Currency substitution 230n, 400–401, 491
Current account 57ff
– – balance on 65

Debt crisis 449, 462–463
Deficit in the balance of payments 64, 72
Deficit in the government budget (see Budget deficit)
Depreciation 4

Subject Index 553

- and absorption approach 159ff, 173–174
- and inflation 293, 294n, 295, 301, 302, 370, 374–378
- and monetary approach 201–202, 247–248
- and the New Cambridge School 292, 293–294
- effects of 87ff, 110ff, 219–220, 277–279, 281, 286, 295, 301, 328
- J-curve 172–173, 178ff
- traditional theory 87ff, 110ff

Determination of the exchange rate (see Exchange rate determination)
Devaluation 4 (see also Depreciation)
Devaluation-inflation (vicious) circle 374–378
- causality tests of 375–376
- structural models of 375, 376–377

Differential
- in inflation rates 378, 379, 394–395, 430–431
- in interest rates 13, 24, 30ff, 104–105, 110, 206, 217, 258, 288, 317, 379, 381, 394, 395, 431

Dirty float 23, 25, 370ff, 468
Discount (see Forward discount)
Disturbances, transmission of, in various exchange rate regimes 285–289, 312–318
Divergence indicator, threshold (see European Monetary System)
Dollar standard 23n, 448, 470
Double entry bookeeping 52ff

Economic growth (see Growth)
Economic transactions (see International transactions)
Economic union 408, 429, 430, 431
ECU or European Currency Unit 28n, 416ff, 430, 431, 432, 443, 444, 453
EC or European Council 429
ECB or European Central Bank 431–432
EEC or European Economic Community 370, 371, 373, 416, 419, 426, 427, 428, 429, 430, 459, 460
Effected transfer 347, 348, 349, 353, 362
Effective market classification 223 (see also Assignment problem)
Efficiency of the foreign exchange market (see Foreign exchange market)
Elasticities
- and absorption 161–164, 173–174
- and Marshall-Lerner condition 95–96, 332
- and stability of foreign exchange market 89, 96ff
- critical sum of 91–101 passim, 110ff, 167, 169–171, 176, 194, 219, 274, 277ff, 298, 305ff, 326, 361, 369, 380

- of exports and imports with respect to price
- – on the demand side 90, 111, 112
- – on the supply side 113, 114
- partial and total 94–95, 159, 361
- pessimism and optimism on 95, 369

EMCF or European Monetary Cooperation Fund 425–426, 430, 462
EMI or European Monetary Institute 425, 430
EMS (see European Monetary System)
EMU or Economic and Monetary Union 430
Equilibrium exchange rate (see Exchange rate determination)
ERM or Exchange Rate Mechanism (see European Monetary System)
Errors and omissions 56, 66
ESCB or European System of Central Banks 431–432
EUA or European Unit of Account 419, 420, 421
Euro-currencies 29, 451
Euro-dollar market 29–30, 450–452, 471n, 472ff, 504ff
- costs and benefits of 478–481
- definition of 29–30, 450–451
- estimated size 451–452
- growth of 451
- – modern theory 476–478, 504ff
- – traditional or multiplier theory 472–476
- origins of 29, 451

European Monetary System 6, 371, 373, 401, 410, 416ff, 439ff, 453, 462
- and optimum currency areas 401, 427–429
- bilateral parity grid 416, 417, 422, 423
- central weights 419, 421
- composition of the basket currency 418–421
- crisis in 1992–1993 428
- definition of the weights 419–421
- divergence threshold 417, 421, 423, 424, 425
- European Unit of Account 419, 420, 421
- exchange rate mechanism 416–417
- indicator of divergence 417, 423–425, 444–445
- monetary cooperation 416, 425–427
- obligatory intervention points 417–418, 422
- realignment 420, 420n, 425

European monetary union 429ff
- convergence criteria 430–431, 433
- Delors plan 430

- European Central Bank 431, 432
- European Monetary Institute 430
- European System of Central Banks 431, 432
- Maastricht treaty 429ff
- various stages of 430
- Werner report 403

Excess demand 68, 70
- for bonds 212, 232, 234, 264
- for goods 134–135, 143, 147, 166, 168, 169, 183, 198, 200, 207–208, 212, 213, 275, 290
- for foreign moneys 491
- for foreign exchange 23, 89, 97, 98, 99, 104, 109, 110ff, 168, 183, 276, 289, 341–342, 359–361
- for money 198, 199, 201, 209, 212, 213, 232, 276, 383

Exchange rate
- and vicious circle (see Devaluation-inflation circle)
- definition of 4
- - cross or indirect 7, 8
- - direct 7, 8
- - effective 28
- - forward 8ff, 9n
- - price quotation system 4
- - spot 6–8, 9, 9n
- - swap 15
- - volume quotation system 4
- determination of (see Exchange rate determination)
- increase and decrease in 4
- interrelations between spot and forward 104ff, 109, 119ff
- role of, in balance-of-payments adjustment (see Balance-of-payments adjustment)

Exchange rate determination 96ff, 168, 274, 295ff, 378ff
- asset market approach 381–386, 394ff
- - interaction between current and capital accounts 384–386
- - interest parity model 381
- - monetary 381–383, 394–395, 397
- - portfolio 383–384, 395–397, 398
- eclectic approach 392–393
- empirical studies 389ff, 397ff
- - and out-of-sample forecasting 390, 393
- - in economy-wide macroeconometric models 386–389, 392–393, 399–400
- - balance-of-payments approach 387–389
- - other approaches 387–389
- purchasing-power-parity approach 378–380
- traditional approach 96ff, 168, 274, 380

Exchange rate forecasting 389–393, 397–400
- alchemists and geologists 389
- out of sample 390, 393, 397ff
- - random walk benchmark and how to beat it 390, 392–393, 400

Exchange rate overshooting 305, 376, 395
Exchange rate policy 25, 28, 289–290, 293, 374, 376, 409, 491–492
Exchange rate regimes
- adjustable peg 23, 372, 449
- Bretton Woods system 22–23, 370, 411, 448–450, 457–459
- crawling peg 24
- currency standard (see pure exchange standard)
- current nonsystem 25–28
- European Monetary System (see European Monetary System)
- fixed 21, 367ff
- flexible 21, 367ff
- gold exchange standard 22, 448
- - limping 22, 448
- gold standard 21–22
- intermediate 23–25
- managed or "dirty" float 25, 370ff, 468
- oscillating exchange rates 25
- pure exchange standard 22
- target zones 491–492, 513–515
- wider band 24–25, 416, 417

Exchange risk 8ff, 396, 510
Expectations 16–20, 31–36 passim, 46ff, 107, 119ff, 296, 482ff
- extrapolative 482, 483
- normal or regressive 482, 483
- rational 46–47, 296, 302ff, 325n, 334ff, 401, 510
- - and news 304–305, 396
- static 35, 296, 300ff, 327ff

Expenditure reducing policy 88n
Expenditure switching policy 88
Export-led growth 354ff, 363ff
- and balance of payments 357–359, 364–365

Factors of production
- and currency areas 405, 428
- and direct investment 345–346
F. a. s. 58
Financial assets (see Assets)
Financial surplus of the private sector 70, 290
Financing versus adjustment (see Adjustment or financing dilemma)
Fiscal policy 220ff, 235ff, 254ff, 279ff, 307ff
- budget constraint 70, 235–236, 238 (see also Budget deficit)
- and monetary policy for internal and external balance 222ff, 254ff, 279ff

Subject Index 555

- in a monetary union 434–439
Fixed versus flexible exchange rates 367ff
Fleming-Mundell model (see Macroeconomic equilibrium)
Flexibility of exchange rates
- limited 21, 22–25
- perfect 21
Floating, dirty or managed (see Dirty float)
Flow and stock disequilibria 73–74, 393
Flows of capital (see Capital movements)
F. o. b. and C. i f. 57–58, 85
Forecasting the exchange rate (see Exchange rate forecasting)
Foreign exchange
- accomodating purchases and sales of 23, 64, 103–104
- demand for and supply of 23, 97ff
- excess demand for (see Excess demand for foreign exchange)
Foreign exchange market 3ff
- and exchange rate determination 380, 387–389, 392–393
- crises in 428, 481ff
- dual or two-tier 370n
- efficiency of 34–35, 46–48, 510
- forward 8ff, 36–37, 108
- interrelations between spot and forward 104ff, 109, 119ff
- official intervention (see Intervention in foreign exchange markets)
- spot 5, 6ff, 36–37
- – multiple equilibria 96, 102ff
- – stability 96ff, 118–119
- swap 14ff
Foreign exchange rate (see Exchange rate)
Foreign (trade) multiplier 123ff
- and balance-of-payments adjustment 124ff, 135ff
- and intermediate goods 137ff
- comparison between the various multipliers 135–137, 149–150, 153–155
- comparison with macroeconomic equilibrium model 217–218, 220, 253, 254
- empirical relevance of 156–157
- without repercussions 124ff, 142ff
- – stability conditions 126, 143
- with repercussions 131ff, 145ff
- – and absorption approach 162–163, 171, 173–174
- – and transfer problem 348–350, 351, 361ff
- – stability conditions 147–149, 152–153
Forward
- arbitrage 15, 37
- covering and hedging 8–10, 9n, 106, 368, 368n
- discount 11–12, 110

- exchange rate 8ff, 36–37, 108
- – outright 11n
- – parity 14
- margin 12, 13
- premium 11–12
- speculation 18–20, 107–108, 121, 343
Full employment (see Internal equilibrium; Macroeonomic equilibrium)
Fundamental disequilibrium 23, 368n, 449

Game theory and international policy coordination 484–488
Gold
- as a commodity or non-monetary 61
- demonetization of
- – in balance of payments accounting 61
- – in international monetary system 449, 460–462
- mobilization of 462
- monetary and non-monetary 61
- monetization of 61
- optimum international distribution of 188, 192
- points 22, 189
- pool 460
- price-specie-flow mechanism 187ff, 241ff
- reserves 453, 454–455, 460, 461–462
- two-tier market 460
- valuation of 460–462
Gold exchange standard 22, 450
- limping 22, 448, 450
Gold standard 21–22, 188, 190
Gold tranche position 453n
Growth
- and the balance of payments 357ff, 363ff (see also Export-led growth)

Harberger-Laursen-Metzler effect (see Laursen-Metzler effect)
Hedging 9–10, 9n, 368, 368n
Hume's price-specie-flow mechanism 73, 187ff, 241ff

IBRD or International Bank for Reconstruction and Development (see World Bank)
IMF (see International Monetary Fund)
Imperfect
- asset substitutability 35–36, 381, 383, 412, 510
- capital mobility 35–36, 282ff, 482, 509
Implicit interest rate 12
Inconvertibility of the US dollar 370, 448, 449, 458
Inflation in open economies 294, 294n, 370, 372n, 373, 374ff, 406, 408, 431, 433 (see also Vicious circle)

Integration between the pure theory of international trade and international monetary economics 517ff
Interest arbitrage (see Arbitrage)
Interest differential (see Differential)
Interest parity (see Interest-rate parity conditions)
Interest rate
- and balance-of-payments adjustment
- - under fixed exchange rates 206, 208–209, 210ff
- - under flexible exchange rates 277–279, 279ff, 305ff
- and capital movements 14, 104ff, 206, 338, 509
- and transmission of disturbances 351–353
- arbitrage (see Arbitrage)
- differential (see Differential)
- implicit 12
- nominal 33, 379, 395
- parity (see Interest-rate parity conditions)
- real 33, 379
Interest-rate parity conditions 30ff, 46ff
- and foreign exchange market efficiency 46–48
- and perfect asset substitutability 35–36, 381
- and perfect capital mobility 35–36, 381
- covered 14, 31, 104–105, 381
- real 33–34, 379
- uncovered 31–32, 381, 383, 509
- uncovered with risk premium 32–33, 396
Intermediate goods
- and foreign multiplier 137ff
- and inflation 294n, 376–377
Internal equilibrium 220, 221
- and external equilibrium 222ff (see also Macroeconomic equilibrium; Macroeconomic policies)
International consistency condition
- on balance of payments 75, 136, 156, 182, 227
- on exchange rates 6
International cooperation (see International policy coordination)
International economics, definition and classifications 3, 517
International investment 338ff
- direct 60, 343–346
- portfolio 60, 343–345, 345n
- short- and long-term 60, 328, 343
International liquidity 452ff, 464ff (see also International reserves)
International management of exchange rates 490ff
- global monetary target 491
- target zones 491–492, 513–515

- Tobin tax 482, 484, 490
International Monetary Fund 23, 27–28, 50, 52, 64, 65, 371, 373, 448, 449, 450, 452–454 passim
International monetary system 22, 27, 448ff
- key events 448–463
- problems of 481ff
International organisations 52
International policy coordination 227ff, 258ff, 294, 484–490, 511–513
- advantages of 485, 486–488
- and strategic interdependence 485
- free rider problem 413, 490
- obstacles to 488–490, 513
- - problem of the reference model 489–490, 513
- theory of games in 485–488
- - Cournot-Nash equilibrium 487
- - Hamada diagram 486, 488
- - policy reaction curves 487
- - Stackelberg equilibrium 488
International reserves (see Reserves)
International transactions 63ff, 67ff, 407
- autonomous and compensatory 64
Intervention in foreign exchange markets 22–23, 103–104, 109–110, 336, 373–374, 409, 416–417, 467
Intrinsic discount, premium 14n
Inversion of balance-of-payments problem 353
Investment income 59, 297n
Invisible trade 58–59
IS 205, 207 (see also RR)
IS-LM apparatus 187, 205n
IS-LM-BB apparatus 205ff

Jamaica Agreement 460, 461–462
J-curve 172–173, 178ff

Key currency 22, 409
Keynesian
- income-expenditure model (see Foreign multiplier)
- transfer problem (see Unilateral transfers)

Labour income 58–59
Labour mobility and currency areas 405
Laursen-Metzler
- effect 181ff, 182n, 284–285, 311
- model 164ff, 174ff
Law of one price 199, 379
Lead and lags 20, 341
Liquidity (see International liquidity)
Liquidity balance 76, 82
LL 209–210, 213, 216, 217, 219, 220, 223, 232, 233n, 234, 248–249, 263, 275–276, 280ff, 287, 301, 302, 303, 313, 352

LM   205, 205n (see also LL)
Long position   18
Long-term capital movements   60, 343ff, 484

Macroeconomic equilibrium under fixed exchange rates   205ff, 248ff
- and portfolio equilibrium   234ff, 265ff
- - budget constraints   237–238
- - long-run equilibrium   239–241, 266–272
- - momentary or short-run equilibrium   238, 266
- - policy interventions   241
- traditional (Mundell-Fleming) model   205ff, 248ff
- - burden of interest payments   215–217, 226, 250–251
- - comparative statics   217ff, 251ff
- - definition of the various schedules   207ff, 248ff
- - determination of equilibrium   210–213
- - policy interventions   220ff, 254ff
- - - assignment problem   222ff, 256–257
- - - coordination problem   227ff, 258ff
- - - redundancy problem   227–228
- - stability   210ff, 249–251
Macroeconomic equilibrium under flexible exchange rates   273ff, 305ff
- and portfolio equilibrium   295ff, 324ff
- - budget constraints   298, 299, 299n
- - long-run equilibrium   302, 304–305, 329ff, 334–336
- - momentary or short-run equilibrium   300–302, 302–303, 327–329
- - policy interventions   301–302, 303, 329, 330–332, 334
- - rational expectations   296, 302ff, 334ff
- - static expectations   296, 300ff, 327ff
- - exchange rate overshooting   305
- - new Cambridge school (see New Cambridge school)
- traditional (Mundell-Fleming) model   273ff, 305ff
- - alleged insulating power of flexible exchange rates   284ff, 312ff
- - - transmission of disturbances   285–289, 312ff
- - definition of the various schedules   274ff
- - determination of equilibrium   273–276
- - policy interventions   279ff, 307ff
- - - assignment problem   279ff, 307ff
- - - effectiveness and ineffectiveness of instruments   279–284
- - stability   276ff, 305ff
Macroeconomic policies   220ff, 279ff, 484ff
- optimizing approach   221n, 484ff, 494ff, 511ff
- traditional approach   220ff, 279ff
(see also Assignment problem; Fiscal policy; International policy coordination; Monetary policy; Macroeconomic equilibrium)
Managed float   23, 25, 370ff, 468
Margin, forward   12, 13
Marginal propensity to domestic demand (or to spend on domestic output), defined   126, 165, 205n
Margins around parity   22, 23, 24, 416, 428, 448
- asymmetry of, in EMS   416n, 445–446
Market for foreign exchange (see Foreign exchange market)
Marshall-Lerner condition   95–96, 332 (see also Elasticities)
Matrix of real and financial flows   67ff
Maturity criterion   60
Meade-Tinbergen approach to economic policy   220, 221n, 500, 514, 515
Mean time-lag   179n, 264, 322, 324, 377, 509
Migrants' remittances   58–59, 60
Models
- n-country   75, 145ff
- one country or small country   74–75, 123ff, 142ff, 164ff, 174–178, 187ff, 199n, 231ff, 235ff, 273ff, 285ff, 297ff, 312ff, 351, 383
- two-country   75, 131ff, 145ff, 181ff, 199n, 227ff, 244–247, 287ff, 315ff, 347ff, 361–363, 484ff, 511–513
Models of exchange-rate determination (see Exchange rate determination)
Monetary approach to the balance of payments   72n, 73, 187, 196ff, 210, 214, 243ff
- basic propositions of   197–199
- and classical theory   196, 196n
- and determination of exchange rate   381–383, 394–395, 397–398
- and determination of price level   196, 196n, 243–247
- and devaluation   201–204
- and growth   357–359, 364–365
- formalization of   243ff
- implications of   199–200
Monetary cooperation within the EMS   425–427
Monetary integration   403ff
- and common monetary policy   412–413
- and common monetary unit   413–416
- and currency areas (see Currency areas)

– and European monetary system (see European monetary system)
– and European monetary union (see European monetary union)
– and fiscal policy   434–439
– various degrees of   403–404
Monetary policy   220ff, 279ff
– and fiscal policy for internal and internal balance   222ff, 254ff
– in a monetary union   412–413
Multiple equilibria in the foreign exchange market   96–97, 102–103, 341–342, 360
Mundell-Fleming model (see Macroeconomic equilibrium)

National income
– and balance of payments   67ff
– multiplier (see Foreign multiplier)
n country models (see Models)
Net acquisition of financial assets   290
Net liquidity balance   82
Neutrality condition
– in covered interest arbitrage   14, 38, 105, 121
– in exchange rate arbitrage   6
New Cambridge school   72n, 289ff, 318ff, 373
– assignment of instruments to targets   290, 292ff, 319ff
– basic assumptions   290–292
– stability   320–321, 322, 324
– various versions of   292–295
New view of money   476, 480
News   304, 396
– and rational expectations   304–305
nth country problem   227

OECD   459
Official settlements balance   82
Offshore   29–30, 452
Oil deficits and surpluses   459–460
One-country models (see Models)
Onshore   29–30
OPEC   459, 480
Open-economy macroeconomics   74
Open-market operations   211n, 233–234, 238, 299, 301n
Open position   9
Opportunity cost of holding international reserves   466, 468, 469, 494, 496
Optimization of economic policy   221n, 484ff, 496ff, 511–513
Optimum
– currency areas (see Currency areas)
– reserve composition   470–472, 501–504
– reserve level   468–470, 493ff

Overall balance   65, 65n, 66
Overeffected transfer   347, 348, 349, 362
Overshooting of exchange rate   305, 376, 395
Own-rate of interest   16, 16n

Partial adjustment   179, 179n, 264, 265n, 322, 393, 506, 508
Par value or parity   22–25
Pass-through period   172, 173
Perfect
– asset substitutability   35–36, 280n, 381, 381n, 383, 412, 509
– capital mobility   35–36, 279ff, 280n, 381, 381n, 412, 482, 509
Peso problem   48
Petrodollars   459–460
Policy multipliers   512
Portfolio equilibrium   38ff, 216, 230ff, 263ff, 295ff, 224ff, 324ff, 470–472, 476ff, 501–503, 504ff, 508ff
– and marginal conditions   39ff
– and speculation   43ff
– under fixed exchange rates
– – integration with macroeconomic equilibrium   234ff, 265ff
– – partial analysis   230ff
– under flexible exchange rates   295ff, 324ff
Portfolio investment   343–346, 345n
Portfolio selection (see Portfolio equilibrium)
PPP (see Purchasing power parity)
Preferred local habitat   383n, 396n
Premium (see Forward premium)
Price-specie-flow mechanism   73, 187ff, 241ff
Productive diversification and currency areas   405–406
Purchasing power parity   33, 34, 199, 202, 244, 378, 381, 382, 383, 394, 395
– absolute and relative   378
– as a theory of exchange-rate determination   378–380
– ex ante   33
Pure theory of trade   3, 517

Quantity adjustment period   172, 173
Quantity theory of money   188, 190, 191

Random walk   36, 390, 392, 393, 400
Rate of foreign exchange (see Exchange rate)
Rate of interest (see Interest rate)
Rational expectations   46–47, 296, 302ff, 325n, 334ff, 401, 510
Recycling of petrodollars   459, 480
Redundancy problem   227

Reserve currency 454–455
Reserve tranche position 453, 453n
Reserves, international 60, 61, 72, 197, 198, 200, 206, 238, 297, 300, 369, 407, 454–455, 464ff
– composition of 454–455, 470ff, 501ff
– creation of 61, 75
– definition of 61, 452–453
– demand for 464ff
– – descriptive approach 465–468
– – optimizing approach 465, 468–470, 493ff
– valuation changes 61
Resident 51–52
Revaluation of exchange rate 89, 281, 298, 333, 334, 395
Revaluation of reserves 61
Risk coefficient 17, 32–33, 44, 45, 46n, 107–108, 344, 396
Risk premium 17, 32–33, 396, 510
RR 166ff, 175, 176, 207, 210–223 passim, 248, 274–287 passim, 300–303, 329
Rybczynski theorem 345

Scarce-currency clause 449
SDRs (see Special Drawing Rights)
Services 57, 58–59
Short position 18
Short-term capital movements 60, 338ff
Siegel paradox 48–49
Small-country models (see Models)
Small country or small open economy (see Models)
Smithsonian agreement 370
Snake 371, 417
Special Drawing Rights 28, 28n, 411n, 449, 452–457
– new suggestions for allocating them 456–457
– substitution account 456
Speculation
– and monetary authorities' intervention 109–110
– bearish and bullish 340–341
– definition of 16ff
– destabilizing 25, 339, 340–341, 342, 407, 414, 428, 479, 481ff
– forward 18–19, 107–108, 120, 121, 343
– one-way option 339, 415
– profitable and non-profitable 340ff
– profits from 341,
– risk-neutral 31–32
– spot 18–19, 120, 338ff
– stabilizing 25, 339, 342–343, 483
– under various exchange-rate regimes 339ff, 369–370
(see also Speculators)

Speculators 16ff
– definition of 16–17
– equilibrium of 16–20, 38ff
– – and portfolio selection theory 38ff
– – excess demand for foreign exchange 107–108, 120, 121, 341–342, 360
– occasional and permanent 483
– short-term and long-term 483
– various types of 16ff
(see also Speculation)
Spot
– covering 11
– exchange rate 6–8, 9n
Sterilization of balance-of-payments disequilibria 210, 211n, 238, 239, 299, 479
Stock and flow disequilibria 73–74, 393
Substitution account 456
Super Marshall-Lerner condition 332
Support points 22
Surplus in balance of payments 63, 71–72
(see also Balance of payments)
Swaps 14ff, 425
Synergetics 519

Target zones 491–492, 513–515
Terms of trade
– and balance-of-payments adjustment 87, 88, 118, 160–161, 181, 195, 296, 298, 300, 348, 350
– definition of 87
Timing of recording in balance-of-payments accounting 56–57
Tinbergen's instrument-target rule 220–221, 221n, 514
Tobin tax 484, 490
Trade balance 65
Transfer problem (see Unilateral transfers)
Transmission of disturbances (see Disturbances)
Triffin dilemma 453, 456, 457–458
Tunnel 371

Uncovered interest arbitrage 20, 31ff
Undereffected transfer 347, 348–353 passim, 362
Uniformity of valuation 57, 58
Unilateral transfers 51, 52, 53, 55, 56, 60, 346ff, 361ff, 460
– and terms-of-trade changes 348, 350
– classical theory of 347–348
– Keynesian theory of 348–350, 361–362
– within the standard macroeconomic model 351–353, 362–363
Unrequited transfers (see Unilateral transfers)

Valuation changes 61
Vehicle currency 470, 471–472
Vicious circle (see Devaluation-inflation circle)
Visible trade 57–58

Walras' law 232, 233, 247, 247n
Wealth
- definition of 230, 230n, 237, 299
- distribution of, and portfolio equilibrium (see Portfolio equilibrium)
- effect 160–161, 237, 298–299, 328, 330, 334
Wider band 24–25, 417
Wider margins around the parity (see Wider band)
World Bank 448

Xeno-currencies 29, 451, 471n
Xeno-markets 29, 472, 478